tween 900 and 200 B.C.: ancient China, India, Israel, and Greece. The fifth major case study examines the rise of the city and the nation—and of tensions between humanists and scientists—in the recent West.

In the final chapter, Professor Martindale summarizes the theory of social and cultural change advanced in the opening section and supported by the five historical studies. The end product is a powerful contribution to the scientific analysis of social phenomena.

THE AUTHOR

DON MARTINDALE, who has been professor of sociology at the University of Minnesota since 1954, graduated from the University of Wisconsin in 1939 and received his M.A. in 1940. He completed work on his Ph.D. in 1947 after serving for four years as an Army officer during World War II. Professor Martindale was an instructor at Wisconsin from 1946 to 1948, when he joined the faculty of the University of Minnesota.

Professor Martindale is author of *The Nature and Types of Sociological Theory*, *American Society*, and *American Social Structure*. He is also co-author of *Elements of Sociology* and editor and co-translator with Hans Gerth and others of four books by Max Weber including *Ancient Judaism*, *The Religions of India*, *The Rational and Social Foundations of Music*, and *The City*.

The present work summarizes and integrates many years of teaching and research in social and cultural change.

Social Life and Cultural Change

Social Life and

DON MARTINDALE

Professor of Sociology
University of Minnesota

Cultural Change

D. VAN NOSTRAND COMPANY, INC.
PRINCETON, NEW JERSEY
TORONTO LONDON
NEW YORK

D. VAN NOSTRAND COMPANY, INC.
120 Alexander St., Princeton, New Jersey (*Principal office*)
24 West 40 Street, New York 18, New York

D. VAN NOSTRAND COMPANY, LTD.
358, Kensington High Street, London, W. 14, England

D. VAN NOSTRAND COMPANY (CANADA), LTD.
25 Hollinger Road, Toronto 16, Canada

Published simultaneously in Canada by
D. VAN NOSTRAND COMPANY (Canada), LTD.

PRINTED IN THE UNITED STATES OF AMERICA

FOR

HERMAN AND CLARA RAMRAS

Preface

THE CRISIS in the current theory of social and cultural change is intimately bound up with the entire history of the social sciences. The social sciences arose in the nineteenth century in a burst of enthusiasm that marked the final stages in the systematic transformation of the outlook of Western man in terms of views pioneered in the natural sciences.

The entire rationale for sociology in the mind of Auguste Comte was its discovery of the laws of a scientific theory of progress. In the words of Bury:

> Auguste Comte did more than any preceding thinker to establish the idea of Progress as a luminary which could not escape man's vision.
>
> The "law of Three Stages" is familiar to many who have never read a line of his writings. That men first attempted to explain natural phenomena by the operation of imaginary deities, then sought to interpret them by abstractions, and finally came to see that they could only be understood by scientific methods, observation, and experiment—this was a generalization which had already been thrown out by Turgot. Comte adopted it as a fundamental psychological law, which has governed every domain of mental activity and explains the whole story of human development. Each of our principal conceptions, every branch of knowledge, passes successively through these three states which he named: the theological, the metaphysical, and the positive or scientific. In the first, the mind invents; in the second, it abstracts; in the third it submits itself to positive facts; and the proof that any branch of knowledge has reached the third state is the recognition of invariable natural laws.
>
> The central aim of Comte, and his great achievement in his own opinion was to raise the study of social phenomena from the second to the third stage.[1]

The idea of progress was quickly combined with the idea of evolution made popular by the development of nineteenth-century biology. The combined progress-evolution formula looked, for a time, as if it would sweep everything before it.

But there were buried problems in the progress-evolution formula. Progress does not mean much unless one decides where it is to start and from what it starts. But the decision as to the origin and the goal of history is capable of very different constructions depending on one's values. Moreover, while it has been assumed that all men travel the same route from sav-

[1] J. B. Bury, *The Idea of Progress* (New York: The Macmillan Company, 1932), pp. 291–293.

agery, through barbarism, to civilization, the very obvious differences in the societies of the world were explained by differential rates of progress. Exponents of the progress-evolution theory felt justified in isolating the institutions in different communities and conceptually reordering them in terms of their private schemes. So many different and partly contradictory pictures of the progress-evolution of mankind were produced by this enterprise that the entire theory of progress collapsed.

Since the primary justification for sociology in the minds of its founders was its theory of social change, the collapse of progress-evolutionism was felt to be a major disaster. As a result, one school of sociological theory (sociological formalism) even completely broke its ties with history, though all the original data of sociology had come from the historians. The collapse also set in motion the search for new, nonhistorical methods. Finally, it left the theory of social change, instead of the strongest and best developed branch of sociological theory, the weakest.

The three main sociological explanations of social and cultural change in the twentieth century, the culture-lag theory, the organic cyclical theory, and the intrusive disturbance theory, have suffered from important defects. The culture-lag theory (which was a disguised form of progress-evolutionism) rested on a distinction between material and nonmaterial culture and the lag of the latter behind the former. However, the distinction cannot be maintained (the idea of a technical process is no more material than the idea of, say, an educational program), and comparative evidence shows that even where the distinction is sustained after a fashion, there are waves of development which may reverse their roles as sources of change. The organic cyclical theories have suffered from the presence of evaluative motives which led them to difficulties similar to the early progress theories. Finally, the intrusive disturbance theory accounts for relatively insignificant aspects of social change: after all, the most important social changes are those caused by social facts juxtaposed to those one is concerned with and not intrusive social or physical events from the outside. In any going system of social life intrusive events from the outside are to be resisted. Talcott Parsons, in *Theories of Society*, a volume which he has edited, tries to remedy this situation by a revival of the evolution hypothesis.

Of all major forms of contemporary social theory, social behaviorism seems to hold maximum promise of a satisfactory new approach to the problems of social and cultural change. The following pages review the various branches of social behaviorism: its theory of social groups and institutions, its theory of community, its theory of civilization. Since the theory of social and cultural change must account for the manner in which social and cultural forms arise and are destroyed, a structural description is a necessary first step in analysis. In the eyes of the social behaviorist, the creation, sustaining, or destruction of such forms is always and only the work of individuals.

The major focus of this study is on the formation of communities and the kind of social thought which arises in connection with communities. No complete examination is undertaken in the present study of the basic formation of social groups other than to note some of the ways by which groups are reconstructed when communities arise; nor is the present study concerned with the synthesis of civilizations, except to make a few occasional observations about aspects of a given civilization which may be consistent with its social thought.

Only the individual creates or destroys social forms. When communities arise and are destroyed, certain persons play a central role in the process. These include the intellectuals of the community. It is their task to provide the ideas and institutions which modify primary institutions sufficiently to make total ways of life possible. Moreover, since social behaviorism assumes that potential human genius is a constant, it is hypothesized that the condition of the community is a factor in either releasing or suppressing the productivity of its intellectuals.

Five major case histories of the interrelation of community, the intellectual, and civilization serve as the basis for testing the hypotheses of the study. Four of these case histories are drawn from the period of the ancient world between 900 and 200 B.C.: ancient China, ancient India, ancient Israel, and ancient Greece. The fifth major case study is the wave of development of society and civilization in the recent West.

The completion of the present study owes much to F. Stuart Chapin and Elio D. Monachesi, who first called my attention to the area and created the circumstances which made possible the researches on which it rests. Special thanks are due to Howard Brotz, Louis Goldstein, Ronald Althouse, Thomas Philbrook, and Balwant Nevaskar, who read parts of the manuscript and gave me the benefit of their advice. For their counsel as unfailing humanists, I owe much to Alex Simirenko and Herman Ramras. I am grateful to Edith Martindale for her careful work on the manuscript in all its stages. For typing the manuscript I am indebted to Mrs. Bette Soderstrom and, particularly, to Miss Louise P. Olsen for her patient work and corrections.

D. M.

Contents

Part I

THE THEORY OF SOCIAL AND CULTURAL CHANGE

In Part I three basic tasks are undertaken: a review of the current crisis in the theory of social and cultural change, a sketch of a social behavioristic theory of social and cultural change, and a general description of the properties of the five specific case studies in the formation of society and civilization which will form the greater part of the study.

Though a great number of theories of social and cultural change have been advanced, they can be reduced to a few basic types. Most have not drawn a sharp line between social and cultural change. However, the practical separability of these two kinds of processes is shown by their occasional independence. A rural society may be transformed into an urban society without basic change in many major items of the culture, such as the language, and vice versa.

The theories of social and cultural change which have been advanced from time to time can be reduced to four: (1) The notion has been held that social and cultural changes are either nonexistent or of little general significance. It holds that no matter how the human social world was established in the first place, since then it has always been much the same. Alterations in human affairs (like good and bad times), whether they be from chance or the whims of deities, etc., have little regularity. (2) The theory has been entertained that social and cultural changes do occur, but primarily for the worse. The Golden Age (Garden of Eden) of society and culture is in the past. Mankind is moving step by step toward some horrible end. (3) The theory has been advanced that social and cultural changes were or are progressive (moving toward some goal attained in the present or to be attained in the future). Such progress has at times been conceived as a development of man's rational life or as an increase in his technical understanding and mastery of nature and man, or as the achievement of social, economic, and political freedom. The implements and vehicles of such progress have been variously conceived as special political institutions, special conceptual tools, the unfolding of man's spiritual potential, and as a by-product of economic, social, and political conflicts. (4) Social and cultural changes have been conceived to be cyclical with the same systems of societies and the same sequences of civilizations following one another in the endless turns of the wheel of fate.

While the theory of social and cultural change has been one of the admittedly weakest branches of recent sociology, at least three interpretations of social change have been advanced. The culture-lag theory—a special brand of type three, the progress theory—has been advanced by one branch of social behaviorism. By certain late members of positivistic organicism, the oldest school of sociological theory, cyclical theories of social change have been developed (Sorokin's, Toynbee's, and Spengler's). And, finally, one of the most influential branches of sociological theory, functionalism, has treated social and cultural change as of little general significance.

The crisis in the theory of social and cultural change has been created as a result of the following reasons: (1) serious objections to the culture-lag theory are unanswered, (2) the cyclical theories have been so vaguely and mystically formulated as to gain few adherents, and (3) the functionalists, by a combination of historical and theoretical considerations, have been placed in the ambiguous position of being unable to accept the one theory of social and cultural change—imminent evolutionism—which would harmonize with their theories.

Of all the schools of sociological theory, social behaviorism seems to hold the greatest promise for an adequate theory of social and cultural change. Social behaviorism treats meaningful social interaction as the primary social reality. It approaches the problem of social structure from the standpoint of the collective problems of socialization, mastery of nature, and social control. It conceives of communities as a secondary reorganization of the institutions in terms of the principles of stability, consistency, and completeness which mold the basic institutions into a complete way of life. It conceives of civilization as a synthesis of cultural forms in terms of the principles of playfulness, aesthetic receptivity, and sublimation. The theory of social and cultural change is, for it, the explanation of how social and cultural forms are established and formed into communities and civilizations, and how these societies and civilizations may decay or be destroyed.

While the social behavioristic theory of social and cultural change accepts some changes as semilinear, some as random and accidental, it places particular importance on those social and cultural changes which are semicyclical in nature. The formation and destruction of communities and civilizations represent such semicyclical changes. The study of these types of changes holds out the special value of supplying a recurrent subject matter for the discovery of the laws, if any, of social and cultural change. While social behaviorism is inescapably wedded to the view that only the individual can initiate or stop change and that any individual is a potential source of change, social conditions often place the primary burden on a special stratum of individuals, turning them into the innovators or conservers of their times. In these semicyclical changes represented by the formation of societies and civilizations, the intellectuals represent such a strategic stratum.

In the present study, five major examples of the interplay between society, civilization, and the intellectual will be examined in the attempt to isolate the factors which evoke or frustrate creative abilities. Four of these cases are drawn from the rich period of social and cultural development between 900 and 200 B.C.: ancient China, ancient India, ancient Palestine, and ancient Greece. The fifth example is our own Western society since the Renaissance.

Four major hypotheses will guide the study: (1) The creative epochs of mankind are periods of community and civilization formation, when the creative individuality of its intellectuals is evoked and rewarded. (2) This creativity is qualitatively shaped by the conditions of local time and place. (3) The periods of maturity of community and civilization largely bring the free creativity of the intellectuals to a close. (4) The standards of the acceptability of thought (truth in this special sense) tends to vary between creative and conservative epochs: (a) in creative epochs the criterion of truth is sought in the proper functioning of the thought process itself; and (b) in conservative or conformist epochs there is a tendency to employ the institutional criteria for determination of truth.

I

THE CRISIS IN THE CONTEMPORARY THEORY OF SOCIAL AND CULTURAL CHANGE

THE IDEA has gained currency in the past thirty years that the theory of social change, the theory which the founders of sociology conceived to be the essence of the discipline and its primary justification, is in crisis. The suggestion has been advanced recently that the entire problem is created by attitudes toward theory:

> The mention of "theory of social change" will make most social scientists appear defensive, furtive, guilt-ridden, or frightened. Yet the source of this unease may be in part an unduly awe-stricken regard for the explicitly singular and implicitly capitalized word "Theory."[1]

Theories of social change put forward by recent sociologists fall into two main types: (1) a specialized conception of social and cultural change as progressive (the culture-lag theory identified particularly with the name of William F. Ogburn[2]) and (2) a version of the cyclical theory of culture (identified with the name of Pitirim A. Sorokin[3]). These particular theories of social and cultural change, however, not only have been subjected to vigorous special criticism,[4] but, more important, have acquired only limited followings. Moreover, all total or large-scale theories have been objected to as empirically weak.

> The current anxious pessimism concerning the topic of social change can readily be traced to several related sources. One such source is clearly the downfall or slight acceptability of global, simplifying theories.

1 Wilbert E. Moore, "A Reconsideration of Theories of Social Change," *American Sociological Review*, Vol. 25, No. 6, December 1960, p. 810. His reference is to "functionalism" or "structure-functionalism."

2 William F. Ogburn, *Social Change with Respect to Culture and Original Nature* (New York: B. W. Huebsch, 1922).

3 Pitirim A. Sorokin, *Social and Cultural Dynamics* (New York: American Book Co., 1937–1941), 4 vols.

4 For a criticism of culture-lag theories, see Pitirim A. Sorokin (New York: Harper & Bros., 1947), pp. 659 ff. For a criticism of Sorokin's theories, see Hans Speier, *Social Order and the Risks of War* (New York: G. W. Stewart, 1952), pp. 202 ff.

> Sweeping evolutionary or cyclical doctrines have provided a relatively poor fit to data. Even where generalization may have been "justified," the loss of information in the process of abstraction has resulted in relevance to only minute segments of observed changes, or in other words, in low predictive power.[5]

Meanwhile, one major recent school of sociological theory, functionalism,[6] which has developed with great speed since World War II, has tended, in many of its authoritative interpretations, to set aside social and cultural change. Moore has formulated this point as follows:

> Now structures and functions, paraphrased as "patterns" and "consequences," are not inherently static. However, the theorists who have been most explicit about their concepts, assumptions, and specific theoretical problems have provided little guidance to the orderly transformation of social systems. Wherever an implicit "equilibrium" model is used, changes in patterns of action and their relationships tend to be viewed as deriving from "external" sources and thus in some sense accidental. The system is viewed as reacting to change either by returning to the *status quo ante* or, more probably, by establishing a new equilibrium. Thus *given* a specifiable change in any component of the system, both the processes and results of social transformation may be traced. But this frame of reference provides little guidance to the occurrence of the initial change, save in the concept of "dysfunction" as a challenge to the notion of perfect integration.[7]

When the system is reified and its state of equilibrium is apotheosized and treated as the cause of all events in it (except for dysfunctions), social change from within the system is in principle excluded. Moore's criticism then becomes quite pertinent; the only possible source of change of the system is by intrusion.

TRADITIONAL THEORIES OF SOCIAL CHANGE

However weakly developed, recent sociological theories of social and cultural change have been, they represented most of the basic positions that have been advanced from time to time. Though elaborated in great detail, these basic positions can be reduced to four:

1. At many times and places the notion has been held that social and cultural change is either nonexistent or of little general importance. Such a view has often been held by thoughtful persons in preliterate societies. They have recognized that every individual is born and lives only for a time. By extension they have usually assumed that there must have been a time when man did not exist. Moreover, preliterates also realized that societies as well as individuals have their ups and downs. However, granting this, the alterations

[5] Moore, *op. cit.*, p. 811.

[6] For a general review, see Don Martindale, *The Nature and Types of Sociological Theory* (Boston: Houghton Mifflin Co., 1960), pp. 441 ff.

[7] Moore, *op. cit.*, p. 811.

in human affairs (such as good and bad times), regardless of cause (natural factors, chance, the whims of deities, the black magic of enemies), are assumed to be merely the temporary deviations from a normal state. Nor have preliterates been alone in theorizing concerning the nonoccurrence of social and cultural change. Some human societies have endured for long periods, giving plausibility to such a theory. Moreover, in every society some strata reap the primary benefits of its social life. These strata are the society's vested interests. Individuals in such position are the given society's natural enemies of changes of many types, at least all changes which would threaten their absolute or comparative position. They are natural adherents of the view that social change is illusory. Intentionally or unintentionally, this seems to be the conception of social and cultural change of the contempoiary functionalists.

2. The second basic position is that social and cultural change does occur, but primarily for the worse. Famous examples of this theory appear in the Western idea that the Golden Age (Garden of Eden) of society and culture is in the past.

There have been times when men, again particularly the vested interests (persons in positions of power and authority) of the society, have experienced the decay of their order without being able to do anything about it. For example, both learned pagan authorities and the intellectual representatives of the rising Christian religion were well aware, at the time, that Rome was declining. The view was widespread that the destruction of Rome was the prelude to the destruction of the world. St. Augustine's famous theory of history attempted to do justice both to the widespread gloom about the historical fate of man and to Christian hope and faith. To this end Augustine developed his conception of the two cities—the secular city and the City of God.

> There is a city of God, and its Founder has inspired us with a love that makes us covet its citizenship. To this Founder of the holy city the citizens of the earthly city prefer their own gods, not knowing that He is the God of gods.[8]

The origin of these two cities was already anticipated in heaven by a separation of good and bad angels. God created the world, and in Eden, at first, there was no division between the earthly and the heavenly city. However, God made Adam different from the angels with a conditional immortality:

> The animal body, . . . in which . . . the first man Adam was made, was, not so made that it could not die at all, but so that it should not die unless he should have sinned. That body, indeed, which shall be made spiritual and immortal by the quickening Spirit shall not be able to die at all.[9]

[8] St. Augustine, *The City of God,* trans. by Marcus Dodds (New York: Hafner, 1948), Vol. I, p. 436.

[9] *Ibid.*, p. 556.

He gave the bad angels something to work with. Man became mortal with Adam's original sin. The separation of the earthly and heavenly cities had been made. It was possible for the earthly city to evolve on its sinful route toward destruction until the time of final judgment, when men would either be "hurled into a second death" and suffer everlasting torment, or, if they had been "embraced by God's grace," "become the fellow-citizens of the holy angels who have continued in bliss," and would never more "sin or die."[10] Thus St. Augustine accommodated the concept of the decay of the secular world by placing it in a framework of the faith in a formula for the history of man which remained the authoritative account of history and social change for Western man for nearly a thousand years.

No sociologists have subscribed to the theories of social change as degeneration. Near approaches to such a theory have been made in recent times by various racialists (for example, Madison Grant and Lothrop Stoddard) who have been convinced that the ethnic mixtures of modern times are bringing about the degeneration of society and civilization, and by cultural *élitists* (for example, José Ortega y Gasset) who attribute similar effects to democratic mass culture.

3. In recent Western history many varieties of the theory of social progress have been advanced. As formulated in a study that has become classic:

> The Progress of humanity belongs to the same order of ideas as Providence or personal immortality. It is true or it is false, and like them it cannot be proved true or false. Belief in it is an act of faith.
>
> The idea of human Progress . . . is a theory which involves a synthesis of the past and a prophecy of the future. It is based on an interpretation of history which regards men as slowly advancing—*pedetemptim progredientes*—in a definite and desirable direction, and infers that this progress will continue indefinitely.[11]

At various times progress has been conceived of as a development of man's rationality, as an increase in his technical understanding and mastery of nature, and as the achievement of social, economic, and political freedom. The implements and vehicles of progress have been variously conceived of as special political institutions, special conceptual tools, the unfolding of man's spiritual potential—as a by-product of social, economic, and political conflicts.

Bury believed the idea evolved through three main stages. In the second it became inseparably linked with sociology:

> During the *first* period, up to the French Revolution, it had been treated rather casually; it was taken for granted and received no searching examination either from philosophers or from historians. In the *second* period its immense significance was apprehended, and a search began for a general law which would define and establish it. The study of sociology was founded, and at the same time the impressive results of

[10] *Ibid.*, p. 557.

[11] J. B. Bury, *The Idea of Progress* (New York: Dover Publications, 1932), pp. 4–5.

> science, applied to the conveniences of life, advertised the idea. It harmonized with the notion of "development" which had become current both in natural science and in metaphysics. Socialists and other political reformers appealed to it as gospel.
>
> The *Origin of Species* led to the *third* stage of the fortunes of the idea of Progress. We saw how the heliocentric astronomy, by dethroning man from his privileged position in the universe of space and throwing him back on his own efforts, had helped that idea to compete with the idea of a busy Providence. He now suffers a new degradation within the compass of his own planet. Evolution, shearing him of his glory as a rational being specially created to be the lord of the earth, traces a humble pedigree for him. And this second degradation was the decisive fact which has established the reign of the idea of Progress.[12]

The most effective fusion of the ideas of progress and evolution was eventually brought about by Herbert Spencer.

While a host of critical difficulties have seriously shaken the theories of progress and social evolution, leading to the overwhelming rejection of the theory by most social scientists, the continuing attraction of the theory is shown by the culture-lag theory of social change. This theory rests on a distinction between material culture (thought to be the spearhead of scientific advance) and nonmaterial culture (where resistance to scientific procedures finds its last stronghold). As the argument is often phrased: in man's material world he has secured all the gains of twentieth century science, but he persists in attempting to harmonize them with a nonmaterial culture which in some respects has not been advanced beyond the Stone Age. The exponents of the culture-lag theory account for our most serious problems by this distinction, even while they remain unshaken in their belief that the strongholds of reaction (nonmaterial culture) will ultimately be transformed by the penetration of scientific habits of mind.

Insofar as he is willing to accept any general position on social change as a whole, Moore subscribes to a version of progress:

> Two generalizations appear justified with reference to adaptation to "external" events or influences. Both are of a long-term and largely unidirectional or cumulative in character. With reference to "natural" influences, accumulated knowledge of methods of prediction and control, together with an increased independence of social systems from the non-human environment, serves more and more to cushion (but not to eliminate) the impact of shifts and crises. With reference to inter-system contacts, on the other hand, the multiplication of agencies of communication serves to reduce the isolation and thus the autonomy of societies, to increase the proportion and rates of changes from external sources, and thereby to increase "cultural" interdependence and even homogeneity.[13]

In brief, social change is unilinear and progressive in two respects: in the accumulation of scientific knowledge and technology, and in the amounts of social autonomy and cultural homogeneity. Despite his objections to it,

[12] *Ibid.*, pp. 334–335.
[13] Moore, *op. cit.*, pp. 812–813.

Moore seems inclined to subscribe to the same basic position which persons, for example, Ogburn and Chapin, advanced to justify the culture-lag hypothesis. As Chapin formulated the problem in 1928:

> The most hopeful approach to the concept of cultural change would seem to regard the process as selectively accumulative in time, and cyclical or oscillatory in character.
>
> Cultural change is accumulative. This has been shown by Wallas, Hobhouse, Bernard, Ogburn, and many others. Ogburn makes the point that cultural change is selectively accumulative. There is a dropping out of elements, but there is also the adding of new elements by invention and borrowing.[14]

4. The conception of social and cultural change as progressive is unique to recent Western civilization. Most civilized areas, such as ancient Greece, ancient China, and ancient India, have been more inclined to accept cyclical theories. Though elements of a theory of progress were present (for example, "Aeschylus represents men as originally living at hazard in sunless caves, and raised from that condition by Prometheus, who taught them the arts of fire"),[15] the Greeks never formulated a general theory of progress. In Bury's opinion, Plato's philosophy typifies Greek inclinations:

> We may take Plato's tentative philosophy of history to illustrate the trend and the prejudices of Greek thought on this subject. The world was created and set going by the Deity, and, as his work, it was perfect; but it was not immortal and had in it the seeds of decay. The period of its duration is 72,000 solar years. During the first half of this period the original uniformity and order, which were impressed upon it by the Creator, are maintained under his guidance; but then it reaches a point from which it begins, as it were, to roll back; the Deity has loosened his grip on the machine, the order is disturbed, and the second 36,000 years are a period of gradual decay and degeneration. At the end of this time, the world left to itself would dissolve into chaos, but the Deity again seizes the helm and restores the original conditions, and the whole process begins anew. The first half of such a world-cycle corresponds to the Golden Age of legend in which men lived happily and simply; we have now unfortunately reached some point in the period of decadence.[16]

The theory of world-cycles was so widely current in the Greek world as to constitute a kind of orthodoxy. Some of the Pythagoreans even argued that each cycle repeats the preceding cycles in the minutest detail. Passed on to the Romans, the theory influenced the thought of Virgil and Marcus Aurelius.[17]

Fundamental to the cyclical theories of the Greeks was their conception of fate, or *moira.*

[14] F. Stuart Chapin, *Cultural Change* (New York: The Century Company, 1928), pp. 202–203.

[15] Bury, *op. cit.*, p. 8.

[16] *Ibid.*, pp. 9–10.

[17] *Ibid.*, p. 12.

> If we were to name any single idea as generally controlling or pervading Greek thought from Homer to the Stoics, it would perhaps be *Moira*, for which we have no equivalent. The common rendering "fate" is misleading. *Moira* meant a fixed order in the universe; but as a fact to which men must bow, it had enough in common with fatality to demand a philosophy of resignation and to hinder the creation of an optimistic atmosphere of hope. It was this order which kept things in their places, assigned to each its proper sphere and function, and drew a definite line, for instance, between men and gods. Human progress toward perfection—towards an ideal of omniscience, or an ideal of happiness—would have been a breaking down of the bars which divide the human from the divine. Human nature does not alter; it is fixed by *Moira*.[18]

Periodically in the West since the days of the Greeks, cyclical theories of social change have been offered. One of the most influential Western political thinkers, Machiavelli, held a cyclical theory of society. With Aristotle he distinguished three good forms of government—principality, aristocracy, and democracy—and three perversions of it—tyranny, oligarchy, and anarchy.

> If any one who is organizing a commonwealth sets up one of the three forms of government, he sets up what will last for a little while, since there are no means whereby to prevent it passing into its contrary, on account of the likeness which in such a case virtue has to vice.
>
> These variations of government amongst men are due to chance. For in the beginning of the world, when its inhabitants were few, they lived for a time scattered like the beasts. Then, with the multiplication of their offspring, they drew together and, in order the better to be able to defend themselves, began to look about for a man stronger and more courageous than the rest, made him their head, and obeyed him.
>
> It was thus that men learned how to distinguish what is honest and good from what is pernicious and wicked, for the sight of someone injuring his benefactor evoked in them hatred and sympathy and they blamed the ungrateful and respected those who showed gratitude, well aware that the same injuries might have been done to themselves. Hence, to prevent evil of this kind they took to making laws and to assigning punishments to those who contravened them. The notion of justice thus came into being.
>
> In this way it came about that, when later on they had to choose a prince, they did not have recourse to the boldest as formerly, but to one who excelled in prudence and justice.
>
> But when at a yet later stage they began to make the prince hereditary instead of electing him, his heirs soon began to degenerate as compared with their ancestors, and forsaking virtuous deeds, considered that princes have nought else to do but to surpass other men in extravagance, lasciviousness, and every other form of licentiousness. With the result that the prince came to be hated and since he was hated, came to be afraid, and from fear soon passed to offensive action, which quickly brought about a tyranny.[19]

[18] *Ibid.*, pp. 18–19.

[19] Niccolò Machiavelli, *The Discourses of Niccolò Machiavelli*, trans. by Leslie J. Walker (New Haven: Yale University Press, 1950), pp. 212–213.

The corruption of the principality and its transformation into a tyranny, runs the argument, led to the establishment of an aristocracy which, after a time, was corrupted into an oligarchy. This, in turn, led to mass action establishing a democracy. But it, too, was eventually corrupted into an anarchy.

> The outcome was inevitable. Either at the suggestion of some good man or because this anarchy had to be got rid of somehow, principality was once again restored. And from this there was, stage by stage, a return to anarchy, by way of the transitions and for the reasons assigned.[20]

In the nineteenth century Nietzsche combined his concept of the superman or, as it has recently been called, "overman" (the vision that the highest type of humanity is represented by people who have achieved complete self-mastery), with the conception of an eternal recurrence. Kaufmann has neatly summarized the argument from the *Will to Power.*

> If science assumes a finite amount of energy in a finite space and an infinite time, it might follow that only a finite number of configurations of the power quanta were possible. In that case, either an end state must be reached or the same configurations must eventually be repeated and recur eternally. If the end state could be reached—and no beginning of time is posited—the end state must have been reached by now; but empirically that is not the case, and there is still change. Therefore, Nietzsche concluded, the doctrine of the eternal recurrence of the same—at great intervals—must be considered "the most scientific of all possible hypotheses." (*Will to Power*, 55, 1062 ff.)[21]

Nietzsche himself indicated in the autobiographical material contained in *Ecce Homo* that he was strongly influenced by the Greeks in his view:

> The doctrine of "Eternal Recurrence"—that is, of the absolute and eternal cyclical repetition of all things—this doctrine of Zarathustra's might also have been taught by Heraclitus. At least, the Stoics, who derived nearly all their fundamental ideas from Heraclitus, show traces of it.[22]

And in *The Joyful Wisdom* he formulated it as follows:

> What if a demon crept after thee into thy loneliest loneliness some day or night, and said to thee: "This life, as thou livest it at present, and hast lived it, thou must live it once more, and also innumerable times; and there will be nothing new in it, but every pain and every joy and every thought, and every sigh, and all the unspeakably small and great in thy life must come to thee again, and all in the same series and sequence—and similarly this spider and this moonlight among the trees, and similarly this moment, and I myself. The eternal sand-glass of existence will ever be turned once more, and thou with it, thou speck of dust!"[23]

[20] *Ibid.*, p. 214.

[21] Walter Kaufmann, *Nietzsche* (New York: Meridian Books, 1959), pp. 281–282.

[22] *Ecce Homo* in *The Philosophy of Nietzsche* (New York: Modern Library, n.d.), p. 869.

[23] Friedrich Nietzsche, *Joyful Wisdom*, trans. by Thomas Common (New York: Frederick Ungar Publishing Co., 1960), pp. 270–271.

It is hardly surprising that with so rich and varied a history behind it the cyclical theory of society and culture should be advanced in sociology in a time when various theories of progress were being seriously questioned.

THE RELATION OF THE THEORIES OF CHANGE TO GENERAL SOCIOLOGICAL THEORY

Even the most elementary review of the current forms of sociological theory of social change, on the one hand, and of the traditional theories of social change, on the other, indicates four things: (1) Theories of social change can be reduced to a few basic models; (2) traditionally theories of social change have been developed in great profusion around these basic models; (3) recent sociological theories have only weakly and uncertainly exploited the traditional models; (4) nevertheless, one of the primary justifications for the development of sociology in the first place was its interest in social and cultural change. The relation between the theory of social change and general sociological theory may help clarify this situation.

Sociological theory attempts to account for the nature and forms of social life; the theory of social change attempts to account for the origin and transformation of these forms. No general sociological theory is complete unless it develops its explanations of social and cultural change. On the other hand, it is also evident that all eclectic theories of social change must prove unsatisfactory in the long run. Only when a decision has been reached as to the nature and forms of social life can the problem of their origin and transformation be systematically developed. The basic types of general sociological theories have very different implications for special theories of social and cultural change.

The types of sociological theory which have been advanced since the origin of science about a hundred years ago have been reviewed elsewhere,[24] making it unnecessary to examine them in detail here. The five types of sociological theory are: positivistic organicism, conflict theory, sociological formalism, social behaviorism, and functionalism. Some of these schools have developed major subbranches: positivistic organicism partly subdivided into traditional organicism, biological organicism; and voluntaristic positivism, before it disintegrated in recent times into pure organicism and pure positivism. Sociological formalism subdivided into a neo-Kantian and a phenomenological branch. Social behaviorism was subdivided from the beginning into pluralistic behaviorism, symbolic interactionism, and social action theory. Functionalism is divided into macrofunctionalism and microfunctionalism. The manner in which these general theories have accounted for human social life have provided them with very different affinities for theories of social and cultural change.

[24] Don Martindale, *The Nature and Types of Sociological Theory* (Boston: Houghton Mifflin, 1960).

POSITIVISTIC ORGANICISM'S LINKAGE WITH PROGRESS AND EVOLUTION

Positivistic organicism, the first general school of sociological theory, created by Auguste Comte, Herbert Spencer, and Lester Ward took mankind as a whole to be the object of study of sociology. Mankind (humanity), or in its major manifestation, society, was thought to be an organic unit. The proper means of study of this organic unit was the examination of the methods and techniques which had proved their worth in the physical sciences.

All of the positivistic organicists were convinced that the happenings of humanity or society were in part determined by the natural and biological environment. However, the primary causes of social events were other social events. Hence, when humanity or the many societies in which human beings were distributed changed, the source of these changes was to be sought in social events themselves. The primary object of the new science, according to its founders, was to explain these same social and cultural changes.

The theories of progress developed broadly and loosely in the eighteenth century, particularly by Condorcet, and advanced in the early nineteenth century, particularly by Saint-Simon, formed the starting point for Comte's thinking which centered in the explicit search for a law of progress which he formulated in his *Cours de philosophie* completed in six volumes between 1830 and 1842. Human progress, he argued, is ruled by the law of the three stages in which men account for the phenomena of the world.

In the earliest attempt by men to explain phenomena, their thinking is theological in nature (events are explained as caused by deities and demons). Later, as men grow more sophisticated, they reject such anthropomorphizing, explaining events in terms of presumed abstract principles or essences. However, in time they recognize that such metaphysical explanations are also inadequate and thinking advances to a positive stage in which explanations are made on the basis of scientific methods. This law of the three stages operates, according to Comte, in every area of human mental life and development.

> The movement of history is due to the deeply rooted though complex instinct which pushes man in all ways to ameliorate his condition incessantly, to develop in all ways the sum of his physical, moral, and intellectual life. And all the phenomena of his social life are closely cohesive, as Saint-Simon had pointed out. By virtue of this cohesion, political, moral, and intellectual progress are inseparable from material progress, and so we find that the phases of his material development correspond to intellectual changes.[25]

Humanity develops in terms of these imminent forces. In the nineteenth century the rise of the biological sciences became a dominant factor in social

[25] Bury, *op. cit.*, p. 293.

thought. Darwin himself had been strongly inclined toward the fusion of the concepts of progress and evolution.

> As all the living forms of life are the lineal descendants of those which lived long before the Cambrian epoch, we may feel certain that the ordinary succession by generation has never once been broken, and that no cataclysm has desolated the whole world. Hence we may look with some confidence to a secure future of great length. And as natural selection works solely by and for the good of each being, all corporeal and mental endowments will tend to progress toward perfection.[26]

The major synthesis of the doctrines of progress and evolution, however, was made by Spencer, who was an evolutionist even before Darwin. Evolution was extended by him to sociology and ethics. Human nature was not conceived to be fixed, but undergoing indefinite variation. This very property made humanity perfectible. Evil is not a fixed element in either the human being or the social constitution, but results from the maladaptation of the organism to the conditions of life. Modification of forms continues until adaptation is complete in the mental and moral, as well as the biological life spheres. Civilization is the end product of the adaptations already accomplished.

> Always towards perfection is the mighty movement—towards a complete development and a more unmixed good; subordinating in its universality all petty irregularities and fallings back, as the curvature of the earth subordinates mountains and valleys. Even in evils the student learns to recognize only a struggling beneficence. But above all he is struck with the inherent sufficingness of things.[27]

One effect of this fusion of the concepts of progress and evolution and of the conception of the evolution of human society toward more progressive forms was to set in motion the employment of societal typologies intended to epitomize early and late stages in the historical process. Examples of famous societal types are the following:

TYPES OF SOCIETY

Thinker	*Early*	*Late*
Auguste Comte	theological society	positivistic society
Herbert Spencer	militaristic society	industrial society
Henry Sumner Maine	status-dominated society	contract-dominated society
Ferdinand Tönnies	gemeinschaft	gesellschaft
Robert Redfield	folk society	secular society

It is unnecessary to trace the rich profusion of progress-evolutionary theories of social change. Nor is it necessary to document in detail the reason

26 Charles Darwin, *The Origin of Species* (New York: P. F. Collier, 1909), p. 528.
27 Herbert Spencer, quoted by Bury, *op. cit.*, p. 340.

for their collapse. It is sufficient to note, simply, that the breakdown of the theory of social and cultural change which at one time was almost coextensive with sociology itself shook the new social science to its very foundations.[28]

The critical difficulties which brought the progress-evolution theory of social change into difficulty and eventually brought about its downfall were: it rested on value premises, its basic propositions were taken as fixed rather than formulated as hypotheses for test, and it lacked an adequate method. Social evolutionism had assumed that human development was unilinear. Contemporary preliterates, who would seem to violate the assumption of the unilinear development of human society, were conceived to have been delayed by local circumstances at an early evolutionary stage in the development of mankind. A potential source of negative evidence against the progress-evolution theory was thus turned into an asset, since one now felt free to use evidence gathered from contemporary preliterates to reconstruct the evolution of society.

Considerable difference of opinion existed between different evolutionists as to where humankind began its ascent and where its odyssey would terminate. These points on the evolutionary series were usually assumed arbitrarily in terms of the value premises of the given thinker. Often some recently reported preliterate group (such as the Australian preliterates which Durkheim considered the lowest stage of surviving primitivism) was taken as the starting point of the evolutionary series. The highest stage of evolution was usually taken to be the sociologist's own society—Paris, London, Boston. A hypothetical line was arbitrarily drawn between these points and various kinds of historical and ethnographic evidence, usually torn out of the social context of particular societies, was arbitrarily strung on this hypothetical line. No mechanism for the social evolutionary process, equivalent to the germ plasm of living species, could be specified which might operate as the foundation of social evolution. Such procedure permitted so many contradictory organizations of the same facts that in the long run the entire progress-evolution theory of social change fell into disrepute.

THE CYCLICAL THEORIES OF THE HEIRS OF POSITIVISTIC ORGANICISM

The downfall of the progress-evolution theory of social change was itself one of the major components in the modification and eventual disintegration of positivistic organicism. From the beginning tension had existed between the positivistic and organismic elements of this school of theory.[29] One result of this tension was the development of voluntaristic organicism which retained the organismic theory of society but placed far greater emphasis on

[28] For some of the details, see Don Martindale, "Sociological Theory and the Ideal Type," in Llewellyn Gross (editor), *Symposium on Sociological Theory* (Evanston, Illinois: Row, Peterson & Company, 1959), pp. 57–91.

[29] See Don Martindale, *The Nature and Types of Sociological Theory*, *op. cit.*, pp. 52 ff.

the *drive* or *feeling* life of man than had the founders[30] of sociology. With this development came the inclination toward a different theory of social change.

Among the philosophic forerunners of voluntaristic positivism, Nietzsche had inclined, in his doctrine of eternal recurrence, toward a cyclical theory of social and cultural change. Among the sociological exponents of voluntaristic positivism, Pareto inclined toward a cyclical theory of social change. The most basic events of social life were found by Pareto in *residues* (the underlying drives of society) and in derivations (variable conscious elements). Two of these residues or powerful voluntaristic proclivities, the residue of combinations (a tendency to innovate) and the residue of persistence of aggregates (the tendency toward conservation), were particularly important.[31] Two principal social types and two major social classes embody these residues: the speculators (the residue of combinations) and the *rentiers* (the residue of persistence of aggregates). *Rentiers* are the lions of society. They are conservative, cautious, suspicious of change, and quite ready to use force to maintain order. However, they also have a fatal tendency to be lazy. They are easily persuaded to allow the foxes (combiners, *entrepreneurs*, schemers, inventors) to penetrate their ranks by craft and trickery. In the end the *rentiers* find themselves dethroned. History is "the graveyard of aristocracies." However, in time the deceit and trickery of the speculators become unbearable, and the lions regain the will to power to put them down by force. History is a "circulation of the Elite."

Not all the heirs of positivistic organicism retained the positivistic elements of the original theory. Certain persons retained and purified the organicism of the original theory, but dropped its positivistic forms.[32] All of the main representatives of a purified contemporary organicism have promoted cyclical theories of social and cultural change. This is illustrated by the works of Oswald Spengler, Arnold Toynbee, and Pitirim Sorokin.[33]

Sorokin is the best example, sociologically speaking, of this trend among the pure organicists toward cyclical theories of social and cultural change. He has developed his doctrines not only in *Social and Cultural Dynamics* but in *Society, Culture, and Personality*.[34] As Speier has noted, Sorokin was as interested in demolishing the theory of progress as in developing an alternative for it:

[30] *Ibid.*, pp. 99–100.

[31] The theories of society based on these were developed in Vilfredo Pareto, *The Mind and Society*, trans. by Arthur Livingston (New York: Harcourt Brace, 1935), 4 vols.

[32] See Don Martindale, *The Nature and Types of Sociological Theory, op. cit.*, pp. 110 ff.

[33] See Oswald Spengler, *The Decline of the West*, trans. by Charles Francis Atkinson (New York: Alfred A. Knopf, 1926); Arnold Toynbee, *A Study of History* (New York: Oxford University Press, 1934–1954), 10 vols.

[34] Pitirim Sorokin, *Society, Culture, and Personality* (New York: Harper & Bros., 1947).

> *Social and Cultural Dynamics* is a very ambitious study. It covers the history of civilization for the last twenty-five hundred years and contains numerous excursions into the history of many civilizations in order to ascertain the forms and kinds of socio-cultural change.
>
> Fundamentally, the work is a gigantic re-examination of the theory of progress which, in popular form, has dominated the philosophic views of many social scientists in the nineteenth century and has exerted a deep influence upon the mores of modern Western society. The theory contained not only the prospect of an ever-increasing efficiency of man's control over nature—making for greater safety and comfort—but also of an ever-increasing liberation of man from prejudices, ignorance, and destructive passions.[35]

Sorokin treats personality, society, and culture as three successively more comprehensive systems of human phenomena. His distinction primarily concerns the third. "The cultural aspect of the superorganic universe consists of meanings, values, norms, their interaction and relationships, their integrated and unintegrated groups ('systems' and 'congeries') as they are objectified through overt actions."[36] When one studies the socio-cultural universe, "the individuals and groups function not for their own sake but mainly as the agents and instrumentalities of meanings, values, and norms."[37] It is Sorokin's contention that this cultural universe of meanings, values, and norms which "contains billions of small systems" forms progressively larger systems:

> Among the comparatively vastest of these systems are the integrated systems of science, philosophy, religion, ethics, law, the fine arts, and the systems of oral and written language as the main vehicles for the objectification of any system or congeries of meanings.[38]

Such vast cultural systems in turn are said to be integrated into the "vastest known ideological super-systems." There are three such great integrations of culture. Their natures consist of their conception of the ultimate nature of truth, reality, and life.

> Some ideological cultures answer that *true reality and true value is sensory*, that beyond the reality and value perceived by our sense organs there is no other reality and no value. Having answered it in this way, such ideological cultures build upon this answer their vastest supersystem in which most of their scientific, philosophical, ethical, and other systems articulate exactly this major premise. Such ideological supersystems can be called *sensate*. Other highly integrated ideological cultures answer the problem by stating that *the true reality and true value is the super-sensory, super-rational God* ("Tao," "World Soul," "Brahman," etc.), *the sensory reality and value being either a mere illusion, or the least important, least real, sometimes even negative, reality and value*. The

35 Hans Speier, *Social Order and the Risks of War* (New York: George W. Stewart, 1952), p. 208.
36 Sorokin, *Society, Culture, and Personality, op. cit.*, p. 313.
37 *Ibid.*, p. 313. The reification of culture should be noted. It uses individuals as its instruments!
38 *Ibid.*, p. 317.

vastest ideological supersystem built upon this premise can be called *ideational.*

Still other highly integrated cultures assume that *the true reality and value is partly sensory, partly rational, partly supersensory and superrational infinite manifold.* The ideological supersystem erected upon this major premise can be called *idealistic.*[39]

Examples of sensate culture are found in Greece and Rome after the fourth century B.C., in the West since the fifteenth century A.D., in some periods of Chinese history, and in some primitive tribes of our day, for example, the Dobu. Examples of ideational culture are found in Taoist China, Greece (prior to the fifth century B.C.), Brahmanistic and Buddhistic India, Christian medieval Europe, and certain modern primitive tribes, for example, the Hopi and Zuni in North America. Examples of idealistic culture are found in Confucianist China, ancient India, ancient Greece of the fifth century B.C., and Europe in the thirteenth and fourteenth centuries.

Perhaps the most significant of all the criticisms that have been directed at Sorokin's constructions is that historical phenomena are not being studied to understand them, but to evaluate them. Moreover, this evaluation is being conducted in terms of a comparatively limited scheme of values. The methodological weakness of Sorokin's procedure has been summarized by Speier:

> In many respects Sorokin's sociological approach to history reminds one of the methodology of the old unilateral evolutionists in ethnological theory, who started out with an assumed and prearranged scheme of universal evolution and then searched for the material to round out the skeleton outline and vindicate the evolutionary scheme, having little regard for the cultural context from which they wrenched their data.[40]

In Speier's view, Sorokin's philosophy is a kind of vulgarization of early Christian thinking.

> The distinction between sense, reason, and faith is retained as a universal principle of division of the types of man, cultures, and "systems" within each culture. The hierarchization of these values, however, is blurred. The idea of a supreme good is given up in favor of a relativistic point of view tempered by eclectic professions of absolute standards. Throughout his work some kind of hierarchy of the three values is implied, as is particularly evident from the expressions of contempt, disgust, and revulsion in which Sorokin indulges whenever he describes the "sensate sewers" of our time.[41]

The substitution in Sorokin's studies of evaluation for scientific analysis is carried further in his relativization of truth and the development of a concept of integral truth, said to be as different from the truths of faith, of reason, and of the senses as each is different from the other. Integral truth is said to

39 *Ibid.*, p. 320.
40 Speier, *op. cit.*, p. 210.
41 *Ibid.*, pp. 211–212.

fuse the empirical truth of the senses, the rational truth of reason, and the superrational truth of faith into a higher unity.[42] This proposal moves Sorokin's theories not only outside of the circle of positivism but outside of science as well.

THE THEORIES OF SOCIAL CHANGE OF CONFLICT THEORY

Long before positivistic organicism had run its course and had begun to modify and eventually abandon the theoretical formula on which the theory first rested, a deeper ground movement in general sociological theory was manifested in the rise of conflict theory. Conflict theory arose as a realistic protest against many superficialities in early organismic theories. By and large, the conflict theorists retained and even intensified the positivism of early sociology. However, in place of the conception of society as an organism, social reality was thought to be a process of conflict of individuals and of groups over scarce values.[43]

It is useful to distinguish various conflict ideologies developed in the nineteenth and twentieth centuries from sociological conflict theory proper. An ideology is a social and political program rather than a scientific explanation. The two main conflict ideologies, Marxian socialism and social Darwinism, were not primarily developed by professional sociologists, but by persons interested in practical economic and political reform. Both major conflict ideologies, however, elaborated interesting theories of social change.

THEORIES OF SOCIAL AND CULTURAL CHANGE OF THE CONFLICT IDEOLOGIES

Marxism, which had in part developed in reaction to Hegelian idealism, took over its theory of imminent development in a conception of dialectical materialism. This was a form of progress theory in which the mechanism of social development was located in economically based class conflicts. As its position was formulated in the *Communist Manifesto*, "the history of all human society past and present has been a history of class struggles."[44] These class struggles in the past occurred under slavery and under feudalism. At the present time they are forming under capitalism. In each stage the nature of social life is determined by the system of social relations which, in turn, rests on the kind of mastery of nature its technology makes possible. Under each system of technology and production in the past, a division arose in time between the owners of the means of production and the workers. The former were able to skim off the surplus productivity of labor. However, in the end, class struggles broke out and the workers took production into their own hands, advancing social development to a new level of efficiency. The cycle of

[42] Sorokin, *Social and Cultural Dynamics*, Vol. IV, p. 762.

[43] See Don Martindale, *The Nature and Types of Sociological Theory*, *op. cit.*, pp. 127 ff.

[44] Karl Marx and Friedrich Engels, *The Communist Manifesto* (New York: International Publishers, 1930), p. 25.

revolutions was accompanied by a rising level of achievement. The positive achievements of capitalism are themselves more extraordinary than the Egyptian pyramids, Roman aqueducts, or Gothic cathedrals. As Marxian theorists saw it, contemporary society is now on the threshold of the next highest step which, through the dictatorship of the proletariat, may open the way to the classless society of the future.

Among the many objections that have been raised against the Marxian theory of social change are the following: It provided a one-factor analysis of social change; its conception of the social classes was oversimplified; it made predictions about social and economic developments (for example, the disappearance of the middle class into the two great classes of capitalists and proletariat) which have not in fact come to pass. However, though Marxism completely failed to establish a general theory of social change, it left no doubts that many social changes are best traced to economic conflicts.

The social Darwinists also developed a conflict ideology in which a concept of social change was involved. The kind of conflict it presupposed was not a struggle of classes but a biological struggle to survive. Moreover, many social Darwinists were inclined to conceive social change in pessimistic terms, presenting one of the few contemporary ideas of change as degeneration. Malthus argued that for all species of living things, including the human species, there is a tendency for population to outstrip the food supply. In the end the effect on population is to drag the level of life down to the point where people are just able to survive. Voluntary methods of population check, he thought, entail an extensive corruption of morals which can be worse than the effects of an excess of population. Moreover, the natural checks on population by vice, unwholesome occupations, poverty, sickness, and war are never sufficient to prevent the encounter of man with his destiny.

> It seems evident that no improved form of government, no plans of emigration, no benevolent institutions, and no degree or direction of national industry, can prevent the continued action of a great check to increase in some form or other; it follows that we must submit to it as an inevitable law of nature.[45]

From Malthus' day to the present, gloomy predictions on the future of human society under the pressures from population have been advanced.

As has been pointed out many times, here again, as in the case of the Marxian theory of social change, only a single factor has been specified. Furthermore, there is a playback from social life on population which has not been adequately accounted for in the idea that the voluntary control of population results in moral corruption. Many societies seem to have stabilized their populations for long periods without either having first reduced the level of life to a starvation level or having permanently corrupted their ethical life. However, here again the proposition was established beyond doubt that

[45] Thomas Malthus, *Essay on Population* (New York: The Macmillan Co., 1894), p. 97.

though demographic factors can never account for the whole of social change, they play a role in it.

EARLY CONFLICT THEORISTS SUBSCRIBE TO A MODIFIED PROGRESS THEORY

By and large, the early conflict theories accepted the dominant interpretation of their period, conceiving social and cultural change as progressive. They differed primarily from the positivistic organicists in attributing social progress to the establishment of equilibria of interests in the course of a struggle for social, economic, and political power. They assumed a more or less constant tendency to shift the scene of the contest to the more comprehensive arenas of power. In one form or another, this is assumed or stated by all the major conflict theorists, among whom are Walter Bagehot, William Graham Sumner, Ludwig Gumplowicz, Gustav Ratzenhofer, George Vold, and Ralf Dahrendorf.

Ratzenhofer, who conceived the social process as a product of conflicting interests, illustrates the tendency in his *Sociological Knowledge*.[46] He argued that conflicting interests lead man successively to form more comprehensive social structures. Or, perhaps, it would be better to say that the contests of men terminate with the formation of structures of increasing size. Any given structure, once formed, becomes the agency in further struggle, hence were formed: the horde, the settled race, the state, the hegemony with world control, and, finally, the international coalition. This societal evolution is accompanied by an ethical and cultural evolution in which the stages are: fellows, community of interests, political self-control in the interest of peace, universal freedom and equality of legal rights, diplomacy, and international peace.

When the theories of progress developed by the positivistic organicists began to tumble into ruins, they tended to cast doubt upon those of the conflict theorists as well. However, the nature of their analytical mechanism did not commit the conflict theorists to value premises in quite the same manner or to unilinear schemes of social development. Most conflict theorists could have accepted the idea that the formation of more comprehensive structures of power may take many different directions at different times and places. The fact that these points have not been made is due more to the fact that conflict theory itself had lacked adherents than to properties of its theories. The comparative lack of adherents to conflict theory is possibly a product of the frequent failure to distinguish between conflict ideology and sociological conflict theory. The conflict ideologists tended to pass over into politics and out of the field of sociology, and sociologically inclined students in distinguishing themselves from the conflict ideologists have usually embraced other types of theory.

[46] Gustav Ratzenhofer, *Die Sociologische Erkenntniss* (Leipzig: F. A. Brockhaus, 1907).

THE LACK OF A THEORY OF SOCIAL CHANGE BY THE SOCIOLOGICAL FORMALISTS

As a movement in general theory, sociological formalism was produced in part by the crisis of positivistic organicism, particularly by the disaster suffered by its theories of social change. Formalism was an attempt to reconstitute sociology by means of the kind of analysis that Immanual Kant employed in his epistemology.[47] The formalists proposed to analyze social life in terms of social relations or forms, as they described them, following Kant's epistemological distinctions. For this purpose they relegated the study of the content of social life to other social sciences. Because of various technical problems in neo-Kantian sociology, formalism tended to shift to the analysis of the presumed depth levels of phenomenal experience along lines outlined by the phenomenologists.

The formalists cut their ties with history, and simultaneously thrust most of the problems of social change aside. The various changes of social life assumed relevance for them only to the degree that social forms or relations were manifested in them. Under these circumstances, though occasional observations about one or another type of social change were made by various formalists, the development of a general theory of social change was not attempted.

THE SOCIAL BEHAVIORISTIC RECEPTIVITY TO SOCIAL CHANGE

Social behaviorism arose in the same atmosphere as formalism and in response to the same problems. However, the school defined the basic materials of sociology as social behavior rather than social structure in the manner of organismic positivism and conflict theory or as social relations in the manner of the formalists.[48] Moreover, while social behaviorism agreed that modification of the positivistic assumptions of the early schools was necessary, it did not accept the antipositivistic inclinations of certain of the formalists. It undertook the development of new empirical methods. Three branches of social behaviorism emerged, differentiated by their peculiar definition of social behavior and their methodological preferences: pluralistic behaviorism, symbolic interactionism, and social action theory. Two of the branches of social behaviorism—pluralistic behaviorism and social action theory—had strong interests in theories of social change.

Pluralistic Behaviorism

Pluralistic behaviorism was developed by Gabriel Tarde in France, modified by E. A. Ross and F. H. Giddings in America, and transmitted in recent

47 See Don Martindale, *The Nature and Types of Sociological Theory, op. cit.*, pp. 211 ff.

48 See Don Martindale, *The Nature and Types of Sociological Theory, op. cit.*, pp. 285 ff.

times to William F. Ogburn, F. Stuart Chapin, and others. As Tarde saw the matter, social life at bottom always consists of the acts of individuals. These acts, in turn, rest on beliefs and desires. Social structures are merely complex arrangements of these unit acts. Nevertheless, one can get his most immediately accurate description of social life by noting the differences between unit acts and counting their frequencies. Such acts will either be repetitions (imitations) of the acts of others or nonrepetitions (innovations). From this perspective, every individual is a potential source of change.

Tarde was convinced that one could establish laws of imitation. For example, he thought that imitations are refracted by their medium. The laws of imitation include the fact that they tend to move from upper to lower classes and from city to country. Finally, considered as a whole, ages of custom- and of fashion-imitation alternate with one another. Such ideas, modified in minor ways by Giddings and Ross, supplied the foundation for the theories of collective behavior in the early twentieth century. The new method of social statistics evolved rapidly in connection with this type of social behaviorism.

Although the pluralistic behaviorists were not committed to the view that only society as a whole changes, since its position emphatically implied that every person was a potential innovator, it became one of the few points in sociological theory where a theory of progress was retained despite the collapse of the progress-evolution formulas elsewhere. The device by which certain recent pluralistic behaviorists managed to save the progress formula was the distinction between material and nonmaterial culture. Culture was defined statistically, rather than structurally, as the accumulated products of human society. With Tarde inventions and discoveries were treated as the specific source of social change.

If the primary source of cultural change is located in the material culture and if nonmaterial culture is assumed primarily to consist of adaptation to this, the illusion of continuous growth can be maintained. If one compares the products of Greek drama with modern movies and asks which is higher, it is no foregone conclusion that the movies will come out on top. However, if one compares the material culture of ancient Greece with that of modern America, the story is quite different. There is little question that classical Greek plumbing was quite inferior to that of modern America. Many times the question has been asked: Why has the cultural-lag theory persisted in the face of all the criticism which over the years has been raised against it? This can only be attributed to the powerful wish by contemporary men to retain the doctrine of progress in the teeth of apparently fatal objections to it.

As Ogburn conceived it, the real source of cultural progress was located in such material inventions as tools, weapons, and technical processes. Adaptive culture consists of all other things which must be adjusted to this material base. Many things may interfere with the easy adaption of non-material to material culture: vested interests in tradition, fear of change, reluctance to change one's habits, lack of education or wrong education, social pressure, and avoidance of the unpleasant. As a result, "material-culture changes force changes in other parts of culture such as social organization and customs, but these latter parts of culture do not change as quickly. They lag behind the material-culture changes, hence we are living in a period of maladjustment."[49] However, Ogburn left no doubt where things had to go.

Unfortunately for the clarity of his argument, Ogburn went on to offer another kind of lag theory, best described as a biological lag. Here the contrast was traced, not between two parts of culture, but between biology and culture. It was argued that "man is the same biologically as he was in the late ice age, while his culture has suddenly become vastly different."[50] As a Stone Age man living in a contemporary city, man is exposed to severe psychological tensions, accounting for such problems as war, crime, sexual aberrations, and disease. Between these two types of theories, cultural and biological lag, contradictory interpretations of the same facts are possible.[51]

The fundamental elasticity of the pluralistic behavioral approach to social change was appreciated much more fully by Chapin than by Ogburn. In his study Chapin retained the culture-lag hypothesis to account for the accumulation of material culture. However, his compromise formula which viewed cultural change as selectively accumulative in time, but "cyclical or oscillatory in character," took account of the possibility that particularly in nonmaterial culture, cycles of varying scope may appear. Cycles of social change, he argued, are of several orders. Cycles of the first order occur in the material culture. They may be minor, illustrated by the displacement of one machine industry by another in a business cycle, or major, illustrated by the rise and fall of a system of technology, for example, the slave system. Cycles of the second order in the nonmaterial culture are illustrated by the rise and fall of religious sects or the rise and fall of social structures. Cycles of the third order relate to large cultural composites, for example, national cultures. These cycles vary in scope from the rise and fall of classes or dynasties to the rise and fall of whole civilizations.[52]

Social Action Theory

Like pluralistic behaviorism, social action theory treated social reality as consisting of particular interhuman acts. Comparable to the pluralistic behavioral insistence that interhuman behaviors have beliefs and desires at their core was the concern of social action theory with the meaningful dimensions

[49] William F. Ogburn, *op. cit.*, p. 193.

[50] *Ibid.*, p. 286.

[51] For a critique, see Don Martindale, "Social Disorganization: The Conflict of Normative and Empirical Approaches," in *Modern Sociological Theory*, ed. by Howard Becker and Alvin Boskoff (New York: Dryden Press, 1957), pp. 340–367.

[52] Chapin, *op. cit.*, pp. 208–209.

of interhuman behavior. For social action theory, too, only individuals innovate, though they often do so in the name of the groups in which they operate. Over and again, for example, new social arrangements were conceived by Max Weber to emerge in the activities of a charismatic leader, that is, a person perceived by his followers as extraordinary and to be followed for this reason. This instance was merely one of many where the role of the individual as innovator was emphasized.

While the social action theorists (Max Weber, Robert MacIver, Thorstein Veblen, John R. Commons, and others) never assembled their many suggestions about social change and their many studies of specific short-time and long-time developments into an integrated theory of social change, various special problems of social change were ever foremost in their thoughts. Veblen, for example, was occupied throughout his life with the rise of capitalism and its consequence for other aspects of contemporary culture. Commons, too, studied the rise of many of the institutions of capitalism—the formation of unions, the development of labor legislation, the influence of immigration on labor conditions. Commons' study of the *Legal Foundations of Capitalism*[53] is a classic in the study of the interrelation and mutual interplay of legal and economic institutions. MacIver was profoundly concerned with the rise and transformation of political institutions.

Finally, Max Weber carried out many profoundly influential studies of specific historical developments. Such was his study of the evolution of the agrarian institutions of antiquity, the role of the religious psychology cultivated among certain Protestant sects in the development of capitalism, the rise of rational musical patterns in Western polyphonic music, the rise and influences of bureaucratic administration in all large-scale modern structures. In the course of these and many other studies, numerous generalizations about social change were established: the emergence of charismatic leaders in times of crisis; the necessity for routinization of charisma, if charismatic change is to be conserved; the influence of the style of life of the stratum which primarily bears it on a social movement as a whole; the interadjustment of major areas of institutional life (such as economics to politics and religion, and vice versa).

While none of the social-action theorists was willing to subscribe either to an unqualified progress theory or to an unqualified conception of social and cultural cycles, all of them were convinced that long-time trends are discernible in certain areas (for example, technology and science), and some social and cultural changes are cyclical in character. The social action theorists have produced a large number of generalizations usually employed by sociology at present to account for various special changes without anchoring these ideas in a single identifiable theory of social change.

[53] John R. Commons, *The Legal Foundations of Capitalism* (Madison: University of Wisconsin Press, 1957).

THE FUNCTIONALISTIC APPROACH TO SOCIAL AND CULTURAL CHANGE

Since the role of functionalism in the theory of social and cultural change has been commented on, it is unnecessary to discuss it in detail. Contemporary functionalism is a return to a modified form of the organicism of the founders conjoined to an up-dated positivism.[54] The observation was made earlier that, in view of the functionalistic assumption of the causal priority of the system over its parts and their reification of the equilibrium states of social systems, the functionalists were put in the position of holding that social change was in principle impossible except for the intrusion of ouside factors.

In terms of the review of the relation between theories of social and cultural change and general sociological theory, this statement appears not altogether true. Functionalism is not in principle prevented from accounting for change arising internal to the system (except for dysfunctions which call for adjustment), but it was put into position where only the imminent evolution of the system adequately accounts for change. In short, the character of functionalistic theory seems to force it into the position where it must account for social and cultural change in the same manner as was originally attempted by the positivistic organicists. However, the memory of the disaster suffered by the early forms of imminent evolutionism is too fresh to make the prospect of a theory of social change which rehabilitates the doctrine of imminent evolutionism very appealing. Functionalism has been left in the unenviable position where the one major alternative open to it is unacceptable.

POSTSCRIPT TO THE FUNCTIONALISTIC THEORY OF CHANGE

Since the above section was written the *magnum opus* of macrofunctionalism, the two huge volumes of *Theories of Society* edited by Talcott Parsons, Edward Shils, Kaspar D. Naegele and Jesse R. Pitts, has appeared. In this "Aristotelian synthesis" of macrofunctionalism a vast number of fragments from pre-1935 sociological writings have been organized exclusively within a functionalistic framework. This enterprise somewhat resembles that of Italian masons of the Renaissance period who chiseled the marbles of the Roman ruins to fragments which they polished and cemented into the entryways and baths of prosperous bourgeois merchants of the cities. Long introductions have been added by the editors to their mosaic tile designs, in which functionalistic theory has been brought to full integration and completeness.

Talcott Parsons, who has grown restive under the frequent observation by contemporary critics that functionalism has troubles with its theory of social change,[55] undertook in his sections of *Theories of Society* to develop the

[54] See Don Martindale, *The Nature and Types of Sociological Theory, op. cit.*, pp. 441 ff.

[55] See Parsons' answer to Llewellyn Gross in the *American Journal of Sociology* for September 1961.

functionalistic theory of social change. His arguments have special interest here; they supply basic confirmation for the contention in the preceding section that the nature of functionalistic theory forces it toward an evolutionary position. At the same time, the judgment expressed earlier—that the memory of the early disaster suffered by social evolutionism was too fresh to make rehabilitation of this theory very appealing—was in error. By way of a series of euphemisms Parsons has taken this very step; he has refurbished social evolutionism.

In "An Outline of the Social System" which compactly summarizes macrofunctionalism, Parsons conceives society as a system surrounded by three others (personality, the organism, and culture). A society is said to be in equilibrium when its boundaries with the other three systems are maintained intact. Social equilibrium consists in "boundary maintenance"; social change consists in boundary-breaking. "If a subboundary is broken, resources within the larger system counteract the implicit tendency to structural change."[56]

Social change conceived as boundary destruction and equilibrium restoration, is said to have two sources, exogenous and endogenous. An exogenous factor is one arising outside the social system; an endogenous factor is one arising internal to the social system. The external (exogenous) sources of social change are internal to the other systems (personality, the organism, culture) which are said to border society. In Parsons' inimitable language:

> The exogenous sources of social change consist in endogenous tendencies to change in the organisms, personalities, and cultural systems articulated with the social systems in question.[57]

Examples of such external causes of social change are properties of the geographical environment, biological heredity, the occurrence of great men, and population pressure. Endogenous sources of social change are strains between the parts of society.

> The most general, commonly used term for an endogenous tendency to change is a "strain." *Strain* here refers to a condition in the *relation* between two or more structured units (i.e., subsystems of the system) that constitutes a tendency or pressure toward changing that relation to one incompatible with the equilibrium of the relevant part of the system.[57]

In other words, a strain is a strain.

There are, Parsons argues, two main types of change depending on the source (exogenous or endogenous) of the model for re-equilibrium once the forces to repair boundary destruction are set in motion.

> The first . . . is the one where the principal model component comes from outside the society. This has been true of the contemporary undeveloped societies. . . .
>
> The second . . . is that occurring when the cultural model cannot be

[56] Talcott Parsons, *Theories of Society* (Glencoe: The Free Press, 1961), Vol. 1, p. 71.
[57] *Ibid.*, p. 71.

> supplied from a socially exogenous source, but must . . . be evolved from within the society. This is the situation to which Max Weber's famous category of charismatic innovation applies.[58]

However whatever the source of its re-equilibrium model, social change normally inclines toward a "functional differentiation" of originally "functionally diffuse" structures. "The process of functional differentiation is one of the fundamental types of social change and has evolutionary aspects."[59]

Elsewhere in the same volume Parsons makes this revived social evolutionism even more explicit. Originally, he argues, all societies were primitive, undifferentiated, and characterized by "ascriptive solidarities."

> In the structure of primitive or relatively undifferentiated societies, ascriptive components are overwhelmingly predominant. The first focus of the ascriptive structure is generally kinship.[60]

"Ascriptive solidarity" is another name for functional diffuseness. The original ascriptive solidarities are said to undergo functional differentiation in time.

> The above outline of comparative social structure has been sketched from a frankly evolutionary frame of reference. We have taken the concept of ascriptive solidarities as not merely designating one structural type, but as a broad evolutionary base line. In the process, old ascriptive solidarities are "whittled away," and in a wide variety of ways new ones are created. . . . However, the *relative* importance of ascriptive solidarity tends to decline, though the process is uneven and reversions are common. . . .[61]

Thus, by way of a series of euphemisms Parsons has rehabilitated the social evolution hypothesis. His very terminology is a thinly disguised version of older formulas. "Ascriptive solidarity" means that individuals are bound to each other by some generalized bond such as by the fact that they are family members, neighbors, or brothers of a fraternal organization. This is exactly what Henry Sumner Maine meant when he described ancient man's relation to his fellows as a "status." By "functional differentiation" Parsons means that individuals are related to one another as interlocked specialists in a division of labor. This is exactly what Henry Sumner Maine meant by the observation that in contemporary societies a man's relation to his colleagues tends to become very precisely defined as in the case of a "contract." In new language Parsons has revived Maine's old formula that human society everywhere evolves, despite occasional setbacks, *from status to contract.*

Since the days when Spencer argued that society evolves from "incoherent homogeneity" to "coherent heterogeneity" to Parsons' argument, nearly one hundred years later, that society evolves from "ascriptive solidarity" to

[58] *Ibid.,* p. 78.
[59] *Ibid.,* p. 76.
[60] *Ibid.,* p. 242.
[61] *Ibid.,* p. 263.

"functional differentiation," the sociological theory of change seems to have made one full circle. Inasmuch as the many objections raised against the evolutionary hypothesis when applied to human society are still largely unanswered, one can expect that they will now be redirected at the functionalists. And sociology is ready for another round.

SUMMARY

Though three major positions on social and cultural change have been sporadically promoted in contemporary sociology, the culture-lag theory, the cultural-cycle theory, and the intrusive-disturbance theory, this branch of contemporary sociological theory is experienced by many sociologists as in crisis.

The great profusion of historical forms of the theory of social change can be reduced to four basic types: (1) the theory that social and cultural changes are nonexistent or of little importance, (2) the theory that social and cultural changes are degenerative, (3) the theory that social and cultural changes are progressive, and (4) the theory that they are cyclical. The three positions in contemporary sociology fall into the first, third, and fourth types.

In contrast to its weak development in current sociology, the theory of social change was one of the most strongly developed branches of theory in early sociology. Five schools of sociological theory have developed: positivistic organicism, conflict theory, sociological formalism, social behaviorism, and sociological functionalism. In positivistic organicism social change was conceived as progressive and evolutionary. However, the theory collapsed when it was demonstrated to rest on value premises and inadequate methods. Later members of this school of theory had recourse to various cyclical theories of social and cultural change. In its early days conflict theory developed specialized forms of the theory of social progress, resting on mechanisms of individual and group conflict rather than on imminent evolution of organismlike structures. Conflict theory has declined for lack of proponents rather than for any structural defect. Formalism was the first school explicitly to renounce its ties with history and to shift the whole theory of social change to an insignificant place in its considerations. Of all contemporary schools, social behaviorism has been most receptive to various theories of social change. The culture-lag theory of the pluralistic behaviorists has attempted to preserve some of the old progress formulas by means of its distinction between material and nonmaterial culture. The social-action theories have been receptive to a variety of explanations of special social changes without, however, integrating its many ideas on social change into a single consistent form.

Contemporary functionalism, which has dominated American sociological theory since World War II, rests on a theoretical formula similar to that of positivistic organicism. However, though its general theory forces it toward an imminent evolutionary theory of change, there has been great hesitation until recently to reconstruct a formula which suffered so severe a disaster in the past.

For all these reasons many contemporary sociologists feel that the theory of social and cultural change is in greater need of reexamination than any other branch of the discipline.

SELECTED BIBLIOGRAPHY

Bury, J. B., *The Idea of Progress* (New York: Dover Publications, 1932).

Chapin, F. Stuart, *Cultural Change* (New York: Appleton-Century-Crofts, 1928).

Commons, John R., *The Legal Foundations of Capitalism* (Madison: University of Wisconsin Press, 1957).

Martindale, Don, *The Nature and Types of Sociological Theory* (Boston: Houghton Mifflin, 1960).

Marx, Karl, and Friedrich Engels, *The Communist Manifesto* (New York: International Publishers, 1930).

Moore, Wilbert E., "A Reconsideration of Theories of Social Change," *American Sociological Review*, Vol. 25, No. 6, December, 1960, pp. 810 ff.

Ogburn, William F., *Social Change with Respect to Culture and Original Nature* (New York: B. W. Huebsch, 1922).

Sorokin, Pitirim A., *Social and Cultural Dynamics* (New York: American Book Co., 1937–1941), 4 vols.

Speier, Hans, *Social Order and the Risks of War* (New York: George W. Stewart, 1947).

Weber, Max, *The Protestant Ethic and the Spirit of Capitalism* (New York: Charles Scribner's Sons, 1958).

2

A SOCIAL BEHAVIORISTIC THEORY OF SOCIAL AND CULTURAL CHANGE

THE EXPLANATION of social and cultural change is the capstone of a sociological theory. In its simplest sense the theory of social and cultural change is the explanation of how social forms are created and destroyed. The theory of change is therefore inseparably linked with general sociological theory.

The previous review of the linkage between the main types of sociological theory and the theory of change establishes their intimacy beyond any doubt. Positivistic organicism, for example, had a natural affinity to imminent evolutionism and to cyclical organic sequences. Conflict theory entailed the view that social change consists in the establishment of sequentially more comprehensive power complexes. Though inclined toward a special version of unilinear evolutionism, conflict theory was not, however, inseparably wedded to the view that change necessarily assumes the form of a single world-wide sequence. Formalism thrust the entire problem of change aside except so far as social forms might be manifested in it. Social behaviorism was so receptive to a variety of special types of social change (linear change of some social and cultural facts, cyclical change of others, unpatterned change in still others) as to cause reluctance on the part of many of its adherents to establish a single theory. Functionalism operated with assumptions committing it in advance either to imminent evolutionism or to organic cyclicalism. However, in view of the downfall of the first theory and the comparative disrepute of the second theory of change, most of the functionalists have left their theories of change undeveloped.

No mystery exists concerning the reasons for the closeness of the linkage between a general social theory and its peculiar notion of social and cultural change. Inasmuch as the theory of change attempts to account for the creation and destruction of social forms, such a theory will be radically affected by one's concept of the nature of these forms in the first place. On the other hand, many of the dispositional properties of the things studied by science only appear under conditions of change. In social life it is also true that until things are studied under such conditions, one's understanding of them remains incomplete. Of all the major types of sociological theory, social behaviorism seems to hold out the maximum promise for a new approach to the theory of social and cultural change.

THE KEY CONCEPTS OF SOCIAL BEHAVIORISM REQUIRED FOR A THEORY OF CHANGE

All branches of social behaviorism, pluralistic behaviorism, symbolic interactions, and social-action theory, conceived of social life in terms of interhuman acts which were meaningful to the parties involved. This meaningful element was accounted for in somewhat different ways. Pluralistic behaviorism thought that the unit acts that made up social life rested on desires and were directed by beliefs; symbolic interactionism thought that human social life was made possible by the fact that human beings possess language which uniquely transforms the structure of an individual's experience, causing him to internalize the attitudes of the others; special action theory maintains that social actions always have a meaningful component which is inseparable from its nature and course. The different ways of accounting for the meaningful components of interhuman behavior are less important in the present context than the fundamental agreement as to the basic subject matter of sociology by the social behaviorists.

Inseparably linked with conception of meaningful interaction of the social behaviorist as the primary subject matter of the discipline was its rejection of the reification of social structures. This does not for a moment mean that the social behaviorists preferred to carry out their analysis of social events without reference to families, churches, economic organizations, political organizations, and the like. However, it does mean that they treated such structures merely as ways in which individuals interact rather than as entities separate from interaction.

Social behaviorism places primary emphasis on what it defines as the basic units of social life. Social behaviorism is thus comparable in sociology to atomism in physics and chemistry and the cell theory in biology. Like these theories, it conceived of other structures in terms of units presumed to be more basic. The concepts required by social behaviorism to account for the major types of social structure and change may be seen in this light. These are:

Social behavior: meaningful interactions of individuals.

Social relation: the arrangement that is present in interaction.

Groups: systems or structures of social behavior which arise when pluralities pursue their separate and collective aims in common.

Institutions: the standardized solutions to the problems of collective life. A group is a shared *strategy* of interhuman behavior, *i.e.*, a plan of action intended to achieve defined objectives. Institutions are fixed elements of such strategies.

Society (or *Community*): a complete system of social interaction, i.e., a set of social groups sufficiently comprehensive to solve for a plurality of individuals all the problems of collective life falling in the compass of a normal year and in the compass of a normal life.

CULTURE: a form (or way or manner or mode) of interaction. Social institutions, the solutions to the basic problems of collective life, are only one though an extremely significant component of culture. Artistic styles or systems philosophy—which do not necessarily represent direct solutions to basic problems of collective life—are also a part of culture.

CIVILIZATION: an integrated system of culture.

SOCIAL CHANGE: the formation and destruction of groups and societies.

CULTURAL CHANGE: the formation and destruction of particular items of culture and of civilizations.

This series of interdefined concepts neither exhausts the conceptual vocabulary of social behaviorism nor exhausts the various ways in which the particular terms have been defined. Other schools of theory define them differently. Finally, the mere fact that a series of terms have been interdefined does not in itself constitute a theory, though a distinction between events, the patterns that may be abstracted from events, and the distinction between events of varying levels of complexity is already contained in the series. This can be represented in tabular form:

Level of Complexity	*Event*	*Abstract Pattern*
Lowest	social behavior	social relation
Intermediate	group	group institution
Highest	society	social organization (interinstitutional relationships)

The basic events of social life, in short, are the meaningful interactions. They are concrete events occurring between two or more persons at particular times and places. A social relation, on the other hand, is not an event but the arrangement of the elements that compose a social act. When two persons interact in such manner that they seek each other's company, assist one another in various ways, take the part of the other when he is not present, and the like, one often speaks of the friendliness that obtains between them. Friendship is an arrangement that obtains between them. It is of great value for some purposes to speak of the friendliness of these persons, for it summarizes an arrangement between them and eliminates the need to speak in detail about the many concrete occasions in which the relation is manifest. The social relation of friendliness, however, is not a new event such that one says, except as a euphemism, whenever these two individuals met friendliness also joined the group.

In a similar manner for events of successively greater complexity, such as groups and societies (or communities), one can speak of abstract patterns, such as group institutions and social organizations. As in the case of social relations, one isolates the abstract pattern because of the analytical power (or economy of thought) one achieves thereby.

While an interdefined set of terms does not of itself constitute a theory, the selection of these terms and the relations between them established by definition already contain some general theoretical implications. Such implications have been built into the terms so far as they are ordered as designations of events of different levels of complexity, and denote concrete and abstract objects. Theory proper, however, consists of the various propositions about social life formulated in terms of its basic concepts.

THE THEORY OF SOCIAL BEHAVIOR

The evolutionary accidents that led to the human animal produced a creature of unusual sensitivity, plasticity, and autonomy. Moreover, man is one of the most social of all the creatures, but unique in the nature of his sociality. He is social by learning and not by instinct.

When life divided into vertebrates and invertebrates, the former division had been pressed upon a course of development in which survival depended upon sensitivity to the stimuli of the world and plasticity of response rather than upon possession of some forms of bodily armament which, while comparatively impermeable to some classes of natural dangers, would permanently bind the creature to a narrow range of environmental conditions. When the vertebrates divided into land creatures and fins were transformed into limbs for land locomotion, a whole new series of possible environmental explorations had become possible to a class of living things. New levels of sensitivities and response plasticities were added to a segment of living things, for a land creature can even live with considerable success on the surface of the waters in a way which cannot be reversed.

When a section of the vertebrates evolved warm-bloodedness, a new kind of environmental autonomy had been gained. A class of creatures had appeared which carried its private climate control mechanisms with it. Without this, creatures are limited to a relatively narrow band of climatic environments. A startling measure of animal autonomy had been attained, for creatures possessing biologically self-regulating temperatures are capable of penetrating a wide range of climatically varied environments.

Among the warm-blooded creatures a further significant series of differentiations were set in motion among those creatures which began to adapt to life in the trees. A creature living on the ground enjoys considerable advantage from the widest possible vision and from a highly developed sense of smell and the speed of his feet related to a horizontal posture. The way of life of a creature living in the trees pulls him into an upright position. Capacity to grasp and to climb are more significant than speed on the ground. The judgment of precise distances is more important than a maximum spread of vision. Greater importance attaches to vision than to the sense of smell. By evolutionary adaptation the eyes are pulled decisively to the front, the posture is emancipated from a horizontal position, the ability to grasp develops, and eye-mindedness dominates sensitivity.

A subclass of those creatures which had begun to evolve in this manner toward an efficient tree life descended to the ground once again, and while they retained and exaggerated some of those traits which could only have emerged during an ancestral tree life, they found the lower part of the body readapted to the ground.

> Man's ancestors will probably be found to have been rather unspecialized creatures possessing a great many primitive characters, creatures that looked very much more like men than they did like apes. Such creatures would have preserved a strong tendency not to develop tusk-like eye teeth, great weight, sagittal chests, or other such specializations, but would have maintained a somewhat conservative tendency to enlarge on the endowments they already possessed. For example, the tendency in the evolution of the primates has been for brain size to increase.[1]

Another aspect of the entire class of creatures out of which man slowly differentiated was a changing foundation of social life. Social life can be an important factor in survival. Groups of creatures capable of acting in common can repel enemies and survive natural hazards fatal to isolated individuals. At first social life everywhere rested on instinct. As long as this was true, instincts narrowly fixed the forms of social life. An instinct-based social life has one great advantage: it can emerge automatically without learning, and is not subject to challenge, but forms an unquestionable basis of social life. However, the creatures out of which men differentiated gradually lost much of the instinctive foundation of social life even while the requirement of social life was growing. Man stands at the extreme of this development.

When attempts were made from time to time in the past to estimate the importance of human biology for man's social life, his upright posture and his remarkably adaptable hands were often singled out as important. With even greater frequency man's lack of specialized properties and his enormous brain capacity have been cited. Moreover, repeatedly from the time of Darwin, the peculiarities of man's biology for his social life have been found in the ways he is able to exercise his great adaptability and intelligence: to construct tools and develop language. Recently man's uniqueness has been estimated as follows:

> The outstanding characteristic of man is that he is the most educable, the most intellectually malleable, the most plastic of all creatures. Everything he knows as a human being, man has had to learn from other human beings. The evidence, as scientists have been able to reveal it, indicates

[1] Ashley Montagu, *Man: His First Million Years* (New York: Mentor Books, 1960), p. 41.

> that the average person in any human society is able to learn just as much as the average person in any other society. Insofar as behavior is concerned, evolution has not proceeded to differentiate human populations into specialists able to meet the requirements of a particular environment and no others, but on the contrary, the evolution of man has proceeded in such a way that he has become a creature capable of adapting to *all* environments.[2]

Thus men have enormous general potentialities with practically no important advance biological commitments. More than any other creature, he is what he makes of himself in the course of his experience. He has an amazing capacity to learn; the one thing unavoidable is that he must employ this capacity if he is to survive. By instinct man is neither egoistic nor altruistic. The degree of self-seeking and sociability which his behavior displays depends upon the personal formula he eventually establishes for his life.

As a creature without social instincts, man could quite conceivably, if he were able to cast off his early social learning from the time of his minority, achieve a degree of purely individual autonomy which is rare in the animal world. To be sure, the sexes would have to associate periodically if there were to be a continuation of the race, but apart from this, there is no reason why an individual could not live out all his days in a manner of his own without reference to anyone else. This has occasionally happened, and human society must contend with a possibility practically nonexistent in any other. At any moment almost any one of its members could set upon a course toward more complete individual autonomy as against everyone else. The imagination of that man must be poorly furnished who has not some time dreamed of departing to some remote corner of the world where no rude elbow would ever jab his ribs. Moreover, there is no reason why any single individual may not take the very techniques and skills that have been perfected in interhuman behavior (for example, language and science) and utilize them as implements in a program of purely personal autonomy. Man may learn language in society. He may also turn it into a powerful tool of his own thoughts to carry out a foundation-shaking critique of his very society.

PROSPERO:

> Abhorred slave,
> Which any print of goodness wilt not take,
> Being capable of all ill! I pitied thee,
> Took pains to make thee speak, taught thee each hour
> One thing or other. When thou didst not, savage
> Know thine own meaning, but wouldst gabble like
> A thing most brutish, I endow'd thy purposes
> With words that made them known. But thy vile race,
> Though thou didst learn, had that in't which good natures
> Could not abide to be with. Therefore wast thou
> Deservedly confin'd into this rock, who hast
> Deserv'd more than a prison.

[2] *Ibid.*, p. 79.

CALIBAN:

You taught me language, and my profit on't
Is, I know how to curse. The red plague rid you
For learning me your language![3]

Man is social only so far as he learns to be so. However, two conditions virtually guarantee that the condition of man will primarily be social: the length of his period of dependency, and the nature of human sex.

As a highly generalized creature lacking both external specialization (claws, fangs, armor plating, etc.) and internal behavioral specialization (a solid core of instincts which prefix the proportions and kinds of behavior assigned to the individual and the group), but with an amazingly extensive intellectual capacity, man was predestined to spend an unusually prolonged period of apprenticeship in the mastery of the tasks of life. Since he was not born with a special set of solutions to the problems of life, man had no other choice but to develop them. Man has the longest period of dependency of any living creature. If one were to imagine optimum conditions for learning to be self-sufficient, and given favorable conditions for survival, once the individual left his childhood groups, the human animal would still have to reach the eighth or ninth year before he could very realistically hope to survive.

This prolonged period of dependency has two consequences. Whatever may happen to certain isolated individuals, the majority of the human population at a given time is certain to be occupying one or the other side of this dependency relation. In our own society many individuals pass directly from the status of dependence on their parents into parenthood with dependents of their own. However, this prolonged period of dependency also means that almost all the early and fundamental learning which man requires for the mastery of the tasks of life occurs under social conditions. There is much to be said for the old folk formula that the learning that occurs in the first seven years of the individual's life is the most fundamental of any that he will receive. Whatever else may happen to man thereafter, his first experiences are irrevocably social. Whatever he does thereafter is an addition to or a subtraction from these beginnings. The individual may become antisocial thereafter, but he can never become completely nonsocial.

In all higher creatures dependent on sexual reproduction for survival, sex supplies a second base of social interaction. In creatures with a rutting period the periodic receptivity of the females to sexual advance alternating with periods of neutrality gives a rhythm to social life. Often creatures with a rutting period alternate between two quite different forms of social life; between female and offspring in which the males have no part (bears, elk, etc.), and between the males (or bulls) and females (such as the elk harems).

[3] William Shakespeare, *The Tempest*, in *The Complete Works of Shakespeare*, ed. by George Lyman Kittredge (Boston: Ginn & Co., 1936), pp. 10–11.

However, among creatures without a rutting period the males and females remain continuously attractive to one another throughout the year. Whenever this occurs, males and females remain in more or less continuous association throughout life. Hence, along with dependency, sex remains one of the permanent reasons for the fact that the natural condition of man is one of society.

In the nineteenth century, under the influence of evolutionism and historicism, the search for origins dominated the students of institutions. With considerable plausibility it was argued that the oldest and most fundamental institution is the family. However, the critical question, "what kind of family?" was not so easy to answer. Two major theories were offered: that the original family was a harem dominated by a patriarch, and that the original family was a matriarchy consisting primarily of women and their children. If the above considerations have any value at all, it must be assumed that in the protohuman society both dependency and sexual dimensions were present from the beginning. The prolonged period of human dependency guaranteed the presence of young of varying ages, while the continuous sexual attractiveness of men and women to one another guaranteed the constant association of men and women.

Of course, what was being sought by the various theories of the origin of society and of the family was not the mere fact of society but the special form it once had. However, the form of society is not a product of natural conditions and of biological instincts, but of learning. Moreover, the possibility was continuously present, even at this early period, that any individual could potentially initiate new social forms which were adopted by others. *There was no single original form of the family or of human society.*

On the other hand, one cannot accept the third position frequently advocated by early social scientists that human society was originally *formless.* The fact that human behavior is intrinsically plastic and adaptable does not mean that the manner of handling dependency and sex was random at any given time and place. While plasticity guaranteed that solutions would vary, only trouble arises when these problems are solved in contradictory ways. A working social life becomes possible only to the degree that some way of settling the problems of dependency and sex can be stabilized. There are many possible ways in which men order their sexual life, but unless in any given case a relatively noncontradictory order of sexual relations is established, sex becomes explosive. When, for example, in present-day society the family sees prostitution as one of its natural enemies, it has correctly perceived that some alternative solutions to sexual problems can cause trouble.

Two major propositions of great importance for the theory of social change are established by the theory of social behavior:

1. *The individual and only the individual is the source of all innovation.* The fact that all patterned behavior is learned carries with it the possibility

that at any time any individual can potentially transform the social patterns in which he participates.

2. *While the biological conditions of dependency and sex virtually guarantee that the "natural" condition of man is one of society, no single form of social behavior can be conceived to be ultimate or basic. Social behaviorism rests uncompromisingly on the position that any given form of social life is relative to the natural and socio-cultural conditions of a given time and place.*

THE THEORY OF GROUPS AND INSTITUTIONS

As has been indicated, man is not born social; rather, he is made social by his experience. What he becomes is a product of his learning, but his early learning is so deeply anchored in social contexts that he will never remove the effects of society from his behavior. The general reason for the crystallization of social behavior into groups and institutions has already been indicated. *Groups* are systems or patterns of social behavior which arise when pluralities pursue their individual and collective aims in common. Groups are *not* something different from social behavior; they are merely special semi-stabilized regularities of social behavior. A number of men, for example, who form a hunting party establish a system of actions binding on each other (who will supply what in the way of camping equipment, food, liquor, etc., where they will go to hunt, whose car will be used, who will drive, and who will lie in wait along the game trails, and how they will divide the kill). This group is not something over and above the social behavior of the men involved; it *is* the way they have ordered their social behavior.

Institutions

Institutions,[4] which have been defined in many ways by other theories, are defined by social behaviorism as the standardized solutions to the problems of

[4] How complicated sociologists have made institutions appear may be seen from Hertzler's review of the definitions of institutions by L. T. Hobhouse, R. M. MacIver, L. von Wiese, R. C. Angel, C. H. Cooley, C. A. Ellwood, W. G. Sumner, and A. G. Keller, F. H. Allport, R. T. LaPiere, W. H. Hamilton, and C. Panuzio. From their various definitions Hertzler drew up a "composite conception": "Thus institutions are: (1) 'apparatus of social life,' 'modes or organs,' 'mechanisms,' 'instruments,' 'forms of order,' and in turn (2) 'part of the social structure,' 'units in the total social organization,' 'component parts of the total structure of a plurality pattern'; they are also, from another angle, (3) 'human achievements,' 'forms of culture,' 'culture complexes,' 'configurations,' 'accumulations of social capital,' (with the elements or 'traits' composing them occasionally set forth), and they have 'considerable permanence, universality'; (4) they meet 'some persistent need or want,' 'supply the fundamental needs of human beings,' 'are necessary to the satisfaction of basic needs,' 'center around the achievement of some human end or purpose,' 'do collectively the things that are right and proper with respect to some particular aspect of life,' 'guide the individual into modes of behavior which assist in one way or another in the maintenance of group life'; (5) they take the form of 'usages,' 'forms of social activity,' 'forms or conditions of procedure,' 'systems of activities,' 'systems of controls,' 'patterns of behavior,' 'Collective Action,' 'collective behavior,' 'patterns of social organization,' or, if social psychologically expressed, 'phase of the public mind,' 'states of mind,' 'configurations or segments of the behaviors of individuals,' 'patterns of attitudes,' 'conceptualizations

collective life. A group, whether it is a hunting party or a family, is a strategy of interhuman behavior, that is, a plan of action intended to achieve common objectives. A group is a concrete system of activities; a group institution is the solution to the problems of social life. The value of distinguishing between institutions and group rests on the analytical power gained by isolating a recurrent pattern from the varieties of specific factual instances in which it may be embedded. When one speaks of the institution of the family (or the hunting party), he is interested in isolating the solution to a specific range of social problems which could potentially be embodied in an indefinite number of specific groups in many of which special circumstances would impair or modify the pattern or solution.

When one is dealing with a creature whose ordered arrangements of social life are neither externally nor biologically fixed but determined by local circumstance, experience, and learning, the potential groups and institutions that may be formed are almost breath-taking in their infinite variety. Nevertheless, the basic task of the theory of groups and institutions is to determine the primary direction that the formation of groups and institutions may take. The social behavioristic theory of groups and institutions approaches this task from the standpoint of the general problems that face every system of social life. There are certain general problems of collective life which must be met if collective life is to continue at all. While one can expect infinite variety in the details of the pattern of collective life, these general problems remain, and may be grouped into three: socialization, the mastery of nature, and social control.

Socialization

If social life is to exist at all, biological and various other phenomena must be transposed into social form. The most important of all forms of socialization is the transformation of the biological individual into a social being. This is a basic function of the family. The modern family has experienced a

---

of behavior and attitudinal relationships'; (6) these are 'established and recognized,' 'incorporated within the social framework,' 'systematized,' 'instituted,' 'sanctioned,' 'have attained some measure of formalization and hence of permanence,' (7) 'by the authority of communities,' or 'by some common will,' and, finally, (8) they are concretely expressed in 'social habits,' 'overt conduct,' 'similar and reciprocal habits of individual behavior.'" Hertzler, for his own part, attempted a summary definition: "Our working definition follows: Social institutions are purposive, regulatory, and consequently primary cultural configurations, formed, unconsciously, and/or deliberately, to satisfy individual wants and social needs bound up with the efficient operation of any plurality of persons. They consist of codes, rules, and ideologies, unwritten and written, and essential symbolic organizational and material implementations. They evidence themselves socially in standardized and uniform practices and observances, and individually in attitudes and habitual behavior of persons. They are sustained and enforced by public opinion, acting both informally and formally, through specially devised agencies." J. O. Hertzler, *Social Institutions* (Lincoln, Nebraska: University of Nebraska Press, 1946), pp. 3–4.

wholesale loss of functions, but the elementary socialization of the child remains. The family carries out a profoundly important structuring of the child's emotional life. The capacity of the individual to depend upon others and to be depended upon by them is largely laid down in early family experience. Children raised in an orphanage seldom experience and, in turn, come to expect emotional ties as deep and unquestioned as those of children from the average family; as a result a limited capacity to enter into emotional relations with others frequently remains typical of the orphan throughout life. On the other hand, children from families of brutal, sadistic parents frequently develop into violent adults. Elementary socialization sets up the ground rules for emotional life.

While the socialization of the child is a particularly dramatic case of the transformation of materials and behavior into socially relevant form, it is not the only one. The facts of disease, illness, and accident, for example, are not in themselves social. Furthermore, they may seriously impair or reverse the efficiency of the individual. However, if the facts of disease, illness, and accident, or, at least, behaviors associated with them, are transposed into social form, society acquires a new and more profound significance for the individual. He turns to it in his time of individual stress. While the socialization of the behaviors and attitudes related to disease, illness, and the like is often a function of the family, a wide variety of specialized health and welfare institutions may develop to serve this purpose.

There were properties of disease and illness that were only incompletely understood before the rise of modern medicine. There were, and are, many other things beyond human knowledge and control. For example man seems to be unique among living creatures in his ability to form a conception of his own death. He is also unique in raising the questions as to where he came from, and where he is going, and why the world itself exists. Moreover, man's very society may generate tensions that it does not altogether resolve. The institution in which in the past these facts were most usually transformed into social forms was religion, which seems to arise out of the human requirement for emotional and conceptual closure with respect to all those problems he cannot otherwise explain. If these emotional and intellectual problems are left unresolved, they may operate like a corrosive agent on other social events. Religion is an institution which carries out the socialization of the events and feelings which arise within and without the sphere of the everyday events man is able to control.

The availability of man for other social activities in considerable measure rests on the success of institutions concerned with socialization.

The Mastery of Nature

As systems dependent on outside sources of energy, living organisms have some capacity to adjust to the intermittent character of the energies they receive from nature. However, the capacity of animal organisms to store up food energy in times of surplus and use it in times of scarcity is limited; the food quest tends to be a more or less continuous process. Furthermore, the number of organisms any given environment can support usually has relatively inflexible upper limits.

What environmental limitations can mean for human society is revealed by the disintegration of the deepest levels of socialization that has occasionally accompanied starvation and other crises. Cannibalism has, at times, appeared among shipwrecked sailors, among inmates of concentration camps, and among pioneer parties stranded in the American West. Also, among the Eskimo in the Arctic, where the margin of life is never far from environmental limits, cannibalism has occasionally occurred.[5]

More rarely the very abundance of nature places strains on society. Partners who have lived together during adversity, find that success destroys what hard times did not. A gold strike or unusual business success can awaken patterns of greed destructive of other social bonds.

In any case, if men are to live in society, the mastery of nature must necessarily become a collective problem. Social orders quickly develop norms to protect themselves against both situations of extreme scarcity and abundance of the material things of life. The lucky hunter may be expected to share his good fortune with the less fortunate. Persons with abundant harvests may be expected to hold parties or to give feasts and distribute gifts to others. In nearly all societies the establishment of foundations, founding of religious institutions, and acts of charity have been enjoined on the rich.

Successful conduct of the food quest is a precondition of collective as well as individual life. Inasmuch as both the scarcity and the abundance of the material things of life can disrupt social life, rules of behavior arise regulating behavior under these conditions. If there were no other reasons, the collective organization of man's relation to nature would proceed from these points. However, there are other reasons why this phase of collective life tends to become organized. Once socialization has been carried to a point where people enjoy each other's company (in fact, they may even come to feel lonely when they do not have it for long), they transform the food quest into a social occasion. Food-gathering, fishing, hunting are often carried on communally simply because it is more fun than performing the same operations alone.

When the mastery of nature is carried on as a communal enterprise, occasions repeatedly appear when obvious efficiencies are produced by a division of labor. While man has no fixed instincts, he has a most elastic capacity to adapt and extensive ability to transform adaptation into habit. Innovation may thus be quickly absorbed and fixed by the conserving complex of social-

[5] Robert F. Spencer, *The North Alaskan Eskimo*, Smithsonian Institution Bulletin 171 (Washington: U.S. Govt. Prt. Off., 1959), p. 95.

ization. William Graham Sumner was so impressed by this that he sought to found the whole of sociology on this process.[6] The mastery of nature is the core of an essential group of institutions of every community.

Social Control

Biological conditions predispose man to a minimum of social life, though they leave open the particular pattern this social life will assume. The task of staying live (the mastery of nature) is converted into a communal activity; accidents of local initiative and natural conditions in considerable measure determine the pattern. The life of any given community represents, so to speak, a selection of one or a few of the many possible patterns of social conduct.

If every possible way of carrying on social life were simultaneously pursued in a given society, the result would be chaos. The fragments of three good plans can bring chaos to a hunt, while the consistent conduct of a single poor plan may yield some measure of success. A military manoeuver that sought to achieve its results by direct vigorous assault and stealthy infiltration simultaneously would probably bring about its own defeat.

Every society faces the task of upholding one or a few of the patterns of social life against the competition of alternatives. Concretely this means that every society must discipline its members: persuading them to observe the accepted forms and dissuading them from pursuing conflicting objections. One of the inescapable tasks of every society is social control.

Social control is not merely a negative task. Life evolves in various events, encounters, and incidents: families are founded, houses are built, fields are plowed, animals are domesticated, military actions are undertaken. Collective decisions are made and executed. The fundamental content of social control is the formation and support of decisions binding on the collectivity.

As in the case of the other basic problem areas of social life, a great number of specialized social institutions may arise to carry out particular phases of social control: status groups form, uniting some members of the society into close-knit units and separating them from others, police forces develop to preserve internal order, military forces develop to repel interference from without and to move against other societies; systems of law, lawyers, judges, courts, and the like develop to interpret and apply the sanctioned rules of a society; governments of various kinds appear specifically endowed with extensive decision-making powers binding on the community as a whole.

The theory of institutions locates the primary areas where social life is unavoidably organized into stable patterns. A number of propositions relevant to the theory of social change are supplied by the social behavioristic theory of groups and institutions. Among them are the following three:

[6] William Graham Sumner, *Folkways* (Boston: Ginn & Co., 1906).

3. *The three main areas of social life that are inescapably organized into groups, in which the solutions to collective problems are embedded, are socialization, the mastery of nature, and social control.*

4. *There are no grounds for assuming that the solutions to the problems in any one of these areas are any more fundamental than the solutions to those in any other.*

5. *The established solutions to any given institutional area define both the circumstances of socially significant innovation in a particular society and the areas of resistance to innovation.*

THE THEORY OF SOCIETY OR COMMUNITY

In the present context the concepts *society* and *community* are used interchangeably, though there is value for some purposes in distinguishing between them as communities of maximum and of lesser comprehensiveness. We can thus distinguish between American society and its communities.[7] A *society* (or *community*) is a complete system of social interaction, that is, a set of social groups sufficient to solve for a plurality of individuals all the problems of collective life falling in the compass of a normal year and in the compass of a normal life.

The problem with which the theory of society attempts to cope concerns the interadjustment of the institutions of one area of social life to influences arising out of another. Under some circumstances these relations of interadjustment may lead to the formation of a distinct way of life. The general principles of community formation are: *stabilization*, *consistency*, and *completeness*. The theory of community locates further sources of encouragement and resistance to institutional innovations beyond the resistance generated by an established institution to alternatives.

Institutional Stabilization

In the various areas critical to life, recurrent human needs guarantee the occurrence of activity. So long as needs remain unfulfilled, activity continues unless frustrated by a force stronger than the need itself. Man's activity, like that of any creature, largely ceases with the satisfaction of the need concerned. However, in the normal course of events, after a time the need arises once again, arousing the activity-pattern of search and satisfaction.

The fact that man lacks the biological foundations of instincts gives an experimental property to behavior arising in response to human needs. It also makes possible a wide range of behavioral solutions to the problem presented by the need. However, as already noted, the variety of possible solutions does not imply that they will always be pursued at once and at the same

[7] Don Martindale, *American Social Structure* (New York: Appleton-Century-Crofts, 1960), pp. 132 ff.

time. Along with an extensive capacity to adapt, man has an amazing capacity to learn and to remember. Hence when a need recurs, one of the most natural of things is to attempt the same solution that worked the last time it arose. Institutions are learned modes of behavior stabilized in habits. When the habit is not merely an individual affair but a collective affair (custom), the stability it represents is many times reinforced.

One must assume that in human society at all times in every major area of behavior, the process of institutional stabilization is at work. Nuclei of successful behaviors are continuously being stabilized into habits.

Interinstitutional Consistency

Social life thus tends to crystallize into stable forms. Once established, the forms that emerge become one of the major conditions for further development. The behavioral landscape, if one may use so crude an image, is not an unmarred plain, but is plotted and pierced by established forms. Further activity must take them into account, much as travelers might take into account such topographical phenomena as rivers, swamps, and mountains. By and large, actions consistent with the established forms are favored over inconsistent ones. Hence in all main institutional spheres rays of consistency radiate from the established solutions to collective problems like waves from the impact point of a stone in a quiet pond.

Furthermore, the time must come sooner or later when the waves of consistent behavior radiating from the solution of the problems of collective life in one area intersect with the behaviors radiating from others. When this occurs, serious interference of one set of behaviors with the other may result. Such interference may be experienced with intense anxiety. For example, a man may discover that his religious ethic and his business ethic are in radical conflict; he may experience his situation as presenting the alternatives of religious damnation or business failure. Most persons, in the long run, are not happy with concealment of the business of the right hand from that of the left. The result is usually to transform business ethic to conform to the religious model or the commercialization of religion. Sumner long ago described the general process as a strain of improvement and consistency in the folkways:

> The folkways, being ways of satisfying needs, have succeeded more or less well, and therefore have produced more or less pleasure or pain. Their quality always consists in their adaptation to the purpose. If they were imperfectly adapted and unsuccessful, they produced pain, which drove men on to learn better. The folkways are, therefore, (1) subject to a strain of improvement towards better adaptation of means to ends, as long as the adaptation is so imperfect that pain is produced. They are also (2) subject to a strain to consistency with each other, because they all answer their several purposes with less friction and antagonism when they cooperate and support each other. The forms of industry, the forms of the family, the notions of property, the constructions of rights, and

> the types of religion show the strain of consistency with each other through the whole history of civilization.[8]

At times the interrelation between the patterns of some one institutional area and the others is conceived as the central fact in social life (for example, the Marxian theory of the primacy of economical phenomena). However, there are no *a priori* reasons for viewing the interrelations of economic and religious behaviors to be more fundamental than, for example, that of political and religious behavior. Patterns are established in particular institutional areas first; they are related to those of other areas later and secondarily.

Institutional Completeness

The stabilization of the solutions of the problems of an institutional sphere and the growth of consistency between the institutions of one area of life and another have quite definite limits. The system of institutions tends to grow until it forms a complete set or, as it is ordinarily formulated, a complete way of life.

There is no mystery as to what constitutes a complete set of institutions. It is a set sufficiently comprehensive to carry out socialization, the mastery of nature, and social control in a manner permitting the community to survive and endure through time. Whenever the basic institutions do not or cannot perform their fundamental functions, the very existence of the community is threatened. Monastic communities and religious communities resting on the disapproval of sex, for example, cannot be self-recruited systems of social life, but can continue to survive only by drawing members from the wider society. Since the Shaker communities, for example, did not permit normal sex relations, preventing the self-recruitment of members by birth, they disappeared just as soon as there was a breakdown of effective recruitment from the outside.

The effect of social arrangements with deficient socialization is revealed by some forms of slavery (for example, those in the American South and Imperial Rome). These slave systems rested on a radical destruction of family life and the reorganization of slave labor in barracks under overseers. Such slave systems were never self-recruited, for despite often desperate expedients, slaves refused to bring children into such a world. In the American South, for example, some slave masters sought to breed slaves; some offered female slaves their freedom if they had sufficient numbers of children (making freedom the price of their children); some slave owners even undertook to breed their female slaves themselves (which meant the ultimate enslaving of their own children). However, all such devices broke down, and in the end such slave systems were dependent for their existence on slave raids to supply the slave markets.[9]

[8] Sumner, *op. cit.*, pp. 5–6.
[9] See Don Martindale, *American Social Structure*, *op. cit.*, pp. 156 ff.

The extreme kind of disaster to social life that can be represented by the failure of the mastery of nature is revealed in the famine of St. Lawrence Island.[10] In the winter of 1879–1880 more than a thousand people perished on St. Lawrence Island because of a supply of whiskey provided by some white traders. The Eskimo, who were unused to liquor, went on a debauch during the period when they normally hunted the herds of walrus that pass the island during their annual migration. By the time the people had exhausted the stock of whiskey, the walrus migration was over, and winter had set in, leaving the Eskimo without their normal food supply. When the traders returned next spring, they learned about the grim sequence. To the effects of starvation were added the ravages of disease. Though in one village there were more than two hundred dead adults, there were no bodies of children. Other villages displayed a similar lack of bodies of children, and all evidence pointed to a recurrence of the cannibalism known among the Eskimo of old. The children, presumably, had been eaten.

The failure of social control may expose a community to schism from within and annihilation from without. The origin of the disaster of St. Lawrence Island actually began as failure of social control. It may be assumed that had there been greater familiarity with the properties of whiskey, indulgence would never have been permitted to work such disaster.

There is another and simpler conception as to what constitutes the completeness of a set of institutional problems, though it adds up to the same thing, that is, solutions to the problems of socialization, mastery of nature, and social control forming a consistent way of life. A set of institutions is complete when it will carry a plurality of individuals through a normal year and through a normal life. The problems of one year are sufficiently similar to those of another to permit one to rely on the same general solutions to life issues for each. Nature itself imposes a kind of cycle on human social life. By the end of a year the same general problems are repeated. Similarly, different kinds of social requirements are imposed on the individual and his fellows at different stages in the organic cycle of life. The dealings of a plurality of individuals with any single member form a kind of cycle from birth to death. With other newborn individuals, the cycle starts again.

The social-behavioristic theory of community provides the basis for understanding a number of types of social change that have mistakenly been generalized far beyond their proper spheres. Moreover, it provides the basis for comprehending the natural terminal points of these same types of changes.

The Marxian theory of social change rested on the notion that the formulas for the mastery of nature (relations of production) were the primary cause

[10] Edward W. Nelson, "The Eskimo about Bering Strait," *18th Annual Report*, Bureau of American Ethnology, Part 1, Washington, D.C., 1899.

of developments in other areas. Political structures, for example, were conceived as a kind of superstructure resting on an economic foundation. The modern state has been described by some Marxians as the executive arm of the *bourgeoisie*. However, the theory of community formation just reviewed indicates beyond any doubt that a range of interadjustments may proceed from any institutional area. There are, to be sure, times and places where developments in the mastery of nature may assume the lead in forcing adjustments elsewhere.

When Weber carried out his brilliant study of *The Protestant Ethic and the Spirit of Capitalism*, he traced a series of influences from the sphere of religion to economics. While he did not intend to present these findings as the sole form of institutional interadjustment, some persons, impressed by the dramatic demonstration of partial alternative to Marxism, tended to view Weber's study as a decisive answer to Marx. However, if one were to trace all institutional interadjustments to religion, he would make the same type of mistake as orthodox Marxism. Moreover, sometimes the primary flow of influence is from the field of social control. Under most circumstances some influences arise from all the major institutional areas and some modifications are brought about in each because of the others.

The social-behavioristic theory of community formation also provides a basis for understanding the natural terminal points in the interadjustment of the major areas of social life. It must be assumed, in the first place, that social life achieves its efficiencies by the appropriateness to their problems of the groups and institutions in the areas of their origin. When the forces of community formation set in motion the interarrangement of the various institutional spheres, this offsets the efficiency of institutions in the areas of their origin. It is sometimes assumed that community formation automatically brings a higher level of efficiency to everyone. This is not necessarily true. The lower limit on the interadjustment of institutional spheres is provided by an impairment of institutions to an extent that they cannot perform their primary functions.

On the other hand, there is an upper as well as a lower limit to the process of interinstitutional adjustment. It does not continue indefinitely. Once a full style of life has been established, the process of interinstitutional adjustment finds a normal stopping place. The theory of community formation thus establishes the following two propositions:

6. *The processes of social life inescapably lead to the interadjustment of the main institutional spheres to one another*. Contrary to some theories of social and cultural change, the main wave of such interinstitutional development may proceed from any of the basic areas.

7. *The social and cultural changes accompanying community formation have lower limits in the impairment of the basic efficiency of the institution and upper limits in the completion of a community's style of life.*

THE THEORY OF CIVILIZATION

By *culture* the social behaviorists mean *all* the forms that arise in the course of social interaction. While social institutions form an important category of culture, they hardly exhaust the stock of cultural forms. Even a basic social institution is capable of sustaining many forms, the relation of which is, at best, indirect to the solution of collective problems. Language, for example, is the oldest and most fundamental means of solving the problem of social control. Without language, the flow of information from the members of the social group which is needed to implement collective decision-making is most whimsical. Without language, it is almost inconceivable to visualize the transmission of any but the most rudimentary decisions to the members of the group. At the same time, once in existence, language is capable of development in many ways of only incidental significance to information assembly and decision execution. One can use language to pass the time and to divert. One can employ it for the construction of jokes, poems, stories, and myths. To reduce all such language forms to socialization, the mastery of nature, and social control is to eclipse much of their significance.

In addition to social institutions, culture includes such things as dance forms, musical systems, forms and style, literary forms, dramatic forms, architectural forms, the styles and forms of the graphic and plastic arts, thought systems (such as logic and science), philosophies, myths, etc. And just as there are forces in social life which lead men to form communities, there are also forces which lead men to transform their ideal life into integrated systems. A *civilization* is an integrated system of culture, a system of man's ideal life.

While the principles of civilization formation have not been explored with the same degree of fullness as those of community formation, three are provisionally discernible: *playfulness*, *aesthetic receptivity*, and the tendency to transfer unsolved social issues to the cultural sphere, or *sublimation*.

Playfulness

Playfulness is a property of the behavior of all higher creatures, a property which increases in importance to the degree that the amount of behavior which is committed on an instinctive basis declines. Unfortunately, most students of play in the past felt compelled either to find some sort of immediate practical purpose in play (such as a practice of the instincts) or to reduce it by one means or another to the instincts, either by finding it to be a kind of recapitulation of the behavior of the race or to be a special instinct—the instinct to play.

There is considerable advantage, however, in treating playfulness as a basic or nonreducible component of the behavior of the higher creatures which emerges whenever the sphere of the instincts is narrowed but the energy for action remains. The advantages accruing to a creature with a fixed scheme of instincts are possession of a box of tricks for survival without having to learn them. The disadvantage of a fixed scheme of instincts, however, is to have a good part of behavior so committed to some special set of conditions that it may be difficult to adapt to environments which vary basically from the one appropriate to his instincts. The world has tended to glide into the sphere of these playful creatures destined for plasticity.

With each loss of instinctive predetermination, the living creature gains a field of uncommitted energy potential. Behavior in this area will automatically be semirandom, experimental, and gradually organized on a foundation of learned habits. To feel compelled to describe the area of behavior so won from the instincts as in some sense instinctive is to miss everything distinctive in it. Its peculiar property is availability for variation.

The higher the creature is along the biological path which leads toward man, the wider the sphere of play and the longer the period in the creature's life when it can play. Normally as these spheres of energy potential are habitually committed, the occurrence of playful activity declines. In man, the spheres available for playful activity are wider than among other creatures, and play activity is almost coextensive with life itself.

The most fundamental of all problems in accounting for the rise of a civilization is the source of the basic stock of cultural forms a civilization synthesizes. As a consequence of playfulness every society comes to possess such a stock of forms over and beyond those directed to the immediate solution of the basic problems of collective life. The comprehensive and durable principle of *playfulness* as the basis of human behavior accounts for the apparently endless figurations constantly cast up in every sphere of human social life.

Aesthetic Receptivity

As in the case of playfulness, there have been numerous attempts to establish aesthetic receptivity on an instinctive or, at least, a physiological basis. As in the case of playfulness, however, all such attempts have failed.

The essential property of aesthetic sensitivity lies in the capacity to discern the form or pattern in events, in the appreciation of such form or pattern, and in the development of preferences for some arrangements over others. Play and courtship (in which the display of form and pattern has a role) have seemed by many students to be natural sources of aesthetic sensitivity. However, if one were to search for biological anticipations of the emerging aesthetic sense of higher creatures, it would seem more primitively rooted in the capacity of many simple creatures to respond to the patterns of experience (the Gestalt psychologists, for example, have demonstrated the response of creatures to patterned wholes). The capacity to discern the order in experience is deep and ancient.

Just as the higher creatures possess a generalized capacity to respond without the instinctive commitment to a special kind of response, the higher creatures possess a capacity to discriminate the forms and patterns of experience without the advance instinctive commitment of its discriminatory power to a restricted set. Perhaps it would be better to describe the higher creature as possessing a general capacity for discrimination. The content of its particular discriminations is learned.

Wherever people are found they enjoy playing with the forms of experience for their own sake. A sense of excitement and satisfaction accompanies the transformation of unordered areas of experience into a unity. A varied internally differentiated unity may be experienced as a dramatic event of heightened intensity. While all attempts to demonstrate the presence of an inherent aesthetic sense have failed, some learned aesthetic discriminations form part of the life of every people.

Aesthetic receptivity plays a role with respect to the general synthesis of cultural forms parallel to that played by the principle of consistency in the formation of communities. In fact, the principle of *consistency* is in some measure a social manifestation of a people's evolving aesthetic sensitivity. Aesthetic sensitivity is in a sense the play-form of consistency. However, there seems to be no good reason for reducing aesthetic receptivity to *playfulness*, though it operates with the forms that playfulness casts up. When it is able, it transforms them into dramatic sequences.

Sublimation

It may at first seem startling to take a concept which has become domesticated in its application to individual psychology and to employ it for the formation of civilization. However, culture does not create itself; it is created by individuals. Civilization, which is a system of culture, can only arise from and within the activities of individual persons. Culture and civilization are merely ways in which individuals work out the problems of their experience.

Among the persons who have developed the idea of sublimation in recent times, Nietzsche and Freud are particularly important. Nietzsche did not hesitate to trace many of the highest manifestations of culture to emotions generally viewed as base.

> Almost everything that we call "higher culture" is based upon the spiritualising and intensifying of *cruelty*—this is my thesis; the "wild beast" has not been slain at all, it lives, it flourishes, it has only been—transfigured. That which constitutes the painful delight of tragedy is cruelty; that which operates agreeably in so-called tragic sympathy, and at the basis even of everything sublime, up to the highest and most delicate thrills of metaphysics, obtains its sweetness solely from the intermingled ingredient of cruelty. What the Roman enjoys in the arena, the Christian in the ecstasies of the cross, the Spaniard at the sight of faggot and stake, or of the bull-fight, the present-day Japanese who presses his way to the tragedy, the workman of the Parisian suburbs who has a homesickness for bloody revolutions, the Wagnerienne who, with unhinged will, "undergoes" the performance of "Tristan and Isolde"—what

> all these enjoy, and strive with mysterious ardour to drink in, is the philtre of the Great Circe "cruelty."[11]

Walter Kaufmann has offered the following summary of the employment of sublimation by Nietzsche:

> Nietzsche believed that a sexual impulse, for example, could be channeled into a creative spiritual activity, instead of being fulfilled directly. Similarly, the barbarian's desire to torture his foe can be sublimated into the desire to defeat one's rival, say, in the Olympic contests; it can even be sublimated into the rivalry of the tragedians who vie with each other for the highest prize, or into the efforts of a Plato to write more beautifully than the poets—and the entire Socratic dialectic could be constructed as a sublimation of the same ancient striving to overwhelm one's foe.[12]

Freud, the most famous modern to develop the concept of sublimation, utilized it primarily to account for the transformation of sex, which he conceived to be fundamentally unsocial, into social forms.

> One amongst these processes serving as protection against illness arising from want has reached a particular significance in the development of culture. It consists in the abandonment, on the part of the sexual impulse, of an aim previously found either in the gratification of a component-impulse or in the gratification incidental to reproduction, and the adoption of a new aim—which new aim, though genetically related to the first, can no longer be regarded as sexual, but must be called social in character. We call this process *sublimation* by which we subscribe to the general standard which estimates social aims above sexual (ultimately selfish) aims. Incidentally, sublimation is merely a special case of the connections existing between sexual impulses and other asexual ones.[13]

In a famous passage Freud utilized the concept of sublimation to explain the psychology of the artist and the creation of all artistic forms. He argued that the capacity to withstand neurotic illness in considerable measure "depends upon the *amount* of undischarged libido that a person can hold freely suspended, and upon how large a portion of it he can deflect from sexual to non-sexual goals in sublimation." However, at this very point, the threshold of complete abandonment to neurotic phantasies, there is a way back to reality.

> The artist has also an introverted disposition and has not far to go to become neurotic. He is one who is urged on by instinctual needs which are too clamorous; he longs to attain to honour, power, riches, fame, and the love of women; but he lacks the means of achieving these gratifications. So, like any other with an unsatisfied longing, he turns away from reality and transfers all his interest and all his libido, too, on to the

[11] Friedrich Nietzsche, *Beyond Good and Evil*, 229, in *The Philosophy of Nietzsche* (New York: The Modern Library, n.d.), p. 535.

[12] Walter Kaufmann, *Nietzsche* (New York: Meridian Books, 1959), p. 190.

[13] Sigmund Freud, *A General Introduction to Psychoanalysis*, trans. by Joan Riviere (Garden City, N.Y., Garden City Publishing Co., 1943), p. 302.

> creation of his wishes in the life of phantasy, from which the way might readily lead to neurosis. There must be many factors in combination to prevent this becoming the whole outcome of his development; it is well known how often artists in particular suffer from partial inhibition of their capacities through neurosis. Probably their constitution is endowed with a powerful capacity for sublimation and with a certain flexibility in the repressions determining the conflict. But the way back to reality is found by the artist thus: He is not the only one who has a life of phantasy; the intermediate world of phantasy is sanctioned by general human consent, and every hungry soul looks to it for comfort and consolation.[14]

The artist understands the way to elaborate his daydreams so that they satisfy the phantasies of many, giving them the satisfaction of their own unconscious sources of pleasure. The artist then receives the gratitude and patronage of many, and by means of his phantasies wins honor, power, and love of women for himself.

That process of sublimation which Nietzsche discerned in the transmutation of socially unacceptable forms of cruelty into forms of high culture, and which Freud discerned in the transmutation of socially unacceptable sexual inclinations into artistic creations are only special manifestations of a general process operating throughout man's social life, constituting one of the primary civilization-forming processes.

All problems arising in the sphere of man's social life, which are not solved in the course of his social behavior, tend to be transferred to the ideal sphere. The constructive forces of the individual's nature then supply ideal solutions to them. These processes are particularly important in connection with community formation. Communities form by the reconstitution of institutions to conform to one another. However, in the reconstitution of institutions their role in the spheres of their origin is modified to respond to influences arising in other institutional spheres. The efficiency of the institution is often impaired. The dynamism a community presents is in some measure tied up with the tensions between single institutions and the whole.

Thus a community is formed only by fixing some pattern and making it binding on the whole. One cannot construct a way of life without curtailing the independence and impairing the original efficiency of at least some of the parts. There are always alternatives, always things left over. The problems represented by these materials—by the principle of *sublimation*—are transferred to ideal and artistic spheres. It is because these materials left over are always partly in opposition to the social formula, that, when they become basic subject matter of art, they place the artist in tension with his times. The civilizational synthesis brought about by the artist, the philosopher, and other workers with cultural forms complements the society (partly in accord and partly in opposition) in which it arises. Again for the theory of social and cultural change, the following propositions are established:

[14] *Ibid.*, pp. 327–328.

8. *The playfulness and aesthetic receptivity of man leads to the multiplication of cultural forms beyond the practical social requirements of their societies.* Creativity always exceeds social requirements.

9. *The transfer of unsolved problems to ideal and artistic spheres in accord with the principle of sublimation keys the civilization to the society around, against which it arises.*

THE THEORY OF SOCIAL AND CULTURAL CHANGE

The theory of social and cultural change attempts to explain the formation and destruction of social and cultural forms and systems. For social behaviorism, the key to these problems always comes down in the end to the creative activities of individuals and the factors which may speed or stay them.

Social behaviorism is not theoretically committed to the view that the products of the creative activity of individuals are necessarily progressive in a unilinear manner, cyclical, or random. Rather, some of the products of its activities fit each of these categories. Some cultural products have been cumulative over long periods (like science and technology) and may continue to accumulate. Some social and cultural changes are cyclical (particularly the formation and destruction of communities and civilizations). Some are random (for example, the responses to natural catastrophes), or unique (for example, the overall drift of human history).

Social behaviorism assumes that lawful regularities are present in at least some social and cultural changes, and the discovery of these is best made in the study of cyclical social occurrences. The formation and destruction of societies and civilizations are thus its ideal subject matter.

In cyclical social and cultural changes the individual—potentially any individual—is innovator. However, since the formation of communities and civilizations represents a regrouping of institutions or of cultural forms around a central point, those individuals who innovate at this core come critically into focus. The core innovators in the formation of social and cultural systems are the intellectuals of the society or civilization in question.

Social and cultural change, on the other hand, is never the exclusive problem of the intellectual. Basic social requirements force men individually and in concert to solve the problems of socialization, mastery of nature, and social control. Action in any one of these areas is a primary social phenomenon, occurring initially without reference to what happens in other areas. However, a train of consequences flows from action in any one of these basic spheres. The solution to the mastery of nature affects socialization and social control, and vice versa. Various innovations may appear in any given area; established behavior in the other two areas operates as a receptive and restrictive matrix for them.

Even relatively simple societies recognize a differentiation of leaders in terms of primary spheres of competence. The sphere of competence of the technical innovator is in the mastery of nature. Tribal communities recognize the talents of an able arrowhead-maker, bow-maker; they adopt the invention of a superior kind of outrigger, or sail, or knife. Tribal communities also recognize persons especially qualified in the sphere of socialization: moral or traditional authorities, priests, and the like. At least occasionally, the tribe recognizes the primary wielder of social control, even if he is only the provisional war chief.

Occasionally, simple formulas have been offered for social and cultural change by designating only one area of collective life as important. The culture-lag theory, for example, places primary importance on the mastery of nature. It assumes that innovations of a technical nature always outrun those of other aspects of culture. This, it has been argued, is the primary source of the problems of modern man: he carries a Stone Age morality and social life into the modern scientific laboratory.

The critical limitation of the cultural-lag theory is its failure to take account of the unavoidable need of human society to resolve the problems of socialization and social control as well as the mastery of nature. It makes the mechanical inventor the sole agent of social and cultural change. In this it even misses the significant fact that any given technology may itself act as a brake on alternatives. In the ancient Roman world, for example, the existence of the plantation resting on slavery prevented the introduction or systematic use of animal and mechanical power for routine work. By contrast the medieval economy resting on serfdom was essentially more technologically progressive—it encouraged the use of the wind and water mills, the invention of the horse collar and nailed horseshoe, and such devices as the spinning wheel and wheelbarrow.

The failure to take account of the potential importance of socialization and social control for the flowering of civilization leaves out of account the significant fact that civilizations have flowered and died without any essential change in the basic techniques for the mastery of nature. In the area of the Indus valley, the civilization which perished for unknown reasons left behind various industrial and economic techniques basic to it, which continued to be practiced into the twentieth century. Similarly, on the same ground where the Maya civilization once flourished, the same industrial and economic forms continue to be employed. In these cases the flowering of civilization cannot be explained in terms of the devices for the mastery of nature but those critical to socialization and social control. Similarly, the brilliant flowering of Arabic civilization rested not on any fundamental change in the mastery of nature, but on masterful developments in the areas of socialization and social control.

One must not, to be sure, underestimate the role in social and cultural change of the mechanical inventor, technical innovator, and organizer, for some level of mastery of nature is a foundation of every community, be it only the pastoral nomadism of the mountain peoples which sustained the

Lamaism of Tibet. However, alongside the inventor and technical expert appear various types of innovators in the fields of social control (politicians, statesmen, officials, administrators, military leaders) and innovators in the field of socialization (moralists, religious leaders, theologians, teachers, philosophers, opinion-makers, propagandists, publicists, and the intellectuals).

The roots of the intellectual seems to be in the area of socialization, for he is fundamentally a teacher, philosopher, artist, and moral counsellor. However, as is dramatically revealed by the invention of writing by the priest-intellectuals of the ancient city, the work and technologies of the intellectual may bring about vast transformations in the areas of mastery of nature and social control. There is some justification for the formula that the pen is mightier than the sword—a formula which has led many a political leader to seek to enlist the intellectual in his cause. At other times and places the intellectual has fused elements across the lines of socialization and the mastery of nature. The combination of institutional elements which enters into the definition of the intellectual role is unique to each community form.

The nature of the role of the intellectual and its unique shaping in each community forms the implicit point of view of one of the major studies of the modern intellectual. Julien Benda[15] has maintained this in his much discussed study, *The Betrayal of the Intellectuals* (*La Trahison des Clercs*).[16]

Benda draws a distinction between those impulses which lead men to pursue the things of the spirit and political passions which lead men to "rise up against other men." The chief political emotions are thought to be those manifest as "racial passions, class passions, and national passions."[17] Benda believes that such political emotions affect a larger number of men at present than at any other time in history. These emotions have, he feels, attained such new coherence as to have become a "habit of discipline."

> How much more uniformity is shown now than a hundred years ago by the emotions known as anti-Semitism, anti-Clericalism, and Socialism.[18]

There has been a condensation of political passions into a small number of simple hates, representing a conquest of modern times.[19] The major form of the organization of political passion is patriotism,[20] which, with its notion of a war of cultures, is an invention of modern times.

> Speaking generally, it may be said that national passions owing to the fact that they are now exerted by plebeian minds, assume the character of

[15] Julien Benda was a Jew by birth (b. 1867) who began his career with some philosophical reflections on the Dreyfus affair (*Dialogues à Byzance*, 1898). Further ethical reflections were contained in *Les Cahiers de la Quinzaine*, 1910. He is also noted for his philosophical and literary criticism of Bergson's philosophy. His greatest work is *La Trahison des Clercs* (first published in Paris in 1927).

[16] Trans. by Richard Aldington (Boston, Beacon Press, 1955).

[17] *Ibid.*, p. 1.

[18] *Ibid.*, p. 3.

[19] *Ibid.*, p. 5.

[20] *Ibid.*, p. 15.

> *mysticism,* of a religious adoration almost unknown in these passions in the practical minds of the great nobles.[21]

Nationalistic passion has come to be the framework of all other political passions, the most powerful of which today are the movement against the Jew, the movement of the possessing classes against the proletariat, and the movement of the champions of authority against the democrats.[22]

Finally, Benda observes that the political passions of race, class, party, and nation have undergone an unusual process of perfection today, for every political passion is supplied with a whole network of doctrines, the sole aim of which is to demonstrate the supreme value of its action. Our age has thus become a time of the "intellectual organization of political hatreds."[23] Whether it be anti-Semitism, Pan-Germanism, French monarchism, or Socialism, each view is developed as a particular form of morality, intelligence, sensibility, literature, philosophy, or artistic apprehension. Every political movement claims to be in line with evolution or historical development; every one claims to be founded on science and to be in accord with precise observation of the facts. All are supplied with the apparatus of ideology claiming supreme value in the name of science or historical necessity. Our present age, Benda concludes, is essentially an age of politics.

Benda finds all this to be of fundamental importance for the role of the intellectual who in the past always stood out in contrast to the layman. By laymen he means not only the masses (whether *bourgeois* or proletarian), but kings, ministers, political leaders, in short, all those persons whose function is the pursuit of material interests and whose actions are systematically realistic. In the past such laymen stood apart from intellectuals—Thomas Aquinas, Roger Bacon, Galileo, Rabelais, Montaigne, Descartes, Racine, Pascal, Leibniz, Kepler, Huyghens, Newton, Voltaire, Buffon, and Montesquieu. The intellectuals of the past were defined as persons whose activity was not directed to the pursuit of practical aims, but who sought intellectual, artistic, or spiritual values for their own sake. They include not only persons engaged in the disinterested pursuit of knowledge, like Leonardo da Vinci and Goethe, but moralists looking frankly at the conflict of human egoism—Erasmus, Kant, and Renan—advocating an abstract principle superior and opposed to such passions.

All this, Benda maintains, is changing in our time. The intellectuals have begun to play the game of political passions. They have adopted political passions as their own (illustrated by Mommsen, Treitschke, Ostwald, Brunetière, Barrès, Lemaître, Péguy, Maurras, d'Annunzio, and Kipling). While in the past the intellectuals opposed the realism of the laymen, today they have entered its service. Even the clergy, in wartime, promote the national cause in the face of shocking excesses of the nation. The modern

[21] *Ibid.,* p. 17.
[22] *Ibid.,* p. 18.
[23] *Ibid.,* p. 21.

intellectual is characterized by xenophobia or hatred of the man from the outside; he attempts to relate the forms of his individual mind to that of the national mind. German science is contrasted with French science; Aryan thought, science, philosophy, art, and music are contrasted with Jewish types.

The intellectuals are said, at present, to bring their political passions to bear even on their intellectual activities, to play the game of political passions with doctrines, to praise the attachment to the particular and denounce the feeling of the universal; to praise attachment to the practical and denounce a feeling for the spiritual. In Benda's summary:

> If I look at contemporary humanity from the point of view of its moral state as revealed by its political life, I see (a) A mass in which realist passion in its two chief forms—class passion, national passion—has attained a degree of consciousness and organization hitherto unknown; (b) A body of men who used to be in opposition to the realism of the masses, but who now not only do not oppose it, but adopt it, proclaim its grandeur and morality; in short, a humanity which has abandoned itself to realism with a unanimity, an absence of reserve, a sanctification of its passion unexampled in history.[24]

Benda feels that the intellectual has been assimilated into the political structure to such an extent that the man of science, artist, and philosopher are as much attached to their nations as the day laborer and merchant. All humanity, including the intellectuals, has become an association of laymen.

It is in the cyclical processes of community and civilization formation that the intellectual becomes particularly important. While the intellectual is never the sole source of change, his peculiarity is that of system innovator. Though his primary institutional location is most often in some branch of socialization, his special tasks include acting as a representative and justifier of the whole. He presents a peculiarly appropriate vantage point to analyze the events in the societal or civilizational system.

SUMMARY

The primary hope for a new attack on the problems of social and cultural change seems to lie with social behaviorism, the view that meaningful social action consists of the primary social reality and that all other forms of social life must be interpreted in terms of social behavior. Since social and cultural change attempts to account for the creation and destruction of social and cultural forms and systems, it is important to take account of the manner in which these are explained before raising the problems of a theory of change.

The core of social behaviorism is its theory of social interactionism, which treats all social behavior as learned rather than instinctive. However, though this entails the view that man is made rather than born social, the nature of

[24] *Ibid.*, p. 143.

human dependency and sex virtually guarantees that man's natural condition is social. Within this social life the theory of groups and institutions accounts for the rise of structures. To social behaviorism, *socialization, mastery of nature*, and *social control* are the inescapable problems of collective life, to solve which structures grow up. However, over and beyond the formation of groups and institutions, three basic principles—*stabilization, consistency*, and *completeness*—are at work leading to the fusion of groups and institutions into a more or less systematic way of life or community. Meanwhile, the principles of *playfulness, aesthetic receptivity*, and *sublimation* lead to the multiplication of social forms outside practical social spheres and their systematization around the unsolved problems are transferred from practical-social to ideal and artistic spheres.

While social behaviorism is not confined exclusively to the linear, evolutionary, cyclical, or random theory of change, it finds some of its most important problems in the analysis of those social processes which are cyclical (community and civilization). These social and cultural changes, like all others (including those stimulated by external physical and demographic factors) are the work of individuals. The natural object of study of these cyclical changes are the core individuals—the intellectuals—primarily responsible for bringing these systems into being, making them work, and justifying them.

SELECTED BIBLIOGRAPHY

Benda, Julien, *The Betrayal of the Intellectuals*, trans. by Richard Aldington (Boston: The Beacon Press, 1955).

Hertzler, J. O., *Social Institutions* (Lincoln: University of Nebraska Press, 1946).

Martindale, Don, *The Nature and Types of Sociological Theory* (Boston: Houghton Mifflin, 1960).

Mead, George H., *Mind, Self, and Society* (Chicago: University of Chicago Press, 1934).

Moore, Wilbert E., "A Reconsideration of Theories of Social Change," *The American Sociological Review*, Vol. 25, No. 6, December, 1960, pp. 810–817.

Weber, Max, *The Theory of Social and Economic Organization*, trans. by A. M. Henderson and Talcott Parsons (New York: Oxford University Press, 1947).

Znaniecki, Florian, *The Social Role of the Man of Knowledge* (New York: Columbia University Press, 1940).

3

SOCIETY, CIVILIZATION, AND THE INTELLECTUAL

THE MOST GENERAL hypotheses of the social-behavioristic theory of social and cultural change are: (1) All social and cultural change is the work of individuals, (2) the major events in human history consist of the formation and destruction of societies and civilizations, and (3) because of their role in forming and justifying communities and civilizations, the intellectuals represent a strategic reference point for the study of these processes.

When we dig into the past and utilize archeological evidence to explore the period prior to written evidence, human development appears not to have progressed smoothly, but as having proceeded by a series of leaps. Before 15,000 B.C. mankind seems to have been distributed in tiny hunting and gathering communities. About 15,000 B.C. a series of social and technical revolutions began to lift much of human kind into a world of peasant villages. A fairly complex development of preliterate civilization accompanied the movement. This process was largely completed by 5000 B.C. Some time between 5000 B.C. and 3500 B.C. a new and more startling series of communities, the world's first cities, were created. During the course of the civic revolution that followed, the world's first literate civilization was shaped. In the areas of its developments, this period lasted to about 1000 B.C.

Shortly after 1000 B.C. a new wave of community formation got under way in all of the major cultural areas of the ancient world. It was the first wave of community formation and civilization synthesis to occur among people literate from the beginning. Hence, for the student it offers the first of a series of communities and civilizations which permit insight from their own accounts into the changing thought processes of men as one traces through an entire cycle.

The cultural creativity of the period, which got under way around 900 B.C. and began to level off and decline in the third and second centuries B.C., was so rich and varied and played so important a role in the formation of all contemporary civilizations as to be described by some scholars as the Axial Period of history. Its great creativity can only be compared to our own. By tracing the role of its cultural elites through an entire cycle, it is possible to isolate the effects of the different requirements placed at different times on the creative talents of an intellectual elite. In the formative period of a society and civilization some—not all—kinds of creativity are rewarded. With completion of the social and civilization synthesis, an epoch of stereotyping ensues. Though Western man is only midway on his destiny, some possible parallels between our society and civilization and those of the Axial Period will be considered.

THE FORMATION OF THE PEASANT VILLAGE

One of the fundamental transformations in society and culture was brought about between 15,000 B.C. and 5000 B.C. At the beginning of this period man lived in the communities of hunters and gatherers; by the end of the period great sections of mankind lived in peasant villages in which food production was actively carried on. The communities of hunters and gatherers were small, fluid, and mobile. Their central institution was the clan, which even dominated the family. The clansmen often traced mystical descent to a totemic ancestor—an insect, plant, or animal important in the tribal economy. They rarely had occasion to develop conceptions of real as contrasted to personal property. Hunting and fishing grounds were usually common. Their arts centered in the tools and weapons for hunting and gathering. Though age and sex grades were important, social differentiation was slight. Religion was adapted to the peculiar hazards of life; it was often magical and animistic, centering in a magician or shamman.[1]

Food production began to replace hunting and gathering as a basis of human economy, perhaps around 8000 B.C., spreading by 5000 B.C. to what became the main cultural areas of the ancient world. The cultivation of grains (probably originally by women) is revealed by the existence of flint sickles in the Old Stone Age.[2] In Palestine emmer was grown, while einkorn cultivation spread through Asia Minor. Domestication was largely carried through after 5000 B.C. (cattle in western Asia, sheep in Egypt, and goats in Asia and Iran; the ass in Africa, the horse in Turkestan).[3] With the transition of mobile hunting and gathering communities into settled communities a considerable development of the crafts was possible: improved leather work, basketry, pottery (around 5000 B.C.), and cloth-making.

In the settled peasant village the food supply became more ample and dependable: granaries were dug, sickles consisting of flint teeth mounted on wooden handles were made, pottery was made, linen was used for clothing.

[1] V. Gordon Childe, *What Happened in History* (New York: Penguin, 1946), pp. 20 f.

[2] F. E. Zeuner, "Cultivation of Plants," *A History of Technology*, Charles Singer, E. J. Holmyard, and J. M. Donaldson (London: Oxford University Press, 1954), Vol. 1, pp. 353–375.

[3] Zeuner, "Domestication of Animals," *ibid.*, pp. 327–352.

The size of the community increased, and women rose in importance. Hoe culture was originally in the hands of women, though it appears that, with the addition of stock-breeding and the use of animals in plowing and hauling, this work was often shifted into male hands. Conceptions of real property developed. Craft specialists appeared, and some differentiation of the social classes occurred. The communal authority structure became in some ways more fixed and formal; a village council and head replaced the tribal chief. Religion underwent elaboration and redefinition, as with great frequency earth cults and fertility rituals of various sorts appeared.[4]

THE WORLD'S FIRST CITIES

Between 5000 B.C. and 3500 B.C., on a foundation supplied by the peasant village, the world's first cities were founded. The importance for culture of this development appears in the fact that the rise of the world's first cities was coextensive with the appearance of a literate civilization. This was one of the great breakthroughs of human culture. It represented a break through the limitations of the community form of the peasant village and its neolithic cultural synthesis to the city and a complex literate civilization.

If the city were to arise, the peasant village had to be destroyed and its elements brought into a new kind of communal synthesis. The process of the metamorphosis is perhaps most completely revealed in the archeological investigations at Tepe Gawra in the upper Tigris Valley, where excavations have revealed twenty-six occupied levels from the peasant village to the fully developed city. In the Tel Halaf-Samarra phase, evidence of the destruction of peasant villages and the new synthesis of their elements into the city is found in such things as the fusion of pottery traditions deriving from Syria and Iran, a synthesis of domestication and cultivation, and the substitution of copper tools, weapons, and ornaments for those of stone.[5]

The first fully developed urban community to be discovered (at Uruk [Erech]) illustrates some of the ways in which the new city community differed from the peasant village. It was dominated by a centrally located sacred hill (*ziggurat*) and a brick temple. The religion was different from that of the peasant village (with its sky cults in contrast to the peasant village earth and fertility cults, with a pantheon of deities, more elaborate and rationalized theology, and a more complex system of specialized priests). In the city, religion held a different place in the social order from that in the peasant village. The temples owned land, slaves, cattle; they made loans, acted as banks, conducted schools, and kept records. Even the fact that the temple was constructed of brick is evidence of major changes. A new industrial era opened when some of the potteries were converted to the manufacture of construction materials. Moreover, already at Uruk writing was not only

[4] Childe, *op. cit.*, pp. 41–60.

[5] Childe, *op. cit.*, Chap. V, pp. 82 f.; Ralph Turner, *The Great Cultural Traditions* (New York: McGraw Hill Book Co., 1941), Vol. I.

known but used for economic and business purposes, indicative of a new kind of organization of social life.[6]

If men were to live in cities, the community of the peasant village had to be destroyed and life reorganized on new principles. The major institution of the peasant village was the (in this area usually patriarchal) family which owned property, carried out basic agriculture and stock-breeding, supplied the members of the village council, supplied soldiers for village defense, raised and trained children, cared for dependents, and served as the primary unit of religious and ceremonial life. The key institution of the early cities was either the temple or the city governor and his retainers (sometimes closely fused with the temple, at other times distinct from it). The key persons in village community life were peasant proprietors; the key persons in the city were usually removed from agriculture: soldiers, bureaucrats, officials, and priests. Corresponding to the synthesis, represented by the city, of fragments of many villages into a new form and the dominance of strata removed from agriculture is the syncretism of the city religions, the decline in comparative importance of fertility and earth cults, and the rise of sky cults. The oral traditions of the village were supplanted by the written traditions of the city; the rise in importance of the scribe accompanied the decline of the village elder and sage.

The city was a new kind of community, finding its point of synthesis in secondary institutions. Accompanying its appearance was a phenomenal cultural development. By the year 3000 B.C. the formation of some of the world's first cities was complete. The expansion of cities eventually brought them into conflict, and an era of city wars and urban imperialism was opened. The wars between the Sumerian cities were opened by Ur around 3000 B.C., leading to its dominance over a number of cities. Other struggles broke out between Lagash and Umma. The Akkadians under Sargon I (*ca.* 2500 B.C.) were the first Semitic people to rise to power in Mesopotamia by overthrowing a Sumerian civic coalition. A Semitic assimilation of Sumerian culture under Babylon occurred between 2100 and 1750 B.C.

Though much less is known about them, there were cities in the Indus Valley which flourished during the late dynastic period of the Sumerian urban communities (about 2500 B.C.). Such places as Mohenjo-Daro, Harrapa, and Chandhu-Daro appear to have been undergoing development similar to those in Mesopotamia. The rise of urban communities in Egypt and Crete was simultaneous with those in Mesopotamia. A period of civic conquests was initiated in Egypt with the founding of the first dynasty (3200–3000 B.C.) under Menes. A series of dynasties followed. The Mediterranean urban coastal cities underwent development from about 4000 B.C. to the beginning of the Iron Age. The three major periods are: the Early Minoan (3000–2200 B.C.), Middle Minoan (2200–1600 B.C.), and Late Minoan (1600–1100 B.C.).

[6] S. N. Hooke, "Recording and Writing," in *A History of Technology*, pp. 744–773.

Some time after the opening of the third millenium B.C. urban communities began to emerge on the basis of peasant villages in China. Ancient Chinese history describes three early dynasties: the Hsia, the Shang, and the Chou. The rulers of the Chinese urban dynasty in the lower Huang Valley appear to have been the Shang (between 1500 and 1100 B.C.). The so-called Axial Period of human history beginning around 1000 B.C. closed an epoch which had opened with city imperialism beginning about 3000 B.C.

The remarkable large-scale construction undertaken by the men who made the transition from preliterate to literate civilization is testimony both to their social organization and to their wealth. Major irrigation works, great fortification projects, and temple and tomb construction even today remain mute witnesses to the enterprise, imagination, technology, and ideas of the new social types and the labor and materials at their disposal. Great technological gains were made. Extensive experiments were made with glazes; a revolution developed in pottery-making with the employment of the potter's wheel. Large-scale construction of a new sort became possible when the potteries were employed for tile- and brick-making. The great gains of the smithies of the metal-workers brought the transition from the Stone to the Metal Age.

Agricultural production was revolutionized. With the production of permanent agricultural surpluses over and above immediate requirements, it became possible for men to support larger numbers of domesticated animals which were assimilated in the structure of human economic life. (Domestication depends on the substitution of an artificially controlled food supply and the artificial protection of the animal—reducing it to dependence upon man). The use of animals for transport and industry, in turn, encouraged further social differentiation. Moreover, with the use of animal labor men were able to increase the size of their landholdings and operations. When the war chariot was invented, the ownership of animals and chariots tended to guarantee control of military life to those able to afford such expensive equipment. (Domestication of the horse and its use with the war chariot may possibly have originated in the Asiatic steppes.)

Not the least of the gains was in the technology of communication. Priests, who were the world's first specialized intellectuals, increased in numbers and differentiated in their religious roles. Religious and political expansion went hand in hand, for religious institutions were crucial in establishing social groupings larger than the family, clan, or tribe. Many varieties of the combined political-religious role appeared. A significant form of intellectual activity of persons occupying such combined political-religious roles was the provision of justifications (ideologies) for political structures. With changing religious and political fortunes intellectual life was forced repeatedly through many successive, specialized adaptations. The invention of writing made possible for the first time a literature destined primarily to be read.

Literary forms were created and fixed. Beginnings were made in the inquiry into the nature of correct reasoning; and a significant accumulation of knowledge was being made.

Social scientists have often observed that once a set of social-physical problems has been solved, the human group tends to expand to the limits of the natural environment concerned. The technology of the Eskimo provided the breakthrough, permitting human occupancy of the Arctic area. They spread over most of the land. The technology of animal husbandry, emerging as a specialization out of ancient agriculture, permitted human beings to thrive in the grasslands of the old world. Pastoral nomadism tended to expand to the limits of these same steppe regions. Similarly, in the ancient world the solution of the problems of the river valley not only permitted the transition from preliterate to literate civilization, but saw the expansion of these civilizations to the limits of their natural environments—to the full extent of the river valleys.

Once the problems of the great river valleys had been solved in a manner permitting the emergence of early civilization, extensive social, economic, and technical differentiation occurred; the geographic area made available thereby was largely occupied. Social development tended to stabilize in an uneasy equilibrium, for though the whole of the river valleys was the scene of a homogeneous culture, a stable community larger than the city had not been developed.

THE LIMITS OF EARLY CIVILIZATION

For a number of reasons the early river-valley civilizations could not rest content either internally or with a surrounding barbarian world. For one thing, they had accumulated great wealth which was a constant temptation to the wild men of the woods, the rugged mountaineers, and the saddle-hardy nomads of the steppes. If nothing else, the enemy outside the walls forced the early civilizations to readjust to themes other than those developing out of their own natures; to militarize where other forces of the civilizations tended to pacify. To keep their populations peaceful and protected, these civilizations developed professional armies, which, in turn, often threatened to transform the society from within. To do neither—arm one's own people or hire others to fight—was to expose civilization to the risk of being overrun from without. On the basis of such facts, it is frequently stated that the advance of civilization was bound up with the conflict between the nomad and the tiller of the soil. At best, however, this is only a partial explanation.

Many of the social and technical developments of the early civilizations were, in some sense, detachable—capable of diffusion to other places. The use of draft animals for plowing, for example, could be adapted to agriculture outside the river valleys. When it was, it caused complex social-economic adjustments in the peasant villages outside the urbanized areas. Or again, use of the skills of metal-working outside the smithies of the river valleys permitted the development of new weapons and tools elsewhere. Adaptations of the agricultural skills, techniques, and weapons to the needs of peoples outside the centers of civilization often added the small net balance over survival, which supplied the foundation of a people's movement and implemented their assault on the centers themselves.

In other words, the conflict of nomad and tiller of the soil was only a surface manifestation of a deeper problem. In the great river-valley civilizations the time-honored solutions found their limits: mankind reached one of the frontiers of social development. The very socio-technical elements which had made the civilizations superior had more and more taken the shape of barriers to further development.

The societies and civilizations of the river valleys had reached a stage where they created problems they could not solve. These problems, far more complex than a breakthrough in scientific research, did not consist in the winning of some single right idea, technique, or formula; rather, it involved the development of new social and cultural syntheses. Moreover, there was no reason why any single solution should work exclusively.

Around the year 1000 B.C. all of the major cultural areas of the ancient world were in ferment. Out of this ferment a series of new societies with their attendant civilizations took shape. Since writing skills were at the disposal of the intellectuals in these communities, it is possible to trace the social and cultural ferment in the minds and emotions of its participants almost from the beginning. Moreover, this more or less simultaneous formation of societies and civilizations in ancient China, India, Palestine, and Greece supplies comparative cases for the qualitative uniqueness as well as comparable features in these semicyclical developments.

THE AXIAL PERIOD OF HUMAN HISTORY

Since the days of Lasaulx, about a hundred years ago, the fundamental parallelism between the social and civilizational movements in the world areas at this period have been noted:

> Denn es kann unmöglich ein Zufall sein, dasz ungefähr gleichzeitig, sechshundert Jahre vor Christus, in Persien Zarathustra, in Indien Gautama-Buddha, in China Konfutse, unter den Juden die Propheten, in Rom der König Numa und in Hellas die ersten Philosophen, Jonier, Dorier, Eleaten, als die Reformatoren der Volksreligion auftraten.[7]

[7] Ernst von Lasaulx, *Neuer Versuch einer alten, auf die Wahrheit der Tatsachen begründeten Philosophie der Geschichte*, ed. by Eugen Thurnher (München: R. Oldenbourg, 1952), p. 137. "It is hardly an accident that almost simultaneously six hundred years before Christ, Zarathustra in Persia, Gautama Buddha in India, Confucius in China, the prophets in Israel, King Numa in Rome, and the first philosophers in Hellas, including the Ionians, Dorians, and Eleatics undertook the reformation of the national religion."

These remarkable coincidences, Lasaulx maintained, could only be produced by a substantial psychic unity of mankind and not by the effervescence of a special folk spirit.[8]

In his commentary on Lao-tse, Strauss made similar observations and came to similar conclusions:

> During the centuries when Lao-tse and Confucius were living in China, a strange movement of the spirit passed through all civilized peoples. In Israel, Jeremiah, Habakkuk, Daniel and Ezekiel were prophesying and in a renewed generation (521–516) the second temple was erected in Jerusalem. Among the Greeks Thales was still living, Anaximander, Pythagoras, Heraclitus, and Xenophanes appeared and Parmenides was born. In Persia an important reformation of Zarathustra's ancient teaching seems to have been carried through, and India produced Sakyamuni, the founder of Buddhism.[9]

Jaspers substantially accepts the same position as Lasaulx and Strauss:

> The mystery of the simultaneous inception of the Axial Period appears to me to be situated at a much deeper level than the problem of the birth of the ancient civilizations. In the first place, the simultaneity is much more exact and, in the second, it relates to spiritual-historical developments in the whole conscious, thinking aspect of humanity. The three regions which, from the beginnings of the ancient civilizations onward, were possessed of a unique character, brought forth creations during the millennium before Christ upon which the entire history of the human spirit has rested ever since.[10]

Describing the period as the axis of world history, Jaspers conceives it as a point which gave birth to everything which man has since been able to be. Its character was determined by a "common frame of historical self-comprehension for all peoples"—in the West as well as in Asia. Man as known today is stated to have come into being at this time.

For Jaspers, and it may well be suspected for most others who have been interested in this period, an essentially religious motive seems to have been powerfully at work at the basis of his reflections, for he maintains that the events of the Axial Period were transrational:

> The fact of the three-fold manifestation of the Axial Period is in the nature of a miracle, in so far as no really adequate explanation is possible within the limits of our present knowledge.[11]

At the same time, the whole purpose of reviewing the facts of the Axial Period is essentially religious; it permits one to experience directly the psychic unity of mankind.

[8] *Ibid.*, p. 137. "Es kann dieses merkwürdige Zuzammentreffen nur in der inneren substantiellen Einheit des menschheitlichen Leben und des Völkerlebens, nur in einer gemeinsamen, alle Völker bewegenden Schwingung des menschheitlichen Gesamtlebens seinen Grund haben, nicht in der besonderen Efferveszenz eines Volksgeistes."

[9] Viktor von Strauss' commentary on Laotse (1870), quoted by Karl Jaspers in *The Origin and Goal of History* (New Haven: Yale University Press, 1953), pp. 8–9.

[10] Jaspers, *op. cit.*, p. 14.

[11] *Ibid.*, p. 18.

> Really to visualize the facts of the Axial Period and to make them the basis of our universal conception of history is to gain possession of something *common to all mankind*, beyond all differences of creed. It is one thing to see the unity of history from one's own ground and in the light of one's own faith, another to think of it in communication with every other human ground, linking one's own consciousness to alien consciousness.[12]

In the end, the whole purpose of Jaspers' reflections is to establish an ultimate religious point of reference beyond all historical religions. History as he sees it is the differentiation of man out of unity, which will terminate with the return to unity once again.

> The One is . . . the infinitely remote point of reference, which is origin and goal at one and the same time; it is the One of transcendence. As such it cannot be, so to speak, taken captive; it cannot become the exclusive possession of an historical faith that could be enforced upon all as truth *per se*.
>
> If universal history as a whole proceeds from One to the One, it does so in such a way that everything accessible to us lies between those ultimate poles. There is a becoming of unities, an enthusiastic seeking of unity; and then again a smashing of unities.
>
> Thus this deeper unity is elevated to an invisible religion, to the realm of spirits, the secret realm of the manifestation of Being in the concord of souls. Historically, however, there remains movement, which always between beginning and end, never attains to, nor continuously is, what it really signifies.[13]

Thus Jaspers closes his reflections on a note of transrational faith.

Jaspers has been quoted at some length in order to clarify the difference between his approach and the one that will guide the rest of this study. It is evident from his own statements that whatever comparative study he makes of the societies and civilizations of the Axial Period and our own are hung in a framework of religious absolutism. It may not be religious in the sense of the existing religions, but there is little doubt of its character. When the *One* begins to be capitalized and the argument acquires the giddy vagueness of a mystic trance as origins and goals become indistinguishable and the *One* acquires a higher form of reality in contrast to the *maya*-like illusoriness of actual historical events, there is little doubt that the world of science has been abandoned.

From the point of view of a social-behavioristic theory of social and cultural change, it is a serious error to assume that, because the first period to have writing at its disposal was able to put into writing the volume of tradition that came to it as well as what it added of its own, it was unusually creative. This would be like giving a publisher credit for writing all the books he published. Nor is there any sound foundation for assuming that because there was a simultaneous social and cultural ferment in the major

12 *Ibid.*, p. 19.
13 *Ibid.*, pp. 264–265.

world areas that they represent a single spiritual ferment in the soul of mankind.

Resting, as it does, uncompromisingly on social and civilizational relativism, social behaviorism provides no basis for making the leap from a similarity of interaction to a spiritual identity. There is one paragraph in Jaspers' account which neatly contains both what the social behaviorist can and he cannot share with Jaspers:

> In the end, the simplest explanation of the phenomena of the Axial Period seems to lie in common sociological preconditions favorable to spiritual creativeness: many small states and small towns; a politically divided age engaged in incessant conflicts; the misery caused by wars and revolutions accompanied by simultaneous prosperity elsewhere, since destruction was neither universal nor radical; questioning of previously existing conditions. These are sociological considerations which are meaningful and lead to methodical investigation, *but ultimately they merely illuminate the facts and do not provide a causal explanation of them. For these conditions form part of the total spiritual phenomenon of the Axial Period. They are preconditions of which the creative result is not a necessary sequel; as part of the overall pattern their own origin remains in question.*[14]

With the unitalicized part of this paragraph, the social behaviorists can agree. It formulates precisely his rationale for treating the societies of the Axial Period and modern times as comparative cases for the study of social and civilizational change. However, in that part of the paragraph that has been italicized, Jaspers abandons sociological science as the social behaviorist sees it.

There is no reason, however, for abandoning the comparative study of societies and civilizations simply because those persons who have most often raised the issue have been cultural and ethical absolutists or have been determined to force historical events into one of the standard religions or into some special religious interpretation of their own. A. E. Burtt, in *The Metaphysical Foundations of Modern Science*, demonstrated that at times religious and ethical motives have operated in the early attempts to solve problems which led to strictly scientific solutions. In the early days of modern physics, for example, some persons, for example, Kepler, were motivated by religion to search for mathematical laws—by the conviction that as God's handiwork the physical world embodies the symmetry of His intentions. Hence, Kepler was in search of the mathematical laws of the harmony of the celestial spheres.

Another error occasionally made is that of assigning such importance to the intellectuals that one attributes almost exclusively to them the gains of an epoch. However, their roles represent only a few of the possible ones in any given society. To be sure, the roles played by the intellectuals have rather special interest, since they are points where tensions in the society are

[14] *Ibid.*, pp. 17–18. (The italics are added.)

mediated. One of the clear indications that a given social stratum is acquiring power in a social order is the emergence of intellectual representation of its interests.

The Marxian theory of social change was one-sided, but it was not altogether wrong. It assigned impressive functions to the intellectuals of a society in times of both conservative reaction and revolutionary upheaval. In the first type of epochs the intellectuals were assumed to turn all their efforts to elaborating ideologies in support of the existing order:

> The ideas of the ruling class are, in every age, the ruling ideas: *i.e.*, the class which is the dominant *material* force in society is at the same time its dominant *intellectual* force. The class which has the means of material production at its disposal has control at the same time over the means of mental production, so that in consequence the ideas of those who lack the means of mental production are, in general, subject to it. The dominant ideas are nothing more than ideal expression of the dominant material relationships, the dominant material relationships grasped as ideas, and thus of the relationships which make one class the ruling one; they are consequently the ideas of its dominance.[15]

However, when class struggles near their climatic stage, all this may change.

> In times when the class struggle nears the decisive hour, the process of dissolution going on within the ruling class, in fact the whole range of the old society assumes such a violent, glaring character, that a small section of the ruling class cuts itself adrift, and joins the revolutionary class, the class that holds the future in its hands. Just as, therefore, at an earlier period, a section of the nobility went over to the *bourgeoisie*, so now a portion of the *bourgeoise* goes over to the proletariat, and in particular, a portion of the *bourgeois* ideologists, who have raised themselves to the level of comprehending theoretically the historical movement as a whole.[16]

In revolutionary epochs the intellectuals were assumed to turn their talents to the creation of Utopian hopes which helped shatter the conservative outlook and vindicated the revolution.[17]

Its theory of interaction commits social behaviorism to the view that every man is a potential innovator. Its theory of groups and institutions commits it to the position that the primary areas, where innovations become generally socially effective, are socialization, mastery of nature, and social control. Both innovations and resistance to it have all their original contests on the firing lines of social experience with respect to these basic problems. The innovators at this level, however, are rarely viewed as intellectuals: the

[15] Karl Marx, *Selected Writings in Sociology and Social Philosophy*, trans. by T. B. Bottomore and M. Rubel, reproduced in Patrick Gardiner (editor), *Theories of History* (Glencoe: The Free Press, 1959), p. 129.

[16] From the *Communist Manifesto*, reproduced from the text, *Karl Marx: Selected Works*, ed. by Adoratsky, in Gardiner, *op. cit.*, p. 136.

[17] These notions became the starting point for Karl Mannheim's sociology of knowledge. See Karl Mannheim, *Ideology and Utopia*, trans. by Louis Wirth and Edward Shils (New York: Harcourt Brace, 1949).

creator of a new industrial process, the founder of a system of chain stores, the politician who promotes a new agricultural policy, the public health official who invents a new sanitation system, etc.

Social behaviorism's theory of society and civilization permits the location of the intellectual precisely in social life. Societies and civilizations are systems which arise in the reconstitution of basic social and cultural forms into ways of life and cultural syntheses. The intellectuals are persons who may well have a special anchorage in the basic social institutions (socialization, mastery of nature, and social control), but their unique functions as intellectuals lie in the innovating or conserving activities in communities and civilizations. They are key persons of the reconstitution of the basic institutions into such more comprehensive systems. Their most fundamental activities usually include accepting or denying the innovations which constantly occur in the basic social and cultural forms.

Eras in which intellectual roles are in ferment are thus indicative of a growth stage in the community and civilization. Such eras in which intellectual roles proliferate have special interests to us. We, too, are in one of the "open epochs" of human history. Apart from the fact that the period 900 to 200 B.C. produced a great intellectual and cultural heritage which is still of importance to us, the activities of the intellectuals of the period have special interest. In their struggle for intellectual freedom, the daring imagination with which they challenged the unknown can be recognized as parallel to the best in our own times.

THE SOCIOLOGY OF CREATIVITY

It is evident that all ages have not been equally favorable for imaginative creativity. Certain periods have honored the intellectual, given him room to develop, welcomed the product of his labors; other ages have suspected him, hedged him about with restrictions, and exercised most careful control over his thought. One of the sociological values of a study of the period Jaspers calls axial is that it permits examination of the kinds of socio-cultural situations in which intellectual development is "needed," "freed," even encouraged.

A creative age is rarely particularly stable or even peaceful. Above all it is not unified in its estimation of its intellectuals. Its participants often experience it as a time of unrest and tension. Just as intellectuals in such periods are given or take credit for all the gains of the epoch, so, occasionally, are they held responsible for all its faults and uncertainties. One need only recall the heated denunciation of the Sophists in classical Greece (paralleled by equivalent changes in the course of the tensions between the Confucian and other intellectual formulations in China, the passionate concern with orthodox and heterodox soteriology in India, the distinction between true and false prophets in Palestine), or present-day scorn for eggheads who are also charged at times with a failure of nerve.

It would hardly do, however, to treat the intellectuals simply as a product of social tensions and crisis. Times of crisis may indeed give rise to acts of desperation. However, the creations of those open epochs of human history never have the property of desperate acts. Instead, the creations of the intellectuals usually have the ease and spontaneity more characteristic of play than of anxiety. An epoch dominated only by a sense of crisis often produces powerful traditional reactions, hesitancy to try the new, attempts to consolidate the past, but hardly the spontaneous venture into the unknown. In a profound crisis one may anticipate even the voluntary sacrifice of the intellect to an institution or a leader blindly followed. (One of the disheartening aspects of Hitler's rise to power was the number of intellectuals who voluntarily abrogated their freedom.)

But an epoch that encourages human creativity seems to combine peculiarly tension and anticipation, crisis and hope. So far as he suggests this, Toynbee's thesis—that the origin and development of civilization lie in a series of "challenges" and "responses"—tends to be attractive. However, Toynbee's thesis is not being argued here. His challenges are often remarkably vague, consisting, for example, of the problem of the desert or the sea; his responses are equally ambiguous, consisting in some sort of development in the soul of mankind, whatever that may mean.

> In our search . . . for the positive factor in the geneses of civilizations, we have been employing the tactics of the classical school of modern physical science. We have been thinking in abstract terms and experimenting with the play of inanimate forces—race and environment. Now that these manoeuvers have ended in our drawing blank, we may pause to consider whether our failures may not have been due to some mistake in method. . . . In our final attempt to solve the riddle let us follow Plato's lead and try the alternative course. Let us shut our eyes for the moment to the formulae of science in order to open our ears to the language of mythology.
>
> It is clear that if the geneses of civilizations are not the result of biological factors or of geographical environment acting separately, they must be the result of some kind of interaction between them. In other words, the factor which we are seeking to identify is something not simple but multiple, not an entity but a relation. We have the choice of conceiving this relation either as an interaction between two interhuman forces or as an encounter between two superhuman personalities. Let us yield our minds to the second of these conceptions. Perhaps it will lead us toward the light.[18]

Toynbee's mind forthwith conjured up the encounter between Yahweh and the Serpent, between the Lord and Satan in the Book of Job, between the Lord and Mephistopheles in Goethe's *Faust*, between the Gods and Demons in the Scandinavian *Voluspa*, and between Artemis and Aphrodite in Euripides' *Hippolytus*. This quickly led Toynbee to his private light:

[18] Arnold J. Toynbee, *A Study of History*, abridgment of Vols. I–VI by D. C. Somervell (New York: Oxford University Press, 1947), p. 60.

> In the language of science we may say that the function of the intruding factor is to supply that on which it intrudes with a stimulus of the kind best calculated to evoke the most potently creative variations. In the language of mythology and theology, the impulse or motive which makes a perfect Yin-state pass into new Yang-activity comes from an intrusion of the Devil into the universe of God.[19]

His argument is at once schematically oversimplified and mystical. Since with a little carpentry on the facts practically any historical sequence can be fitted to it, the theory has limited explanatory power. The dangers inherent in Toynbee's procedure have been compactly summarized by Kaufmann:

> Surely, Toynbee is not more than a historian. Toynbee is less than a historian; he is a symptom: a symptom of the worship of size; a symptom of the eclipse of scruple; a symptom of the widespread hunger for vast spectacles, for men of learning who come out for any version of religion whatsoever, and above all for assurance that history has a meaning. Sparked by the futility of so much human suffering, by a deep ambivalence over the mechanization of modern life, and by profound confusion in the face of more and more specialized experts, there is a desperate demand for a royal road to meaning. And, while men of impeccable methods generally avoid questions of meaning, vast masses of people who will not be put off turn to commentators, columnists, and editorials; and to popular accounts by men who have consulted experts; and to Toynbee. As long as there is even some small promise of significance, people willingly put up with vagueness, inconsistencies, and errors.[20]

In this context it may be assumed that Kaufmann is denouncing the idea that history has a meaning, not in the sense that it is unexplainable or that its materials cannot be employed to establish general knowledge of social life, but in the sense that it has a special moral or religious significance. Furthermore, it may be assumed that Kaufmann does not intend to promote a special kind of scientific irrationality in denying historical or other materials to any except "experts" who, because they are "men of impeccable methods," usually "avoid questions of meaning." Rather, it may be assumed that Kaufmann is objecting to some types of "popularization" which tear facts out of context and fit them to moral, ethical, or propagandistic purposes.

From the beginning social behaviorism works with assumptions contrary to those of Toynbee (and as indicated earlier, of Jaspers): all questions of value, of ethics, and of religious significance are relative to the particular societies and civilizations which sustain them. Social behaviorism does not seek ethically to evaluate human history, but to explain as far as possible the unique and recurrent features of human social life. The general social con-

19 *Ibid.*, p. 63.

20 Walter Kaufmann, *From Shakespeare to Existentialism* (New York: Doubleday Anchor Books, 1960), pp. 406–407.

ditions which promote or frustrate the creative potentials of individuals are its legitimate object of study.

The theory of social change of social behaviorism which locates the intellectual as a key figure in the formation of communities and civilizations had an ideal subject matter in the so-called Axial Period with its tremendous flowering of intellectual activity. The theory hypothesizes that such a time should be characterized by a simultaneous breakdown of old communities and civilizations and the move to establish new ones. This seems to have been the case. In many areas of life elements that had formerly been bound into societal and civilizational systems were broken out of their contexts to be pressed into service as constructive forces in new contexts.

Plow culture, which made possible the cultivation of far larger holdings than before, became generally diffused from Greece to India, from India to China. Agriculture thus acquired greater stability and a higher level of productivity. The diffusion of cattle breeding which was very important from Greece to India (less so in China) also had significant implications. With the systematic use of animal products the cattle nomad was developed. He penetrated the steppes, the arid grasslands, and even (among the camel nomads) the desert.

Both plow culture and cattle-breeding, individually and with special force when they appeared together, tended to result in a strong consolidation of the patriarchal household which accordingly acquired basic importance for the inheritance of both land and animals. Such households often became fairly large in size and, in some measure, economically autonomous. The institutionalization of plow culture and cattle-breeding within the patriarchal household not only raised the level of productivity and prosperity, but simultaneously created a strong, socially decentralizing force, which penetrated all areas of the great river valleys and acted as a powerful corrosive acid to the unity of its social life.

A third technology—horse-breeding—exaggerated all the effects noted, particularly when it was accompanied by the skill of chariot-making. Social differentiation and decentralization resulted. Only the powerful family could afford to breed horses and manufacture war chariots; automatically, such a family acquired a virtual monopoly of the instruments of warfare. It might fortify itself within its castles and fortress walls and defy imperial power itself, meanwhile reducing to serfdom the free peasants on its lands. The able-bodied men of the noble family monopolized the arts of war and cultivated social graces appropriate to their eminence. The importance of the patriarchal family increased, and with its heightened productivity (or, at least, greater local concentrations of property and wealth), even more powerful, socially decentralizing forces developed. These were intensified by the fact that conquest became an additional source of wealth. Complex and constantly changing petty conflicts became the rule.

With the full emergence of the eminent household and its development of cultivated standards of taste, a further source of social differentiation appeared as well as the development of a fourth technology: the manufacture of and the commerce in luxury goods intended for consumption in the genteel household. These added another series of activities that might in themselves be a source of wealth. Foreign trade in such luxury items tended to be accompanied by the diffusion of alien social influences; in any case it tended to weaken the insular cultural unity of the local area. Here again a complex appeared which simultaneously heightened prosperity and operated as a force for social and cultural division.

With the consolidation of the patriarchal household, the development of the weapons monopoly by the noble sib, the restriction of warfare to the aristocracy where it became an honorable ceremonial arrangement among gentlemen, together with the disintegration of former political military structures, the social order was laid open to a rather unexpected hazard. The warfare of the barbarian outside the pale of civilized society lacked gentlemanly refinement. When the barbarians learned the lessons of disciplined warfare of the individual foot soldier, the warfare of the panoplied individual charioteer was no match for them.

In all these respects the Axial Period showed simultaneously a heightened prosperity in newly formed communities and a new series of adversities for old ones. The distinctive institutions of the early river-valley civilizations were being dissolved; at the same time, new problems appeared. And in all areas, as the time period opened, there was a constant, changing kaleidoscope of warring petty kingdoms, princedoms, states, tribes, and city-states. In all areas the struggle between settled groups and barbarians was a source of anxiety; and everywhere the issue was unsettled between the noble warfare of men on horseback (charioteers) and disciplined foot soldiers.

THE SOCIOLOGY OF CANONIZATION AND INTELLECTUAL STEREOTYPING

The sociology of creativity will be completed only when the study of the opposite process—the stereotyping of thought—is carried through. Nothing signals more quickly the end of a creative period than the *canonization* of thought: the emergence of one pattern of thought from the many available, its sanctification, its labeling as official. And once the distinction between orthodoxy and heterodoxy is drawn, the most varied external pressures are brought to bear to maintain the official view.

Human needs still change, of course, and new ideas develop, but once the stereotyping process is carried through, a new idea must disguise itself as a commentary on or an interpretation of the canon. Sometimes, in fact, men have gathered in formal ceremony to announce solemnly that the age of discovery, the time of prophecy, has ended.

In such a period of stereotyping, conservative forces come into play against innovation. Far from feeling a need for free thought, the community feels the need to control it. Every device may be employed to restrict it to carefully defined limits. Actually, as the fate of heretics reveals, thinking is not so much eliminated as fixed. There may be considerable effort to maintain the form of thought accepted as canonical, and a training program may be carried through to guarantee a supply of practitioners. But the role of the intellectual is carefully and rigidly institutionalized.

In the Axial Period the same processes that represent a kind of solution to the problems of the time are seen in retrospect to signal the decline of creative thought. In China the close of the period of free thought could hardly have been more dramatically heralded than by the burning of the books under Shin Huang-ti after the conquest of Ch'in. To be sure, Confucianism was not at once made into official canonical doctrine—this occurred only under the Han Dynasty—but the founding of the Imperial Academy was clear enough indication that henceforth some form of an official doctrine was to prevail. In India the advent of Buddhism under Asoka in the Maurya Dynasty was indicative of similar types of forces and displacements. The first great councils held under Asoka ushered in the determination of accepted thought on the basis of social criteria. Here, too, the process was not accomplished immediately. Only later, with the restoration of orthodox Hinduism, was Buddhism itself defined as heterodox. But there is little doubt as to the increasing stereotyping of thought. In the Palestine area the fertile intellectual rivalries between prophet and priest and between true and false prophets were violently concluded with the Babylonian Exile. Later, with the reestablishment of the Jewish community, the religious community was held tightly under socio-religious control, while the political structure remained under foreign domination most of the time. The age of prophecy was formally declared at an end. Canonization of the holy texts proceeded rapidly during this time, and new religious thought was increasingly confined to interpretations and commentaries. In the Hellenistic world the beginning of the end was introduced by the emergence of the Alexandrian and Roman empires. Greek thought flowered for a time, and was officially sanctioned and brought under political patronage in the Museum at Alexandria. But this was also a kind of omen, for henceforth official needs were to determine what would prosper or perish.

The period which opened with the encouragement and freedom of the intellectual ended everywhere in the canonization and stereotyping of thought and the careful fixing of the intellectual in an institutional context. These were also periods when the period of growth of the distinctive societies and civilizations of the respective areas were completed and stabilized as uneasy equilibriums, which, if anything, showed a tendency slowly to deteriorate.

COMPARISONS AND CONTRASTS IN THE SOCIAL ROLES OF THE ANCIENT INTELLECTUAL

The single most striking parallel among the various cultural areas is the simultaneous emergence of outstanding men. Even at this level it is easiest to assume that their genius was called forth by their respective social situations; the only sound biological supposition is that the proportionate potential genius is a constant in mankind. Its manifestations vary with the capacity of society to evoke it. In Greece after Homer there appeared a series of brilliant philosophic schools: the Mileasians, Electics, Pythagoreans, the Atomists and the Sophists, within which flourished an array of outstanding individuals from Thales through Heraclitus and from Parmenides to Socrates, Plato, and Aristotle. In the arts a shining series of stars appeared, including Aristophanes, Euripides, Sophocles, and Aeschylus; among the historians, individuals of the talent of Herodotus, Thucydides, and Xenophon.

In China there appeared such men as Confucius, Mo Tzu, Yang Chu, Mencius, Hui Shih, Kung-sun Lung, Lao Tzu, Chuang Tzu, Hsun Tsu, Han Fei Tsu, and such historians as Ssu-ma T'an, Ssu-ma Ch'ien, and Liu Hsin among many others. In India a profound antihistorical tendency made all but the most outstanding names irrelevant. But in addition to an outright sophisticated materialism, such as that of Carvaka or Lokyata, Indian mentality created the great heterodoxies of Jainism (Vardhamana and Mahavira) and Buddhism (Buddha). The readaptation of *Upanishad* doctrines led to the gradual isolation of the "six traditional systems": Nyaya, a system of logic (founded by Gautama); Vaisesika, a system of atomism (Kanada); Samkhya (founded by Kapila); Yoga (founded by Patanjali); Mimamsa (Jaimini); and Vedanta (attributed to Badarayana). In Palestine the appearance of the scriptural prophets was heralded by Elijah, and followed by such splendid figures as Isaiah, Jeremiah, and Deutero-Isaiah. In nearby Iran, Zarathustra was developing his doctrine of light and darkness.

The same general range of problems was shared in each area, and all encouraged intellectuals. But from this point the culture areas tended to vary. Physical, historical, and social-historical differences were eventually to effect the development of a qualitatively distinct intelligence in each culture. China, for instance, possessed a relatively uniform river valley; northern India, two river valleys separated by deserts. In each nation there was a different distribution of tribal peoples. Palestine was characterized by a much-fissured plateau divided by mountains, and represented an interstitial area between two great powers. Greece was formed of many mountains and valleys and extended coasts.

The areas varied historically. In China a feudal state triumphed eventually among the principalities, in part as a result of a military technique borrowed and adapted in the course of border-state warfare with the steppe nomads.

In India a long period of penetration of cattle-breeding Aryan peoples into a land of tribal groupings gradually gave way to the formation of numerous petty states. India witnessed the temporary triumph of a dynasty linked to Buddhism rather than to the older formations of Aryan society. Palestine in the time of Judges saw the gradual conquest of settled lands by armed peasant confederations. The early period terminated in an oriental despotism under David and Solomon, and was destroyed between the colliding world powers of Babylonia and Egypt. In Greece the disciplined Spartan hoplite and the Athenian sailor turned back the Persian hordes, opening the way for politically autonomous city-states. These were never able to form into genuinely permanent associations until Philip and Alexander of Macedon finally reduced them by force.

In addition, there were many social and cultural elements peculiar to the special areas. Reference to them is intended to underline the fact that the areas produced not only a creative intellectuality but one selectively responsive to the peculiarities of the special area. For example, India produced a distinct historical and other-worldly type of thought. China, however, showed a preoccupation with the everyday affairs of empire. One found in Palestine a kind of concern with morality and religion that the Greeks would have called crudely unsophisticated.

It is a risky task to try in a phrase or two to epitomize the general character of the mentality of an entire area; it is done only with the qualification that it represents a high level of schematization. While emphasizing these limitations, however, it may still be observed that each cultural mentality is quite distinct.

THE UNIQUE CHARACTER OF THE CULTURAL MENTALITY IN THE FOUR MAJOR CULTURAL AREAS OF THE AXIAL PERIOD

Area	*General Character of the Mentality*
China	practical rationality and pragmatic traditionalism
India	metaphysical salvation consciousness ascetic other-worldliness ahistoricality
Palestine	emissary prophetic orientation revolutionary social Utopianism
Greece	methodological rationalism

This sort of unifying thematic quality of the intellectual is not, of course, the only way to distinguish the intellectual production of different areas. Nor is it completely trustworthy. If the intellectuals are permitted real freedom they will hardly seek out a restricted pattern to imitate. (This does not, of course, mean that they will not steal each other's brightest ideas. The time honored way of doing this is to take over the ideas of another by disguising them in a new terminology.) But the very nature of creative activity demands that it move in the area of the unexpected; when the unstandardized human imagination is allowed free range it seems to have at once a prying and impudent quality. It delights in forbidden areas and in upsetting the accepted.

Responsible members of ancient Greek society were often shocked by what appeared to them as brazen impudence of their intellectuals to whom nothing seemed sacred. Aristophanes, for instance, who shared profoundly the contemporary conservative suspicion of unlicensed thought, was able, nevertheless, to make a daring artistic connection between the cry for peace and feminine coquetry. In *Lysistrata* the women of Athens, having seized the Acropolis, meet with female representatives of the various city-states. Lysistrata's plan is at once bold and direct. The women of Greece will force their men to make an end to war by the expedient of refusing to lie with them.

> Of course we should, by the goddesses twain! We need only sit indoors with painted cheeks, and meet our mates lightly clad in transparent gowns of Amorgos silk, and perfectly depilated; they will get their tools up and be wild to lie with us. That will be the time to refuse, and they will hasten to make peace, I am convinced of that![21]

It would be difficult to find a more impudent conceptualization than one that approaches the most solemn problem of the sacred order through the comedies of the boudoir! In another of his comedies Aristophanes, with somewhat similar idealistic social ends in view, suggests that the men have made such a mess of running the state that it should be placed in the hands of women.

These observations, however, only reemphasize the risks in trying to characterize such creative epochs in terms of some generally pervasive quality. All creative periods resist narrow characterization. Later ages in human social development sometimes make the astonished discovery that their own requirements have been anticipated. This fact has led to the rather ironic observation that everything of value to an age has been discovered by some other age which did not appreciate it. However, this does not mean that the qualitative characterization of the creative activity of an epoch is only unfounded intuition. Even the freest epochs have their own problems. Creative activity tends always to exceed any special set of requirements, but some of its products are fitted more closely to the needs of the time than others. It is the adjustment between creativity and social needs that stylizes and gives direction to thought. Some things are encouraged, some are discouraged. Such stylizing processes can be seen most directly in the operation of the social roles of the intellectual.

A social role is the unit of activity forming the *individual's share* in some

[21] Aristophanes, *Lysistrata*, in the *Complete Greek Drama*, edited by Whitney J. Oates and Eugene O'Neill, Vol. II (New York: Random House, 1938), p. 816.

system of interactive life. With respect to the individual performing in it, the role offers certain guaranteed opportunities or values. A sphere of social life and the rewards adhering to it belong to him by virtue of his occupancy of the role. With respect to others participating in the total activity, the value of the role is that *specific responsibility for certain activities* is assigned to the role occupant. In any system of social life any given role is not necessarily of equal importance to other roles in the social life of the whole. This statement may be clarified from the comparable situation in play-acting from which the whole figurative language of roles was taken in the first place. The leading role in a stage play has certainly far more importance to the play as a whole than that of some bit part. Not only in recognition but in actual monetary rewards, the player of the leading role is differentially rewarded for role performance.

Intellectual roles are not basically dissimilar from any others. They represent the stable patterning of individual behavior with respect to conceptual activities and skills. They provide certain rewards to their occupants. They are assigned certain responsibilities toward other members of the social order. Intellectual roles are unique only with respect to their peculiar content and their concern with intellectual activities and skills. However, to pursue the stage analogy a bit farther, even when they are not the lead roles of the social drama the intellectual roles still have a special kind of interest. The intellectual in the role of advisor to a prince may not be in the lead position, but, in terms of the entire operation of the social order, he may be even more significant. As formulator of policy, he may even determine the fate of the prince. Or again, the intellectual in the position of teacher of the young may have more long-range influence on the social order than many persons wielding more direct forms of power.

Among the most important properties of intellectual roles are those derived from the social strata and institutions they most immediately serve. This raises two questions: Which social strata supply the individuals for the intellectual roles in question, and which social interests do the activities of the intellectuals represent? It is clear that the content of intellectual performance will differ if the intellectuals are drawn from the top or the bottom of society, or if their activities serve a restricted elite, or the masses, or some combination of interests between such extremes.

In all respects, in terms of the social roles of the intellectual, it is possible to follow most directly those individualizing forces in a social order which tend to stylize creative life, rewarding some things, ignoring or punishing others, leading in the long run to a prevailing trend.

As they emerge historically, in the time of the Warring Kingdoms the Chinese intellectuals seem originally to have had rather specific social derivation and institutional standing, for in the feudal period they formed a homogeneous status group. They were a politically oriented stratum of aristocratic intellectuals who were, at the same time, experts in ceremonial matters. One may guess that these two sets of requirements—the more purely political and more purely religious—may at one time have been separate. But in the time of the feudal kingdoms the mandarins were drawn primarily from the lower levels of the nobility. For example, Confucius' father died when the boy was three years old. It appears that the family suffered reverses, and Confucius was educated in part to provide the means of a livelihood.

The most striking property of the Chinese intellectuals during this period was a social plasticity that matches the variety in their thinking. Their thought was bold and original; it is reported of some, on occasion, that they defied the princes themselves. This could only be due to the fact that in their role as ceremonial experts they had a general status (like that occasionally found in priests and magicians), making the touching of their persons magically and socially dangerous. This stratum possessed valuable writing skills of importance to administration. They served as the repository of administrative wisdom. Among the primary roles of the Chinese mandarins of the feudal period were their services as administrative officials in a variety of capacities (librarians, justices, accountants, etc.) and as founders of schools—for fees. Their official roles varied from that of princely advisors and policy-makers to that of mere technicians.

In India in the time designated here as the Axial Period, the intellectual emerges from a prehistory that had already drawn a distinction between the house priest (*purohita*) and the village priest. The former had far greater prestige than the latter, which was in part based on his ties with aristocratic houses. Moreover, there are indications that the *purohita* had evolved from magician guilds which received members on the basis of special training and ascetic practice calculated to provide the (twice-born) individual with special magical powers. The heads of magician guilds were already guardians of a special holy lore orally transmitted to novices. In the feudalization process aristocratic households attached priests to their staffs, a process important to their elevation above the older village priests. As house priests the *purohita* were also, in part, teachers of genteel youth. Moreover, in the crucial time period in Indian history, characterized by successive and varied movements toward political consolidation, roughly comparable to those accompanying the wars of the Chinese feudal states, other intellectuals appeared as rivals of the Brahmans. They were anchored in the eminent nonpriestly strata, playing a powerful role in the foundation of the heterodox religions of Jainism and Buddhism, and serving as a nonpriestly stratum of intellectuals that could be utilized for administrative purposes by the political powers. In the main social roles of the Aryan priests, the Brahmans were those of (1) house chaplains and (2) teachers of sacred lore, to both novitiate priests and nobles. The most striking role of the eminent heterodox intellectuals was that of (3) founder and religious leader (monk) of a religion. Both the Brahman and heterodox (Jain and Buddhistic) intellectuals were drawn into administration as (4) officials.

In Palestine during the time of the peasant Yahweh confederacy, the religious war association, there was no permanent priesthood. The Levites originally appeared to have been a group of Yahweh exponents especially qualified for their position by training rather than birth. In the course of the repeated covenants that accompanied the conquest of Canaan, Yahwehism grew increasingly more important. Finally, with the monarchy, Yahwehism became a state religion. At this time the priest of the temple took the place of the Levite as a house priest or as the priest installed at the shrine established by an eminent household. The priest became distinct as one of the major intellectual types. During this period, which was unlike either the older *ro'eh* and *nabi* (though somewhat more closely akin to the latter), the scriptural prophets emerged. They seem to have been sustained by those eminent rural households existing partly outside the civic structure and resisting its domination. The scriptural prophets themselves were cultivated intellectuals familiar with the intellectual traditions and foreign problems of their day. Unlike the king's prophets of good fortune or the popular sellers of oracles, they were outside the church structure. Their programs were essentially Utopian, representing a profound sublimation of the socio-religious ethic of their culture.

In classical Greece during the period of creativity the key intellectual roles were constructed around the *citizens'* roles of the autonomous city-state. The intellectual appears as (1) political administrator, (2) lawyer or legal counselor, (3) the founder of a genteel religious sect, (4) teacher, particularly of urban sophistication and the art of rhetoric, and (5) physician. (Not to be forgotten is the amount of intellectuality appearing in the drama and historical writing.)

Again and again members of the aristocracy who had lost their fortunes turned to the cultivation of intellectual skills as the source of a livelihood. Displaced intellectuals (like Pythagoras or the Sophists) founded schools in the cities to which they migrated. Formerly ascendant members of older aristocratic strata also founded schools and functioned in part as propagandists for the older type of social order. (Plato's view of the ideal society, as one under the control of the philosopher-king and based on carefully limited education—which was confined primarily to music and the approved myth—and resting on disguised breeding policies, belongs here.) Some, like Demosthenes, found work in the law courts.

Greece seems, in any case, to have provided the richest variety of available intellectual roles of any of the major areas. The primary intellectual roles during the creative period in these four cultural areas may be presented in tabular form.

PRIMARY INTELLECTUAL ROLES OF THE MAJOR CULTURAL AREAS DURING THE AXIAL PERIOD

Area	*Primary Intellectual Roles during the Axial Period*	*Epitomized by*
China	official (a) advisor and policy-maker (b) clerk and scribe founder of a private school and teacher	learned official and wandering scholar
India	house priest teacher founder of a school official in the patrimonial state	ascetic
Palestine	Yahweh priest prophet	prophet
Greece	official of the city-state founder of a genteel sect lawyer teacher and public lecturer physician	philosopher

It is at the level of their comparative social roles that both similarities and differences among intellectuals become clear. As Jaspers had observed, "a sociological parallel can be drawn between Confucius' failure at the court of Wei and Plato's failure at Syracuse; between the school of Confucius, which trained future statesmen, and the academy of Plato, which served the same purpose."[21a] Between the various culture areas hundreds of such parallels appear.

SOCIAL STABILIZATION, CANONIZATION, AND THE FIXING OF SOCIAL ROLES

An important property of the intellectual activity in all areas of the ancient world was its high level of social responsibility. However, it should not be assumed that members of other social strata were either uncreative or that they worked only for themselves. The intellectuals were no more unselfish than any other group. Their roles, of course, guaranteed them certain values which, like other groups, they attempted to increase. Their actions were in this respect no different from those of a modern labor union which attempts to maximize benefits to its members, or the actions of a group like the American Medical Association in attempting to improve and protect the situation of the doctor.

The critical property of the intellectual role however, is such that as the intellectual pursues his own interests he must take into account the interests of other groups. The intellectual role is keyed into the societal and civilizational systems and not solely in a single institutional area. Generally, the more indispensable he is thought to be, the higher the return he can demand.

[21a] Jaspers, *op. cit.*, p. 5.

One need only observe the mounting prices commanded by atomic physicists in our day.

In all the major cultural areas of the ancient world at this time, intellectuals were valued as teachers of the correct life, suppliers of administrative and writing skills, persons who might provide the rationale for various new social arrangements, and persons who might pacify the masses.

In most general sociological terms and in all major cultural areas of the world, out of the destruction of older communities and civilizations new communities and civilizations were rising. When social decentralization goes to any length, there is an advantage in even the smallest forceful combination which is able to prey on other weaker social units. Hence, both within and outside of society there were constant encounters, conspiracies, and wars. The decentralizing forces in all areas were manifest in the mounting strength of the patriarchal sib, which not only strove for military and economic autonomy but developed its own powerful family religiosity as well. At the dawn of the Axial Period, household religion and ancestor worship were already strongly developed in China. In India, Aryan priests, originally the singers of praises of the gods of the eminent household, depended for their livelihood on the gifts of the generous ones (*maghavan*) in return for conducting essential rituals and performing appropriate magical rites. In Israel, too, the Yahweh war confederacy did not succeed without conflict with the religion of the household, and even in times of greatest military danger the individual often departed for performance of the rituals of the home. In Greece in Homeric times, the singer to the warrior deities of the noble house was a familiar fixture. In all areas of the ancient world in the early part of the Axial Period there was a confused battle between older decaying social forms and new and expanding social forces. The task of the intellectual was to find a solution to the problem of social disintegration with all its attendant wars and human suffering.

The intellectuals of these ancient societies were quite aware of the problems of the day—to secure peace, to establish the forms of a wider civil order, and to counteract the tendencies toward social decentralization. To the ancient thinker, his social responsibilities were beyond doubt.

In China the canny wisdom of Confucius is seen in his attempt to widen the traditional relations of the family to the realm. Mo-Tzu formulated a semidemocratic, semisocialistic conception of social order. The legalists with almost Machiavellian ruthlessness reviewed every device for the maximization of state power.

In India the social responsibility of the intellectual formulations appears in the many varied organismic theories of society. While at all times the emphasis was placed upon ultimate salvation from the world, the Indian intellectuals also attempted to stabilize in a most permanent way the relations among the social classes.

In Palestine priestly intellectuals developed an established religion out of the religion of a war confederation to meet the requirements of the larger social forms of an oriental despotism. And in the face of major social crisis, the prophets restylized its content in an ethically superb fashion.

In Greece, from the theories of social origins by the Sophists through the political inquiries of Plato and Aristotle to the politically sensitive writing of the dramatists and the historians, a philosophic literature was created belonging to the significant bodies of thought of the world.

In the various areas of the world the great need was for the development of institutional forms adequate to counteract the disintegrating and decentralizing tendencies of the times. It is difficult to imagine what, under the conditions of the time, could have brought about the new integration other than religious structures. The new socially integrating forces could not be found in the family or clan. In fact, the factors that strengthened the family and clan tended to disorganize the wider society. The larger social unity had to be religious or political. New political structures were needed and the intellectuals were everywhere active in creating them. One does not build political structures by force alone. A precondition of the peaceable formation of adequate political structures lay in the emergence of the religious institutions. At least the establishment required a system of loyalties stronger than those involved in the family or clan. Political structures could hardly have established such a system of loyalties on their own under the conditions of the time. Only religious institutions seem to have been capable of this.

In any case, the stabilization of the society proceeded most speedily when political and religious development went hand in hand. The emergence of Confucianism and Taoism in China; Jainism, Buddhism, and Hinduism in India; Yahwism in Palestine—all went together with the building of larger social forms. All the great religions of the world were either evolved during this period or constructed out of materials already present. The epoch saw the development of Confucianism, Jainism, Buddhism, Hinduism, and Judaism; out of the materials of Judaic religiosity Islam emerged, and in combination with Greek philosophy Christianity as well.

The political events that roughly mark the transformation of the social order—the triumph of the dynasty of the Ch'in under Shih Huang-ti, the emergence of the Maurya Dynasty under Asoka, the Babylonian Exile in Palestine, and the triumph of the empires of Macedonia and Rome—can easily conceal the most important point. The larger social forms and relative stability that emerged suddenly or gradually in the major areas were not political phenomena alone. In China the legalist intellectuals provided much of the technical knowledge that made the empire a success and provided the outlines of the bureaucracy. However, the empire did not achieve full internal stabilization until consolidation of Confucianism under the Han. Similarly in India the Maurya and Buddhism were linked. The consolidation and restoration of Hinduism occurred only after Buddhism and Jainism had done their work. All were linked with changing political fortunes. Stability was eventually found in the caste system. In the period following return from exile, social stability was found with an intensified lay religiosity. In the areas of the West, real stability was not found until, through Christianity, a new social homogeneity was won.

Among the developments in intellectuality and the intellectual accompanying these developments was the establishment of the canonical literatures which, in large measure, are still accepted from the respective cultural areas. A great simplification and consolidation of social roles occurred, roles which became fixed in quite a new sense.

THE COMPARATIVE SOCIAL ORDER AND SOCIAL ROLE WITH THE CLOSE OF THE AXIAL PERIOD

Area	*Institutional Order*	*Primary Intellectual Role*
China	bureaucratic empire	mandarin bureaucrat
India	caste system	Brahman *purohita*
Palestine	parish community centering in the synagogue	rabbi
Greco-Roman	imperium	moral counselor and jurist

SOCIETY, CIVILIZATION, AND THE INTELLECTUAL IN THE RECENT WEST

When the Axial Period came to a close in the third and second centuries B.C., the societies and civilizations that had been established did not suddenly disintegrate. They stiffened and lost their elasticity, perhaps in considerable measure as a product of the attempt by their members to prevent an insidious decay which was setting in. The communities and various aspects of the civilizations were subject to occasional revivals. In China there were moments when the old fire was periodically manifest in the revivals of court culture. In India, too, there were periodic attempts to reverse the general drift into a deepening caste system. The Judaic community was slowly hardened in a process still continuing in the first two centuries of the Christian era but in a manner permitting the creation of an internally high level of intellectual life perhaps never before equalled. At the same time the Jews were becoming an internationally settled guest people. Hellenic culture was hardened into a form so different from its original fluidity that the scholars coined the term Hellenism for its status at the time it was converted into a tool of imperial policy by the Macedonians and later by the Romans. However, ancient society in the West was decaying from within, Hellenism was hardening into a mechanical shell, and it was not long before the invaders from the north were able to pillage the ruins of the Roman Empire almost at will.

There were some movements to establish new societies and to bring about civilizational syntheses (such as the Islamic) in the long period between the

Axial Period and the present. However, nothing of quite the same scope and intensity of the societal movements of the Axial Period occurred before the events of the recent West. The cycle of society and civilization in which we are embedded has not run its course. However, both parallels and differences with the social developments of the Axial Period are already evident.

When the ancient world fell apart, responsible Roman administrators were well aware that something was wrong. The symptoms were everywhere evident: masses of formerly free men were turned into a proletariat in the cities without means to support themselves, the urban centers were tending to be depopulated, rural areas formerly cultivated by free yeoman farmers were either enclosed in slave-operated latifundia or abandoned to waste, and civic officials were finding their responsibilities impossibly burdensome.

Representatives of the new Christian congregations, which were growing despite sporadic persecutions, were also aware that the once resplendent society around them was falling into decay. It was fitted into the presuppositions of their theology, and the decline of Rome was visualized as the last stage of a process in the decline of the sinful secular world which began with the original sin in the Garden of Eden. St. Augustine synthesized the conceptions of the decline of Rome and Christian hope in his philosophy of history and the doctrine of the two cities (the worldly city and the City of God), one of which would suffer destruction because of man's sin; the other represented those who had received the faith. This philosophy of history dominated the interpretations of Western social history for a thousand years.

> The medieval churchmen had written history from a universal point of view, *sub specie aeternitatis*. Their world chronicles were constructed on a basis of theology and were shaped by concepts of a divinely ordained universal church with its secular counterpart in a universal empire. They divided human history either into Six Ages, corresponding to the six days of creation, or into the Four Monarchies mentioned in the prophecy of Daniel (2:40). The fourth and last of these monarchies had been definitely identified by St. Jerome with the Roman Empire. Under the influence of Augustine and Orosius the idea of the Roman Empire as the last of the world monarchies, which should continue until the beginning of the reign of Antichrist, was transferred from the pagan to the Christian empire.[22]

Though in the eleventh century new urban communities were rising in the West, it was not until the fifteenth century that these conceptions were reversed. According to Ferguson, it was Leonardo Bruni, a scholar and chancellor of the Republic of Florence, who more than anyone else perceived the role of the new urban communities in the development of modern Italy.

> Having broken with the theory of the continuity of the Roman Empire, Bruni was free to break also with the tradition of continuous de-

[22] Wallace K. Ferguson, *The Renaissance in Historical Thought* (Boston: Houghton Mifflin, 1948), p. 6.

> cline. The whole tenor of his work indicates an awareness of the rising fortunes of Italy after the break-up of the Carolingian Empire. . . . The cities of Italy gradually began to be mindful of their freedom and to think less of the imperial authority. Thereupon "such cities throughout Italy as had survived the various barbarian floods began to grow and flourish and return to their original power."[23]

Later historians and scholars were to confirm the correctness of Bruni's judgment that the cities were a new societal formation capable of bearing a cultural synthesis, the like of which had not been seen since the days of classical Greece.

The new urban communities rising in the West were to produce their own unique intellectuals in the humanists who often acted as tutors in noble households and ransacked antiquity for guidance in the affairs of the expanding urban communities. In one of his classic studies, Burckhardt spoke of them as follows:

> We have here first to speak of those citizens, mostly Florentines, who made antiquarian interests one of the chief objects of their lives, and who were themselves either distinguished scholars, or else distinguished *dilettanti* who maintained the scholars. They were of peculiar significance during the period of transition at the beginning of the fifteenth century, since it was in them that humanism first showed itself practically as an indispensable element in daily life.[24]

From the beginning the humanists of the Western city had properties that differentiated them from their counterparts in Greek antiquity. There was a close fusion of humanist and artist unknown in ancient times. As Burckhardt phrased it:

> In Italy at the time of the Renaissance, we find artists who in every branch created new and perfect works, and who also made the greatest impression as men. . . . Dante, who even in his lifetime was called by some a poet, by others a philosopher, by others a theologian, pours forth in all his writings a stream of personal force by which the reader apart from the interest of the subject, feels himself carried away.
>
> The fifteenth century is, above all, that of the many-sided man. There is no biography which does not, besides the chief work of its hero, speak of other pursuits all passing beyond the limits of dilettantism. The Florentine merchant and statesman was often learned in both the classical languages; the most famous humanists read the ethics and politics of Aristotle to him and his sons; even the daughters of the house were highly educated. It is in these circles that private education was first treated seriously. The humanist, on his side, was compelled to the most varied attainments, since his philological learning was not limited, as it is now, to the theoretical knowledge of classical antiquity, but had to serve the practical needs of daily life.[25]

[23] *Ibid.*, p. 11; L. Bruni, *Historiarum Florentini populi libri xii*, in Muratori, XIX, 3 (New ed. by E. Santini, Citta di Castello, 1914), p. 23.

[24] Jacob Burckhardt, *The Civilization of the Renaissance* (New York: Oxford University Press, 1945), p. 128.

[25] *Ibid.*, pp. 84–85.

So far, the social and cultural events of the recent West traced a path approximately similar to the developments in the main culture areas of the Axial Period. The Western city began to take shape in the tenth century, and began to achieve autonomy on a foundation of revolutionary movements in the eleventh century. By the twelfth century the free granting of urban rights had become the rule. The high point of this urban revolution was reached in the sixteenth century, after which the city began to harden from within and to be threatened from without.

Western cultural development was set into accelerated motion in connection with the events of the city. The new cultural demands of the emerging urban communities led to the so-called Renaissance of the twelfth century with its rapid recovery of ancient science. By the thirteenth century the cities had become the scene of conflict between medieval theology and the learning recovered from antiquity. By the fifteenth century the new communities had begun to evolve a cultural synthesis of their own. However, at this very time the nation-state was rising. It was to find its key intellectuals in a new kind of humanist-scientist, and to evolve a unique civilizational synthesis of its own.

Since we are now living in what may be the climactic period of Western society and civilization (the last great wave of the crystallization of the world into nation-states is now in process), it is not possible to say where these developments will end, though some persons[26] believe they see a hardening of intellectuality which may be an omen of incipient decline.

SUMMARY

There are the outlines of great creative periods in human culture before the time period of our study. Some time between 14,000 and 8000 B.C. humankind moved out of a world of the tribal communities of hunters and gatherers into a world of peasant villages within which active food production was carried on. In these neolithic peasant villages of the old world, the domestication of plants and animals was carried out, pottery-making was discovered, a great advance in textile manufacture was made, social units of larger size were created, and a new differentiation of institutions was achieved.

A second great creative period of human culture, one conventionally identified with the rise of civilization, was carried out between 5000 and 3500 B.C., when the first cities of the ancient world were formed as new kinds of communities on a foundation of neolithic peasant villages. The new urban communities were synthesized around secondary rather than primary institutions. They provided the context for the emergence of many new urban types: priests, administrators, specialized craftsmen, mercenaries, and the like. A new specialization of institutions occurred with city religions, city governments, complex economic institutions, social classes. New develop-

[26] For example, see Julien Benda, examined earlier.

ments in the arts, in architecture, and in literature were made possible. With the invention of writing, human history dawned. However, it seems that by the time of the Axial Period the first cities of the world had reached the limits of their development, and had begun to crystallize into comparatively inelastic forms.

The specific period of our study, the so-called Axial Period of human history, represents the third great wave of human cultural creativity or the second wave of civilization. The figure of speech for the period, the axis or hub of civilization, is, of course, only appropriate from the standpoint of the present. Like spokes of a wheel, the underlying forms of contemporary civilization spring from the solutions to the institutional problems of this period. Nevertheless, there are certain misleading aspects of the figure, for it suggests that the period from about 900 to 200 B.C. was the starting point of all civilization. However, the Axial Period itself was preceded by the earlier wave of civilization accompanying the early city formation, which terminated in the civic imperialisms of the river valleys. These, in turn, were preceded by the world of peasant villages. Every wave of social and cultural creativity works with social and cultural materials already in existence; the so-called Axial Period, so to speak, also had its axis.

The comparative review of the social structure, and the intellectual and his product in the four major areas of the ancient world, adds strong confirming evidence to the general hypotheses of our study. The Axial Period opens in all areas with the bankruptcy of the previous civilizational movements. In ancient China the empire of the Shang which is discernible in the last half of the second millennium, while supporting a civilization of considerable refinement, seems to have passed its apex. It was not able to maintain itself in the face of more vigorous barbarians on its frontiers. When it was eventually conquered by the Chou, the deterioration of the empire into feudal particularism occurred at a rapid rate.

Similarly the ancient Mohenjo-Daro and Harappa civilizations of northern India appear to have grown so rigid and inelastic that it required only a minor push by the more barbaric invading Indo-Europeans from the north to complete their destruction. A period of cultural backwardness followed in which even the techniques of writing were lost.

On the borders of Palestine the ancient civilizations of Babylonia and Egypt were bogged down in their own internal problems at the time of the opening of Jewish history. This deterioration of the great powers had gone so far that they were unable to protect their frontier outposts in the Palestine area against the uprisings and conquests of confederations of peasants and stock-breeders or against new invaders like the Philistines from the sea coast.

In the eastern Mediterranean the ancient civilization of Crete had passed its peak. It, too, found itself in such a state of decay as to be unable effectively to defend itself against the piratical raids of barbaric sea raiders who roved the Mediterranean in search of booty.

In all areas, the Axial Period opened a world partly structured by preexisting civilizations which, though possessing refined culture and writing, had reached some type of inner societal limitations. In all these areas the forces for particularism seemed at any moment ready to triumph over the forces for universalism. It was almost as if new institutions were in need of being invented, but the creativity was prevented from emerging from their own midst. In all areas the future lay in the hands of more primitive peoples lacking the refinements of the old centers of culture but free of their limitations as well. There was a freshness, a dawn quality, a naive self-confidence, about the more barbaric peoples who created the high civilizations of the Axial Period. At the threshold of modern times in the West, we again find an ancient empire in decay, overrun by barbarian revolutions, and ready for a new societal and civilizational synthesis.

In all cases except the last we are able to trace the course of societal and civilizational development through the period of its formation and completion with its very different effects upon the creative or conservative talents of its intellectuals. The creative eras are those in which extensive space is allowed for the play of individuality. This, in turn, seems to be related to the formative stage in the communities and civilizations concerned, which brings us to the four specific hypotheses that will guide our study:

1. The creative epochs of humankind are the periods of the formation of new communities. At such times the sphere permitted for individuality of the intellectuals tends to be widened, and its products tend to be rewarded.

2. The quality and quantity of creativity are related to the type of community in which they occur. In general, the brilliant creative periods have coincided with the creation of the more complex human communities.

3. During the periods of the maturity of a community and the completion of its cultural synthesis, the encouragement of free creativity tends to come to an end. The sphere of social life left open for the free construction of individuals is narrowed, and a restricted array of intellectual forms tends to be fixed.

4. The standards of the acceptability of thought, or truth in this restrictive sense, tend to vary as between the creative and conformist epochs of human civilization: (a) During creative epochs there is a strong tendency to determine truth in terms of standards and criteria established in the proper conduct of the thought process, and (b) during conformist epochs of human civilization there is a tendency to establish socially acceptable truth by institutional procedures.

SELECTED BIBLIOGRAPHY

Burckhardt, Jacob, *The Civilization of the Renaissance in Italy* (New York: Oxford University Press, 1945).

Childe, V. Gordon, *What Happened in History* (New York: Penguin Books, 1946).

Jaspers, Karl, *The Origin and Goal of History* (New Haven: Yale University Press, 1953).

Mannheim, Karl, *Ideology and Utopia*, trans. by Louis Wirth and Edward Shils (New York: Harcourt, Brace, 1949).

Sorokin, Pitirim, *Society, Culture, and Personality* (New York: Harper & Brothers, 1947).

Spengler, Oswald, *The Decline of the West*, trans. by Charles Francis Atkinson (New York: Alfred A. Knopf, 1926).

Toynbee, Arnold J., *A Study of History* (New York: Oxford University Press, 1947), abridgement of Vols. I–VI by D. C. Sommervell.

Weber, Max, *The Religion of China*, trans. by Hans Gerth (Glencoe, Illinois: The Free Press, 1951).

Weber, Max, *Ancient Judaism*, trans. by Hans Gerth and Don Martindale (Glencoe, Illinois: The Free Press, 1952).

Weber, Max, *The Religions of India*, trans. by Hans Gerth and Don Martindale (Glencoe, Illinois: The Free Press, 1958).

Part II

THE CHINESE MANDARIN

THE SOCIAL forces which created the Chinese mandarin and his influence upon these forces supply the first of the series of empirical studies in society, the intellectual, and civilization which will constitute the greater part of our study. The theory of social and cultural change and the general manner in which it seems to apply to developments in ancient China were outlined in the preceding section. It is the purpose of the present and later sections to test these suggestions by a more thorough examination of the facts.

Social behaviorism assumes that while the same general principles operate in behavior at all times and places, this does not imply that any historical series can be exhaustively explained in terms of these principles or that events in one time and place must be identical with those in another. While the human struggle always has two basic forms, the contest of man with nature and of man with man, nature presents man with different obstacles and opportunities from case to case, and cultural traditions accumulate in ways unique to the given area.

In order to estimate both the unique drift of ancient Chinese society and culture and elements which are paralleled elsewhere because they were produced by the principles of community and civilization formation, a brief review is made of natural and cultural backgrounds of ancient China in the periods of particular interest to us. The unique elements in Chinese development extend back at least as far as the neolithic period and accumulate in the period of the Shang or Yin, China's first historically determinable civic period.

The period of greatest interest to us is the Chou or feudal period, during which political and religious institutions were fragmented and particularized. It was a period of agricultural improvement, of expansion, and of commercial and industrial development. It was also a period of wars, revolutions, and political consolidations. Step by step the states moved toward the consolidation eventually effected by the Ch'in. The Ch'in also completed the liquidation of the feudal system, which was under way by this time, and laid the foundation for those policies which were, in the following century or two, to bring the Empire substantially into the form maintained until modern times. The feudal period was thus a time of transition, of wars, of revolutions, of economic and technical growth, of rapid change, and of dramatic contrasts.

In the following section these societal developments are sketched first, for they provide the *milieu* of the intellectual. The changing social role of the intellectual is then traced as it arises and responds to societal changes. Finally, while no complete examination of the civilization of ancient China, which arose in connection with these societal formations, is presented, the social thought, the most immediate contribution of the intellectuals to that civilization, is outlined.

4

THE DEVELOPMENT OF ANCIENT CHINESE SOCIETY

THE CORE of China is made up of the valleys of the Yellow and Yangtze rivers which traverse the tablelands from the western mountains. Northern China, comprising the provinces of Shantung, Hopei, Honan, Shansi, Shensi, and Kansu, is traversed by the Yellow River, which rises in the mountains that fringe Tibet. The river carries much of the sediment lodged in shifting bars, which have built the alluvian plain that borders Shantung. The Yellow River presents an almost impossible problem of flood control, for in the course of its sedimentation it tends to build natural dikes which rise above the plain until eventually the river bursts its natural banks, flooding the plain and changing its course. The soil of the plain is loess, a wind-deposited soil, the product of thousands of years of dust storms, which blankets regions of North China from the borders of Mongolia on the north to the Yangtze Valley in the south. It is fertile and easily cultivated and has been subject to the extensive agricultural exploitation.

The Yangtze breaks into two general regions. The river rises in the Kunlun Mountains, cutting great canyons in its precipitous course. It traverses Szechwan, bordering on Tibet, and part of Yunnan, bordering on Burma. Much of the area along the upper river is well watered by lakes and smaller rivers. Part of the province of Szechwan extends over the hilly region known as the Red Basin, toward the western edge of which there is a fertile plain watered by an ancient irrigation system. The Red Basin has abundant rainfall and a subtropical climate and has long supported a dense population. The lower river traverses a valley and delta region.[1]

Except for its three southernmost provinces, China lies in the temperate zone. In the arid northwest the land masses are very warm in summer, and moisture-laden winds sweep northward from the ocean. In winter the process is reversed. In the south, where the coast is mountainous, the precipitation is heavy. The rainfall is monsoonal, in central China averaging about 40

[1] For a review of China's geography and the defense of the theory that it is the basis for a southern movement of China's civilization, see Harold J. Wiems, *China's March Toward the Tropics* (Hamden, Conn., The Shoestring Press, 1954).

inches a year and declining to less than 20 inches in the north. The north, which suffers periods of drought and famine, grades off into true desert.

PREHISTORY

Man has long inhabited this area. The bones of an ancient race closely allied to *Pithecanthropus* of Java have been found in caves near Peking.[2] Peking man (*Sinanthropus pekinensis*), sometimes asserted to show characteristics peculiar to the yellow race, lived in caves, had crude stone implements, knew the art of fire-making, buried his dead, and possibly practiced cannibalism. It is assumed that he lived in the area about 500,000 years ago. At that time the climate of North China was warm and moist, with great lakes and rivers in what are now dry steppes, supporting a variety of wild life: elephants, rhinoceros, some species of cattle, antelope, and tapirs.

In the ancient lake region between 20,000 and 10,000 B.C., a paleolithic culture flourished with implements similar to those of Europe (Mousterian, Aurignacian, and Magdalenian cultures appear). This culture was borne by men ancestral to ourselves.[3] This Stone Age culture appears to have spread over North China, Mongolia, and Manchuria. The lack of evidence of implements in the south may be due to use of perishable implements of wood and bamboo rather than to lack of people.

In North China in the modern period there has been an increase in aridity consequent upon the gradual recession of the latest glacial age. The formation of loess soils accompanied these changes, and various branches of a neolithic culture make their appearance. Around 4000 B.C. interpenetration of cultures is evident.

In the west a combination of pastoralism and agriculture was practiced, the chief animals being horses. The people were not Mongols. It has been suggested that this was the original home of the Turks (Shensi and Kansu). In the western (Szechwan) and mountainous regions (Kansu and Shensi) lived a shepherd people, wandering with their flocks. There were at least four distinct cultures: in the south, the Liao culture of Austro-Asiatic hunters; the Yao culture to the east, mountaineers who hunted and practiced some agriculture; the Tai culture of southern rice growers; and the Yueh culture, a northeast (Hopei, Shantung) people ancestral to the Tunguses who hunted, practiced primitive agriculture, made a crude pottery, and raised hogs.

TRADITIONAL HISTORY

Continuities appear between these neolithic cultures and the culture of historical China. In the earliest written documents extant, for example, the

[2] Franz Weidenreich, *Apes, Giants, and Man* (Chicago: University of Chicago Press, 1946).

[3] Franz Z. Weidenreich, "On the Earliest Representatives of Modern Mankind Recovered on the Soil of East Asia," *Bulletin of the Natural History Society of Peking*, XIII (1939), pp. 162–174.

Shi Ching (Classic of Poetry) and the *Shu Ching* (Classic of History), there is evidence of a far from primitive agricultural people. Archeological finds in the regions of Honan reveal a people of neolithic culture (the skeletons seem to belong to the same stock as the contemporary Chinese), with implements like those still manufactured in China in modern times.

Traditional Chinese history begins with the age of the five sovereigns (Wu T'i),[4] and the three august ones who ruled in a golden age of perfect virtue. Each of the five sovereigns was held to be a successive embodiment of one of the five elements. Each represented a center of civilization. Hu-hsi and Nü-kua invented marriage; Shen-nung, a sovereign with the head of an ox, made the plow and invented agriculture; Huang-ti invented weapons; Shun made porcelain vases; Hsi-ho regulated the solar year; K'i taught men to sow and transplant; and Kao-yao formulated the penal law.[5] The sovereign ruled over space, because he was the master of time. Huang-ti, for example, established the order of the sun, moon, and stars. Acting in accordance with the seasons, the sovereigns guided their influence. The age of the five sovereigns, according to traditional history, was followed by the three royal dynasties. Yü the Great followed Shun, the last sovereign, and founded the dynasty of the Hsia. When it fell from virtue, it was displaced in turn by the Yin, or Shang, which was later displaced by the Chou.[6]

Among dates supplied for these periods are the predynastic period, 2357–2206 B.C.; Hsia dynasty, 2205–1766 B.C.; and the Shang, 1766–1122 B.C.[7]

While many of the things assigned by traditional Chinese history to the pre-Shang period must actually have occurred (new modes of house building, domestication, development of musical instruments, invention of writing, developments in medicine, development of a calendar, the use of uniform weights and measures), historical traditions have so clearly been retouched and reworked to conform to the needs of later ages as to be unreliable in detail. Granet observed that in all ages in China, at the moment that writings or objects have been shown to the public, they become the possession of a circle or syndicate which uses them as a means of influence or of fortune. As editions become perfect and criticism more learned, the work is brought into accord with ancient tradition.

> The work of the Chinese critic strongly resembles touching up. It is directed to the purification of the texts and to making sure that nothing contradicts the official version. An infinite amount of erudition has been expended, in such a way as to make all research aiming at what a European would call truth almost impossible.[8]

[4] Marcel Granet, *Chinese Civilization* (London: Kegan Paul, 1930), pp. 9 ff.
[5] *Ibid.*, p. 11.
[6] *Ibid.*, p. 14.
[7] Edward Thomas Williams, *A Short History of China* (New York: Harper & Brothers, 1928), p. 28. Another chronology places the dates of the Shang dynasty at 1558–1051 B.C. Carl Whiting Bishop, "The Chronology of Ancient China," in *Journal of the American Oriental Society* (1932), 52, pp. 232–247.
[8] Granet, *op. cit.*, p. 51.

One must be equally suspicious of archeological finds the moment they become important.

On the banks of the Huan River near the village of Hsiao T'un in the district of Anyang, farmers noted after rain and after plowing the appearance of bones of a peculiar type and smoothness. At first they were thought to be dragon bones; these were ground up for medicinal purposes and prescribed for various ailments, especially nervous disorders. However, when some of these bones with markings came into the hands of Chinese antiquaries, the markings were recognized to be a form of Chinese writing older than all forms known at the time. They were the scapulas or leg bones of cattle or the shells of tortoises, used in divination. Questions were written on them, and applied heat caused cracks to appear on them, from which the diviner determined the answer of the spirits to the questions. Hardly had the bone inscriptions become known when mass forgeries began to appear.

> The Chinese are masters at counterfeiting antiquities, and they began counterfeiting these inscribed bones almost as soon as it was learned that archeologists would pay for them. Thousands of them have been turned out, most of them quite near to the site where the genuine ones are found. The fakers use the bones without writing . . . which are practically valueless, for their work, and some of it is very good indeed.[9]

Thus, for example, when traditional Chinese history attributes to Yü the Great the draining of the waters of a great flood and the founding of the first dynasty of Hsia, there is a general plausibility in the report. Undoubtedly major works of irrigation and flood control were as important to early Chinese civilizations as to those of the Near East. However, in a land with so much retouching of history and invention of antiquities, the acceptance of detail must be undertaken with caution. At the same time the gradual deciphering of the language on the oracle bones has confirmed most of the names which traditional history attributed to the Shang, gradually lifting it out of the sphere of mythology to the realm of historically established fact.

The first archeologically and historically determinable literate urban Chinese civilization is the Shang or Yin, centering at Anyang in the fourteenth century B.C. Though some Western scholars represented the Bronze Age culture of China as established by Western invaders who came already equipped with bronze, horses and chariots, and cattle to establish themselves as an aristocracy over enslaved neolithic populations, there is little support for this in the facts. Had they been of foreign derivation, the Shang aristocrats would hardly have employed their skills in bronze-making to cast vessels for sacrificing in patterns copied from the cooking pots of humble natives. In terms of archeologically established cultural continuities, it is much more plausible to assume that Chinese urban development was pri-

[9] Herrlee Glessner Creel, *The Birth of China* (London: Jonathan Cape, 1936), p. 25. It was during the excavations begun at Anyang under the direction of Li Chi that the inscriptions on the oracle bones were proved to be genuine. Li Chi, *The Beginnings of Chinese Civilization* (Seattle: University of Washington Press, 1957).

marily a native growth, possibly spurred on by some things diffused from the West.

THE SHANG DYNASTY

The Shang was a city dynasty; hence a period of city formation preceded it in ancient China. In Mesopotamia, when the successive archeological layers are isolated from the neolithic peasant village to the city (as at Tepe Garwa), the city appears as a new synthesis of neolithic cultures. Li Chi's excavations near Anyang similarly reveal successive deposits. At many sites, for example, painted pottery, black pottery, and the products of the historical Shang culture are found in successive layers.[10] Shang culture represented a new synthesis of cultural elements:

1. New developments in the ceramic industry
2. Employment of bronze to cast tools, weapons, and sacrificial vessels
3. The presence of a highly developed writing system
4. Chamber burials and human sacrifices
5. The use of chariots
6. Advanced stone carvings[11]

This synthesis rests on long-time indigenous developments. For example, though the Hsia-t'un script is some 1800 years later than the earliest Sumerian writing, and though the idea of keeping written records may have migrated from the Tigris and Euphrates to the Yellow River, Chinese writing at this time was composed of more than 2000 characters quite unlike those of the cuneiform scripts.

One must beware of the tendency in historical reconstruction to project a possibility from a general principle, then to make deductions from it which are taken as facts. However, if one never forgets their hypothetical status, it is not unfair to apply the sociology of community formation to the materials of ancient Chinese history. When China clearly emerges in the historical accounts, it has the form of a city dynasty. However, one cannot have city dynasties without the initial formation of cities. When the city appears as a new community synthesis of the materials of peasant villages, it is so much more powerful, with its professional soldiers, superior weapons, materials, and fortifications, than any peasant village that at first its only rival is another city. In both Egypt and Babylonia the competition of the cities for dominance of the countryside opened an epoch of city imperialism. The Shang dynasty has all the properties of such a late stage of civic development. According to tradition, supported by archeology, around 1400 B.C. P'an Keng moved his people to Anyang and built a city on the banks of the Huan River. This suggests the prior existence of other cities.

Huge buildings of wood were erected on pounded earth foundations. A

[10] Li Chi, *op. cit.*, p. 14. Creel has also noted this fusion, *op. cit.*, p. 50.
[11] Li Chi, *op. cit.*, p. 15.

section of the city was occupied by royal artisans who manufactured bronze. Another section of the manufacturing area was occupied by artisans working in stone, carving mother of pearl, jade, and bone. Knife- and utensil-making were thriving industries. Surrounding the city was a pounded-earth wall. Agriculture, animal-breeding, and hunting supplied the livelihood for the citizens. Hunting parties were organized by the royal family. Possibly elephants were used.[12] Horses were kept in large numbers and used to draw chariots. Possibly carts were also drawn by oxen, and water buffalo were used for routine hauling. Among the domestic animals kept by the Shang were cattle, pigs, sheep, dogs, and chickens. Cattle were the principal domestic animals. Wheat and millet were the primary grains from which liquor was manufactured. Irrigation was practiced; a textile plant (probably hemp) was grown. Plows were made of wood; silk culture was practiced; a wine industry was developed.[13] Cowry shells were used as money; tribute from vassal cities was often in the form of cowry shells or bronzes.

Shang society seems to have comprised, in addition to the royal family and aristocrats, free individuals and slaves. The status of women of the upper classes was high. Chariots and armor made of leather reinforced by wood were possessed by warrior aristocrats. Ministers and officials of a professional sort were employed by the Shang kings in their government along with members of the royal clan and aristocracy.

The Shang people buried quantities of objects with their dead in a manner suggesting concepts of another world and its needs. However, ancestors were not the only deities. There was a Dragon Woman as well as an Eastern and Western Mother, and a Ruler of the Quarters. A number of functional deities, for example, King Wind, were the assistants of Ti, who was possibly the highest ruler of the gods. Among the subjects of divination were the determination of what sacrifices should be made, announcements to be made to the spirits, and decisions on matters of state, on journeys and rests, on hunting and fishing prospects, on war manoeuvers, on the prospects of crops, and on the state of the weather.

When one examines the established facts about the Shang dynasty in the light of the theory of the city community, a number of additional possibilities are suggested: merchant strata must have developed and enjoyed royal favor (or represented a royal monopoly), for a considerable number of things, such as mother of pearl and cowry shells, had to be transported great distances. The high development and standardization of writing suggests the existence of temple schools in which literary culture was taught and monopolized. The close association of writing with religious and political requirements not only shows the ties between priest intellectuals and the royal administration, but suggests that writing, here as elsewhere, was being

[12] Tsui Chi, *A Short History of Chinese Civilization* (New York: G. P. Putnam's, 1943), p. 25.

[13] *Ibid.*, p. 27.

brought into the service of secular administration. Although there is a tendency to project the religious forms of a later time into the Shang period, attributing to its religion the form of ancestor worship, it is more plausible to assume that religion was, in some measure at least, a civic cult rather than a domestic, tribal, or peasant village cult, as was the case of the religion of the early cities of the Near East.

CHOU FEUDALISM

When the ancient city in both the West and the East reached a stage of development where city faced city across an intervening space of peasant villages, an era of city imperialism set in. Moreover, in time the new improvements in weapons technology diffused to tribal circles outside the cities, where nomads and mountaineers could often become a threat to the cities. Thus the ancient city was unavoidably set upon a course of city imperialism. When this occurred the organization of the city community was often taxed beyond its limits, and sooner or later conflict with increasingly formidable barbarians tended to break out. In China this event occurred at the time the Chou displaced the Shang.[14]

The Chou was a principality in the Wei valley on the western frontier of the Shang. Its people were perhaps racially and certainly culturally somewhat different from the Chinese of the time, though intermarriage occurred with the Shang royal families perhaps as a part of ancient oriental harem politics. When Chou Hsin successfully revolted against Wen Wang, the change of dynasty was brought about (1122 B.C.).

According to traditional history, the Chou tribe which conquered the Shang was the leader of a military coalition of tribes less civilized than the Shang people. The first Chou rulers introduced a feudal system of political control,[15] and as many as 1,773 states were established. However, a consolidation by conquest or other means set in almost immediately, so that by the opening of the Spring and Autumn period (named from the Ch'un-Ch'iu annals of the State of Lu), 722–381 B.C., they had been reduced to 170.

> Already by the start of the Ch'un Ch'iu period a process of consolidation had taken place. Towns pushing out their areas had come into contact and conflict, and the weaker ones were absorbed by the stronger. Some alliances were formed, but the allegiance to the Chou ruler still formed the main bulwark against the ruder tribes which roamed outside the pale of Chou civilization to the West. . . . By the beginning of the

[14] See E. T. C. Werner, *A History of Chinese Civilization* (Shanghai: *The Shanghai Times*, 1940); E. T. Williams, *op. cit.*, pp. 54 f.; Creel, *op. cit.*, pp. 219 ff.; Granet, *op. cit.*, pp. 23 ff.

[15] E. Stuart Kirby, "Introduction to the Economic History of China," *Far Eastern Economic Review*, Hong Kong, 1951–1952, Chaps. V–VI. Elements of Chou feudalism which trace to Shang times are indicated by K. A. Wittfogel, "The Foundations and Stages of Chinese Economic History," *Zeitschrift für Sozialforschung*, IV, 1935, pp. 26–58. Otto Franke, *Geschichte des Chinesische Reiches*, Vol. I, Berlin, 1930, pp. 133–150, traced the rise of the early Chou feudal states.

> Lu chronicles of 722 B.C. there were only about 170 states in the area of Chou control. . . . At the end . . . there were only 13.[16]

Chou feudalism established a number of ranked social classes, and the various states were ranked at diplomatic functions and conferences according to the original patents given their heads: Kung, Hou, Po, Tzu, and Nan were respectively duke, marquis, earl, viscount, and baron. The trends evident by the beginning of the Spring and Autumn period indicated the extent in which the growth of local autonomy had proceeded independently of the original rank of the states by the Chou.

RANK AND COMPOSITION OF CHOU STATES

State[17]	*Chou Rank*	*Sub-States Consolidated according to Li Tung-fang*
Lu	marquis	12
Sung	duke	9
Wei	marquis	7
Ch'i	marquis	14
Chin	earl	43
Ch'u	viscount	32
Wu	viscount	6
Yen	earl	1

The Chou initiated a definite cultural break in Chinese development. For a time the monarchs of the Chou were able to extend their domains, and even gained a foothold in the Yangtze Valley. However, by the ninth and eighth centuries it was clear that the kingdom, long divided into principalities, was growing progressively weaker, and the local principalities had begun to increase in size. Eventually, out of fear of barbarian inroads, the capitol had to be moved from the valley of the Wei eastward. Thereafter the real point of development was in the separate states.

Though the empire persisted in name for five more centuries, from the eighth to the middle of the third centuries B.C., China was in fact a collection of independent feudal principalities. In theory the princes owed homage, tribute, and military service to the Chou monarchs; in fact, alliances and leagues of individual states won hegemony. Warfare between the individual feudal aristocrats was more an affair of honor and an excuse to exhibit individual skill and gallantry than to annihilate the enemy. Warfare between the feudal states and between feudal states and barbarians was another matter.

By the seventh century B.C., five states had emerged as more powerful than the rest, and at various times first one and then another managed to achieve hegemony. Monopolies over various natural resources and also

[16] Richard Louis Walker, *The Multi-State System of Ancient China* (Hamden, Conn.: The Shoestring Press, 1953), p. 20.

[17] *Ibid.*, p. 27. Following Li Tung-fang, "The Ch'un-ch'iu and Chan-kuo," in the *Complete Discussions of Chinese History* (Chungking: Commercial Press, 1944), pp. 114–125.

over commerce, which was beginning to develop rather rapidly, were important in the rise of princes of these feudal states. Walker has compactly reviewed some of the evidences of growing prosperity in the seventh and sixth centuries B.C.

With increasing frequency there is mention of building and castle construction, such as Tso's report that the Duke Hsiang erected a castle after the style of those in the Ch'u, where he had visited two years earlier (542 B.C.). Increasing numbers of items of clothing, carriage ornaments, and other items of material wealth are mentioned in the literature deriving from the latter years of the Ch'un-Ch'iu. Bronze vessels which in Shang times had been reserved for sacrificial use became household fixtures in the palaces of aristocrats. The increased use of slaves was reported.

> In 679 B.C. 66 slaves were killed to accompany Duke Wu of Ch'in to his grave. A little over fifty years later almost three times that number (177) accompanied Duke Mu to his grave.
>
> Of course the main reason for the increasing prosperity was the great improvement in the means of production and distribution. The Spring and Autumn Period witnessed the utilization of iron on an extensive scale both for weapons of war and in agriculture. The introduction of the ox-drawn plow marked a great advance, increasing commerce made greater specialization possible, and made available a greater variety of products in the market place. . . . In the year 493 B.C. . . . the ruler of Ch'i was helping support a revolution within Chin. . . . At one point the leader of the rebellion was in the town of Chao-ko and in dire straits. Ch'i sent a convoy of grain to help meet his needs. The convoy was intercepted and over 1,000 wagon-loads of grain were seized. Chao-ko was at least 300 miles from Ch'i.
>
> Undoubtedly much economic growth was fostered by state action. One of the key activities . . . was the construction of large-scale waterworks projects for irrigation and flood control.[18]

The disintegration of peaceful relations was progressive. The Chin which had managed to gain hegemony and form a federation eventually disintegrated. The principal combatants were the frontier principalities: the Ch'in, Ch'u, and Yen. In the fourth century B.C., the Ch'in conquered Shu (Szechwan). By shrewd policies of treaties and alliances (which were kept only so long as they served their purpose) and warfare, the Ch'in increasingly advanced its fortunes. Most decisive for success were military innovations developed by the Ch'in in its struggles with the barbarians. Reliance was less exclusively placed on chariots. Disciplined foot soldiers were used with telling effect. When Ch'u, its last great rival, was eliminated (221 B.C.), the conquest of the Chinese culture area by the Ch'in was completed.

CHOU (FEUDAL) SOCIETY

The break between the Shang and Chou periods of ancient China seems to have been as great as that between the Roman and Holy Roman Empires

[18] Walker, *op. cit.*, p. 17.

in Europe. When the Chou conquerors had gained the empire, they parceled out territory to relatives and allies of the royal family, giving to the prebendaries the power of life and death over the individuals occupying these lands. The nobles were held in a kind of vassalage to the king. The disintegration of political unity that flowed from this practice is thoroughgoing proof of extensive departure from the Shang system of administration. Creel observes that though there is at least one bronze inscription telling of the appeal to the king by a man for protection of his lands against a stronger neighbor, in the nature of the case an individual's power determined what he could or could not hold.[19]

On the basis of a study of inscriptions Hsü Chung-shu argues that in the early period of the Chou there were four, not five, feudal ranks which later became traditional. Two, marquis and baron, were remnants of Shang times. According to the *Book of History*, four ranks (marquis, count, baron, and knight) were distinguished as outer ranks, indicating that they were territorial officials in contrast to the inner ranks serving the central administration. The duties of holders of outer ranks were as follows: the marquis patroled for the king; the count remitted the land tax; the baron performed king's services; and the knight defended the king.

> In accordance with their specific functions . . . the distribution of fiefs was as follows: the knight's fiefs were located at the capital, the fiefs of the barons farther out, those of counts were still farther away, and the fiefs of the marquises were situated on the borders of the country, since the function of the marquises was to patrol the borders.[20]

Chang Yin-lin maintains that the Chou was feudal in the strict sense of the word. The king had exclusive control only over his royal *demesne*. The rest of the land was granted to a number of states constructed in like manner. In each territory the lord had his own tax system, labor force, army, administrators, and capital city. The states were of three kinds: those established from conquered territory over which from the beginning the Chou placed relatives (the Ch'u and Lu in Shantung, and Chin in Shensi); those established later by subdivision of the royal demesne (Ch'in in Shansi, and Cheng in Honan); and those surviving from the period of the Shang but which surrendered to the Chou (the Sung in Honan and Hsü in Anhwei).[21]

Only aristocrats, called *tai-fu*, qualified as minor lords of the states. The men were known as *shih*. There was a maximum of six in a state. They usually, but not always, possessed land grants. The social strata consisted of the Chou king and feudal lords, the officials and warriors, the common people (chiefly farmers), and the slaves owned by the aristocrats.

[19] Creel, *op. cit.*, p. 276.

[20] Hsü Chung-shu, "The Well-Field System in Shang and Chou," *Chinese Social History*, by E. Tu Zen Sun and John de Francis (Washington, D.C.: American Council of Learned Societies, 1956), p. 7.

[21] Chang Yin-lin, "Feudal Society of the Chou Dynasty," in *Chinese Social History*, *op. cit.*, p. 21.

The primary source of slaves was war. Except for those new captives which were sacrificed, most slaves were retained in the feudal household and on the lord's demesne. For military exploits the Duke Ching (599–581 B.C.) was given a thousand families of barbarian slaves. Wealthy *tai-fu* may at times have possessed as many as ten thousand.

> Every feudal household from the king down to the official was a self-sufficient economic unit. Slaves produced all the necessary goods, from food, clothing, salt, and timber to chariots, weapons, and musical and ritual implements. Labor was supervised by a special official.[22]

If the same forces were operating on slavery under the Chou as elsewhere (in Rome at the time of its decline, or in the Southern United States prior to the Civil War), the system was tending to decline, being replaced by a serf system. Slavery is a wasteful method of economic production, yielding only slight profits over costs. Moreover, no slave system has ever been self-producing. Hence, the system can be maintained only so long as wars or a slave traffic sustain it. The numerous wars of the feudal period undoubtedly maintained a large and continuous supply of new slaves, much as the black market in slaves in the United States from 1808 to 1860 made such a practice possible. The slave system was a heritage of the Chou from Shang times, just as slavery was a heritage from Rome of the early Western Middle Ages. Early medieval slavery, inherited from Rome, was sustained for a time during the wars that accompanied the peoples' movements, only to disappear under conditions that made it unprofitable.

In any case, during the early days of the Chou new territories and cities were occupied and partitioned between the lords and *tai-fu*. Persons pressed into slavery worked on the estates. The remaining land was cultivated by the peasants who originally had occupied it. From the peasants exactions in agricultural produce, manufactured articles, and *corvée* service were made. Though the peasants had a status higher than that of the slaves, their lot was so hard that they were often driven to revolt.

> But the peasants and other common people sometimes did not behave properly when the aristocrats proved too callous toward their sufferings. King Li (878–842 B.C.), the tenth monarch of Chou, lost his throne in a popular uprising when he was chased out of the capital.[23]

In a similar manner the peasants under the Wei (643 B.C.) engaged in a great popular uprising that drove the ruler into exile.

Specialists for war were called *shih*, a term originally meaning warrior and only later, a man of letters. The warrior's training included archery, charioteering, weapons handling, dancing, music, and ritual. The ideal warrior, like the Western feudal knight, was supposed to be skilled in arms and motivated to place the claims of fealty and honor above those of life. The military system was tied to the land system.

[22] *Ibid.*, p. 23.
[23] *Ibid.*, p. 25.

In early times the well-field system (eight families constituted a well) appeared in the territories of counts and barons. Four wells were a town, four towns a ch'iu, four ch'ius a county, and four counties a district. In wartime each ch'iu provided one war horse and three head of cattle, each county provided one long chariot, four horses, twelve head of cattle, three armored warriors, and seventy-two foot soldiers with weapons. Under the Chou dynasty local administration and military organization came to rest on units of five. Five men made one company, five companies one brigade, five brigades a division, and five divisions an army.[24]

> Sons of the king, feudal lords, and *tai-fu* received education of warriors. There was a "School Palace" in the royal household, where the prince and his aides learned archery, and in which the Chou king and his officials also sometimes held archery tournaments. In addition there was an "Archery Hut" where the king practiced archery, music, and dances.[25]

The status of warriors was second to that of the *tai-fu.*

The majority of feudal lords, the *tai-fu,* formed a landlord-ruler class. In Lu there were three houses of Huan; in Cheng seven houses of Mu; and in Sung at least twelve noble houses. The noble house computed its domain in terms of towns or districts (which also included any cities lying within them). Fiefs might vary from as few as one hundred to as many as three hundred towns:

> *Tai-fu* were free to dispose of their land. Some wealthy ones at least set apart portions of their fiefs with which their younger sons might establish new hereditary houses called "secondary lineage." Other persons favored by a *tai-fu* could also receive, or petition for, land grants from him. For example, in 500 B.C. Prince Ti of Sung gave five-elevenths of his fief to a favored follower.[26]

The *tai-fu* had great freedom. They could receive grants from sovereigns of another state, or desert to other states with their fiefs. The *tai-fu* employed a variety of officials for their household administration. Fief administrators included a household manager (prime minister), officer of prayers, historian, director of commerce, minister of war, and numerous others.

> Although nominally there was a difference in status between the ducal houses and the noble families which possessed land, people, and armies, actually they were opposing forces. The head of a noble family acted as though he were the absolute ruler of a certain area.[27]

The only special powers of a ruler consisted in sacrificing on behalf of the entire community, receiving tribute from noble houses, commanding the armed forces of the state, and granting and taking away fiefs and attendant ranks.

[24] Hsü Chung-sho, *op. cit.*, p. 7.
[25] Chang, Yan-lin, *op. cit.*, p. 30.
[26] *Ibid.*, pp. 33–34.
[27] *Ibid.*, pp. 34–35.

Agriculture was fundamental to the economy. Millet, rice, wheat, and barley were basic cereals. A major improvement in agricultural implements was made under the Chou with application of the art of metal-casting to a forked stick used for breaking up the ground. In the Chou period most effective results were gained by so-called "pair plowing."[28] In the early Chou period oxen were used for drawing carts, but not for plowing. Ox-plowing possibly appeared in the fifth century B.C.[29] Fruits and vegetables were cultivated with greater efficiency under the Chou than previously. The silk-worm industry had grown in importance. Pigs and chickens were universal livestock; irrigation on a large scale was practiced; iron was introduced, and metal money came into use.

Hsü Chung-shu maintains that the well-field system, *ching t'ien,* which was widely employed, was not as progressive as has at times been thought. The original meaning of the word *t'ien* (field) was a battlefield or a hunting field. Long into the Chou period hunting, pastoralism, and agriculture existed side by side.

> During Shang and Chou the rise of pastoralism had not entirely replaced hunting, nor had agriculture replaced pastoralism. The result was a prolonged stagnation in social evolution. Critics usually glorify the nominal equal distribution of landed property under the well-field system, not realizing that such a system was actually the tool with which the ruling tribes enslaved other peoples.[30]

While it may have contributed little to agriculture, the well-field system helped preserve the feudal system for centuries.

Eight plots were cultivated by eight families around a central plot reserved for residences and the raising of produce for the lord. The land title, of course, was vested in the lord. Much of the work of bringing wastelands under cultivation, draining swamps, and constructing canals was performed under instigation of the lords of the feudal states. The feudal lords had an interest in such development both for increasing their own resources and as a means of producing new estates for their children. The peasants lived on the land while it was under cultivation; during the winter they gathered into villages, which were usually walled and clustered about the residence of an aristocrat or official. An extensive development of the towns occurred. The feudal princes of the Wang dominated the towns, which had a market place, an altar, and an ancestral temple of the ruling lord. As in the Western Middle Ages, merchants and artisans fell outside the scheme of agricultural labor. They were supervised by the nobility. In 650 B.C. five-sevenths of the capital city of the State of Ch'i was composed of *shih* (mainly army

[28] Hsü Chung-shu, "Some Agricultural Implements of the Early Chinese," *Chinese Social History,* op. cit., p. 19.

[29] Arthur Waley maintains that ox-plowing did not occur before 95 B.C. "Note on Iron and Plough in Early China," *Bulletin of the School of Oriental and African Studies,* XII, Parts 3 and 4 (1948), pp. 803–804.

[30] Hsü Chung-shu, *op. cit.,* p. 6.

officers), while two-sevenths were artisans and merchants. Under Chinese feudalism the merchants were permitted to trade freely, and occasionally amassed fortunes.[31]

Married women of the aristocracy supervised their households. Often they were educated and able to quote the *Book of Poetry*. At times the wives of kings and rulers competently ran the feudal states in the absence of their husbands. Aristocratic families acquired considerable importance in this period. The family of a minister of the State of Chin in the sixth century B.C. possessed wealth equal to half of the treasury of the state and an army of retainers half the size of that of the state.[32] As in the Western Middle Ages, the knights often counted on family ties more completely than on their vassals. Land was the chief form of wealth. A vassal acquiring title to lands developed his private armies and was often able to defy the king. The actual tillage was done by the peasants and the slaves. A fief not only raised vegetable crops but kept animals for food and sacrifice; at times oxen, sheep, pigs, and dogs were eaten. Hunting was the sport of the aristocracy. Artisans were needed for the manufacture of weapons, chariots, and fine clothing; artisans and merchants were generally better off than the peasants. Merchants carried luxury goods, salt, fish, furs, and cloth. Tariffs were collected at the borders of each feudal state. In some places silks, varnishes, and ivory were the main items of trade. Metals, particularly copper, were imported.

The ancestral temple was the center of the life and affairs of the family—sacrifices, proposals of marriage, and the like. The temple of a ruler was the center for the affairs of the state. Nobles with lands covering many villages had large mounds representing all their territory. There was no organized priesthood; a variety of officials, retainers, and servants specialized in religious activities.[33] The Chous seem to have had a conception of heaven (a chief deity was called Heaven) and a place called Yellow Springs similar to the Sheol of the Hebrews.[34] However, there was no general unity of faith. By and large a fragmentation of religious life had occurred under the Chous comparable to the fragmentation of economic life and political administration.

Administration and law were similarly fragmented. Government was farmed out to the feudal lords who were able to rule their territories as they pleased. After 771 B.C. the power of the Chou kings practically vanished.[35] A wide variety of local codes developed, for each petty aristocrat was the sole arbiter of the conditions of the persons under him and able to do as he pleased short of precipitating a revolt among his subjects. He was, in turn,

31 Creel, *op. cit.*, p. 284.
32 *Ibid.*, p. 308.
33 *Ibid.*, p. 338.
34 *Ibid.*, p. 339.
35 *Ibid.*, pp. 346 ff.

subject to those above him. This, again, suggests a condition similar to the growth of manorial law in the Western Middle Ages.

THE EMPIRE

The triumph of the Ch'in occurred under one of the most unusual men in Chinese history. The social and political order established at this time was not the work of Shih Huang-ti alone, but had long been developing in the state of Ch'in. However, to him fell the task of imposing it on the Empire, and it remained (with some changes) characteristic of the Middle Kingdom till 1912 A.D.

Cheng, or Shih Huang-ti, assisted by his legalist chief minister, Li Ssu, set out to abolish the remnant of the feudal order.[36] The realm was redivided into satrapies governed not by members of the imperial family but by an elaborate bureaucracy with graded honorific titles. The administrative staff of the capital was divided into departments with a military chief, chief of provincial officials, chief of archery, a chief justice, and a number of others. The Empire was divided into thirty-six provinces (*chun*), and these into prefectures (*hsien*). A member of the bureaucracy was placed in charge of each. A number of devices were employed to destroy the power of the feudal nobles. Arms were collected and melted into bells and statues. Powerful and wealthy men were required to move to the capital, getting them off the estates on which their semiautonomous power rested. Local fortifications were raised, and the building of the Great Wall around the realm was begun. The economic base of feudal power was liquidated when, as had long prevailed in the Ch'in, private ownership in land by the peasants was encouraged. At the same time because of vast public works, *corvée* labor was reorganized to conform to the new requirements of the state. A system of roads was built around the capital, canals were improved, and irrigation projects were undertaken.

The emperor and his ministers looked askance at the varied literature of the time, disapproving of everything other than scientific texts. A burning of books was undertaken, which included official chronicles of feudal realms, even the *Shih Ching* and *Shu Ching*. Only books on divination, medicine, and agriculture, and the chronicles of the Ch'in were permitted. Copies of the forbidden books were preserved in the imperial library; the death penalty was prescribed for anyone having forbidden books in his possession.

A new style of script, the lesser Seal, was promoted. Colonization was extended, and the seminomadic Hsiung Nu in the north were defeated. By enforced movement of the population into the frontier areas, ethnic and cultural unity was promoted.

Resentment of the dictatorial policies of Shih Huang-ti was intense. The imposition of heavy taxes and *corvée* labor was particularly burdensome. The severe persecution of anyone daring to criticize the emperor was a

[36] Derk Bodde, *China's First Unifier* (Leiden: E. J. Brill, 1938).

source of anxiety to every official. Displaced intellectual strata were embittered. The remnants of the feudal order were ready for revolt. Some of the former political rivals of the Ch'in who had not been completely crushed were ready to spearhead revolution.

Upon the death of Shih Huang-ti, partly through the connivance of the palace eunuch, Chao Kao, Erh Shih Huang-ti succeeded to the throne rather than the emperor's chosen son. Though he favored the policies of his father, he did not have the personal authority to make them succeed. He soon fell under the influence of Chao Kao, who set about the consolidation of power in his own hands. The experienced advisors of the realm were disposed of one by one. Meng T'ien, commander-in-chief of the frontier armies, was ordered to commit suicide; Li Ssu, who had headed the "brain trust" of Shih Huang-ti, was thrown into prison and later executed. When revolts broke out, the opportunity was seized to have Erh Shih Huang-ti killed (207 B.C.), and Chao Kao himself was soon killed.

The rebellion terminated the Ch'in dynasty, bringing a new group into prominence. Among the armies that defeated the Ch'in, those of Hsiang Yu eventually rose to power. The realm was parceled out among the generals of the victorious rebels, who gave the title of Wang to Hsiang Yu's chief. However, Hsiang Yu soon lost favor with the new emperor, and a struggle broke out among the rival generals. In it Liu Pang was the chief opponent of Hsiang Yu, and eventually defeated him.

Liu Pang became Wang of the Han in 202 B.C. Kao Tsu, or Kao Ti, as he was called, declared a general amnesty of prisoners, repealed many of the laws of the Ch'in, and decentralized the political structure. He gathered Confucian scholars about him, for he loved ceremonies in which they were expert. Everything traditional seemed good to him, hence even tribal and local cults were recognized. Members of his family and commanders who had performed noteworthy military service were placed in charge of the principalities into which he divided the realm. A partial restoration of feudalism resulted. On Kao Tsu's death his wife placed Wen Ti on the throne. Surviving structures of the Ch'in were still further weakened. A general recovery of prosperity was experienced throughout the Empire.

The high point of the early Han dynasty was reached under Han Wu Ti (140–87 B.C.). China's frontiers were expanded in all directions, and the Hsiung Nu were defeated. One of Wu Ti's envoys, Chang Ch'ien, journeyed to the Western world, exploring the possibility of setting up trade routes through India. Chang Ch'ien is supposed to have introduced alfalfa and grape cultivation into China.

Wu Ti reversed the trend toward feudalism, strengthening the imperial bureaucracy. Imperial representatives were appointed over each Wang to report on the actions of these local magnates. Great fiefs were divided by the simple expedient of partitioning them on the death of the lord among all sons. Meanwhile, men were recruited for official service according to ability rather than birth. Wu Ti instituted competitive examinations for office. A school was established at the capital for the training of officials. Schools of lower order were encouraged in the provinces.

Internal commerce flourished during Wu Ti's reign, and foreign trade increased. An official supervised and regulated commerce for state profit buying staples when they were cheap, selling them when prices advanced. A state monopoly was established in salt and iron. Among other expedients employed by Wu Ti for raising money were the creation of a special military nobility in which titles were sold, the substitution of fines for punishments, and levies on princes for supporting official sacrifices. Coinage was turned into an imperial monopoly.

The immediate successors to Wu Ti were rather indifferent personalities. In 48 B.C., through a concubine of the heir apparent, the Wang family came into prominence; one of the Wang daughters, having become a favorite, was made Empress. A nephew of the Empress Dowager, Wang Mang, was made regent of the new emperor. The boy emperor died, and Wang Mang disposed of the puppet put in his place.

Wang Mang attempted agrarian reform of the Empire. He nationalized the land, breaking up the huge estates, and he also abolished slavery. The land was to be divided into equal tracts and given to the cultivators. He continued the royal monopolies of salt, iron, and coinage, adding monopolies of wine and mines. The currency was reorganized and tokens of several denominations were introduced. State loans to encourage business were provided on which no interest was to be charged. Dormitories were built for students and education was encouraged. However, in the insurrection which eventually broke out Wang Mang was killed.

The Liu family led the armies which revolted against Wang Mang. One of their number established himself on the throne. The capital was moved to Loyang (in the present Honan). This was the beginning of the Later Han.[37]

SOCIETY UNDER THE EMPIRE

In the years between the triumph of the Ch'in and the rise of the Later Han, Chinese society assumed the social composition it was to maintain until 1912 A.D., and in some fragments, into the present. In feudal times, as Weber noted,[38] the peasants were serfs of feudal lords to whom they owed taxes and labor. One must take care not to assign the categories of European feudalism too exclusively to China, for at the time of Shih Huang-ti the peasants had some ability to bear arms. In any case the situation of the peasants under the Ch'in was not completely duplicated by that of peasants elsewhere. The Ch'in was a border state which in its conflicts with the

[37] Granet, *op. cit.*, pp. 124 ff.

[38] Max Weber, *The Religion of China*, trans. and edited by Hans H. Gerth (Glencoe: The Free Press, 1951), p. 64.

barbarians was forced to depart from the typical feudal pattern more completely than most states.

During the feudal period most of the peasants were serfs subordinate to a stratum which monopolized not only the land but slave-holding as well. Typical feudal structure is evident in the fact that only the *kuan* families who were qualified for office owned serfs. Individual families often owned as many as forty serfs, suggesting that the estates of the time were relatively moderate in size. The very devices for social and economic reorganization employed by Shih Huang-ti testify to the extent of feudalism at this late period: he disarmed the lords, instituted a general system of private property, and provided for inheritance of estates by all sons in order to break the back of their military and economic power. Shih Huang-ti also generalized the procedure of making land available by purchase. It is useful to trace the changes in the land system which the Ch'in policies helped bring about.

> This practice of absorbing the landed property of self-cultivating farmers and small landowners through buying and selling was . . . noticed and utilized in the warring states period by Shang Yang, a radical utilitarian. It was . . . protected and extended under the political auspices of the Ch'in state, and became one of the state measures of the new Ch'in, which was strengthening itself through reforms.[39]

According to Han history,

> Duke Hsia (371–338 B.C.) of Ch'in, employed Shang Yang, who destroyed the well-field system and erased the paths between fields. Thus the imperial way was lost, and there was no limit to excesses and discrepancies. Among the people the property of the rich was counted by the myriads, while the poor subsisted on chaff.[40]

And according to Tung Chung-shu, as quoted in Han history:

> In the Ch'in . . . Shang Yang's laws were used, and the system of the empire was changed. The well-field was abolished, and the people were free to trade (in land). The fields of the rich lay one beyond another, while the poor did not have enough land to stand an awl.[41]

In short, the effect of these policies, was to promote tremendously the absorption of the small by the large and wealthy property owners, and to promote the subjugation of neighboring states, assuring hegemony to Ch'in landlords.

> In the era of monetary trade, the absorption by local magnates of small peoples' land through economic pressure was as easy as the manoeuverings of a tiger in a flock of sheep, particularly in view of the encouragement given by the government and the emperor. . . . This finally led to a fervent examination into the problem of land distribution by those men of all ages who were perceptive.[42]

39 *Ibid.*, p. 79.
40 Quoted by Wu Ch'i-Ch'ang, *op. cit.*, p. 79.
41 Quoted by Wu Ch'i-Ch'ang, *op. cit.*, pp. 79–80.
42 *Ibid.*, p. 80.

In other words, the destruction of the feudal system of property and the rise of the property system which came to prevail under the Empire was long anticipated by developments in the Ch'in and accomplished in stages: first, the policies of free purchase of property were promoted, which led to the aggregation of properties on a plutocratic rather than a feudal basis; finally, various devices of inheritance and land distribution broke up these aggregations.

A continuation of these trends completed the movement of the Chinese land system out of feudal context with hereditary holdings by aristocrats and with ordinary persons in a serflike situation of hereditary bondage. Though under the early Han dynasty a partial return to feudalism was experimented with, it was soon perceived to be destructive to central power and was therefore reversed, and a modified return to the political and economic policies of the Ch'in was made. Thus the emergence of the kind of land distribution which would transform China into a world of peasant villages on the local level was completed.

By the Later Han, local structures were approximately in the condition still observed in modern times by Yang of Taitou, Shantung Province.[43] Yang observed that the extended family (perhaps with two or three smaller units composed of married sons with their wives and children), so long as the members live under the same roof and eat and work together, is the primary unit. The village is secondary; between it and the family are the clan, neighborhood, school, and family associations. The land is much divided, and one field may be only 1/10 *mow* (4.3 *mows* equal 1 acre) or as large as 5 *mows*. The land is divided equally among sons (with an endless process of division), while there is continuous buying and selling. Purchases are made when a large family with large holdings is in decline. The largest families have from 30 to 40 *mows*. The main crops are wheat, millet, barley, soy beans, corn, sweet potatoes, peanuts, and a variety of vegetables. The fields are plowed with a team (ox and donkey or ox and mule). The plow, wooden harrow, and other implements are of ancient construction. The family is not only the basic land-owning but also the basic ceremonial and religious structure. Village solidarity appears in such things as methods of cultivating, threshing, storing, preparing foodstuffs, and ceremonies which are ideal for every family of a village. Villagewide organizations include: the village defense programs in which every village participates, the village school, the villagewide organization for collective protection of crops and the crop watcher, and the common concern for social control.

The peculiarity of the Chinese village[44] lay in part in the unusual power of the family, which was the smallest political as well as economic unit and the source of most secret societies. Villages were often named after powerful families, and the village societies were confederations of families. The village

[43] Martin C. Yang, *A Chinese Village* (New York: Columbia University Press, 1945).
[44] Weber, *op. cit.*, p. 86.

head was usually elected from the most powerful family, and sib elders stood beside him and retained the right to depose him. Cohesion of the family rested in considerable measure on the ancestor cult. The village temple was a central agency of Chinese law, and often took care of defense against robbers or neighboring villages; it provided schools, doctors, burials (otherwise not provided for), and even contained the armory of the village.

While the base of Chinese society was composed of semiautonomous peasant villages, the apex was composed of the community of the palace.[45] In the course of his consolidation of imperial power, Shih Huang-ti transferred to the capital of Hien-yang rich and powerful men from the empire. When he destroyed an overlordship, Huang-ti had a palace (modeled on the noble's own) built for him in the capital, where his women and trophies were relocated. The imperial town thus contained hostages from the entire realm. At court the nobles received honorary offices, while newcomers wielded actual power. Ruined nobles and men newly arrived to positions of power confronted one another in the court.

The palace personnel was centered in the emperor, an empress consort, various secondary wives, and numerous ranks of concubines. The harem of the emperor seems to have been an instrument of foreign policy consisting in considerable measure of women from the rulers of various dependencies and rival states (they were, thus, in effect hostages). Much of the palace administration was in the hands of eunuchs, castrated boys of humble origin without hope of founding families of their own and hence, presumably, in a position of enforced loyalty to the palace.[46] Granet observed that the emperor provided great feasts in the museum of his palace at which high officials, celebrated provincials, rich merchants, and ambassadors from subject barbarians attended.[47] Entertainment was provided by companies of jugglers and musicians under the direction of the emperor's eunuchs. Crowds of singers and dancers were affiliated with the harem. A vast building, the palace kia-yi was furnished for opera, and the Chinese theatre arose for the great jousts taking place in it. Members of the imperial family had estates granted to them. The nobles, high dignitaries, and officials often rivaled the prodigality of the emperor with their dwellings, country seats, and equipages.

Intermediate between the peasant village and the imperial city with its palace and court were the provincial capitals. However, the Chinese city went into a comparative decline in the imperial period. The city was characteristically a walled fortress and, in contrast to the village, the seat of a mandarin and the center for imperial administration. Caught between the peasant village on the one hand and the imperial court on the other, the

45 See Granet's summary drawn primarily from Ssu-ma Ch'ien, *op. cit.*, pp. 406 ff.

46 Chinese history many times displayed the phenomenon of the conspiracy of eunuchs for power, as in the case of Chao Kao at the death of Shih Huang-ti.

47 Granet, *op. cit.*, pp. 408 ff.

cities of China, as Weber notes,[48] could never achieve full development. The city lacked political autonomy. It had no citizenry representing a self-equipped military estate bound into sworn confederations. Craft and merchant guilds, city leagues, and city guilds appeared, which imperial officials had to reckon with, but they did not fuse into autonomous structures.

The imperial bureaucracy was the mediating structure between the palace and the village communities. In time it found its synthesis in two councils and numerous bureaus and boards charged with the business of the state (the board of civil office, board of revenue, board of ceremonies, board of war, board of punishment, etc.). A critical institution originating in the Ch'in was the censorate (Tu Ch'a Yüan) which kept correspondence and documents, examined officials, investigated financial corruption, and kept critical watch on the affairs of government. Outside the capital in the provinces (*sheng*) were a number of officials—viceroys, governors, lieutenant governors, provincial judges, salt comptrollers, and grain intendants. The heads of various local structures were in contact with the masses (judges, persons in charge of police and the performance of religious rites, and tax collectors).[49]

The mandarin bureaucracy acted as the equilibrating mechanism in the system. Its ranks were almost universally open by way of competitive examinations to the whole of Chinese society, except to certain persons, for example, actors. Potentially, therefore, almost every Chinese family had a stake in the government; the government, meanwhile, though often tempted to by-pass its own bureaucracy and go directly to the people, had more to gain in the long run by working through it. Though the salaries of imperial officials were so small that numerous family members, clients, and others exploited the opportunities for profits provided by imperial position, such devices as the censorate, investigations, and the rotation of mandarins in office and prevention of officials from holding offices in their home districts prevented the bureaucracy from absorbing final power. Chinese society was a rough but durable equilibrium resistant enough to endure all major disturbances, even foreign conquest, for nearly two thousand years.

SUMMARY

The present chapter has traced some of the main features in the transformation of ancient Chinese society from the days of the Shang, or Yin, through Chou feudalism which terminated in the struggles of the Warring Kingdoms, to the establishment of the Chinese Empire which endured for nearly two thousand years.

The Shang appears to have been a city dynasty very similar to those which arose in the Near East—Egypt and Babylonia in the early period. The

[48] Weber, *op. cit.*, pp. 13 ff.

[49] For a general summary, see Kenneth Scott Latourette, *The Chinese* (New York: The Macmillan Co., 1946), pp. 513 ff.

Shang had a fused hierocratic and political structure and very possibly rested on a foundation of slavery. It developed a literate civilization in the hands of a priestly class, which suggests that other paraphernalia of the ancient priest-intellectual were also present, including temples, schools, and the like. This Shang civilization flowered in the midst of a barbarian world, much of which still remained largely in a tribal or peasant-village condition.

The Chou conquerors of the Shang opened a feudal period in ancient China. This entailed the gradual disintegration of central hierocratic and political authority into a large number of semiautonomous local structures. Though there is clear evidence of slavery in the early Chou period—probably inherited from the Shang—and though it was periodically well-supplied by the wars of the feudal period, the progressiveness of the technology, the amount of wasteland brought under systematic cultivation, and the incorporation of formerly free tribesmen into the system as peasant serfs, suggests that a technology resting on slavery was being replaced. Considerable development in commerce and in town life occurred.

Though the Chou period opened with a division of the empire into perhaps as many as 1,773 states, by the opening of the Spring and Autumn period they had already been reduced to 170, and by the end of the period they were reduced to 13. After the final great period of conflict, the state of Ch'in triumphed under Shih Huang-ti, whose policies completed the liquidation of feudalism already in progress in the period of state consolidation. Local fortifications were raised, and the building of the Great Wall around the realm was begun. Ownership of land by the peasants was encouraged. An attempt to consolidate the ideal world was even made with a great burning of the books. The rise of the imperial bureaucracy, the conversion of the base of Chinese society into a world of peasant villages, and the synthesis of Chinese civilization were under way.

SELECTED BIBLIOGRAPHY

Bodde, Derk, *China's First Unifier* (Leiden: E. J. Brill, 1938).

Chi Li, *The Beginnings of Chinese Civilization* (Seattle: University of Washington Press, 1957).

Chi, Tsui, *A Short History of Chinese Civilization* (New York: G. P. Putnam's Sons, 1943).

Creel, Herrlee Glessner, *The Birth of China* (London: Jonathan Cape, 1936).

Granet, Marcel, *Chinese Civilization* (London: Kegan Paul, 1930).

Kirby, E. Stuart, "Introduction to the Economic History of China" in the *Far Eastern Economic Review* (Hong Kong, 1951–1952).

Sun, E-tu Zen, and John de Francis, *Chinese Social History* (Washington, D.C.: American Council of Learned Societies, 1956).

Walker, Richard Louis, *The Multi-State System of Ancient China* (Hamden, Conn.: The Shoestring Press, 1953).

Weber, Max, *The Religion of India*, trans. by Hans H. Gerth (Glencoe, Illinois: The Free Press, 1951).

Weidenreich, Franz, *Apes, Giants, and Man* (Chicago: University of Chicago Press, 1946).

Wiems, Harold J., *China's March toward the Tropics* (Hamden, Conn.: The Shoestring Press, 1954).

5

THE CHANGING ROLES OF THE CHINESE INTELLECTUAL

In the time period of interest to us, Chinese society evolved through three major stages: the civil imperialism of the Shang, or Yin, the feudalism and court society of the Chou and Warring Kingdoms, and the imperial civism and peasant village culture of the Ch'in.

There was never a single type of community in any of these periods, though each was dominated by a major community form. In the Shang period the early city was the major community. The area dominated by the early imperial city was divided into peasant villages, tribes, and rival cities. The period of Chou feudalism witnessed a decline, for a time, of civic life and the rise to dominance of the self-sufficient fief of the noble family. These evolved into feudal towns of various types and sizes. Forces were at work from the earliest days of the Chou which tended to incorporate the formerly free tribes and peasant villages into the Chinese feudal complex. The feudal towns were agencies of this fusion. As time went on, a considerable flowering of civic life occurred under feudalism, and the courtly cities of the Warring States rose to prominence in societal life: Eventually the imperial government liquidated the feudal structure and promoted a community development in which a new kind of imperial and provincial city dominated Chinese society on a national and regional level, which the peasant village dominated on the local level.

Intellectual types played a role in the formation and maintenance of the complex communities in each of these periods. Each period offered distinct opportunities, and made a distinct demand upon its intellectuals.

THE INTELLECTUAL UNDER THE SHANG

There are theoretical reasons to suppose that the literati of the Shang were similar to the priest intellectuals of Egypt and of Mesopotamia in the time of city imperialism in those areas.

The city is a complex community resting on secondary social institutions, that is, institutions that grow up in the course of a kind of secondary differentiation of the activities by which men solve their problems. In the city, for example, considerable numbers of men make a living not by agricultural production but by a variety of other activities, such as commerce, administration, or the profession of arms.

The formation of a city was originally possible only so far as the structures of a plurality of previous communities had been, so to speak, melted down and cast into something new. Only so far as old tribal and village communities had been transmuted into a new complex of loyalties could the city arise. In Shang, as in Babylonia and Egypt, religion seems to have performed this function. The centrality of the religious system of the Shang people to their way of life has been summarized compactly by Tsui Chi.

> Among their other civilized habits, the Shang people evidently elaborated a religious system, and this might be called the characteristic feature of the dynasty. Sacrificial vessels and oracle bones, which have been dug up in the thousands from the Mounds, and which far outnumber the practical instruments of living, such as tools and household pottery, point to the all-important part which religion must have played in their lives. Yet in spite of this wealth of material, the exact form of their religious rites is not known, nor can the Shang pantheon be enumerated. However, the deities seem to have been somewhat intimate ones, chiefly ancestors who lived in "heaven" but who would participate in human actions, helping or hindering according to whether they received the proper sacrifices. A god who is familiarly termed "Emperor" and seems to be a sort of First Ancestor of the race is frequently mentioned on the shell and bone inscriptions: every kind of trouble, great or small, private disasters and the fortunes of war, are all brought before him. In addition there are gods of agriculture, mountains, and rivers, and natural elements, though it is likely that these too were identified with ancestors, for we read one interesting record which says, "Pray for rain from Grandmother Yi."[1]

The plausibility of conceiving the Shang pantheon in terms of ancestor worship derives, of course, from the prominence of ancestor cults in later times. An ancestor cult usually accompanies employment of the family, particularly the patriarchal family and gens, as a major principle of social organization. On the other hand, the first cities of the world arose only by a wholesale breakdown of family cults of all sorts. In the Near Eastern city, as a sort of symbolic detachment from earth (agricultural) and family cults, various sky cults headed up the pantheon even though many familistic and agricultural deities occupied the lower ranks. Some indications that in the Shang a sky cult also played an equivalent role in the restructuring of civic allegiance may be indicated by elements of the "Six Odes" of the Shang preserved in the *Book of Poetry* compiled by Confucius. One, "The Mystic Swallow," accounts for the origin of the Shang as follows:

[1] Tsui Chi, *A Short History of Chinese Civilization* (New York: G. P. Putnam's Sons, 1943), p. 29.

Heaven sent the Mystic Swallow down to earth,
From Whom sprang the ancestor of Shang,
Who chose his dwelling in the land of Yin.
By Heaven's will, his grandson, glorious T'ang,
Assigned each State its formal boundary. . . .[2]

Such evidence suggests that the great initial problem of the priest intellectuals under the Shang was to create the ideal synthesis which fused loyalties into a new complex. Creel has made a major attempt to pull together the evidence for the nature of the Shang literati.[3] He argues that there is evidence that officials who were also diviners and priests served as envoys and were sent on diplomatic missions. The oracle bones indicate that the talents of the writers were employed in the service of the rulers of the Shang. Nor were the oracle bones the only literature of the period, for the early writers of the Chou were familiar with Shang books that have since perished.[4] In Shang times correspondence was actively carried on with distant points and in wartime reliance was placed on written commands to insure that there would be no mistakes.[5] The spirits addressed by the augurers and diviners of the Shang clearly belonged to a sky cult (such as usually evolves when religion is borne by strata who have been emancipated from the soil), for in the oracle bones they are spoken of as descending and sending down blessings.[6] The divination ceremonies in which oracle bones were used took place in the civic temple, and were conducted by a small group of official diviners.[7] Creel believes that they were able to manipulate the oracles to suit their purposes.[8]

Among other things, the Shang priest-intellectuals seem to have supervised human sacrifice. It has, according to Creel, long been known from the oracle bones that the Shang people practiced human sacrifice.

> Many scholars, especially among the Chinese, have strongly resisted the conclusion that human sacrifice was practiced in Shang times. Complete data on this point must be reserved for a later paper, which will deal with human sacrifice exclusively. But any doubt which might have existed previously was finally removed by the excavation, in the Shang grave field at Anyang excavated by the National Research Institute in the fall of 1934 and spring of 1935, of more than a thousand headless skeletons, and a corresponding number of skulls buried separately. From the manner in which they were buried, there can be no doubt that they were sacrificial victims. Ten headless skeletons, neither more nor less, were buried together in an oblong pit. In some cases the wrists were crossed behind the back, indicating that the hands were tied in this position before decapitation. Near this rectangular pit is a square pit,

[2] Quoted by Tsui Chi, *op. cit.*, p. 30.
[3] Herrlee Glessner Creel, *The Birth of China* (London: Jonathan Cape, 1936), p. 129.
[4] *Ibid.*, p. 171.
[5] *Ibid.*, p. 173.
[6] *Ibid.*, p. 179.
[7] *Ibid.*, p. 188.
[8] *Ibid.*, p. 190.

> containing ten skulls, standing upright in regular rows, and all facing north. I have seen a number of these skulls and skeletons *in situ*, in the process of excavation. That the burials are always of ten individuals together is significant in connection with the fact that the numbers of human beings mentioned as being sacrificed, in the oracle bone inscription, is commonly divisible by ten. Along with the skeletons are found various small objects, such as bronze knives and ax-heads, small grinding stones, etc., always in sets of ten, as if there was one for each victim. Possibly these were a part of some ritual equipment or ceremonial garb with which the victims were accoutered before being slain.[9]

All such details suggest that the Shang intellectual either belonged to a semihereditary stratum of priests or to special magician guilds. In any case there is no doubt about his high rank and the intimacy of his relation to higher administration in which he served not only as priest and diviner but as historian, clerk, and administrator.

THE INTELLECTUAL UNDER CHOU FEUDALISM

The Chou rose to power gradually among the tribes of the Wei basin, intermarrying with women of the Shang royal families before the conquest.[10] Such intermarriages may possibly have consisted of an exchange of women for the mutual harems of the royal families of the Shang and Chou, as was customary for the oriental sultanate. As Weber has indicated for the Near East, a royal harem presented the possibility of establishing kinship ties and alliances with other monarchs. He observes that at the time of the setting up of the royal Jewish state:

> A regular harem appeared with kinship ties and alliances with the rulers of the great powers, above all, with Egypt and Phoenicia, affording opportunity to engage in world politics. This led to the import of foreign cults, in part only in the form of court chapels for the strange princesses; in part, however, it also led to the incorporation of strange gods into the home cult. Such were the prompt ramifications of kingly power. Thus kingship acquired the typical features of the great war powers of the Orient.[11]

In any case the intermarriage of Chou and Shang men and women must have created some familiarity on the part of Chou nobles with the advantages of the superior Shang culture. In a period of weakness the Shang kings were unable to deal with the vigorous barbarians. The Shang king is said to have fled to his favorite pleasure place, dressed in rich clothes, decked himself with jewels, and then set fire to the building in which he perished.[12]

There is little doubt of the initial cultural inferiority of the Chou people

[9] Herrlee Glessner Creel, *Studies in Early Chinese Culture* (Baltimore: Waverly Press, 1937), p. 215.
[10] *Ibid.*, p. 223 ff.
[11] Max Weber, *Ancient Judaism*, trans. by Hans Gerth and Don Martindale (Glencoe, Illinois: The Free Press, 1952), p. 99.
[12] Creel, *Birth of China*, *op. cit.*, p. 230.

to their predecessors. In the art objects from the first period of the Chou conquest, a sharp deterioration of taste is evident. Nor does there seem to be evidence that the Chou possessed independent writing traditions of their own. Rather, it appears that the people of the Chou set about to appropriate Shang culture, including its literary culture, and in time began even to trace their ancestry to the people of the Shang.

Chinese feudalism does not seem to have been bound up initially with a manorial complex to the same extent as in Medieval Europe. According to Weber, family ties and their military obligations were of primary importance.

> In China, as far as one can judge, political feudalism was not primarily connected with landlordism in the occidental sense. Both emerged from the "state organization of the *gentes*," as in India, when chieftains' sibs escaped ancient fetters of the bachelor house and its derivatives. The sib, which according to a documentary note originally furnished the war chariots, was basic to the ancient status structure.[13]

Though Chinese feudalism seems to have had special beginnings in the militarily competent family (sib) rather than in the ties between a war chief and his associates in the war bond as among Teutonic peoples, it tended to develop the other features of a feudal structure. Moreover, as Weber notes, as in other places where feudalism appeared, men who did not bear arms because of economic or educational disqualification also lost their political rights.

Also, as Weber points out, the unity of the feudal empire was more cultural than political and rested on the homogeneous status-mores of chivalry, religious or ritual unity, and the homogeneity of the literati.[14]

> In point of ritual and status, the forms of homogeneity among chariot-fighting, chivalrous vassals, and castled fief-holders were similar to the Occident. Just as "barbarians" and "heathens" were identified in the latter, so in China a lack of ritual correctitude was considered a mark of the barbarian or semi-barbarian. When at a far later time the prince of Ch'in made mistakes in offering sacrifices he was considered a semi-barbarian. Warfare against a ritually incorrect prince was considered meritorious work. In later times every one of the numerous conquering Tartar dynasties of China was considered "legitimate" by the depositories of ritualist tradition when they correctly adjusted to the rules of ritual and thus to the authority of the literati caste.[15]

The social stratum in feudal China in which this combination of distinctive elements was anchored was one of patriarchal noble families. The ancestral cult of its ruling family provided the core of the religious life of a given feudal state.

[13] Max Weber, *The Religion of China*, trans. by Hans Gerth (Glencoe, Illinois: The Free Press, 1951), p. 33.
[14] *Ibid.*, p. 40.
[15] *Ibid.*, p. 40.

Unless one recognizes that this feudal emphasis on the family in every area of social life, including religion, represents a considerable departure from practices among the Shang, a number of things do not make sense. All the evidence from the Shang period suggests that the intellectuals were priests. When the literati emerge into historical light in the Chou period, however, though they are experts in ceremonials and ritual, they are not priests. Of the Chou literati, Weber observes:

> It has been of immeasurable importance for the way in which Chinese culture has developed that this leading stratum of intellectuals has never had the character of clerics of Christianity or of Islam, or of Jewish Rabbis, or Indian Brahmans, or Ancient Egyptian priests, or Egyptian or Indian scribes. It is significant that the stratum of literati in China, although developed from ritual training, grew out of an education for genteel *laymen.* The "literati" of the feudal period, then officially called *po-shih;* that is, "living libraries," were first of all proficient in ritualism. They did not, however, stem from the sibs of a priestly nobility, as did the Rishi sibs of the *Rig-Veda,* or from a guild of sorcerers, as did in all likelihood the Brahmans of the *Atharva-Veda.*[16]

If one assumes, however, that the rise of the Chou at the expense of the Shang was only possible by the destruction of its nerve center, that is, its religious institutions, and the replacement of these religious structures by the ancestral cults of feudal clans, the literati would tend, in the nature of the case, to retain the aura of magico-religious efficacy as of old. However, their loss of spiritual monopoly would be counterbalanced by their importance as experts in matters of ritual for purposes of secular administration in feudal household administration.

The most immediate effect of the transition from the Shang to the Chou must have been a serious temporary loss of status by the former priestly intellectuals, for the evidence from the Shang suggests that they possessed a monopoly of religious life under a situation in which religion touched almost every other sphere. Under the Chou with its emphasis upon the ancestral cults of the feudal clans, this religious monopoly was broken, giving the Chou literati, as Weber notes, a very different character from the Egyptian priests.

On the other hand, as Walker has pointed out, the Chou conquerors and their successors are traditionally reported to have set up no less than 1,773 states.[17] Moreover, each one of these newly established states immediately proceeded to develop its feudal city. Chang Yin-lin maintains that the towns and cities of the Chou period were of two types, walled and unwalled:

> The walled towns again can be classified into three groups: first the capitals of the Chou king and of the various states; second the metropolises

[16] *Ibid.*, p. 108.
[17] Richard Louis Walker, *The Multi-State System of Ancient China* (Hamden, Connecticut: The Shoestring Press, 1953), p. 20.

> of feudal lords within the royal demesne and states; and third the ordinary walled towns.[18]

The size of the towns varied. Lo-Yang, capital of Eastern Chou, was said to have measured 81 square *li,* about 21 per cent of the area of modern Peking. Most of the capital cities of the states were much smaller.

> The principal inhabitants in a capital city were the ruler and his guards, the artisans of the "hundred crafts," and the ministers and *tai-fu* and their guards. Like the royal court, most state courts had the following officials of importance: Grand Minister of War, in charge of military affairs; Grand Minister of Crime, in charge of the judiciary and police; Grand Minister of Finance, in charge of taxation and corvée; and Grand Minister of Works, in charge of public works, such as the construction of city walls, roads, and ancestral shrines (of the ruling house). Within the capital of a state the principal buildings were as follows: The palace, pleasure gardens, hunting parks, treasury, and granaries, and ancestral temples of the ruler, the *she* shrine for sacrificing to the God of Earth, and the *chi* shrine for sacrificing to the God of Grains; residences of the ministers and officials; and hostels provided for envoys of other states.[19]

Under such circumstances it is evident that a stratum of priestly intellectuals trained in writing might have lost many of their former religious functions, but they must have found themselves in new demand for secular political and administrative purposes.

Walker has observed, however, that though the Chou began its career with a wide distribution of states, almost from the beginning a consolidation began. The 1,773 states set up at the beginning of the Chou period were reduced to 170 within the areas of Chou control by 772 B.C., the Ch'un-ch'iu period of the state of Lu.[20] The effect of this was to displace many literati and other types of administrative personnel from some centers and to consolidate them into larger aggregations at others.

The various ranks of personnel in the fiefs and states of the feudal period were still hereditary or semihereditary. The *Tso Chuan,* a detailed history probably written in the third century B.C., covering in more detail the materials of the *Ch'un Ch'iu* than does the Lu annal, divides the various ranks into ten:

> As the days have their divisions in periods of ten each, so men have their ten ranks. It is by these that inferiors serve their superiors, and that superiors perform their duties to the spirits. Therefore the king has the ruler (of each feudal state) as his subject; the rulers have the great prefects as their subjects; the prefects have their officers; the officers have their subalterns; the subalterns have their multitude of petty officers; the petty officers have their assistants; the assistants have their employees; the employees have their menials. For the menials there are helpers, for

18 Chang Yin-lin, "Feudal Society of the Chou Dynasty," in *Chinese Social History: Translations of Selected Studies* by E-Tu Zen Sun and John de Francis (Washington, D.C.: American Council of Learned Societies, 1956), p. 26.

19 *Ibid.*, pp. 26–27.

20 Walker, *op. cit.*, p. 20.

> the horses there are grooms, and for the cattle there are cowherds. And thus there is provision for all things.[21]

Long before the Warring States period (403–221 B.C.), the repeated consolidations of states must have tended to break up the hereditary character of these various feudal ranks. Fung Yu-lan has conceived of this process as the most significant in liquidating feudalism itself.

> The outstanding characteristic of the Warring States period (403–221 B.C.), however, was the gradual collapse of the feudal system, resulting in marked changes in the earlier rigid social system. This phenomenon was marked, on the other hand, by the rise during the Warring States period of many men, of comparatively lowly origin, to positions of great political importance; while on the other it was marked by the fall from power of many of the former ruling families. This movement reached a climax in 221 B.C., when Ch'in Shih-huang succeeded in unifying all China under the rule of the House of Ch'in, and dealt feudalism a decisive blow by relegating the royal families of all states except that of Ch'in to the level of the common people.[22]

The fact that nobles were losing their formerly hereditary positions to men of lowly origin meant that ability and chance were beginning to count more than hereditary claims in the achievement of positions of eminence. As Fung Yu-lan observes, Confucius himself had belonged to the nobility of the Sung state and was forced by poverty to enter literati service. Old institutions, Fung Yu-lan observes, were breaking down:

> From the age of Confucius onward, there arose men who criticized or opposed these institutions; who wished to revise them; who wished to establish new institutions in their place; or who were opposed to all institutions whatsoever. The age was one of transition, during which the institutions of the past had lost their authority, and those of the new age had not yet been definitely formulated. It was inevitable, then, that it should also be one of uncertainty and divergence. Thus when the Confucians had advanced their arguments for the preservation of the past, other philosophers, holding divergent views, were forced, if they wished to gain a following, to explain in their turn the reasons why they considered their own doctrines superior.[23]

In short, new institutions serving the needs of the literati also had to be created.

Under the Shang the training of the literati was possibly under the control of schools dominated by the priesthood. Under the Chou with its typical feudal emphasis on the principle of heredity, the training of the intellectual must have been primarily a family affair. However, with the decline of family as a principle for the organization of social life, and the failure it must have entailed of family apprenticeship in supplying the literati needed

[21] Quoted by Fung Yu-lan, *A History of Chinese Philosophy* (Princeton: Princeton University Press, 1952), p. 9.
[22] Fung Yu-lan, *op. cit.*, pp. 9–10.
[23] *Ibid.*, p. 14.

by the times, the school organized by the literati themselves made its appearance. Fung Yu-lan believes that this was first done by Confucius.

> I would . . . maintain that: (1) Confucius was the first man in China to make teaching his profession, and thus popularize culture and education. It was he who opened the way for the many travelling scholars and philosophers of succeeding centuries. It was also he who inaugurated, or at least developed, that class of gentleman in ancient China who was neither farmer, artisan, merchant, nor actual official, but was professional teacher and potential official. (2) The activities of Confucius were similar in many ways to those of the Greek Sophists. (3) The activities of Confucius and his influence in Chinese history have been similar to that of Socrates in the West.[24]

Though it is easy to understand why the transition from the hereditary literati to the professional literati by training should be attributed to Confucius, the conditions which turned Confucius into a professional teacher were operating throughout the states. It is much more plausible to assume that the practice of establishing private schools was dramatized by Confucius' example rather than created for the first time by him.

In any case, private schools arose in great numbers and became bearers of special intellectual traditions. The number of schools was so great that the Chinese have referred to them as the hundred schools and from ancient to modern times the attempt has been made to account for them. One of the most recent summaries of the attempt in China to account for the development of schools has been made by Fung Yu-lan, who has offered a theory of his own.[25] He maintains that the first historian to try to classify the hundred schools was Ssu-ma T'an (d. 110 B.C.), father of Ssu-ma Ch'ien (145–86 B.C.). Ssu-ma T'an classified the philosophers into six major schools: the Yin-Yang, or school of cosmologists, who believed all things to be an interaction of female (yin) and male (yang) principles; the Ju Chia, or school of literati, that taught the ancient classics (Confucians); the Mo Chia, or school following Motse; the Ming Chia, or school of names, which distinguished between names and actualities; the Fa Chia, or legalist school, which sought reform of the law (*fa*) as the means to good government; and the Tao-te Chia, or school of the way, which taught a philosophy of individual self-concentration.[26]

The second historian to classify the schools was Liu Hsin (46 B.C.–23 A.D.), who added four schools to the six distinguished by Ssu-ma T'an. The four schools were: the Tsung-heng Chia, or school of diplomaticists; the Tsa Chia, or school of eclectics; the Nung Chia, or school of agrarians; and the Hsiao-chu Chia, or school of storytellers. Liu Hsin's theories were elaborated by later historians. He argued that before the social institutions of the Chou

[24] *Ibid.*, pp. 48–49.
[25] Fung Yu-lan, *A Short History of Chinese Philosophy*, edited by Derk Bodde (New York: The Macmillan Co., 1948).
[26] *Ibid.*, pp. 30–31.

dynasty disintegrated there was no separation between officers and teachers. The officers of a certain department of government also transmitted the branch of learning pertinent to it. Like other feudal lords they held their posts on a hereditary basis. There was no private teaching; only official learning. However, when the Chou dynasty lost its power, the officers of the governmental department also lost their positions, and began to teach the special branches of their knowledge on a private basis. The separate schools were said to have originated in former departments of government: the Ju school in the ministry, the Tao school in official history, the Yin-Yang school in official astronomy, the legalist school in the ministry of justice, the school of names in the ministry of ceremonies, the Mohist school in the guardians of the temple; the diplomaticists school in the ministry of embassies, the eclectic school in the councillors, the agricultural school in the ministry of soil and grain, and the school of storytellers in the petty offices.

Fung Yu-lan is in essential agreement with Liu Hsin's attempt to trace the origin of the schools to political and social circumstances.[27] As he sees the problem in the tenth century B.C. under the Chou royal house, there were hundreds of states, each owned and governed by its princes. Within each state the land was subdivided into fiefs, each with its feudal lord. The political and economic masters were the *chün tzu* (sons of the princes) in contrast to the *hsiao jen* or *shu min* (ordinary people or serfs). Under such circumstances Fung Yu-lan contends there was no chance for the serfs to become men of learning. However, between the seventh and the third centuries B.C. the entire social system disintegrated. Former official representatives of the various branches of the common people, he believes, became scattered among the common people. Former nobles or officials often maintained a livelihood by carrying on private instruction in their private schools. The various private schools were in the areas of the specialty of the former officials: the classics, ceremonies and music, ju or literati, war, speaking, debate, divination, astrology and numerology, and the occult arts. Fung Yu-lan believes that Ssu-ma T'an was correct, that the six major schools he isolated originated from six different kinds of officials (the Ju school originating with the literati, the Mohists school originating with the knights, the Taoist school originating with the hermits, the school of names originating with the debaters, the Yin-Yang school originating with the practitioners of occult arts, and members of the legalist school originating with men of methods).

Fung Yu-lan's theories are perhaps significant of the persistence into the present of attitudes of the traditional Chinese scholar, of piety toward the classics. He confines his account to rearranging the theories of Liu Hsin and Ssu-ma T'an. However, it seems necessary only to modify some of the details. First, the actual biographies of the scholars of the later feudal period in China do not show the schematic origin of special schools from special branches of official administration; rather, the scholar-teacher administrators are often

[27] *Ibid.*, pp. 34 ff.

plastic, holding a variety of positions. Second, Weber seems essentially correct concerning this period of late feudalism in his view that the literati were educated in a school for genteel laymen (who were then called *po-shih* (living libraries) and had to be, first of all, proficient in ritualism, suggesting that the positions had evolved out of those of court astrologer. They were not recruited at this time from the ranks of ordinary people or serfs.[28] In the early feudal period strong trends were in motion to create a hereditary stratum of scholar officials; the degeneration of feudalism broke up these hereditary configurations.

Confucius (551–497 B.C.) was born in the state of Lu. The fact that his father was a soldier meant that he was either a feudal lord or the retainer of one. The latter seems to have been the case, for when his father died and Confucius was but three years old, the family was impoverished. Confucius seems to have been trained for the literati rather than for the knighthood so that he would be able to support himself. Confucius married at the age of nineteen, taking first employment as keeper of the stores of grain; later he was in charge of public fields and lands. At the age of twenty-two he became a public teacher. In 516 B.C., because of confusion in his native state, he migrated to the state of Ts'e, where he served as political advisor. He later returned to his native state and served as magistrate and minister of crime. After later political upsets in his home state, he set upon a period of wandering.

Similar patterns are evident in the biographies of other thinkers. Laotse, for example, a contemporary of Confucius, was born in K'uksien in 571 B.C., the son of an old cultured family. He was keeper of the imperial archives (official librarian) and a teacher until, in the course of the decay of the empire, he left in disgust and lived the life of a hermit. Mencius (371–289 B.C.) was, like Confucius, born of one of the great clans of Lu. His father, like the father of Confucius, died when Mencius was a child. His mother was one of the celebrated women of Chinese history. Mencius became the center of a school, and for twenty years wandered from court to court, where he occasionally accepted office and often received gifts. Motse (468–390 B.C.) traveled extensively among various of the feudal states, serving as a teacher (at one time with as many as 300 students), and for a time held the ministry of defense and fortifications in the state of Sung. Chuangtse (369–286 B.C.), the greatest of the early Taoists, was a native of the state of Meng, where he lived as a hermit. He formed a private school, and if he did not hold office, it is at least transmitted that King Wei of Ch'u sent a messenger with gifts and the offer to make him chief minister of the state.

As Weber has indicated, the literati in China's feudal period were ritualistically trained politicians concerned with problems of internal administration ranging from power politics to correspondence and diplomacy.[29]

[28] Weber, *op. cit.*, pp. 108 ff.
[29] Weber, *ibid.*, pp. 110 ff.

Far from remaining confined to any single branch of administration, they showed great plasticity in facing the problems of a variety of administrative roles. Moreover, with considerable adeptness, when for any of a variety of reasons they lost their positions in the administration of the states, they either opened private schools or migrated to other states. This practice led Weber to observe that a stratum of vagrant Sophists (*che-she*) appeared who were comparable to the knights and scholars of the medieval period under conditions which made them bearers of schools of antagonisms comparable to those of India, Hellenic antiquity, and the Middle Ages.[30]

In these times of change the literati were often most valued for their capacity to innovate, which they sometimes did with considerable audacity. They did not hesitate on occasion boldly to criticize the official government or even, as is said of Motse, openly oppose the policies of princes. Motse on one occasion is said to have heard of the intention of a prince to try out a new weapon of war, whereupon he quickly trained his disciples in appropriate defense strategy and rushed to the beleaguered state to save it from attack. The very unstable conditions that often sent the literati migrating from state to state must have considerably increased their comprehension of the socio-political problems of the time, further enhancing their value.

THE INTELLECTUAL UNDER THE EMPIRE

Among the policies adopted by the Ch'in was the deliberate unification of thought. Its prime minister, Li Ssu, submitted a memorandum on the point to Shih Huang-ti:

> Of old, the world was scattered in confusion. . . . Men valued what they had themselves privately studied, thus casting into disrepute what their superiors had established. At present, Your Majesty has united the world. . . . Yet there are those who with their private teaching mutually abet each other, and discredit the institutions of laws and instructions. If such conditions are not prohibited, the imperial power will decline above and partisanships will form below.[31]

A great burning of the books followed in 213 B.C.[32]

Though repelled somewhat by the violence of the Ch'in, the Han rulers followed the same general policy. Upon the recommendations of his minister, Tung Chung-shu, Emperor Wu (140–87 B.C.)[33] announced that Confucianism in which the Six Classics were dominant was henceforth to be the official state teaching. The first national university was founded in the same dynasty for the teaching of the Confucian texts.[34] Yang Lien-sheng notes that it quickly became a primary avenue to officialdom. The interest of candidates in securing official positions and the imperial government for personnel

[30] Weber, *ibid.*, p. 111.
[31] *Historical Records,* Chap. 87. Quoted by Fung Yu-lan, *op. cit.*, p. 204.
[32] Bodde, *op. cit.*, pp. 80 ff.
[33] Fang Yu-lan, *op. cit.*, p. 205.
[34] Tsui Chi, *op. cit.*, p. 58.

coincided, and though the fate of the academy wavered at first, it tended to grow.

> The National Academy was actually an avenue to officialdom. At first fifty fellowships were created by Emperor Wu of Western Han. The Fellows were selected by the Minister of Rites, or recommended by local officials, and all were exempt from labor service. Examinations were held once a year, out of which a number of Fellows were sent to fill official posts. Gradually the number of Fellows was increased, until it reached three thousand in the time of Emperor Yüan (48–32 B.C.). Extra quotas were added in the reign of Emperor P'ing (1–6 A.D.) for sons of officials of the *yüan-shih* rank. Placements through examinations thenceforth were divided into three classes, with a total of one hundred a year.
>
> In the early years of Eastern Han the scholarly traditions of the former period were maintained in the Academy, but the spirit of learning declined sharply after the reign of Emperor An. The professors neglected their teaching, the fellows neglected their studies, and the Academy premises were turned into a vegetable garden. Later Emperor Shun, followed the advice of high officials, restored and expanded the physical plant of the Academy, which now possessed 240 buildings with a total of 1850 rooms. The Fellows at this time numbered some 30,000, ten times that of Western Han.[35]

The content of knowledge was fixed at the same time so that after passing the imperial examinations democratic access to office by way of literary education became possible. The beginnings of examinations for public office extend back into the feudal period. In the Han dynasty they were made into a principle.[36] The examinations were intended to determine that the candidate was steeped in the literature and had the outlook of a cultured man. The examinations were concerned with political affairs. Instruction was given in part by individuals and in part by college foundations. This education, Weber notes, served the interest in prebends. It was tied to a script even while it was a pure lay education of ritualistic and traditional-ethical character.

For two years before he was introduced to their meaning, the student learned to paint about two thousand characters. The examiners were concerned with style, the art of versification, and a firm foundation in the classics. Chinese learning was addressed to the eye. "In China the very finest blossoms of literary culture lingered, so to speak, deaf and mute in their silken splendor."[37] The Chinese bureaucracy was concerned with conventional propriety. Even justice was a summary Star Chamber procedure in which high officials ruled solely on documents, permitting no oral pleading.[38] In the popular mind, successfully examined candidates were proved holders of magical qualities. It was possible, always, for a candidate without office

[35] Yang Lien-sheng, "Great Families of Eastern Han" in *Chinese Social History* (Washington, D.C.: American Council of Learned Societies, 1956), p. 127.
[36] Weber, *op. cit.*, p. 116.
[37] *Ibid.*, p. 124.
[38] *Ibid.*, p. 127.

to teach in a village school. However, the preferred position of the mandarin was a political post determined by the number and rank of examinations he had passed. Here he remained under control of the school and the surveillance and criticism of the censors who, according to Weber, valued impeachment of officials as meritorious, in the way of the Roman Catholic confession of sins.[39] Periodically (usually every three years) the record of the officeholder was examined and a list of his merits and demerits was published in the *Imperial Gazette*. According to his published grades he was either permitted to remain, promoted, or demoted.[40]

There were a number of basic ways in which the literati under the empire differed from their counterparts in the earlier period. Under feudalism and the period of the Warring Kingdoms, the intellectual had been of aristocratic derivation; under the empire, by way of officially sponsored education and the examination system, the mandarinate was opened to every stratum in Chinese society except the despised classes, for example, actors.

In the previous period education was gained in the school of a private teacher under conditions which promoted the sharpening of the contrasts between one school and another and which favored the emergence of charismatic teachers who enhanced the individuality of their persons and doctrines. The alternative educational opportunities between one state and another partly appear in the following table.

STATES, DOMINANT SCHOOLS, AND FAMOUS TEACHERS[41]

State	*Dominant School* (*if any*)	*Famous Teachers*
Chao		Hsün Tzu, Kung-sun Lung, Shen Tao
Ch'i	Confucianism five elements school	Ch'en Chung Tzu, P'eng Meng, Tien, P'ien, Tsou Yen, Yen Wen
Ch'in	legalism	Shang Yang Han F'ei Tzu
Ch'u	Taoism	Hsü Hsing Lao Tzu
Han		Han Fei Tzu Shen Pu-hai
Lu	Confucianism	Confucius Motse
Sung	Mohism	Ch'en Hsiang, Chuang Tse, Hui Shih, Sung K'eng
T'eng		visited by Mencius Hsü Hsing, Ch'en Hsiang
Tsou		Mencius
Wei		Shang Yang
Yen	five elements school	

39 *Ibid.*, p. 128.
40 *Ibid.*, p. 129.
41 Following Fung Yu-lan, *A History of Chinese Philosophy*.

In contrast to the emergence of famous schools and outstanding teachers in the period of Warring states, scholars of the imperial period achieved importance because of their political function rather than their learning or originality. Yang Lien-sheng observes that before the system of the censorate stabilized, the fellows of the national academy found it to their advantage to create favorable public opinion to insure their selection to significant political posts. Since the literati were *corvée*-exempt and enjoyed high status, they were also in a position to employ deceitful devices to create favorable public opinion for themselves. The censurers appeared, he maintains, in order to stabilize this relation.

> For example, Hsü Shao at the end of Eastern Han was director of official selection at Ju-nan. He and his cousin Hsü Ching were both fond of censuring the local people and published their comments once every month.
>
> Another famous censurer and contemporary of Hsü Shao was Kuo T'si (127–169 A.D.), leader of the National Academy Fellows. At that time the Academy Fellows were restless, and spent their time in criticizing current affairs or political personages.
>
> The Grand Ministers often solicited advice from censurers before reaching decisions on the selection of officials. This opened the way for opportunists and impostors.[42]

Moreover, the content of instruction in the imperial period tended to consist more and more in detailed textual criticism of the classics. So far as the system of education under the Empire elicited original philosophic activity, it was thrust in the direction of an eclectic synthesis of alternative points of view from the classical period.

SUMMARY

In the time period of interest to us, Chinese society evolved through three main forms: early civic imperialism (the Shang, or Yin, period, 1766–1122 B.C.), the Chou period of feudalism (112–255 B.C.) (perhaps distinguishable into three subperiods: the early period of pure feudalism, 1122–721 B.C., the Ch'un-Ch'iu period or Spring and Autumn period, 722–481 B.C., the period of Warring States, 480–221 B.C.); and the imperial period 221 B.C.–220 A.D. (covering the Ch'in dynasty, 221–206 B.C., and the Western and Eastern Han dynasties with their capitals at Ch'angan, 206 B.C.–25 A.D., and Loyang, 25–220 A.D.).

These three periods presented very different *milieux* for their respective intellectuals. One thing, however, was shared in common by all. As complex communities composed of the elements of many simpler ones, all of them presuppose a breakdown in the loyalties that had originally been tied to the institutions of the tribe and peasant village and their consolidation into more

[42] Yang Lien-sheng, *op. cit.*, p. 126.

comprehensive forms. In this reconsolidation, the intellectuals played an indispensable role.

The comparative lack of precise evidence from the Shang period makes full reconstruction of the intellectual role impossible. However, such evidence as is available closely fits the hypothesis that at this time the literati were comparable to the theologian-priests of ancient Egypt. The oracle bones indicate that they formed a most important class of official augurers. There is also indication that they kept official records and handled official correspondence. Their performance at religious rites involving human sacrifice are indicative of the intimacy of their position with the political structure, for no religious rituals involving human sacrifice are possible without the full cooperation of the political institutions of the community.

In the Chou period the literati had many properties which ordinarily belonged to theologian priests, but they were without anchorage in special religious institutions. This fact suggests that if the reconstruction of the role of the Shang literati has been correct, a major revolution in the intellectual's role was brought about in the transition from Shang to Chou-feudal society. A number of forces were at work during the early Chou period which would tend further to secularize the literati's role: the multiplication of feudal states increased the demand for literati to perform essential ceremonial and administrative tasks of the feudal towns and cities; the consolidation of feudal states separated numbers of literati from their local setting and reconsolidated them in larger centers. Throughout the early feudal period the recruitment of intellectuals and their training rested on hereditary or semihereditary family practices. The training and recruitment of literati under the Shang, on the other hand, were most probably consolidated either in official training centers and schools or the training facilities of augurer and magician guilds.

By the Ch'un-Ch'iu period, however, the competition of the feudal states had become so brisk as to shatter many of the forms of the hereditary principle which organized so much of early feudal life. In many cases, noble families experienced hard times and individuals who, in other periods, would have enjoyed careers as warriors were forced—as was Confucius—to struggle for literary educations. The professional teacher and self-organized school appeared as institutions replacing the family apprenticeship of the early Chou. It was an age of highly individualized scholar-*entrepreneurs* who moved freely from state to state and in and out of civil service.

In the imperial period, opened with the triumph of the Ch'in, the self-organized schools by brilliant scholar-*entrepreneurs* were closed. A great burning of books signalized a new relation between the state and the content of learning. An Imperial Academy was set up, and education was officially sponsored and controlled. By means of the Imperial Academy and the opening of the civil service system to almost all classes through the examination system, the relation between the literati and the state was organized. In a comparatively short time special institutions, like the censorate, made their appearance, and served to keep the individual literati under surveillance for life.

SELECTED BIBLIOGRAPHY

Granet, Marcel, *Chinese Civilization* (London: Kegan Paul, Trench, Trubner, 1930).

Hughes, E. R., editor and translator, *Chinese Philosophy in Classical Times* (New York: E. P. Dutton, 1942).

Legge, James, translator, *The Shu King, The Shih King, and The Hsiao King* in *The Sacred Books of China* (Oxford: The Clarendon Press, 1879), Vol. 3.

Levenson, Joseph R., *Confucian China and Its Modern Fate* (London: Routledge and Kegan Paul, 1958).

Lu-chi, Liu, *Confucius: His Life and Time* (New York: Philosophical Library, 1955).

Sun, E-to Zen and John de Francis, *Chinese Social History* (Washington, D.C.: American Council of Learned Societies, 1956).

Tsui, Chi, *A Short History of Chinese Civilization* (New York: G. P. Putnam's Sons, 1943).

Weber, Max, *The Religion of China*, translated by Hans H. Gerth (Glencoe, Illinois: The Free Press, 1951).

Yu-lan, Fung, *A History of Chinese Philosophy* (Princeton: Princeton University Press, 1952).

6

CHINESE SOCIAL THOUGHT AND THE SYNTHESIS OF CHINESE CIVILIZATION

THE HYPOTHESES which have guided this study suggest that periods of the destruction of old communities and the formation of new ones encourage creativity. This creativity is socially relevant only insofar as it is addressed to the unique elements in the social *milieu.* Furthermore it was assumed that in the formation of complex communities much of the burden of the creation of new institutions falls upon the literate strata of the society.

The examination of the society and literati of ancient China has supplied powerful confirmation of these hypotheses. The feudal period was, above all, one in which the destruction of old complex communities and the formation of new ones occurred. It was also the period when literati emerged as intellectual *entrepreneurs* and as charismatic founders of schools. In the period of the Shang before this, and of the Empire that followed it, the institutions directly involving the literati were embedded in political structures. The factual foundation for the hypotheses concerning the uniqueness of the intellectual's product, however, remains to be examined.

It is unnecessary to prove that the Chou period evidenced a great flowering of ancient Chinese thought. However, one can ascertain the extent to which Chinese social thought was adjusted to the unique requirements of Chinese society only by a specific review of its main forms. In the present chapter a review of Chinese social thought developed during the Chou period will be undertaken. An estimation will be made of its general character and of the changes in it most directly traceable to social change. Finally, as Chinese society began to harden into the forms of the imperial period, the place of Chinese thought in Chinese civilization will be briefly examined.

CHINESE SOCIAL THOUGHT OF THE CHOU PERIOD

Confucianism

One of the oldest and most fundamental schools of Chinese thought is that of Confucius (551–497 B.C.). A doctrine of human nature or of "the human heart," lies at the basis of Confucianism, according to which men are born with intuition and native intelligence which can be developed to attain the supreme good. In words attributed to Confucius:

> The ancients who wished to illustrate virtue throughout the empire first ordered well their own States. Wishing to order well their States, they first regulated their families. Wishing to regulate their families, they first cultivated their persons. Wishing to cultivate their persons, they first rectified their hearts.[1]

Social reconstruction rests on moral reformation, which begins with the individual who must be a gentleman toward himself if he is to become an adjusted family member and a reliable participant in society.

A concept of personal virtue lies at the basis of the so-called five universal moral obligations of man. They define a hierarchy of deference or respect of persons toward one another. As summarized in the *Doctrine of the Mean:*

> The duties of universal obligation are five, and the virtues wherewith they are practiced are three. The duties are those between sovereign and minister, between father and son, between husband and wife, between elder and younger brother, and those belonging to the intercourse of friends. Those are the duties of universal obligation. Knowledge, magnanimity, and energy, these are the virtues universally binding.[2]

Confucian teaching is strongly familistic. The pivot of the entire Confucian system is filial piety. In the Analects the rules of a most exacting familism are formulated, for example:

> XIX. The master said, "while his parents are alive, the son may not go abroad, to a distance. If he does go abroad, he must have a fixed place to which he goes."
>
> XX. The master said, "if the son for three years does not alter the way of his father, he may be called filial."
>
> XXI. The master said, "the years of parents may by no means not be kept in memory, as an occasion at once for joy and fear."

The system requiring utmost deference from the individual to the family head was extended to the state in the conception of family and state as a single unified order. Familism was also the primary area of application for the Confucian form of the Golden Rule. Tzao-kung said: "What I do not wish men to do to me, I also wish not to do to men."[3] At no time did Confucius sanction individual revolt against family or state, but he proposed an attitude of resigned fatalism. Confucius insisted that life and death are matters of fate, and to be rich or poor is determined by heaven.

Confucius was not inclined toward abstract speculation either theological, eschatological, or metaphysical. Moreover, while Confucianism is pragmatic, practical, and social-minded, it was reformist only in a special sense. The

[1] James Legge, *The Life and Teachings of Confucius* (London: Kegan Paul, 1909), p. 226.
[2] Legge translation, p. 300.
[3] *Analects*, Legge translation, p. 141.

patriarchal family was conceived to be the one fixed and eternal source of social stability. The political sovereign was treated as patriarch of the realm. The five fundamental duties were addressed to the preservation of this politico-familistic hierarchy. Customary behavior and ceremonialism were conceived as primary instruments of family solidarity. The classics were, among other things, valuable because they were old. Innovations were discouraged. The only acceptable type of reform was a return to the good old days when peace prevailed, because the subject was obedient like a pious and dutiful son and the sovereign was like a kindly father. One's lot and his misfortunes were the will of heaven.

Mencius

Like Confucius, Mencius (371–289 B.C.) was born of one of the great clans of Lu. His father died when he was three years old. Mencius' mother was one of the celebrated women of Chinese history, indicating his genteel derivation. Mencius was forty years old before, like Confucius, he became founder of a school. For more than twenty years he wandered from court to court, occasionally accepting offices and receiving gifts. Eventually he withdrew from politics, and spent the last twenty years of his life with his disciples.

As with Confucius, a conception of human nature (*jen*) was central to Mencius' teaching. According to Suzuki, *jen* means "broadly speaking . . . sympathy, or loving kindness, or friendly feeling, or better, feeling of fellowship."[4] *Jen* was theorized to be the foundation of society. As the source of all virtue, it is Tao, the proper way to the good life–kindheartedness, charity, sincerity, sympathy, and self-control.

Mencius isolated, clarified, and systematized one of the interpretations of human nature implied by Confucius. *Jen* as compassion, or "not being able to bear what others should suffer . . . responsibility for the suffering of others,"[5] is roughly equivalent to sympathy or altruism. If *jen* is its core, human nature must be innately good. Society rests on altruism or sympathy. As Suzuki interprets him, Mencius even formulated the rudiments of a metaphysics of world order based on altruism. The movements of the heavenly bodies, the cycle of the seasons, and the growth and transformation of all living things on earth were conceived to be manifestations of *jen*.

However, Mencius was interested in the operation of human goodness, or *jen,* as a practical moralist rather than as a metaphysician:

> Man's impulse is to do good, for his nature is good. That he does not do good is no fault of his natural faculty. A feeling of sympathy everybody has; a feeling of shame everybody has; a feeling of deference everybody has; a sense of discrimination everybody has. The feeling of sympathy is humanness (*jen*); the feeling of shame is justice (*i*); the feeling

[4] Daisetz Teitaro Suzuki, *A Brief History of Early Chinese Philosophy* (1914), p. 51.
[5] Arthur Waley, *Three Ways of Thought in Ancient China* (London: George Allen & Unwin, 1939), p. 115.

> of deference is (*li*); and the sense of discrimination is intelligence (*chi*). Humanness, sense of justice, propriety, and intelligence are not what is moulded into us from without. They are inherent in us, only men are not conscious of them.
>
> Therefore, a man without a feeling of sympathy is not human; a man without a feeling of shame is not human; a man without a feeling of deference is not human; a man without a sense of discrimination is not human; the feeling of sympathy is the starting point of humanness; the feeling of shame is the starting-point of justice; the feeling of deference is the starting-point of propriety; and the sense of discrimination is the starting-point of intelligence. A man has these four starting-points as he has four limbs; and those who, having these four starting-points, plead incapability are mutilating themselves.[6]

In Book XI Mencius had compared the *jen* in human nature as equivalent to the property in running water which causes it to seek its lowest level.

> Now, that water, when whipped and tossed, could be passed over one's forehead, or that, when arrested and driven in another direction, it could be made to go over a hill, is not in the nature of water. It is due to the force of circumstances. Man could be made to do not-goodness, for his nature is as susceptible as water.[7]

Mencius believed that experience often tends to erase one's natural sentiments. He recommended breath-control (suggestive of Yoga) as one way for maintaining one's composure in the face of such experiences.[8]

The Rousseauesque suggestion is contained in Mencius' argument that while man is born good, institutions may corrupt him. As a practical moralist, Mencius thus argued that goodness depends on economic security as well as peace of mind. "If beans and millet were as plentiful as fire and water, such a thing as a bad man would not exist among the people."[9]

Mencius tended to modify Confucianism in an idealistic and reformist direction. Whatever else may be said of Confucius' original position, he certainly did not advocate a democratic political order—emphasis on the sanctity of hierarchical ranks is too fundamental. However, when *jen* is interpreted to refer to a universal innate goodness of human nature, it thrusts Confucianism toward democratic conclusions. Man is born good; institutions corrupt him. Economic reform is a precondition of virtue. Mencius himself was not afraid to challenge the rulers of principalities and denounce princes for their lack of virtue.

Mencius was led to question the basis of sovereignty. He agreed with Confucius that the right to govern was by virtue of heaven. However, he thought the decree of heaven could only be determined by the will of the people. This shifted emphasis within Confucianism toward a conception of the "consent of the governed," making the doctrine equivalent to the con-

[6] Quoted by Suzuki, *op. cit.*, pp. 67–68.
[7] Quoted by Suzuki, *op. cit.*, p. 67.
[8] Waley, *op. cit.*, p. 118.
[9] Quoted by Waley, *op. cit.*, p. 119.

cept of the sovereign people (Rousseau's general will) of eighteenth-century occidental thought.

In the end, however, Mencius' reformism was traditionalistic. He advocated the revival of the old system of agriculture in which eight families worked together on a common plot. He did not like the tribute system under which each householder paid a fixed tribute in grain determined by average yield. He advocated abolition of market and frontier taxes, a minimum of parks and enclosures, and the restriction of conscript labor to periods when agriculture was slack. Finally, he proposed a system of state education for moral instruction of the people.[10] Mencius' ideal state was a monarchy in form ruled by a sage king in accordance with the principles of benevolence and righteousness.[11]

Hsuntse

Like many other scholars of the period, Hsuntse (360–260 B.C.) traveled extensively and gathered a school about him. For a number of years, as an old man, he was district magistrate of the state of Ts'u. After a change of administration, he lost his position and sustained himself in his last years as a private teacher. In contrast to Mencius who toyed idealistically with the concept of the welfare state, Hsuntse represented the realistic branch of Confucianism.[12]

Hsuntse, whose position is orthodox Confucianism, saw an inconsistency between the notion of the innate goodness of human nature and the goals of the Confucian system. He revised the estimate of human nature and carried out its implications with systematic practical rationality. He taught that the essential characteristic of human nature is sociability, in which lie the origins of society. Thus far the position appears to be similar to that of Mencius. However, the core of sociability is not sympathy (*jen*) but desire. "There are two elements in desire in the sense of an impulse to seek for certain *objects*, and there is desire in the sense of a seeking or a purpose."[13] Egoistic and self-oriented drives rather than sympathy and altruism provide the clue to human behavior. In a manner suggestive of Hobbes, Hsuntse suggests, according to Dubs, that human nature is fundamentally evil:

> To Hsuntse . . . "The nature of man is evil; his goodness is only acquired training." In support of this contention he alleged a number of facts, viz., that there are evil tendencies in human nature, such as strife, rapacity, the desires of the ear and eye, etc., and that these seem to be innate; that the civilizing influence of teachers, laws, and virtues are necessary; that character development is through the overcoming of contrary impulses . . . ; that in the states, such as the state of Ts'in, which

[10] For details, see Waley, *op. cit.*, pp. 121 ff.

[11] Francis C. M. Wei, *The Political Principles of Mencius* (Shanghai: Presbyterian Mission Press, 1916), p. 55.

[12] Fung Yu-lan, *A Short History of Chinese Philosophy*, edited by Derk Bodde (New York: The Macmillan Co., 1948), p. 68.

[13] Homer H. Dubs, *Hsuntse* (London: Arthur Probsthain, 1927), p. 51.

> are simpler and where the people follow their feelings more than in the cultivated districts of central China, the people are ruder and less refined. . . . Hsuntse went so far as to speculate what would be the result if the authority of the prince and the influence of the codes of conduct were removed, and said that the whole country would be in turmoil, in the same condition as Hobbes' State of Nature. . . . But Hsuntse had no theory of any state of nature; he was merely taking a view of what would happen if men followed their evil nature alone.[14]

While human nature is fundamentally evil, human behavior is capable of modification and improvement. Men are everywhere basically the same. The man on the street as much as the sage has the capacity to understand virtue and the ability to achieve it. It is training that makes one man a criminal and another a sage.

Hsuntse was not particularly interested in denouncing human nature for its depravity but, like the Protestants who think man was born in original sin, in socializing it. Western Protestantism also maintains that human nature is innately evil, but with Protestantism the responsibility for its control is individualized. This is quite different from the Confucian solution. For Hsuntse the whole rationale for society lay in securing human virtue. The evil in human nature is the reason for education, ceremony, and ritual.

The two basic principles in Confucian thought were propriety (*li*) and sympathy (*jen*), referring respectively to outward conduct and inward sentiment. They received somewhat contrasting emphasis in the works of Mencius and Hsuntse. The reform of the state for Confucius began with a reform of the human heart (*jen*). In Mencius' conceptions *jen* acquired a subtlety of meaning, becoming *altruistic* social sentiment. Social reform aims at removing the fetters of *jen*. Outward conduct will then be good as a matter of principle. In Hsuntse's teachings the emphasis upon *li* and *jen* was reversed.

> Li, which is standards of conduct and ceremonies to be performed, fits Hsüntse's conception of virtue much better than any other and so we are not surprised to find that he emphasized it almost to the complete exclusion of Jen.
>
> "The principle of *Li* is truly deep. . . . Its principle is truly great. . . . Its principle is truly high. . . . When the superior man has investigated into *Li*, he cannot be cheated as to what is false. . . . *The rules of proper conduct* (*Li*) *are the utmost of human morality* . . . the student who resolutely studies *Li* becomes a Sage; without especially studying it, he becomes a directionless person."
>
> In Hsüntse's teaching, *Jen*, has almost disappeared. It remains only as an attribute of the benevolent and kindly prince who seeks the welfare of his people; it has become characteristic of the Sage alone, who, because of his highly developed character, can rise superior to the ordinary man, and can himself be the source of authority. For him morals can proceed from within.[15]

[14] *Ibid.*, pp. 80–81.
[15] Dubs, *ibid.*, pp. 134–135.

The only other virtue of which Hsuntse makes much is *yi*. In the *Doctrine of the Mean* by Confucius this has been explained as follows: "*Yi* is doing what is right and proper or correctness; its greatest exhibition is in honoring the worthy. (D.M., XX 5.)

Hsuntse took *yi* to be basic. "Men are able to form social organizations . . . through *Yi*. For *Yi* are harmonized through social distinctions. When people are harmonized, they can unite . . . and have greater strength."[16]

Yi are rights. *Yi* are social inequalities which men accept and recognize. Hsuntse sometimes uses *yi* in conjunction with *li*, but also at times employs it alone. In general *li* is the all-embracing principle. It is ceremony, it is ritual, it is moral and legal order; in fact, it is even interpreted on occasion as natural order. *Li* is the total order of social relations; *yi* is an important subclass.

Hsuntse was profoundly conservative. He nowhere speculated about the future of the state or its basis. He advocated an intensified observance and extension of rituals, ceremonies, and all outward forms of conduct. He specifically discouraged philosophic and theological speculation.

> Although the Way of Heaven be deep, . . . man will not reflect on it; although it be great, he will not use his ability for its investigation; although it be mysterious he will not scrutinize it—this is what is meant by refraining from contesting Heaven.[17]

Heaven, for all practical purposes, was reduced to its manifestations. It becomes simply natural law, the impersonal order of *li*.

Hsuntse categorically denied the existence of spirits and wrote a book against fortune-telling. Having a kind of tongue-in-cheek skepticism, he hardly mentioned the ancient practice of divination. In accordance with his general positivistic bias, he reduced the problem of destiny to what one meets at the moment.

The pragmatic rationalization of everyday conduct, so central to Confucian thought, was brought to a systematic instrumentalism by Hsuntse. Speculation, on the one hand, and superstition, on the other, were swept aside. The conception of the evil of human nature justified the traditional absolutism in government and ethics. Society was conceived as a fixed hierarchy of classes established by systematic education and maintained by conformity to ritual and ceremony. As in the case of Hobbes, a skeptical conception of human nature implemented social and political conservatism.

Taoism

The second major school developing during this period was Taoism. Here only two of the Taoists will be discussed—Laotse and Chuangtse.

[16] Quoted by Dubs, *ibid.*, pp. 155–156.
[17] Quoted by Dubs, *ibid.*, p. 57.

Laotse

Laotse, the founder of Taoism, was, at least according to legend, a most unusual philosopher. After a supernatural conception, his mother carried him in her womb sixty-two years, so that when he was born his hair was white as with age. Other myths attributed to him extraordinarily great age, some 160, others over 200 years. This great age was attributed to his practice of *Tao*. With mild skepticism the Chinese historian of the Han, Ssu-ma Ch'ien, assigned to Laotse the lesser of his reputed ages.

Laotse was born in K'uksien in 571 B.C., being thus an older contemporary of Confucius. He came from an old and cultured family and served as keeper of the imperial archives (official librarian) at the capital of the Chou. Confucius visited him and reported to his disciples:

> I know how birds fly, how fishes can swim, and how animals can run. But the runner may be snared, the swimmer may be hooked, and the flyer may be shot by the arrow. But there is the dragon. I cannot tell how he mounts the wind through the clouds, and rises to heaven. Today I have seen Laotse, and can only compare him to the dragon.

According to tradition Laotse, seeing the decay of the empire, planned to depart, but upon the request of his disciples left behind a book on Tao in 5,000 characters. In the *Book of Tao* Laotse identifies Tao as the nameless essence of reality:

> The Tao that can be told of
>   Is not the Absolute Tao;
> The Names that can be given
>   Are not Absolute Names.
> The Nameless is the origin of Heaven and Earth:
> The Named is the Mother of All Things.[18]

The Taoists developed a monistic conception of the universe. Tao was conceived as a metaphysical reality superior to, back of, and the source of all other things. In almost Hegelian fashion this "absolute" underlying all distinctions gives rise to opposites. It was the source and cancellation of all distinctions. No matter where a distinction is drawn, there rises a conception of an antithesis. The absolute (*Tao*) represents the point at which all antitheses meet.

> When the people of the Earth all know beauty as beauty,
>   There arises (the recognition) of ugliness.
> When the people of the Earth all know the good as good,
>   There arises (the recognition) of evil.

Therefore:

> Being and non-being inter-depend in growth;
> Difficult and easy inter-depend in completion;

[18] *The Wisdom of Laotse*, trans. by Lin Yutang (New York: The Modern Library, 1948), p. 41.

Long and short inter-depend in contrast;
High and low inter-depend in position;
Tones and voice inter-depend in harmony;
Front and behind inter-depend in company.[19]

This reasoning might seem to be a most unpromising foundation for a popular philosophy of conduct. However, the Taoists were convinced that their view of nature was accurate.

> "Nature is unkind: It treats the creation like sacrificial straw dogs." The sage, through the practice of Taoism, achieves a state of personal impartiality like that of nature, for it is said, "The Sage is unkind: He treats the people like sacrificial straw dogs."

Nature is one of infinite manifestations of power of Tao.

The universe is like a bellows!
Empty, yet it gives a supply that never fails;
The more it is worked, the more it brings forth.[20]

Human nature possesses some of the same power.

Taoism is a proposal for conduct in a world conceived as impersonal, cruel in its impersonality, indifferent to human striving and suffering, and endless in its snares. The core of Taoism is the practice of *wu wei*—nonstriving. Through appropriate practice of *wu wei* one may rise superior to the snares and entanglements of the world. Above all else, the Taoist avoids the entanglements of the world.

Therefore the Sage:
Manages affairs without action;
Preaches the doctrine without words;

All things take their rise, but he does not turn away from them;
He gives them life, but does not take possession of them;
He acts, but does not appropriate;
Accomplishes, but claims no credit.[21]

Against the Confucian proposal to exalt the scholar to key positions in government, Laotse suggested that this only leads to endless ambitious scheming. Better than the Confucian cultivation of intelligence are full bellies and empty heads. However, the most fundamental proposal of Taoism is denial of self:

In his dwelling, [the Sage] loves the [lowly] earth;
In his heart, he loves what is profound;
In his relations with others, he loves kindness;
In his words, he loves sincerity;
In government, he loves peace;
In business affairs, he loves ability.

[19] *Ibid.*, p. 47.
[20] *Ibid.*, p. 63.
[21] *Ibid.*, p. 47.

In his actions, he loves choosing the right time.
It is because he does not contend
that he is without reproach.[22]

Contention, ambition, seeking for praise, egoism, all things arising from desire, are quite vain. Only he can be trusted in government who does not want to govern at all and hence is beyond ambition, praise, and blame. Only by withdrawal from the world can one become superior to it.

While Laotse compactly formulated Taoism, he did not in any real sense invent it. The practice of apathetic ecstasy and the achievement of inner (magical) power through ascetic practices are ancient. It is, however, unusual to find magical asceticism sponsored by a high state official. One may assume that, when the secular urbanity more usual in state officials is replaced by the magical asceticism more natural to a monk, special hazards threaten the officials' situation. It is in keeping with this that Laotze was shocked by the decay of public life.

Chuangtse

In the closing days of the Chou, the subtle skeptic and poet Chuangtse consolidated and expanded the doctrines of Laotse in somewhat the same fashion as Mencius and Hsuntse had expanded those of Confucius. Extremely little is known of Chuangtse. He died around 275 B.C. He was a contemporary of Mencius, and a native of Mengshien. That he was of "noble" derivation is suggested by his position as an "officer of the varnish grove."

His conceptions of Tao and Taoist are an elaboration of the ideas of Laotse:

> Tao is real, is faithful, yet does nothing and has no form. Can be handed down, yet cannot be passed from hand to hand; can be got, but cannot be seen. Is its own trunk, its own root. Before Heaven and Earth existed, from the beginning Tao was there. It is Tao that gave ghosts (*Shen*) their holy power, that gave power to dead kings. It gave lift to Heaven, and life to earth.[23]

More clearly than Laotse, Chuangtse sees Tao as a mystic substance or perhaps inner principle of the world.

The Taoist is impervious to the hazards of nature.

> The great bushlands are ablaze, but he feels no heat; the river and the Han stream are frozen over, but he feels no cold. Fierce thunders break over the hills, winds rock the ocean, but he is not startled. He can climb high and not stagger; go through water and not be wet, go through fire and not be scorched.[24]

By practicing *wu wei*, the Taoist concentrates the magical power of Tao in himself and thus becomes impervious to the fortunes of the world. Chuangtse

22 *Ibid.*, p. 76.

23 Waley, trans., *op. cit.*, pp. 78–79. See also *Chuang Tzu, Musings of a Chinese Mystic* (London: John Murray, 1920), p. 60.

24 *Ibid.*, p. 80. See also *Chuang Tzu, op. cit.*, p. 86.

sat on the ground singing and beating time with a basin, while his wife's body was lying in her coffin in the house awaiting burial. He was not acting from happiness, but from the futility of all grief.

Reason was renounced by the Taoist in favor of antirational practices. Taoism was, in fact, antilogical. Chuangtse undertook to demonstrate the vanity of reason by proving "that the sky is lower than the earth, that the mountains are no higher than the marsh lands, that the sun at noon is standing on the horizon, that what lives is at the same time dead."[25] Such disputes aroused anxiety in the Confucians, as did the attempt by Taoists to prove the uselessness of learning and the emptiness of the classics. However, though they were anti-intellectual, the Taoists were not pessimists. The Taoists proposed techniques for conserving one's vital powers, which in later times developed into four distinct branches: the secrets of the chamber, which permitted the Yellow ancestor to enjoy 1,200 concubines without injury to his health, breath-control, physical exercises, and special dietary practices.

The Confucian thought of the individual as immersed in the practical affairs of the family and the state. The Taoist withdrew, if not physically, psychologically from both; he hid his inborn powers from the world. *Pau* is the soul in its natural condition and is the symbol of man's true pure state. It is an inward vision, a state of pure consciousness which "sees without looking, hears without listening, knows without thinking."[26] Preoccupation with the world of the senses is the death of this pure state.

The Taoist, however, does not require actual physical withdrawal from society. The Taoist merely seeks anonymity. He seeks to live in the world, but not of it. There are, however, stories of Taoists who renounced the highest positions to seek actual physical withdrawal.

Another point at which Taoism was at variance with Confucianism was in the evaluation of rites, customs, and ceremonies. To Taoism, they were useless. Even the elaborate ritual of mourning, central to the rites of the ancestor cult, was renounced by the Taoist. In a dialogue between Chuangtse and a skull, the skull said, "In death there are no kings and no subjects and no change of seasons. One is completely free, regarding heaven and earth as spring and autumn. Such happiness exceeds even that of a king."[27] When Chuangtse was found singing after his wife's death, he answered to a query, "She merely goes through a process resembling the rotation of spring, summer, autumn, and winter."[28] And at the time of his own approaching death, he renounced a sumptuous funeral:

> "I regard the heaven and earth as my coffin and outer coffin, the sun and moon as a pair of jade gifts and the constellations as my buried jewels. And the whole creation shall come to my funeral. Will it not be a grand funeral? What more should I want?"

[25] Waley, *op. cit.*, p. 28.
[26] *Ibid.*, p. 97.
[27] Lin Yutang, trans., pp. 179–180.
[28] *Ibid.*, p. 180.

> "We are afraid that vulture crows will come and eat our master," said the disciples.
>
> "Above the ground, I shall be eaten by the vultures, and underground I shall be eaten by the ants. Why rob the one to give it to the other? Why are you so partial (to the ants)?" Chuangtse replied.[29]

The political orientations of the Taoists were consistent with their other theories. War was denounced, not on moral or humanitarian grounds, but because of the absolute insignificance of all conquest and defense. Chuangtse thought that only a king exclusively preoccupied with Tao could be trusted with a kingdom. Since to such a king the affairs of state were meaningless, this was merely a quick route to anarchism. Taoistic anarchism makes most Western varieties appear rather shallow. The sages were viewed as misguided altruists. Philosophical wisdom was thought to be simply one more additional snare of the world. Conventions and laws were conceived as forms of hypocrisy.

The ideal society was pictured as one without books and with no records except knotted ropes. People were to have only the simplest foods. Such complete lack of mobility was to be maintained that villagers could hear the crowing of the cocks of the next village without even visiting it. The ideal society rested on such primitive agriculture that even machines were to be excluded. Above all, the sages, as inventors of goodness, duty, and laws, were to be prohibited. Plato might keep out poets from the good society; the Taoists would keep out Plato. Tyrants, as inventors of tortures and inquisitions, could have no place in such a society.

Two primary dimensions of Chinese feudal thought were demarked by Confucianism and Taoism, the one emphasized conventional order, the other anarchistic withdrawal. A quite distinct direction was taken by Motse.

Motse

Motse (468–390 B.C.) was born in the state of Lu. Like many of the scribes of the time, he traveled extensively among the various feudal states, alternating between private teaching and public service. He was one of the most popular teachers of ancient China. It is reported that at one time he had up to three hundred students. For a time he held the position of minister of war in the state of Sung, and was in charge of defense and fortifications.

Motse was unusual among the Chinese philosophers in giving explicit attention to the problem of method and proof. Except for the Taoists who were radically antihistorical, argument from precedent was common to most philosophers of the time, but Motse made it self-conscious. The aims of Motse's methodological reflections according to Mei were threefold:

> . . . it is to demonstrate (1) that what he was teaching was practicable, because it had been done before and therefore could be done, (2) that it was right because it was confirmed by the conduct and ideals of the

[29] *Ibid.*, p. 181.

ancient sage-kings, and in conclusion, (3) that therefore it should be followed here and now.[30]

Like the Confucians, Motse identified ethics and politics. His position was somewhat similar to that of Hsuntse, but he sought elsewhere for the answers to the problems this posed. Convinced that human problems arise from selfishness, he felt the only cure was to be found in the principle of love.

> Disorders arise from lack of mutual love among men. A thief loves what is his and cares not what belongs to others. Consequently he steals to enrich himself. . . . If peoples of the world will only love one another, nations will no longer attack one another; families will no longer harm one another; and individuals will no longer rob one another.[31]

Motse sought theological sanction for this principle, urging that love is the wish of heaven.

> I know it is so because the wise emperors before us were blessed with happiness and prosperity by following this sacred decree. . . . Whereas those who continue to dislike and harm one another were invariably punished by the consequences.[32]

Only the principle of love is able to bring the ideal society into being. Motse's ideal is expressed by Suzuki as follows:

> The ideal of Mu Ti is universal peace and universal prosperity. Whatever his teachings, they are all intended to bring about this state of things. He declares that the business of the holy man consists in promoting peace among his people, in developing all the resources of nature, and in avoiding all the possible causes of evils that befall our community.[33]

Following the implications of this idea of the greatest happiness of the greatest number, Motse developed a logically consistent utilitarianism. He profoundly objected to the implications of poverty which he thought had negative ethical significance. Man, he urged, is dependent on himself for economic salvation, a fact which should be turned to a principle of public policy.

> Those who do not exert themselves cannot live. When the gentlemen do not attend to government diligently, the jurisdiction will be in chaos. When the common men do not attend to work, supply will not be sufficient.[34]

The same elements found in Veblen's contrast between conspicuous consumption and the instinct of workmanship runs through Motse's doctrines.

[30] Yi-yao Mei, *Motse; The Neglected Rival of Confucius* (London: Arthur Probsthain, 1934), p. 63.

[31] Quoted by Huang-hsing Wang, *The Chinese Mind* (New York: John Day, 1946), p. 77.

[32] Quoted by Wang, *ibid.*, p. 78.

[33] Suzuki, *op. cit.*, p. 94.

[34] Quoted by Mei, *op. cit.*, p. 129.

He proposed an ideal society consistent with this reformist utilitarianism. The key elements of it were: (1) the reduction of consumption to a minimum, (2) the elimination of luxury, including reduction of the time spent in mourning, expensive burials, the use of silks and embroideries, and other nonutilitarian items (he even proposed banning the fine arts, for example, music, dancing, and painting); and (3) the increase in the production of necessities.

Warfare was condemned by Motse, but for practical reasons.

> Now about a country going to war. If it is in winter it will be too cold; if it is in summer it will be too hot. So it should be neither in winter nor in summer. If it is in spring it will take people away from sowing and planting; if it is in autumn it will take people away from reaping and harvesting. Should they be taken away in either of these seasons, innumerable people would die of hunger and cold.[35]

Motse was not a pacifist, however. He believed defensive wars were necessary and unavoidable. He was a master of defense and fortification, and taught courses in the art. In one instance it was transmitted that, to dissuade an aggressive king from ambitions inflamed by the invention of a new offensive weapon utilized in scaling city defenses, he hurriedly trained some of his disciples and repulsed every attack, thus dissuading the king from undertaking a series of wars.

Motse gave a practical twist to his concept of the welfare state. Political measures were to be judged by their capability to "enrich the poor, increase the few, remove danger, and regulate disorder."[36] He desired a redistribution of wealth, an increase of population, and a condition of political peace.

Motse's utilitarian inclinations were also evident in his interpretation of religion. He treated belief in ghosts in a manner suggestive of William James' *Will to Believe*. The existence of ghosts was a matter of indifference to him. However, he thought that belief in ghosts had an important social function. Fear of spirits could be a useful coercive measure to dissuade ignorant people from evil actions.

All political measures were brought to the test of utility to the state and contribution to the general welfare. Motse thus condemned luxurious habits in all spheres as an unproductive consumption of wealth. On the other hand, he thought the masses should be encouraged in all activities which increased the production of wealth. Concubinage was seen as an overproduction of both bachelors and old maids, hence a threat to population growth. Confucian sentimentalism was rejected and denounced, because it led people to support funerals far beyond their means. Such things waste wealth, paralyze administration, and check the progress of industry and commerce.

[35] Quoted by Mei, *The Ethical and Political Works of Motse* (London: Arthur Probsthain, 1929), p. 61.

[36] Quoted by Mei, *ibid.*, p. 130.

The School of Fa Chia

At the opposite pole from the mystical irrationalism of the Taoists and the anarchistic individualism it engendered was the philosophy of Fa Chia (the Legalists) which proposed the rational strengthening of the state. They agreed with the Moists that political reform was necessary, but in no case was political reform encouraged in the name of the general welfare of the masses. Moreover, the conduct of such a program in the name of love was radically contrary to their principles. Fa Chia were sustained in their views by a conception of human nature even more cynical than Hsuntse's.

Legalist thinking was based on the theory that the essence of society and human relations is force. The primary principle of social and political program of Legalism was the replacement of morality by law. With the Confucians, the essential characteristic of an emperor was not virtue but power (*shih*). Power adheres to an emperor, again contrary to the Confucians, not by the decree of heaven, but by virtue of his position.

The position at bottom was Machiavellian. Right is what the ruler wants; wrong is what he does not want. Human nature is not basically good. The people hate toil, and fear danger and punishment. Yet these are the only ways of securing genuine conformity. Hence the Legalists proposed a program of reform, not by moral instruction but by a rigorous system of laws and punishments. Not anarchism, but a totalitarian state was implied by their reforms. They objected to the welfare program of the Moists, advocating, in modern terms, "not butter, but guns."

The Legalists sought the systematic building of state power. The basic means for this were: (1) punishment for anyone who did not conform to the laws, (2) systematization of the law, (3) support of only two types of activities—agriculture and military preparation, (4) division of the entire population into the able-bodied and the old and weak, (5) elimination of all privileges except those gained by military distinction, (6) elimination of merchants and harmful moralists "who protect parents and friends who have disobeyed the law,"[36a] and (7) suppression of all learning except handbooks on war and agriculture.

The school of Fa Chia was the closest approach in the period to a group of thinkers with a completely scientific approach to social issues in the sense that it divorced the analysis of social issues from magical consideration (like those of the Taoists) and from ethical considerations (like those of the Moists and Confucians). They proposed problems in purely technical terms; they produced the numerous scientific texts which appeared in the late Chou period. China's classical treatise on war, written during this time, illustrates the detachment the Legalists could achieve in posing problems free of ethical considerations.

Sun-wu lived sometime between 722 and 481 B.C. In his thirteen-volume

[36a] Arthur Waley, *Three Ways of Thought in Ancient China* (London: George Allen and Unwin, 1939), p. 226.

study on warfare, he discussed such topics as strategy, supplies, attack, topography, timing, combat organization, manoeuverability, incendiary art, and spying. War, Sun-wu admitted, was a brutal business. But for this very reason, he urged, there was no point in not practicing every trick, scheme, or dishonorable practice that would work.

Looking at warfare in technical terms, he fully appreciated the fact that loyalty (morale) was usually essential to military success. He advocated constant military preparedness. He proposed that armies in the field should use the resources and supplies of the occupied country as completely as possible. In a manner suggestive of Clausewitz he viewed war as a political expedient to be resorted to only after diplomacy had failed. However, once a war operation started, he emphasized the values of manoeuverability and speed. "A good arm should move like an arrow from a bow." Other things being equal, the quickest decision is least costly. However, this did not mean that superior manpower and techniques should be neglected. Sun-wu thought it would be a major military blunder to permit civilians to participate in military decisions. Because of the danger of encouraging inferior officerships, he was even opposed to the emperor interfering with generals.

Sun-wu distinguished five types of spies: (1) native spies (fifth columnists), (2) inside spies (men in the enemy ranks with a grievance), (3) spies in reverse (spies sent by the enemy who were fed false information), (4) dumb spies (persons given false knowledge and sent to spy on the enemy in full knowledge that they would be caught and interrogated), and (5) daring spies (propagandists, rumor manufacturers, saboteurs). Sun-wu's treatise is an example of ethically neutral analysis.

THE GENERAL CHARACTER OF CHINESE THOUGHT

The review of Chinese social thought just completed was not intended to be complete, but only to outline its central properties and to illustrate the bold spirit of free creation that inspired it during this period. An examination of its central character quickly reveals how closely it was shaped to social needs.

The Confucians visualized a conventional stabilization of the socio-political order. Though Confucius insisted that he was not an innovator, his program was a critique of contemporary tendencies. By making filial piety of central importance, Confucius constructed a unified system out of the heritage of the past. The system he proposed was practical, easily comprehensible, and with general appeal. Hardly anywhere else has the father-son relation been made so completely the most significant element in the entire ethical system. The elevation of the human heart (*jen*) to central importance gave a rational base for the position, emphasizing the profoundly pacifistic character of the Confucian system.

While accepting Confucian doctrine as orthodox, both Mencius and Hsuntse exercised full freedom in interpreting it. They accepted the general objective of conventionalization and stabilization of social order. In explaining the Confucian stand, Mencius turned the notion of *jen* into an innate quality. The effect of this was to carry the position toward a more democratic and social-critical orientation than appears to have been Confucius' intention. Continuous development in that direction could result in a position akin to that of Motse. Mencius may, in fact, have been influenced by Moism. Through his reinterpretation of human nature, Hsuntse brought the Confucian position to full development. By the interpretation of human nature as evil and by emphasizing propriety (*li*) rather than human goodness (*jen*), the necessity of conventional and ceremonial order was vindicated and legitimized.

In contrast to Confucianism, the Taoists presented a rather extreme form of anarchism quite distinct from the idealistic anarchism of the West. The Confucian *jen* represented a kind of yielding to society; the Taoist *wu-wei* was a psychological withdrawal. Conventional morality was suspect to the Taoists, because it legitimized existing social relations, and the Taoists were fully aware of the fact that the existing order was breaking down. The problem for the Taoist was the achievement of individual self-sufficiency and power in part against society. Between them, Confucianism and Taoism explored the major alternatives of sociability and individualism for ancient China in the period of the Warring Kingdoms.

In its general value, orientation, Moism stands closer to Confucianism than to Taoism. It looks forward to the attainment of highest values in society rather than through freedom from it. Motse's general theoretical position is closer to that of Mencius than Hsuntse. However, what was only a tendency for Mencius became a primary theme for Motse. Moreover, with Hsuntse he agreed that the difficulties of mankind arise from various tendencies in human nature. Motse's answer was the development of love.

The Moists evolved a consistent utilitarianism leading toward a semi-socialistic theory of the state. Personal happiness was the primary objective of individuals. The general happiness should be the primary political objective. Social and political programs ought to be judged in terms of their satisfaction of fundamental needs. In an almost puritanical vein Motse did not hesitate to propose the elimination of luxury, the arts, music, in fact everything that did not directly promote the general welfare.

The interests of the Legalists, like the Moists, were in socio-political reform. However, their program centered not in love but in power. Their aim was not to develop a welfare state, but a totalitarian order. They proposed a reconstruction of social forms even more sweeping than Motse's proposed elimination of such things as concubines and parasitic social classes that consumed but did not produce. The Legalists also wished to eliminate most other social ranks, for they thought efficiency was the only adequate basis for political structure. In contrast to the Moists, and in accordance with the doctrine that the state (and civil society) was a power complex, they wished to strengthen the military and the police.

Thus there was a rich variety of alternative positions: conventionalized ceremonialism, individualistic anarchism, utilitarian socialism, and totalitarianism. During the feudal period, however, as interesting as the variety were the common elements running throughout. One problem dominated them: the relation of the individual to society and particularly to the state. The Confucians answered the question in familistic terms. The individual is related to political superiors as is a family member to its patriarch. The Taoists answered in terms of what must certainly have been one form of ancient magic. It is an answer out of the hurt and suffering an individual may experience in the withdrawal of the individual from society. Through magically effective asceticism the Taoists hoped to obtain all the values really conceived to be important—long life, inner peace, etc. The Moists proposed a welfare state, fusing utilitarianism and puritanism in a way familiar to occidental thought. The school of Fa Chia discounted the individual except insofar as he was incorporated into a totalitarian order.

Despite such interesting variations, there were some basic similarities for all schools. An underlying ethical preoccupation was shared by all, even when formulated negatively. This ethical preoccupation varied from the family ethic of the Confucians, which was universalized, through the utilitarian ethic of Motse. The Taoists differed not so much in the values to which their thinking was addressed as in their conception of the means by which it might be achieved. And finally, even the Legalists posed social stability as the highest value.

The schools are similar, however, in more than their general problem and the general character of the solution. The special terms in which the problems are conceived are also similar. It is particularly interesting that in a time when there were no major limitations on speculative inquiry, purely theoretical speculation was almost completely lacking.

The lack of theoretical speculation is emphasized by the fact that it was necessary to legitimize positions in the face of alternative stands. There is no particular problem for a point of view so long as it is the only one in the field. It is simply unchallenged. But the moment there is a variety of points of view the question may be raised—why accept one rather than another? Hence we find the Confucians and Moists relying on the decree of heaven. The more radical of the two, Motse, begins to reinterpret the will of heaven in a manner which would bring it into line with a concept of the sovereign people and also incidentally that would encourage the use of public opinion as a sanction of political policy. The Legalists and Taoists eventually, though in different ways, legitimized their argument by results. The need to explain their stands is felt. But such justifications are remarkably primitive. All the arguments are practical rather than theoretical in character. The problem for the Chinese thinkers is one of how to secure the desired value. Sudden shyness tends to seize all of the thinkers when on the verge of drawing a major theoretical conclusion.

Despite the essential instrumentalism of all approaches, it is noteworthy that its intellectuality is not scientific. Pure scientific research is as far from the minds of all the thinkers as was theoretical speculation of other types. The Confucians emphasize conventional order, the Taoists self-control. The most instrumentally oriented of all were the Moists and Legalists. The Legalists went so far as to propose the elimination of all books except those on such problems as agriculture and warfare.

Still another common point is the absence of the theological elements usual to ancient speculation. This is particularly noteworthy in view of the semireligious vindication of the positions. The problems of an eschatology or theodicy are completely lacking. The very manner of phrasing any number of religious issues displays a good deal of religious skepticism. The Confucians had a difficult time deciding whether spirits existed. Moreover, the Confucians waged a more or less continuous struggle against superstition. This is the more noteworthy when it is realized that to the popular mind the Confucians were charismatic magicians, and individual literati were often consulted as priests and employed in the conduct of family ceremonies. Motse disposed of all the issues involved in the question, Do spirits exist?, with the observation, Fear of ghosts is socially useful. The Legalists rejected the whole popular demonology, but were willing to use it for social control.

Tied closely to this skepticism of religious propositions is the thoroughly this-worldly orientation of the thought systems. None of them proposes a recompense in a future world as an answer to the suffering in this one. Even the Taoists, in the usual sense the most religious of them all, propose purely this-worldly values: good fortune, long life, freedom from pain and disease of all types, and imperviousness to natural and human ills and dangers.

SOCIAL THOUGHT AND SOCIAL CHANGE IN ANCIENT CHINA

The Social Basis of the Variety of Feudal Thought

Most decisive for the varieties of thought was the presence during troubled times of a stratum of genteel intellectuals, strategically necessary to the social order. Later on China was to elevate an aristocracy of talent to key position, such talent being recruited from almost all strata. This was not the case during the feudal era. A feudal hierarchy was not inclined to seek its scribal talent among the artisans or the peasantry. Moreover, at the time the artisans and peasants were hardly in a position to secure literary educations. On the other hand, there was no churchly structure, equivalent to the Christian Church of the Middle Ages, that could supply clerks for secular needs. Administrative needs had developed to a point where record-keeping was essential, to say nothing of complex ceremonial and religious needs.

Moreover, noble families were being broken up—it being one of the policies of later empires to split them up by insisting that all sons inherit equally. It appears that sons other than the heir of feudal families or members of impoverished families often undertook literary training to survive. In contrast to the clerk of the Middle Ages, the scribe had a rank which would give him a hearing by princely administrators.

The literati were aristocrats who were at least partly secularized. They were used in a wide variety of positions—magistrates, ministers of justice, ministers of defense, supervisors of tribute levies, record-keepers, and librarians. Again and again they were relied upon for administrative advice and policy determination.

The feudal literati were repositories of ceremonial and political lore. Moreover, they had sufficient prestige of a semireligious, seminoble sort to make difficult their liquidation if they became critical of the social order. A feudal lord would think twice before he had a scholar executed. Moreover, the more famous scholars were often sought by other administrations. Hence we frequently hear of the scribes leaving one administrative post in one province for that in another. This mobility, in turn, provided a source of comparative knowledge of different social practices.

Even when the scribes were received coldly by a regime or deposed from office, they were not at a loss for a livelihood. They could always set up schools and teach for student fees. However, though this tended to provide access for the upward mobility of all classes, only the aristocracy or rich merchants could pay for the education of their sons.

The desired situation of the literati was official service. This paid more than an often-uncertain private school, and certainly carried more prestige. It was a rather unhappy accident for the ordinary scribe to lose his post. Sometimes, to be sure, it is transmitted that a sage condescended to accept a post. The individual scribe had both the possibility of cultivating a unique point of view and the situation to sustain it. If he was at odds with the administration, he could establish a school or else migrate to a new state. His prestige was normally sufficient to prevent personal harm. When his prestige developed, he was sought after as advisor and official.

Differential Receptivity of the Intellectual Programs

One of the most interesting problems for the theory of social change is the changing fate of the schools as between the feudal and imperial periods. During the feudal era, a variety of positions was simultaneously possible and the clash of alternative ideologies often accompanied the clash of arms. The wish for peace, particularly as the struggle became increasingly more grim, was endemic. The Confucian program could hardly have been other than popular with feudal princes. It accepted as given the principle of hierarchy. It proposed for the subject the pacifistic reconciliation of the individual in his own heart (*jen*) to his life fate. It legitimized feudal hierarchy in terms of family hierarchy.

The Taoistic program, on the other hand, could hardly serve the political needs of the princes directly. It answered the problems of the individual, not those of the political group. Most ceremonies which serve as a socially binding force were shrugged off as useless. One does not build an order on subjects who withdraw into individual anarchism. The proposal for eliminating all record-keeping in writing and substituting knotted ropes, or steering clear of all developed implements, are hardly means of maximizing the wealth of the state. At the same time Taoism promised magical access to many important values (longevity, good fortune, etc.) to the masses which it helped to pacify. A Taoistic state program was out of the question. But it could and did become a mass religion. In contrast to Confucianism it eventually developed a system of churches.

Meanwhile, in the highest circles of court society Taoism never completely lost its popularity. It could become a source of secret strength for the individual subject to the uncertainties of high politics. The eunuchs of the royal harem, with their characteristic magical inclinations and their derivation from the masses, were always a stronghold of Taoism. Taoism also eventually became a component in the intellectual orientations of the painters; its contemplative intensity was an element in the development of the exquisite landscape paintings of later times, presenting the ideal of the ascetic and withdrawn life, surrounded by magic mountains and waterfalls. In the very heart of agitated courtly society, Taoism nourished the ideal of meditative, ascetic withdrawal.

The potentialities, however, for a possible short-circuiting by the palace of the mandarinhood by a direct linkage of the court with Taoistic masses did not appear until later. It never succeeded in deposing Confucianism, which became the intellectualism of the civil servants.

Of all the intellectual positions, Moism was least able to win general acceptance. Moism proposed nothing short of eliminating altogether the leisured strata and all of their characteristic rites and ceremonies as well as their arts. It was the most democratic and least feudal in inclination. It contemplated a welfare state in the interests of the average individual. But there was no stratum powerful enough to serve as its foundation. The peasantry was neither militaristic nor politically effective. And the feudal hierarchy was, no more here than elsewhere, self-liquidating. Moreover, the artisan groups were bound to the household industries of the aristocrats and did not form a free demos in the manner of the cities of the Occident. It required a different age and time even to perceive the Moist program as interesting and to see in it hope rather than danger. Had there been a better developed middle class, the story could have been different. As it was, the Ch'in under Shih Huang-ti began the curtailment of the growth of the middle class. As the program of Wang Mang indicates, however, Moism remained a minor tendency for some centuries.

As the feudal struggle became increasingly more grim, typical rationalization occurred. Emphasis was inevitably placed on efficiency. The Confucians began to be visualized as proponents of outmoded ceremonialism ill-adapted to the challenge of the times. The border state of Ch'in learned its lessons the hard way, adopting the decisive military innovations that were to transform the political landscape. The military tactics of the barbarians were partly taken over. Combinations of cavalry and disciplined foot soldiers were introduced. This meant a partial rearming of the peasantry. When the Ch'in triumphed, the peasantry experienced a tremendously significant gain in social and economic importance, acquiring the right of land ownership. China gradually ceased to be a land of feudal estates and serfs, and became a land of free villages.

Thus there is evidence of a general decline in importance of Confucian thought modes during the late stages of feudalism and an increasing importance of the rationally expedient thinking of the Legalists. When Shih Huang-ti eventually succeeded, it was under the Legalistic guidance and advice of Li Ssu. When Li Ssu counciled Shih Huang-ti to avoid putting his relatives in charge of the provinces, he was employing the Legalist principle of avoiding all ranks other than those earned through efficiency. When Confucianism was forbidden, and Confucian scholars were prevented from holding office, it was, in part, out of the Legalist realization of the danger of counterpropaganda and traditional resistance to political rationalism. The burning of books, except for those on agriculture, merely put teeth into a fundamental Legalist tenet. The establishment of a bureaucracy based upon the principle of efficiency and the deliberate by-passing of aristocratic ranks in the recruitment of official personnel were both Legalistic.

Legalism was the midwife for the birth of the empire. With the triumph of the empire, under the principles of Legalism, China's most highly creative period was brought to an end. The Legalists even forbade the Confucians to teach their doctrines. Only later, under changed needs, when it became necessary to mitigate the harshness of the earlier totalitarianism, under Wu Ti, could Confucianism be substituted for Legalism.

Legalist doctrines played their role in the birth of the Empire. However, when continued they became a disorganizing force. The constant critique of policies and practices in terms of the principle of efficiency can become annoying; the development of armies (justifying themselves in the same manner that the Legalists used, in terms of power *per se*), which could turn on the state itself, was a danger. Once it was established, the central administration had far more to gain by cultivating passive acceptance of the *status quo*. Of all of the previous intellectual positions, Confucianism was most completely adaptable to this need.

Emperor Wu Ti, who was personally inclined toward ceremoniousness, appointed a Confucian as his chief advisor. However, it would be a mistake to conceive of the revival of Confucianism as a mere whim of the ruler. The value of traditionally binding ceremonies for social stability was perceived. There was every reason to conventionalize political relations.

CHINESE SOCIAL THOUGHT AND THE CRYSTALLIZATION OF CHINESE CIVILIZATION DURING THE IMPERIAL PERIOD

No attempt will be made in this or in the following case studies of society, civilization, and the intellectual to trace the step-by-step formation of a system of civilization in terms of the principles of playfulness, aesthetic receptivity, and sublimation. The playfulness which casts up the fundamental stock of cultural forms with which the civilization operates is manifest most completely in the same period of transition which saw the development of its social thought.

In a recent attempt to present a synthetic picture of Chinese civilization, Riencourt argues that the artistic development of China follows a curve similar to the evolution of its social thought with a blaze of creation of forms, styles, and symbols in the Chou period, followed by a period of simplification and synthesis beginning in the Han dynasties.[37]

During the Han period Confucianism was not only reinstated, but made the orthodox position of the realm. Other positions, in turn, were banned. The study of the classics was encouraged. Officials henceforth were chosen from the ranks of the Confucians. Restylization of Confucian doctrine was unavoidable. The conventional order that Confucius had attempted to underpin was feudal. The political myth of the ruler as father to his people had been addressed by Confucius to the relation between prince and vassals. It was now reinterpreted to apply to the relation between emperor and subject.

Confucius had been a member of the gentry. The new Confucian scholars were recruited in increasing numbers from humbler segments of the population. The Confucians formed a genteel stratum, but as an aristocracy of learning and achievement rather than as an aristocracy of birth.

The noble of feudal times largely monopolized the right to bear arms. The Confucians, retaining the image of the past, characteristically practiced archery as a sport. For a time in the examinations of the Confucian schools two sets of examination questions were made, and were placed on tablets. The easier set was on a small tablet, the more difficult one on a large tablet. The student shot at them with a bow and arrow, taking the examination of the tablet he hit. The study of music, characteristic of the leisured aristocracy, also remained a status activity of the mandarin. The long fingernails

[37] Amaury de Riencourt, *The Soul of China* (New York: Coward-McCann, 1958), p. 94.

of the sage were an external symbol of his detachment from manual labor. In the feudal period, this would have been unnecessary. One may assume that this increased in importance when access to the mandarinate was broadened to include persons who would otherwise have had to labor.

An extensive conventionalization of thought occurred on all levels, and new ideas were discouraged. Nor was it possible any longer for the sage who disagreed with the government simply to pack up and move to another town, or to set up a school in opposition to the government.

Rote memory of the classics and use of the classics as style models typified the new emphasis. Typical examination tasks required composition in the style of the ancients. The accent thus shifts from the substance of classical thought to its forms. This change was also evident in the tremendous emphasis upon pure mastery of the brush technique. The equivalent would be the establishment for our own civil service examinations of a special test on handwriting. An incidental effect of the emphasis upon brush technique was its influence on Chinese painting, which developed many of its basic features from the application of writing techniques to graphic problems.

While the civil service system thus placed tremendous emphasis upon rote memory, it should not be forgotten that by and large only the most intelligent persons managed to surmount the years of difficult preparation. The recruitment of talent still occurred. Moreover, a stratum of administrators arose with a remarkably homogeneous cultural background.

The control over the life conduct of the scholar-official did not cease when he had passed the highest examinations and received an official appointment. He was required to present accounts of his work, which was kept under surveillance of the censorate. His conduct in office was periodically reviewed in the *Imperial Gazette*, exposing him to continuous criticism by his peers and superiors.

In their relations to the masses, the mandarins had great prestige. Writing had anciently been pressed into the service of divination. It retained much of this character for the masses. Moreover, the state itself required the mandarin to conduct local ceremonies: to make sacrifices to the spirits of local mountains, rivers, etc. Furthermore, the mandarin was frequently appealed to by the population to conduct various religious ceremonies. Yet the decisive element in the mandarin's situation was his role as a public official. He could not establish a church of his own; he would be subject to official censure and reprimand if he did. He never developed into a priest.

Nevertheless, the elaboration of the state cult of Confucius reflected the semireligious relation of the mandarin to the general population. Confucius himself was deified. His descendants formed one of the few hereditary aristocracies in China. Temples were built to Confucius and to some of his more important descendants. Moreover, the state cult began to develop a pantheon of deities in which various ancient and local deities were incorporated in rank order. However, the official in his wider relations both to the imperial government and to the masses opposed superstition and magic. The development of mass cults could threaten the prestige and situation of the mandarin. There was never a time when the very existence of spirits was not held to be improbable by a considerable number of the literati. However, the mandarins also perceived fear of spirits as an implement of social control.

The Confucians thus defended their positions against the development of mass cults on the one hand and court Taoism on the other. They formed a pacifistic middle stratum in the empire. They served as a meeting point, where two converse systems of values represented by the peasant village and the palace could meet and be resolved.

In the system of civilization that was beginning to emerge, the form and content of a traditionalized Confucianism supplied the central style note and the status ethic of the genteel cultivated literati, forming a kind of central reference point for other features of the emerging cultural synthesis. As Riencourt observes, the developments in literature and art tended to proceed along the lines laid down before the triumph of the Ch'in. And while encyclopedias were compiled and history was recorded with care, works such as the *Shih Chi* were almost always the model. Even the great assemblies of scholars, for example, the Shih Ch'u conference of 51 B.C. and the Pai Hu Kuan conference of 79 A.D., were primarily intended to establish beyond question the interpretation of the classics.[38] Thus they served a function like the church council which fixes dogma.

The lines were so completely fixed against intellectual innovation of a fundamental sort which criticized basic suppositions that the activity of major scholars tended to be limited to the eclectic synthesis of the classical forms. Riencourt attributes to Chu Hsi (1130–1200 A.D.) the carrying through, a thousand years later, of the final Neo-Confucian synthesis of Chinese thought. As he sees it, Chu Hsi's achievement was primarily eclectic: fusing Taoistic cosmological speculations, Buddhist metaphysics, a commonsense approach to reality, and the fundamental dualism of yang and yin extending back to mythological prehistory.[39]

SUMMARY

Three main stages of ancient Chinese society were isolated: the period of the early imperial city, the period of the feudal town and city, and the period of the empire. The literati held somewhat different positions in the primary communities of each period. In the Shang the literatus was probably augurer and theologian priest; during the Chou he was, at first, a hereditary literarily trained expert in ritual and administration and later a professional teacher and administrator; during the imperial period he was a literarily trained

[38] *Ibid.*, pp. 93 ff.
[39] *Ibid.*, p. 100.

office candidate and bureaucrat. Of these periods it was the Chou, with the destruction of older types of complex communities and the formation of new ones, that held out the major promise of a maximum differentiation and individualization of the literati.

The product of the literati was uniquely molded by the times that called it forth. Among the major forms of social thought to appear in the later days of the Chou were Confucianism, Taoism, Moism, and Legalism. All these social philosophies shared the objective of securing social and political stability. Confucius visualized a conventional stabilization of the socio-political order modeled on filial piety. Taoism visualized a rather extreme form of anarchism counterbalanced by the preoccupation of the individual with a magically attained self-sufficiency. Moism visualized a program of semisocialistic utilitarianism and developed a concept of the welfare state. Legalism visualized an order achieved by a program of rationally organized political and military power.

Circumstances in the Warring Kingdoms caused a varying emphasis on these social philosophies and the types of social and political reconstruction they suggested. Confucianism and Taoism dominated in the early days. However, as the struggles between the various kingdoms grew more intense, the welfare-state program of the Moists and the power-state program of the Legalists increasingly came to the fore. There was never a sufficiently strong middle class to constitute Moism into a realistic possibility. Eventually the Ch'in with its legalistic philosophy was in a position to consolidate the empire and liquidate the remaining elements of feudalism.

Though the legalistic consolidation of the empire had been effected, many dissatisfied elements remained in the Chinese social order. A socio-political outlook modified by Moism endured at least until the attempted socialistic reforms of Wang Mang. Eventually Confucianism with its conventionalization of the socio-political order in terms of the generalization of filial piety proved to be most adapted to imperial conditions.

With the emergence of a transformed Confucianism (adapted to the needs of an empire which integrated a world of peasant villages) and the mandarin bureaucracy under the control of the Imperial Academy, the censorate and an army of official spies and informers, the key elements for the synthesis of Chinese civilization were at hand. The mandarin bureaucrats were the primary bearers of Confucianism. Taoism evolved into a mass cult with churches and a religious hierarchy and into a refined outlook adapted to the requirements of the court. When movements, for example, Buddhism, penetrated into China, they found an elastic system already at hand, capable of accommodating them without change.

Meanwhile, the mode of deportment proper to a literary, humanistic stratum offered itself as a basic reference point for painting (which borrowed its most basic technique from Chinese writing) and literature and other elements of a crystallizing civilization.

SELECTED BIBLIOGRAPHY

Chih-yi Cheng, Andrew, *Hsüntzu's Theory of Human Nature and Its Influence on Chinese Thought* (Doctoral Dissertation, Columbia University, 1928).

Chuang Tzu, *Musings of a Chinese Mystic,* Selections by Lionel Giles (London: John Murray, 1920).

Dubs, Homer H., *Hsüntze: The Moulder of Ancient Confucianism* (London: Arthur Probsthain, 1927).

Legge, James, translator, *The Shu King, The Shih King, and The Hsiao King* in *The Sacred Books of China* (Oxford: The Clarendon Press, 1879), Vol. 3.

Levenson, Joseph R., *Confucian China and Its Modern Fate* (London: Routledge and Kegan Paul, 1958).

Mei, Yi-pao, *Motse, the Neglected Rival of Confucius* (London: Arthur Probsthain, 1934).

Mei, Yi-pao, *The Ethical and Political Works of Motse* (London: Arthur Probsthain, 1929).

Riencourt, Amaury de, *The Soul of China* (New York: Coward-McCann, 1958).

Silcock, Arnold, *Introduction to Chinese Art* (London: Faber and Faber, Ltd., 1959).

Waley, Arthur, *The Way and Its Power* (London: George Allen & Unwin, 1936).

Wu-chi, Liu, *Confucius: His Life and Time* (New York: Philosophical Library, 1955).

Part III

THE INDIAN GURU

In the first of the case studies of societal and civilizational change to be made, the hypotheses formulated in the theoretical part of our study seems to be borne out. The literati were found to play a particularly significant role in the formation of the larger systems of social and cultural life. Their greatest creativity occurred in the period of Chinese feudalism and the Warring States, China's great age of transition. The products of the literati were seen to be uniquely shaped in terms of special natural environmental and social-historical conditions. And, finally, even the standards of truth varied between the period of creative innovation and the period of conservatism. In the first period the test of the truth of a proposal was found in its pragmatic utility; however, in the imperial period the content of thought was in part determined by the censors and by scholarly assemblies, for example, the Shih Ch'iu Conference of 51 B.C. and the Pai Hu Kuan Conference of 79 A.D. Institutional criteria were increasingly being advanced for the test of the acceptability of thought.

One cannot, however, establish a system of hypotheses on the basis of a single case. In the present and following sections the hypotheses will be brought to the test of additional examples of community and civilization formation under locally distinct circumstances.

Ancient India presents an interesting series of parallels and differences with ancient China. While China possessed great internal fertile river valleys which were comparatively isolated by mountains, deserts, and ocean, India possessed an exposed subcontinent marked by important internal divisions. China's climate is largely temperate; India's is tropical and subtropical. While ancient China benefited by a cultural continuity between the ancient civic society and its feudal period, India's cultural history was marked by major mutations. On the other hand, just as a new wave of community formation and civilizational synthesis was brought about in China by a people more barbaric than those they displaced, so in India the wave of development in the Axial Period was carried by a more barbaric people. Moreover, though its terms were somewhat different than those in China, India experienced at approximately the same time the breakdown of older types of communities and the formation of new ones. In both areas these were times of trouble.

As in China, Indian society moved toward an equilibrium of great stability which was maintained after a fashion for nearly two thousand years. However, while the synthesis in China consisted of imperial and provincial cities and peasant villagers mediated by a mandarin bureaucracy, the Indian synthesis consisted of caste-organized village communities and patrimonial courts mediated by Brahman *gurus*.

7

THE CHANGING FORMS OF ANCIENT INDIAN SOCIETY

Ancient Chinese territory comprised an extensive area capable of relatively uniform economic development. This was hardly the case with India. The subcontinent is divided on the north from Asia and the Near East by the Himalayas, the highest mountain range in the world. It is broken in the middle by the Vindhya Mountains which vary from about a fifth of a mile to a mile in height. They are heavily wooded, presenting a barrier of mountain and jungle. The mountains extending to the coasts of India from the Vindhyas are known as the Ghats. The Western Ghats rise abruptly from the sea, averaging about 3,000 feet in height, with some higher peaks. The Eastern Ghats are more broken, and have an average elevation of only about 1,500 feet. They are traversed by broad passes which serve as a drainage area for the plateau contained within them.[1]

In the north the Himalayas extend for a distance of 1,500 miles; in the mountain regions lie the states of Nepal and Bhutan. The tableland of Tibet extends behind them. Though the Himalayas afford access to the river valleys in both the extreme east and west, subranges serve partly as barriers. In the northeast, for example, India is partly cut off from Assam and upper Burma. In the west, mountains extend from the Himalayas to the sea.

The average elevation of the Himalayas is almost 20,000 feet. The broad plain at the foot of the mountains forms the dry region of alluvial deposits, saline swamps, and rolling sands of a desert. On the margin of the northern Punjab, on the other hand, rain occurs in a monsoonal pattern. The alluvial plain north of the desert area traversed by the Indus and the Ganges is also swept by monsoons.

The southern climate is patterned by the monsoon and the mountain system. The plateau of Deccan is swept by the southwest monsoon. Along

[1] Sir Halford J. Mackinder, "The Sub-Continent of India," in *The Cambridge History of India,* Vol. 1, ed. by E. J. Rapson (New York: The Macmillan Co., 1922), pp. 1–36. See also *Census of India,* 1951, Vol. 1.

the Western Ghats rainfall is heavy over the mountain barrier itself, but light beyond the range. However, the winds through Palghat Gap between the Eastern and the Western Ghats bring the southwest monsoon. In the north, India's climate is continental; in the south it is oceanic.

With the highest mountains on earth, great plains hardly above sea level, a continental land mass behind it, and tropical oceans on its sides, India offers almost every type of climate from desert to tropical jungle to the arcticlike conditions in her mountains.

PREHISTORY

Though no skeletons of fossil men have been found there, India lies in the arc where eastern Asian representatives of fossil men dating from the Middle Pleistocene have been found, including *Pithecanthropus* of Java and *Sinanthropus* in Choukoutien China. Artifacts from both branches of Old Stone Age technology (the core and flake industries) have been found in India. The flake industries, perhaps developed by Paleoanthropic men (including *Pithecanthropus*), have been found in south India; artifacts from the core technique (perhaps developed by early representatives of *Homo sapiens*) have been found in the north.[2]

Between 6000 and 5000 B.C. in the Near East, the transition was made by humankind from hunting and gathering to food-producing.[3] Either simultaneously with or soon after the domestication of plants, animals were also domesticated. The two technologies soon fused, supplying considerable economic resilience to new-neolithic peasant communities of the time. Weaving and pottery-making were highly developed in these peasant communities. By 3000 B.C. agricultural communities of this type appeared in northwestern India. In the regions of the west comprising present-day Afghanistan and Pakistan, the climate was once much more moist than it is today. Human settlement goes back at least to the third millennium B.C. Significant ties were maintained in this area with the Bronze Age culture of regions farther west.[4]

The quantities of kiln-fired bricks in the Harappan cultural area indicate a plentitude of wood in the early period. Excavations in the area have confirmed the existence of two major pottery cultures, a buff-ware and a red-ware culture.[5] Features of the pottery traditions and of the Bronze Age were developed in a manner suggesting diffusion from the fertile crescent.

Though the steps have not been isolated, the cities of a Bronze Age civilization flowered in the Sind and the Punjab, on the soil of these peasant villages some time before 2500 B.C.[6] From the Makran coast to Katiawar and

[2] Stuart Piggott, *Prehistoric India* (Harmondsworth: Penguin Books, 1950), p. 22.

[3] V. Gordon Childe, *What Happened in History* (New York: Penguin Books, 1946), p. 41; William Howells, *Back of History* (Garden City: Doubleday & Co., 1954), pp. 135 ff.

[4] Piggott, *op. cit.*, p. 66.

[5] *Ibid.*, p. 72.

[6] Childe, *op. cit.*, p. 117; Howells, *op. cit.*, p. 528; and particularly Piggott, *op. cit.*, p. 132.

the Himalayas, more than 400 settlements built on a similar plan have been located with houses made of standard-sized baked bricks. Similarly, engraved stamp-seals were manufactured. A uniform script and a standard system of weights were employed. Towering over the sites of towns and villages, but some 350 miles apart, were two cities—Harappa in the Punjab and Mohenjo-daro in Sind. Each formed a dense settlement covering more than a square mile.

Since the valley was lacking in the raw materials necessary for extensive manufacture, a regular trade developed: wood from the Himalayas, copper from Rajputana, and shells from southern India were imported. Tin, gold, and precious stones were obtained from other countries. Manufactured products from the Indus reached Mesopotamia, and some Sumerian devices were copied by the Harappans.

Certain features of the ruins suggest a bazaarlike organization of retailers. The size of the magazines attached to private houses indicates the existence of a developed merchant class, though it may have been under temple control. Both cities were dominated by an acropolis or citadel. However, in contrast to heavily fortified Mesopotamian cities, evidences of defenses around the cities are scant. This has led Wheeler to believe that the armed citadel was an affirmation of domestic authority rather than a safeguard against external aggression.[7]

There may have been religious significance in the civic hygienic practices. Public bathing pools were constructed, and two-storied houses were provided with bathrooms. There were also rows of mud-brick tenements, consisting of two rooms and a court, suggesting the stratification of the population into priests and officials, rich merchants and businessmen, and laborers (probably slaves). While a large quantity of gold, silver, and precious stones has been collected by archaeologists, nothing suggesting royal treasures has been found.

It has been suggested that the citadel builders may have been innovators imposing themselves on pre-existing urban civilizations.[8] However, this is unlikely if the ancient Indian city followed the same course as cities did elsewhere. The streets of the cities were planned, which suggests an ancient system of central control. Drainage systems were in operation and in apparent good repair up to the time the cities were destroyed. A conventional script (not deciphered), a number system constructed on a decimal basis, and standard weights and measures, were in use. While the script is pictographic and hieroglyphic in the manner of the early Sumerian, it is distinctive, showing autonomous development.

Some scholars have thought to see in this pictographic script the origin of Brahmi (Sanscrit), but the mass of evidence is against this hypothesis.

[7] Sir Mortimer Wheeler, *The Cambridge History of India* (Cambridge: Cambridge University Press, 1953), p. 52.

[8] *Ibid.*, p. 93.

The script which appears on seals carried as amulets reflects a long evolution, for the signs were standardized and simplified; 396 were listed. (Early Dynastic Sumerian employed twice as many.) Though the script remained in a hieroglyphic state (not having degenerated into conventional summaries), accent marks suggesting phonetic maturity were added to a large number of letters.[9] Whether the civilization developed science in the manner of the Sumerians and Egyptians is unknown.

The Indus Valley civilization shows close resemblances to those of Sumer and Babylonia (particularly the pre-Sumerian culture of Kish). However, the products of the craftsmen were quite different, and the ax, saw, and dagger are clearly distinguishable from those of Mesopotamia. The evidence suggests that the two civilizations differentiated from the same original base with only occasional borrowing later. Clay figures of men and women, the seals, and the large stone *lingas* and *yonis* from this civilization seem to foreshadow later practices of Hinduism. Dress fashions popular in these cities are still followed in the same area by the people retaining many of the technical processes of old. There are unsolved problems of cultural continuity between these cities and the civilization of later India.

Though the Indus Valley cities were subject to floods, this fact does not seem to have been decisive in their disappearance. After bad floods, the lower floors of the houses were filled with bricks until sections of the city rose on a platform 20 feet high. Among the suggestions as to the unexplained catastrophe which brought this civilization to an end are climatic changes, changes in the course of the Indus River, malaria, or invasions by tribes from the north and west. Invasions played a role, for Mohenjo-daro was sacked and burned, but there are also indications that a general decline had preceded this event.

Harappa and Mohenjo-daro have all the properties of a late development of ancient urbanism which has reached the stage of city imperialism. A high level of centralized control of socio-economic life is evident: city planning was carried through, bricks were made of standard size, labor was regimented, and commerce was probably under centralized control. Wheeler believes this regementation was religious as in Sumer.

> In a vague sense the artificial mountain of the ziggurat and the artificial mountain of the Indus citadel may be thought to reflect a comparable hierarchical policy. The regimented cantonment of Harappa may suggest the priest-controlled industries of Sumer.[10]

Extensive regimentation correlated with a low level of militarism are the earmarks of theocracy. Though the suggestion has been made that small dome-shaped pieces of copper perforated with two holes, discovered in quantities, were probably sewn on garments to achieve the effect of mail,

[9] *Ibid.*, p. 82.
[10] *Ibid.*, p. 94.

their is no supporting evidence for this.[11] Neither body armor nor helmets were present.[12] The Harappans had no shields, and the tanged spears were so thin and flat that most would have buckled on impact. The military aspects of the ancient Indus civilization seem to have functioned more as a symbol of authority than as an efficient force hardened by continuous use. The entire civilization gives the impression of a theocratic rather than a military regimentation, for there was clearly a large, pacific population. The developed script presupposed the standardizing work of a school which was elsewhere always the work of priests. If anything, the Indian script does not show properties which emerge when pressed into the service of free commerce.

There are clear suggestions that religion in the Indus civilization was undergoing the same general kind of syncretism that accompanied the emergence of the urban community elsewhere. There are terra-cotta figurines of almost nude females and other evidences of fertility cults. However, such cults were subordinate to a hieratic cult suggested by the seated male figure of stone statues which may have been the archetypes of the great god Siva of historic India. Phallus worship is evidenced in the polished stone *linga* and *yoni* associated with Siva worship. The prevalence of the bull also suggests later forms of Siva worship.[13] A semihuman monster attacking a horned tiger may perhaps represent the counterpart of the Sumerian Enkidu who combatted Gilgamesh. Moreover, the Babylonian tree of life may have had its counterpart in the astral trefoil of Harappa seals which portray a sacred tree enshrining a three-horned deity. The great bath of the citadel of Mohenjo-daro and the provision for bathing and drainage suggest the use of bathing in modern Indian ritual. Such things suggest the religious organization of life and a syncretism of previous religious elements into the new ideological unity of the city.

It is possible that some day the peculiar ratio of continuity and discontinuity between the ancient Indus Valley civilization and that of later India will be worked out with greater precision than at present. The greater part of the historical evidence points toward a major discontinuity between the Indus Valley civilization and the one arising around the Indo-Europeans who came as conquerors. The break was far deeper than the one between the people of Shang and those of Chou in China.

The Indo-Europeans did not intermarry with the people of the Indus Valley civilization, nor did they take over the intellectuals or their literary culture or their arts. They did not set up sections of the river-valley civilizations as subordinate parts of their states in return for proper and due acts of submission. At the same time the more carefully the remains of

[11] J. Marshall, *Mohenjo-daro and the Indus Civilization* (London: 1931), Vol. II, p. 533.

[12] As Wheeler observes, such military equipment was well known in early dynastic Sumer, *op. cit.*, p. 53.

[13] *Ibid.*, p. 83.

the Indus Valley civilization are studied, the greater the number of parallels that appear between its items and those of historical Indian culture.

It is possible that both the evidence for discontinuity and the evidence for continuity are correct. It could well be true that the Indo-Europeans who came as conquerors destroyed the remnants of the early great cities without being influenced by them except to add, by pillage, to their store of material things. On the other hand, the native population with which the Indo-Europeans were reluctant to fuse could have continued to bear major elements once present in a great cultural synthesis in the cities. As time went by and the slow integration of the native population and the Indo-Europeans was brought about, it carried with it a late triumph of the once-rejected cultural elements of the Indus Valley civilization.

AN OUTLINE OF INDIAN DEVELOPMENT FROM THE VEDIC TO THE SUTRA PERIOD

India's combination of barriers, open areas, and multiple climates have encouraged cultural diversity. The physical types of India have also complicated the picture. In the *Census Report* for 1901, Sir Herbert Risley suggested that the type of Dravidians that occupy the peninsula south of the United Provinces represents the aboriginal population.[14] These people are short, dark, with plentiful wavy hair, dark eyes, round heads, and broad noses. Somewhat distinct from the Dravidians are the tribes occupying the hills and jungles. They seem to be related to the Veddas of Ceylon, the Todas, and possibly the Australians. Perhaps the Dravidians were themselves a conquest group that came to dominate an older native population. In any case, Dravidian language was common throughout India at the time of the Indo-European invasion.

The Indo-Europeans are concentrated in the Punjab from Kashmir to Rajputana. They are tall and have fair complexions, dark eyes, long heads, narrow and prominent noses. These people came from Bactria over the passes of the Hindu Kush into Afghanistan. Turko-Iranians are distinguishable on the northwest frontier in the Province of Baluchistan and the lands west of the Indus. They are above average in stature, with fair complexions, dark or gray eyes, broad heads, and narrow, long, prominent noses. In the Sind are persons transitional to the Turko-Iranians and the Dravidians; the Aryo-Dravidians in the plain of the Ganges are transitional between the Aryans and Dravidians. Mongoloid types in Burma, Assam, Bhutan, and Nepal are characterized by broad heads, dark yellowish complexions, scanty facial hair, short stature, fine to broad noses, and occasionally eyefolds. This type has been produced by the invasions of peoples from Tibet and China. The Mongol-Dravidian (Bengali) type again represents a kind of transition between them and the Dravidians. While the present account is concerned

[14] See the summary by E. J. Rapson, "Peoples and Languages," in the *Cambridge History of India,* Vol. I, pp. 37 f.

directly with the Indo-Europeans (who may not have been a single race) and the Dravidians, one key to Indian society is the plurality of competing racial and ethnic groups from prehistoric times to the present.

The first sources permitting some insight into Indian historical development after the fall of the Indus Valley civilizations are the literatures of the Aryans, the interpretation of which was a *coup* of modern comparative philology. Sir William Jones, who was chief justice of Bengal, perceived that the sacred language of India (Sanscrit) was bound up with the language of the Celts, Germans, Slavs, Greeks, Romans, and Persians.[15] This epoch-making suggestion did not require that an original single race be postulated as bearers of the language. However, it did indicate that there was a time and place when the language was common property of people later widely separated. By isolating core words (words common to all, and therefore presumably present before differentiation from the original language occurred), scholars have tried to establish the location of the original bearers of the language.[16] Indian scholars have often claimed India itself as the original home of the Indo-Europeans, treating the Europeans as immigrants.[17] However, this assumption creates more problems than it solves, while the weight of the evidence is in favor of the non-Indian origin of the Aryans.[18] Various cases have been made for the location of the original language group in the steppes of Russia north of the Caspian Sea, in Hungary, in Germany, and in Scandinavia.

The migrations of the Indo-Europeans began some time between 2500 and 2000 B.C. The Nashili dialect of Hittite, which belongs to the Indo-European group, left traces in the historical documents of the urban cultures of Asia Minor and Mesopotamia around the beginning of the second millennium B.C. In the sixteenth century B.C., the Kassites, whose monarchs had Indo-European names, set up a new dynasty in Mesopotamia, bearing many evidences of cultural affinity with the Indo-Europeans. In a treaty dating around 1380 B.C., the names of the Indian gods Mitra, Varuna, and Indra are recognizable. A Boghaz Keui document on chariot construction contains terms with

[15] A. L. Basham, *The Wonder That Was India* (New York: Grove Press, 1959), p. 5.

[16] For example, the words "father" and "horse" appear in the following distribution:

	Father	*Horse*
Sanscrit	pitár	aśva
Latin	pater	equus
Germanic	fadar	—
Tocharian	patar	yakwe
Armenian	hair	—
Anglo-Saxon	—	ehu
Celtic	—	ech
Lithuanian	—	aszwà

[17] See, for example, S. V. Venkateswara, *Indian Culture through the Ages* (London: Longmans Green, 1928), pp. 12 f.

[18] P. Giles, "The Aryans," *Oxford History of India,* Vol. I, pp. 65 ff.; see also Piggott, *op. cit.,* pp. 244 ff.

Sanscrit counterparts. The Mitani people, in fact, were as enthusiastic about chariot-racing as were the Indo-Europeans.

Apart from a few archeological evidences,[19] however, the dating of the Indo-Europeans before, and particularly within, India is mainly based on analysis of literary evidence from a magically stereotyped religious tradition. Many Hindu religious expressions written down in the Indian Middle Ages were transmitted in unbroken tradition as inviolable magical formulas by the Indo-European priests to their successors. The oldest of these, the *Rig-Veda*, contains material generally agreed to go back to the second millennium B.C.

On the basis of internal evidence, Müller divided the Vedic period into four parts: The Chandas, representing the oldest Vedic hymns prior to 1000 B.C.; the Mantra period, covering later portions of the *Rig-Veda* dating from 1000 B.C. to 800 B.C.; the Brahmana period, 800 to 600 B.C.; the Sutra period, 600 to 200 B.C.[20] The general chronology of India in the period of our study as estimated by the *Oxford History of India* is as follows:

CHRONOLOGY

Date	*Event*
2500 B.C.	beginning of movement of Indo-Europeans
1400 B.C.	inscriptions of Mitani at Boghaz Keui
1200–1000 B.C.	earliest hymns of Rigveda
1000–800 B.C.	mantras of early Brahmana period (Purana tradition places the war of Kurus in this period)
800–600 B.C.	later Brahmanas and period of earliest Upanishads (not later than 600 B.C. Story of the Ramayana may have originated at this time)
600–200 B.C.	sutra period
564–483 B.C.	Buddha (contemporaries of Buddha include Parsenajit, king of Kosala, Bimbisara of Magadha)
558–530 B.C.	Cyrus, king of Persia
522–486 B.C.	Darius I, king of Persia (Persian domination of Northern India under Darius I and other Persian kings)
336–323 B.C.	Alexander the Great of Macedon (Conquest of Persia, 330 B.C.)
321–184 B.C.	Maurya dynasty
321–297 B.C.	Chandragupta
274–237 B.C.	Asoka
184– 72 B.C.	Sunga dynasty[21]

19 Piggott, *op. cit.*, pp. 250 f.; Giles, *op. cit.*, pp. 72–76.

20 See F. Max Müller, *Rigveda, Samhita, and Pada Texts with Sayana's Commentary*, edited by F. Max Müller, Vol. IV, *Sacred Books of the East*, pp. vii ff.; see the summary of A. Berriedale Keith, "The Age of the Rigveda," in the *Oxford History of India*, Vol. I, pp. 77 f.; and Piggott, *op. cit.*, pp. 254 f.

21 *Oxford History of India*, pp. 697 f.

The Rig-Veda indicates that the Indo-Europeans entered India through the Hindu Kush. They collectively called themselves Aryans (nobles) in contrast to the Dasyus (enemies) with whom violent struggles were undertaken. Federations of Indo-European tribes were occasionally formed for military ventures against the Dasyus. Struggles also occurred between Aryan tribes. From place names it appears that the Aryans were familiar with Afghanistan. In many of the earliest hymns there are references to a mountainous territory and violent thunderstorms not characteristic of the Punjab. The Aryans appear not to have followed the Indus River to the ocean, for fishing plays no part in the economy. The tiger of the Bengal jungles was unknown to the *Rig-Veda*, though the elephant of the lowland jungle of the Himalayas was. Rice which belongs to the southeastern part of the area is not mentioned. Cities were unknown, and kingship was relatively undeveloped.

By the period of the Brahmanas (800–600 B.C.), Aryan society and civilization had grown more complex. Eastern lands increasingly came into focus, and the Punjab declined in comparative importance. Mention of tribes, such as the Bharata, which played a central role in the *Rig-Veda*, are either omitted altogether from the accounts or are reduced in importance. New tribes, such as the Kuru, had become important.[22] On the other hand, the people of Magadha, which were to furnish the core of Buddhism, were still alien, even though Brahmans were found among them. The Andhras, who were to play an important role in Indian history, later appear still to have been completely Dravidian in blood and speech.

By the sixth century B.C. numerous states had formed in northern India. There were at least sixteen independent states in addition to a number of monarchies and tribal republics. The four monarchies were those of Kosala (modern Oudh), Magadha (Modern Bihar), Vamsas, and Avanti. Kosala was initially pre-eminent, domination later shifting to the Magadha. Powerful new religious movements, Jainism and Buddhism, appeared in India at this time. Both found primary reception successively in the kingdom of Magadha.[23]

In 327 B.C., Alexander the Great entered India and carried on a two-year campaign in the Punjab and Sind.[24] He established garrisons in key places, and formed alliances with various Indian states. A body of troops remained in Bactria, which fell to Seleucus Nicator after Alexander's death in 323 B.C. Meanwhile, interesting developments were to occur in the Magadha, which had gradually disintegrated under the Nanda dynasty. Chandragupta Maurya, who appears to have been among the Indian adventurers in Alex-

[22] A. Berriedale Keith, "The Period of the Later Samhitas, the Brahmanas, the Aryanarkas, and the Upanishads," *Cambridge History of India*, pp. 114 f.

[23] Jarl Charpentier, "The History of the Jains" in *Cambridge History of India*, Vol. I, pp. 150 f.; T. W. Rhys Davids, "The Early History of the Buddhists," *ibid.*, Vol. I, pp. 171 f.

[24] George Macdonald, "The Hellenic Kingdoms of Syria, Bactria, and Parthia," *Cambridge History of India*, Vol. I, pp. 391 f.

ander's camp in the Punjab, founded a kingdom in 322 B.C. Chandragupta is said to have maintained an army of 60,000 infantry, 30,000 horsemen, 36,000 men with elephants, and 20,000 men with the chariots, regulated by a military bureaucracy.[25]

Under the Maurya, apart from the royal domain, the land was under the control of the king. In default of taxes, he was accustomed to place on the land a cultivator of his own. The king's officials supervised irrigation. They encouraged the recovery of new lands. Regulation of water supplies and revenue therefrom was consolidated in the hands of the state. Roads were constructed under the supervision of royal officials. Communications were maintained by couriers, and state rangers supervised the forests.

Towns had grown numerous, ranging from the rural village to the great city, port, and royal capital. There were also frontier forts. Guardhouses for troops were located in the towns. Attending the royal palaces were workshops, storehouses, arsenals, and prisons. The population, according to Megasthenes, was divided into seven classes. Trades and crafts were numerous. State officials traded in royal merchandise. The guild was officially recognized. In workshops, artisans were engaged on contract, and combinations of workmen at times had corporate responsibility for contracts.

Under Chandragupta's son, Asoka,[26] the empire was extended to include much of Afghanistan, Baluchistan, Sind, Kashmir, Nepal, and Bengal.[27] Asoka's administration grew with the problems he imposed on it. In the midst of his conquests, Asoka was converted to Buddhism, which he transformed into a state religion. Under its influence the Maurya developed many features of a welfare state. However, after Asoka's death the Maurya dynasty declined.

During the second century B.C., northern India was invaded and partly conquered by Antiochus III and, in turn, by Demetrius, Eucratides, and Menander. Pushyamitra Sunga waged successful war against Menander, driving him from the valley of the Ganges, and established the Sunga dynasty which lasted 112 years.[28] This was succeeded by the Kanva dynasty, which was, in turn, overthrown in 27 B.C. by the Andhra dynasty. During this period an extensive reaction against Buddhism by the Brahmanical forces occurred. The reversal was touched off by a savage persecution of Buddhist monks by Pushyamitra Sunga.

In the time period of concern to us, Indian society evolved three major forms: a semifeudal society of manorial communities, the society of the

[25] F. W. Thomas, "Chandragupta: The Founder of the Maurya Empire," *Cambridge History of India*, Vol. I, pp. 467.

[26] V. R. Ranachandra Dikshitar, *The Mauryan Polity* (Madras: University of Madras, 1932).

[27] F. W. Thomas, "Asoka: The Imperial Patron of Buddhism," *Cambridge History of India*, Vol. I, pp. 495 f.

[28] E. J. Rapson, "Indian Native States after the Period of the Maurya Empire," *Cambridge History of India*, Vol. I, pp. 514 f.

patrimonial kingdoms which was composed of a loose texture of cities and peasant villages, and the caste system.

EARLY ARYAN SOCIETY

The Aryans played a role in the development of India comparable to the Chou in ancient China. For a time it was thought that the Indus Valley civilization had declined before the appearance of the Aryans, but more complete archeological evidence has revealed the fact that the Harappa civilization came to a violent end. The cities were sacked and burned, and Harappans were left dead among the ruins of their baths and drains.[29] The reverse side of the picture of a barbarian people attacking a superior civilization is told in the *Rig-Veda.* Their greatest deity, Indra, to whom the greater proportion of early hymns is addressed, is a powerful, bearded, heavy drinking, heavy-eating, battle-intoxicated warrior-hero fighting in the midst of his warrior band, the Maruts. He is a cattle raider and destroyer of the fortress strongholds of the wealthy Dasyus who live in fortifications with hordes of treasure.

> With all-outstripping chariot-wheel, O Indra, thou
> far-famed, hast overthrown the twice ten kings of men
> With sixty thousand nine and ninety followers . . .
> Thou goest on from fight to fight intrepidly,
> destroying castle after castle here with strength.[30]

Like the Shangs in China, the rulers of the Indus Valley civilization were destroyed by more vigorous barbarians. However, the contrasts are important. The Chou people had lived on the frontiers of the Shang, receiving Shang women into their harems and presumably sending women from their own harems. As a consequence they became aware of and admired the achievements of the Shang. The Chou victory was quickly followed by the attempt to take over major blocks of Shang civilization. In many respects the cultural continuities between the Shang and Chou were even more important than the discontinuities. The Aryans, however, did not crystallize as a frontier state on the edge of the Indus Valley civilization, but came over the mountains from a distance. They did not learn to appreciate Harappan civilization nor attempt to adopt it. The war bands which plundered the citadels of the Harappa civilization belonged to people who had never known a city.[31]

The ultimate units of the tribes into which the Aryans were organized were patriarchal families. Child marriage was unknown. Both dowries and bride prices were employed. Women lived under the protection of the men in charge of the family—fathers, husbands, and brothers as the case might be. The solidarity of the family and the intimacy of family and re-

[29] Piggott, "Time of Troubles and the End of the Cities," *op. cit.*, pp. 214 f.
[30] *Rigveda*, I, 53. Quoted by Piggott, *op. cit.*, p. 261.
[31] Piggott, *op. cit.*, p. 263.

ligion are indicated by the keen desire of the Vedic Indian for a child who was required to perform his father's funeral rites.[32]

There were considerable similarities between the society of the Vedic Indians and that of the Greeks of the Homeric period. A nucleus of families formed the village (*grama*), and kings ruled over the subjects as a whole (*jana*). Confederations of tribes were occasionally formed for military action. The economic basis of the society was mixed agriculture. Herds of cattle and flocks of sheep and goats were kept; in fact, the most important form of wealth was cattle. Oxen were used for drawing carts and for plowing. Barley seems to have been the most important grain crop. Irrigation was practiced. Horses were bred for chariot-racing and warfare.

Among industrial specialists the carpenter was particularly honored because of his work on chariots. The metal workers were valued for their ability to manufacture weapons. Kettles and other domestic utensils were made of bronze. Tanning was important to the manufacture of harnesses. The Aryan chariots were developed independently of the native Indian tradition. They seem only to have invented superior weapons and the eight-spoked iron-tired wheel. The horse-drawn battle chariot carried the driver and a warrior armed with a composite bow. The charioteers formed a light-armored force of aristocratic warriors accompanied by hand-to-hand fighters of the war band.[33]

The social classes were divided into knights, priests, and commoners (who tilled the soil and practiced industrial trades). In war the kings and nobles fought from chariots, the common people fought on foot. Social standing depended on the ownership of the weapons of war and also of cattle. The fact that the commoners had not been completely disarmed indicates that feudalism had not attained full development; nevertheless, the presence of the nobles with more expensive weapons and superior holdings in land cattle as well as serfs and slaves, signifies an emerging manorial system. However, the tradition of infeudation with quasi-contractual ties between princes, vassals, and subvassals was at best weakly developed. The system was quasi-feudal.

Feudalism achieves its fullest development when a peculiar system of political control is a part of a manorial system of agricultural subsistence economy. The political structure, as illustrated by medieval Europe, consists in a contractual system of loyalties and military obligations between vassals and subvassals in return for investment of vassals with fiefs for their support. Political control and military competence are consolidated in the class of landlords. The system tends to transform the lower classes of agricultural workers into serfs rather than slaves or free peasants, with hereditary claims to their positions and hereditary obligations to the lord.

The forces in Indian society which prevented the quasi-feudal system from

[32] A. B. Keith, "Age of the Rigveda," *op. cit.*, pp. 88–89.
[33] Piggott, *op. cit.*, p. 273.

achieving all of the features of the European system were in part related to the tensions between the thin stratum of Indo-Europeans stretched over massive conquered populations. The historical tensions between these two groups gave the Aryan society the properties of a semiunified conquest group which stood over and against the conquered as a whole. This custom operated against reduction of Indo-European commoners to serf status. It also tended to reduce the Dravidian population to the uniformly low status of slaves of the Indo-European community.

INDIAN SOCIETY AT THE TIME OF THE PATRIMONIAL KINGDOMS

During the early period of expansion in which movement was made by entire communities composed of patriarchal households under their warrior-husbandmen and priests, Aryan society began to undergo internal differentiation. The three major points of conflict were between the Aryans and the natives (Dasyus), between the nobles and the common people, and between the nobles and the kings. The relations between the nobles and the common people tended to evolve toward full feudalism. Since they were superior in weapons and wealth, the nobles were inclined to disarm the free peasantry and turn them into serfs. A rise in status of the former enemy population (Dasyus) to serf status and a fall in the status of former free peasants was started. However, so long as the conquest of India was still in progress, it was impossible to disarm the free peasants completely. It was also impossible to take away their political rights.

In the period of the *Rig-Veda* the center of Aryan civilization was in the land between Sarasvati and Drishadvati, but in the Brahmana period it was located east in Kurukshetra.[34] While the Aryans had not yet reached the Vindhyas, there is reference in the literature to new areas and places. Old tribes disappear from the accounts, and new ones arise. Moreover, the Aryans increasingly met organized opposition from the states against which they moved. In carrying out the conquest, the kings increased in importance, for as the organizers of increasingly larger and more professional armies the kings were freed from the dominance by the nobles. Thus these three sources of tension interacted and modified each other. Just before the rise of Buddhism, North India was divided into no less than sixteen independent states, monarchies, and tribal republics. The four major monarchies, as noted, were Kosala, Magadha, Vamsas, and Avanti.

Extensive social changes occurred. While in the first period only the nobles (Kshatriya) were hereditary, in this second period the priests (Brahmanas) were on the way toward becoming hereditary. Two classes of priests had become distinct—the house priests (*purohitas*) of the king and the priests of the village.[35] A great difference in rank separated the king's priests from

[34] A. Berriedale Keith, "The Period of the Later Samhitas," *op. cit.*, p. 117.
[35] *Ibid.*, p. 127.

those of the village. The persons outside the pale of society had largely disappeared; they had become Sudra at the base of the class system. The incorporation of former enemy aliens into Aryan society may have been partly responsible for a tendency evident at this time to introduce endogamy into the ranks of the former freemen, *Vaishya*.[36] In the face of a threat, there is always a tendency to close ranks. The fusion of the Aryan and native populations could possibly mean a serious loss of status by the formerly free commoners (*Vaishya*) of the Aryans.

The kings were developing increasingly complex administrative structures. Among the king's officials appeared the royal priest (*purohita*), village headman (*gramani*), chamberlain (*kshattri*), treasurer (*samgrahitri*), and tax collector (*bhagadugha*). These officials were concentrated in the capital city. The rural nobles faced a serious loss of status in favor of the king's officials. Mercenary soldiers of the king, often recruited for his private armies, partly displaced the older *kshatriya*.

The village people's assembly (*samati*) passed into oblivion, indicating a decline of the village in the affairs of state. On the other hand, an extensive growth of cities occurred–Sravati and Ayodhya, capital of Kosala, Baranasi (modern Benares), capital of the Vamsas, Rajagriha, capital of Magadha (built by Bimbisara), Roruka, capital of Sovira, and Ujjayini, capital of Avanti. Extensive trade was carried on (mostly by native Dravidians) between these and foreign cities overseas. Overseas traders of the seventh century B.C. may have brought back the Semitic alphabet from which those of modern India evolved. A unified growth of civil law occurred within and between the cities.

The rural economy, however, had grown more complex. The large plows, sometimes drawn by as many as twenty-four oxen, were used. In addition to irrigation, fertilization was practiced. Barley, wheat, beans, and rice, as well as sesame (from which oil was extracted) were grown. The later Samhitas speak of hunters, fishermen, plowmen, charioteers, jewel-makers, basket-makers, chariot-makers, barbers, weavers, slaughterers, goldsmiths, cooks, fish peddlers, smelterers, and blacksmiths. The merchant was frequently mentioned, and the usurer had a special name.

In this new context of urbanism and partrimonialism, Jainism and Buddhism, two great religions later to become heterodox, flowered. Mahavira (founder of Jainism) and Gautama Buddha preached in Magadha during the reign of Bimbisara (520 B.C.). For two hundred years Buddhism spread over northern India, until it reached its early height under Asoka (264–227 B.C.). After Asoka's death, the Maurya dynasty began to fail. In the second century B.C., northwestern India was invaded successively by Antiochus III, Demetrius, Eucratides, and Menander. In the course of a successful war against Menander, Pushyamitra Sunga developed an efficiency which permitted him to establish dominion over northern India. He spearheaded the

[36] *Ibid.*, p. 128.

Brahmanical reaction against Buddhism with bloody persecutions of Buddhist monks. However, Buddhism and Hinduism remained rivals for several hundred years before the eventual complete triumph of Hinduism.

THE CASTE SYSTEM

Pushyamitra Sunga's persecution of Buddhist monks marked the beginning of a restoration of Brahmanism, a movement reaching its height in the Gupta period (320 to 480 A.D.), often described as the Golden Age of Hinduism. The social order corresponding to developed Hinduism was that of caste, which approached final form during this period.

Caste is an hereditarily closed class and status order reinforced by religious sanctions. A class is a plurality of persons sharing a common economic situation. A status group is a plurality of persons sharing equal claims to social honor, or a lack of it. The right of intermarriage and sharing of table community are among the most important indications of shared status honor. However, special terms of address, possession of titles, the claims to special kinds of treatment, are also important status items. Hereditary closure of a class or status group simply means that access to those desirable categories of social values is determined by legitimate birth. A Hindu caste is fully developed when an endogamously closed group follows a fixed occupation, practicing a unique way of life and receiving special social honors which are magically or religiously sanctioned. Even in twentieth-century India the distinctions of caste have been maintained. Blunt places functional castes at the top of his list:

> (i) The functional caste . . . is composed of persons following the same occupation. Instances are numerous; by far the greater number of castes are functional. The Barhai (carpenter), the Sonar (goldsmith), the Lohar (blacksmith), the Nai (barber), the Teli (oil presser), the Thathera (coppersmith), are a few examples.
>
> (ii) The tribal or racial caste . . . is composed of persons who are, or believe themselves to be, united by blood or race. Such cases are less common: the Jat, the Gujar, the Bhar, the Pasi, the Dom are the best known.

Of minor varieties may be mentioned:

> (iii) The sectarian caste . . . composed of persons united by a common belief. There are only four examples in the United Provinces—the Atith, Goshain, Bishnoi, and Sadh.
>
> (iv) The hill castes . . . are subject to restrictions much less severe than their neighbors in the plains.
>
> (v) The outlaw castes . . . were originally as a rule, groups of broken men and outcasts who had banded together for purposes of self-defense or of crime, and subsequently became a caste. Instances are the Badhik, Barwar, and Sanaurhiya.
>
> (vi) The Muhammadan castes.
>
> There are castes which it is difficult to classify. The Ahir has a well-defined occupation (cattle-owning), yet it appears to be a tribal

> caste in origin. The Kurmi is certainly formed of different racial elements, but has no traditional occupation, unless agriculture can be regarded as such; but there are many castes of cultivators, whilst there is only one caste of carpenters, blacksmiths, barbers, etc. The Khattri caste, according to its own account, would be an offshoot of an old occupational caste—the Kshatriya—which had given up the Kshatriya's occupation. The gypsy castes appear to be in origin tribal castes, whose blood has been much modified by free recruitment of outsiders.[37]

The Indian caste system was a social order of castes of varying degrees of ascendancy, forming a hierarchy of honor and economic opportunity reckoned in terms of the social distance of any given caste from the Brahman caste. Such reckoning of social distance has often been carried to the most minute regulation, even of degrees of physical approach. For example, if a member of the lowest caste came nearer than 30 feet, the Brahman was polluted and was required to undergo various purification rites. If the shadow of a lower-class man falls on the Brahman's food, it becomes inedible. For a lower-class man even to look at the food of a member of high caste is to defile it. In reverse, the very excrement of the Brahman has powers of divination for some of the lowest castes. The diversity of caste forms, indicated by Blunt, reveals the power of a caste system, once formed, to pull other social groups into its structure.

The peculiarities of the caste system lie in the elevation of the occupational and status group of priests to central position in the social order, and extreme application of the principles of class and status closure with reference to them. Though the orthodox Hindu holds caste to be divine, caste was not known to the *Rig-Veda* which did, however, distinguish between priests (Brahmans), nobles (Rajanyas or Kshatriyas), tillers of the soil (Vaishyas), and slaves (Sudras). There was a great gulf between the first three (Aryans) and the last (Dasyus)[38] who were differentiated in part by color (*varna*). These classes form a caste system only if they become hereditary and are ranked with respect to the priests. Then, as the law books state, new castes can arise by intermarriage.[39] However, while the priest is the key to the caste system, the fundamental unit of any individual caste is the family rather than the congregation.[40] While the priest is ascendant, caste does not presuppose a theocracy with a church organization of priest rulers. The component elements of caste are tendencies found in every society, for example, the aspiration by persons well-placed in the social structure to monopolize their advantages for themselves and their children. In India the motives for

[37] E. A. H. Blunt, *The Caste System of Northern India* (London: Oxford University Press, 1931), pp. 2–3.

[38] Rapson, "Peoples and Languages," *op. cit.*, p. 54.

[39] See the *Laws of Manu*, X, 6 f. Among the classical studies of the caste system are those of C. Bougle, *Essai sur le Regime des Castes* (Paris: 1908); S. V. Ketkar, *The History of Caste in India* (Ithaca, N.Y.: 1909); E. Sennart, *Les Castes dans l'Inde* (Paris: 1896).

[40] Rapson, *op. cit.*, p. 55.

social and economic closure were given special poignancy by the presence of racial and ethnic tensions. The initial role of the priests seems to have been the sanctioning of marriages. The elaboration of ritualistic reinforcement of appropriate marriages appears in the Sutras. In time not only improper marriage but defilement by the touching and eating of unclean things are the earmarks of caste. In the Sutras appear the beginnings of a formal theory of defilement. However, at that time India was still a long way from a caste system. A Brahman, according to Gautama,[41] was allowed to eat food from any of the twice-born castes or even from a Sudra in case of necessity. Primitive magic still predominated among food taboos. Forbidden food is that defiled by hairs or insects, by being touched by a woman during her courses, by being given by a prostitute, a hermaphrodite, or a police officer. At the time of the Sutras, the marriage of a Sudra woman was even permitted to members of the highest caste (Kshatriya) if she were the last of four wives.[42] However, though incompletely developed, the process of endogamous closure was operating from the top classes of Indian society to successively lower ones. The process of priestly tabooing and magical fixing of traditional society was going on.

The situation of the Brahmans as house priests put them in a position to impose the typical features of the caste system on the Indian population while simultaneously preventing the development of the Brahmans into an institutional priesthood in the usual sense. The Brahmans were elevated to the top position in Indian society only as a product of repeated foreign invasion. As noted earlier, in the second century B.C. Antiochus II, Demetrius, Eucratides, and Menander invaded and partly conquered northwestern India. About 200 B.C. the first of three foreign tribes from the north established themselves in northern India. Around 165 B.C. the Yueh-chi crossed the Hindu Kush and established a dynasty, annihilating what remained of Greek domination. Barbarian invasions in the fifth and sixth centuries A.D. dismembered the Gupta empire, and converted India into a Hun province. Later the Mohammedans conquered India. Weber has argued that the superior status of the Kshatriya would tend to crumble under foreign conquest, while that of the Brahmans (valued for their capacity to pacify the population) would tend to be elevated. Thus foreign conquest probably supplied the final conditions for the emergence of caste.

Perhaps the most skillful account of the changes in time of the composition of the castes and their ultimate fixing is that of Weber.[43] He maintains that the Kshatriya of classical literature lacked the character of the medieval knighthood. They did not constitute a feudal hierarchy, but were kings and subkings and village notables, protecting the people politically and mili-

[41] Dharma Sutra, XVII, 1 f. See E. Washburn Hopkins, "Family Life and Social Customs as They Appear in the Sutras," *Cambridge History of India,* Vol. I, pp. 227 f.

[42] *Ibid.*, p. 235.

[43] Max Weber, *The Religion of India* (Glencoe: The Free Press, 1958), pp. 3 ff.

tarily. Warfare was the *dharma* of the Kshatriyas, who were expected to practice force and fraud in war and politics and die with their boots on.

The original Kshatriya groups rivaled the Brahmans in education. However, their ranks were penetrated by the Rajputs, a derivation of a tribe of mercenary knights which emerged as conquerors in the north, who were inferior to the Brahmans in culture. In Rajputana the raja had the right to tax part of the harvest yield, dispose of wasteland, control mining, and receive fines for punishments.

The Kshatriya were changed further when the patrimonial kings installed their representatives alongside the old village chieftains and when military posts were sometimes combined with territorial fiefs. The royal armies were partly staffed by self-equipped knights, while the peasantry was disarmed.

Under kingly administration, changes important for the Vaishya were also brought about. Rural occupations lost much of their ancient prestige. The social prestige of animal husbandry also declined. While the peasantry was depressed, commercial strata rose in esteem. Trader castes collected great fortunes, and at times became moneylenders of the king. Merchants were called on to finance the wars and other enterprises of the princes. The typical Vaishya became a craftsman or trader rather than a peasant.

On the other hand, the monopoly of arms by the king together with an extensive pacification of the cities prevented the development in India of anything like the hoplites of Greece or the militant citizenry of the European Middle Ages. In time the power of caste was turned against that of the city guilds.

Among the Sudras, the industrial castes, two groups were important: the degraded castes and the pure Sudra. The Sat-Sudra (pure Sudra) engaged in such urban industries and trades as oil-vending, baking, and pottery-making. The lower caste stratum comprised a number of trades almost always despised: physically dirty work like street-sweeping, and such ritualistically impure trades as slaughtering, tanning, and leather work.

This caste, too, had a complex history, being gradually constructed out of the enslaved native population which appears as either helots (slaves of the community) or slaves of the household, practitioners of ancient crafts and crafts developed in the course of division of labor, practitioners of crafts that were at times honored and sponsored by the princes (jewelry-making, goldsmithing, work as masons) and practitioners of tribal industries which were incorporated into the Aryan economic order over a period of time.

Since India was repeatedly subject to foreign invasions and conquest, the Hindu community assumed a dependent political existence. Members of the Hindu community then participated in political power only insofar as was permitted by foreign conquerors. The manner in which the Hindu community secured comparative self-regulation fell to the castes.

At times little more than public opinion was operative in the self-control of castes, but most castes possessed a ruling body, a council, or *panchayat*, with some measure of judicial power as well as power to investigate and punish (primarily ritualistic) offenses. It also acted as a licensing authority for economic activities of caste members.

The *panchayat* normally ruled not the caste as a whole but the local endogamous group; the *panchayat* of one endogamous group was independent of that of another of the same caste. The local boundaries of a jurisdiction were clearly marked; sometimes it covered a part of a village or town, sometimes a whole village, and at times a group of villages.

Even today in rural areas there are two main types of *panchayat:* the permanent type possesses permanent officers who bring offenses to its notice and serve as members of a sort of legal and administrative committee. Most *panchayats* have a permanent official as headman. At other times the office is hereditary or elective for life. *Panchayats* may also possess a variety of elected officials. They meet in different ways: at feasts of the brotherhood, on special summons (for example, when called by the headman), or on a fixed occasion (such as a fair or a religious festival). Their meetings may follow a kind of legal format with a charge, a plea, a hearing of evidence, a sentence, etc. Caste jurisdictions include breaches of commensal law, breaches of marriage law (seduction of a wife, immorality, refusal to carry out a marriage after agreement, refusal of the *gauna* ceremony, and refusal to maintain a wife), breaches of caste feasting or trade customs, the killing of certain animals (a cow, etc.), or insulting a Brahman. Castes also have jurisdiction over criminal and civil cases which do not come before the regular courts (assault and debt). *Panchayat* punishments include fines, the giving of feasts to the brotherhood or to Brahmans, overcasting, degradation, and at times, corporal punishment. The temporary *panchayats* have no official responsibility for calling offenses to public notice; only the offended persons are likely to do so.

The family was the place where central caste influence was felt. Family and caste became inseparable, for it was the family where the occupation became traditional and where commensalism and connubium were all-important. The *purohita* was a family priest. Family rites were elaborated by priests and held under priestly supervision, paid for by traditional fees. A large number of the offenses judged and punished by the caste *panchayat* were and are family offenses.

Caste originally secured for eminent families a monopoly of desirable marriage opportunities for their daughters. This was undoubtedly a major reason for the development of child marriage, the aim being to secure a monopoly on proper marriage opportunities as soon as possible. Moreover, caste was easily accommodated to the custom of *suttee* which eliminated the widow as a contender for the inheritance. Significantly, both of these typical Hindu customs were not present in early times.

At all times occupation has had an influence upon social status. The tendency in India was evident in Buddhist times toward hereditary closure of economic activities. Inheritance of economic functions monopolized a class situation for one's children. By the time of Manu, the endogamous closure of most classes was far advanced. Movement toward economic closure was a defensive gesture, evidencing serious internal stress.

In recent times it has almost always been possible to distinguish any given caste in terms of the occupation or group of allied occupations it monopolizes. Not all occupations are equally capable of traditional closure. In agricultural, laboring, hunting castes, traditional fixing of functions is not frequent, but in herding, the learned professions, carrying and peddling, trade and industry, and begging, for example, it is.

New skills develop, however, despite all resistance, and old ones die out. A typical result in India is for the new group to form a new caste, to affiliate itself with another caste, or for a new group to become endogamous as a subcaste within an older caste. The Bhuinhar and Taga are Brahmans who took up agriculture. The Singhariyas and Kahars deserted domestic service for agriculture. The astrologers (Dakaut) and funeral priests (Mahabaraman) may be of Brahman descent. The Belwars are Sanadh Brahmans who took up the carrying trade. The Gaul Nats, formerly singers and dancers, have taken to trade and call themselves Badi Banjaras. Many Kahar subcastes are occupational: the fisherman (Dhimar), women's servants (Mahar), drawers of water (Kamkar).

In the ancient trade guilds, matters of professional labor were regulated by the guild authorities. However, with the development of the castes, the *panchayats* took over such matters. One mode of control was through boycotts and sympathetic strikes. Two Chamars were fined by the *panchayat* for removing dead cattle from the premises of another Chamar's clients. When a Chamar woman worked as a midwife on another's client, her husband was fined. The general economic implications of caste were extensive, for caste regulated methods of manufacture, and limited the clientele, types of tools, and prices of goods.

Caste custom controlled expenditures on marriage, restrictions on trade and industry, caste penalties, repayment of ancestral debt, and maintenance of social prestige. Caste was thus an important factor in fixing the level of economic consumption. It was a religious duty to marry, which by custom was through purchase. Moreover, apart from the dowry, or bride price, the expenditure on the ceremony itself was extensive. Customary ornaments, entertainment, fees for officiating priests, and the like added to the expense. Often the groom represented a higher status with a style of life higher than the bride's family dared to aspire to. Hence these and various other ceremonies (the *Sraddha* and *Upanayana* were especially bad) led to extravagance and debt. Combined with the restrictions on trade and industry, penalties by the brotherhood, repayment of ancestral debt, and the maintenance of social prestige, the weight could be crushing. Nevertheless, a high-caste woman was unable to give assistance in the field; a Brahman or Rajput could not handle a plow; a high-caste man coming in physical contact with a lower-caste man became impure. The magical stereotyping of economic processes fixed the individual in the system with special strictness. It is little wonder that progressive Indians today often see caste as a vicious form of the dead hand of the past.

SUMMARY

In contrast to the large area in ancient China susceptible to relatively uniform economic development under conditions of a temperate climate, the Indian subcontinent was rimmed by huge mountains in the north and broken by mountains in the middle, cut by valleys, and bounded by coasts. Its climate varied from continental to tropical to oceanic types.

These natural geographic and climatic conditions perhaps played a role in the major cultural discontinuities of Indian development extending as far back as the middle Pleistocene. Periodically waves of men penetrated India through the mountain passes of the northwest and, perhaps, northeast. They made their way slowly through this much subdivided subcontinent. It was quite possible for various representatives of these waves of migrants to live on in more or less isolated sections of India only to come in contact with each other at much later times. However, at least by 3000 B.C. agricultural communities of a peasant-village type were forming in northwestern India.

Around 2500 B.C. in the Sind (now Pakistan) and Punjab a formation of cities on a foundation of peasant villages occurred. It is highly probable that there was stimulation in this development from events in Mesopotamia. However, the civic development was largely autonomous. This Bronze Age civilization was dominated by the cities which have been named Harappa and Mohenjo-daro. They constructed buildings and walls of baked brick. They developed a uniform script and standard system of weights. They exported manufactured products to distant places, and imported wood, copper, shell, tin, gold, and precious stones. They constructed citadels and baths. Their streets were planned, and a drainage system was in operation.

The Harappa and Mohenjo-daro civilization seems to have been decaying at the time of the movement of the Aryans into India. However, it is quite possible that the invading Indo-Europeans attacked and dismantled its remnants. In any case, in major contrast to Chinese developments, where the people of the Chou partly fused with those of the Shang, and took over much of Shang culture as their own, there was a sharp break in the cultural continuity of India from pre-Aryan to Aryan times.

The Indo-Europeans who began to migrate into India some time after 1500 B.C. came into repeated struggles with the natives. The tension between these conquerors and the conquered was one of the main characteristics of early Aryan society. A thin stratum of conquerors spread like oil over the surface of the native population. Out of these conquests an amalgamation of populations slowly got under way. Between the eighth and sixth century

B.C. a number of states had begun to rise. Between them, in turn, various conflicts were waged and federations were formed. During the same period numerous cities were in the process of development. Thus the period bears many similarities to the conditions in China during the Spring and Autumn and the Warring Kingdom periods. During this same time new powerful religious movements took shape in India.

However, India never achieved an imperial system like that of China, but beginning in the second century B.C., with the invasion and partial conquest by the Greeks, India was repeatedly unsettled by foreign conquests. At later periods the so-called White Huns and still later the Mohammedan conquests operated the same way. In this last period India gradually achieved a stability in which the key communities were the courts of patrimonial kingdoms and peasant villages, through both of which ran the structure of the caste system.

SELECTED BIBLIOGRAPHY

Blunt, E. A. H., *The Caste System of Northern India* (London: Oxford University Press, 1931).

Childe, V. Gordon, *What Happened in History* (New York: Penguin Books, 1946).

Dikshitar, Ranachandra V. R., *The Mauryan Polity* (Madras: The University of Madras, 1932).

Howells, William, *Back of History* (Garden City: Doubleday & Co., 1954).

Ketkar, S. V., *The History of Caste* in India (Ithaca, N. Y., 1909).

Müller, F. Max, *Rigveda, Samhita, and Pada Text with Sayana's Commentary* in *The Sacred Books of the East* (Oxford: The Clarendon Press, 1879), Vol. IV.

Piggott, Stuart, *Prehistoric India* (Harmondsworth: Penguin Books, 1950).

Rapson, E. J., editor, *The Cambridge History of India* (New York: The Macmillan Co., 1922).

Venkateswara, S. V., *Indian Culture through the Ages* (London: Longmans Green, 1928).

Weber, Max, *The Religion of India*, trans. by Hans Gerth and Don Martindale (Glencoe, Illinois: The Free Press, 1958).

Wheeler, Sir Mortimer, *The Cambridge History of India* (Cambridge: Cambridge University Press, 1953).

8

THE CHANGING ROLES OF THE ANCIENT INDIAN INTELLECTUAL

In the time period of interest to us, we have the barest glimpse of an early city imperialism which was tumbled into ruins possibly in part by invading Indo-Europeans who came down into India around the year 1000 B.C. and made a new beginning of society and civilization. In contrast to China, where there are demonstrable continuities between the society of the Shang and the Chou, the Indus Valley cities played no determinable role on the structure of the early Aryan communities. These were tribal communities modified by their position as conquerors over a large alien subject population. This tended to convert the Aryan communities in their earliest period into a quasi-feudal form.

The movement of Indo-European peoples continued down into historical times. A confused, two-sided conflict was in progress. There was, in the first place, an increasing crystallization of the socio-political structures of Indo-European and non-Indo-European tribal societies into states and tribal republics, between which the conflict assumed an increasingly more comprehensive and organized form. Within the societies formed by the Indo-Europeans, a slow process of assimilation and reorganization was going on. The former enemy population was slowly being fused into the Indo-European social order, and the kings were consolidating their positions by the development of administrative staffs and professional military forces paid out of royal resources. Royal resources also were being consolidated and developed by means of new fiscal and tax policies. In this period a rapid growth of towns and cities, particularly of the capital cities, was occurring.

However, while successively larger consolidations of political power were being formed, in India this did not terminate, as it had in China, with a single empire imposed over the whole of India. Perhaps the internally varied geographic and climatic conditions of India made this more difficult than usual. Certainly one important factor was the persistence in India of an unusually complex series of ethnic and racial groups making the internal homogenization of Indian society a far more complicated task than in China.

Also, the periodic disruption of native Indian trends by invasions from without had its influence.

In any case, out of the plurality of forces arising from such diverse sources as the internal ethnic and racial conflicts, the continuous conquest activities of Indian states and the activities of outside conquerors, India eventually found a high degree of social stability in the caste system which emerged gradually over time. Wherever the caste system took root, the trends toward urbanism were reversed.

Each of these types of communities, the early city, the quasi-feudal conquest community, the civic capital of the patrimonial states, and the caste communities presented very distinct *milieux* for the intellectual.

THE EARLY CITY PRIESTS

While there are no continuities between the early city literary groups and the Vedic priests, it is of some value for purposes of contrast to consider what they must have been like. We know far less about the Indus Valley intellectuals than we do about those of the Shang in China. However, the high degree of regimentation (which could only have been produced by military or hierocratic coordination) was clearly priestly in view of the weak evidence of militarism. The high development of writing testifies to the existence of an active, schooled class of priest-scribes. The lack of archeological evidence of royal or princely treasures does not suggest any great differentiation in the Indus Valley civilization between a secular political and a priestly class. It is quite possible that Harappa and Mohenjo-daro were under the domination of semiascetic priestly rulers to an extent unknown in other areas of the ancient world of the time.

It is interesting to speculate concerning the very different course later Indian social history might have followed if a fusion had occurred between the militarily more vigorous Indo-Europeans and the ruling strata of the Indus Valley civilizations. The Indo-Europeans would have had at their disposal a considerable stock of information about the organization of industrial and commercial enterprise and about the administration of large masses of people. They would have had access to a considerable literary culture. It it doubtful whether the intense social conflict between conquerors and conquered populations would have been permitted to take the same course.

Such idle speculations aside, the Vedic priests were very different from the literarily trained priest-scribes (who may also have been hierocrats) of the Indus Valley civilization.

THE VEDIC PRIESTS

Weber maintains that though more than half of them lived in the upper Ganges Valley and in Bengal, the Brahmans were never a tribe but a guild of magicians who developed into a hierocratic caste of cultured men.[1] Even in classical times they had to undergo a course of instruction in sacred literature and ritualistic practices in which rote learning of the Vedas orally was required under the guidance of freely chosen gurus in a manner bearing traces of ancient magical asceticism. A somewhat similar position has been taken by Deshmukh:

> The word *brahmán* which is considered by Scrader to have originally meant a magician in the Rigveda, denotes at first "poet," "sage," and then "officiating priest" or still later "a special class of priests," and this is not questioned by Sanskrit scholars. The authors of the *Vedic Index* think that the word does not mean merely "poet" or "sage" but can in the Rigveda almost always be translated by the word "priest," "since the priest was of course the singer": but they do not say that the original meaning was a priest, and that it came to mean a "poet" or "sage" later on. Thus the meaning of the word undoubtedly shows that the Brahman was originally a singer of the hymns and probably also a composer, who was revered for these admirable virtues of his. The simple folk of that time easily believed that prayers thus sung and sacrifices offered by such learned men would gain a quicker response than the crude manner in which they would do it. So, although it was allowable for every householder to perform his own religious rites and ceremonies, he voluntarily fell into the practice of asking the professional singer of the hymns to do it for him. Very soon after the community of these singers came to have a sort of vested interest in maintaining the hold of sacrifice on the popular mind, and also they believed in the increased efficacy of the rites when performed by them. The simple people who had fallen into a trap set by their own ignorance were easily imposed upon, and thus the bases of the hereditary indispensable priesthood were securely laid. It is possible that the office of the *purohita* came into existence as a result of the same process.[2]

In the Vedic period a hereditary priesthood did not exist, though the spiritual eminence of some priestly families seems to have been well established.[3]

The apparent conflicts over whether the Vedic prototype of the later Brahman was a priest or a magician and whether the office was hereditary (on all of which points there is disagreement) fall away the moment one takes into account the fact that the religion of the Indo-Europeans in the Vedic period was still largely familistic or a matter of household observance. The single most powerful institution of the Aryans was the patriarchal household. So far as there were originally hereditary members directly associated with the household cults, they were the heads of the household rather than a special class of priests. On the other hand, poets or singers,

[1] Max Weber, *The Religion of India,* trans. by Hans Gerth and Don Martindale (Glencoe: The Free Press, 1958), p. 58.

[2] P. S. Deshmukh, *Religion in Vedic Literature* (London: Oxford University Press, 1933), p. 156.

[3] A. B. Keith, "The Age of the Rigveda," *Oxford History of India,* Vol. I, p. 93, believes that the Vedic priests were largely hereditary.

who were engaged to render the hymns and prayers of the household cults, were undoubtedly hired because of their reputations for magical efficacy.

There must undoubtedly have been a tendency for families with a reputation for magical efficacy in hymn singing or prayer rendition to pass it on to the next generation. Deshmukh has a point in reasoning from Indo-Iranian examples:

> From the fact that we find sure beginnings of a hereditary priesthood in the Indo-Iranian period, we infer with great probability that the Indo-Europeans also were in the habit of offering prayers and sacrifices through some men who were believed to possess qualities peculiarly suited to this purpose. This must for a long time have depended only upon personal qualifications but later tended to become hereditary.[4]

However, so long as the patriarchal families of the Indo-Europeans remained the primary bearers of the religious cult, the priests who were arising must have belonged to priestly or magician's guilds rather than special religious institutions which represented the cult of the entire community.

There were tensions between priests who came in fact to serve the entire community and those who served the household cults. It was of particular importance for the course of Indian social and intellectual development that the house priest rather than the community priest won out.

In the estimation of the composers of the Vedic hymns the position of *purohita*, or domestic priest, was the height of ambition. As Keith indicates, the Vedic *purohita* was the forerunner of the Brahman statesman.[5] He accompanied the king in battle, for his prayers and spells were thought to be essential to victory. In reward for his services he received generous gifts, at times a portion of the king's revenues. The sacrificial fee (*dakshina*) was originally a cow placed at the right hand of a singer.[6]

The factors that led to the dominance of the house priest (*purohita*), rather than the tribal or community priest, in Vedic times were probably complex. Within Indo-European ranks at the time a significant economic, political, and status difference existed between the chariot-owning, horse-breeding, noble families and commoners. The constant warfare sustained their importance for long periods. It is not surprising that such families should have been reluctant to submerge their household cults in a community cult which could only have implied a loss of status.

Moreover, above all else one could hardly have expected the Indo-Europeans to take over the religious institutions and tribal priests of the conquered populations. Finally, the Indo-European commoner might not be in the position to add a *purohita* to his household, but if he chose a model for his own religious practice it was more apt to be that of the nobles of the Aryan group than that of the Dravidians. He probably hired the services

[4] Deshmukh, *op. cit.*, p. 158.
[5] Keith, *op. cit.*, p. 95.
[6] *Ibid.*, p. 99.

of members of the priest-magician's guild as he needed them for births, marriages, sickness, crop failure, or death. This would tend to perpetuate the Vedic religious figure in two main situations: as the house priest in a noble or kingly household, or as a member of an independent priestly guild to be called on for occasional special services in major ceremonies of the noble household or in the ceremonies of Aryan commoners.

While composed of relatively simple elements, the religion administered by the Vedic priests[7] bears all the signs of considerable priestly work and wholesale syncretism. Beside Indra, Agni (fire) and Soma were important to the priests, for they were the objects of sacrifice (milk, grain, ghee, meat, and soma were sacrificed). The soma sacrifice was particularly elaborate. The labor for it was divided among several priests: the *Hotri* (who recited the hymns), the *Adhvaryu* (who performed manual actions to the accompaniment of muted incantations), the *Udgatri* (who sang the soma chants), and several assistants.[8] Only a very rich man or a king could afford the ministrations of such an array of priests. Such patrons were *Maghavans* (bountiful ones) to the priests.

Weber believes that the historical dominance of the Brahmans was a product of the increasing importance of the family priests of nobles and princes as opposed to those administering the community sacrifice. Such a change suggests the diminished importance of the military association before the military forces of the prince and his vassals.[9]

In Vedic times education tended to glide into the hands of the Brahmans. A careful review of Vedic education has been made by Venkateswara.[10] The student (*brahmacharin*) underwent a three-day initiation ceremony during which he worshiped the fire and wore the *munja* girdle as a sign that he was a twice-born boy. Initiation incorporated him into the teacher's family, the *guru* who stood in *loco parentis*. There were a number of types of teachers. The *Achara* and *Kulaguru* were in charge of a number of pupils; *Srotriyas* were teachers in whom the basic passions had been subdued by Vedic study; *Tapsas* practiced austerity; *Vatarasanas* were ascetics. At this time there were also wandering scholars who went about the country engaging in disputations.[11] There were also less orthodox scholars, the *Sthavirs* and *Sramanas*. A pupil was required to do service, menial and otherwise, such as begging for alms, tending the teacher's household chores and affairs.[12] Studentships lasted from twelve to thirty-two years. Brahmans began study between eight and sixteen; Kshatriyas eleven to twenty-two;

[7] *Ibid.*, p. 103.
[8] *Ibid.*, p. 107.
[9] Weber, *op. cit.*, p. 58.
[10] S. V. Venkateswara, *Indian Culture through the Ages* (London: Longmans Green, 1928), Vol. I.
[11] *Ibid.*, pp. 75–76.
[12] *Ibid.*, p. 81.

Vaishayas twelve to twenty-four.[13] When the studentship was over, a ceremonial bath was taken, the vows taken as *Brahmacharin* were terminated, and the teacher was given a substantial present. The Brahman was then expected to establish a household and become a *grihastha* (householder) while he took up active work.[14] The Brahman's work consisted of performing the sacrifice and giving instruction. In both kinds of activities he received gifts (*dakshina*)—never pay. The minimum value of gifts was traditionally stipulated, and unfair competition among Brahmans was prohibited. At the birth of his grandson, the Brahman was expected to retire from the household and become a forest dweller. Through proper ascetic exercises at this time he was able to acquire the power to enchant deities and men. Thus he concluded his life as an apotheosized superman. This, Weber notes, is a survival of the ancient magician's organization of age classes.[15]

THE INTELLECTUAL IN THE CLASSICAL PERIOD OF THE PATRIMONIAL KINGDOMS

The role of the priest-intellectuals had to change with the transformation of northern India from a land of semifeudal manorial communities to one of patrimonial kingdoms. In the early Vedic period the trend toward feudalism sharpened the distinction between the nobility and the free peasants who were being transformed into serfs. The attendants of the nobles, including representatives of ancient magicians' guilds, shared the honors and privileges of the nobles. The nobility and the priesthood were evolving into closed hereditary groups. The movement was well under way at the time of the later Vedas.

The formation of the kingdoms, however, introduced new elements. The kings with their private armies were inevitably suspicious of the armed nobility, for the nobles were serious competitors as well as allies. Moreover, the priests of the king were inevitably the spiritual competitors of the priests of the nobles. In the *Aitareya Brahmana*,[16] the highest of the classes is the Kshatriya. The Brahman is a receiver of gifts, a drinker of soma, a seeker of food, and liable to removal at will. Two classes of Brahmans were distinguished. The Brahmans of the king who performed great sacrifices, some of which lasted a year, and village priests. The priests of the village were more humble, waiting to be called by a rich noble or merchant to serve at a sacrifice.

The conflict between semifeudal nobles and their priests on the one hand and the kings and their priests on the other was a major factor in the crystallization into endogamous groups by the Kshatriya and the Brahmans.

[13] *Ibid.*, p. 82.
[14] Weber, *op. cit.*, p. 59.
[15] *Ibid.*, p. 61.
[16] *Vedic Index*, Vol. II, p. 255. See the summary of A. B. Keith, "The Period of the Later Samhitas," *op. cit.*, p. 127.

This crystallization was similar to the tendency on the part of the medieval guilds in Europe, which had at one time been comparatively open, to turn into closed hereditary groups in the face of the competition of the domestic system and other forms of early capitalism which tended to destroy the economic monopolies they had once enjoyed. All social strata tend to remain open on the way up, economically and socially, but once they have arrived at the top, they tend to close. Hereditary closure of the ranks of Kshatriyas and Brahmans as against the inroads made in their social standing by the princes and their priests is quite understandable.

However, the rise of the kingdoms had far more extensive bearing on the role of the intellectual than forcing of traditional-priest intellectuals toward endogamous closure. Cities were beginning to form, and in the eighth century B.C. writing was introduced by overseas merchants. Writing was of such great value to business and administration that it was quickly made a part of the educational curriculum of the Brahmans. The urban communities required new ideas as well as new skills. The administrative requirements of patrimonial governments were far more complex than in the Heroic Age. Venkateswara establishes the occurrence of a considerable expansion and differentiation of education in the period of the epics and of the sutras.

The educated woman made her appearance, evidencing a breakdown of the patriarchal subordination of women. Buddha's proposal of marriage to a girl was accomplished in writing. She was not only able to read but composed poetry and was familiar with the rules of the sutras. In the *Ramayana*, Sita possesses fluent command of Sanscrit, and Draupadi in the *Mahabharata* is a brilliant conversationalist. Educated women played a considerable part in the early history of Buddhism. Dhammadinna surpasses her husband in knowledge of Buddhist doctrine. Kautilya reports that women unable to earn their living in other ways were helped by the state. Women teachers even became common.

In the epic period home education ceased at the age of five, when formal school began. The Siksha lists the course of study as comprising writing, prayers, word meanings, and elementary grammar. Kautilya reports that the boys learned the alphabet and arithmetic. In Brahmanical schools the formalization of Vedic schooling is apparent. The Grihya Sutras regard the eighth year as the time of initiation for a Brahman, the eleventh year for a Kshatriya, and twelfth for a Vaishya. In the initiation ceremony (*Upanayana*) a sacred girdle was placed around the boy: sacred grass for a Brahman, a bow-string for a Kshatriya, a woolen thread for a Vaishya. The clothing was different for each caste: linen or hempen cloth for a Brahman, cotton for a Kshatriya, woolen for a Vaishya. The student received a new name at initiation. Student duties included frequent bathing, begging for alms, offering sacred fuel to the fire, speaking the truth, avoiding garrulity, avoiding gambling, forbidden food, and drink. Studentship theoretically lasted twelve years for each Veda. On completion of his formal studies the student sacrificed in the water his girdle, staff, sacred thread, and departed after giving a special present to his teacher.

Among the classes of teachers were the *Arharya* (spiritual teacher of the highest grade who accepted no fees), the *Gurua* (who also taught gratis, particularly in moral matters), the Upadhaya (who demanded pay, and gave instruction in some particular subject), the *Sikshaka* (who gave instruction in arts, such as dancing). Teachers who had given up the world also included the Buddhist *Bhikkhus*, Jain *Nirgranthas*, and the *Ajivikas*.[17]

In this period specialization of centers and agencies of industrial and vocational education occurred. Special localities in the cities were occupied by master craftsmen organized into guilds: ivory-workers, weavers, dyers, perfumers, florists, potters, carpenters, blacksmiths, and mariners.[18] In addition to guild-supervised technical training, some development of higher technical education took place.

The school was usually in the teacher's home, but there were often many more students than a teacher could control. A monitorial system was employed, with senior boys teaching the juniors. Similar methods were employed in monastic schools. As learning increased, more specialized classes of schools dealt with different subjects.[19] Moreover, specialized study was carried on in the "forest colleges." Benares, Ujjain, and Taxila were early university centers.

According to the great Indian grammarian, Panini, the various classes of subject matter studied in his time included the *Vedic* texts, arrangements and commentaries on them for convenience in exposition and recitation for purposes of ritual, works of original thinkers and system-makers, and ancient tales or works of fiction dealing with mythological subjects. Among the sciences (*kalas*) distinguished by Patanjali were augury from the observation of the habits and activities of crows, interpretation of omens, knowledge of marks in men and women, horses, and cows, military science, and archery.[20] The *Jaina Sutras* mention sixty-four achievements of ladies. Among the seventy-two *kalas* are eighteen scripts corresponding to eighteen vernacular tongues, arithmetic, impersonation, dancing, singing, instrumental music, gambling, chess, conversation, composing verses and riddles, and rules regarding the preparation and service of food and drink.[21]

During the patrimonial and civic period many forces were at work toward the separation of education from the household of the *guru* and the

[17] S. V. Venkateswara, *Indian Culture through the Ages* (London: Longmans Green, 1928).
[18] *Ibid.*, p. 156.
[19] *Ibid.*, p. 159.
[20] *Ibid.*, p. 173.
[21] *Ibid.*, p. 174.

formation of specialized schools. There may even have been, according to Venkateswara, some government schools:

> Comparing the Indian education of this period with that of other countries, it strikes one as possible that there may have been in Kautilya's day government schools of the kind there were in Egypt, where instruction was given by one of the higher officials under whom the pupil served a sort of apprenticeship.[22]

The *Arthasastras,* which primarily concern the education for princes, give some indication of the content of instruction expected of upper-class persons. Princes studied not only the Vedas but various accessory sciences, such as economics (including agriculture, cattle-breeding, and merchandise) and politics. From three to five years of age the princes were supposed to have learned the alphabet and arithmetic. After the Upanayana they learned the three Vedas (logic, economics, and politics). Princes were permitted to marry after sixteen. They then studied military arts in the morning, and tradition, history, mythology, ethics, politics, and economics the rest of the day and night. In their sixteenth year, princes were sent abroad for instruction to complete their educations.

> The Arthasastras were regarded not only as the curricula for princes and servants of governments, present or prospective, but as accomplishments of cultured people. We find in the *Sukasapati* merchandise, story-telling, painting, and the Arthasastras included among the Kalas.[23]

A review of the various special educational institutions which he believes were established at this time (600–500 B.C.) is contained in the account by Tribhuvandas L. Shah:

> Primary education was imparted in the village schools, as it is done to-day. There were separate colleges and institutes for different branches of study. When primary education and higher education were so carefully attended to, it is reasonable to conjecture that secondary education was not neglected. We have to admit that not many references are found of institutes imparting secondary education. Sons of rich men were specially trained—by what to us would seem a very peculiar system of education—for acquiring sound common sense and a perfect social behavior, by courtesans. . . .
>
> There were many 'Gurukulas' or residential schools. Such institutes must have filled the place of the secondary schools of to-day. Students in such boarding schools had naturally two advantages over the boys going to the non-residential high schools of to-day: (1) up to the time they studied in such schools, they could not marry; *e.g.*, they reaped all the advantages of leading a celibate life; (2) they could come into contact with boys hailing from various provinces, and thus could acquire a sound knowledge of the ways of the world. . . .
>
> In universities, special classes were conducted for special branches of knowledge. The world famous universities of those times are mentioned

[22] Venkateswara, *op. cit.*, p. 176.
[23] *Ibid.*, p. 169.

> in various books concerning those times: (1) The university of Nalanda, situated in the town of Nalanda, which was near Rajgrhi, the capital of Magadha, (2) the Taksasila University situated in Taksasila, the capital of Gandhara country, the modern Punjab. In the time of King Srenika, *e.g.*, in the time of Mahavira and Gautama Buddha, the Taksasila University was of greater importance than the Nalanda University. (The Taksasila University was famous for its medical education. This may be due to a close contact with the Persian traders, whose country was far advanced in medical science.) But when the ninth Nanda king conquered Gandhara and brought the learned trio of Panini, Chanakya, Vararuchi, from Taksasila to Nalanda, the Nalanda University came into the forefront.[24]

During the time that the Indian world was being transformed from one of semifeudal manorial communities to loosely knit kingdoms comprising a series of forms varying from peasant villages to thriving cities, the Brahmans were in a strategic position to monopolize the intellectual roles. As Weber observed, the Brahmans infiltrated the learned occupations, particularly administrative posts, which demanded writing skill and education, as did the clerics of the Middle Ages.[25] However, the restrictive monopolies of the Brahmans and the groups they represented met with serious resistance from the kings. Resistance was particularly strong in the kingdoms east of the lands where the Brahmans enjoyed traditional strength. In the course of the sixth century B.C., both the Buddhist and Jain orders took shape in this area.

The extent to which the life of the Jain ascetic was modeled after the Brahman has been shown by Jacobi in his comparison of the rules of the two disciplines.[26] Though Jain monks were responding to the same role requirements as the Brahmans, they offered a different solution. The birth story of the founder of Jainism (Mahavira) was intended to prove that it was a greater honor to be born of a Kshatriya than of a Brahman mother. Mrs. Stevenson[27] has observed that throughout the Jain sacred books antagonism to the Brahmans is evident in such things as bathing, divination, and sacrifice.[28] In contrast to the exclusiveness of birth and caste emphasized by the Brahmans, the Jains lay stress on the consequences of this action (*karma*).[29]

Mahavira (599–527 B.C.), the charismatic hero of Jainism, was the second son of a Kshatriya chieftain of Magadha. While generally viewed as the

24 Tribhuvandas L. Shah, *Ancient India* (Baroda: Shashikant & Co., 1938), Vol. I, p. 21–22.

25 Weber, *op. cit.*, p. 57.

26 H. Jacobi, Introduction to Vol. XXII of the *Sacred Books of the East*, pp. xxii ff.

27 Mrs. Sinclair Stevenson, *The Heart of Jainism* (London: Oxford University Press, 1915).

28 *Sutrakritanga, Sacred Books of the East*, XIV, p. 294; *Uttaradhayana, Sacred Books of the East*, XLV, pp. 136 ff.

29 In fact, it was by one's actions that he became a Brahman or member of one of the other castes. *Uttaradhayana, Sacred Books of the East*, XLV, p. 140.

real founder of Jainism, the Jains claimed that before Mahavira there were no less than twenty-three prophets (*tirthakaras*).[30] The adherents of Mahavira, according to Stevenson, were drawn chiefly from the Kshatriya aristocracy with which Mahavira was connected by kinship. Mahavira organized his followers into a regular community containing lay members as well as monastic followers of both sexes. At his death the order was said to contain more than fourteen thousand monks.[31]

Both Mahavira's successors and disciples were primarily drawn from the ranks of the Kshatriya.[32] When Mahavira visited the great towns of Magadha, he was well received by all the nobility. He frequently met with Bimbisara and Kunika, kings of Magadha. While the Jains did not insist on such long training of candidates as was true of Vedic schools, they did not intend that their monks should be ignorant. The way of life of the Jain was built around the principle of asceticism. A Jain initiate had his hair torn out by the roots (an operation performed once a year). If he were a Digambar, he took a new name; if a Svetambar, he changed his name or added a new one. He became a homeless wanderer subsisting on alms. He carried pieces of cloth to strain off any insects from water he boiled or drank. He rose at four in the morning to perform Jain rituals, beginning his round of begging at ten. Female ascetics (*sadhyi*), held in great reverence by the Jains, followed much the same practices as male ascetics.[33]

Laymen and monks were organized into a religious community. The Jain lay gentleman strove to develop twenty-one qualities: serious demeanor, cleanliness, good temper, striving after popularity, fear of sinning, mercy, straightforwardness, wisdom, modesty, kindness, moderation, gentleness, care of speech, sociability, caution, studiousness, reverence for old age and old customs, humility, gratitude, benevolence, and attention to business.[34] The Jain monks took five great vows: (1) *Ahimsa* (never to destroy a living thing), (2) *Astya tyaga* (against untruthfulness), (3) *Asteya vrata* (nonstealing), (4) *Brahmacarya vrata* (*chastity*), and (5) *Aparigraha vrata* (renouncing all love for anything or any person). The Jain monk cultivated twenty-seven qualities: he must keep the five vows, never eat at night, protect all living things, control his five senses, renounce greed, practice forgiveness, possess high ideals, and inspect everything he used to make sure no insect was injured.[35]

The Jain sect enjoyed the support of the Magadha kings. Not until the Maurya dynasty gained ascendancy was royal preference decisively shifted to Buddhism. Around 300 B.C. a great split in the Jain church occurred,

30 See the summary of "The History of the Jains" by Jarl Charpentier, *Cambridge History of India*, Vol. I, pp. 150 ff.

31 *Ibid.*, pp. 8–9.

32 *Ibid.*, Chap. IV, "Mahavira's Predecessors and Disciples," pp. 48 f.

33 *Ibid.*, pp. 225 f.

34 *Ibid.*, p. 224.

35 *Ibid.*, p. 238.

dividing the community into *Svetambaras* (monks dressed in white clothes) and *Digambaras* (the sky-clad or naked).

The powerful competitor of Jainism among the heterodoxies was Buddhism. Despite Senart's[36] brilliant treatment of Buddha as a sun-myth, which Oldenberg took seriously and answered at length,[37] there has never been a serious doubt of the historical existence of the war prince of the Cakyas family of Nepal. Siddhartha (died perhaps 483 B.C.) received a somewhat indifferent Vedic education, as was not unusual for a member of the Kshatriya. Buddha appears to have been on the road toward the normal life of a noble, when he became obsessed with the examples of age, sickness, and death about him. Despite his father's protests, he left home and family, giving up all Kshatriya advantages for the practice of asceticism. After six years he gave this up, in turn, announcing his own doctrine of the "Middle Way." Buddha appears initially to have been obsessed only with his own salvation. In Hopkins' words,

> The founder of Buddhism did not strike out a new system of morals; he was not a democrat; he did not originate a plot to overthrow the Brahmanic priesthood; he did not invent the order of monks. There is, perhaps, no person in history in regard to whom have arisen so many opinions that are either wholly false or half false.[38]

Hopkins observes that in Buddha's day asceticism was customary for persons of all the twice-born castes. Moreover, it was a time when all ascetics were looked upon as equal to priests. Hence Buddha had no very important public opinion to struggle against, when he declared that Brahman birth and wisdom were of no value.[39]

Buddha, however, found asceticism to be empty—not an unexpected finding for a well-bred noble. Salvation was rather to be achieved by the four truths and the eightfold path:

> I. Birth is sorrow, age is sorrow, sickness is sorrow, clinging to earthly things is sorrow.
>
> II. Birth and rebirth, the chain of reincarnations, result from the thirst for life together with passion and desire.
>
> III. The only escape from this thirst is the annihilation of desire.
>
> IV. The only way of escape from this thirst is by following the eightfold path: right belief, right resolve, right word, right act, right life, right effort, right thinking, right meditation.[40]

Against both the rigorous asceticism and prolonged training program of Hinduism and the extreme asceticism of Jainism, Buddha offered a position more calculated to appeal to the aristocrats and rising wealthy strata of the

[36] Émile Senart, *Essai sur la légende du Buddha* (Paris: 1875).

[37] Hermann Oldenberg, *Buddha: His Life, His Doctrine, His Order,* trans. by William Hoey (London: Luzac & Co., 1928), pp. 71 f.

[38] Edward W. Hopkins, *The Religions of India* (Boston: Ginn & Co., 1895); pp. 298–299. See also Oldenberg, *op. cit.,* p. 73.

[39] *Ibid.,* p. 303.

[40] *Ibid.,* pp. 305–306.

time. Significantly, it was the rich youth of Benares that first flocked about him. At an early period more than sixty young nobles joined the movement, and were sent to teach in all lands in their own tongue.[41]

> The Buddhist theory acknowledged the equal right of all persons without distinction to be received into the order . . . if even Brahman exclusiveness was not maintained in its full extent, still a marked leaning to aristocracy seems to have lingered in ancient Buddhism as an inheritance from the past. . . . Buddha speaks . . . of the highest consummation of religious aspirations, for the sake of which "the sons of noble families (*kulaputta*) leave their homes and go into homelessness." The disciples who gathered round the teacher coming from the noble house of Sakyas, the descendant of king Ikshvaku, were themselves for the most part "sons of noble families." If we review the ranks of personages . . . we . . . meet in the texts, we find . . . young Brahmans like Sariputta, Moggallana, Kaccana, nobles like Ananda, Ruhula, Anuruddha, sons of the great merchants and highest municipal dignitaries, like Yasa, invariably men and youths of the most respectable classes of society, and with an education in keeping with their social status.[42]

Buddhism denied the existence of a permanent soul, describing the individual as an aggregate of aspirations. Buddhistic salvation rested on the renunciation of desire as the one certain means of achieving release from the wheel, or rebirth, and all the trials of the world. Buddhism was well received by the kingdoms of India. Pasenadi, the king of Kosala in Buddha's time, while never actually converted, was favorable to the movement. He adopted its elementary teachings and called on Buddha for advice.[43] On Gotama's second visit to Rajagaha, Bimbisara, just as he had endowed the Jains, presented him with a bamboo grove, where he was able to build an accommodation for the order.[44] Avanti became an important center of Buddhism from the first.[45] However, Buddhism found its most brilliant sponsor in Asoka, who made it the official religion of the Maurya. Asoka is said to have supported 64,000 Buddhist priests and established many religious foundations. Buddhism developed monasteries with both monk and nun orders. The congregational confession and partial remission of sins appeared. Missionaries were sent forth and the conversion of India to the state religion was undertaken. Councils were held to determine orthodoxy. Eventually a great schism took place between the northern canon (the greater vehicle) and the faith as originally supported by Asoka (the lesser vehicle).

Thus, during the classical period of the patrimonial kingdoms in India, an intellectual ferment was manifest, comparable to that in the period of

[41] *Ibid.*, p. 307.
[42] Oldenberg, *op. cit.*, pp. 155–156.
[43] T. W. Rhys Davids, "The Early History of the Buddhists" in *Cambridge History of India*, Vol. I, p. 180.
[44] *Ibid.*, p. 184.
[45] *Ibid.*, p. 186.

the Warring Kingdoms in China. The sphere of intellectual activity was enormously widened. Hinduism found itself faced by powerful rivals in Jainism and Buddhism, which received varying kinds of official support and threatened for a time to displace Brahmanism altogether.

The existence of cultivated strata of laymen in this period, able to promote religious movements outside Hinduism, was a major fact in the intellectual life of the period. The organization of universities and other institutions of higher learning outside of the *guru* households and in the service of the emerging urban communities was initially the work, directly or indirectly, of the heterodoxies.

> A very remarkable achievement of this period is the organization of higher education in some of the prominent centers of India. The earliest and the greatest institutions were those of Benares and Taxila, which were the resort of people from all parts of the world, from at least as early as the Buddhist period. But Fa-Hien does not mention any monasteries in Taxila. In his time the chief place of Buddhist education was the Jatavana monastery near Pataliputra, which had a regular succession of teachers extending over a thousand years.[46]

The earliest traces of a school building have been found in Sarnath. The most famous university of the period between Fa-Hien and I-Tsing was Nalanda, which is also identified with fine specimens of sculpture. "Yan Chwang informs us that the grounds of Nalanda had formed originally a mango park which was bought by five hundred merchants for ten crores of gold coins and presented by them to Buddha."[47] However, higher education centers were by no means confined to places like Taxila and Nalanda. But wherever they were formed, it was either by the Buddhists or orthodox Hindus in competition with the Buddhists.

THE CASTE SYSTEM AND THE GURU

Despite the bloody persecution of Buddhists under the Sunga dynasty which followed the Maurya, signaling the beginning of a counterattack on the heterodoxies, the rise of the caste system and the attendant close of India's most creative period were not brought about with the same incisiveness as in China with the establishment of the Empire and the burning of the books under the Ch'in. Rather, it was a slow process. Weber has summarized it as follows:

> Buddhism in all its forms in the course of the first millennium of our era was pressed back step by step and was almost completely exterminated. In South India it gave way to Jainism. This may . . . be correlated with the superior community organization of this confession. However, Jainism, too, shriveled within the area of its diffusion, finally being reduced to the cities of West India, where it still lives on today.[48]

[46] Venkateswara, *op. cit.*, p. 225.
[47] *Ibid.*, p. 228.
[48] Weber, *op. cit.*, p. 291.

Even during the height of the heterodox religions of India, Brahmanism never completely disappeared. Brahmans continued to perform various rites for the laity at times, to supervise temple service, and to appropriate temple prebends for themselves. The caste order was weakened, but it never completely disappeared in north Indian territory.

Buddhism was linked to a growth of cities, and it implemented the social and political aspirations of urban strata, this could have involved the restriction of the activities of the princes by the urban plutocracy. The princes revived the ties with the Brahmans and encouraged the caste organization as a countermeasure to the Buddhistic monkdom and the urban guilds.[49]

The Brahmans themselves played an important role in the orthodox restoration of Hinduism, for as a noble secular priesthood they wished more than anything else to free themselves from a position subordinate to the congregation of heterodox monks.

> The restoration took place with the decay of the heterodox intellectual soteriologies, on the one side, in the stereotyping of caste ritualism. . . . On the other side, the restoration occurred in the propagation of the ancient classical Hindu sects, dating to the epoch prior to the great kingdoms. And indeed it took place through the same means which the heterodox communities owed their success: an organized professional monkdom.[50]

With the rise and hardening of the caste system, the place of the intellectual came to be epitomized by the *guru*.[51] As established during the Brahmanical restoration, the position of the *guru* was modeled after the relation of the Vedic teacher to the student of the Vedas (*Brahmacharin*). In early times such experts in Vedic lore were employed by the kings and nobles as house chaplains and tutors. However, in the course of the restoration of Hinduism their ranks were interpenetrated by plebeian mystagogues and soul-helpers,[52] who were often quite aliterary. They became a stratum of trained, monastically organized, wandering mendicants who cooperated with the court to bring about the restoration of Hinduism. They established religious orders and achieved spiritual domination over the masses. The majority of the mendicant *gurus* were Brahmans. Their income, however, was considerable, and they came into conflict with the more traditional Brahmans whose places they usurped. They were not the bearers of a new religious interpretation, but of a new kind of religious authority.

> Quite apart from the Krishna and Rama cults which it embodied, it was a "redeemer" religiosity in a special sense. It offered the masses the corporeal living savior, the helper in need, confession, magically therapeutic, and above all, an object of worship in the form of a dignity-bear-

[49] *Ibid.*, p. 292.
[50] *Ibid.*, p. 293.
[51] The single, most compact account is contained in Weber, *op. cit.*, pp. 380–428. Except where otherwise noted, the present review follows Weber.
[52] *Ibid.*, p. 319.

ing *guru* or *gosain*—be it through the designation of successors, be it hereditary.[53]

The apotheosis of the *guru* is dramatically illustrated by the fact that even religious reformers who turned every effort toward the destruction of idolatry were deified in their turn. Hopkins, for example, gives the following account of the fate of the religious reformer, Kabir, a nominal adherent to the Ramanand sect.

> Kabir, probably at the beginning of the fifteenth century, the most famous of Ramanand's disciples, has as religious descendants the sect of Kabir Panthis. But no less an organization than that of the Sikhs look back to him, pretending to be his followers. The religious tenets of the Kabir Panthis may be described as those of unsectarian Unitarians. They conform to no rites or *mantras*. Kabir assailed all idolatry, ridiculed the authority of all scriptures, broke with Pundit and with Mohammedan, taught that outer form is no consequence, and that only the "inner man" is of importance. These Panthis are found in the South, but are located chiefly in and about Benares, in Bengal in the East, and in Bombay in the West. There are said to be twelve divisions of them. Kabir assailed idolatry, but alas! Discipline requires subordination. The Guru, Teacher, must be obeyed. It was not long before he who rejected idolatry became himself a deity. And in fact every Teacher, Guru, of the sect was an absolute master of thought, and was revered as a god.[54]

In this particular sect, according to Hopkins, a *guru* was examined before election. If the faithful were not satisfied, they could reject him, but if they once elected him, they were bound to obey him without question. Among the powers of the *guru* was the right to excommunicate, though not to administer corporal punishment.

> This deification of the Guru was retained by the Sikhs, and the office was made hereditary among them (by Arjun), till Govind, the tenth pontiff, who left no successor, declared that after his death the *Granth* (bible) should be the sole authority of the church.[55]

When as a *guru* the Brahman was conceived to be a living god (*thakur*), no correct *sudra* would fail to drink water in which a Brahman had touched his toe. There was even a sect (the *Satnami* established by a Kshatriya) in which the eating of the excrement of *gurus* was practiced as a sacrament.

> The leading *guru* in a territory is similar to a bishop of a Western church, visiting his diocese accompanied by his following. He had power to excommunicate individuals in the case of grosser sins. He bestowed absolution for penitence, placed a tax on believers.[56]

According to Weber, every sect believer had his *guru* who taught him the *mantra*. The diocese of the *guru* was so completely his personal property

[53] *Ibid.*, p. 319.
[54] Hopkins, *op. cit.*, pp. 510–511.
[55] *Ibid.*, footnote, p. 511.
[56] Weber, *op. cit.*, p. 319.

that it was not only hereditary but unalienable. As a living savior, the *guru* replaced all transcendent objects of worship. However, since the Brahmans lacked exclusive political support, heterodox mystagogues were also able to practice soul-healing and gather adherents about them.

Related to the popularization of Hinduism which accompanied the restoration was a change in the structure of Brahmanhood. Only in Rajputana did the Brahman remain the house chaplain of a king or noble. There high-caste Brahmans were permitted to receive fees only from aristocratic castes. The *Vaidika* (an aristocratic Vedic culture of Brahman caste) claimed an exclusive monopoly of fees. In medieval India great prebend foundations were established by princes and nobles for these Brahmans in return for ritualistic and administrative services. Meanwhile, all temple priests, whose services did not require Vedic learning, were demoted.

> Among the full Brahmans the highest ranking individual, according to his own claims, took the ranked position of *pandit*. They were responding jurists and judges; the highest among them in the time before the foreign dominations was often held to be the first man in the land.[57]

In the ancient time Brahmanical positions depended on the possession of holy wisdom. However, after the restoration, popular Vishnite sects, in which Vedic learning plays little if any role, have tended to displace these ancient forms of Brahmanical power on a more or less permanent basis.

> Emotional confessional agitation and competition in public, with its specifically plebeian means of recruiting and assemblage, appear. . . . Processions and folk festivals, collective pilgrimages and similar forms, made their appearance as well.[58]

When the number of small burghers in the towns and cities increased, and their growing wealth offered increasing opportunity for fees, it was inevitable that the demagogic *guru* would be oriented toward them. Under such circumstances the incorporation of tantristic (magical) and other such elements into Brahmanical circles was inevitable also. The authority of the pandits declined in the face of the growing popularity of aliterary representatives of the masses. Hence Weber insists that adoration of the living savior was the final stage in Hindu religious development.

The political power of the clergy was also great. The mendicants served the king as spies, while Brahmans served as officials and advisors. However, as long as the kings retained their positions, the full apotheosis of the *guru* was not permitted. It was only toward the end of the fifth century that extreme forms of *guru* deification appeared. Before that, regardless of how useful the *gurus* were in pacifying the masses, the kings were hardly inclined to allow the power of the heads of the religious sects to exceed their own.

[57] *Ibid.*, p. 321.
[58] *Ibid.*, p. 323.

> It was first the foreign domination of Islam which shattered the political power of distinguished Hindu castes, which gave the development of the *guru* power free reign, permitting it to grow to grotesque heights.[59]

SUMMARY

When the Indo-Europeans began to pour down as a conquest group into India between 1500 and 1000 B.C., they found the remains of an Indus Valley civilization which they pillaged and helped to destroy. However, they do not seem to have been directly affected by it, other than to be temporarily enriched by booty from their pillage. The Indo-Europeans spread as a thin stratum of conquering tribes over a large alien population, forming into quasi-feudal conquest-communities. However, both the Indo-Europeans and the peoples to the East against which they moved were beginning to crystallize into larger political aggregations, making warfare an increasingly more comprehensive business. Meanwhile, some integration of the once alien population into the social order was progressing. The cities and patrimonial courts became the critical communities during this phase of Indian development. However, when—as a product of increasing conquests of the states, of the policies of the princes who found it advantageous to play the Brahmans off against the urban masses which were being integrated by the heterodox faiths, and finally of foreign conquest—the orthodox restoration of Hinduism was brought about, the caste system emerged as the definitive Indian community.

Each of these communities sustained a type of intellectual peculiar to its needs. The early Indus Valley cities seem to have supported literarily trained hierocrats of a type similar to those of Egypt. However, between them and the later intellectual types of India, there was no direct continuity. In the quasi-feudal communities of the Vedic period the key intellectual strata consisted of house chaplains and tutors in the service of royal and noble households. During the period of the patrimonial Warring States, new strata of intellectuals arose, particularly in the capital cities, out of educated aristocratic circles. These strata of intellectuals founded new mass religions adapted to the needs of an urban society. They also founded new educational institutions. Meanwhile, the conversion of the masses of Indians proceeded rapidly as a result of the activities of the mendicant monks who bore the heterodox religious faiths.

In the period of the orthodox restoration, Hinduism itself was transformed from an aristocratic and intellectual religion to a religion adapted to the salvation needs of the Indian masses. Also, the structural role of the priests was transformed. The key intellectuals of the Neo-Hindu restoration were no longer the chaplains of royal and noble households (though remnants of these ancient roles remained) but apotheosized leaders of mass salvation cults, the *gurus*.

59 *Ibid.*, pp. 324–325.

SELECTED BIBLIOGRAPHY

Deshmukh, P. S., *Religion in Vedic Literature* (London: Oxford University Press, 1933).

Hopkins, Edward Washburn, *The Religions of India* (Boston: Ginn & Company, 1895).

Oldenberg, Hermann, *Buddha: His Life, His Doctrine, His Order,* trans. by William Hoey (London: Luzac & Co., 1928).

Shah, Tribhuvandas L., *Ancient India* (Shashikant & Co., 1938).

Stevenson, Mrs. Sinclair, *The Heart of Jainism* (London: Oxford University Press, 1915).

Venkateswara, S. V., *Indian Culture through the Ages* (London: Longmans Green, 1928).

Weber, Max, *The Religion of India,* trans. by Hans Gerth and Don Martindale (Glencoe, Illinois: The Free Press, 1958).

9

INDIAN SOCIAL THOUGHT AND ITS PLACE IN INDIAN CIVILIZATION

Because of the lack of other means of dating historical periods, ancient Indian history tends to be ordered to an unusual extent in terms of its literary remnants. Radhakrishnan accepts the general periods of Indian thought as follows:

Vedic period	1500 B.C. to 600 B.C.
Epic period	600 B.C. to 200 A.D.
Sutra period	200 A.D. onward[1]

He subdivided the epic period into finer gradations:[2]

Systems of revolt (Carvaka, Jainism, Buddhism)	600 B.C.
Theistic reconstruction of the *Bhagavadgita* and later Upanishads	500 B.C.
Speculative development of the six systems,	300 B.C.–200 A.D.

The Vedic literary period designates at least a thousand-year interval of Indian history, and covers a mass of literature. It has been argued that some of the hymns of the earliest collection of songs and hymns, the *Rig-Veda Samhita*, perhaps date to 2000 B.C. The lower data of the Vedic period has been placed at 600 B.C., because the major Upanishads were composed by then. Between these limits appear the other *Samhitas*, the Brahmanas (which developed the ritualistic aspects of Vedic religions and elaborated the mechanical details of the sacrifice (*yajana*)), the Aranyakas and the Upanishads (which developed the philosophical ideas contained in the Vedas and literatures developing out of them).[3]

If one looks at the development of ancient India sociologically in terms of its distinctive communities, however, he observes that the excited creativity occurring in the later phases of the Vedic literary period was a product

[1] S. Radhakrishnan, *Indian Philosophy* (New York: The Macmillan Co., 1922).

[2] *Ibid.*, p. 276.

[3] C. Majumdar, "Evolution of Religio-Philosophic Culture in India," *The Cultural Heritage of India*, edited by Haridas Bhattacharyya (Calcutta: The Ramakrishna Mission, 1956), Vol. IV, p. 33.

of the new communities arising at the time. The earliest sociological period of ancient India was the period of the quasi-feudal conquest community which began to decline between 800 and 700 B.C.—the time when the composition of the first Upanishads began.

SOCIAL THOUGHT IN THE PERIOD OF THE CONQUEST COMMUNITY

There are four collections in the Veda: *Rig*, *Yajur*, *Sama*, and *Atharva*. The *Rig*-Veda is oldest, representing inspired songs which the Aryans in part brought with them from their non-Indian homeland. The *Sama*-Veda and *Yajur*-Veda serve liturgical purposes. The *Atharva*-Veda is a late addition to the Veda, containing elements suggesting compromises between the views of the Aryans and the people they were conquering. Each Veda has three parts: *Mantras* (the hymns constituting the *samhita*), the *Brahmanas* (including precepts and religious duties), and the *Aranyakas* (the concluding portions of which, the *Upanishads*, discuss philosophical problems). The Upanishads contain the materials from which the whole subsequent philosophy of India is derived.

The thirty-three deities mentioned in the Vedas were classified as gods of the earth (like Agni, and Soma), gods of the midair (like Indra and Maruts), and sky gods (like Mitra and Varuna). Vedic thought was built around the worship of these and various functional deities, for example, Agni and Parjunya (gods of fire and of cloud), and practices resting upon *rita* (the uniformity of nature and moral order). The gods sustained the natural and moral order of *rita*. Vedic thought was thoroughly this-worldly. Milk, grain, and ghee were sacrificed to the gods to obtain important worldly ends: long life, prosperity, or special favors. Sacrifice formed no ironclad ritualism as in later times, nor were symbolic substitutions employed for it. It was frankly a means of influencing the gods.

In late *mantras* many deities were fused as if the inclination toward a kind of monotheism was felt. At various times both Varuna and Indra were elevated to the rank of supreme gods. However, more characteristic than any genuine monotheism was the tendency by Vedic seers to magnify the importance of the particular deity to whom the worship was addressed at the moment. This practice was called by F. Max Müller henotheism to separate it from both monotheism and polytheism. Another tendency was manifest in those passages of the *Rig-Veda*, where the goddess Aditi (the boundless) was identified with the sky and with "whatever is or shall be," suggesting pantheistic monism.

At no time was the reality of nature and the external world questioned in the Vedas. The deities themselves were a part of nature. Ideas of the origin and development of the universe appeared, but the later notion of endless creations and dissolutions did not. Sometimes the world was treated as generated with heaven and earth as parents. Or again, the world was conceived as a sacrificial act. At one time Varuna appeared as a cosmic architect. Again, when a transcendental being was sacrificed, the moon was born from his mind, the sun from his eye, Indra and Agni from his heart, Vayu from his mouth, the middle region emerged from his navel, the sky from his head, the earth from his feet.

The Vedas did not develop a theodicy of suffering. They were joyous and optimistic toward life. The notion of recompense in heaven or hell for unrewarded virtues and unpunished failings in this world was absent, at least in the early *mantras*. The objective of the religion was health, happiness, and a plenitude of the good things of the world. Their conceptions corresponded to a world of semifeudal conquest communities in which young warriors carried the brunt of pioneering and conquest.

The Vedic priest was a member of a magician's guild who derived his fees for his service from the conduct of household sacrifices. The two primary situations of the Vedic priest were those as a practicing expert in ceremonies or house chaplain and as a *guru* within the circle of his colleagues and students. The Brahmanas, with their strong emphasis on ritualistic practice, seem addressed to the first requirement; the Upanishads seem addressed to the intellectual requirements of priestly circles and students.

THE PERIOD OF URBANISM AND THE PATRIMONIAL STATES

The family was the most important institution of Vedic society, but it was very different from later Indian forms. Child marriage was unknown.[4] Though the family was patriarchal, women had a much better position than in later periods. Girls received an education similar to boys, and underwent the *brahmacarya* discipline. Women had control over their dowries, and were not secluded as they were later. While ascetics were known in Vedic times, renunciation of the world was not popular. The main social divisions were between Aryas and Dasyus: the Aryas were sacrificers and fire-worshipers; the Dasyus were phallus-worshipers. Agriculture and cattle-breeding were the mainstays of economic life. The professions known at this time included: the blacksmith, goldsmith, physician, carpenter, weaver, tanner, stonemason, basket-maker, warrior, and priest. The main class divisions among the militarily pre-eminent cattle-breeding Aryans were Brahmana, Kshatriya, and Vaishya. These classes, however, were not hereditary, and intermarriages were possible not only between them but also with the Sudra. Commensalism, too, was possible even with the Sudra. Agriculture was the basis of economic life; trade and commerce were undeveloped. Cows were a medium of exchange; silver was almost unknown, and currency did not exist. The Vedic Indians were in process of abandoning a nomadic state, and the rulers of such tribes as the Kurus, Pancalas, and Yadus were not described as rulers over particular regions. Monarchy was the normal form of

[4] See the review of Vedic society by A. S. Altekar, "Vedic Society," in *The Cultural Heritage of India, op. cit.*, Vol. I, pp. 221 ff.

political organization, but the kings were often elected and, like the Homeric monarchs, only the first among peers.

By the eighth century B.C., many changes were under way. The foundation of territorial states involved an important differentiation between former aristocratic circles and the kings with whom they had enjoyed equality. The kings developed the tax resources of their kingdoms to free themselves from dependency on the nobles and to build administrative staffs and armies loyal to themselves alone. It was to their advantage to promote commerce and to encourage the development of a money economy. With the rise of urban society, merchants became more important to the kings than peasants and even, at times, the nobles, for they produced more taxable moneyed wealth than the latter.

These social changes inevitably placed a series of strains on the bearers of Vedic religion. A division grew up between the priests of the rural aristocrats (the most direct heirs of the Vedic priests) and the priests serving the kings and the new urban strata. There were unavoidable ideological conflicts accompanying these social conflicts. The intensified intellectual activity evidenced by the Brahmanas in developing and fixing the ritualistic aspects of Vedic worship and the elaboration of the mechanical details of the sacrifice (*yajña*) was probably produced by the growing threat to the situation of the rural aristocrats.

At the same time, the total content of instruction required of the *purohitas* was being expanded by changing social needs, for they served not only as house chaplains but as tutors in the knowledge and skills required of genteel strata. The lines between those Vedic priests who obtained work in royal and noble households and those who did not grew sharper and assumed a new character. Moreover, the social changes must have demanded a religious reinterpretation of Vedic literature. In any case, the Upanishads have every appearance of a series of religious reconstructions of the tradition evoked by the dramatic social changes which accompanied the transition from a quasi-feudal conquest society to a world of settled patrimonial states in which the new urban communities were increasingly crucial.

The Conceptual Ferment of the Upanishads

The strong tendency toward idealistic monism in the Upanishads, and their conception of reality as a kind of spiritual animation, are among the kinds of tendencies one could expect on the part of thoughtful, spiritual teachers pressed by social changes to attempt to consolidate their religious tradition. The terms Brahman and Atman, for example, early assumed importance as conceptions of ultimate reality in Upanishadic speculation.[5] In spite of their mystic character, Majumdar insists, the *Upanishads* formulated numerous conceptions which became fundamental for later thought.[6] The

[5] Radhakrishnan, *op. cit.*, pp. 137 ff.
[6] Majumdar, *op. cit.*, p. 34.

first was the idea of one all-powerful, all-pervading, self-existent, eternal, and incomprehensible *absolute* (*Brahman*) in which all creatures originate and dissolve. The Upanishads also formulated the idea that the miseries of life are due to our own action, or *karma*, and perpetuated by transmigration. This is quite different from the Vedic location of human ills primarily in nature or in the activities of spirits or demons. However, once the source of misery is located in human action, so, too, is the possibility of remedial action, and the Upanishads had faith in a salvation (*mukti*) possible through knowledge of Brahman. Purity of life and intensity of meditation were basic to achievement of such knowledge. In elaborating these ideas, the Upanishads laid the foundation for the dualistic formulations of later heterodox and orthodox thought.[7]

Underlying all other distinctions in Indian thought was the contrast between *dharma* and *mata*, the equivalent of Christian conceptions of ritualistic duty and doctrine, or dogma. *Dharma* meant order or law, both natural and moral law which in India, in contrast to the West, always tended to fuse. To the individual, *dharma* was manifest as duty; a man's total *dharma* was a system of eternal, unconditionally valid duties. *Dharma* comprised all things essential to a given style of life. *Dharma* differed for each social status; it constituted the order of caste and depended upon where the individual was born. *Mata*, on the other hand, was a system of teaching or beliefs. In Christian parallels, the sacraments are Christian *dharma*, but the doctrines of the Bible and teachings, such, for example, as those of St. Augustine or Thomas Aquinas, are Christian *mata*.

Hinduism recognized the necessity of both *dharma* and *mata*. To perform sacrifices, and to study the Vedas, were major elements of the *dharma* of the Brahman; his particular *mata* was the system of philosophy he accepted. The rules of caste constituted the *dharma* of the ordinary person, who also subscribed to some system of beliefs. One of the major differences between Hinduism and the other world religions was the emphasis on *dharma* rather than *mata*. It was quite possible for a father and a son to believe in very different deities without the slightest effect on caste standing. Sect adherence reflected the teaching of the particular *guru* under whom each studied. So long as the rules of one's *dharma* were rigidly maintained, there was, in fact, an amazing tolerance in Hinduism to varieties of individual belief. This stands in sharp contrast to Western experience, where bloody persecutions have at times followed the expressions of heretical opinion, even though the person who expressed them lived like a saint. On the other hand, in the West there has often been tolerance of quite iniquitous behavior, so long as the individual expressed the proper pious sentiments.

A second pair of related concepts of almost equal importance was the

[7] Max Weber, *The Religion of India*, trans. by Hans Gerth and Don Martindale (Glencoe, Illinois: The Free Press, 1958), pp. 21 ff.

atman and *maya*.[8] The concept *atman* expressed the inmost essence of man, sometimes conceived as equivalent to mind, spirit, soul, or consciousness. *Atman* was the Self, freed from all the distractions and shackles of the world. However, *atman* was not in man alone, but in the universe and all its objects. Brahma was *atman*. *Maya*, on the other hand, was the phenomenal world as it appeared and was experienced. Nature, the objects of ordinary experience, the ordinary desires, the person's physiological responses to the world, his sense experience, all were *maya*.

The ideas of *atman* and *maya* are somewhat similar to the Western *spirit* and *flesh;* in part they also suggest the dualism of mind and matter. However, in contrast to the West, the distinctions were consistently applied to the interpretation of everything. Moreover, while the West has usually conceived of matter as real, and mind as epiphenomenal, with some noteworthy exceptions, the Hindu tendency is to reverse the order of reality—*atman* is real; *maya* is illusory.

A third powerful dualism in Indian thought is that between *karma* and *mukti*.[9] *Karma* was responsibility for one's deeds. It suggests the Christian conception of moral consequences or the wages of sin. The concept of *karma* implied that every act of an individual was frought with fateful consequences for better or worse in the next life. Not to behave (*karma*) in terms of one's *dharma* was to incur a debt that must be paid. Salvation (*mukti*) was understood with reference to the *karma* doctrine. There are various avenues to *mukti*—ascetic practice, ritualistic conformity, study, and particularly the attainment of the proper self-knowledge. In the *Upanishads*, when a man knows his true self he obtains *mukti;* he becomes *Brahman*.

Closely related to the last dualism are the complementary concepts of *samsara* and *nirvana*.[10] Underlying a good portion of Indian thought was the very ancient and fairly widely diffused primitive belief that when a person dies his spirit enters various other living things or persons—which was called *samsara*. When linked to the concept of *karma*, the concept of transmigration of souls developed into the notion of a wheel of rebirth. Hence in terms of the total consequences of one's actions (*karma*), he is born in the next life in a state appropriate to his just dues. By negative *karma* the individual may be depressed in the social scale, being born as a slave or even as an animal or insect. Like a standardized curse is the formula that an individual may behave so badly in this life that in the next he will be born as a worm in the intestine of a dog. On the other hand, by meritorious behavior the individual may be born in a higher station in the next life. He may, in fact, even be reborn in one of a variety of heavens, in the presence of God or even as a god. But the wheel of birth rolls on endlessly, and after

[8] Radhakrishnan, *op. cit.*, pp. 151 f.; 184 f.
[9] *Ibid.*, pp. 245 f.
[10] *Ibid.*, pp. 146 f.

a time he will be born in some new form. *Nirvana* is the state achieved when one realizes salvation or *mukti.* It is an eternal state, conceived as one of pure undisturbed bliss secured by escaping from the wheel of rebirth.

The Heterodox Ferment in the Urban-Patrimonial Period

Vedic thought had developed within the framework of a rural society. It presupposed the primacy of the family in the social system and added powerful magical and religious reinforcement to it. Toward the close of the Vedic period, however, this was changing. The courts of the kings were growing at the expense of the courts of the nobles, and the city was emerging. The structures of rural society had to be modified radically to make this possible. The rural family in particular declined in importance.

In the society of the court and urban community, new institutions were taking up functions that the family was losing. If the kingdoms were to grow, it was necessary to weaken the monopoly of weapons held by the former nobles; it was also necessary to break the ordinary citizenry out of the context of semimanorial communities, incorporating them into more comprehensive structures. Meanwhile, the royal administration, the court, and the city were providing new opportunities for wealth and power. In the long run it would be difficult to deny to persons who had achieved power and wealth through these new routes the honors that normally accrued to the occupants of high social positions. The monopoly of the Brahmans over spiritual life and over various administrative and other positions requiring education could hardly be felt as other than restrictive by those persons.

The kinds of speculations which fill the Upanishads have the appearance of last ditch attempts to adapt Vedic religiosity to changing circumstances. However, they failed. By 600 B.C. the forces in Aryan society which were separating its urban-patrimonial from its rural, traditionally Aryan component had grown powerful enough to spawn new intellectual and social movements of its own. This has led Majumdar to characterize the period 600 B.C. to 300 A.D. as an age of revolt. The chief characters of the religious and intellectual trends in this period he summed up as follows:

> (1) Belief in a personal God to be worshipped with devotion (*bhakti*) rather than an impersonal Absolute (Brahman) to be realized through meditation and knowledge (*jñana*).
>
> (2) Broad practical view of everyday life, laying stress on morality and discounting the metaphysical discussions about God and soul. Emphasis is laid on the control of will and emotions, and the right actions of a man are regarded as the only means to his salvation.
>
> (3) A rational interpretation of all the problems of human life and an attempt to solve them by a coordinated system based on analytical reasoning.
>
> (4) Aversion to mechanical sacrificial performances as detailed in the Brahmanas, and regard for the sanctity of animal life.[11]

[11] Majumdar, *op. cit.*, p. 35.

The revolt of the heterodoxies was, in part, a revolt of new social strata against the monopolies of the Brahmans and their sponsors.

Materialism

Though the main work of an ancient system of Indian materialism, the *Brhaspati Sutra* (600 B.C.), is not available, this philosophy achieved sufficient importance to be mentioned in the Epics, in the *Dialogues of Buddha*, and in the *Bhagavadgita.*[12] The position must be reconstructed from the statements by thinkers critical of it.

The materialistic position is called *Carvaka*, after the name of its founder, and *Lokayata* on the basis of its view that only the physical world (*loka*) exists. The materialists believed that only what was arrived at by means of perception could be accepted as existing; the testimony of others was of no value. As sense perception was the only valid basis of knowledge, matter was the only true form of reality. Reality was made up of four elements: earth, water, fire, and air. The usual Indian fifth element (mind) was denied. Intelligence was thought to be a modification of the four elements, and was destroyed when the elements from which it arose were dissolved. Neither souls nor gods existed. Consciousness existed only as a product of the concatenation of the elements of the living body, which it could not survive. Feeling also arose as a characteristic of the physical body. Pleasure and pain were the central facts of life and the only legitimate foundation of ethics. The postulates of religion, god, freedom, and immortality were illusions. In nature there was no distinction between good and evil; vice and virtue were relative to pleasure and pain and to social conventions.

In its skepticism and urbanity, in its denunciation of the Vedas as humbug and the priests as charlatans, in its refusal to put anything in the place of the religious views it denied, *Carvaka* was clearly not a view of priests. It was an emphatic demonstration of the existence of thoroughly secularized intellectual circles in India at this time.

Jainism

As was noted earlier, Jainism found support in non-Brahman strata. Like the school of *Carvaka*, the Jains did not believe in God; to some extent the apotheosized founders (*Tirthankaras*) of the faith who have achieved liberation and have become free, perfect, omniscient, omnipotent souls, substituted for a belief in the gods.[13] The influence of the same intellectual current

[12] See Madhava Acrya, *Savadarsnaasamgraha*, trans. by E. B. Cowell and A. E. Gough (London: Kegan Paul, 1904); S. C. Chatterjee and D. M. Datta, *An Introduction to Indian Philosophy* (Calcutta: University of Calcutta, 1939), pp. 63 f.; M. Hiriyanna, *The Essential of Indian Philosophy* (London: George Allen & Unwin, 1949); pp. 57 f.; Radhakrishnan, *op. cit.*, pp. 277 f.

[13] See J. L. Jaini, *Sacred Books of the Jains* (Arrah, India: The Central Jaina Publishing Co., 1920); M. Hiriyanna, *op. cit.*, pp. 59 f.; Chatterjee and Datta, *op. cit.*, pp. 83 f.; Radhakrishnan, *op. cit.*, pp. 286 f.

which produced factors present in *Carvaka* perhaps accounts for Jain materialism. Though the Jains did not deny the existence of spirits, they accounted for them materialistically. This led Radhakrishnan to describe their philosophic position as a form of "pluralistic realism."

According to the Jains, the universe was made up of two ultimate realities: spirit (*jiva*) and nonspirit (*ajiva*). *Jiva*, which corresponds to the idea of *atman* or *purusa* in other schools, was the metaphysical principle underlying animate existence. The number of *jivas* was infinite. Union of *jiva* with matter constituted *samsara*. Knowledge was intrinsic to the *jiva*, hence there were two kinds of knowledge—inner knowledge of the *jiva* as such and empirical knowledge mediated by the senses.

Ajiva was divided into *kala* (time), *aksa*, *dharma*, and *adharma* (space), *pudgala* (matter). Both time and space were thought to be infinite (though there were cycles in time and space divided into two: space where movement was possible and where it was not). Matter possessed color, flavor, odor, touch. Sound was a mode rather than a quality of matter. Matter was eternal, consisting of atoms.

Reality was characterized by birth, death, and persistence. Though eternal in itself, the particular modifications of reality were not. Change was produced by the fact that though collocations of qualities appeared to remain unchanged, new qualities were generated, and old ones were destroyed. At every moment qualities were coming into or going out of existence. The changes of the physical world were traced to atomic aggregations which gained and lost qualities.

According to one basic doctrine of Jainism (*syadvada*, the relativity of knowledge), the universe was relative to one's point of view. The total number of possible points of view were infinite, for reality admits all predicates. Every proposition was conditional, all absolute affirmations and denials were false. The best that could be done was to approach a true statement through a series of partial ones; this provided the sevenfold formula:

1. Maybe, is
2. Maybe, is not
3. Maybe, is and is not
4. Maybe, is inexpressible
5. Maybe, is and is inexpressible
6. Maybe, is not and is inexpressible
7. Maybe, is, is not, and is inexpressible.[13a]

In speaking of an object, Jainism demanded that the statement include its place, time, and state.

According to Jainism, things were in the first instance made up of gross

[13a] See A. L. Basham, *The Wonder That Was India* (New York: Grove Press, 1959), pp. 502–503.

matter, but there was also thought to be a subtle matter which was transformed into different kinds of *karma*. *Karma* was conceived to be a kind of sticky substance which filled all space. In its commerce with the world, the soul became variously obscured by it. This had fateful consequences, for the kinds of *karma* determine such things as the length of life, the peculiar body with its special qualities, nationality, caste, family social standing, and energy. *Karma* compelled the soul after death to assume some one rather than another body.

The essence of the soul, consciousness, cannot be destroyed. Freeing the soul from *karma* entanglements constitutes the primary task of religion. Jainism urged that this required special conduct, enlightenment, and faith. These were the three gems of Jainism. Right knowledge was knowledge of the principles of the religion and philosophy; right conduct was the application of this knowledge.

The five basic vows of the Jain were not to injure any living thing (*ahimsa*), not to utter falsehood (*satya*), not to steal (*asteya*), to lead a celibate life (*brahma-charya*), and to renounce the world (*sparigraha*). *Ahimsa* occupied the central place. Construed strictly, it led not only to renunciation of meat-eating, but to the avoidance of bringing death to any living thing. The correct Jain even objected to the destruction of plants and microscopic animals; he did not engage in any trade that might destroy living things; he swept the ground before him as he walked; he went about veiled lest he inhale insects; he refused meat and honey; and he did not eat fruits which might contain worms. Jainism recognized a twofold training, one for monks, the other for the laity. For the latter the vows had to be relaxed, and were called the lesser vows (*anu-vrata*). For example, while only continence was required of the layman, absolute renunciation was required of the monk.

With considerable skill Weber has traced the relation between the Jains and the wider community.[14] With painstaking casuistry the requirement was laid on the Jain monk to wander restlessly from place to place, living by begging in such a manner as to free himself from all *karma* engendering the actions of his clients. The Jain lay person, on the other hand, was only able to travel under the rigid supervision of the monks. Thus the monks rapidly developed a comprehensive general knowledge of the trade opportunities, routes of trade, and political conditions.

Meanwhile the various restrictions laid on monk and lay person alike rigorously limited the trades into which the Jain could engage. *Ahimsa*, for instance, was pushed to extremes. During the dark season the correct Jain could burn no lights which would destroy moths, nor kindle a fire that would kill insects. He had to strain water before boiling or drinking it. He went about with his mouth and nose covered with a cloth, and carefully swept every bit of earth with a soft broom before walking on it. He

[14] Weber, *op. cit.*, pp. 193 ff.

plucked his hair from his head by the roots, for fear that the use of scissors or razor would cut a louse in two. Such restrictions excluded the Jain from all industrial trades using fire or sharp instruments. Agriculture was completely out of the question. He was forced into urban administrative positions and into retail trade, where the rules of his order, as in the cases of some branches of Protestantism, transformed him into an industrious, honest, and reliable businessman.[15]

Buddhism

As in the case of Jainism, Buddhism represented an interpretation of the Upanishad doctrines.[16] While it was strongly disinclined to metaphysical speculation, it rested on an interesting metaphysic concerned with the traditional problems of the soul, the nature of reality, and the problem of knowledge.

The starting point of Buddhistic theory was similar to David Hume's analysis of self. Jainism had thought of the soul (*jiva*) as underlying the flux of sense experience. Buddhism reversed the relation. At any moment of experience we perceive a particular quality of heat or cold, light or shade, love or hatred, pain or pleasure. Buddha admitted the reality of these, but denied that they belong to an entity such as the self. A similar explanation was given of matter. Various sensations, size, color, weight, are usually assumed to refer to real things. However, we only experience these qualities, never some substance apart from them. This doctrine was described as *nairatyma-vada* (teaching of no-self).

At a later time, in a reputed conversation between Menander and Nagasena, the Buddhistic sage, the sage explained the meaning of the doctrine as follows:

> "Great king, hast thou come on foot or on a chariot?"
> "I do not travel on foot, sire: I have come on a chariot."
> "If thou hast come on a chariot, great king, then define the chariot. Is the pole the chariot? Are the wheels the chariot?"[16a]

Continuing in this fashion, the sage demonstrated that the chariot was not one of its parts nor the whole, but a mere label for the assembly. The self is also a pure label for a complex. Neither soul nor matter exists except as such temporary assemblies.

The ancient concepts of *rita* and *dharma* were reinterpreted to fit these suppositions. Since the chariot is neither its ingredients nor the sum of its parts, it was argued, it can only be the relation of the parts to each other.

15 *Ibid.*, pp. 199–200.
16 H. C. Warren, *Buddhism in Translations* (Cambridge: Harvard University Press, 1915); S. Radhakrishnan, *The Dhammapada* (London: Oxford University Press, 1954); F. L. Woodward, *The Minor Anthologies of the Pali Canon* (London: Oxford University Press, 1935).
16a T. W. Rhys Davids (tr.), *The Questions of King Milinda*, 2 vols., *Sacred Books of the East*, xxxv–xxxvi (Oxford University Press, 1890–94).

Similarly, the self arises as a relation between the elements of experience due to meaning or purpose. This unity of the self consists in ceaseless striving. The self is merely the form or order of change of experience, like the shape in a stream or a flame. The examples given by Buddha are somewhat similar to those of Heraclitus, though Buddha's conclusions were closer in some respects to those of the eighteenth century empiricists.

The real point of gravity in Buddha's doctrine, however, lay not in the elaboration of this view of the no-self, but in his use of it for the explanation of religious life. His primary aim was to account for the suffering of life, for all the waters of all the seas are not to be compared with the flood of tears which had flowed since the universe first was. Worldly pursuits cannot give man final happiness. Neither can a life of sensual indulgence or self-torture be the answer.

Evil was a product of ignorance of the fact that the self is the source of all suffering. The only reprieve from suffering was the negation of the self. The Four Truths concerned suffering, its origin, its removal, and the way to remove it. Suffering originated in ignorance. The steps in the appearance of suffering consisted of ignorance, of action, of consciousness, of names and forms, of the five senses, and of the mind together with its objects, of contact between the sense and objects, of sensation, of desire, of clinging to existence with its birth, rebirth, pain, old age, and death. Ignorance leads to desire, desire to activity, giving rise to rebirth and fresh desire. (The circle of *samsara*, the wheel of rebirth, was thus accounted for by the Buddhists.) Suffering can be eliminated only by the removal of ignorance via the eightfold path: right faith, right resolve, right speech, right action, right living, right effort, right thought, and right concentration. The discipline aspires to *nirvana* (blowing out, or annihilation).

As in the case of Jainism, the Buddhist system assumed a dual form: one for monks and one for the laity. Though an ascetic system for the monks, the ethical doctrine evolved a general conception of moral improvement. Teachings concerning noninjury, forgiveness of enemies, and friendliness to all men diffused outside the monastic structures. By playing down the importance of ritual, sublimation of moral principles and practice was under way. Buddhism found its point of gravity in the achievement of a kind of universal detached compassion: universal friendship, universal pity, and indifference to every type of preference for one's self, his friends, for enemies, or third parties.

It is not difficult to see why Buddhism was Jainism's most active competitor, for while appealing to the same groups it did not require from its adherents the kind of behavioral excesses that could appear quite unbecoming to an aristocrat or rich merchant: going unwashed, pulling out the hair by the roots, taking care not to injure a body louse. Moreover, the principle of *ahimsa* could lead the Jains to other types of excess. Hopkins observed that in almost every city of west India there were beast hospitals, where animals were kept and fed. Such a hospital, Pinjra Pol at Saurarashtra, Surat, supported five thousand rats.[17] Prominent social persons in an age of comparative secularism could easily react against such practices as undignified and even downright foolish. Moreover, Buddhism did not require from its laity the radical reorganization of behavior of Jainism. It was thus possible for Buddhist recruitment to outrun the Jains very rapidly. Buddhism, of course, also had the striking good fortune of a brilliant sponsor in Asoka. However, in the long run, because the reorganization of behavior demanded by Buddhism was relatively superficial, it was easily deposed in the land of its birth. On the other hand, Jainism, and still more completely Hinduism, involve such complete reorganizations of behavior that once they were established they were hard to uproot.

Bhagavatism

A fourth heterodox movement in this period, but later to be pulled within the framework of orthodoxy, was represented by the Bhagavata sect. Gautama Buddha and Vardhamana Mahavira were once thought to be legendary, though they are now admitted to be historical personalities. As yet there are still persons who doubt that Krishna-Vasudeva was a historical personage. Some have argued that he was a solar deity, a vegetation deity, and even a tribal deity.[18] However, recent research has left no doubt in the minds of numerous major scholars that Krishna-Vasudeva was a teacher deriving from the republican Kshatriya family known as Satvatas, of the famous Yadu or Yadava clan which played an important role in the activities of Vasudeva-Krishna as narrated in the epics and *Puranas*.[19]

The roots of Vishnu worship have been traced to sections of the *Rig-Veda*, where he is regarded as the greatest deity by one section of the Vedic Indians. In the *Rig-Veda*, Vishnu is identified with the sun and worshiped with sacrifice, devotion, and grace. Vishnu worship is characterized by the *bhakti* doctrine, which has been traced to the Upanishadic idea of fervent meditation, *upasana*, as the highest form of worship. Sircar maintains that the earliest reference to devotion to a personal god is traceable to Panini's *Ashtaghyayi*, which offers a rule for the formation of the word *Vasudevaka* in the sense of a person whose object of devotion, *bhakti*, is *Vasudeva*. This would indicate that *Vasudeva* was an object of such devotion, at least by the fourth century B.C. Moreover, since a reference to Krishna-Vasudeva has been traced to the *Chhandogya Upanishad*, this teacher must be located some time before the sixth century B.C.

Sircar argues that the Bhagavata religion was probably the development of sun worship. Only later, he believes, was a pastoral character attributed

[17] Hopkins, *op. cit.*, p. 296.
[18] Majumdar, *op. cit.*, p. 37.
[19] D. C. Sircar, "Vaishnavism," *The History and Culture of the Indian People*, ed. by R. C. Majumdar (Bombay: Bharatiya Vidya Bhavan, 1953), p. 532.

to Krishna, perhaps partly developed out of the Vedic legends about Vishnu, called *gopa* or protector of cows in the *Rig-Veda.* Also the mythology of the cowherd Krishna may have been related to the fact that the Yamuna region was famous for its cows.

Sircar believes that the first step in the evolution of Vishnuism was identification of Vasudeva-Krishna with the Vedic Vishnu. This had been accomplished by the time of the *Bhagavadgita.* Still later he believes a deified sage or hermit named Narayana was identified in the combination of Vasudeva-Krishna-Vishnu.

> The Bhagavata religion, which originated with the Yadava-Satvata-Vrsni people [of the Mathura area appears to have] spread to western India and northern Deccam with the migration of the numerous Yadav tribes. . . . Vasudeva was probably deified, at least partially, and worshipped by his own people as early as the age of Panini. . . . It cannot be ignored that the identification of Vasudeva with the highest god is not recognized in the earlier parts of the *Mahabharata.*[20]

Buddhism, Jainism, and Bhagavatism were the three major heterodox religions that arose at this time. In his comments about social similarities in the circumstances of their origin, Majumdar has isolated some of the sociological factors:

> All these three constitute a revolt against, or at least a decided break from, the accepted religious creeds of the day. And it is not perhaps a mere accident that all of them originated in the free atmosphere of independent republican clans, the Sakyas, the Licchavis, and the Satvatas. The history of the world has again and again demonstrated that nurseries of political freedom often tend to develop freedom in the domains of thought and beliefs. Besides all the three clans lived in regions which may be described as the outer fringe of the stronghold of Vedic culture and therefore comparatively free from its rigid control.[21]

The Bhagavata sect substituted a personal god for an abstract universal soul. Since Vasudeva-Krishna could only be worshiped with intense personal devotion, the efficacy of sacrifice, of asceticism, and even of abstract knowledge were moved to second place to devotion (*bhakti*). While Buddhism did not acknowledge a personal god or any god at all, hence setting aside both *bhakti* and metaphysical abstract knowledge, it went even further in opposition to sacrifice, asceticism, and upholding the sanctity of animal life. Buddhism also rejected the Vedas and divine revelation, and opposed the emerging caste system. The Jains accepted every individual soul as eternal, but viewed asceticism as the essential means of salvation. They opposed the Upanishadic view that each individual soul is ultimately merged into the world soul. The Bhagavata sect was therefore the most conservative of the three heterodox religions.

[20] *Ibid.*, pp. 116–117.
[21] Majumdar, *op. cit.*, p. 38.

The Orthodox Counterattack

Philosophies, such as that of Carvaka, and even more the religions of revolt—Jainism, Buddhism, and Bhagavatism—were strongest in the eastern areas of northern India in the seventh and sixth centuries B.C. The strongholds of Brahmanical culture to the west, however, were adjusting internally to changing conditions. As Majumdar sees it, the revolutionary sects were a major factor in shattering the complacent dogmatism of Brahmanism. The orthodox leaders attempted to meet the threat by codifying and systematizing their religious and philosophical doctrines and by accepting elements from the heterodox systems which would permit them to struggle on a more equal footing.[22] Among the major developments which Majumdar traces to the period of orthodox reaction (400 to 200 B.C.) were the winning of the Bhagavata sect for the orthodox faith by identification of Krishna with the Vedic god Vishnu, popularization of the remodeled religion and philosophy by means of epics such as the *Ramayana* and the *Mahabharata*, and the formulation of the six systems of philosophy—Nyaya, Vaisesika, Samkhya, Yoga, Purva-Mimamsa, and Vedanta. This left only Jainism and Buddhism outside the fold.

The *Mahabharata* relates the events of a great war presumably fought in the twelfth century B.C.[23] The *Ramayana* deals with the conflicts between the natives and the Aryans in the Vedic period. The orthodox concern with social conduct and politics during the time of the epics is revealed in *The Law of Manu* and Kautilya's *Arthasastra*, a treatise on the sciences of economics and politics.[24]

The appearance of the *Bhagavadgita* and *Mahabharata* at this time (500 B.C.) in India bears comparison with the appearance of authoritative Athenian texts of Homer in the second half of the sixth century B.C. Homer, too, celebrated early events in the history of the people. The epics of the Greeks also served political and social purposes—in this instance insuring Athenian leadership of the league of Greek cities. The Indian epics in part served the purpose of bolstering the unity of traditional Brahmanism in the face of the heterodoxies. In the case of the *Mahabharata* there was deliberate seeking of popular appeal to counteract the use of the vernacular by Buddhism.

The *Bhagavadgita* accepts the cult of the Vedas and in some measure elaborates the Upanishadic teaching of absolute Brahman. However, it also presents a theistic interpretation of a god at once transcendent and individual. New deities, particularly Siva, Sakti, and Vishnu, were elevated to importance beside the older Vedic gods. Devotion (*bhakti*) to a personal god

22 *Ibid.*, p. 39.

23 Radhakrishnan, *op. cit.*, p. 478.

24 S. Radhakrishnan (trans. and editor), *The Bhagavadgita* (New York: Harper & Bros., 1948); *The Mahabharata*, trans. by Pratap Chandra Ray (Calcutta: Bharata Press, 1890); *The Laws of Manu*, trans. by G. Buhler: *Sacred Books of the East* XXV (Oxford: Clarendon Press, 1886); *Kautilya's Arthasastra*, trans. by R. Shamasastry (Mysore: Wesleyan Mission Press, 1923).

was advanced as a primary religious means. The orthodox social code was elaborated with its four aims: righteousness, wealth, worldly enjoyment, and spiritual freedom. The four states of life (student, householder, forest dweller, and ascetic) were described. The four castes (priest, warrior, trader, and worker) were visualized as comprehending the social world. The world was visualized as the stage for a struggle of good and evil. The paths (*yogas*) to salvation were knowledge, devotion, asceticism, and work. Thus the epics were compounds of new and old elements. The integration of the older forms of Brahmanism with new popular themes was under way.

The *Laws of Manu* have been dated variously from 200 B.C. to 500 A.D. It is perhaps most accurately dated after the latest epic.[25] As already noted, according to the orthodox position the four aims of human life are righteousness, wealth, enjoyment, and spiritual freedom. The *Laws of Manu* deal with the rules of righteousness, or with *dharma*. Though it discussed philosophical doctrines, its primary aim was to support the customs and conventions transmitted from the past. *Manu* held the four caste divisions of society to be absolutely essential for social cooperation. By means of the castes each person performed the function for which he was best suited. The *Laws of Manu* was an important product of orthodox thought during the period when the heterodoxies were contending for dominance. The treatise reflects a considerable hardening of the caste system.

Kautilya's *Arthasastra*, like the *Laws of Manu*, represents a product of orthodox thinking at a time when heterodox rivalry was keen. It deals with wealth (material advantage or *artha*), one of the four orthodox aims of life. Kautilya, who had been a minister of the first Magadha emperor, developed an account of the law and administration of the empire; the work is dated 321–296 B.C. The theory was offered by Kautilya that wealth (*artha*) is the chief aim of life. The work is comparable to that of Machiavelli in its discussion of efficient administration, the selection of administrators, the principles of taxation, political economy, and military discipline. The state was conceived as established by the strong for the protection of the weak. Kautilya seems personally to have preferred an enlightened monarchy in which the king assumes responsibility for the welfare of his subjects. It is quite clear that orthodox Hinduism was rising to meet the crises presented by the great heterodoxies, developing theistic interpretations of the Upanishads, social codes (for example, the *Laws of Manu*), and a political theory (for example, the *Arthasastra*) with which to combat the heterodoxies.

The Orthodox Systems

Under Asoka Buddhism became the official religion of nearly the whole of India, but long before this the counteraction of the orthodox Brahmans against heterodoxy was under way. Under such circumstances, it was almost inevitable that when other Indian dynasties arose they would look for sup-

[25] Radhakrishnan, *op. cit.*, pp. 515–516.

port from the elements of Hinduism that had been suppressed during the ascendancy of the heterodoxies. Moreover, from the standpoint of a ruler, Hinduism offered the possibility of a far more thorough pacification of the population than did the heterodoxies. Under the Sunga dynasty a direct counterattack on Buddhism by force began. In various ways and at later periods, foreign conquest operated the same way. Heterodox thought movements either disappeared (as did Carvaka and Buddhism in India) or were reduced to the status of minor sects and partly Hinduized (as was Jainism). The orthodox positions were rapidly codified into the famous six systems of orthodox Hinduism. Even in a superficial review, their sophistication is evident.[26]

Nyaya

Nyaya was a system of logic and disputation. It carried forward the problem of knowledge which in one form or another was raised by every body of thought since and including the *Upanishads*. The founder of Nyaya was said to be Gautama, who has been placed in the third century B.C. He was born at Gautamasthana, where a fair was held in his honor. Most of his life was said to have been spent in a hermitage with his wife. Most of the literature assembled in the name of Nyaya belongs to the post-Christian era.[27]

The primary purpose of reason, according to Nyaya, was salvation from a world of ignorance, misapprehension, and grief. It did not examine fundamental propositions, but developed a logic and epistemology in the conviction that if all error was destroyed only the truth would remain.

The means to right knowledge were four: perception, inference, comparison, and verbal testimony. Perception may be either determinate or indeterminate (offering direct and indirect knowledge about objects). Perception arises from contact of the sense with its object. The primary requirement of valid perception, if it is to produce knowledge, is that the object be clearly perceived. The name has nothing to do with the reality of an object. Inference is knowledge preceded by perception and using its materials. Comparison is knowledge of a thing derived from its similarity to another. Verbal testimony is the assertion of a reliable person.

The objects of right knowledge are: the soul, the body, the senses, intelligence, intellect, activity, faults, rebirth, pain, and release. The soul is recognized by the presence of desire, aversion, effort, pain, and knowledge. It is intangible and can be known only by verbal testimony or inference. The body is the site of motion and the object of pleasure and pain and the field of the soul's experience. The senses are the powers of smell, touch, taste,

26 See Chatterjee and Datta, *op. cit.*, pp. 185–455; Rene Guenon, *Introduction to the Study of the Hindu Doctrines*, trans. by Marc Pallis (London: Luzac & Co., 1945), pp. 177–296; F. Max Müller, *The Six Systems of Indian Philosophy* (London: Longmans Green, 1899); Radhakrishnan, *op. cit.*, Vol. II; Heinrich Zimmer, *Philosophies of India* (New York: Pantheon Books, 1951).

27 Radhakrishnan, *op. cit.*, Vol. II, pp. 36 f.

sight, and hearing, and are associated with the five elements: earth, water, fire, air, and ether. The objects of the senses are the qualities of odor, flavor, color, and sensation. The intellect is the capacity for reflection, inference, testimony, doubt, cognition, and memory.

Inference consists of the derivation of a conclusion from ascertained facts. The model syllogism illustrating correct inference contains a proposition (to be proved), a reason (vehicle of inference), an example (object of perception), an application (a comparison), and a conclusion. Thus:

1. The hill is on fire
2. Because it smokes
3. Whatever smokes is on fire as is a kitchen
4. This hill smokes
5. Therefore it is on fire.[28]

The elements of right reason include familiar examples (examples with which the average man and expert would agree) and tenets (dogmas resting on the authority of a school). The forms of reason include: confutation (establishing the character of a thing not known, by eliminating all alternatives), ascertainment (the removal of doubt by hearing both sides), and discussion (the adoption of one side of an argument and proving it to arrive at the truth). Spurious forms of reasoning include: controversy (gaining victory by quibbles) and cavil (mere attacks on the opposition). Both spurious forms of reasoning are useful for debunking pretenders. Among the fallacies of reason are: the erratic (reasons leading to more than one conclusion), the contradictory (a reason opposite the one to be established), equal to the question (*petitio principii*), and reasons which stand as much in need of proof as the proposition.

Universal propositions are reached, according to the school, by intuition, enumeration, and indirect proof. The school recognized three different kinds of causes—material, nonmaterial, and efficient.[29] The appearance of a plurality of causes was assumed to be due to defective analysis. Comparison depends upon the perception of a similarity between things, and involves knowledge of the object.

To Nyaya the individual self is a real substantive being possessing the qualities of knowledge, feeling, and desire, and differing from the body, the senses, and the understanding. It is unique though there is an infinite number of souls. Its cognition, however, cannot be self-evident, for there would otherwise be no possibility of doubt.

Vaisesika

According to the Vaisesika system, individuality arises from underlying realities (imperceptible souls and atoms). True knowledge is only possible

28 *Ibid.*, p. 75.
29 *Ibid.*, pp. 92 f.

by comprehending the properties of these eternal realities. The founder of Vaisesika, at least in its contemporary form, was said to be Kanada (atom-eater) or Kanabhuj or Kasyapa. Practically nothing is known about him or his personal life. He presumably lived in the third century B.C. Since atomic theories appear in the *Upanishads*, the position may be as old as Buddhism-Jainism (6th–5th centuries B.C.). However, Vaisesika is not mentioned by Kautilya, which would seem to put it after 300 B.C.[30]

Vaisesika developed a classification of objects which would be conceived, consisting of substance, quality, movement, generality, particularity, inference, and nonexistence. Qualities are found both in pluralities of objects and in individuals. The former are general, the latter are either permanent or transitory. In the course of time a distinction between these qualities developed in India somewhat similar to that between primary and secondary qualities in Western thought, the first inherent in things, the second in the act of perception.

All the phenomena of nature are accounted for in terms of nine fundamental realities: earth, water, fire, air, ether, time, space, soul, and mind. Matter is composed of infinitely small divisions not further divisible. Hence the components cannot be produced and destroyed. They have no magnitude; they are not visible. Extension and visibility are produced by combinations of atoms. At least two atoms must combine to create length, three to produce thickness. Very similar theories were held by the Pythagoreans in Greece.

Each type of atom was thought to possess inseparable qualities of flavor, form, and touch. The things of the world are identified by their peculiar combination of qualities. Earth has odor, flavor, form, and touch; water, flavor, form, and touch; fire has form and touch; air has touch. These are recognized by the senses. Ether is postulated to account for sound. *Kala* (time) is the force residing in things that accounts for change. It cannot be reduced to the basic qualities or to sound. Space must be postulated to account for orderly relations and position. *Atman*, the soul or self, is indicated by the breath, the movement of the eyelids, and the affectations, such as pleasure and pain. The soul is the substratum which accounts for memory and personality. Finally *manas* (free to think) is mind, mental power, intellect, understanding, consciousness, and will. The *atman* requires an instrument for perception; this is the mind (*manas*).

In accordance with his conception of atoms, Kanada maintained that at the level of the atoms the world exists forever, and cannot be created or destroyed.

Samkhya

Samkhya, which may be the oldest school of Hindu philosophy, represents a reaction to the idealistic monism of the *Upanishads*. The presumed

[30] *Ibid.*, pp. 177 f.

founder of Samkhya, Kapila, has been placed as early as the sixth century B.C. Tradition has it that though his father was a sage, he learned the rudiments of philosophy and the nature of the soul from his mother. He is supposed to have spent the latter part of his life on Sagara Island in the mouth of the Ganges. However, despite early antecedents, the position was pulled into final shape only in the post-Christian era.[31]

Like the others, the system was addressed to the problem of suffering which, according to the theory, proceeded from intrinsic, extrinsic, and supernatural causes. Release from suffering was obtained through right knowledge.

Samkhya developed a dualistic philosophy, positing two ultimate realities: spirit (*purusa*) and matter (*prakrti*). Cause and effect are merely the developed and underdeveloped aspects of one and the same process. Development consists in the unfolding of what is implicit. The processes of cosmic evolution may be summarized in terms of (1) that which is neither produced nor produces (cosmic spirit), (2) that which is not produced but produces (cosmic substance), (3) that which is produced but does not produce (cosmic intelligence), and (4) that which is produced and does not produce (cosmic mind).

Purusa, the animating principle of nature and the source of consciousness are frequently identified with Brahma, Vishnu, Shiva, and Durga. The existence of *purusa* is sustained by the argument that everything is produced for something else, hence there must be a spirit to use the products of cosmic substance. Since cosmic substance is composed of constituents, something must control the powers (*gunas*). Moreover, cosmic substance cannot account for experience, hence something else must. Finally, scriptures promise release which is only possible if something transcending cosmic substance guarantees it. *Prakrti* must be accepted on the grounds that nothing can come from nothing. Furthermore, since cause and effect are states of the same thing, they must be grounded in more ultimate substance.

The constituents of cosmic substance, the *gunas*, are three: *sattva guna* is the power that illuminates and is responsible for lightness and upward movement. It appears as fire. *Rajas guna* is exciting force responsible for motion and change. It appears as wind. *Tamas guna* is the restraining power of nature and the source of the downward pull of the earth. It is the cause of mass and inertia.

Before the objective manifestation of the world the *gunas* were in a state of equilibrium. When their balance was disturbed the phenomenal world appeared. The predominance of one or another *guna* defines the stages in cosmic evolution. Spirit and matter thus constitute the soul and substance of the universe; the one is the action, the other is the vehicle. The original polarity appears as consciousness and unconsciousness, subject and object, knower and known. The process of creation and dissolution unceas-

31 *Ibid.*, pp. 249 f.

ingly recurs in the rhythm of life and death. As a result of past action (*karma*), the great cosmic substance quickens, setting the world in motion.

The first product of the evolution of nature is cosmic intelligence (*mahat*), which appears out of the stress upsetting the equilibrium of cosmic substance. Individuality arises next, as variety develops out of harmony. In the state of consciousness that appears, the "I" is distinguished from "Not-I." Schopenhauer's "principle of individualization" makes such ideas familiar in the West. From this manifestation of *sattva guna* arises the *manas* (mind) the five organs of perception and five organs of action. From the manifestation of *tamas guna* arise the five fine elements from which the five gross elements are produced.

Purusa is the intelligent self for the experience of which nature evolves. *Purusa* is conscious; nature is unconscious, depending for its manifestations upon the light of consciousness, which depends on nothing else. Freedom is salvation from *prakrti*.

Yoga

Samkhya and Yoga were traditionally so closely bound that they are frequently treated together as, respectively, the theory and practice of a single system. Yoga differs from Samkhya in its insistence on behavioral discipline and its religious theism. The founder of Yoga was Patanjali, who elaborated very ancient conceptions into a system. There is no reliable information about him. He is assumed to have lived between the third century B.C. and the fourth A.D.[32]

Our ills arise from our own conduct, external nature, and supernatural powers, as was made familiar by Samkhya doctrine. Release from human bondage is achieved through nonattachment to the world and mental restraint. The method proposed by Yoga is described as the eightfold path: abstention (*yama*) and observance (*niyama*) are ethical preparations for self-control; posture (*asana*) and breath control (*pranayam*) discipline the body. *Pratyahara* is the withdrawal of the senses from their outward functioning. However, these are only preparations. Contemplation (*dharana*) and more profound contemplation (*samadhi*) are the crucial elements of *Yoga*.[33]

Yoga discipline seeks to reorient man's faculties which are habitually adjusted to the preservation of ordinary experience. The object is to concentrate the power of mind. There are several stages in achieving Yoga perfection, divided into a higher and a lower form: *samprajnata* and *asamprajnata samadhi*. In the former, consciousness (*buddhi*) continues to function though absorbed in the contemplation of a particular object. In the latter, consciousness disappears along with self-consciousness. In final form only *purusa* remains. There are three levels of life determined by pre-

[32] *Ibid.*, p. 349.
[33] *Ibid.*, pp. 353 f.

dominance of different *gunas: rajas, sattva,* and *yajna guna.* A person achieving the final stage of *Yoga* concentration at death attains complete absorption (*kaivalya*), in which *purusa* is related to a *buddhi* fully enlightened and perfect. Such a man lives in this world, but is not of it.

The general rules for Yoga purification practice are: the noninjury of all living things (*ahimsa*), nonstealing, absolute sexual restraint, rejection of anything not absolutely necessary, the practice of internal cleanliness, contentment of mind, bearing privation, remaining silent in speech. Yoga meditation is initially assisted by placing one's self in external circumstances, where disturbance is lacking. The Yogin assumes a prescribed posture, and fixes his mind on some object. Breath-control is practiced. As the Yogin develops, he attains miraculous power, but this is played down in Patanjali's account. The primary aim remains the disintegration of ordinary consciousness into its constituents and the achievement of *purusa.*

Mimamsa

Mimamsa, which specialized in the study of *dharma,* was founded by Jaimini in the fourth century B.C.[34] It is said that Jaimini was a pupil of Badarayana, founder of the Vedanta system. Mimamsa treats action as the essence of existence and the precondition of knowledge, happiness, and destiny. Right action is the prerequisite of spiritual life. Hence it sets out to examine the character of *dharma.* According to Mimamsa, *dharma* is an object distinguished by a command, and refers to anything which holds, maintains, and preserves. Metaphysically, it comprises the law of nature as well as the code of conduct which sustains the soul and permits it to fulfill its destiny.

Since the six means of knowledge employed by other systems are not infallible when dealing with the effects of ritual, Jaimini accepts as the true source of knowledge only verbal testimony based upon a magical conception of language. The words were thought to possess inherent power to convey eternal meanings. Teachings consist in knowledge derived from the words which serve as an infallible guide in the invisible realm of the spirit. Words are self-sufficient, and not dependent upon anything else for their meaning.

The problem of proof central to Nyaya was brushed aside. Jaimini attempts to refute various objections raised against the eternal character of the word. As against the view that the word is a product of verbal utterance, it is urged that it existed before the utterance. As against the idea that the word vanishes after it is pronounced, Jaimini urges that this applies only to the sound. The metaphysical reality of meaning was maintained against all objections.

Mimamsa took salvation rather than liberation as its goal. Salvation, it maintained, cannot be achieved by knowledge, for the soul must first exhaust its potentiality through action. It emphasized ethical rather than

[34] *Ibid.,* pp. 376 f.

philosophic correctness. Jaimini's purpose was essentially practical, to interpret the Vedic texts for purposes of religious observance. The contents of the Vedas were classified under injunctions, hymns, names, prohibitions, and explanatory passages. In view of the ever-increasing emphasis on ritual practice that was occurring, Mimamsa was in some ways the most influential of all the orthodox systems.

Vedanta

The *Vedantasutra* attempted to set forth the Upanishads in a consistent manner. Traditionally the *Vedantasutra* is attributed to Badarayana, whose dates range somewhere between 500 B.C. and 200 A.D.[35] Vedanta attempted to survey the existing Vedic knowledge, to sum it up, and to arrive at a view that resolved all conflicts. It was urged that the ultimate principle (*Brahman*) lies outside the ken of mind, and can be known only by intuition. Reason, however, can be used in other matters. A special case was made for the study of Vedanta as well as the Vedas, Upanishads, and other philosophic systems. The illumined mind depends on right discrimination (between eternal and noneternal, real and unreal), right disposition (indifference to the transitory and renunciation of desire), and right conduct (involving tranquility of thought, self-restraint, tolerance, endurance, faith and a balanced mental disposition, and right desire).

In its analysis of other systems, the *Vedantasutra* raised the question of the cause of primal motion, urging that the design of the world must presuppose a designer. In this, and against other systems, except Yoga, a theistic position was taken. However, the Vedanta system was so cryptic as to permit various interpretations ranging from monism through dualism to theism.

ORTHODOX HINDUISM AND THE CASTE SYSTEM

Long before the caste system hardened into final form and moved to the center of the stage as the primary form of the Indian community, an inner transformation of Hinduism was under way. The philosophic systems which claimed to be authoritative interpretations of Vedic literature from the Samhitas to the Upanishads were codified, tightened up, and put on as sound a methodological foundation as possible. Moreover, Hinduism was beginning to develop popular sects of its own to rival the popular heterodoxies.

Vishnuism

One of the major popular Hindu sects which paved the way for the rise of Neo-Brahmanism and the emergence of the caste system, Vishnuism, represented the winning of the Bhagavata sect to the cause of orthodoxy. The worship of Vasudeva as an object of *bhakti* goes back at least to the time of Panini (the fifth century B.C.), and was reported by Megasthenes at the end of the fourth century B.C. An account of the system appears in the

[35] See Radhakrishnan's arguments against this, *op. cit.*, pp. 432 f.

Narayana section of the *Mahabharata*. The *Mahabharata* itself was a primary foundation of popular Hinduism. The Bhagavata sect did not, like its more radical counterparts (Jainism and Buddhism), reject the authority of the Vedas and was more easily won to the side of orthodoxy.

> It was . . . a comparatively easy task to win over this school to the orthodox side. This was effected first by regarding Vasudeva as an *avatara* or incarnation of the Vedic god Vishnu, and secondly by the identification of Vasudeva with Narayana who came to be regarded as the supreme Being in the later Brahmanical period. It is worthy of note that the first point was not generally conceded, and the second had not taken place at all, when the *Bhagavad-Gita* was composed. Vishnu grew to be the supreme god in the epic age, and the identification of Vasudeva with Narayana and Vishnu completed the transformation of the *Bhagavata* religion as the great religion of the orthodox Hindus.[36]

Shivaism

The other great Hindu sect which had beginnings during the epic period was Shivaism. As in the case of Vishnuism, it was in part worked up out of ancient materials, particularly those centering in the Vedic Rudra. However, according to Mahadevan,[37] the rise of a sect honoring Shiva as the supreme god and having a philosophy and organization of its own, cannot be traced earlier than the Christian era. Shivaism was gradually put together out of a variety of elements. Megasthenes, as Greek envoy to Pataliputra around 300 B.C., described two Indian deities under the names of Hercules and Dionysus, who are generally identified with Krishna and Shiva respectively. From the evidence of the *Mahabharata*, it appears that Vishnuism and Shivaism had become more popular than other cults, and were beginning to divide the allegiance of great masses between them.[38]

The general character of the orthodox restoration of Hinduism in India and the changes being brought about in its course have been summarized with unusual compactness by Max Weber.[39] The restoration of Hinduism proceeded out of Kashmir as a two-sided process involving the decay of the heterodox religions and the stereotyping of caste ritualism along with the propagation of the classical Hindu sects (Vishnuism and Shivaism), dating from the previous period. Though elements of the Brahmanical restoration were already manifested in the final editions of the epics, this was hardly the motive of the epics. It did constitute the primary motive of the Purana literature. The Puranas were not composed by ancient bards, but by temple priests and mendicant monks. The Puranas, as Weber sees them, were organized eclectically and crammed with the teachings of particular sects. However, Weber notes that the epics, particularly the *Mahabharata*, became

[36] Majumdar, *op. cit.*, p. 42.
[37] T. M. P. Mahadevan, "Shivaism," in R. C. Majumdar, editor, *The History and Culture of the Indian People* (Bombay: Bharatiya Vidya Bhavan, 1953), p. 453.
[38] *Ibid.*, p. 457.
[39] Weber, *op. cit.*, pp. 291–298.

a kind of interconfessional, ethical paradigm recognized by all great sects.[40]

During the orthodox restoration, the personal gods, Vishnu and Shiva, who, though known of old, acquired a new importance. Moreover, the sects with hierarchical organizations which characterize medieval and contemporary Hinduism arose. The content of Hinduism was also changed. While ancient Brahmanism had been elaborated in accordance with the requirements of cultivated intellectuals who either ignored or eliminated orgiastic and emotional religious and magical practices, in *tantra* magic, folk religious practices were introduced into Brahmanical literature. The *tantra* writings were even viewed by many as the fifth Veda. Weber described the *tantra* writings as follows:

> *Tantra*-magic was originally a form of orgiastic-ecstasy called forth through common indulgence of the five *nukara* (in later terminology known as the "holy circle" *puruabhishaka*) the five things beginning with the letter "M": *maida*, alcohol; *mamsa*, meat; *matsya*, fish; *maithura*, sexual intercourse; *mudra*, holy finger gestures (presumably originally pantomimes). The most important was alcohol bound up with sexual orgies, and next, the bloody sacrifice beside the concluding meal. The goal of orgy was doubtless ecstatic self-deification for magical purposes. He who has attained possession of god, *Bhairava* or *Vira*, has magical power. He has united with the feminine creative power of *sakti*, which later appears under the names of Lakschmi, Durga, Devi, Kali Sana, etc., represented by a naked woman eating meats and wine (*Bhairavi* or *Nayika*).[41]

One of the continuous dramas of the restoration was the adaptation of ancient Hinduism to folk elements of many sorts. The Vedas, for example, despised the phallus (the *lingam* symbol, a combination of male and female genital parts) cult. When Hinduism received the symbol and its attendant sexual orgiasticism, it also, to the degree that it remained orthodox, carried out an extensive sublimation of its cultic sexual practices.

During the amalgamation of ancient Hinduism with such popular cults, ancient feminine fertility spirits were often received through the device of elevating them to the status of wives of Brahmanical gods: Lakshmi was made the bride of Vishnu; Parvati of Shiva, Sarasvati (as patroness of lovely music and writing) of Brahma.[42] Similarly, in receiving a folk element, such as demons, the normal mode of reception was identifying the folk spirit with a Hindu god.

A two-sided modification accompanied the process of adjustment to popular religious practices. Hinduism was modified by receipt of popular religious forms. The popular religious practices, on the other hand, were, whenever possible, sublimated and rationalized. When, for example, the Brahmanical reception of the feminine fertility goddess of the Sakta sect, sublimation of the one-time sex orgy was turned into meditative worship of

[40] *Ibid.*, p. 293.
[41] *Ibid.*, p. 295.
[42] *Ibid.*, p. 296.

the holy circle which took the place of the feminine sexual organs.[43] However, Weber urges, distinguished Brahmans continued to look askance at the accommodation to popular elements, even though they, too, had to adapt themselves to the folk cults. Thus, during the course of the Brahmanical restoration, there were to be found different states of cryptoerotic sublimation along the way to complete ascetic reversal of sexual orgiasticism.[44]

As the caste system was clamped down on Indian society in a manner somewhat suggestive of the bureaucracy of China in the imperial period, the trends toward urbanism were reversed. Comparable to the clans and peasant villages of China were the castes in India. Comparable to Confucianism and Taoism in China were the systems of orthodox Hinduism in India. In India the relativizing of ethics and the organic conception of society were carried to their extreme consequences until a given way of life, while absolutely binding on one caste, had no bearing whatsoever on another, and the only way of transforming one's social station was through exemplary religious conduct and the wheel of rebirth. The orthodox philosophies thus supplied the metaphysical legitimation of the caste system in the course of the new fusion of social and religious elements into a vast organic whole.

INDIAN THOUGHT AND CIVILIZATION

There is general agreement among Indian and Western scholars that the two major reference points of Indian civilization are the social system of caste and peculiarities of its religion. As Ruthnaswamy phrases it, "Next to caste and the society which made it, religion filled the largest place in the history of the individual . . . in India."[45] Elsewhere he argued:

> "Of the three powers–state, religion, and culture–which according to Burckhardt form the theme of history, religion and culture fill much the larger part of ancient Indian history. The political history of the Hindu period may be written out in a page or two. . . . Nor is there a history of civilization . . . for civilization has to deal with the customs and institutions that produce a refined social life and manner. It is produced by and in cities, and in ancient India, cities were scarce."[46]

While all people have a society and a religion, in India they have been distinctive. The religious essence of Hinduism has been unique as was its social system of caste, unique not in the sense that it contains elements not found elsewhere, but in the sense that it carries tendencies present in every society to an unusual kind of logical conclusion. In the caste system class and status differences were transformed into the sole reference points of styles of life which were then religiously closed. Then the whole of society was organized into a system of caste-communities ranked with respect to

[43] *Ibid.*, p. 298.
[44] *Ibid.*, p. 298.
[45] Mariadas Ruthnaswamy, *India from the Dawn* (Milwaukee: The Bruce Publishing Co., 1949), p. 47.
[46] *Ibid.*, p. 64.

one another and in terms of social distance from the Brahman caste. In Hindu religion world-fleeing individualistic salvation-striving was developed to its ultimate logical conclusions in terms of an array of specific religious beliefs. The distinctive features of Indian religious thought, in contrast to the religious thought of Western civilization, has been formulated by Bharataratna Bhagavan Das as follows:

> The Semitic mind is preoccupied with the power aspect of God and, hence, the constant dread of offending His majesty and the need of intercession through prophets to make peace with God play such a large part in the Semitic religious consciousness. The Indian mind was latterly turned more inward and was, so to say, afraid of the blandishments of nature; it felt the greater need of self-discipline and indifference to the attractions of sense for realizing the inner Self. It is these that have given the distinctive twist to the Indian religious mind resulting in the abnegation of the lower self and reliance on the higher Self. Each man has been called upon to fight his lonely battle with the solicitations of the flesh and to conquer his lower self almost unaided. Buddhism, Jainism, Samkhya, Yoga—all exhort the individual to be self-reliant in his spiritual struggles, to avoid the bondage caused by evil action, and to resist the temptation of even a pleasurable heavenly existence, where the senses are regaled by agreeable enjoyments. There is no spiritual advancement in heaven as held by many types of theism.
>
> The boldness of the creed of self-help has proved baffling to those who have been brought up in the belief that at every step the helping hand of God is indispensable for the attainment of spiritual heights. . . . The Indian mind . . . posited the impersonal Brahman that could be contemplated and realized but not loved or reverenced in the ordinary sense. . . . From this absolutistic position the Indian mind has drawn the logical conclusion that everywhere the universal Consciousness is present, images are not expected, and that therefore all the earth is equally sacred, and all souls are identical in essence through their common identity with Brahman.[47]

One consequence of the joint operation of the caste system and the peculiar structure of Indian religious interpretations was to fasten an extreme form of organic conception of society on India and to bring about an unusual relativization of ethic and outlook. Weber observes that apart from a few absolute ritualistic prohibitions, such as the killing of cows, there was no universally valid social ethic that obtained for all classes, only a compartmentalization of social ethic along the lines of caste and status. The idea of *karma* (as the compensation for previous deeds) not only explained the caste organization (every person was in this life born into a situation in accord with the merits and demerits of his actions in a previous life), but the rank order of all animals, humans, and divine beings. From this standpoint of ethical relativism, there was even a vocation *dharma* for thieves, robbers, and prostitutes, as well as for kings and Brahmans. Extreme conservatism

[47] Bharataratna Bhagavan Das, "Introduction," to *The Cultural Heritage of India*, Vol. IV, *The Religions*, ed. by Haridas Bhattacharyya (Calcutta: The Ramakrishna Mission, 1956), pp. 27–28.

toward existing social arrangements was simultaneously established, for though all men have equal opportunities for ascent, it cannot be in this life, but only through rebirth when they rise and fall in the scale of beings in terms of the principles of *karma*.

These doctrines, Weber notes, eliminate any possible conception of original sin, for no absolute sin can exist. Only ritual offenses against the *dharma* of the particular caste are possible. Moreover, the concept of natural law is impossible. The social critical implications of a concept of some natural equality of men, either by nature or before a superworldly god that could be turned into a device for social criticism, was out of the question.

> It excluded forever the rise of social criticism, of rationalistic speculation, and abstractions of natural law types, and hindered the development of any sort of idea of "human rights." Animals and gods, at least, in consistent elaborations of doctrine, were only different, *karma*-conditioned incarnations of souls, thus common "rights" were obviously out of the question and could exist for these beings as little as common "duties." The concepts "state" and "citizen," even of "subject," did not appear. Only status *dharma* was recognized—the rights and duties of kings and other estates to themselves and others.[48]

At the same time, the extreme relativization of the social ethic permitted any given social stratum to develop whatever activities were thought peculiar to it (its *dharma*), with complete inner freedom from considerations arising in other spheres. So, for example, the *dharma* of the Kshatriya was war, protection, and political administration. Weber notes that Indian princes were able to practice naked machiavellianism without any objections from the kind of political ethic which arises from various forms of ethical universalism and natural right. Since the *dharma* of the prince was to wage war for the sole purpose of attaining power, he was free to destroy his opponents by any kind of cunning, fraud, or unknightly ruse. "All political theory was a completely oral technology of how to get and hold power."[49]

Until such time as the trends in Indian society and religion were to clamp the caste system on society and a popularized religiosity, consisting of a complex system of compromises between the old literary culture of refined aristocratic Brahmans and the orgiastic-ecstatic religious elements of the masses, the cultural *milieu* of India was not unreceptive to major developments in the sciences, letters, and arts. The great creative period of Indian civilization in these fields was the time of struggle between the heterodox and orthodox forces in India's urban, patrimonial-state period.[50]

In this time not only was the philosophic literature systematized and developed, but the *Dharma-sutras* and *Dharma-sastras* were written, laying the

[48] Weber, *op. cit.*, pp. 144–145.

[49] *Ibid.*, p. 146.

[50] See M. A. Mehendale, "Language and Literature," in R. C. Majumdar, editor, *The History and Culture of the Indian People* (Bombay: Bharatiya Vidya Bhavan, 1951), pp. 243–286.

foundation of modern Hindu law and customs. The most significant of ancient India's literary efforts, the epics, were completed; they were to exercise a major influence on Indian society and letters for centuries. Similar advances were made in the drama and in poetry:

> The dramas of Asvaghosha are only fragmentary, and those of Bhasa are no doubt thrown into the background by later masterpieces of Kalidasa and Bhavabhuti, but the *Mrichchhakatika* of Sudraka has ever remained popular on account of its variety of incidents and quick dramatic appeal. The poems of Asvaghosha, though not widely read these days, had strength enough to influence the diction and incidents in the works of Kalidasa.[51]

Moreover, Mehendale maintains that the achievements of this period in many departments of science remain unsurpassed until modern times:

> There did not appear at a later stage any grammarian who had the critical acumen of Panini or the remarkable observation of Patanjali; and whatever the merits or demerits of the *Arthasastra*, no work of a later period has been able to oust it from the high position adorned by it in the branch of polity. Similarly in medicine most of the important works were written in this period. Important works were written on astronomy, the knowledge of which was considerably advanced by contact with the western world.[52]

As the multiplicity of cultural forms cast up by the creativity of the urban, patrimonial period were being brought into a civilizational synthesis in which the caste system and neo-orthodox Hinduism were the central points, its literature, art, and architecture came to be dominated by religion to an unusual degree. "Religion," Ruthnaswamy observes, "dominated Hindu culture. Its literature was sacred scripture."[53] The epics, *Mahabharata* and *Ramayana*, he observes, are filled with the activities of *rishis* and *gurus*, and centered in matters of religion, philosophy, and morality to a degree strikingly different from the *Iliad* and *Odyssey*. The drama of ancient India, he maintains, was religious in origin. It did not center in social problems or the contests of strong men or the struggle of man with fate or in the romance of love or the beauties of nature; the worship of God was its subject. "Very little secular literature hails from ancient India."[54]

Hindu architecture, he observes, is first and last temple architecture. There are few notable domestic buildings or feudal castles, royal palaces, town halls, colleges, or university buildings. Moreover,

> . . . the excessive decoration and ornamentation, the tier upon tier of gods and goddesses that they pressed on the *gopuras* (entrance towers) and the *vimanas* (*sanctum sanctorum*), on the walls and pillars of these temples, were the very fantasia of religion. Its popular polytheism . . .

51 *Ibid.*, pp. 277–278.
52 *Ibid.*, p. 278.
53 Ruthnaswamy, *op. cit.*, p. 60.
54 *Ibid.*, p. 61.

> and its aristocratic pantheism . . . the colossal size of the temples, the mixture of man and animal in the sculptured figures, the welter of ornamental flora, and the confusion between the human and the divine, between sense and spirit, are characteristic of Hindu art.[55]

Ruthnaswamy maintains that Indian music and the dance also have religious origin. Apart from the folk and tribal music, vocal and instrumental music originated in the temples. "Like most religious music, the Gregorian, for instance, it is homophonic, simple melody sung by a single voice. The dance in India, too, had its stage in the temple."[56] For example, the Radha-Krishna dance sequence which may have originated as a pastoral dance expressing the love of the cowherd Krishna with the Gopis or shepherd girls is interpreted as the mystical approach of the soul to God.

> There is no negation. All is harmonized. All the forces of life are grouped like a forest, whose thousand waving arms are led by Nataraja, the master of the Dance. Everything has its place, every being has its function, and all take part in the divine concert. . . . Whereas in the West, cold, hard logic isolates the unusual, shutting it off from the rest of life into a definite and distinct compartment of the spirit, India, ever mindful of the natural differences in souls and in philosophies, endeavors to blend them into each other, so as to recreate in its fullest perfection the complete unity. The matching of opposites produces the true rhythm of life. Spiritual purity may not shrink from allying itself with sensual joy, and to the most licensed sexualism may be joined the highest wisdom.[57]

SUMMARY

The three major periods of community formation in ancient India were the early Aryan quasi-feudal conquest community, the urban, patrimonial-state period, and the system-of-caste communities.

The four major hypotheses which have guided this study are borne out by the materials from Indian thought. These hypotheses are: (1) the creative epochs of mankind are periods of community destruction and formation; (2) this creativity is qualitatively shaped by the conditions of local time and place; (3) the periods of the maturity of communities are times when the civilization comes into synthesis and the amounts of creativity decline; and (4) the standard of truth shifts from intrinsic to extrinsic grounds as between creative and conservative epochs.

The conquest community corresponds to the first period of Vedic thought. Vedic thought was this-worldly, naturalistic, and poetic. Its attitude toward life was basically joyous and optimistic. A theodicy of suffering was absent as well as notions of recompense in heaven or hell or of complex consequences for action in an eternal cycle of rebirth.

[55] *Ibid.*, pp. 61–62.
[56] *Ibid.*, p. 63.
[57] Romain Rolland, "Foreword" to *The Dance of Siva* by Ananda Coomaraswamy (London, 1924), p. iii.

The period of urbanism and patrimonial-state formation was a time of much community transition, when the semifeudal conquest communities broke down, when urban communities arose, and when these, in turn, were in process of transforming into the communities of caste. It was also the major period of creative innovation of India. It was in this period that the great heterodoxies were born—Carvaka, Jainism, Buddhism, and Bhagavatism. It was also the period of the orthodox counterattack on the heterodox faiths, in the course of which Carvaka was thrust aside and Bhagavata religiosity was won to the cause of orthodoxy. Moreover, in addition to Vishnuism and Shivaism, which arose as orthodox sects, both of which represented theistic forms of Hinduism, the six orthodox systems of thought—Nyaya, Vaisesika, Samkhya, Yoga, Mimamsa, and Vedanta—were brought to completed form. During the same period there were also brisk developments in literature, the arts, and science.

During the period of the rise and crystallization of the caste system, the most important event was the process of accommodation of the rich intellectual heritage of the Brahmans to the orgiastic-ecstatic culture of the Indian masses. Neo-Hinduism differed from its ancient aristocratic counterpart in its accommodations to popular culture. Its bearers, too, differed from the aristocratic house chaplains and *gurus* of early times, becoming apotheosized miracle workers viewed by their followers as living saviors. In the same period, in contrast to the reliance on intrinsic standards of truth as illustrated by the emergence of the Nyaya system of logic, recourse was to such institutional devices as decisions of the caste *panchayat* or the unquestioned decisions of the *guru* or the *pandit*.

The unique shaping of the course of Indian developments has been accounted for in many ways. One of the frequent arguments in the past has been based on the nature of the Indian landscape and climate. Ruthnaswamy attempted to account for its peculiar course by two factors: the contact with the Dravidians by the Aryans, and the natural landscape of India. He argues that while at first it appeared that the religion of India was developing into a belief of one supreme being, this was modified by contact with the Dravidians, which brought with it ideas of the transmigration of souls and a world of spirits. However, he feels that the real turning point came from the Indian climate and landscape. The Indian mind was turned from its theistic tendencies by the experience of "coming from the thin air of the hills of Kubulistan and the simple, straightforward plains of the Punjab." The Aryan conqueror was impressed by "the rich, varied, thick, overwhelming vegetative forest life of the valleys of Madhyadesa." The philosophy that emerged was developed by the solitary *rishis* of mountains and forests. "The Hindu philosophy of life," he argues, "was a forest philosophy. It was influenced and determined by the thick, confused, and mixed growth of vegetation in an Indian forest."[58]

[58] Ruthnaswamy, *op. cit.*, p. 50.

There is no evidence that social behavior is ever affected by nature in any such direct and immediate way. Besides, India was quite capable in its urban period of producing a philosophy like Carvaka which certainly represents about all in urbanity, skepticism, and empiricism that one could wish. There are far too many evidences that the uniqueness of Indian civilization was determined by response to the peculiarities of its social experience to require resort to climatic or geographic determination.

The caste system and neo-orthodox Brahmanism represent a comparatively complete synthesis of a variety of cultural phenomena arising from social historical peculiarities and a variety of adjustments to different natural environments. Early India's social and cultural history was marked by the number of cultural variations that entered into consideration: the sharpness of the cultural discontinuities (as between the Indus Valley civilization and the Aryan civilization that followed it) and the sharpness of the antagonisms (such as those between the Aryans and Dasyus).

The variety of Indian environments undoubtedly played a role in Indian socio-cultural developments, for it was not easy to invent any single set of institutions capable of solving problems in such very different types of environments. Moreover, institutional variety specifically means that the basic problems of social life are being solved in different ways. The problem of unification grows more complex when there is a plurality of competing centers of dominance. Under the circumstances of the time, India could not have achieved unity, as did China, with an imperial system. The caste system seems to have been one of the few ways by which many varied social tensions could have been mediated by a single social order without the mass liquidation of major parts of them.

SELECTED BIBLIOGRAPHY

Bhattacharyya, Haridas, editor, *The Cultural Heritage of India* (Calcutta: The Ramakrishna Mission, 1958).

Coomaraswamy, Ananda, *The Dance of Siva* (London: Simpkin, Marshall, Hamilton, Kent & Co., 1924).

Majumdar, R. C., editor, *The History and Culture of the Indian People* (Bombay: Bharatiya Vidya Bhavan, 1953).

Radhakrishnan, S., *Indian Philosophy* (New York: The Macmillan Co., 1922).

Raza, Hamid, *The Cultural Role of India* (Anakari, Lahore: Minerva Book Shop, 1944).

Ruthnaswamy, Mariadas, *India from the Dawn* (Milwaukee: The Bruce Publishing Co., 1949).

Shahani, Ranjee, *The Indian Way* (New York: The Philosophical Library, 1951).

Weber, Max, *The Religion of India*, trans. by Hans Gerth and Don Martindale (Glencoe, Illinois: The Free Press, 1958).

Part IV

PRIESTS AND PROPHETS IN PALESTINE

In the same general time period when great social and cultural changes were under way in ancient China and India, a dramatic series of changes were also in motion in the interstitial area between the great early river-valley civilizations of the Nile and of the Tigris and Euphrates. In some ways the social and cultural events that were to lift ancient Israel to its unique place in the history of mankind were all the more interesting, because all portents seemed so unpromising for any such result.

The bearers of this wave of social and cultural creativity were originally more crude, barbaric, and less civilized than the persons whose society and culture they replaced. To be sure, the ancient Jews were comparable to the Chou, who were originally semibarbarians compared with the refined urbanities of the Shang; they were, in this one respect, also comparable to the Indo-European Aryans who were certainly less refined than the members of the Indus Valley civilization. However, the Chou and Aryan peoples possessed weapons and, possibly, even economic superiority over the people they were to displace. This certainly could not be said of the humble peasants and ass-nomads who made up the bulk of the ancient Jews who were to carve out a kingdom and found one of the great religiously stylized civilizations of the world.

Moreover, if anything, the Holy Land in which these social and civilizational changes were to be staged was immeasurably less promising than the areas already studied. The central valleys of the Yellow and Yangtse rivers may be subject to great floods, but they also represent huge areas of vast potential agricultural richness. The Indian subcontinent was much divided and subdivided by special features of climate and terrain, but there was no question of the vast and varied wealth of the natural opportunities it offered to cultural devices that would unlock them.

In contrast to all this, while there was enough moisture in Palestine to make it a link in the Fertile Crescent, its mountains and deserts and periodic threats of drought, its dust storms and intense summer temperatures (sometimes rising as high as 130° F), made the area far more important to the great civilizational centers of the ancient world as a land bridge for the caravan routes than as a place for occupancy.

One cannot account for the brilliant creative achievements of the Jews on the basis of race any more than one can account for the creative achievements of China and of ancient India on such grounds. There is no Jewish race; the Jews are Caucasians. One cannot account for them on the foundation of some presumed genius of Jewish culture, for the story concerns the emergence of that very culture.

That such an apparently unpromising people under such unpropitious circumstances should achieve such a brilliant synthesis of the cultural forms cast up in the course of their social experience is a confirmation of the observation that there are tides in the affairs of men which, seized at the flood, may carry them on to dramatic adventures. In all these respects the developments of society and civilization in ancient Palestine offer a challenging case study for our hypotheses.

10

THE CHANGING FORMS OF ANCIENT ISRAELITE SOCIETY

In contrast to the rich plains of the Yellow River and the tropical abundance of India, Palestine presented a most moderate mien. The ridge of mountains forming the west wall of the great rift running south from the Taurus Mountains causes the winds to drop their rain, creating a comparatively fertile area between the Mediterranean Sea and the Jordan River. Lowlands parallel to the fracture lines from Galilee to the Dead Sea form subareas, for example, the rich valley of Esdraelon.

North of the Esdraelon Valley the Galilean Mountains break into Upper Galilee, made up of rich wooded mountains, and Lower Galilee, consisting of low hills enclosing elevated plains running largely east and west. Eastward the country falls off the Jordan rift. The hills of Judea, forming the central core of Palestine, eventually disappear into the desert. A mountainous district on the west extends halfway to the sea. The southern district including Beersheba is a wide steppe. The maritime plain extending along the Mediterranean Coast from Lebanon to Egypt is fertile, being formed of raised beaches and sea beds varying from 4 to about 20 miles deep.[1]

In winter westerly winds bring rainstorms which touch the eastern scarp of the Jordan rift but deposit the moisture on Gilead. The winter rains last until Easter. In summer local thunderstorms occasionally explode out of the interaction of land and sea air. However, when the desert dust storms blow over Palestine, the temperature may rise as high as 130 degrees in the Jordan Valley, and people yearn for the rains that usually start in October. Nevertheless, there was sufficient moisture to make Palestine a link in the Fertile Crescent and the land bridge for the caravan routes between ancient Asia and Africa.

HISTORICAL DEVELOPMENT

Prehistory

The archeological finds of Acheulian flints from the second interglacial period (180,000 to 230,000 years ago) indicate human occupancy of Pales-

[1] Sir G. A. Smith, *Historical Geography of the Holy Land* (London: Haddon & Stoughton, 1910).

tine at a time when rhinoceroses, hippopotamuses, elephants, and cave-oxen still roved its semijungles. From earliest times it seems to have been a cross-road, for skeletons found in a cave near Nazareth belonged to a mixed race midway between Neanderthal and Mousterian man.[2] Even then, a hundred thousand years ago, Palestine was an intercontinental bridge across which *Homo sapiens* came—apparently from the southeast.

There were few stages, if any, of material culture which did not leave their mark on the other area. The Levalloisian-Mousterian flint culture was replaced by the Aurignacian culture of the upper Paleolithic period. Then, approximately ten thousand years ago, a mesolithic culture appeared in Palestine with sickle-blades and picks of an agricultural culture. Other cultures followed after 6000 B.C. Around 5000 B.C. the art of making pottery became known. About the same time, men in the Near East began to live in settled peasant villages around permanent shrines.

Throughout Palestine, and particularly in Transjordan, there are numerous dolmen fields with megalithic stone constructions dating between the fifth and third millennia.[3] The Chalcolithic (copper and stone) Age began in Palestine around the end of the third millennium B.C., followed by the Bronze Age which corresponds to the patriarchal age of the Bible.

The Great Powers of the Ancient Near East

The first wave of civilization found its natural limits in city imperialism. As a community replacing the rural village, the city extended its control over the rural area which supplied food for its subsistence. Sooner or later it found itself confronted by other cities also engaged in extending control over their rural hinterlands. These encounters launched the cities upon a period of conquest and defense. In the course of such conquests, the early city lost its flexibility. (This was also evident in the early Chinese empire of the city of Shang, and in the Indus Valley civilization under the dominance of Mohenjo-daro and Harappa.)

Meanwhile, such technologies as metal-working, horse-breeding, chariot-making, plowing, which skills were either invented in the city or perfected in it, diffused beyond the confines of the city, giving a new vigor to less civilized peoples. The high culture of the Shang underwent serious decline under the conquest of the more barbaric Chou in China; in India the high culture of the Indus Valley civilization was replaced by that of the invading Aryans. The same processes were at work in the cradle of human civilization, the valleys of the Tigris and Euphrates and the Nile, between which Palestine was a natural roadway.

[2] Ernest Albert Hooton, *Apes, Men, and Morons* (New York: G. P. Putnam's Sons, 1937), pp. 100–101; Franz Weidenreich, *Apes, Giants, and Man* (Chicago: University of Chicago Press, 1946), pp. 34, 40, 83.

[3] Stephen L. Caiger, *Bible and Space* (London: Oxford University Press, 1947), pp. 48–49.

In Mesopotamia powerful cities in time began imperialistically subduing the hinterland and contending with one another for dominance. At an early date the Northern (Akkad) and Southern (Sumer) dynasties formed. The non-Semitic Sumerians of the South invented the cuneiform script, once so widespread in the Near East. The northerners were augmented by immigrant Semites, from the ranks of whom the later Jews may have formed. About 3000 B.C. military domination was shifting from city to city. A stage was reached comparable to the Shang at the time the Chou appeared on its borders, or comparable to the Indus Valley civilization in the immediate pre-Aryan period. Augmented by incoming Semitic people, north Mesopotamia militarily reduced the south. The newcomers, *Ammurru*, established their chief center in Babylon. (The first dynasty of Babylon was founded by Summu-abu about 2050 B.C.) The sixth member of this dynasty was Hammurabi, who called himself king of the Westland and who was its greatest king, identified with the legal code promulgated in the course of administrative reorganization. His domination extended over Syria and Palestine, and was perhaps one of the first influences that shaped the future Jewish nation.[4]

During the reigns of later kings of the first dynasty of Babylon, there were indications of decline. An invasion of Hittites (c. 1754 B.C.) resulted in the capture and sack of Babylon. Though the Hittites soon retired, raiding bands of Kassites (Indo-Europeans) followed, establishing the Kassite dynasty (c. 1750) which lasted 576 years. The Kassites were able administrators who gradually assimilated the best of Babylonian culture.

The Nile Valley, too, supported a typical river-valley civilization in which a variety of peoples (Ethiopian, Semitic, Mediterranean) were formed into the Egyptians. A period of contending city-dynasties led to the establishment of two great kingdoms. Meanwhile hieroglyphic, syllabic, and partly alphabetic writings had been developed. The two kingdoms (possibly partly resting on ethnic differences) were eventually united; the first of thirty-one dynasties was established about 3500 B.C. The period between dynasties I and VI (c. 3500–c. 2500 B.C.), known as the Old Kingdom, included the time of the pyramid builders. After several centuries of discontent, civil war, and unsettlement, the Middle Kingdom was formed with dynasty XI, reaching in dynasty XII (c. 2000) a kind of Golden Age. After a period of decline, the Hyksos, or shepherd kings, established themselves as invaders in the delta in perhaps 1800 B.C.

The Hyksos were probably Semitic, perhaps partly accounting for the friendly reception of the Jews in Egypt at this time. Toward the close of the seventeenth century B.C., the Egyptians arose against a domination they found hateful. South Egypt was delivered from Hyksos control around 1580 B.C., following which Egypt entered upon a new career of conquest. By

[4] For Babylonian influence on the Jews, see J. Garrow Duncan, *New Light on Hebrew Origins* (New York: The Macmillan Co., 1936), pp. 15–74.

taking advantage of the weakness of Babylon, Palestine, and Syria, Egyptian domination was extended to the Euphrates.

The Palestine province (evidenced by the *Amarna* letters) was ruled by native princes whose sons were taken to Egypt as hostages. Egyptian troops were stationed throughout the province, and Egyptian officials maintained vigilance over the native princes. Regular tribute was exacted. During this period, Amenhotep IV (c. 1376 B.C.) initiated one of the most publicized religious reforms in history. Ikhnaton (as he called himself) built a new capital, advocated a spiritualized form of monotheism, and attempted the education of the masses and the reform of the clergy.[5]

With the weakening of the Egyptian empire once again and the recovery of Hittite power, the provinces began to shake loose from Egypt's grasp. Not only Syria and Phoenicia but also Palestine, which had been invaded by Aramean tribes who joined the Canaanite princes, began to resist Egyptian domination. Around the middle of the fourteenth century B.C., Assyria entered upon a career of conquest, and gradually achieved domination over a good part of the Near East.

Periods of expansion alternated with periods of weakness. The first period began about 1350 B.C., lasting nearly a century. A peoples' movement during the next century halted expansion, causing Assyria to lose her hold on west and northwest Mesopotamia. From 1180 to 1150 B.C. a revival carried Assyria forward again. North Babylonia was conquered and to the west penetration was made to the Mediterranean but another recession followed, providing a period of relative freedom from foreign threat for Palestine. Shortly before 900 B.C., Assyria entered upon a third period of expansion (c. 911–782 B.C.). Her armies campaigned farther than ever before, bringing her into conflict with the Chaldeans, the Medes, and Urartu, before she once again receded.

In 745 B.C. Assyria entered her fourth period of expansion. After a period of terrifying, bloody conquests, she once again declined, losing out to Babylon. The Medes struck the final blow in the first half of the seventh century. During the penetration of the Scythians, a barbarous people from north of the Crimea, Syria and Palestine were lost, and the Assyrian Empire was divided between the Medes and the Babylonians. To Nebuchadnezzar (604 B.C.) fell the task of consolidating the position of Babylon. His siege ended in the capture of Jerusalem and the deportation of its inhabitants. The revolt of Jehoiakim of Judah checked the conquest for a time. In 586 B.C. Nebuchadnezzar again besieged and recaptured Jerusalem. A large number of Jews were carried off into captivity, and the city was plundered and razed.

The movement to establish the Persian Empire began in 553 B.C., when Cyrus made himself master of the Median Empire. He defeated Croesus of Lydia, and established supremacy in Iran. In 539 B.C. Babylonia, Syria, and Palestine were brought under Persian control. At Marathon (490 B.C.),

[5] For Egyptian influence on the Jews, see Duncan, *op. cit.*, pp. 75–159.

Salamis (480 B.C.), Plataea (479 B.C.), and Eurymedon (466 B.C.), the Persians were stopped in their conquest of Greece. Under Cyrus' sociopolitical policy the treatment of the Jews began to improve, and the missions of Ezra and Nehemiah were carried out under Artaxerxes I.

Persian power collapsed under Artaxerxes III (359–338 B.C.). The movement which overthrew Persia was initiated by Philip of Macedonia, and was carried out by Alexander (336–323 B.C.) who subdued the Persian Empire, conquered Egypt, founded Alexandria, and extended his conquests to the Indus. Alexander's death was followed by the disintegration of the Empire. The Jews were then caught between the Ptolemys of Egypt and the Seleucids of Syria. Greek domination and the attempted Hellenization of Palestine continued to the time of the revolt of the Maccabees.

An Outline of Ancient Jewish History

The *Tell el-Amarna* letters[6] and those from Ras Shamra[7] and excavations at Lakish,[8] Gezer,[9] Megiddo,[10] and Beth-shan[11] indicate that the Biblical picture of the Jews as a relatively backward people moving into a land with a developed trade, fortress cities, and urban culture is essentially correct.

Though, like the Chous of China or the Aryans of India in representing a more primitive people than those they were displacing, and destined to become bearers of splendid new developments of human civilization, the Jews presented certain interesting developmental peculiarities. While the Chous of China rose to power as a frontier state of the Shang, exchanging women for their respective harems and eventually stepping into the place of the Shang, and while the Aryans moved as conquering barbarians into the area of a superior culture that they did not choose or were in no position to copy, the Jews gradually became a seminomadic people in an area alternately subject to the influence of two great powers. While there were clearly many influences on the Jews from both cultures, it is doubtful if there was much extended contact with the upper strata of the great powers.

Even if not integral to the oldest document of Genesis, the Biblical tradition of Abraham's connection with Ur of Chaldees is, as Caiger indicates, supported by archeological evidence.[12] Woolley's discovery (reported in *Ur of Chaldees*) that Ur had experienced a great flood and that its people

6 Correspondence sent to Amenhotep IV (Ikhnaton) by his regent in Palestine. In this correspondence dating from 1400 to 1360 B.C., invaders to the south, called Habiru are mentioned, often identified with the Hebrews and the mention is taken as evidence of the conquest of Canaan from a different point of view than that of the Jews. Sir Frederic Kenyon, *The Bible and Archaeology* (London: George G. Harrap & Co., 1940), pp. 71 f.

7 *Ibid.*, pp. 156 f.

8 *Ibid.*, pp. 190 f.

9 *Ibid.*, pp. 200 f.

10 *Ibid.*, pp. 198 f.

11 *Ibid.*, pp. 198 f.

12 Caiger, *op. cit.*, pp. 30 f.

thought of themselves as the people of the flood possibly established the origin of the Biblical story.[13] The law of Moses shows close similarities with the code of Hammurabi.

Exodus	*Hammurabi*
xxi. 16. He that stealeth a man . . . shall surely be put to death	14. If a man has stolen a man's son under age, he shall be slain
xxviii. 28. If an ox gore a man or a woman that they die, the ox shall be surely stoned . . . but the owner of the ox shall be quit	251. If a man's ox is known to be addicted to goring, and he hath not blunted his horns, nor fastened up his ox: then, if his ox hath gored a freeman and killed him, he shall pay half a mina of silver
xxii. 2. If the thief be found breaking in, and be smitten that he die, there shall be no blood guiltiness for him	21. If a man hath broken into a house, before the breach shall he be slain, and there buried[14]

There is much additional evidence of the formative influence exercised by Babylonian culture on the Jews. However, the Old Testament attributes directly and indirectly even greater influence to Egypt. Out of necessity Abraham is reported to have gone to Egypt, and Jacob's family was well received there. Among the famous stories of the Egyptian experience of the Jews is the rise of Joseph to importance.[15] Duncan traced Egyptian influence on such Old Testament narratives as the creation and paradise stories. Moreover, not only do the Biblical writers display a most intimate knowledge of terms, idioms, and administrative roles of Egypt, but in the reaction of the Jews to the changing patterns of Egyptian treatment the foundation for a new stage of Jewish development was laid.[16]

Whenever Babylonian and Egyptian influences on Old Testament literature are traced, this has often been misunderstood by both pious Christians and Jews. To trace the multiple social and cultural influences on the Bible is not to deny its significance but to understand it more fully. Maurice Samuel quite correctly refused to be dismayed because the conception of One Universal God was no exclusive vision of the Jews. It has emerged many times and is found, for example, in Ikhnaton, Cleanthes, Epictetus, and Marcus Aurelius. It was, Samuel argued, not the discovery of God that constituted the importance of the Jews, but what they did with the discovery. "One may properly say that Judaism is meaningless

[13] Duncan, *op. cit.*, pp. 15 f.; Caiger, *op. cit.*, pp. 20 f.

[14] Caiger, *op. cit.*, pp. 88 f.

[15] Caiger, *op. cit.*, pp. 56 f.; Duncan, *op. cit.*, pp. 74 f.

[16] For details on the ancient history of the Jews and for some of the main types of interpretation, see Salo Wittmayer Baron, *A Social and Religious History of the Jews* (New York: Columbia University Press, 1952), Vol. I: *Ancient Times;* Theodore H. Robinson and W. O. E. Oesterley, *A History of Israel* (Oxford: The Clarendon Press, 1934), 2 vols.; J. N. Schofield, *The Historical Background of the Bible* (London: Thos. Nelson & Sons, Ltd., 1938); W. L. Wardle, *The History and Religion of Israel* (Oxford: The Clarendon Press, 1936); J. Wellhausen, *Sketch of the History of Israel and Judah* (London: Adam & Charles Black, 1891).

without the Jewish Bible, not because it tells of the discovery of God, but because it mirrors the struggle of recalcitrant man with the consequences of his discovery."[17] One must know something about the cultural materials with which a people worked to comprehend what they themselves did with them.

It would be equally wrong, of course, to assume that, since many items which had worked up into the earlier civilizational syntheses of the Babylonians and the Egyptians eventually made their way into the structure of Old Testament thought, they here acquired their true significance in this context for the first time. From the standpoint of one or another apologist, there is no doubt about the issue. Sociologically, however, it is of importance that a variety of cultural materials—legends, stories, myths, customs, ethical prescriptions, and the like—are capable of functioning in different civilizational syntheses. They could be expected to be given very different interpretations in different cases.

While the legends of the patriarchs mention a time of Babylonian influence, the Exodus and Moses stories assign special importance to Egypt in the acceptance of Yahwehism as a religion and the formation of the Israelite Confederacy. It has been conventional to locate the early Egyptian phase of Jewish history at a time when Egypt was under the domination of the Hyksos (who were presumably Semitic). The Egyptian administration was initially sympathetic to the Israelite clans settled within the borders. Perhaps new and more severe repressive measures were taken against such alien tribes as the Jews by the Egyptians, once the Hyksos had been driven out. In any case, the imposition of forced labor on alien tribes was a custom of ancient states. Moses was the charismatic leader who organized the Jewish opposition to Egypt and directed their escape. Moses' origins are obscure. While he has an Egyptian name, he was friendly with the Kenites, a Midianite clan, and he married the daughter of the Midian priest Jethro.

Moses led the flight of the Israelites across the Goshen marshes into the Sinai peninsula, and was aided in his escape by the Red Sea miracle, (possibly crossing a lake of reeds on a patch of sand laid bare by the wind). Violent thunderstorms and possibly a volcanic eruption made a major impression on the refugees of the Exodus. A band of mixed tribes were led by Moses to the mountain abode of Yahweh, where they were formed into a sworn confederation. Into the confederacy were also drawn tribes settled in the neighborhood of Kadesh. Moses caused them to enter into a solemn covenant to worship Yahweh.

The conquest of Canaan was carried out by tribal confederation at times fired by the conception of holy war, at others practically falling to pieces. Joshua represents the confederation in holy war with an aim no

[17] Maurice Samuel, *The Professor and the Fossil* (New York: Alfred A. Knopf, 1956), p. 106.

less than the extermination of all Canaanites. However, the picture is not one of a unified nation in continuous operation with a single purpose, though in major crises the confederation was periodically rededicated. The Israelites were weaker than the Canaanites, and were forced to utilize peasant militias against the war chariots and professional knights of fortified cities. Their efforts were only occasionally crowned with success.

The conquest was actually a gradual infiltration into the mountain areas and around the fringes of the richer settled agricultural areas accompanied by occasional military encounters. The various tribes, which were by no means constant, became three groups: the southern group included Judah, Simeon, Levi, and Reuben; the central group consisted of Ephraim, Manasseh, and Benjamin; the northern group was made up of Issachar, Zebulun, Naphtali, Asher, and Dan. Rarely was there concerted action by more than a few at a time.

In the period of Judges, various of the sheiks enlarged their spheres of power, at times preying on the caravan routes and occasionally invading the plain. The Moabite king, Eglon, dominated the district around Jericho and exacted tribute from it. He was assassinated by Ehud, who conducted the caravan bearing the tribute, whereupon every Moabite found west of the Jordan was slain. Barak (in Song of Deborah), at the head of the contingents of six tribes, routed the enemy at Taanach. The Midianites harassed the Manassites, but Jerubaal (Gideon) collected troops, surrounded the enemy, and disorganized it in a night attack. The Gileadites invited Jephtha (a freebooter) to take command against the Amonites; he defeated them. Abimelech, the half-caste son of Gideon by a Canaanite wife, attempted to make himself king of Shechem. Meanwhile, a new threat in the form of the Philistines appeared. Samson was a folk hero of the Israelites during the war against the Philistines.

Under the leadership of Saul, David, and Solomon, the Israelites repelled the Philistines, and established an oriental sultanism. The old peasant army of the confederacy was replaced by a professional army of fighting knights with chariots. Foreign craftsmen were imported for palace and temple construction; and a royal harem (as, in part, the instrument of foreign diplomacy, and with it the importation of foreign cults and deities) made its appearance. Centralization of worship was undertaken, patrimonial administrative structures were formed, and a territorial system of taxation was set up.

But this most munificent of Jewish royal periods was not without its internal and external problems. The heavy taxation associated with palace-building and other projects was a great burden. The demilitarization of the old army and the formation of a new, foreign-modeled army of knights was feared. The importation of foreign cults (along with the wives of the harem) and the building of special cult temples were experienced in some quarters as an abomination. Meanwhile, external relations were far from easy. The Edomites had regained power, and sought revenge. Damascus threatened Israel in the north. Under Rehoboam, after Solomon's death, domestic tension mounted. Israel renounced affiliation with Judah, and Jeroboam, one of Solomon's former officers, became its king (937 B.C.). Of the two kingdoms, the career of Israel was the more hectic, for it was more exposed to dangers from surrounding areas.

Syria, which had been defeated by David, recovered in power. A whole series of conflicts with varying results occurred between it and the northern kingdom. Some territories changed rulers several times. Meanwhile, Assyria began her western movement. When, in 722 B.C., the northern kingdom fell, whole groups of the population were deported.

Judah enjoyed a more unbroken dynasty, and its priesthood under the Zadokites increasingly developed in prestige. But the story is similar, for Judah too was pressed by the Assyrians. Moreover, the Chaldeans were rising in power. In 607 B.C., following the defeat of Necho by Nebuchadnezzar at Carchemish in 604 B.C., the determination of Judah's fate was clearly shifted from Egypt to Babylonia. Judah became tributary to Babylon, but in 597 B.C. Jehoiakim revolted. His son Jehoiachin had been king only three months when the Chaldeans besieged the city. The king surrendered, and was carried off to Babylon with the most important elements of the city, including the military and a thousand artisans.

Despite indication of the occasional harsh conditions of the exiles (Isaiah 14:3, 6, 47), they were not treated very severely. They were permitted to make money (Isaiah 55:1 f.), to marry (Jer. 29:6; Ezek. 24:18), to possess homes (Ezek. 22:1–7), to settle in colonies, and to maintain a semiautonomous common life. While forced into various types of conscript labor, for example, canal digging, they were allowed to farm and enter a wide variety of trades and professions.

Among the exiles, temple priests from the highest aristocracy of Jerusalem turned their efforts to the cult needs of the community. In the Babylonian exile the Jews became painfully conscious that their religion was one of the few things left from the old life. This realization led to the elevation of old moral and ritualistic codes contained in the old Law of Holiness to a new intensity of observance. While remaining culturally autonomous, the Babylonian Jews gradually improved their socio-economic situation, entering into the mercantile pursuits of this city of merchants and even acquiring influence in court circles.

Babylonia was conquered by the Medes. In turn, the Medes were vanquished by the Persians under Cyrus, who became master of Babylon in 539 B.C. Upon assumption of power, Cyrus granted the Jews permission to return to Jerusalem and rebuild the temple. In the first group of returning exiles there were about 42,360 free persons and 7,337 slaves. Religious leadership was in the hands of Joshua, the high priest, who made a beginning of temple construction in 538 B.C. The Samaritans offered assistance which was refused. They retaliated by sabotaging the construction. In the end, the work of reestablishing the community fell to Ezra and Nehemiah.

Ezra, a scribe (*sopher*) or student of the Book (*sepher*), and well-versed in the Torah, was granted permission by King Artaxerxes (465–426 B.C.) to tackle the problems of the reconstituted community. Under his leadership a new group of refugees secured funds from the Babylonian Jews and settled in Jerusalem. Ezra was shocked by the number of intermarriages which had occurred in the community. He convoked an assembly of the entire community in Jerusalem and dissolved all unlawful marriages. A commission was appointed to draw up a list of the transgressors. Ezra also started preparations for rebuilding the walls of Jerusalem, but was opposed by the many groups which his policies had alienated. He was denounced by his enemies to the king, and orders were issued for razing the section of the wall already constructed.

When he heard of the disaster, Nehemiah, a cupbearer of Artaxerxes, obtained permission to go to Jerusalem to restore the walls. He was granted the title of governor of Judah. In spite of the force and fraud of his opponents, he succeeded. Nehemiah also assumed a central role in reconstructing the socio-religious life of the community. He secured the release of poor Jews from debt slavery. He bound the community in a general oath to observe the Torah, to abstain from foreign marriage, to refuse traffic on the Sabbath, to observe the sacred seventh year commanded in the Law, to pay the tax to the temple as well as first fruits and tithes (Nehemiah 9:38–39).

In the Exile the detachment of Judaism from politics and the relocation of its point of gravity in the cult community had been brought about, and Ezra and Nehemiah continued this transformation. During the remainder of the Persian period the political concerns of the community remained in the hands of the Persian regent. The same was true under the Greek and Roman periods. Judaism was destined to remain in the situation of a subordinate religious community until the success of contemporary Zionism.

Rowley has made one of the most recent attempts to establish the chronology of the ancient Jews to the time of the Exodus. Hippisley has summarized the overall chronology:[18]

CHRONOLOGY

Date	*Event*
2050–732 B.C.	First Babylonian Empire
1950 B.C.	Hammurabi's Code
1650 B.C.	the migration of Abraham from Harran

[18] H. H. Rowley, *From Joseph to Joshua* (London: Oxford University Press, 1950), p. 164; Evelyn W. Hippisley, "The Old Testament Chronologically Arranged," in W. L. Wardel, *The History and Religion of Israel*, *op. cit.*, pp. 229 ff. The differences in chronology by the various students cannot be taken up here.

Date	*Event*
1440 B.C.	Hebrew groups at Kadis become associated with Yahweh worshipping Kenites. Tell el-Amarna Letters (1450), northward pressure of Kenite groups (Habiru)
1370 B.C.	Joseph taken into Egypt and rises to high office in reign of Ikhnaton
1300 B.C.	the oppression of Jews under Rameses II
1290 B.C.	the birth of Moses
1260 B.C.	Moses flees to Jethro, a Kenite kinsman of his mother
1230 B.C.	the exodus from Egypt under Moses in the name of the Kenite god, Yahweh; the covenant by Exodus tribes and the formulation of Ethical Decalogue
1200 B.C.	Philistines (refugees from destroyed Cretan empire) begin settling in Canaan
1025 B.C.	Saul
1000 B.C.	David
970 B.C.	Solomon
933 B.C.	the divided kingdom
721 B.C.	the end of the kingdom of Israel
586 B.C.	the fall of Jerusalem
549 B.C.	Cyrus overthrows the Medes (Persian Empire)
538 B.C.	the capture of Babylon by Cyrus
537 B.C.	the return of Zerubbabel and Joshua; the building of the temple, 530 B.C.
445 B.C.	the return of Nehemiah
397 B.C.	the return of Ezra
331 B.C.	the conquest of Palestine by Alexander (Ptolemaic and Selucid Empires)
311 B.C.	Palestine under the Ptolemies of Egypt
198 B.C.	Antiochus II conquers Palestine
167 B.C.	the Maccabean revolt against Antiochus (The independence of the Jews after 142 B.C.)
65 B.C.	Pompey enters Syria, and conquers Jerusalem

THE CHANGING FORMS OF THE JEWISH COMMUNITY FROM THE CONFEDERATION TO THE POST-EXILE PERIOD

The formation of a community is a slow process. However, when the inconsistencies between one institutional area and another are gradually worked out so that a consistent way of life has taken shape, a community presents formidable resistance to change. To be sure, every community offers some elasticity and a capacity to tolerate alternatives and semiconflicting forms. If it were not for this property of communities, it would be almost impossible for a community to meet a crisis. However, when a crisis arises and old community forms break down, the reconstitution of the community may begin from the stock of alternatives.

Folk myth often reports the birth of a new community in some dramatic event—a volcanic eruption, the actions of a semidivine leader, or a war of the gods. Great skepticism is necessary concerning such legends. However, most of the time a very real crisis is the basis of the birth of a new community, for example, the American Revolution marked the formation of a distinct American community, the French Revolution marked the emergence of modern France, and the Russian Revolution made possible the formation of Soviet Russia. A new community often seizes upon details of the crisis attendant on its birth and finds in them the symbol of itself.

There is no reason to doubt the general accuracy of the Biblical record which presents a major crisis at the turning point of each of the major community forms of the ancient Jews: the community of the confederation period was presented as born in the course of the dramatic events attending the Exodus, the organization of the monarchy with its distinct community form resulted from the wars of the Philistines, and the Babylonian defeat and deportations were responsible for the formation of the ethnic community.

THE JEWISH COMMUNITY IN THE PERIOD OF THE CONFEDERACY

As Baron sees it, the period of the origins of Israel falls into three phases:

> "The period of the patriarchs"—the appearance of the first Hebrew groups in Palestine, some of them penetrating down into Egypt; the "Mosaic period"—their Exodus from Egypt and migration through the desert under Moses; and the period of the final conquest of Canaan and settlement under the "Judges."[19]

At one end of a scale of social and economic contrasts in Palestine at the time of the confederation was the Bedouin who had no agriculture, who lived on camel milk and dates, drank no wine, and tolerated no form of state organization. The clan's head, the sheik, was the one permanent authority along with the family head. The clans formed tent-communities which traced descent to a common ancestor, and were bound together by requirements of blood revenge. Tent-communities were occasionally formed into tribes, though they were unstable, for the clans were able to join and leaves the tribes at will. At times a charismatic prince managed to elevate his clan to a position of semipermanent military authority, though this was possible only when the clan received a fixed income—perhaps from tribute

[19] Baron, *op. cit.*, p. 32.

levied on oases, from tolls, caravan fees, or from plunder. In such a community unrelated brothers were without rights, while tribal claims to grazing grounds were respected out of mutual fear.[20]

Albright maintains that there is no clear archeological evidence that the domestication of the camel proceeded far enough before the thirteenth century B.C. to have a decisive effect on nomadism.[21] However, he opines that pressure from camel-riding nomads may partly account for the Israelite invasion of Canaan shortly after this time. Though the Israelites show few traces of Bedouin forms,[22] the pressure from the Bedouins on the Israelites may have helped start them on the first step of their development.

The Hebrews were ass-nomads rather than camel-nomads. According to Albright,[23] in contrast to the Hebrew nomad the true Bedouin can cover long distances on camelback and live in places where the shepherd cannot, for the camel eats desert shrubs and bushes that grow without a direct supply of water, which a sheep or goat cannot touch. The Bedouin drinks camel's milk, uses camel's skins and camel's hair for his tent and equipment, and is self-sufficient wherever a camel can survive. The ass-nomad cannot move more than a day's journey (20 miles) from water. Even today the seminomad lives in tents or temporary houses, he owns goats and sheep, and raises some crops. In ancient times his territorial sphere was much more limited than that of the true Bedouin. He constantly engaged in intertribal warfare because of crowding and competition.

At the other end of the social scale from the Bedouin were the cities, which Weber maintains were castles of warrior chiefs established as places of refuge for cattle and people. Often a city was no more than a small fortified agricultural community with a market. However, the Tell el-Amarna correspondence indicates that there were also large cities with an urban stratum appearing beside the vassal kings of the Pharaoh. Such kings were equipped with magazines and arsenals. The urban group controlled the administration.

Fortified cities often controlled a number of rural towns as dependencies. In these cities, clan structure often remained strong, though land ownership had assumed major importance as a foundation of rights. The most powerful strata of the cities were the *gibborim* (warrior knights) who were also called *bne chail* (sons of property). The city princes shared power with the elders of the clans. Other clans were settled interlocally, and occasionally held power in several small towns or tent villages. At times a

[20] Max Weber, *Ancient Judaism*, trans. by Hans Gerth and Don Martindale (Glencoe: The Free Press, 1952), pp. 10 ff.

[21] William Foxwell Albright, *Archeology and the Religion of Israel* (Baltimore: The Johns Hopkins University Press, 1953), p. 96.

[22] Weber, *op. cit.*, p. 13.

[23] Albright, *op. cit.*, p. 97.

charismatic warlord succeeded in making himself independent of the elders of the city by means of a personal following.[24]

According to the Bible, the patriarchs were the original nucleus of the Israelites. They were seminomadic stock-breeders occupying a position midway between the Bedouins and the peasants. In addition to the pure types of itinerate stock-breeders (like the Rechabites), there were numerous transitional strata. Occasionally alliances with cattle-breeders and Bedouins were formed. On the other hand, the relation of the small stock-breeders and the tillers and urban populations normally rested on a contractual basis with respect to meadow and traverse rights. In periods of peace and favorable climatic cycles, an expansion of tillage occurred, and concomitantly, a restriction of land available for grazing. Because of the tensions such developments producted, however, the size of the social units also tended to be reduced at such times.

The social organization of the small stock-breeder, Weber believed, was somewhat similar to that of the Bedouins: the large family formed an economic community, the clan guaranteed personal safety through blood revenge, and the tribe was a military organization of clans to protect grazing grounds. Like those of the Bedouin, the political structures of the small stock-breeders were quite unstable.[25]

Albright[26] has pointed out that even today traveling smiths or tinkers of modern Arabian areas follow regular trade routes with asses and tools, depending for a livelihood on craftsmanship, music, and divination (in which women excel). They resemble the Kenites of the Bible (with a name derived from *quain*, meaning smith). Cain's descendant, Lamech, had three sons who were credited with creating occupational specialties (tents and herds, musical instruments, and copper and iron utensils). It is probable that the ancient Hebrews were in part composed of the same or related types.

A section of ancient Jews settled for a time in Egypt, where they first experienced friendly relations and even, as the story of Joseph illustrates, had opportunity to acquire considerable power. Later, however, they were subject to increasing repression. The Egyptian branch of the Jews found its great charismatic leader in Moses, who led them out of Egypt and formed them into the Yahweh confederacy.[27]

Israel was not originally a tribe or nation, but a confederation of tribes which developed into a nation through repeated ritualistic resolutions in the name of Yahwehism, which led in time to the establishment of the pure Yahweh cult in Jerusalem. The confederate idea which assumed major importance in ancient Israel originally had no existence apart from the

[24] Weber, *op. cit.*, pp. 13–23.
[25] Weber, *op. cit.*, pp. 36 f.
[26] Albright, *op. cit.*, pp. 98 ff.
[27] Weber, *op. cit.*, pp. 61–117.

contractual relations between warrior clans, guest tribes, and legally protected metics (including itinerant herdsmen, guest artisans, merchants, and priests) conjoined by Yahwehism. Not only was the covenant with Yahweh basic to Israel's judgment of its place within the nations, it was also the essence of its unity.[28]

Only such a cult organization was able to provide a basis for semipermanent political and military structures in this world of small stockbreeders. This is illustrated by the tenacity of the organization of the Rechabites of the Yahweh cult in contrast to the plastic way other tribes and clans organized and dissolved. Once religious fraternization proved to be an efficient political and economic instrument of power, the motive for its diffusion was powerfully intensified. The Israelite synoecism was a war confederation under a war god who guaranteed its social order and its material prosperity. Israel originated not as a tribal name, but as a cult league. In contrast to the city-states which participated in the Deborah war, Israel was a nonurban association; its army of peasants on foot followed the princes who rode on white asses against the armies of chariot-riding knights of the city kings. The confederacy, moreover, became formally active only in wartime, when the legal body of the army assembly meted out justice to offenders of the law of war or of the ritual and social commandments of Yahweh.[29]

Religious confederation was the sole device which permitted an otherwise loose composition of peasants, itinerant stock-breeders, and artisans to coalesce into a fighting force with sufficient unity to carry out the conquest of Palestine. A series of covenants thus created Israel; indeed, they were its essence. Perhaps the greatest of all the Acts of the Covenant was that of Moses. As summarized by Baron:

> Appearing in the minds of one of the great Semitic migrations, the Hebrew tribes settled in Canaan after a process of penetration, partly martial and partly pacific, extending over several centuries. In the meantime, the respective tribes reflected striking antitheses: semiprimitives touched by the age-old civilizations of Babylonia, Egypt, or Canaan; seminomadic herdsmen, whose eyes were turned toward the rich agricultural settlement of Palestine; clans and tribes held together by strong blood ties but surrounded by often hostile aliens; finally, a people without state or territory which wanted both but could not regard either as essential. A politically wise consciousness of unity, indispensable for survival, encountered strong disintegrating forces.
>
> At that critical juncture arose a man who through his supreme genius in statesmanship and religion resolved these conflicts into a new religious expression, an historical monotheism centering in the history of God's own, the chosen, people. Through his religious adeptness he created a unifying social force, with the capacity of developing beyond the desert or Palestine, beyond all natural boundaries, beyond state and territory.[30]

[28] *Ibid.*, p. 79.
[29] *Ibid.*, p. 90.
[30] Baron, *op. cit.*, pp. 61–62.

URBAN COMMUNITIES OF THE ROYAL PERIOD

The religious confederation of nonurban tribes and peasant villages of Palestine permitted the Israelites to carry out the conquest of Canaan. Once an area had been conquered it was not unusual for the Hebrews and the conquered Canaanites to enter into a religious covenant which stabilized their relations with each other. Such arrangements encouraged the fusion of the formerly discrete social elements and speeded the urbanization of the Hebrews. The successful conquest of Canaan inevitably opened a new era of community formation.

A national catastrophe and "a great national revival,"[31] however, also provided the occasion for the establishment of the monarchy of ancient Israel and accelerated the transformation of its social structure. The Philistines composed of Lycian-Carian and Cretan sea peoples were set in motion by troubles in the eastern Mediterranean. When the Philistines were turned back by Egypt around 1187 B.C., they began to settle in western Palestine, soon undertaking the conquest of Canaan. In the counterattack against this new enemy, the Israelites, led by Samuel, Saul, and David, were transformed into a unified nation.

Before the advent of the Philistines the differential successes of the various tribal groups during the Israelite conquest of Canaan tended to create internal conflicts. The social composition of the tribes was growing more varied. The tribes of Asher and Dan were urbanized at an early period. Ephraim, Issachar, Zebulun, and Naphtali had the greatest admixture of settled peasant proprietors. Other tribes varied between these extremes. Though the city patricians, peasants, and herdsmen made common cause in the pacification of the desert, there were frequent clashes of interest between peasants and cattle-breeders (Jud. 8:1 f.).[32] The old unity of the confederation was rapidly being replaced by a diversity of partly conflicting interests.

The external threat of the Philistine invasion, however, overcame the diversity, and forced the Israelites together again. According to Biblical tradition, the beginning of the resistance to the Philistines started with the peasants—the Benjaminite Saul left his plow to become king. Only later were the herdsmen from the Judaic mountains drawn into the struggle. David, who was launched on his career as a charismatic leader of a mountain band, did not become independent of the Philistines until he became city prince of Jerusalem. The establishment of a unified military monarchy and the formation of a body of chariot-riding soldiers ended the career of the militia of free peasants and herdsmen in Israel. The military forces of Solomon were organized along the lines of other royal forces, and were furnished with chariots and horses imported from Egypt.[33]

[31] Baron, *op. cit.*, p. 63.
[32] Weber, *op. cit.*, p. 53.
[33] *Ibid.*, p. 56.

The history of the Israelite state under David and Solomon was substructured by a conflict between the tribal separatism of early Israel and the centralizing tendencies of the crown. David selected Jerusalem for his capital to secure a site near the geographical center of Israel which was not identified with any tribe. He installed his officials, retainers, and mercenaries there. Solomon actively pursued similar policies, supplanting the amphictyonic tradition by attaching the chief priest and his family to the court. Abiathar, as high priest of the Shiloh line, was placed at the head of the official cult establishment in Jerusalem. However, Solomon was forced to remove him for suspected political activity, and Zadok was placed at the head of Israel's priestly organization.[34]

The social transformation of the Israelites in this period has been aptly summarized by Max Weber:

> Social formations hitherto essentially discrete and standing side by side as stock-breeding tribes, peasant tribes, cities, now became fused; the capital and its ruling sibs became politically paramount. . . .
>
> The old stratification of Israel into armed sibs of peasant proprietors or herdsmen, on the one hand, sib clienteles of guest artisans, day laborers, and musicians, on the other, was gradually displaced by a quite different stratification. Urbanized patrician landlords as the champions of training for chivalry appear on the one hand, on the other, indebted or landless, hence proletarized Israelites and metic proselytes of the Yahwe ritual, who now, in the eyes of the priest, formed a homogeneous stratum of "the poor" opposite the patriciate. The poor were not a socially or economically homogeneous stratum but comprised all who did not belong to the military sibs.[35]

Israel was being transformed into a world of city communities.

THE ETHNIC COMMUNITY

In the period of the kingdom the internal and external problems of the Jews in Palestine complemented one another in a peculiar manner. Internally, the major problem was the continuing clash between the residues of the old tribal confederation and the new forces of the royal city. The disarming of the free peasants was resisted. People groaned under the imposition of new taxes and work levies for the projects of the princes. Meanwhile, the external situation of Palestine was becoming grim. The military power of Israel was inferior to that of Assyria, Egypt, or Babylonia, and they were swinging into action once again. In the minds of the representatives of the elements of the former confederacy, the two situations were linked in the prophecy that God would chastise Israel by military defeat at the hands of the great powers for the sins of the kingdom.

The spiritual ferment in the Near East at the time was not confined to the Jews, for Parsiism was flowering in Iran. However, Judaism faced unusually

[34] See Albright's summary, *op. cit.*, pp. 138–139.
[35] Weber, *op. cit.*, pp. 56–57.

serious problems. Baron describes the event of the destruction of the first temple and the loss of national independence (586 B.C.) as the crucial test of Judaism to survive the destruction of the state:

> The Jews themselves were confronted with . . . epochal changes in the outside world at a crucial period of their own national history. The deportations, life during the exile, the partial restorations under Zerubbabel and Ezra-Nehemiah, the change in the status of the Jews under Persia in and outside Palestine, created unprecedented situations. Again there arose such able leaders as Ezekiel and Deutero-Isaiah, comparable to the noblest of the prophets before them, to make a new intellectual advance in explaining new perplexities.[36]

In Babylonia the danger of assimilation and of the complete extinction of the Jewish culture was great. Nearly one-third of the prewar population of Judah was forcefully removed, while thousands were killed or died of hunger and disease.[37] One of the clearest perceptions of the sociological implications of the Exile for the Jewish community is that of Max Weber. He saw, as Baron put it, that the new community, having lost its territorial basis, could only be built around an ethnic principle.[38] The materials for the formation of the ethnic community were provided by elements from the historical development of the Jews.

> Prophecy together with traditional ritualism of Israel brought forth the elements that gave to Jewry its pariah place in the world. . . . This transformation of the Israelite community began, to be sure, under the influence of the Torah and prophecy even before the exile.[39]

In place of the ancient organization of settled warriors bound by covenant with guest tribes and in place of the urban institutions of the capital of the nation, there appeared a purely ritualistic organization with Jerusalem postulated as a symbolic capital. Though soon after the first deportation Jeremiah advised the exiles to make their homes in Babylon, Ezekiel (30:35) opposed this, insisting that Jerusalem was the only proper place to worship.

> Thus, almost at the moment when Israel lost its concrete territorial basis, the ideal value of the political territory was definitely and ritually fixated for henceforth developing internationally settled guest people.[40]

Though neither commensalism nor connubium with the stranger was originally prohibited in the confederate and royal periods, all this changed in the ethnic community. True prohibitions against mixed marriages began

[36] Baron, *op. cit.*, p. 103.

[37] *Ibid.*, p. 105.

[38] *Ibid.*, p. 124. Max Weber (*op. cit.*, pp. 336 ff.) described the ethnic community as a pariah community. Because of the unfortunate connotations of the word "pariah," the term "ethnic" community will be employed here.

[39] Weber, *op. cit.*, p. 336.

[40] *Ibid.*, p. 338.

during the Exile. The story of Ruth, however, indicates that intermarriage with a stranger was still possible even for David's lineage.[41]

Although he was reluctant to do so, for he had hoped to use Jerusalem as a stronghold against Egypt,[42] Nebuchadnezzar entirely destroyed Jerusalem when he had to. He deported many artisans, royal officials, members of the standing army, and urban patricians. After the initial disaster, the Jews did not suffer particularly, either economically or socially, in exile. They encountered an active industrial and commercial life in Babylon. Being bilingual and derived from urban strata in the first place, they found a rich field for their skills, and they prospered. Baron believes they may have been responsible for the appearance of large-scale private banking which replaced temple credit in the Assyrian empire during the latter part of the seventh century B.C.—three generations after the arrival of the first deportees from Samaria. The founder of the House of Egibi, the largest private banking firm, had a Hebrew name.[43] The emergence of the Jewish financier may have been brought about in part by Jewish abhorrence of dealing with the pagan temple treasuries. However, the Jews were not limited to finance and usury. The records of the commercial establishment of the House of Murashshu show that for a century after the Exile many men with Hebrew names became landowners, merchants, contractors, and rent collectors. The Jews at times even gained public office.[44] A considerable section of the exiles became wealthy, as was evidenced by the magnificent contribution to the temple construction with return from the Exile.[45]

However, the Babylonian community was a cultural island. The great cohesion acquired by the community in the course of the Exile was in considerable measure the work of the priests who had been abducted *en masse* with the last deportation. Authority among the exiles was held by the elders and priests, who remained the permanent representatives of the community responsible to Babylonian administration (Jer. 29:1). Ezekiel's plan for an Israelite state did not assign much importance to kingship. The king was conceived as merely the patron of the theocratic community.[46] The high priest was unknown before the Exile, but by raising the demands for purity and qualifying the high priest alone for performing the essential rites, he was made central to the cult.

Meanwhile new cultic commensal (dietary) and connubial (marital) restrictions were imposed on the congregation. The prohibition of mixed marriages by Ezra was so severe that even the family of the high priest was found guilty of the abomination (Ezra 10:18 f.). Castelike commensal clo-

41 *Ibid.*, p. 340.
42 *Ibid.*, p. 346.
43 Baron, *op. cit.*, pp. 108–109.
44 *Ibid.*, p. 110.
45 Weber, *op. cit.*, p. 347.
46 *Ibid.*, p. 348.

sure was carried out, prohibiting consumption of the hip nerves, fat, blood, fallen and lacerated meat. Ritually controlled and regulated butchering became necessary. Jews living in isolated or small communities soon found it almost impossible to obtain Kosher food or to perform proper religious rituals, forcing the settlement of orthodox Jews into the city. The casuistic elaboration of dietary and butchering rituals began in the Exile.[47] The Jews became a ritualistically distinct congregation recruited by birth and the reception of proselytes.

In his study of the formation of Judaism in the first Christian centuries, Moore confirms the continuing development of ethnic distinctness, the origins of which Weber and Baron trace to the Exile. By the second century A.D., he observes, a remarkable and enduring unity had been established in the Jewish community:

> The ground of this remarkable unity is to be found not so much in a general agreement in fundamental ideas as in community of observance throughout the whole Jewish world. Wherever a Jew went he found the same system of domestic observance in effect. This was of especial importance in the sphere of what are now called the dietary laws, because it assured him against an unwitting violation of their manifold regulations. If he entered the synagogue he found everywhere substantially the same form of service with minor variations.[48]

Flowing from its emphasis on an ethnic rather than a territorial principle, the exile community had still other traits. The family and clan again became the "primary cohesive force in Jewish life."[49] Because of a determination to retain their Jewishness, whole families and clans tended to cling together, and from these family groups came the elders of the community at large. At communal gatherings psalms, hymns, and poems were sung and historical events remembered. This custom gave rise to the institution which became the core of Jewish life in the Diaspora, the synagogue.[50] Other institutions quickly began to cluster around it.

His perception of the closeness of the tie between traditional Judaism and the ethnic community led Baron to see various activities of the state of Israel in our time as one of the potential threats to Judaism:

> Developments favorable to individual Jews have frequently proved detrimental to Jewish group life, and consequently to Judaism. The "Emancipation" itself which raised the economic and social status of millions of Jews . . . was attended by the destruction of Jewish self-government . . . and a partial disintegration of traditional religious and cultural patterns. From another angle, Russian Communism, while relieving the Jewish masses of the severe oppression suffered under the czars, also becomes a serious menace to the survival of traditional, per-

47 *Ibid.*, pp. 351 ff.

48 George Foot Moore, *Judaism in the First Centuries of the Christian Era* (Cambridge: Harvard University Press, 1927), Vol. I, pp. 110–111.

49 Baron, *op. cit.*, p. 125.

50 *Ibid.*, p. 126.

haps of all Judaism. More recently, the projected separation of state and church in the new state of Israel would formally divorce the destinies of the people from those of its religion.[51]

The issue, to be sure, may not be so much the survival of Judaism as the form such survival will assume. The formation of the state of Israel means that two major communities have become bearers of contemporary Judaism (the nation-state and the internationally settled ethnic communities). The process of community formation insures that religion will have a quite different position in each.

An ethnic community finds its point of integration in religion and culture. This does not mean that religious and cultural innovation are impossible, but it does mean that the very existence of the community rests on the unquestioned location of religion and culture as the point of synthesis of the community. The nation-state, on the other hand, shifts religion to a peripheral relation to the whole, and locates the point of community synthesis in a core of political and economic institutions.

The formation of the state of Israel thus potentially represents a turning point in the structure of the religion and culture as major as the shift from the religion of the tribal confederacy to the religion of the oriental state under Solomon and David. Or again, it potentially represents as dramatic an internal restructuring as the shift from the religion of the royal period to the religion of the exile community. Samuel calls attention to the fact that the institutional core of the community, in the time of Ezra and Nehemiah, began to shift from its core in the royal period.

> From the time of Ezra and Nehemiah onward the synagogue and school were slowly taking over the survivalist function for the Jewish people; the spiritual predominance in Jewry was with the Pharisee teachers, not the Sadducee Temple functionaries. Alexander Jannaeus, who had insolently united in his own person the offices of King and High Priest, earned the hatred of the Pharisees, and when a throng of worshippers objected to his desecration of the ritual, and pelted him with citrons, he turned his troops loose on them and slaughtered some thousands.[52]

An ethnic community is a minority community within a semialien majority. By its very nature it is in an underprivileged position, held together by two forces: prejudice and persecution from the outside, and some faith or vision or even, perhaps, a sense of desperation on the part of its members who believe that they must either hang together or hang separately. The unifying vision of the Jewish ethnic community has been phrased brilliantly by Samuel:

> What, then, is the Jewish people? It is a continuing association of individuals, now some thirty-five hundred or four thousand years old, working out an experiment in the relationship to God. It is partly a

[51] Baron, *op. cit.*, p. 3.
[52] Samuel, *op. cit.*, p. 87.

hereditary association, though not on principle or by deliberate choice. . . . Judaism in Jewry is an experiment in time; when the Messiah will have come, when all peoples will have accepted the faith, the experiment will have been successfully concluded. We shall be beyond history, and we cannot picture to ourselves in secular terms the post-historic condition of mankind.[53]

The two forces which tend to hold an ethnic community together are: (1) the inner faith in the significance of its culture and (2) persecution and prejudice from the outside. Whenever either, and particularly, whenever both of these forces weaken, the ethnic community tends to dissolve. On the other hand, persecution and prejudice recall the members of the ethnic community to their faith.

> Many peoples have been persecuted, though none as persistently as the Jewish people, one obvious reason being that none has stood up to persecution—and in exile, at that—as long as the Jews. Persecution is one of the factors that have contributed to the Ashkenai ethos.[54]

To ask that Judaism retain all and only those properties it possessed as the religion of an ethnic group at the time the nation-state is becoming one of the primary vehicles of the culture is to ask something impossible on scientific grounds. That they are possibly faced with major religious change is seen by some Israelis.

> There does exist in Israel today a very small group, the *Neturei Carta*, which is still opposed on superorthodox grounds to the idea of the Jewish state. Its supporters do not believe that Judaism is compatible with present-day governmental functions.[55]

That Judaism will undergo some inner transformation as a product of the success of modern Zionism is a sociological certainty. The values or disvalues of this inner change, however, are not a sociological issue but a matter of faith.

SUMMARY

As in the case of the Chou people of ancient China and the Indo-Europeans in ancient India, the ancient Jews represented a more primitive people who moved into the cultural sphere of a more advanced civilization and created a brilliant new civilization of their own.

A number of peculiarities of the events in the Jewish cultural sphere provides a special challenge to the theory of the interrelation of society, the intellectual, and civilization. The Jews started from humbler beginnings, as far as is known, than did either the Chou or the Indo-Europeans. The Jews were militarily inferior to the chariot-fighting semiprofessionals in the land they undertook to conquer. By contrast, the people of the Chou

[53] *Ibid.*, p. 176.
[54] *Ibid.*, p. 206.
[55] *Ibid.*, p. 186.

and the Indo-Europeans seem to have been in possession of the most advanced military technology (chariot warfare) of their time. It was a component in their success. Moreover, the area the Jews undertook to conquer was only semifertile by comparison with the rich plains of China or the Indian subcontinent—it was a most humble "promised land." Finally, the Jews moved into the space between two of the great world powers of the day. The rush of social and cultural events that formed its ancient social history were crowded into a comparatively short interval of weakness of these great world powers. The imminent possibility that they would rise to activity again and crush the developments in their borderlands hung like a storm-clouded destiny over the course of events.

The ancient Jews made the most of the little time available to them, and out of materials which they shared profoundly with the cultural world about them, fashioned a unique societal and cultural synthesis of their own. Samuel was most certainly correct when, in the course of his brilliant refutation of Toynbee's thesis on the Jews, he refused to quarrel over whether the Jews were the first to conceive monotheism.[56] Moreover, he was also correct when he refused to quarrel about cultural borrowings between the Jews and the surrounding civilizations, but, instead, placed the emphasis on the unique manner in which the cultural materials available to the Jews were put together.

> It is the proper task of the archaeologist of ideas to try to identify the fragments: Was the *t'hom* ("the deep") originally *Tiamat*, the Babylonian dragon? It is worth thinking about, though not worth losing sleep on. Whence the story of the sons of God mating with the daughters of man to produce a race of giants? To what particular or general source may we trace the serpent? and so on, through not merely Genesis, but many of the Biblical books. Here is, indeed, a fruitful field for study of cultural interrelationships. But these very fragments bring into bolder relief the unique nature of the effort which, beginning with the trumpet peal of the first sentence, gives the Book of Books its perdurable position among human utterances. In the ancient world that effort, so far as we know, is unique; as Professor Toynbee himself says, neither the "Syriac," nor the Egyptic, nor the Babylonic, nor the Minoan civilizations participated in it; and that effort, bound up with the everlasting struggle against inertia, relapse, and apostasy, expressed itself in the record that constitutes the Bible.[57]

However, whether or not one accepts the apologist's explanation of these events is a matter of faith, not of science. Few persons have expressed this faith more convincingly than Samuel:

> We are dealing not with a discovery, but with a process. The Biblical record is a continuing drama. It is fragmentary, a sacred anthology of excerpts in which there is frequent reference to other records, now lost. And yet, with all its incompleteness, it is magnificently consistent

[56] Samuel, *op. cit.*, p. 105.
[57] *Ibid.*, pp. 107–108.

> and instructive. The theme is struggle: inspiration, defection, return, near-obliteration, re-emergence against all probability, the picture of a people possessed by a divine destiny reluctantly assumed, everlastingly repudiated, everlastingly reclaimed.[58]

The sociologist must leave such formulations to the sphere of faith; it is sufficient for his purposes to know that the great creativity of the ancient Jews occurred in a time of community destruction and re-formation, as in the case of the creativity in other areas of the ancient world of the time. The ancient Jewish community moved from a world of tribes and peasant villages to a world of cities and oriental despots, and finally, to a world of ethnic communities. The creative forces of the participants in these dramas were assembled and released in the course of these social transformations.

SELECTED BIBLIOGRAPHY

Albright, William Foxwell, *Archeology and the Religion of Israel* (Baltimore: The John Hopkins University Press, 1953).

Baron, Salo Whittmayer, *A Social and Religious History of the Jews* (New York: Columbia University Press, 1952).

Caiger, Stephen L., *Bible and Spade* (London: Oxford University Press, 1947).

Kenyon, Sir Frederic, *The Bible and Archaeology* (London: George G. Harrap & Co., 1940).

Moore, George Foot, *Judaism in the First Centuries of the Christian Era* (Cambridge: Harvard University Press, 1927).

Smith, G. A., *A Historical Geography of the Holy Land* (London: Haddon & Stoughton, 1910).

Weber, Max, *Ancient Judaism*, trans. by Hans Gerth and Don Martindale (Glencoe, Illinois: The Free Press, 1952).

Weidenreich, Franz, *Apes, Giants, and Man* (Chicago: University of Chicago Press, 1946).

Wellhausen, J., *A Sketch of the History of Israel and Judah* (London: Adam & Charles Black, 1891).

[58] *Ibid.*, p. 106.

II

THE CHANGING ROLES OF PRIEST AND PROPHET

THE CONDITIONS presented by the appearance of the Israelite priest-intellectuals in Canaan were somewhat different from those of the Chous of China and the Aryans of India. The Chous established themselves as a conquest state over a culturally superior predecessor into the footsteps of whom they quickly began to move. The Aryans came into northern India as barbaric conquerors, clearly militarily superior to the populations they were displacing. They spread as a conquest stratum, as a thin layer of oil on water, over a more numerous conquered population. They tended to close ranks and solidify in this relation rather than to mix fluidly with the conquered population. The ancient Hebrews, on the other hand, represented a militarily inferior amalgam of peasants and small stock-breeders opposed by a militarily and culturally superior settled population. Only when the Israelite tribes were fused into the sworn war confederation were they able to carry out the various phases of the conquest of Canaan. No equivalent role was played by the religion of the Chous in the conquest of the Shang, or by the religion of the Aryans in the conquest of Mohenjo-daro to that played by Yahwism in the conquest of Canaan. Israel was a creation of its religion in a unique sense.

RELIGIOUS FIGURES OF THE PREMONARCHICAL PERIOD

It has been argued that some of the oldest religious forms of the ancient Jews show traces of primitive totemistic and animistic forms. Totemism has been suggested by the names of early tribes—Caleb (a dog), Leah (a cow), Rachel (a sheep). Totemism is also suggested by the appearance of the bull as a symbol of Yahweh (in Ex. 32, when Aaron set up a molten calf to be worshiped and I Kings 12:28 ff., when Jereboam instituted worship of the calf in the northern kingdom). Animism has been suggested by such things as the sacred stones at Bethel, where Jacob dreamed of a ladder to heaven (Gen. 28:11–18),[1] or in sacred trees which gave out religious

[1] Brooke Peters Church, *The Private Lives of the Prophets and the Times in Which They Lived* (New York: Rinehart & Co., 1953), pp. 14–15.

messages, as in the story of the burning bush in Exodus or the diviner's oak at Shechem.[2]

Methods of divination practiced among the ancient Hebrews included interpretation of the movements of the stars, clouds, and flights of birds; the sacrifice and divination from entrails and livers of animals, employment of sacred arrows, appealing to the deity by lot, and employment of forms of ordeal; use of the diviner's cup (in the Joseph stories); and suggesting residues of ancestor worship, the belief that the spirits of the dead could be consulted (Saul's visit to the witch of Endor, I Sam. 28). It has been argued that in connection with such practices a variety of religious figures appeared:

> Hence there arose a great host of augurers, soothsayers, astrologers, wizards, diviners, and necromancers: some knaves and some doubtless faithful to their light. They and the priests, who usually interpreted the omens and took charge of the sacred lot and oracles, were the first forerunners of the prophet.[3]

The two poles in the range of experience, synthesized and religiously interpreted by these early religious figures, were represented by dreams (the interpretation of which was looked upon as determination of the will of God) and by various abnormal psychic states (taken as evidence of divine possessions) and often artificially induced, as is done today by the whirling dervishes.

At the time that such preprophetic figures appeared in abundance in Palestine, the prophetic impulse in both Babylonia and Egypt was eclipsed by the functions of the priest who interpreted oracles or determined the will of the gods by various standardized institutional means. In Canaan, on the other hand, as shown by the contest between Jehovah and Baal on Mount Carmel (in which they danced about the altar and cut themselves in a state of frenzy—I Kings 18:26–29), religious figures equivalent to the modern dervish were a dominant type.[4] Dervishes similar to those of the oriental religions also appear among the Baccantes of Greece,[5] and the Hindu Shiva.

It is maintained by certain interpreters that the two types of religious specialists, the clairvoyants to whom God was directly revealed (I Sam. 9:15 f.) and the Corybantic ecstatics (sometimes using artificial devices like the group met by Saul, which employed music and dancing as a means to prophetic ecstasy; see also II Kings 3:15), originally represented two separate types of religious figures. The seer (*ro'eh*) and the prophet (*nabi*)[6] were dream interpreters and Corybantic ecstatics respectively.

[2] Charles Foster Kent, *The Sermons, Epistles, and Apocalypses of Israel's Prophets* (New York: Charles Scribner's Sons, 1921), pp. 3–4.

[3] *Ibid.*, p. 4.

[4] *Ibid.*, p. 5.

[5] *Ibid.*, p. 6.

[6] W. L. Wardel, *The History and Religion of Israel* (Oxford: The Clarendon Press, 1936), p. 175; Weber, *op. cit.*, pp. 106 ff.

On the basis of dream interpretation, the seer (*ro'eh*) gave oracles in a state of apathetic ecstasy in solitude. His patrons sought him out for his counsel. Dream interpretation often became a private business. All sorts of everyday questions were brought before the seers, who were compensated by gifts (I Sam. 9:6–7).[7] By contrast, as magical ecstatics the *Nebiim* were a religious counterpart to the Nazarites, or warrior ecstatics. The Nebiim may have been recruited largely from laymen on the basis of personal charisma. They tattooed themselves on the forehead (I Kings 20:41) and wore a special costume. They pursued a common course of study in special places (for example, Carmel). Their practices included not only ecstatic dancing, but wounding one another and producing nonsense speech. The cataleptic states into which they worked themselves by their practices were thought to have magical power. The miracles of Elisha (II Kings 4:1 f., 4:8 f., 4:18 f., 4:38 f., 4:42 f., 6:1 f., 8:1 f.) were typical of the kinds of powers claimed for the professional sorcerer.[8]

Free prophecy, that is, prophecy occurring outside the framework of existing social and political institutions, can be socially disruptive, as Ahab and Jezebel were well aware every time Elijah spoke. In Egypt and Babylon it was prohibited. Its persistence in Israel was a testimony of primitivism and of the weakness of official organizations. Prophecy had been important at the great crises of the forming nation; at such times it had come to the support of the social order. In Moses' desert experience the spirit of God touched him and he had a vision of Yahweh ready to deliver the oppressed. The vision, typical of the seer, constituted Moses' call, and he became a man of action.[9] Moses united the roles of *ro'eh* and *nabi* in his person. At the second major crisis of Israel during the conquest of Canaan, when the Canaanites formed a coalition under Sisera, the prophetess Deborah rose to deliver her people, placing the mantle of military leadership on the shoulders of Barak. In the third great crisis, Israel was threatened by the Philistines. Samuel, the *ro'eh* of Ramah, found in Saul the hope of the Israelites, as Deborah had found it in Barak.[10] Saul was destined to be overcome by nabi ecstasy.

> As you approach the town, you will meet a band of dervishes coming down from the height with lutes, drums, flutes, and lyres playing in front of them while they prophesy; the spirit of the Eternal will then inspire you till you prophesy among them and become a different man. (I Sam. 10:5 Moffatt translation.)

The person possessed with the spirit of Yahweh was thought to become capable of unusual feats. The kind of magical power attributed to the prophet is evident in Elijah:

[7] Max Weber, *Ancient Judaism, op. cit.*, p. 106.
[8] *Ibid.*, pp. 96–99.
[9] Kent, *op. cit.*, p. 10.
[10] *Ibid.*, p. 11.

> Now Elijah the Tishbite of Tishbe in Gilead said to Ahab, "As the Eternal the God of Israel lives, whom I serve, there shall be neither dew nor rain these years except as I give orders." (I Kings 17:1)

He was even thought to be able to perform such miracles as raising the dead (I Kings 17:19). At times of crisis in Israelite history the talents of seer and Corybantic ecstatic were fused.

PRIESTS AND PROPHETS UNDER THE MONARCHY

The general character of the period of the monarchy has been ably summarized by Wellhausen.[11] Writing which had been introduced at an early period came into general use. A new epoch in the literature opened with the collection and writing down of such songs as the *Book of Wars of the Lord* and the *Book of Jashar*. With the aid of legal documents and family reminiscences and legends, prose history was written, parts of which are preserved in the Old Testament in the Books of Judges, Samuel, and Kings.

Though agriculture and gardening were normal occupations (Gen. 4:3), and implied in the laws (Exod. 21–22), and though industry was undeveloped, the economy was changing. Merchants became influential, and the use of money increased. Solomon engaged in commercial competition with the Tyrians for control of seagoing commerce. Large estates were formed, and the number of mortgages testified to a decline in the number of free peasant proprietors. Free Hebrews were often forced to sell themselves into slavery to pay their debts. Meanwhile, towns were fortified, horses and chariots became indispensable to warfare, the bow became the primary offense weapon, and a professional military class was formed. However, the monarchy remained primarily a kingdom imposed on the tribes. Despite catastrophes to the monarchy, ordinary life went on almost as usual. Though a national religion placed spiritual life on a unified basis, new and old forms of social life coexisted.

A simplification and consolidation of the social roles of the religious figures of the ancient Jews had necessarily accompanied the formation of the monarchy.[12] In the course of the consolidation of the kingdom, David transplanted the priests of Shiloh to Jerusalem. Because of suspicion of subversive activity, Solomon replaced its representative by Zadok. The objective of transforming religion into an official support of the monarchy was clear. Eventually by reorganization of the provision of prebends for its priests, the cult monopoly of Jerusalem was asserted. The Deuteronomic law book designated the Levite priests as the sole legitimate representatives of Yahweh.

Weber believes that the Levites originally came from the southern steppe region bordering the desert, specifically from the Oasis of Kadesh near Seir.

[11] J. Wellhausen, *A Sketch of the History of Israel and Judah* (London: Adam and Charles Black, 1891).

[12] See particularly Weber's chapter, "Priests and the Cult Monopoly of Jerusalem," *op. cit.*, pp. 169–193.

They made their appearance first as a personal following of Moses. At that time they may have been a guild of magicians, for, according to Moses' blessing, one had to deny father and brother to be a Levite. This would be true of a trained status group, not of a hereditary caste. Biblical tradition also reports the existence of a tribe of Levi whose members were not Levite priests. Hence, Weber believes either a tribe of Levi was dispersed by a political catastrophe, its members then taking up work as Yahweh priests, or an occupational group became, in time, a hereditary group of priests, as the Brahmans did in India. In Deuteronomic times Levitical priests belonged to families which possessed hereditary monopolies of oracular formulas, priestly teaching, and at times priestly positions. At least in the south the Levites managed to monopolize priestly positions.

Weber suggests that because of their superior ritualistic training the Levites evolved into a kind of guest tribe within the Israelite community. Their knowledge of sacrifice and training for the cure of souls placed strong demands on their spiritual ministrations. Though originally at home in South Israel, they diffused northward.

> In this manner, the Levites by gradual expansion attained their position as cult monopolists which in Deuteronomic times was essentially recognized in Judaic territory. Deuteronomy presupposes in every territory a resident Levite, living off sacrificial offerings.[13]

From the first, Weber maintains that the Levites segregated themselves ritualistically from the laity, opposing the Egyptian cult of the dead. In Moses' blessing the Levites had the duty of instructing people in rights and in the Torah. In legal disputes they activated the oracle by lot. The source of their prestige was rational knowledge of Yahweh's commandments. Sins were confessed to them (Numb. 5:6 f.), and they mediated between the guilty and Yahweh (Lev. 4:20, 31).

During their rise in importance, Weber maintains the Levites adjusted to existing conditions, even conforming to the idol cult of the northern kingdom. It is probable that those Levites who were later disqualified for priestly office and degraded to the status of temple servants were from idolatrous Levite clans.

As the Levites diffused from the south to the north, they must have met increasing resistance from the priests with vested interests in the ancient northern sanctuaries. On the other hand, many of the northern priests could hardly have viewed with equanimity the temple construction of Solomon and the predominance of that sanctuary over all others. The secession of the northern kingdom may have been in part determined by the antagonism within the priesthood. In any case, Jeroboam took prompt action to certify Dan and Beth-El as sanctuaries for the northern kingdom, and when the northern kingdom was destroyed, the Jerusalemite (Zadokite) priesthood quickly decreed that the worship of Yahweh in mountain shrines and under

[13] *Ibid.*, p. 174.

trees, and at the ancient and rural provincial sanctuaries at Beth-El, Dan, Shechem, and other places should stop.[14]

Deuteronomic law claimed a religious monopoly for the Jerusalem priesthood. However, this created the problem of providing for the Levites and other priests who had officiated at the sanctuaries. Simply to disqualify them but otherwise permit them to go their way would have been to create a stratum of agitators. Hence it was stipulated that these priests should move to Jerusalem, where they would be permitted to participate in the cult.

While the Levitical religiosity of the south was evolving to the point where it could claim monopoly of the cult for itself, it encountered opposition from the orgiastic ecstatics, the Nebiim. The Nebiim were strong in other areas and partly under the influence of Phoenician and Canaanite Baal cults which supported charismatic ecstatics organized into guilds, or schools, such as that of Elisha. Levitical and Nabi forms of religiosity inevitably came into conflict.

> The mass ecstatic Nebiim, under the influence of Canaanite orgiasticism and the irrational and emotional forms of magic, came from the North. The rational Levitical Torah and rational ethical emissary prophecy came from the South.[15]

These formed, for Weber, the foundation of a dualism which he felt runs through Israelite history from the time of the invasion.

One aspect of the religious life of the ancient Hebrews during the period of the monarchy was represented by the diffusion of Levitical religiosity and the evolution of a cult monopoly by the Jerusalem priesthood. Other religiously important events were happening in the free expression of Israelite religious sentiment outside official circles. The brilliant flowering of prophecy occurred at this time in the course of the intersection of these two types of development.[16]

The pre-Exile prophets, from Amos to Jeremiah, have been conceived as political demagogues and pamphleteers,[17] though they did not form parties or try to seize power. Their form of free prophecy was able to arise only with the developing external foreign threats to the country and to royal power, and in a time when the internal coordination of institutions had been only incompletely achieved. Elijah publicly opposed both the king and his prophets, and was forced to flee. Amos complained of the suppression of his prophecy by the strong government of Jeroboam II in a manner comparable, according to Weber, to the modern demagogue's cry for freedom of the press. The prophet was a private citizen, but one of considerable significance because of his potential influence on the masses who often viewed

14 *Ibid.*, p. 183.
15 *Ibid.*, p. 193.
16 See Church, *op. cit.;* Kent, *op. cit.*, pp. 13–38; Wardel, *op. cit.*, pp. 174–193; Weber, *op. cit.*, pp. 267–296; J. M. Powis Smith, *The Prophets and Their Times* (Chicago: University Press, 1925).
17 Weber, *op. cit.*, p. 267.

> . . . ay, sacrifice in the morning,
> and every third day pay your tithes,
> burn your dough as a thank-offering,
> announce your freewill gifts—
> oh, make them public,
> for you love that, you Israelites! (Amos 4:4 f.)

But the trouble was not with the cult; Yahweh did not seek a reform of the cult. "Your sacred festivals? I hate them, scorn them; your sacrifices? I will not smell their smoke" (Amos 5:21). Yahweh did not want sacrifice but justice "like fresh water" (Amos 5:24). For lack of it he would send Israel into exile "beyond Damascus." On the Day of Yahweh the devastating justice of the Lord would arrive. The city would be abandoned, houses would be pulled down, famine and drought would scourge the land. No one would survive. Added later to Amos' prophecy was the qualification that "the house of Jacob will not be wiped out" (Amos 9:9).

Hosea, son of Beri, in the northern kingdom, began to prophesy under the reign of Jeroboam II (782–743 B.C., probably the major part of the book of Hosea originated in years between 750 and 735 B.C.). He was a member of a prosperous household, perhaps of a priestly family. From the tragedy of his personal experience, Hosea formulated the image of the relation between Yahweh to Israel as that of a loving bridegroom to his bride. Even as Hosea's wife proved untrue to him, so Israel decked herself with rings and jewels and ran after her lovers, the Baals, forgetting Yahweh. But even as Hosea loved his faithless wife, Yahweh loved Israel still. If she would only come back, all would be forgiven:

> On that day, the Eternal declares, she shall call me, "My Husband," no more "My Baal"; I will betroth her to me for ever, betroth her in a bond of goodness and of justice, in kindness and in love; yes, loyally will I betroth her, to let her understand the Eternal (Hos. 2:16–20).

On the day of reconciliation there would even be a covenant of peace with the animals:

> On that day I will make a league for them with the wild beasts and birds and creeping things of earth; and I will wipe out of their land bow, sword, and all munitions, to let them lie down in security. (Hos. 2:18)

Meanwhile in Israel, however, there was "no fidelity, no kindness, no knowledge of God . . . nothing but perjury, lying, and murder, stealing, debauchery, burglary—bloodshed on bloodshed!" (Hos. 4:2). Israel pursued false religions, employed oracle poles, enjoyed temple prostitution, sacrificed on mountains and supported the cult of oak and terebinth (Hos. 4:12). Particularly abominable was the gold and silver calf of Samaria (Hos. 8:4). Israel's foreign policy was a major target for Hosea's blasts:

> Ephraim is like a silly, senseless dove, crying to Egypt, flying to Assyria. (Hos. 7:11)

This could only lead to disaster.

> Ephraim herds the wind and hunts a sirocco piling up fraud and falsehood daily, striking a bargain with Assyria, carrying presents of oil to Egypt. (Hos. 12:2)

These foreign nations were to be the implement of Israel's chastisement.

> In my wrath I will chastise them, gathering nations to attack them, in chastisement for their two-fold offense. (Hos. 10:10)

There was no help from a priesthood which rejected the knowledge of Yahweh (Hos. 4:6). The prophet was God's watchman, yet in the very temple of God men were hostile to him (Hos. 9:8). There was no answer but to reverse the Exodus or carry the people off to Assyria.

> They must go back to the land of Egypt or Assyria must be their king; the sword shall ply within their towns and lay them low within their fortresses (Hos. 11:5–6).

This statement was inspired by the vision of the Exodus as a kind of honeymoon of God with Israel—God's just love for his people. Sacrifice was not demanded by God, who approved mercy rather than sacrifice (Hos. 6:6). Religion was an affair of the heart, not of outward protestations (Hos. 7:14). Like a father Yahweh taught Ephraim to walk (Hos. 11:1–4). Forgiveness was held out wherever Israel sought its father's face.

Isaiah was a Judean of Jerusalem from an upper-class household of perhaps royal blood. The period of his prophecy extended from around 740 B.C. to 701 B.C. Isaiah's prophecy was inspired by the vision of the Lord in his temple and the seraphs singing:

> Holy, holy, holy, is the Lord of hosts, His majestic splendor fills the whole earth (Isa. 6:3).

One of the seraphs took a hot coal and touched the lips of the prophet, consecrating him for prophecy (Isaiah 6:6). Isaiah was an ecstatic man overwhelmed by the splendor and majesty of God.

Sacrifice counted as little for Isaiah as for the other prophets. "What care I for all your lavish sacrifices?" the Eternal asks (Isa. 1:11). Zion, once so true, was a haunt of murderers, its rulers were unruly and conspired with thieves. Everyone was fond of bribes, while careless of the orphan's rights and the widow's cause (Isa. 1:22–24).

The woes of the city were produced by the kingship. The Lord had no use for all the types of persons who populated the kingdom: the warrior, governor, official seer, sheik, counselor, expert magician, or exchanger. Isaiah dreamed of the confederacy of old, where a mere lad could be leader (Isa. 3:2–5). The detailed complaints that Yahweh had against Judah included unjust accumulation of wealth (Isa. 5:8), reveling and drinking (Isa. 5:11), haughtiness (Isa. 5:15), irreligion (Isa. 5:19), accepting bribes (Isa. 5:23), and depriving the innocent of their rights (Isa. 5:24). The foreign powers were the implements of God's wrath:

> He signals to a foreign power, whistling for them from the ends of the earth (Isa. 10:26).

Assyria would be the specific instrument of Yahweh's wrath:

> He is my club in anger, the rod I wield in wrath; I speed him against an impious nation a people with whom I am wroth, bidding him plunder and spoil them, trample them down like mud in the street (Isa. 10:5–6).

The nation was condemned, because it had become a land full of horses, war chariots, idols, gold and silver, traders, and bargains with foreigners (Isa. 2:6–8). All these things were of no avail, for they could not stand against the fury of Yahweh. Isaiah condemned the policy of seeking help from Egypt, and foretold the disaster of Assyria.

The only possible hope for Israel lay elsewhere than in military resistance. Isaiah foretold of a Messiah who would be chosen by God to deliver His people:

> "Listen, you royalties, I am tired of you!—And will you insist on tiring my God as well as a man like myself? An omen you shall have, and that from the Eternal Himself. There is a young woman with child, who shall bear a son and call his name 'Immanuel.'" (Isa. 7:13)

Moreover, a remnant would be saved on the day Yahweh visited destruction on the land:

> A remnant, a mere remnant of Jacob
> shall come back to the Mighty God;
> for though your folk, O Israel, are
> like sea-sands in number,
> only a remnant of them shall return,
> destruction is decreed, a flood of
> retribution,
> for the Lord of hosts will carry out
> doom fixed and final over all the
> world. (Isa. 10:21 f.)

Micah was contemporary with Isaiah, living in the countryside of Judah. He gained a special importance because of an incident in the life of Jeremiah (Jer. 26:18 f.), for when Jeremiah was endangered because of his prophecy of the destruction of the Temple, the elders reminded the prince that there was a precedent for such prophecy. Micah condemned the social ills with special force: bribing judges, giving oracles for pay, divining for money (Mic. 3:11 f.). One of the criteria of true prophecy was its gratuitous character in contrast to false prophecy for pay (Mic. 2:11, 3:5). Assyria was the agent of Israel's punishment (Mic. 1:6, 1:10–11). Even the temple of Jerusalem must be destroyed.

Zephaniah's prophecies around 630 B.C. are most important for his portrayal of the Day of Yahweh (Zeph. 1:14:18) and his doctrine that a righteous remnant would survive (Zeph. 2:3–7). More important is Jeremiah, who began his work at the same time and prophesied in Jerusalem until the kingdom came to an end. He was a member of a priestly family of Anathoth and a man of property with influential friends in Jerusalem.

The reforms of Josiah to whom he pays tribute (Jer. 22:15 f.) occurred during this time. However, in the end he emphatically repudiated the sacrificial cult (Jer. 6:2, 6:20, 7:21–6). Of all the prophets Jeremiah provides fullest insight into his inner experience. He was a sensitive, shy person, experiencing the prophetic call as an unhappy fate: "I am too young!" (Jer. 1:6). But when the prophetic call came, Jeremiah felt he must speak before he burst:

> O my heart, my heart! It writhes!
> O how it throbs!
> My soul is moaning!
> I cannot hold my peace. (Jer. 4:19)

He was not always sure of his judgment or of his own courage when he was taunted and insulted because of his prophecy:

> I am tired of this,
> so tired I cannot bear it any longer
> At every turn I am in terror,
> for I hear many whispering,
> Denounce him! Let us denounce him! (Jer. 20:10)

Yet it was the sign of a false prophet—a distinction which Jeremiah sharpened—that he told people what they wanted to hear:

> I have heard what the prophets say,
> who prophesy falsely in my name—
> "I've had a dream," they cry, "I've had
> a dream!"
> Will they never give over
> these prophets of falsehood,
> who preach their own illusions? (Jer. 23:25 f.)

Jeremiah brooded over the suffering of the poor and of the oppressed, the metic, the orphan, the widow, the innocent (Jer. 22:3 f.). However, he was no mass leader. Responsibility lay with the upper classes who knew better.

> "But these are the poor," I said, "Mere
> ignorant folk,
> who never learned the rules of
> the Eternal
> of the religion of their God.
> I will turn to the upper classes,
> I will talk to them;
> for they have learned the rules
> of the Eternal,

and the religion of their God."
But they had flung off all restraints,
and broken every bond. (Jer. 5:5)

Jeremiah was hated and reviled by both the people and the king whom he accosted in the streets of the city with his oracles. He was cast into prison, and threatened with death as a traitor. However, he sincerely believed the foreign powers were God's instruments. All military resistance was useless. The foreign powers were the scourge with which Yahweh chastised his people. When the Babylonians were at the gates, he advocated nonresistance. Because the Babylonians saw him as an ally, they did not deport him with other city notables. However, Jeremiah was no traitor; he sent a curse to Babylon and ordered it thrown into the Euphrates, and subsequently joined the flight to Egypt.

Nahum and Habakkuk were contemporaries of Jeremiah. Nahum was intensely nationalistic, being something of the type of prophet Jeremiah denounced. Habakkuk prophesied during the reign of Jehoiakim (Hab. 1:2–11), though most of the book bearing his name dates from the end of the Exile. He was primarily concerned with the question of why the righteous suffer (Hab. 1:13). He found no answer, and was only able to counsel patience (Hab. 2:2–4).

THE RISE OF THE SCRIBES

In the Exile and Postexile periods, the Jews were transformed into an ethnic community. This transformation was located by Weber at the center of the whole problem of contemporary Judaism.

> All the essential traits of Jewry's attitude toward the environment can be deduced from this pariah existence—especially its voluntary ghetto, long anteceding compulsory internment, and the dualistic nature of its in-group and out-group morality.
>
> The differences between Jewish and Indian pariah tribes consist in the following three significant circumstances:
>
> 1. Jewry was, or rather, became a pariah people in a surrounding free of castes.
> 2. The religious promise to which the ritual segregation of Jewry was moored differed essentially from those of the Indian castes. Ritually correct conduct, *i.e.*, conduct conforming to caste standards, carried for the Indian pariah castes the premium of ascent by way of rebirth in a caste-structured world thought to be eternal and unchangeable. . . .
>
> The whole attitude toward life of ancient Jewry was determined by the conception of a future God-guided political and social revolution.
>
> 3. This revolution was to take a special direction.[24]

This peculiar combination of an ethnic community, and a social revolutionary promise, did not arise all at once. It represented a new synthesis of elements cast up in the course of successive experiences of the people. The

[24] Weber, *op. cit.*, pp. 3–4.

ancient Jews had been formed into an effective fighting force by means of a religious confederation (with its critical feature of a covenant between the chosen people of Yahweh). The experience of the monarchy added new elements of legal codification and the sublimation of the socio-religious ethic by the prophetic critics of monarchy. Finally the formation of the ethnic community during the Exile and politically subordinate status of the community at the time of the Second Temple, supplied the conditions for a new kind of religious synthesis.

A radical transformation in the rôle of the priesthood was under way during the last days of the monarchy. It has already been observed that the weakness of the priesthood was one of the conditions for the flowering of prophecy. However, consolidation of the priesthood was also occurring. With the downfall of the northern kingdom the cult monopoly of Jerusalem was asserted. The distinction between priests and Levites was drawn; nevertheless the Levites were guaranteed a share in the cult of Jerusalem (Deut. 24:19–21, 14:28 f.; 16:10–14). This may well have been more a product of political acumen than of weakness, for to have left the Levites outside the official cult would have involved loss of control over them. The abduction of the priesthood and the transportation of priests into exile, however, did not reduce its significance, but increased it. There the priests became the backbone of the ethnic community, and carried through ritualistic consolidation of the community.

In Ezekiel's vision of a restored community, the kings declined in importance except as patrons of the priests who were in command. In Ezekiel's code, the Levites, for whom the Deuteronomic code had provided a share in the cult, were reduced to the position of menials performing the duties of temple servants. In the priestly code, probably codified toward the end of the fifth century B.C., the distinction drawn between priests and Levites was even more sharp. Only in the central sanctuary might the cult be practiced.[25]

As Weber indicated, in the Postexile period the spirit of prophecy rapidly went into eclipse before the priest:

> It vanished because the priestly police power in the Jewish congregation gained control over ecstatic prophecy in the same manner as did the bishopric and presbyterian authorities over pneumatic prophecy in the early Christian congregation.[26]

Ezekiel, the prophet deported to Babylon with the exiles in 597 B.C., was famous for oracles. His prophecies of doom, at first not taken seriously, were confirmed by news of the final destruction of Jerusalem. He brilliantly synthesized in his person the roles of both priest and prophet. Once the task of preserving the community fell on his shoulders, Ezekiel, the priest, shifted the emphasis from inner religiosity to community of ritualistic observance.

[25] See Wardel's review, *op. cit.*, pp. 164–173.
[26] Weber, *op. cit.*, p. 380.

God was conceived to be transcendently holy. The nation had profaned this holiness. Hence, God punished the people by the destruction of the state. The foreign nations that invaded Israel were the instruments of God. However, God would create a new nation out of the nucleus of restored people from the exiles.

The ancient notion of the collective responsibility of all for the guilt of some was transformed by Ezekiel. "What do you mean by quoting this proverb in the land of Israel, 'The fathers eat sour grapes, the children's teeth are set on edge?' By my life," says the Lord the Eternal, "you must never quote that proverb again in Israel" (Ezek. 18:2–4). Out of the cleansed remnants of the people, on the basis of individual religiosity, the new people would be formed.

Ezekiel's bizarre visions were an intimation of later angelology. His apocalyptic teaching of the future also anticipated later development. Nations led by a mysterious figure called Gog would descend on Israel to ravish it. Yahweh would annihilate them with hail, fire, and brimstone from heaven. The corpses would be so numerous that it would require seven years to clear the land of their pollution. Eventually a golden age shared by both northern and southern kingdoms (fused into one) would arrive.

An anonymous prophet (Deutero-Isaiah) of the Exile added his oracles to those of Isaiah (Isa. 40–55). He wrote while Cyrus was in the ascendant (about 540 B.C.). While sensitive to the faults of the people, he was filled with pity for them, consoling them as having suffered enough and atoned for their sins. He elaborated an ideal of absolute monotheism. God the creator of the universe was not only all powerful but all kind, caring for his people like a shepherd. In the "Servant Songs" (Isa. 42:1–4, 49:1–6, 50:4–9, 52:13–53), which may symbolize Israel, the conception of vicarious suffering was developed.

Haggai and Zechariah were primarily important for their work in the rebuilding of the temple in Jerusalem. In apocalyptic visions Zechariah formulated a conception of a Messiah. Trito-Isaiah exalted the cult, the temple, the sacrifices, and festivals. Malachi, his contemporary, was noted chiefly for his hatred of the Edomites and indignation over moral laxness. Joel (400 B.C.) was primarily concerned with a locust plague.

Charismatic ecstatic prophecy, Weber notes, lived on after a fashion as indicated by the visions of Daniel and Enoch and other apocalyptics. However, literary art forms began to dominate the actual emotional experiences. The activities of the seers became an affair of sects and mysteries. The priests succeeded in destroying the prestige of Nabi ecstasy. Deutero-Zechariah's scorn of the prophets as representatives of the spirit of uncleanness (13:1 f.)[27] was symptomatic of the change. The age of prophecy was held by the priests to be ended.

Yet even while, under priestly influence, ecstatic prophecy was be-

[27] Weber, *op. cit.*, p. 381.

ing pushed outside the pale, a new contrast began to appear which was to affect the priests. The Book of Jesus, Son of Sirach (Ecclesiasticus), is of considerable importance in tracing this change.[28] Sirach was a cultivated scholar and teacher of religious morals to young men, active around 200 B.C., a teacher of the law and representative of the class of *soferim* (scribes). In his portrait of the scribe Sirach observes:

> Learning is the privilege of leisure. Husbandmen and artisans are the support of the social structure, but, occupied as they must be in their several callings and often highly expert in them, they have no time for the wide-ranging studies that make the scholar.
>
> Different is the case of the man who gives his whole mind to it, and concentrates his thought on the law of the Most High. He will seek out the wisdom of all the ancients, and occupy himself with the study of prophecies, and pay attention to expositions of famous men, and will penetrate into the elusive turns of parables. He will search out the hidden meaning of proverbs, and will be versed in the enigmas of parables.[29]

Ezra and the men of the great synagogue were the forerunners of the scribes. Not only did Biblical scholars and teachers attain great proficiency, but they achieved an independent place beside the priesthood in the interpretation of the law.

A new differentiation of social classes was occurring. The Pharisees, the great body of pious members of the community, were growing distinct from the patriarchal aristocracy composed of the wealthy families and the priestly nobility, the Zadokites, or Sadducees.[30] Flowing from the character of an ethnic community, there were many temptations for the Sadducees, who occupied top positions in the Jewish community, to cooperate with and to imitate the foreign powers which dominated the secular administration. The temptation was particularly strong under the Greeks. As Moore observes:

> After Simeon the Righteous . . . high priests who bought their appointment from the king were willing tools in his hellenizing plans, and turned the Scribes, with all the Jews who were zealous for their own religion (the Hasidm) against them. The national high priests, from John Hyrcanus in his later years, went over to the Sadducean party, and the priestly nobility under Herod and the procurators were of the same stripe. The Scribes, on the other hand, had the support of the Pharisaean party, to which many of them belonged.[31]

When the priests came to be thrust aside as traitors to the cause of Jewish orthodoxy, the successors to the scribes (*soferim*), sustained by the Pharisees, came to be known as rabbis.[32] The formal legitimation as rabbi

[28] George Foot Moore, *op. cit.*, pp. 317 ff.
[29] Quoted by Moore, *ibid.*, pp. 40–41.
[30] Weber, *op. cit.*, p. 387.
[31] Moore, *op. cit.*, p. 43.
[32] *Ibid.*, pp. 391 ff.

appeared only with the establishment of the patriarchate after the fall of the temple. The rabbinical teachers derived their prestige solely from education, like the Roman jurisconsults and Indian *gurus*. They were a stratum of plebeian intellectuals. Aside from a few merchants and artisans, they were blacksmiths, sandal-makers, carpenters, shoemakers, tanners, architects, boatmen, and wine-testers. The first two famous founders of schools, Hillel and Shammani, were artisans,[33] and although Jewish municipal law of talmudic times privileged the rabbis in various ways (exemption from taxes, freedom from *corvée* labor, the right to sell their products in the market before others sold), it came to be expressly understood that a rabbi earned his livelihood through work. They became the plebeian bearers of that aspect of the religiosity resting on learning. In the last analysis, Weber notes, the rabbis rejected asceticism as well as the intellectual mysticism of a salvation aristocracy.[34]

SUMMARY

In the three major time periods of ancient Jewish history, the period of the confederation, the royal period, and the period of the Exile and Post-exile, three very different kinds of communities were present. In the confederate period the basic communities were tribes and peasant villages held together in a war confederation by Yahwism; in the royal period the dominant form of community was the city; during the Exile period and the times following it, the major form of society was the ethnic community.

These various communities sustained quite different types of intellectual roles. In the first period a wide variety of augurers, soothsayers, astrologers, wizards, diviners, and necromancers were present. They tended to fall into two major types—the seer (*ro'eh*) who interpreted, and the Corybantic ecstatics who prophesied. Both the *ro'eh* and *nabi* played important roles in the repeated dedication of the tribal confederation to its task.

In the royal period the *milieu* for the development of religion was quite different because of the attempt by the newly formed Jewish monarchy to consolidate its institutions. Jerusalem was established as a capital with a central location on tribally neutral land. Along with the centralization of the administration in the capital city, Yahwism was transformed into the official religion of the monarchy, and the Temple was located at the capital. Such consolidation of the religious position of the monarchy transformed the religion into a central monopoly, but left many rural elements in Israel which opposed these centralizing tendencies of the official cult.

The combination of unsolved internal tensions and the weakness of the monarchy compared to the great powers on whose borders it had taken shape provided a fertile ground for the emergence of two major types

[33] *Ibid.*, p. 393.
[34] *Ibid.*, p. 400.

of religious figures: the official prophets and priests of the kings, and the free prophets who were supported by the rural clans.

With the destruction of the Jewish monarchy and the deportation of a large segment of the influential citizens to Babylon, a radical reconstruction of the community was required if the Jews were to retain their identity as a people. This was accomplished by the formation of an ethnic community, a community which found a new point of synthesis (for its old political and economic core) in religion and culture. The priests and elders rose to a position of authority in the ethnic community, the like of which they had not enjoyed since tribal days. The institutional synthesis of the ethnic community was found, not in the temple, but in the synagogue and school. Moreover, since, as time went by, there was a natural temptation on the part of the upper classes and the priests of the ethnic community to enter into commerce with and to be influenced by the social practices of the surrounding world, the point of gravity of the community tended to shift to the pious middle-class, the Pharisees. In time, pioneered by the scribes (*soferim*, learned lay persons), the rabbis evolved into the representatives of the ethnic community.

SELECTED BIBLIOGRAPHY

Baron, Salo Whittmayer, *A Social and Religious History of the Jews* (New York: Columbia University Press, 1952).

Church, Brooke Peters, *The Private Lives of the Prophets and the Times in Which They Lived* (New York: Rinehart & Co., 1953).

Kent, Charles Foster, *The Sermons, Epistles, and Apocalypses of Israel's Prophets* (New York: Charles Scribner's Sons, 1921).

Moore, George Foot, *Judaism in the First Centuries of the Christian Era* (Cambridge: Harvard University Press, 1927).

Smith, J. M. Powis, *The Prophets and Their Times* (Chicago: University of Chicago Press, 1925).

Wardel, W. L., *The History and Religion of Israel* (Oxford: The Clarendon Press, 1936).

Weber, Max, *Ancient Judaism*, trans. by Hans Gerth and Don Martindale (Glencoe, Illinois: The Free Press, 1952).

12

THE SOCIAL THOUGHT AND CIVILIZATION OF ANCIENT ISRAEL

The canonization of the Old Testament transformed choice elements from a millennium of the literature of a people into the symbol of the community. Considerable rearrangement of the various historical strata of literature accompanied this canonization, bringing it into conformity with propaganda needs. The fascinating story of the analysis of these various historical levels by literary criticism, however, belongs elsewhere.

The literature was created by the bearers of social processes operating under very different conditions. The three major stages in this development were represented by the tribal and peasant communities of the war confederation (1260–1025 B.C.), the city community of the monarchy (1024–586 B.C.), and the period of the formation of the ethnic community (585 B.C. into the present).

The social roles of the creators were quite distinct. In the earliest period, the bearers of the religious tradition were augurers, diviners, and necromancers of various kinds who were of two major types (seers and prophets). Of these the Yahweh prophets were particularly important, for they were bearers of a form of religion which in the case of the Rechabites had proved its capacity to give the tribal association a remarkable and enduring permanence under conditions where the tribe was normally unstable.

From all indications, Moses was a man of genius. The Jews were being pressed from a number of directions at once, and perhaps cast into the position where they either had to carry out the conquest of Canaan or be swallowed up. Possibly because of a change of administration in Egypt, those tribes settled inside its borders were oppressed in a manner which they considered intolerably burdensome and a threat to their very existence. Meanwhile, there is evidence that by about 1300 B.C. the domestication of camels by the Bedouins had proceeded far enough that the people could greatly widen their life sphere. The combination of tribal groups which occupied the narrow band of environmental conditions between the

Bedouins and the settled agricultural populations must have created problems; the group either had to enter upon a course of conquest or be swallowed up. At the same time, the traditional difficulty of forming such unpromising social structures into anything like an effective war association made such a course of events *a priori* quite implausible.

Moses' genius lay in the fact that he consciously or intuitively took the one way of welding these miscellaneous elements into a unified structure that held out a promise of permanence, turning them into an oath-bound religious confederation.

SOCIAL THOUGHT IN THE TIME OF THE TRIBAL CONFEDERATION

The oldest literary productions of the Israelites were poems which at a later period were incorporated into the historical books. As isolated by literary analysis, the materials belonging to the premonarchical period (before 1000 B.C.) include:

1. *War and march songs:* Songs of Lamech (Gen. 4:23 f). Song of Miriam (Ex. 15:21). Eternal War with Amalek (Ex. 17:16). Incantations to the Ark (Numbers 10:35 f). List of Stations (Numbers 21:14 f). Taunt Song of the Amorites (Numbers 21:27–30). The Song of the Well (Numbers 21:17 f). Joshua's Appeal to the Sun and the Moon (Joshua 10:12 f). The Song of Deborah (Judges 5).
2. *Proverbs, riddles, and fables:* David's Proverb (1 Samuel 24:13). Samson's Riddles (Judges 14:14) and Taunt (Judges 15:16). Jotham's Fable (Judges 9:7–15).
3. *Prophetic blessings and oracles:* The Blessing of Noah (Gen. 9:25–27). The Oracles of Balaam (Num. 23 f).[1]

The literature of the Israelites from the premonarchical period compares with the literature of India and Greece from earliest times. All three literatures reflect an ancient conflict between peasant or seminomadic peoples and more settled urban communities. All literatures were maintained by guilds of magicians or shamans or bards (Vedic bards, Homeric bards, or singers, and Levites).

There does not seem to have been a Chinese literature quite parallel. Although ancient China had its epic period, the legends of conquest of the Chou people of the Shang were perhaps too quickly swallowed up in the literary traditions taken over from the Shang to permit the elaboration of a typical epic literature. In India, Greece, and Israel, on the other hand, the gap between the more primitive conquerors and the conquered was great. Amalgamation between the old and new did not proceed too speedily to prevent the elaboration of a characteristic heroic literature. There were, however, important differences between the heroic literatures of these three areas. Of the three, the Homeric epics were the least religiously stylized. The Indian literature from its heroic period was partly con-

[1] Following Julius A. Bewer, *The Literature of the Old Testament* (New York: Columbia University Press, 1933), p. xii.

tained in the Vedas and partly maintained as an ancient oral tradition to be worked up later in their epics. Indian development moved through henotheism toward a peculiar kind of syncretism. In Israel socio-religious development was uniquely centered in the concept of a covenant between God and His chosen people.

Israel arose as a sworn confederation. In the minds of the later interpreters, its unity was achieved through a series of covenants between God and Noah, Abraham, Isaac, and Jacob, reaching a climax in the covenant of Sinai. It is more plausible to assume that the pre-Mosaic covenants were legendary. The decisive covenant was the Mosaic. The terms of the covenant of Moses were said to be inscribed on stone (Deut. 27:8) and confirmed by a solemn ceremony.

> The Levites shall proclaim aloud to all the men of Israel: "A curse on the man who carves or casts an idol—which the Eternal detests—the work of a craftsman's hands, erecting it in secret," And all the people shall answer. "So be it." "A curse on the man who dishonors his father or mother!" And all the people shall answer "So be it!" (Deut. 27:14 ff. Moffatt translation).

There seems to be no question about the frequent recourse to the covenant device thereafter. The Joshua tradition, for example, reports that after the conquest a covenant was made with the people of the land:

> And Joshua said unto the people, "Ye cannot serve the Lord; for he is an holy God; he is a jealous God; he will not forgive your transgressions nor your sins.
>
> If ye forsake the Lord, and serve strange gods, then he will turn and do you hurt, and consume you, after that he hath done you good."
>
> And the people said unto Joshua, "Nay: but we will serve the Lord."
>
> And Joshua said unto the people, "Ye are witnesses against yourselves that ye have chosen you the Lord, to serve him." And they said, "We are witnesses."
>
> "Now therefore put away," said he, "the strange gods which are among you, and incline your heart unto the Lord God of Israel."
>
> And the people said unto Joshua, "The Lord our God will we serve, and His voice will we obey."
>
> So Joshua made a covenant with the people that day, and set them a statute and an ordinance in Shechem (Josh. 24:19–25. King James version).

Events in this period moved forward from one covenant to another. The idea of the covenant was transmitted as a model for the interpretation of later social and political events.

The important events in the historical organization of the law were typically conceived in terms of a renewed covenant such as the Deuteronomic law (II Kings, 2 ff.) dating from 621 B.C. When Ezra brought the Book of the Law from Babylon (Neh. 8–10), it was solemnly sworn to by the people in a renewed covenant with God. The prophets assumed that the obligation of the people to God rested on their covenant with Him.

The Israelites were repeatedly reminded of their sworn relation to God.

> Thou wilt sink all our sins deep in the sea; Thou wilt prove faithful to Jacob and loving to Abraham, as of old Thou hast sworn to our fathers. (Mic. 7:19–20. Moffatt translation).

Jeremiah hoped that in the end Yahweh would again conclude a new covenant with His people, though under more lenient conditions than of yore.[2]

When an agreement, the terms of which are decided in advance and to which the parties bind themselves by oath, is made central to socio-religious experience, a number of related social and religious consequences follow. The relation of the Israelites to their God was particularized; they became a "chosen people." The events of the social and political order were conditionally dependent on observance of the terms of the covenant. The development of the nation was transformed into a specific system of time-bound hopes and aspirations. Since the covenant concerned a war confederacy of seminomadic stock-breeders and peasants, its efficacy depended upon the avoidance of too intimate an involvement of the God of the covenant with the gods of the tribes. In fact, it was necessary to assert the superiority of the God of the covenant to them.

Thus the covenant idea set in motion the trend toward the religious penetration of the this-worldly socio-political relations of a people developing in time. With almost every step the development moved toward monotheism.

THE PERIOD OF THE MONARCHY

The completion of the conquest of Canaan and the consolidation of the nation achieved in the course of the counterconquest against the Philistines opened the urban and monarchical period of Israel's history. It was a period of great literary productivity with the appearance of major historical and prophetic work. As analyzed by the literary critics, the Old Testament sources produced in this period include the following:

1. The Time of David, Solomon, and Jeroboam I (1000–910 B.C.):
   a. *Poems:* Paean over David's victories (1 Sam. 13:7). Sheba's war cry (2 Sam. 20:1). David's Lamentation over Saul and Jonathan (2 Sam. 1:10 ff.) and over Abner (2 Sam. 3:33 f.). Nathan's parable (2 Sam. 12:1–4). Solomon's Dedication of the Temple (1 Kings 8:12 f.). The Books of Yashar and of the Wars of Yahweh. The Blessing of Moses (Deut. 33).
   b. *Narratives:* The Story of the Founding and Establishment of the Kingdom by Saul, David, and Solomon (Parts of 1 and 2 Sam. and 1 Kings 1 f.). The Book of the Acts of Solomon (1 Kings 3–11 in part). Beginnings of the Royal Annals of the Temple records.
   c. *Laws:* The Book of the Covenant (Exodus 20:33–23:19). The so-called Cultic Decalogue of Exodus 34.

[2] See Weber's summary, *op. cit.*, pp. 75 ff.

2. The Ninth and Eighth Centuries B.C.:
   The Elijah stories (1 Kings 17–19:21). The Elisha stories (2–8 Kings in part, 13:14–21). The history of the rise and fall of the Dynasty of Omri (1 Kings 20:22, 2 Kings 3:6–24, 7:20, 8:7–15, 9, 10). The Yahwist (about 850 B.C.). The Elohist (about 750 B.C.). Amos (about 750 B.C.). Hosea 7:45 (735 B.C.). Isaiah (780–700 B.C.). Micah (725 to around 700 B.C.).
3. The Seventh and Early Sixth Centuries B.C.:
   Combination of the Yahwist and the Elohist. Deuteronomy (published in 621 B.C.). Zephaniah (about 627–626 B.C.). Jeremiah (after 626 B.C.). Nahum (about 615 B.C.). The first edition of the Books of Kings (between 620 and 608 B.C.). Jeremiah (after 585 B.C.). Habakkuk (between 600 and 590 B.C.).[3]

The brilliant flowering of socio-religious thought during the period of the monarchy took two major forms–law and prophecy.

Law

In Israel special importance was attached to a clearly formulated code, since the protection by Yahweh of His chosen people was conditional on observance of the terms of the covenant. A number of legal or semilegal distinctions were made. *Chuk* (binding customs and legal usages established through precedent, Judg. 11:39), *gedah* (resolutions of the army assembly), and *mishpat* (decision on disputed points) were formed into the Torah (from "to direct" or "to cast," perhaps representing the ancient priestly function of presiding over ordeals). The establishment of a judicial system was attributed to Moses as a result of the advice of his father-in-law, Jethro, who was reported to have advised him to set up a popular court to take care of ordinary conflicts (Gen. 18:21 f.). The religious code of Moses, on the other hand, was said to have been received direct from Yahweh and solemnized either by a burnt offering and the reading of the law to the assembled people (Ex. 24:2 f.) or in a solemn ceremonial meal eaten by seventy elders with God after they met Him (Ex. 24:1–11).

The oldest code in the Old Testament, the Book of the Covenant (Ex. 20:33, 23:19), had many similarities with the Code of Hammurabi dating from a thousand years earlier. The code was adapted to the needs of an agricultural economy: damages were prescribed for householders who, in burning fields or vineyards, permitted the fire to get out of hand, destroying neighboring property. Sacrificial offerings of grain and wine were specified; agricultural festivals (the festival of unleavened bread, the festival of in-gathering, etc.) were regulated; rules for borrowing animals and for damage to them or by them were set down.

Slavery was taken for granted, though the code opposed permanent slavery of Hebrew by Hebrew (Ex. 21:2). Hebrew slaves and their wives were to be freed without ransom in the seventh year. However, if the

[3] Paraphrased from Bewer, *ibid.*, p. xiii.

master had supplied the wives, these were to remain as slaves. Though the freeing of female slaves was not required (Ex. 21:7), a woman's family was permitted to buy her back if the master was not satisfied with her. Slavery could be established through voluntary pledge by the slave, through sale by the family (in the case of the young or of daughters), or involuntarily because of indebtedness.

Though an agricultural economy was presupposed, money was also used (Ex. 22:7). However, oppression of debtors by creditors was controlled (Ex. 22:27), particularly the oppression of widows and orphans. The charitable treatment of aliens was enjoined, and injunctions were set down against usury. Political ordainments were directed against circulating rumors, joining a mob to do wrong (Ex. 23:2), impairing a poor man's legal rights, and bribing judges.

Cultic and religious prescriptions were intermixed with civil and criminal regulations. The altar was not to be built of undressed stone (Ex. 20:25); mounting the steps of the altar was prohibited, lest it expose the limbs (Ex. 20:26), and the death penalty was prescribed for sacrificing to other gods (Ex. 22:20).

Women were viewed as wards of their menfolk. The seduction of a maiden was treated as a property damage. The seducer must pay for her, and marry her. If the father was not willing to let the seducer marry his daughter, the marriage fee had to be paid any way. The law of *talion*—an eye for an eye (Ex. 21:24)—was only occasionally invoked. The death penalty was prescribed for murder (Ex. 21:12), sorcery (Ex. 22:13), pederasty (Ex. 22:19), and as already noted, for sacrifice to alien deities (Ex. 21:20).

Though the Book of the Covenant was probably codified in the time of Solomon, there was no reference to the king or to the nation. Its most significant feature was its attempt to centralize the cult in Jerusalem. Its novelties included refinements in the problem of evidence. The code anticipated the reorganization of the religious and legal life that had to accompany the birth of the nation.

Prophecy

A consolidation and redirection of the religious code inevitably accompanied the formation of the nation. Very different requirements were placed on the codes of an oriental state from those placed on a sworn religious and military confederation. The monarchy also presented a new context for other socio-religious forces.

Before the formation of the monarchy, the Yahweh confederation was activated only during times of crisis. In times of peace it tended to disintegrate. Now the Israelites had a permanent center and more enduring unity. David deliberately chose Jerusalem as the location for the monarchy, not only because it was centrally located but because it was not identified with any of the former tribes. Now a section of the most influential Israelites worked out its destinies in the royal city. This did not automatically eliminate the tensions between centralizing and particularizing forces, such as had existed earlier between the war confederations and the separate tribes; it merely transposed their form. There now arose the internal tension between the residues of the former tribes settled in rural areas and the monarchy and its attendant elements.

The monarchs pursued the policies of the typical oriental despotism of the time; they placed reliance on chariot warfare. After disarming the peasantry, they formed an army of professional soldiers; they imposed new taxes and *corvée* labor for national needs; they formed a harem as an item in foreign policy; they advocated royal industry and commerce. However, as if this were not enough, in the minds of the former tribal confederates the monarchs permitted the typical process of syncretism of the oriental monarchy to get under way. Ahab married Jezebel of Tyre to seal relations between Israel and Phoenicia. Jezebel was not for a moment ready to abandon her religion, so brought her Baal priests and prophets with her. She vigorously promoted Baal worship in Samaria. Elijah was aroused to opposition against Jezebel and Ahab, representing the conscience of the old confederates in reaction to the syncretistic tendencies of the kingdoms. It is so usual to see the story from Elijah's point of view that it is sometimes forgotten that Ahab and Jezebel had a point. Ahab was only trying to run a state, and Jezebel seems to have been sincerely religious. Ahab was trying to keep peace with Phoenicia.

Perhaps if the monarchy had been more powerful or even if it had had more time to wipe out internal dissension, the story would have been different. However, before the internal problem was solved the external situation worsened. When the great powers threatened the kingdoms, the prophets increasingly linked this fact to the internal conflict. The true prophets were spokesmen for the conscience of the old confederacy in contrast to the royal prophets, the lying prophets who represented the king.[4] According to the scriptural prophets, along with their moral failure to exhort the people and threaten disaster, the sure indication of the lying prophets was their failure to be converted and to obey the divine law.

The true prophets developed a form of emissary prophecy. However, they did not belong to any sort of esoteric association, nor did they found congregations. They appeared in the midst of their people as spokesmen interested in the fate of the political community. However, they formulated its ethics rather than its cult, and preached a reformation of morals and not one of social and religious institutions.

The environment helped determine the form of their prophecy. The popular fears of war and social unrest were uppermost in everyone's

[4] Weber, *op. cit.*, p. 299.

mind.[5] The reason for the misfortunes to come, the prophets maintained, was God's will. The fulfillment of the promises of Yahweh for His people was conditioned on their remaining contractually faithful to Him and His Commandments.[6] Yahweh ordained terrible misfortunes for moral and social-ethical trespass of the terms of the Covenant. However, the misfortune to be visited by Yahweh was not absolute or irrevocable; He could repent His decisions.[7]

Thus Yahweh was ever and again gracious and forgiving. An element of tenderness runs through the prophecies of grace, especially those of Hosea and Jeremiah, but also those of Isaiah.[8] Moreover, a God who could use the great kings as a means for punishing a sinning Israel (manipulating them, so to speak, at His pleasure) was conceived as possessing a new universalism and majesty unknown to the old war god of the confederacy. However, like him, He was a god of action, not eternal order.[9] Prophetic expectation of the future was Utopian. The substance of the eschatological message consisted in sublimation of the traditional religion into ethical absolutism.[10]

Further Development of the Law

Under the circumstances of the monarchy with its systems of internal and external conflicts, the path of the pious Yahweh priests could not be smooth. The forces within the monarchy toward syncretism must have fallen heavily on them. Their lot was cast in part with the kings; their hearts must have been with the prophets. After the fall of the northern kingdom, the next development of the law appears in the Deuteronomic Code which was presumably found in the Temple of Jerusalem during the reign of Josiah. It was based on the Book of the Covenant and upon laws that had grown up meanwhile.

The Deuteronomic Code carried out the centralization of the cult in Jerusalem with injunctions to destroy non-Yahwistic cult places (Deut. 12:2) and to sacrifice only in legitimate places (Deut. 12:13). A blow was struck at the cult of the home, and it was provided that sacrificial meals were to be eaten only in accepted places (Deut. 12:17 f.). Older religious forms (and Canaanite religious practices) were rejected. Sacred poles and obelisks were no longer to be set up (Deut. 16:21). Persons sacrificing to other gods were to be stoned outside the city gates (Deut. 17:2 f.). Even though their prophecies might be fulfilled, the prophets of other deities were to be put to death (Deut. 13:2).

As perhaps could be expected of a life adapted to more settled condi-

[5] *Ibid.*, p. 302.
[6] *Ibid.*, p. 301.
[7] *Ibid.*, p. 306.
[8] *Ibid.*, p. 308.
[9] *Ibid.*, p. 311.
[10] *Ibid.*, p. 335.

tions, an elaboration of cult prescriptions was evidenced and a list of acceptable and unacceptable foods was drawn up: the camel, hare, and pig were not to be eaten; fish were acceptable, but no water animal without fins or scales; prohibited birds including the griffon, vulture, eagle, glede, buzzard, kite, raven, ostrich, nightjar, and seamew; insects were treated as unclean, and no creature that had died a natural death was to be eaten. A tenth of the yearly produce was to be dedicated to God (Deut. 14:22); a tightening of tithing and ceremonial prescriptions occurred; and the Passover was to be kept (Deut. 16:1 f.) but only in approved places (Deut. 16:5). The festival of booths was required after in-gathering (Deut. 16:13).

The political order received more systematic treatment in the Deuteronomic Code. Governors and officials were to be appointed throughout the clans (Deut. 16:18). Trials were to be held before priests and presiding judges. Cowardice in warfare was made punishable (Deut. 20:2 f.). New homeowners, newly married persons, and the fainthearted, however, were to be excused from military service (Deut. 20:5–9). It was prescribed that an enemy who yielded should be spared and put to forced labor (Deut. 20:11 f.). However, if any enemy village resisted, every male inhabitant was to be killed. In a city under attack, the fruit trees were not to be destroyed (Deut. 20:19 f.). Concubines taken in battle could become wives (Deut. 21:10 f.). The polygamous family was taken for granted.

Woman's lot was improved over previous codes. However, Hebrew women slaves as well as men slaves were now to be freed in the seventh year (Deut. 15:12). Women taken in battle and made into wives were not dishonored (Deut. 21:12 f.). The children of other than the favored wife were not to be discriminated against (Deut. 21:15 f.). It was forbidden that women be forced into temple prostitution (Deut. 23:17). If they displeased or were immodest, wives could be divorced (Deut. 24:2), but they were free to remarry. However, women were still subject to the levirate system, and men were denounced if they did not marry the wives of dead brothers (Deut. 25:7 f.). If a wife assisted her husband in a fight with another and seized the assailant by his private parts, her hand was to be cut off without pity (Deut. 25:12). Adultery was punishable by death (22:23 f.), but the violation of a virgin was still viewed as property damage and the man responsible was required either to marry her or to pay the usual marriage fee.

The charity ethic became more comprehensive. The poor were recognized. "Though indeed there should be no poor among you (for the Eternal your God will prosper you in the land which the Eternal your God assigns to you as your own possession), provided that you are attentive to the voice of the Eternal your God, and mindful to obey all these commands laid down by me today" (Deut. 25:4). The seven-year remission of debts for Israelites (Deut. 15:2) was to be observed. So, too, was the release from slavery (Deut. 15:12). Loans were not to be withheld from the poor (Deut. 15:7 f.), nor was help withheld from a countryman (Deut. 22:2 f.). Workmen, including foreigners, were not to be exploited (Deut. 24:14 f.). Oppressed orphans, widows, and metics were to be treated with consideration; and the gleanings of field, orchard, and vineyard must be left for them (Deut. 21:19–21). Every third year the tithes were to be devoted to the poor and to the Levites (Deut. 14:28 f.) who were to be invited to share in feasts (Deut. 16:10–14). Essential implements necessary to domestic life (Deut. 24:6) were not to be used as pledges for loans. The taking of interest from a fellow countryman was forbidden (Deut. 23:19).

A refinement of the standards of evidence in criminal and religious cases had occurred: to condemn a person for observing non-Yahwistic rites, the testimony of two witnesses was required (Deut. 17:5 f.), but one witness could exonerate him; a single witness could not count against a man in connection with any crime or sin (Deut. 19:15 f.). The judges were to investigate carefully affairs with conflicting testimony; false or malicious witnesses were to be punished. The Deuteronomic Code limited the principle of *talion*, restricting revenue to the person committing the offence (Deut. 24:16).

During the period of the kingdoms, *law* and the *prophecy* took shape at the two poles of Israelite thought, each serving to elicit the best qualities of the other.

THE PERIOD OF THE ETHNIC COMMUNITY

During the Exile Israel lost its territorial standing and was transformed into an ethnic community. During this period the canon was gradually established. The last literatures to be accepted dated from the second century.

1. The Sixth Century B.C.:
   Jeremiah (till after 588). Habakkuk (between 600 and 590). Ezekiel (593–571). The Holiness Code (Lev. 17–26). Lamentations (586–550). Isaiah 63:7, 64:12. The combination of the Yahwist and Elohist with the Deuteronomist in the Hexateuch. The second edition of the Books of Kings (about 550). The Deuteronomistic editions of the stories of Joshua, Judges, and Samuel. The song of Moses (Deut. 32). Isaiah 13:2 ff; 14; 4–21. Deutero-Isaiah (Isa. 40–55, between 546 and 539). Haggai (520). Zechariah I–VIII (520–518 and after). Isaiah 56:9–58; 12, 59:1–15a, 65:1–16, 66:1–6 and 15–18a (from 520 on). The priestly code (about 500).
2. The Fifth Century B.C.:
   Isaiah 59:15b–63; 6, 65:17–25, 66:7–14 and 18b–23. Jeremiah 3:14–18. Isaiah 34 f. Obediah. Isaiah 15 f. Amos 9:8b–15. Zephaniah 2:72, c8–11. Isaiah 11:10–16. Malachi (about 460). The memoirs of Nehemiah (after 432), and of Ezra. The Book of Ruth. The Aramaic story in Ezra 4:8–6:18. Joel (about 400).

3. The Fourth Century B.C.:
   Joel (later elements). Isaiah 19:1–15, 23:1–14. Proverbs (older portions). Job. Isaiah 24–27.
4. The Third Century B.C.:
   The Chronicler (300–250). Genesis 14. 1 Kings 13. Esther. Song of Songs. Proverbs 1–9. 30 f. Jonah. Isaiah 19:18–25. Ecclesiastes (about 200).
5. The Second Century B.C.:
   Daniel (165–164). Zechariah 9–11 and 13:7–9. Isaiah 33. Zechariah 12 and 13:1–6 and 14. Completion of Psalter.[11]

The Code of Ezekiel

A new phase of code construction was opened in Ezekiel's Utopian vision of the reconstructed community. In spirit he was carried off to a valley of dry bones. The spirit

> . . . set me down in a valley. It was full of bones: he made me go all round them, and I saw that they were very many on the surface of the valley, and very dry. "Son of man," he said, "can these bones live?" (Ezek. 37:2)

Ezekiel then outlined his Utopia. Israel was to become a single kingdom with a single king (Ezek. 37:22). The reconstructed temple was visualized in detail and elaborate regulations for the altars were set down. They were to be in the hands of the Zadokite priests (Ezek. 43:18). No foreigner (uncircumcized in heart as well as in flesh) was to enter the sanctuary (Ezek. 44:9).

The Zadokite priests in charge of the temple were to wear special garments. No priest was to marry a widow or a divorced woman, but only an Israelite virgin (Ezek. 44–22). Except under very special conditions, the priests were never to touch a dead body (Ezek. 44:25). The priests were to own no property (Ezek. 44–28). The best or first fruits and first-baked products belonged to the priests (Ezek. 44:30). No creature that had died a natural death or had been lacerated was to be eaten by them (Ezek. 44:31).

The realm was to be divided into sacred districts. The Levites, now reduced to temple menials, were to be paid by income from one of the strips of land (Ezek. 45:5). The prince held the land outside the sacred holdings (Ezek. 45:7). Ezekiel proposed standard measures and weights, fixed the value of the shekel, and established price regulations.

Contributions by the people were to be made to the prince who provided for festivals. The prince was denied permission to dispose of property (for more than a year) to any other than his sons (Ezek. 46:16). Nor could he seize the people's lands (Ezek. 46:18) or otherwise dispose of them.

The Code of Ezekiel reflected the elevation of religious practice to central importance in the national life. The regulations of cult were becoming more important than law in the strict sense.

[11] Paraphrased from Bewer, *op. cit.,* XIV.

The Holiness Code

The holiness laws (Lev. 17:26 and possibly 11) were spiritually akin to the Code of Ezekiel. While this code had many points of contact with the Deuteronomic Code, its chief concern was with cult. It traced the priesthood primarily to Aaron.

Examples of the increased concern with purity regulations are found in Leviticus 17, where the tasting of blood (the seat of the soul) was strictly prescribed. Anyone who did so or who ate lacerated flesh or meat from a creature that had died of natural causes became unclean. In avoidance of impurity, sexual regulations were elaborated (Lev. 18). Intercourse with the wife of a father, daughter of a mother, a daughter, a son's daughter, a granddaughter, a paternal aunt, maternal aunt, an uncle's wife, with a sister of the wife while the wife was alive, with a neighbor's wife, with a male, with a beast, with a woman during menstruation was prohibited.

Parental piety was emphasized (Lev. 19:2). Not only was gleaning to be left to the poor and the metic, but fallen fruits and sheaves were not to be picked up; a corner of the field was to be left unharvested for them (Lev. 19:9 f.). The deaf were not to be cursed, nor the blind tripped; people were not to be slandered, and grudges were not to be borne. One was enjoined to "love your neighbor as you love yourself" (Lev. 19:18).

The Priestly Code

The Priestly Code, forming a part of a document beginning with Genesis I, was known to Ezra and probably was formulated toward the end of the fifth century B.C. It attempted to account for the manner in which God brought the church into existence. One major purpose of Genesis was to justify the Sabbath. In this document the elements of the cult were projected into the distant past. The Priestly Code sharpened the distinction between priests and Levites. Centralization of the cult was assumed. The distinction between clean and unclean animals, which could not be sacrificed, was made. Forgiveness of sin was obtained by a sin offering. The Passover (in contrast to the trend evident in Deuteronomy) was turned into a family ritual.

In the Priestly Code the increased importance of cult and of the family of the ethnic community was reflected. Bertholet's summary of it and its tendencies is worth noting.

> To a certain extent the so-called Priest's Code (middle of the fifth century) marks the end of the evolution of Hebrew jurisprudence. On the one hand, conceiving the Jewish community to be of divine constitution, it completely shut off Israel from non-Israel, thus widening the gulf between the two. At the same time, however, it constructed a bridge across which non-Hebrews, at least those residing among Israel, might be admitted to religious, though not to complete civil, equality.

> The sole condition was the adoption of the law, including, if possible, circumcision.
>
> It is this union of law and religion that constitutes the specific peculiarity of the development of Hebrew jurisprudence. . . . The deeper knowledge and recognition of Jahveh's legal and moral character was the growth of time, and though it would be an error to place the highest interpenetration of law and religion at the beginning of the process of development, it is undoubtedly true that in the Priest's Code (which was practically its ultimate phase) the process of development did not altogether escape the danger which only too often accompanies an increasing legalizing of religion. That danger is that when men conceive of themselves in their conduct to be related to God exclusively by a definite external law the differences between great things and small things in the law inevitably disappear. "Whoso keepeth the whole law and is guilty in one point, the same is guilty of all." It is significant that, intensifying an earlier commandment, the law ultimately decreed that intercourse with a menstruous woman should be punished by the death of both parties, as if their offence were on a level with murder or any other crime adjudged worthy of death.[12]

The process involved in such a leveling of ritualistic offences was not so much the legalizing of the religion as of reversing the process which most usually occurred in transforming customary ethical or religious rules into legal rules.

The main stream of human social development has tended to substitute more complex for less complex communities. When this occurs, areas of social behavior, which had at one time been regulated by custom or religion, break loose from these contexts unless new institutions specifically charged with their regulation and implemented with coercive sanctions take over. One source of law is previous ethical or religious custom.

The formation of an ethnic community, however, moves in the opposite direction. During the Exile, for example, the authorities that had once guided the state were no longer effective, and the exile community revived the old democratic constitution and restored the elders to a position of authority, the like of which they had not enjoyed since confederation days. In the years following the Exile, a political governor (often a Persian) was supreme head of the state. However, in the minds of the Jews the governor lost prestige compared to the priests whose position had, in a sense, been confirmed when the Persian king ratified the Priest's Code of Ezra. Moreover, since the Persian domination the Jews had had considerable powers of self-government, and the elders had retained a prominence they had acquired in the Exile. They controlled the administration of secular jurisprudence. Elders from the provincial towns met in the capital and formed the rudiments of the later Sanhedrin.

Moreover, as Bertholet noted, there were repeated public assemblies in

[12] Alfred Bertholet, *A History of Hebrew Civilization*, trans. by A. K. Dallas (London: George G. Harrap & Co., 1926), pp. 283–284. The references are to Lev. 25:24 and 22–18.

the Postexile community, which indicated that ecclesiastical customs were being shifted to the secular sphere. The political and religious institutions of the community were merged with one another.

Prophecy

The great period of prophecy falls within the time of the national crisis, at the time when the weakness of the kingdoms was increasingly evident. The period terminated in the national disaster of the Babylonian captivity. Prophecy continued for a time after this, but its greatest period was over.

The later literature illustrated, in the collection of proverbs, the growth of simple faith and everyday rationality. The Psalms, collections of songs and hymns, despite occasional expression of exotic passions, were valuable for liturgical purposes. The Book of Job, one of the most able examples of story-telling in the literature, with its provocative question of why the good should suffer, perhaps reflects a growing influence of Hellenic skepticism. The Song of Songs, with its glowing eroticism, consists in good measure of songs for weddings and other festive occasions. Canonization of such materials served to bring these spheres under cult control. Perhaps similar motives were at work in the canonization of such literature as Ecclesiastes, which is obviously inconsistent with the spirit of simple piety and faith.

Ecclesiastes is profoundly skeptical. Everything is vain: human labor, the generations, the course of events (Ecc. 1:2 f.). Wisdom is sometimes said to be a value, but who knows the difference between wisdom and folly? (Ecc. 2:13 f.). Everything has its place including death, stealing, murder, tears, hate, and war (Ecc. 3:2 f.). Oppression of the poor, perverted justice, and human avarice are only what can be expected (Ecc. 5:8). The evil thrive, and the good die young (Ecc. 8:12 f.). The dead "know nothing, they have nothing for their labor, their very memory is forgotten, their love vanished with their hate and jealousy, and they have no share now in anything that goes on in the world" (Ecc. 9:6). Men toil to satisfy insatiable hunger. A wise man is no better than a fool (Ecc. 6:7–8).

> For men, I find, there is nothing better than to be happy and enjoy themselves as long as they are alive; it is indeed God's very gift to man, that he should eat and drink and be happy as he toils. (Ecc. 3:12)

Incorporated in the Canon from the third and second centuries B.C. was not only the urban skeptical, utilitarian hedonism of Ecclesiastes which was strongly influenced by Hellenistic thought, but the bizarre visions of the clearly apocalyptic book of Daniel. It is difficult to escape the impression that deep wisdom was manifest in the incorporation of samples of Hellenistic skepticism, on the one hand, and popular apocalyptics, on the other. In the religion of an ethnic community they could serve as signposts pointing the way from popular religiosity to the main body of the teaching.

The two great bodies of teaching in this period, the Apocrypha (and Apocalyptic) and Rabbinical, however sharply in contrast, had their source in the Old Testament and developed side by side with little contact with one another. Scholars dealing with Jewish literature of the period have often observed the difference between them. In the words of Herford:

> Christian scholars have extolled the Apocryphal writings as being representative of the ancient free prophetic spirit, the "true child of prophecy" . . . and they have contrasted it with the legalistic character of Rabbinical teaching. . . .
>
> Jewish scholars, on the other hand, have quite naturally placed a high value on the Rabbinical teaching, and paid but little attention to the Apocryphal literature. They have always maintained that the real essence of Judaism is expressed in the Rabbinical literature and that the Apocryphal literature is by comparison of very small importance.
>
> Both these literatures are undeniably products of Judaism . . . part of antagonism to which the study of these literatures has given rise is due to the fact that the Apocryphal literature has a much more direct bearing upon the rise of Christianity than could be claimed for the Rabbinical.[13]

While this quotation is something of an oversimplification, it calls attention to the fact that at the very time the religion of the Old Testament was brought into a synthesis in connection with the events of the Exile and the Postexile circumstances, the foundations of modern Judaism and Christianity were laid.

THE GENERAL CHARACTER OF HEBREW THOUGHT AND ITS RELATION TO HEBREW CIVILIZATION

The knowledge of ancient Israel was characterized by a lack of abstract, theoretical, or scientific tendencies. Even the idea of theoretical knowledge hardly existed, and wherever the verb translated "to know" is used its objects do not form a part of a theoretical or scientific system.[14] When, as in the Book of Job, questions of the ultimate nature of things are raised, it is usually implied, if not stated, that such knowledge is reserved to God alone. The knowledge always has a practical moral intent; the descriptions of the hippopotamus, ostrich, and crocodile illustrated the glory of God. Scientific questions, such as the nature and source of the rain, often represent little more than naïve folk ideas. The source of rain presented little problem. God, like man, kept water in skins which he simply tipped to make the rainfall. In the creation, light was conceived to be independent of the sun. The stars were thought to be inhabited by spirits; the morning stars burst into song when creation occurred. God ordered the stars like a military commander. His voice was the thunder, and the lightning consisted of arrows from his bow.

[13] R. Travers Herford, *Talmud and Apocrypha* (London: The Soncino Press, 1933), p. 3.

[14] Bertholet, *op. cit.*, p. 285. The following discussion draws heavily on Bertholet's able summary, pp. 284–306.

Geographical and ethnological information of the ancient Jews was primitive. In the law codes all men were conceived in a single genealogical scheme (which, incidentally, contained the implicit thought that mankind was ultimately one). Ethnology, Bertholet observes, was transformed into genealogy; the people of each city were thought to have arisen from a single family. Geographical information was vague. In the story of paradise the Gihon River had the same source as the Euphrates and Tigris, and was made to circle around the whole of Cush. In a later source the Nile was thought to arise in Asia. Jerusalem, like Delphi for the Greeks, was conceived to be the center of the universe: the word for the Mediterranean Sea became the word for west; the Negeb for south, etc.

The Hebrew ideas of history were no more scientific than their geography or ethnology. However, in the concept of the Jews as God's chosen people and of foreign nations as instruments of His will, the concept of the unity of mankind and progress to a destined goal contained the roots of a concept of universal history.[15] A series of legends proposed to account for the origin of human callings: Noah was the first wine-maker, Cain was the founder of cities. Since it was important for the holy season, the calendar was important. In the story of paradise this was said to be the purpose of the stars—to signify coming events and fix the times of religious ceremonies.

Both a decimal and a sexagesimal system of numbers were known. The priests employed their skills in calculation to determine the amounts of the poll tax, redemption of the first-born, tributes on war booty, and the weights of votive offerings.[16] Medicine was held in high esteem, but the healing arts were primarily developed with respect to the treatment of wounds.[17] The physiology of human birth was primitive: it was thought that the male seed coagulated in the womb like milk to form cheese. God then clothed the embryo with skin and flesh and strengthened it with sinews and bones.[18] A wide variety of ailments and sicknesses had been isolated. The soul was identified with the breath, and thought to enter the body at birth and leave it at death through the nostrils.

As Bertholet sees it, the mentality of the ancient Israelite was practical and concrete rather than abstract and speculative.

> One would scarcely look for anything like speculative science in ancient Israel; the Hebrew was far too much of a realist, incapable of abstract thinking, and unable to get away from the sensuous. . . . The connection between thinking and its vocal utterance was axiomatic. . . . The mind of the Hebrew was not directed to the universal. We have already spoken of his inability to form a comprehensive view of the universe and of the lack of a word for the "world." This is characteristic

[15] *Ibid.*, p. 293.
[16] *Ibid.*, p. 297.
[17] *Ibid.*, p. 298.
[18] *Ibid.*, p. 299.

of his whole mentality. His whole tendency is to emphasize striking details.[19]

Bertholet observes that thought tends to move from one striking image to another, being united by the personality of the man who conceives it rather than by any inner logical relation.

> Some scholars have even gone the length of saying that subjectivity is a fundamental feature of the Semitic mind, and this is often adduced as explaining why lyric poetry is so predominant in Hebrew poetry, and why the more objective types, epic and drama, are to all intents and purposes absent. This being so, the more the writer's presuppositions determine his estimate of the world and of all things, all the more, in view of the strong religious tendency of Hebrew thought, does this estimate take on a religious color.[20]

From this point of view, the Book of Ecclesiastes marks a fundamental turning point in ancient Hebraic thought. It is the first "attempt of a philosophic Jew to come to terms with the Greek spirit."[21]

The peculiar circumstances of the genesis of ancient Israelite civilization forced an increasingly intense synthesis of religion, politics, and social order rather than their differentiation and specialization. Furthermore, Israel originated as a war association and in time was converted into a pacifistic ethnic community. Moreover, throughout its early history, Israel was never free of internal and external pressures long enough to permit any great differentiation of the arts or the development of high culture. It was, for example, never in possession of the kind of material wealth and conditions which permitted the great pyramid and temple construction in Egypt and Babylonia. So precipitously had the transition been made from agriculture and pastoral nomadism to civic life that the kingdom followed foreign architectural styles and imported carpenters and masons to do the work. To build his palace, for example, David imported carpenters and masons from King Hiram of Tyre (2 Sam. 5:11).

In their early stages the fine arts elsewhere found a natural home in religion. The elevation of the fine arts out of the practical arts had repeatedly been brought about by stages; initially artistic motives were pressed into the development of cultic objects and infused with a new intensity as vehicles of simultaneous spiritual and sensuous interests. Then the separation of the fine arts from religious contexts left them in possession of a semiautonomous sphere of their own as vehicles of a refined way of life.

The socio-religious development of Israel, however, reversed this process. In elevating the war god of the confederacy above the gods of the tribes and of the household (usually intermediated and symbolized by

[19] *Ibid.*, pp. 304–305.
[20] *Ibid.*, p. 305.
[21] *Ibid.*, p. 306.

a multiplicity of cultic images), the power and invisibility of Yahweh were emphasized, not the material symbols of Him. Wischnitzer observes that "The attribute of invisibility was thus fundamental to the Jewish conception of God. To identify Him with any material form whatever would be to confuse the Creator with His creature."[22]

Karl Schwarz notes that when the Israelite tribes entered history they encountered mighty empires in which religion was celebrated in temples embellished by the arts. The Israelites also had their idols. However,

> . . . out of the desert they brought the mission of a new faith; faith in a spiritual God who could not be portrayed. And it was possible for them to establish their own culture only by banning from their midst everything that was connected with the physical imagery of gods. Thus was born the taboo on pictorial portrayals. . . . Since it had no chance to be active, the artistic sense within the Israelite nation was necessarily stunted.[23]

As the commandment was laid down in Exodus: "Thou shalt not make unto thee any graven images, nor any likeness of anything that is in heaven above, or in the earth beneath, or in the waters under the earth." (Ex. 20:4)

During the royal period artistic skills were repeatedly pressed into the service of religion and the embellishment of the life style of the upper classes. There were almost always conventional reactions against such developments. The prophets engaged in violent tirades against such practices. This ambivalence was experienced in another form by the Jews of the Postexile period. According to Wischnitzer, however, art was accepted in time:

> From the point of view of Judaism it is important to discover that the art practices by Jews was a national, popular art dedicated to problems of Jewish interest. This art offered a counterpart to the Rabbinical interpretation of Jewish history and Jewish behavior. Art, a companion of literature, shared in the responsibility for the cultural and political education of the community. . . . The Rabbinical leaders seem on the whole to have tolerated art with some misgivings. . . .[24]

In view of the frequent Biblical references to it and the fact that there did not seem to be an equivalent religious taboo against it, music was, perhaps somewhat more fully developed among the ancient Jews than were the graphic arts. Werner maintains that:

> . . . the biblical period, in general, created an abundance of musical forms and institutions which, later on, through Christianity, became the adored and incessantly imitated standards of Western civilization. The

22 Rachel Wischnitzer, "Judaism and Art," Finkelstein, ed., *op. cit.*, Vol. II, p. 984.

23 Karl Schwarz, "The Hebrew Impact on Western Art," in Runes, ed., *op. cit.*, p. 411.

24 Wischnitzer, *op. cit.*, p. 994.

> principal form, of course, was the psalm and the principal institution was the musical service of the Temple in Jerusalem.[25]

However, though the Levites seem to have served as professional musicians of the Temple of Jerusalem, and though various instruments such as the silver trumpet (*chatzotzra*), the pipe organ (*magrepha*), the cymbals (*tziltaal*), the finger-played harp (*nevel*), the lyre (*kinnor*), and the ram's horn (*shofar*) are mentioned, only the ram's horn remains. Moreover, with the destruction of the Temple (70 A.D.), the music of the Hebrews fell into oblivion, though chanting was preserved in the synagogue. However, the investigation of the musical traditions of Jewish tribes in Yemen, Babylonia, Persia, Syria, and Spain have revealed a similarity of melodies which suggests a common origin in the temple song.[26]

Without examining other features of Hebrew civilization, it may be observed that the pattern already indicated is repeated over and again. So far as a social or general cultural life sphere was in accord with its particular religious point of view (such as music and literature), it tended to be developed; so far as a life sphere was defined as outside or antagonistic to Judaism's particular religious point of view (like painting and the graphic arts), it tended to be curtailed.

The peculiarities of the socio-religious synthesis of Judaism crucial to the ethnic community were: (1) pacifism, (2) an unusual development of the charity ethic, (3) the dualism of in-group, out-group morality, (4) monotheism, (5) institutionalization of the concept of the chosen people with a historical relation to God conditional on observance of the terms of the covenant, and (6) institutionalization of the spirit of the prophets in the form of the Messianic hope.

Israel originated as a tribal confederation sworn to mutual loyalty in the name of Yahweh, its war god. In the royal period, however, this was changed, and war-making became a monopoly of the kings and their knights. A partial pacification of the lower classes was carried through in connection with this change; the old peasant militia was disarmed. The Exile then destroyed the political and military elements of the Royal period. Following Wellhausen,[27] Bertholet notes the transformation of the old military vocabulary into technical religious terms.

> From the Exile some returned, but not as they had gone away. Their life now was that of a regular religious community, gathered round their sanctuary and the interests of their cultus. It is instructive to observe how, under the altered conditions, the ancient stock phrases of war were increasingly converted into religious technical terms. The word for war-service itself took on the meaning of holy service, *militia sacra;* the ancient war-cry became the call to worship; the war-trumpet, at

[25] Eric Werner, "The Jewish Contribution to Music," in Finkelstein, ed., *op. cit.,* Vol. II, p. 951.

[26] Paul Nettl, "Judaism and Music," in Runes, ed., *op. cit.,* p. 365.

[27] Wellhausen, *op. cit.,* p. 184.

> whose sound the nation gathered, ready for battle, became the instrument of peace, blown by the priest as a call to worship.[28]

So complete was the pacification of the Jews that when foreign armies crossed their land they were permitted to exercise their arts of war unopposed, while the nation waited for the intervention of God. This pacification was an invaluable asset to the ethnic community, forced over and again to survive under most unpropitious circumstances, particularly being deprived of all means of political and military power.

Of special interest was the manner in which the Hebrew charity ethic came to be one of the most powerful bonds of the ethnic community. In the confederation period the basic communities of the Jews were tribes and peasant villages. Within the families that composed such tribes, joint responsibility (particularly blood vengeance) established the claims of the individual. Development of social responsibility outside the sphere of the patriarchal family, however, could occur when friendship as a category of covenant developed. Because of an oath before God between David and Jonathan,

> David spared Jonathan's son when he delivered the survivors of Saul's house over to the blood vengeance of the Gibeonites. The consummation of the friendship between David and Jonathan occurred when Jonathan removed his mantle, coat of mail, sword, and bow and gave them to David. (I Sam. 18:3)

However, generally in this period the injured, poor, sick, widowed, and orphaned were joint responsibilities of the extended patriarchal family and not of the community at large.[29]

During the transition from nomadic to urban conditions, the rise of a distinction between rich and poor cut the lines of family and clan, and the official religion (centralized and made responsible to royal requirements) replaced the religion of the war confederation. The royal court sustained a style of life of hitherto unknown luxury. As a rich class was formed, the common free peasant was seriously pressed. The greed of those who seized fields by force, took away homes, and deprived men of their heritage (Mic. 2:2), who pyramided properties (Isa. 5:8), and consolidated wealth into their hands (Isa. 2:7), were denounced by the prophets.

The conflict between rich and poor was basic to the evolution of the charity ethic. The conservative and prophetic elements under the kingdom modified the charity ethic from tribal days to apply to the class of the poor under these new conditions. Examples of such a developing charity ethic were the injunction against usurious oppression of the poor (Ex. 22:24), the encouragement of modification of legal proceedings against the poor (Ex. 22:25), the injunction to turn the fruits of the seventh

[28] Bertholet, *op. cit.*, p. 258.
[29] *Ibid.*, p. 231.

(fallow) year over to the poor. (Ex. 23:11), the granting of permission of the poor to eat as many grapes as they wished in the vineyards (Deut. 23:25), allowing the poor to glean wheat fields, vineyards, and olive groves (Deut. 24:19); the leaving of a tenth of the yield every third year to the Levites who had lost their occupations outside of Jerusalem, strangers, widows, and orphans (Deut. 24:28).

In India and Egypt two areas where charity classically developed supplied a different foundation for charity. In India charity rested on the conception of the unity of all life and the belief in *Samsara;* in Egypt charity was influenced by the bureaucratic structure of the welfare state and its economy. On the other hand, in Israel,

> Charity was continuously developed in increasingly systematic fashion through the moral exhortation of the Levites; the Shechemite cursing formula was influenced by them; the *debarim*, joined to the Book of the Covenant; and then Deuteronomy and the priestly law.
>
> Despite many striking and hardly accidental similarities, the substantive demands of Israelite charity differed in tenor from Egyptian charity demands. It rested on a priestly influenced community of free peasants and herdsmen sibs, not on a priestly influenced patrimonial bureaucracy.
>
> In Israel . . . the primary evil to be fought was not oppression by a bureaucracy but by an urban patriciate.[30]

With the Exile the destruction of official structure of the state shifted the point of gravity of the community nearer to those circles in whose name the charity ethic was evolving. One of the effects of this was to produce a new kind of clannishness.

> In post-Exilic days there must have been a pronounced development of clannishness, small circles banded together against others. Actual cliques arose, which became the breeding-grounds of endless evil-speaking and wicked gossip. . . . The tongue must have been the cause of an incredible amount of harm; on the one side intrigues and slanders, talebearing, and falsehood, and on the other cringing flattery and obsequiousness, seem to have been universal. There was no privacy; tale-bearing and scandal-mongering were rampant.[31]

This state of affairs led to a new evolution of the injunctions concerning the poor. Weber notes:

> Only the pacifistic, urban epoch of the Torah directly prior and during the Exile produced the abstractions of the Holiness Code. We note the injunction of replacing candid discussion by hatred and vindictiveness against one's "neighbor," that is (Lev. 19:18) against the children of one's people and, according to 19:34 against the *ger*. This is related to the principle: "thou shalt love thy neighbor as thyself" (Lev. 19:18).[32]

[30] Weber, *op. cit.*, p. 259.
[31] Bertholet, *op. cit.*, p. 232.
[32] Weber, *op. cit.*, p. 259.

In this same period the evolving charity ethic was picked up from the earlier period (Deuteronomy) and strengthened: leaving a corner of a field uncut for the poor is enjoined (Lev. 19:25–28); the sabbatical year is to be turned into a year of Jubilee intended to abolish all poverty (Lev. 25:25–28). The writers of the Proverbs urged that mercy to the poor was like lending to God (Prov. 19:12), while mockery of the poor was blasphemy (Prov. 17:5).

The foundation was being laid for the powerful in-group ethic of the ethnic community. Karpf maintains that the giving of charity to the poor, the widow, orphan, and stranger, came to be looked at not only as elementary social justice but as something of benefit to the group.[33] Eventually, he maintains, charity was institutionalized:

> The institutionalization of charity among the Jews during the Middle Ages was due to two important factors. First, the persecutions, expulsions, and wanderings imposed upon the Jews by their Christian neighbors created hordes of penniless wandering individuals and families—the "displaced persons" of a former day, who had to have help if they were to survive. But it was not only the wanderers who needed financial and other types of assistance for survival. Many of the older residents of the ghettos, limited as they were to a few pursuits with the many restrictions against land ownership, tilling of the soil, and most of the occupations controlled by the guilds, were forced to resort to charity to maintain themselves. This required some concrete organizational forms for collecting and administering charitable funds. At first there were two such funds: the general Fund *Kuppah* and the soup-kitchen fund, *Tamhui*. Later seven well organized funds became the practice, and each community established them.[34]

Thus the charity ethic evolved under the ethnic community into institutions of mutual help which were repeatedly important for community survival.

The other side of the coin of a developing in-group morality with powerful injunctions against usury and other exploitive activities toward in-group members was the freeing of the out-group ethic from ethical consideration. In Weber's summary,

> There was no soteriological motive whatever for ethical rationalization of out-group economic relations. No religious premiums existed for it. That had far-reaching consequences for the economic behavior of the Jews. Since Antiquity, Jewish pariah capitalism, like that of the Hindu trader castes, felt at home in the very forms of state- and booty-capitalism along with pure money usury and trade, precisely what Puritanism abhorred.[35]

[33] Maurice J. Karpf, "Jewish Social Service and Its Impact upon Western Civilization," in Runes, ed., *op. cit.*, p. 162.

[34] *Ibid.*, pp. 163–164.

[35] Weber, *op. cit.*, p. 345.

This, too, was extremely important for the survival of the ethnic community. The restriction of religious and ethical consideration primarily to the in-group permitted the Jews to take up in an ethically neutral fashion all sorts of marginal and semidisreputable trades and activities which permitted them to survive in the lands in which they were a guest people.

Meanwhile, the positive core of beliefs which served as an integrating philosophy within the ethnic community was the conception of the Jews as God's chosen people, the interpretation of historical events as a contractlike relation to God such that their fate was conditioned on their observance of the terms of the covenant, and the prophetic vision of a Messiah who at some time would bring about the socio-religious fulfillment of the religious promise. The ethnic community was powerfully equipped to survive an almost unbelievable number of shocks.

SUMMARY

The three main periods in the development of ancient Israelite society were: (1) the time of the tribal confederation, (2) the time of the settled urbanism of the royal period, and (3) the time of the Exile and Postexile ethnic communities. Very different intellectual types were bearers of the community synthesis in each period. During the tribal confederation period, the chief types of religious figures were the seers and prophets. During the Royal period the most important division was drawn between the priests of the temple and the free prophets. In the Exile and Postexile period the priests first gained, then declined in prestige, and the educated layman gradually evolved into the rabbi.

The evolution of socio-religious thought of ancient Israel reflects the circumstances of communities to which it was addressed. Although the formation of complex communities is usually accompanied by religious syncretism, the peculiar conditions of its early development sent Yahwism on the opposite path. Yahweh was the war god of a confederacy related to the people of the various nomadic tribes on the basis of a sworn covenant. Hence, insofar as the confederation unity was to be maintained, the identification of Yahweh with the many forms of local, tribal, and family gods had to be resisted. Yahweh became an invisible god, and the first steps were taken toward monotheism.

Under the circumstance of the urban and royal period, Yahwehism was restylized. An attempt was made to establish a cult monopoly for the Jerusalem priesthood. Meanwhile, however, there was also a powerful tendency toward the religious syncretism which so often accompanies the formation of more complex socio-religious structures. At this point the residual social tensions of Israel between the traditional, rural, as yet incompletely assimilated tribal elements, and the royal city, taken together with the weakness of the monarchy in the face of foreign threat, provided the stage for the emergence of priestly code-making on the one hand and prophecy on the other. The priestly code-makers integrated the history, formulated the codes, and carried out an adaptation of the charity ethic to the new social conditions. The prophets carried out a political-religious critique of the internal social conditions and external political relations of Israel, linking these two phenomena in a dramatic manner. The ethical sublimation of the religious tradition was carried through, and the Messianic hope for the future was developed.

In the Exile and Postexile ethnic community the pacification of the socio-religious ethic was completed, the development of the in-group charity ethic into a systematic philosophy of mutual aid implemented by specific institutions was accomplished, the out-group ethic was detached from in-group religious and ethical forms in a manner promoting plastic capacity to survive under difficult conditions, and the concepts of a chosen people, of the mission of the Jews, of their specific historical destiny in time, of the covenant relation of the Jews to God, and the Messianic hope, were all institutionalized as a powerful in-group philosophy.

With certain modifications, the general hypotheses of the study seem borne out. The great period of creativity falls within the time of the destruction of old and the formation of new communities. In ancient Israel this high point was represented by the periods of the destruction of the urban communities and the formation of the ethnic community. The profound shaping of the directions of Israelite creativity by the special circumstances of its origin was evident in the peculiar manner in which religion and politics fused rather than separated in time. As the ethnic community came into synthesis, the attempt to bring the kind of creativity which would overthrow basic premises was shown by the repeated movements toward the canonization of the holy literature. Such canonization was powerfully promoted by the official adoption of the Priest's Code under Ezra, but was not completed for another two hundred years. Eventually most of the apocalyptic literature and most of the new literature influenced by Hellenistic thought (of which Ecclesiastes is a sample and the effects of which may be manifest in Job) were set aside. However, while one may canonize the holy literature, social change continues. Hence, beginning in the time of Ezra a body of oral interpretations of the law (the *Mishma*) grew up. Two *gemaras* also developed: (1) the *Talmud Jerushalmi* in Palestine and (2) the *Talmud Babli* in Babylon.

At a time of great crisis, when Jerusalem was razed by the Romans in 70 A.D., the rabbis created the *Talmud*, or teaching, for it looked as if everything was about to be destroyed. A number of fragmentary notebooks containing new ordinances derived by interpretation of the Torah were collected. The original 613 were supplemented in 200 A.D. by a digest, the *Mishna*, consisting of four thousand legal decisions covering every phase of Jewish life. These, in turn, came in time to be supplemented by other interpretations, the *Gemaras*, which were finally reduced to writing and consolidated with the *Mishna* around 500 A.D.

In contrast to the method of prophecy, which found its criteria of truth in special personally interpreted signs, the establishment of truth in the period of the ethnic community had a strongly institutional and authoritative character and tended to assume the form of an interpretation of an infallible text.

SELECTED BIBLIOGRAPHY

Bertholet, Alfred, *A History of Hebrew Civilization*, trans. by A. K. Dallas (London: George G. Harrap, 1926).

Browne, Lewis, *The Wisdom of Israel: An Anthology* (New York: Random House, 1945).

Finkelstein, Louis, ed., *The Jews: Their History, Culture, and Religion* (New York: Harper & Bros., 1949).

Oesterly, W. O. E., and G. H. Box, *A Short Survey of the Literature of Rabbinical and Medieval Judaism* (New York: The Macmillan Co., 1920).

Runes, Dagobert D., ed., *The Hebrew Impact on Western Civilization* (New York: Philosophical Library, 1951).

Samuel, Maurice, *The Professor and the Fossil* (New York: Alfred A. Knopf, 1956).

Waxman, Mayer, *A History of Jewish Literature* (New York: Bloch Pub. Co., 1930).

Weber, Max, *Ancient Judaism*, trans. by Hans Gerth and Don Martindale (Glencoe, Illinois: The Free Press, 1952).

Part V

PHILOSOPHERS AND SOPHISTS IN GREECE

THE ANCIENT GREEKS presented a series of similarities and differences with other peoples of the Axial Period. Before the appearance of the ancestral Greeks, the comparatively high civilizations of Crete and Mycenae had developed in the area. Thus there were comparisons with the civilization of the Shang in China, the Indus Valley civilization in India, and the civilizations of Babylonia and Egypt which dominated Palestine. However, the complex civic imperialism against which the ancestral Greeks moved was a sea empire. The natural environment, too, was unlike the great inland plains of China, the varied Indian subcontinent, or the semiarid interstitial land of Palestine. In terms of one predominant use, the area was, perhaps, most like Palestine. As Palestine stood astride the caravan routes of the Fertile Crescent, classical Greece controlled the sea routes of the eastern Mediterranean.

The ancestral Greeks, like the Chous of China, the Indo-Europeans of India, and the ancient Hebrews of Palestine, represented a primitive people moving against a more advanced civilization. The ancestral Greeks were least like the Hebrew nomads and peasants, and most like the Aryans of India. In fact, the Greeks seem to have been a branch of the same movement of Indo-Europeans who swept down into northern India.

In their relation to the peoples against whom they moved, the ancestral Greeks again showed a combination of similarity and difference with the other areas. Though belonging to the same people's movement that swept into India, they had no such relation of absolute hostility to the Minoan civilization as did the Aryans to the Indus Valley civilization. On the other hand, their conquest was carried out in a manner closer to that of the Aryans, and hardly in the form of a tribal confederation like the Jews. Conjoint military actions by the ancestral Greeks were more like feudal operations. At times, as in the case of Sparta with relation to the helots, the ancestral Greeks reduced the subject population to the status of slaves of the conquest community. However, all in all, the integration of the ancestral Greeks with the previous civilization bore far greater similarities to that of the people of the Chou than to the Shang.

Thus, while there were many elements in the Greek situation which paralleled those of other cultural areas in the Axial Period, they existed in a unique combination of their own, which offers a special case for the test of the hypotheses of our study.

13

THE CHANGING FORMS OF ANCIENT GREEK SOCIETY

SOUTHERN GREECE is a land of olives, northern Greece a land of oaks. Though there are basins adaptable to cultivation, the Epirus is an upland area primarily suitable for sheep-raising. Thessaly, consisting of two lowland basins linked by the Peneios River, is capable of cultivation, though it occasionally experiences the typical continental threat of drought and crop failure. Mount Olympus stands in the north, dividing Thessaly from Macedonia, the plains of which bear some similarities to those of Thessaly, except that they open onto the sea.

Central Greece, the area extending from the Gulf of Corinth and the Gulf of Aegina to the Othrys Range forming the southern boundary of Thessaly, is dominated by the mountains running down its center, which cut off the fertile lowland plains of Aetolia, Boeotia, and Attica from one another.

The Peloponnesus, separated from the rest of Greece except for the narrow isthmus, is insular to Greece proper. It is divided into the fertile plains of Sparta and the upland of central Arcadia which is surrounded by alternate mountains and lowland basins. The basins sustain wheat and maize; on the upland areas grow vines and fruit trees. Beyond the mainland, the Aegean Islands, which extend like steppingstones toward Asia Minor, contain a variety of useful rocks and minerals (obsidian from Melos, marble from Paros and Naxos, emery from Naxos, metallic ores from Seriphos, and potter's clay from most of them.

The climate of central and southern Greece is subtropical, subject to ocean-controlled wind and rain patterns. With its combination of plains and mountain barriers, the mainland tends to separate rather than unify social life. The rushing mountain streams are too rarely accessible for transportation to permit easy integration of the whole. From antiquity the people of Greece have been oriented outward toward their much divided coast and ocean islands.[1]

[1] A. Jarde, *The Formation of the Greek People* (New York: Alfred A. Knopf, 1926), pp. 7–35.

PREHISTORY OF GREEK SOCIETY

Though a paleolithic culture has not been established for Greece, in the plains of Thessaly a distinctive neolithic culture flourished at the same time as in Crete.[2] From at least 4000 B.C. in neolithic peasant villages there was a variety of cultivated crops (wheat, barley, oats, rye, olives, and grapes). The oxen, sheep, goats, and pigs had been domesticated, pottery was made, and textiles were woven.

The Bronze Age civilization which grew up on this neolithic foundation centered in the islands, particularly Crete. This civilization possessed a monarchical form of political structure (indicated by palaces and fortified citadels), a developed religion with an elaborate iconography, developed social classes, an administration staffed by scribes, and a developed commerce (traceable through the distribution of island-manufactured objects). The Aegean civilization developed an indigenous script, peculiar architectural styles with labyrinthine arrangements of rooms around central courts, a unique art (including sculpture, ceramic work, reliefs, and fresco painting), and a peculiar type of beehive tomb. Minoan art objects were actively exchanged for those of Egypt. The archeological study of the Bronze Age civilization on Crete and on the Greek mainland was opened up by the businessman-archeologist, Heinrich Schliemann,[3] and by Sir Arthur Evans.[4] Because of differences between Bronze Age culture on Crete and the mainland, the periods have been called Minoan and Helladic respectively.

CHRONOLOGY OF THE GREEK HEROIC AGE

Time	*Form*
2900–2100 B.C.	early Minoan
2500–1900 B.C.	early Helladic—earliest settlements at Mycenae by non-European inhabitants related to those of Crete
2100–1580 B.C.	middle Minoan
1900–1500 B.C.	middle Helladic first Indo-European tribes at Mycenae—gradual extension of Indo-European settlements
1580–1000 B.C.	late Minoan
1500–1100 B.C.	late Helladic
1350 B.C.	Perseus becomes king of Mycenae

[2] George Willis Botsford and Charles Alexander Robinson, *Hellenic History* (New York: The Macmillan Co., 1956), pp. 13–15.

[3] H. Schliemann, *Mycenae: A Narrative of Researches and Discoveries at Mycenae and Tiryns* (New York: 1880); C. Schuchardt, *Schliemann's Excavations* (London: 1891).

[4] Sir Arthur Evans, *The Palace of Minos at Knossos,* i-iv (London: 1921–1935); *The Shaft Graves and Beehive Tombs of Mycenae and Their Interrelations* (London: 1929).

Time	*Form*
1200 B.C.	Agamemnon rules over Mycenae
1183 B.C.	traditional date of fall of Troy, followed by return and death of Agamemnon
1100 B.C.	destruction of Mycenae by Dorian tribes.[5]

Helladic and Cretan cultures, which were originally very similar, began to differentiate after 1900 B.C., in part because of the intermixture on the mainland with Indo-Europeans, the Achaeans, who absorbed Minoan culture.

In the second millennium, when the mainland branch of Minoan culture was being transformed, Minoan culture was also changing in the islands. Around 1800 B.C. bronze and the potter's wheel were introduced. Trade increased and the center of political power was established at Knossus. A network of roads and forts linked the Minoan towns on Crete. An elaborate centralized administrative bureaucracy developed to run the overseas empire. This civil imperialism, however, was violently overthrown around 1450 B.C.; Knossus and other cities of Crete were razed.[6]

On the mainland the Mycenaeans were also scheduled for trouble. Around 1200 B.C. large numbers of ancestral Greeks left the Balkan peninsula, moving eastward across the Aegean Sea. These Aeolian and Ionian migrations were followed a century later by the new and more violent movement of the Dorians.[7]

AN OUTLINE OF GREEK HISTORY TO THE HELLENISTIC PERIOD

Homeric Period

The neolithic people who first absorbed elements of the Minoan civilization are conventionally described in Greek sources as Pelasgians.[8] The Achaeans, who in the nineteenth century B.C. began to displace and assimilate the Pelasgians, were sea raiders who hammered against the ramparts of Egypt. In Egyptian documents they were known as "peoples of the sea."[9] The Achaeans had no writing. Their warrior gentry was composed of neither traders nor diplomats; they have been compared to the Goths in the Roman Empire as vigorous, illiterate barbarians, bent on plundering the treasure of existing civilization.[10] With them Greek history proper begins.

The Homeric epics indicate that toward the close of the second millen-

[5] Following George E. Mylonas, *Ancient Mycenae: The Capital City of Agamemnon* (Princeton: Princeton University Press, 1957), pp. 181–182.

[6] Botsford and Robinson, *op. cit.*, pp. 9–33.

[7] *Ibid.*, pp. 34–35.

[8] Strabo, ix, 5.19, ix. i. 18; Jarde, *op. cit.*, pp. 72–73.

[9] Jarde, *op. cit.*, p. 73.

[10] A. R. Burn, *Minoans, Philistines, and Greeks B.C. 1400–900* (New York: Alfred A. Knopf, 1930), p. 199 ff.

nium the Achaeans were in the process of consolidation. They were formed into an uneasy confederation under Agamemnon, King of Mycenae.[11] Sea-raiding and aggressive wars were frequent. The confederation was intended both for defense and for the undertaking of large-scale sea-raiding expeditions. The siege and sack of Troy was the last and perhaps the most spectacular destructive achievement of the confederacy.[12]

About the time of the Trojan War new waves of Indo-Europeans moved down from the Balkan peninsula. The first two waves moved comparatively slowly. Those who colonized the large islands of Lesbos and Chios came to be known as Aeolians. Those who colonized Attica, Euboea, and the central littoral of Asia came to be known as Ionians. The Dorians crashed over much of the same area later. Technical innovations gave these northerners their striking power. Iron-working had been adopted by the central European tribes who had access to a large supply of raw material. The Dorians possessed not only superior iron weapons but a more compact social organization than the people they overcame.[13] The Achaeans were a less cultivated people than the Minoans with whom they began, in time, to amalgamate; the Aeolians, Ionians, and Dorians were even more barbaric than the Achaeans.

> With the Dorian and Ionian migrations the age of the sea-raids, which the Greeks called the Heroic Age, draws to an end. The piracy universal in the society which Homer describes had ended by killing the goose that laid the golden eggs. The age of the great "Sackers of Cities," as they proudly called themselves, ends for lack of civilized cities and palaces to sack.[14]

The Formation of the City-States

The next major development in ancient Greece was the formation of the city-states. Any study of the historical development of the city in Greece is faced with the problem that first posed itself to Aristotle when he set out to study the constitutions of the Greek states and found it necessary to survey no less than 158 of them. There was an amazing number of variations between them. However, there is no distortion in viewing the two major forms of the Greek city-state in terms of the two historically most important ones—Sparta, the land power, and Athens, the sea power.[15]

Sparta was made up of Dorian settlers who established a number of

11 The Iliad opens with the disagreement of Agamemnon and Achilles. See Andrew Lang, Walter Leaf, Ernest Myers, *The Iliad* in *The Complete Works of Homer* (New York: The Modern Library, n.d.), pp. 1–38.

12 Burn, *op. cit.*, p. 211.

13 Botsford and Robinson, *op. cit.*, pp. 34 f.; Jarde, *op. cit.*, pp. 56 f.; Burn, *op. cit.*, pp. 222 ff.

14 Burn, *op. cit.*, p. 235.

15 A compact review of Athens and Sparta appears in M. Rostovtzeff, *A History of the Ancient World* (Oxford: The Clarendon Press, 1925), Vol. I, pp. 205–228.

village communities which dominated the Eurotas Valley.[16] A city-state formed out of the settlement of the Lacedaemonians, as they called themselves. Other communities formed of preexisting elements called *perioicoi* (dwellers round about), were free in all but political respects.

By the end of the seventh century Sparta had developed a constitutional aristocracy, which, however, conservatively retained elements of the earlier kingship. The functions of hereditary dual kingship (possibly originally the kings of two discrete tribes) were, however, much curtailed. They served as priests, prepared special sacrifices for expeditions and battles, and acted as spiritual leaders of the community. Though they were supreme commanders of the army in wartime, they were responsible to the people for the consequences of their military decisions. Their actions were subject to legal control. They retained judicial powers in adoption cases, over the marriages of heiresses whose fathers had died before the betrothal, and in conflicts concerning public roads.

In Sparta the old Homeric council of elders (*gerontes*) was transformed into a fixed body (the *gerousia*) with thirty members (including the two kings) subject to special age requirements (over sixty years of age except for the kings). Members were chosen by acclamation in the assembly, and held office for life. Only nobles could become members. The council had political advisory powers, and served as a court in criminal cases. Every Spartan over thirty years of age was a member of the *Apella*, the assembly of citizens which met every month. It elected the *gerousia*, the *ephors*, and other magistrates.

The most significant part of the Spartan constitution, the five *ephors*, perhaps originated as representatives of the five *demes*, or villages, that had formed the city. The ephors were elected representatives of the people. They kept the actions of the king under surveillance, served as a supreme civil court, and acted as criminal judges in cases involving the *perioicoi*.

Sparta soon undertook the conquest of Messenia to increase the land lots for the citizens. The Messenians were reduced to helot status (slaves of the Spartan community), and were required to pay tribute amounting to half of the produce of the land. The Messenians staged a revolt against such oppression which for a time succeeded, at the end of the seventh century, but which the Spartans in a bitter fight put down.

The constant threat of helot revolts led Sparta to undertake a basic reconstruction of her civic institutions. The Spartans bound their population under an iron discipline in which everything was subordinate to the art of war. Every citizen was freed from the necessity of providing for himself. The condemned land was divided into lots, one lot being assigned to every citizen. The original inhabitants were reduced to serf-

[16] K. M. T. Chrimes, *Ancient Sparta* (Manchester: Manchester University Press, 1949).

dom. A fixed payment was demanded from each helot, the remainder of the produce being allowed to him. A secret police (*crypteia*) was set up to keep a constant check on the helots.

The Spartan's life was organized around the military barracks. From the age of seven a boy was in the care of a state officer and trained in the skills of war and endurance of hardship. At the age of twenty he could marry, but must continue to live in the barracks. At thirty he became a full citizen. Public messes were established for the men. Public discipline was extended to women who went through gymnastic training. However, once this was completed, Spartan women enjoyed a freedom unusual elsewhere. Except for being enjoined by the state to have children in or out of marriage, they lived independently on the estates of their husbands, often consolidating even more of the land into their hands.

The struggle of Messenia had been assisted by Arcadia and Pisa. Sparta's success changed the balance of power of the Peloponnesus. As she emerged as the primary power, Argos, formerly preeminent, receded.

Just as the city-state of Sparta arose as a new military community out of a number of village communities, so Athens represented a new community synthesis of formerly small independent villages of Attica.[17] The new Athenian community was located 5 miles from the sea and hence was not subject to immediate invasion. Its natural defenses were in the Acropolis which became the dwelling place of the city goddess Athena.

According to mythology, the lords of the Acropolis subdued the plain. This statement seems to be essentially correct, for Athens originally had the form of a kinship. Athens assumed its historical form, however, with an act of *synoecism* (a sworn association of knights who were interested in sharing civic power with the king), which played a role for Athens equivalent to Lysander's militarization of Sparta. In historical times a feast celebrated this *synoecism* as a kind of founders' day celebration. From the beginning there were marked contrasts to Sparta, for the members of the sworn association were free citizens of Athens, where they exercised their political rights and were subject to military service, but were not transformed into permanent professional soldiers as in Sparta.

Athens passed into the status of an oligarchical republic at an early date. A military commander (*polemarch*) was soon instituted alongside the king, while the kingship was reduced to a religious office. An *archonship* took over most of the functions of the king. The archonship was at first for life, but was later reduced to ten years, and finally made into a yearly office. The state was organized into four tribes and twelve *phratries* (three to a tribe). However, these were tribes and phratries in name only, as the old tribal community had long since vanished. The nobles were members

[17] William Scott Ferguson, *Hellenistic Athens* (London: The Macmillan Co., 1911); G. Glotz, *The Greek City* (New York: Alfred A. Knopf, 1930); Sir W. Young, *The History of Athens* (London: W. Bulmer, 1804).

of clans which had their clan gods, though the public cult was common to all. Peasants and craftsmen without clans, called *orgeones,* were organized according to their worship of a common diety.

By the seventh century Athens was a republic with its executive branch in the hands of three annually elected officers. The *archon* was supreme judge in all civil suits, the *polemarch* was a supreme military official who also held court for noncitizens, the king was chief priest of the state religion. A council of elders (*areopagus*) which presided over cases of murder, violence, etc., was the governing body presiding over elections of the *ecclesia* (the citizens' assembly). During this period Eleusis was annexed to Athens.

The Athenians recognized (among the free population) three classes: the *eupatridae* (nobles), the *georgi* (free peasants on their own farms), and the *demiurgi* (public workers, traders, merchants, etc.). A group of noncitizens, who were nevertheless still free men, comprised agricultural laborers who acted as tenant farmers and craftsmen. Slaves composed a good part of the laboring population.

The influences of commercial and industrial development were clearly felt in changes in the class structure. By the end of the seventh century, the population was divided on the basis of wealth into the nobles (*pentacosiomedimni*) with incomes of over five hundred *medimni* of corn, the knights (*hippes*) with incomes of more than three hundred but less than five hundred measures, and the teamsters (*zeugitae*) with a minimum income of two hundred measures.

Pressure from the new wealthy classes is indicated by the institution of the *Thesmothetae,* a college of six judges who managed the judicial system and together with the magistrates composed the "Nine Archons." Free laborers without land of their own (the *thetes*) retained some significance, particularly as mariners in the *penteconters.* The growth of naval power is indicated by the division of the four tribes into *naucrariae,* each bound to supply a ship. Naval affairs were governed by an important administrative council.

Strong tensions clearly existed between the new and old class structures. The peasants were ground down under urban creditors. The adoption of coined money accelerated the rate of exploitation. So great was the discontent that Draco was appointed extraordinary legislator with power to do whatever was necessary to clear up the situation. Unfortunately, most of Draco's famous code (621 B.C.) was lost. It appears to have been harsh, but it reduced current economic practices to a standard form, and established a special body of fifty-one judges (*ephetae*) who systematized court procedure. Draconian laws on debt, however, were severe, even providing for debt slavery.

The Draconian Code slowed without preventing the absorption of the estates of small proprietors by large creditors. Both the free peasants and the formerly free laborers were rapidly transformed into slaves. The unrest continued until Solon, who appears to have been a merchant, was appointed as mediator. Solon was charged with the reform, and was granted extraordinary powers (592–591 B.C.).

Solon took more drastic action than Draco. He cancelled old debts, passed legislation against debt slavery, fixed a legal limit on the amount of land ownership, and inaugurated a native coinage. He retained the classification of people according to property, but granted the *thetes* some political rights. They were to be used as light-armed troops or marines. The *ecclessia* was opened to them.

Solon constituted a court of all the citizens. Thereafter the archons gradually lost judicial powers. The *Areopagus* was given broad supervisory powers and made the body into which all archons, after their year of service, entered for life. Meanwhile a new council (the Four Hundred) was created to prepare business for the citizen's assembly. Its members were chosen by quota (one hundred from each tribe) and from the tribes by lot. Lot was also used for appointment of minor public officials.

Though Solon's reforms brought about some permanent improvement, party strife broke out, and ended thirty years later in the tyranny of Pisistratus. Meanwhile, Salamis was conquered and divided into lots among the Athenian citizens. Pisistratus first established the tyranny in 561 B.C. He was exiled, restored, exiled again, and restored once again. He held office by means of private mercenaries and the seizure of hostages from noble families. He secured support by dividing the vacant lots of estates and giving them to peasant proprietors in return for a land tax. As a part of self-advertisement as a public benefactor, he may have been the first person to commission the establishment of an authentic Homer text. For the same reason, he promoted the Panathenaic feast. Under Pisistratus a shrine was built to Dionysus and the festival, the "Greater Dionysia," was instituted. He sponsored public works, improved the water system of Athens, and undertook temple construction in part to provide labor for the indebted classes.

While Pisistratus was occupied in Athens, Sparta was extending her power through successes against Tegea and Argos, becoming predominant in the peninsula. After the death of Pisistratus, Sparta interfered in Athens' affairs, forcing her to enter the Peloponnesian League. Out of the conflicts that followed this move, Cleisthenes eventually came into prominence.

Cleisthenes believed the difficulties of Athenian politics were a consequence of the power of the clans. He divided Attica into three regions—city, coast, and island. In each he divided the *demes* into ten groups (*trittyes*). He then formed ten groups of three, in such a manner that no group contained two *trittyes* from the same region. Both tribes and *demes* were corporations with officers, assemblies, and corporate property. The organization of the army depended on the tribes; each contributed a regiment of hoplites and a squadron of horses. This system of gerrymandering cut across all the old antagonisms. Conforming to the new organization, Cleisthenes devised a Council of Five Hundred based on the ten new tribes; it was the supreme administrative authority of the state. Finance was in its hands, it had judicial powers in matters of public finance, and it had initiative in all law-making. Through such developments democracy assumed its classic form in Athens.

The Persian War

In contrast to Palestine, over whose history looms the continuous threat from surrounding great powers, Greece was able to pursue its internal self-development untroubled by equivalent foreign interference. Even the rise of Babylonia that brought the fall of Jerusalem hardly caused more than faint echoes throughout the Greek world. However, the Medes who were rising in the north attacked Lydia in 585 B.C. Lydia, in turn, under Croesus (560–546 B.C.), attacked and subdued the cities of eastern Greece. Croesus sacrificed to the oracle at Delphi. The combined Medes and Persians turned on Lydia, capturing Sardis in 564 B.C. The Persians then instituted the systematic policy of reducing the Asiatic Greeks one after another. The Aeolians and Ionians appealed to Sparta for aid, but to no avail.

When Darius came to the Persian throne he continued the policy of his predecessors. Thrace and Macedonia were soon conquered. Meanwhile, the Ionians revolted, appealing for aid from both Athens and Sparta. Only the Athenians responded. However, the revolt was put down by Darius, and preparations for the invasion of European Greece began. This terminated in the Battle of Marathon. For ten years no further invasion of Greece occurred, but under Xerxes systematic preparation for the conquest of Greece was again undertaken. In the battles of Salamis (480 B.C.), Plataea (479 B.C.), and Mycale, the Persians were decisively repulsed.[18]

The Persian wars had dramatized the need for wider Greek unity, and had left Sparta in a primary position to achieve it. It was the Athenians, however, who formed a voluntary confederacy of Ionic and Aeolic cities for the dual purpose of defense of the rescued cities and plundering Persian lands to offset war losses. A treasury of the league was established at Delos in 478 B.C., when the Council of the league met.[19] However, the league was dominated by Athens, which soon turned it into an Athenian empire and transferred the treasury to Athens.

The Peloponnesian War

In 461 B.C. the First Peloponnesian War broke out between Athens and her rivals, Corinth and Aegina.[20] Sparta was eventually drawn into these

[18] The fundamental source for the Persian wars is Herodotus' *Persian Wars*, trans. by George Rawlinson in *The Greek Historians* (New York: Modern Library, 1942).

[19] W. A. Laidlaw, *A History of Delos* (Oxford: Basil Blackwell, 1933), pp. 62 ff.

[20] The fundamental source for the Peloponnesian War is Thucydides, *The Peloponnesian War*, trans. by Benjamin Jowett, *The Greek Historians, op. cit.*, Vol. I.

struggles. This war was the prelude to the Peloponnesian War (431–404 B.C.), which was in part a struggle between sea and land power. When Lysander managed to line the oligarchies against the democracies, the fate of Athens was sealed. The Spartans attempted to integrate the mainland, but within a year after the surrender of Athens, Thebes and Corinth rose in opposition. The Corinthian War (394–387 B.C.) was brought about by an alliance of the secondary powers (Thebes, Athens, Corinth, Argos) against Sparta. Sparta emerged victorious, but with the destruction of her sea power. The Battle of Leuctra transferred hegemony to Thebes, but the elements for a union of Greece were even less favorable than in the case of Athens or Sparta, for Thebes was exclusively a land power and had no revenue comparable to Athens.[21]

The Empire

Under Philip of Macedon the basis was laid for the exploits of his illustrious son. Alexander was an extraordinarily brilliant military strategist. The Macedonian army was unparalleled in the world at the time. Through it he coordinated a large part of the Near Eastern world into an empire.[22] With the formation of the Macedonian Empire, whose place was eventually taken over by the Roman Empire, the old world came to an end. The chronology of important events in this period was as follows:

CHRONOLOGY OF THE CLASSICAL GREEK PERIOD

Date	*Event*
1100 B.C.	Dorian invasion
730 B.C.	Spartan conquest of Messenia
700 B.C.	Synoecism at Athens
560–546 B.C.	Pisistratus
545 B.C.	Persian conquest of Asiatic Greeks
490 B.C.	Battle of Marathon
480 B.C.	Battle of Thermopylae and Salamis
431–404 B.C.	Peloponnesian War
336–323 B.C.	Alexander the Great
184 B.C.	Macedonia becomes a Roman province
27 B.C.	Peloponnesus becomes a Roman province

THE CHANGING FORMS OF THE ANCIENT GREEK COMMUNITY

The ancient Greek community went through three general stages: the feudal manors of the heroic period, the autonomous city, and the imperial city. At no time did the peasant village deriving from neolithic prehistory completely disappear, but remained as a subordinate community under the domination of the more complex communities.

21 Xenophon's *Hellenica*, trans. by Henry G. Dakyns, is the best source for this period.

22 See Arrian's *Anabasis of Alexander*, trans. by Edward J. Chinnock.

The Feudal Manors of the Heroic Period

Homeric society consisted of a world of peasant villages under the domination of castle-dwelling warrior kings. That the peasant villages were looked upon as a source of wealth is shown by Agamemnon's conception of them as an appropriate dowry for his daughter.

> Three daughters are mine in my well-builded hall, Chrysothemis and Laodike and Iphianassa; let him take them which he will, without gifts of wooing, to Peleus' house; and I will add a great dower such as no man ever yet gave with his daughter. And several well-peopled cities will I give him.[23]

The nearest approach to a portrait of the peasantry which formed the foundation of the Homeric world is found in Hesiod's *Works and Days*. Hesiod lived at Ascra under Helicon Hill in southern Boeotia toward the end of the ninth century B.C. The plasticity of the class from which he was derived is shown by the fact that his father failed in business as a merchant sailor before going back to Boeotia, where he bought a farm. When Hesiod's father died, he left the farm to his two sons, Hesiod and Perses. Some aspects of the relation between the free peasant and the castled notables appear in the course of Hesiod's quarrel with his brother. He accused his brother of having bribed the local nobles with timely presents and so received more than his share of the paternal inheritance.[24]

The poem described the difficult life of the free peasant, the character of farming at the time, and the star lore thought to control it. Hesiod stressed the necessity for hard work:

> First, get a house and a woman and an ox for the plough, and have your tools all ready in the house, that you may not try to borrow from another, and he refuse, and you be without one, and the season be going by and your work come to nothing. And do not put things off till tomorrow and the day after . . . a man who puts off his work is always at hand-grips with ruin.[25]

In Homeric times much of the land was held in common.[26] While no reference to land being sold appears in the Homeric poems, this had become possible in Hesiod's time. Private ownership of land appeared whenever tribes conquered territory, at which time land was allotted for homes, grain fields, and orchards. However, in Lacedaemonia in historic times large tracts were reserved as commons for pasture. Grain and fruit fields were enclosed by hedges or stone walls. Oxen and mules were used for plowing,

[23] *The Iliad*, in *The Complete Works of Homer*, *op. cit.*, p. 230.

[24] Andrew Robert Burn, *The World of Hesiod* (London: Kegan Paul, Trench, Trubner & Co., 1936), p. 34 ff.

[25] Hesiod, *Works and Days*, trans. by Evelyn-Whyte. Quoted by Burn, *ibid.*, p. 37.

[26] Thomas Day Seymour, *Life in the Homeric Age* (New York: The Macmillan Co., 1908), p. 235.

horses being too honorable for such menial tasks. In the Homeric Age wealth consisted largely of flocks and herds; cattle were the chief form of wealth and served as the standard of value. Villages were small, manufactures were domestic, and every man was a farmer. Even princes tended cattle, and dug in their gardens.

Outside of beans and chick-peas, few if any garden vegetables were grown. Barley and wheat were the main grains (rice, rye, oats, and buckwheat were unknown). Flax was less important than later. Most bedding and clothing were made of wool. Irrigation was practiced, and the use of manure was understood. Fields were periodically allowed to lie fallow. Agricultural implements were simple: the scratch-point plow, the mattock, and the hoe. Only in classical times was the plowshare tipped with iron. Grain was reaped with a sickle. Wheat was threshed by a team of oxen, which tramped the threshing floor. Grapes, olives, figs, pears, apples, and pomegranates were cultivated.[27]

The chiefs of the castles bearing the hereditary title of king (*basileus*) claimed to be of divine descent. Agamemnon, Menelaus, Achilles, Odysseus, and Idomeneus, for example, claimed descent from Zeus, Ajax from Apollo, Nestor and Alcinous from Poseidon.[28] They were charismatic figures whose supernatural powers had to be confirmed from time to time. Every nine years in Crete, Minos entered the cave of Zeus to render account and be reinvested. At intervals on a clear night in Sparta the *ephors* kept silent watch of the skies for a shooting star which signified that the kings had committed some sin against the gods, and had to be deposed.[29] However, even when the monarchy was in jeopardy the hereditary right of the son, for example, Telemachus,[30] was not generally questioned, though it was necessary occasionally, through exceptional exploits, to verify fitness for the office.

The badge of kingly office was the scepter.[31] According to tradition, Agamemnon's scepter had been made by Hephaestus. As a symbol of domination it was employed in the formalization of debating procedure before the assembly. Handing over the scepter was formal recognition of the right of a speaker to the floor.

A high priest of the community, the king performed its sacrifices, cut the throats of sacrificial lambs, and clipped hair from the heads of victims and cast it into the fire. With the scepter he had received knowledge of the *themistes*, the principles of justice. A commander-in-chief in war, the king also planned campaigns, chose officers, and had power of life and death over

27 *Ibid.*, pp. 323 ff.
28 *Ibid.*, p. 82.
29 Plutarch, *Agis,* 11.
30 Op. I, 387.
31 Weisenborn, *Homeric Life,* trans. by Gilbert Campbell Scoggin and Charles Gray Burkitt (New York: The American Book Co., 1903), p. 58.

cowards. Since his palace and hearth were the public hearth, he represented the community to foreigners and received ambassadors.[32]

The king's personal staff consisted of freemen and slaves. Officials from noble families (*therapontes*) who bore official titles and dwelt in or near the palace, also served the kings. In first rank were the heralds, who assisted the king in religious duties, served as public ministers, convoked the council and the assembly, served as police to keep order, and gave the scepter to the speakers. Another section of the *therapontes* had domestic duties. The cupbearer was chief in the palace. The domestic staff comprised a variety of assistants and attendants ranging from those who assisted the king to don his armor to those who looked after the horses and chariots.

Beside the Homeric king appeared the chiefs of the clans who formed a council (*boule*) of elders or "elders of the people." At times a smaller council of the king's closest peers (table companions) was separated from the larger council of all the chiefs. In council meetings the eldest customarily spoke first (like Nestor in the Achaean council). The elders (*gerontes*) were consulted in all matters of importance. At the assembly they sat in a place apart. They participated in foreign relations; they were consulted before dispatching embassies. In the field they formed a council of war; their oath confirmed treaties. In their own clans the elders were the highest legal authorities, possessing the scepter and the *themistes*.

The assembly, the gathering of all those who had no place in the council, consisted of full though not privileged members of Homeric society. At the typical assembly, the gathering of all qualified warriors, decisions of the king and his advisors were announced. The assembly was normally held in the morning, though in the field it might be held in any open area near the military camp at any time. When not in the field, a specified place (usually near the temple) served for assembly meetings. Before the assembly were brought actions on pestilence, rewards for services to the state, repatriations, news of the battlefield, and proposals of peace negotiations. To speak in the assembly it was necessary to be invested with the scepter by a herald. Ordinarily only the elders took part in discussions; the opinions of the people were manifest only in signs of agreement or dissent.[33]

From this general type of social structure, consisting of castle-dwelling nobles exercising dominion over peasant villages, the two most frequent historical developments have been either toward full feudalism or toward patrimonial administration. The development into full feudalism is possible when the primary claims to power rest on landed wealth and control of military implements, both of which characterized the members of the council of the Homeric kings. All that was required for the appearance of full feudalism was the regulation through contractual agreement (*enfeoffment*)

[32] Seymour, *op. cit.*, pp. 83 ff.

[33] Bonner, Robert J., and Gertrud Orlin Smith, *The Administration of Justice from Homer to Aristotle* (Chicago: University of Chicago Press, 1930), pp. 5 ff.

of tribute and military service of the relation between kings and subkings. The actual control over his situation by the individual subchief would guarantee him relatively complete autonomy in his own sphere.

On the other hand, the development to patrimonial kinship could have been facilitated by the strengthening of the king's administrative staff at the expense of the council. The establishment of sources of tribute for the king in independence of the general council permitted him to equip a personal army and provision a private official staff exclusively loyal to himself. The use of mercenary soldiers, for example, or of lay persons as military personnel, shortcircuiting the relation between king and subject, might have weakened the powerful council.

The development toward feudalism in China occurred in the transition from the Shang to the Chou dynasty, and was completed in the Chou. Something very similar was well under way in India before the rise of the patrimonial states. In Palestine, however, the victory of the Israelites was the work of an armed peasantry, and the monarchy was established over a semifeudal Canaanite population. In China the feudalization process was reversed by the Ch'in implemented by a peasant army modeled in part on nomadic military practice. The feudalization process was reversed in India under princes who built up their private staffs in large measure from nonnoble elements, as Shi Huang-ti had done in China. None of these developments occurred in Greece. Rather, the semifeudal castles of the Homeric kings were replaced by city-states.

The Greek City in the Classical Period

If the city was to appear as an autonomous social and political unit, it had to be able to defend itself. Already in the Homeric period the feudal fortress was not only the place from which the countryside was dominated and exploited but the place from which the community could seek refuge.[34] The city had an inner fortification and temple on an acropolis. The acropolis had usually been fortified first. Later growth led to the development of fortifications around the extended city. Aristotle had observed that the defensive fortifications of the acropolis favored monarchy and oligarchy, whereas democracy preferred fortresses in the plains.[35]

The city was composed of the acropolis and the *asty*, the lower city that grew around it.[36] The heart of the ancient city was the city hearth (*prytaneum*) under the tutelage of the god or goddess of the city.[37] When a

[34] Max Weber, *The City*, trans. by Don Martindale and Gertrud Neuwirth (Glencoe: The Free Press, 1958), pp. 75 ff.

[35] Aristotle, *Politics*, IV, 10.

[36] G. Glotz, *The Greek City*, trans. by N. Mallinson (New York: Alfred A. Knopf, 1930), pp. 10 ff.

[37] To Coulanges the indispensable foundation of the city was the act of religious synoecism. Fustel de Coulanges, *The Ancient City* (New York: Doubleday Anchor Books, 1956), p. 127.

colony was founded the emigrants took embers from the hearth of the mother city to light the sacred fire of the new *prytaneum*.[38]

In addition to the *prytaneum*, and usually near it, was the building where the council (*boule* or *gerousia*) of deputies (*prytaneis* or *aisymnates*)[39] met. Before the synoecism in Attica, every subcommunity had its own council. When these disappeared the representatives of the subcommunities met in the newly constituted council.

The most frequent place for the gathering of the people was the *agora*,[40] traditionally the market place or the street where men came to gossip and talk politics. The *agora* was the breeding ground of public opinion in the Greek city. In some cities (Delphi, Naupactus, Gortyna) the assembly retained the name *agora*, but in most cities the usual terms for the assembly of the people were *ecclesia*, *haelia*, and *apella* (in Sparta).

Communities around the cities fell under their domination. Their dependence included tribute-paying and, at times, serflike dependence (as in the case of the Spartan *perioicoi*). At times administrators from the mother city (in Elis) supervised the local authorities of dependent towns.[41]

The substructure of the cities was called *gens*, *phratries*, or tribes. However, though as the terms indicate, these divisions were inherited from earlier community forms (the tribe and the peasant village), they were readapted to the needs of the city community. Aristotle found, as noted, that he had to deal with no less than 158 city constitutions; there were probably three times that many. In all of them, the former structures of tribe and peasant village had been transformed into something new.

The broadest class distinctions that emerged in civic Greece during the Hellenic period were between cities and noncitizens, and between free persons and slaves. As a full member of the city-state, the citizen was able to hold office and to share in city booty. However, resident aliens (*metics*) also played an important role in the cities. Many of the richest merchants, best craftsmen, and finest artists of Greece were *metics*. Since the *metic* could not appear in court, he had to enter clientage to a citizen who represented him. At times *metics* penetrated the ranks of the citizenry.[42] They also bought or married their way into citizen circles, where adopted into a clan, or were awarded citizenship for meritorious wartime service to the state. The status of the citizen was prized. Slavery supplied the foundation of commercial economy.[43] To Aristotle, society was literally inconceivable without slavery, though he had his doubts as to the morality of pressing fellow-Greeks into bondage.[44]

38 Glotz, *op. cit.*, p. 20.
39 *Ibid.*, p. 21.
40 *Ibid.*, pp. 21 ff.
41 *Ibid.*, p. 24.
42 Alfred Zimmern, *The Greek Commonwealth* (Oxford: The Clarendon Press, 1931), pp. 383 ff.
43 *Ibid.*, pp. 380 ff.
44 Aristotle, *Politics*, Bk. I, 3–13.

In Athens income-based classes in time became more important than the hereditary landed nobility. In the Athenian classification the knights (*hippes*) were in second place. Athenian development was only one of the possible forms of class formation. Two other types were represented by Thessaly and Sparta.

The cities in Thessaly remained until late in a rather abortive state. Horse-breeding remained the primary claim to social significance. Thessaly, in fact, evolved toward complete feudalization throughout most of the period. More important than typical urban classes were feudal princes and vassals, while the population of the land was increasingly reduced to serf status under the feudal lords. Not until the middle of the fifth century did urbanism make serious inroads into the social structure.[45]

In Sparta, as noted earlier, a series of crises were precipitated by the revolts of the oppressed populations, which led to the full militarization of the dominant population.[46] The three important classes were constituted by the members of the royal families (of which there were two), the nobles (who retained their estates even under the military dictatorships), and the mass of the soldiery. Since in Sparta the practice of trade was specifically prohibited to citizens by law, the emergence of classes of citizens based on commercial wealth was impossible, and it did not suffer the same kinds of class conflicts as Athens.

Classical Greek class structure was in considerable measure influenced by the evolution of military techniques.[47] At the time of the Achaeans, the chariot had recently been introduced. The twin military forms—chariot warfare and walled fortifications—diffused through Greece as they did through China, northern India, and the land of the Canaanites. Cavalry was at first not important, though it took shape toward the close of the classical period. Summons of peasant warriors played an important role in the conquest of Palestine, but once they attained power, the Israelite monarchs paid tribute to the superiority of chariot-fighting by demilitarizing the peasants and developing professional armies along Egyptian models.

In China the Ch'in led the way in the evolution of militarism by the introduction of armed peasants against other feudal principalities. In the treatises of Sun Wu, quite advanced military theory was apparent. The military structures evolved by the Ch'in had proved to be remarkably successful in putting down revolt, rounding off the empire, and putting a stop to barbarian inroads. However, the further development of military techniques was not particularly necessary in China, and military technology declined.

The tiny city communities of classical Greece became the bearers of new

45 H. D. Westlake, *Thessaly* (London: Methuen, 1935), p. 29.

46 K. M. T. Chrimes, *Ancient Sparta* (Manchester: Manchester University Press, 1949), pp. 348 ff.

47 Weber, *The City, op. cit.*, pp. 208 ff.

developments in military technology. Under the requirements of civic defense, the individual warrior assumed a new importance. When properly disciplined, the hoplite proved to be more than a match for chariot-fighting individual heroes and cavalry. Meanwhile, in connection with naval warfare the individual sailor became important. Since it is rarely possible to deny militarily competent persons a voice in political affairs, the individual hoplite and the individual sailor were received more and more into full membership in the political community. The former *thetes* were thus elevated in status.

It also became possible for the successful military commander to bid for highest civic positions, and for the political demagogue to develop a mass (or a class) following and to elevate himself into prominence in the local city-state. In the cities a complex array of classes emerged with differently situated persons in highest rank in different places.

The political structure of the city-state was extraordinarily variable, with subtle transitions from type to type. The two main forms (or types) of political order were oligarchy and democracy. Aristotle distinguished four principal types of oligarchy, varying from extreme to moderate types. These need not concern us.[48] In general, oligarchy varies from the semi-feudal type characterized by centralization of political influence between superior and subordinate nobles to a type so broad it merges into democracy. The oligarchical dynasties of Thessaly exemplified the first, with its organization of masters and serfs (*penestai*) and its rigid fixing of the difference between proprietors (who monopolized political power) and free peasants, merchants, and artisans. The middle class here had no place in the state.[49]

In Corinth the shipowners formed a semidynastic order, naming the *prytaneis* from its own class.[50] At times the chiefs of noble families were not subordinate to one another, but shared political power. In Elis, a small core of families monopolized the political power, though different members were rotated through the offices.[51] Where the old landed families had been partly displaced by the *nouveau riche*, the number of families participating in government tended to increase. In response to such pressures, attempts in a number of places were made to limit the number of citizens by law.[52]

In the evolution of the city, only the first stages were similar throughout the Greek world. The beginning was always with a feudal monarchy. In monarchical society the king was surrounded by personal retainers, but was forced to share power with the nobles. In all cases the first step toward the city was the taking over of power by the aristocracy. The administration of the city-state was not under the king but under the council (the *timouchei*,

48 Aristotle, *Politics*, Bk. IV, 5.
49 Westlake, *op. cit.*, p. 47.
50 Glotz, *op. cit.*, p. 71.
51 *Ibid.*, p. 72.
52 *Ibid.*, p. 270 ff.

prytaneis, or *aisymnetes*). Initially there was little need for a great number of magistrates. By placing its own leader on a level with the king, the aristocracy reduced the king to the level of an administrator. In Athens a polemarch was given the war powers formerly held by the king.[53] Later on, six *thesmothetai* were made responsible for the administration of justice. However, beyond this initial step in common, various city-states took quite different directions.

Under the oligarchies the assembly (*ecclesia*, *helia*) made some, though not considerable, gains. Sometimes the assembly could only discuss motions initiated from above. At times it could confirm but not reject decisions. Sometimes it served purely consultative functions. At times the assembly of citizens was not evoked at all. At Sparta, membership in the assembly (*apella*) was rigidly limited to those over thirty, who were enrolled in tribes, having taken public instruction and been admitted to public messes.

The real core of the political structure in the oligarchies was the council (*gerousia*), which could acquire a dynastic character. In Sparta it consisted of only twenty-eight members who had to be over sixty years of age, candidates being chosen from the narrowest circle of privileged persons. There were ninety *gerontes* in Elis chosen from three tribes. Sometimes the council was composed of magistrates who had completed their term of office (as in Athens); sometimes the great council was replaced by a restricted council (*probouloi*). This was a frequent development whenever the number of councilmen increased.

Not all city-states went through the next stage of development in which the council itself became subordinate to the *ecclesia*. However, again there were variations. Athens was the most famous example.

Just as in the transition to oligarchy, when the magistracy became dependent on the council, so with movement to democracy both council and magistracy became dependent on the sovereign people. They still needed executives, however. These were qualified to act in accordance with the laws or on consultation of the other groups; they could pass compulsory measures and punish delinquents, and in special cases, they had judicial competence. Magistracies were generally of short duration: Most were annual, though a man could be appointed for two years to the council, and military offices were capable of indefinite reappointment. The various magistracies were generally independent of one another, being secured through the council.

A distinction was made between major and minor offices. Those with extensive responsibilities were not paid; lower ranking citizens did not aspire to them. Magistracies were almost all computed in terms of the tribes. There were, for example, thirty tribal judges in order that each tribe and each division of the tribe might be represented. Magistrates were appointed by

[53] Botsford and Robinson, *op. cit.*, p. 79.

election or lot which grew in popularity toward the end of the fifth century. However, this was not as serious as might appear, since incompetent persons were withheld from participating in the lot drawing by public ridicule. All magistrates were required to have professional knowledge or monetary backing. Furthermore, whether appointed by lot or election, magistrates did not take office until they had been subjected to the test of the *dokimasia*.[54] It established the position of the individual in his family and his *deme*, inquired into his cult participation, the possession of family tombs, and the individual's family and public life. Magistrates took an oath of investiture. They were solemnly confirmed, and harbored in a special building. Some magistrates had assistants, who were also forced to undergo examination. Business was dispatched either by the special group or by members acting in its name.

Magistrates enjoyed special privileges (for example, freedom from civil action) necessary to the performance of their duties. They also enjoyed special honors, for example, special places in processions and ceremonies, and reserved seats at the theatre. They were usually not interfered with until the end of the term, when a public examination awaited them. Their responsibility was moral as well as political. A sworn account of disposition of public funds had to be made and audited. Legal action could be taken in case of delinquency. Restitution was required for misappropriated public funds. Few groups have ever been more carefully watched than the Greek magistrates.

Just as oligarchy begins at the point where the council appoints magistrates beside or in place of the king, democracy begins when the appointed council takes the place of the hereditary council. In Athens, as noted, this did not take place all at once. A succession of expedients was tried until a satisfactory one was found. Cleisthenes[55] replaced the old council of the five hundred which was to endure for a long time. The five hundred seats of the councillors were divided among the *demes*—fifty to each tribe. The councillors were elected by lot from candidates of at least thirty years of age. They were paid five *obols* a day. Candidates were subject to the *dokimasia*, and were limited to two terms. It was quite possible (almost necessary in fact) for every qualified citizen to serve some time during his life. The body was self-disciplining. At the end of the period of office the whole council had to render an account to the people. The *prytaneum*,[56] a directing committee of the council, was composed of ten sections, one for each tribe, and was housed in a special building where members took their meals (for which they were paid). The council prepared for the assembly drafts of decrees of the people. It also issued special decrees of its own. (These were executive decrees not deemed worthy of the assembly's atten-

[54] Bonner and Smith, *op. cit.*, p. 268.
[55] *Ibid.*, pp. 187 ff.
[56] *Ibid.*, p. 63.

tion.) It possessed authority over the magistrates. The *Boule*[57] held audiences with ambassadors before introducing them to the assembly, conducted negotiations with them, gave instructions to Athenian embassies, sometimes appointed them, received correspondence, honored guests, supervised military functions, and supervised civic defense.

The council garrisoned and provisioned the navy and was responsible for naval construction and preparations. The council also looked at the resources of the budget, supervised state contracts (like tax farming), kept state accounts, scrutinized the use of public funds, supervised public works, and watched over religious administration (took care of temples, etc.). Originally the penal jurisdiction of the *boule* had been extensive, but this in time was reduced. Under the democracy it could not condemn without appeal, nor punish with fines of more than five hundred drachmas—beyond that, cases were taken by the *thesmothetai.*

The *ecclesia*[58] was limited to Athenians, according to a Periclean law of 451 B.C., with Athenian parents on both sides, eighteen years of age, who had completed two years of military service. Copies of citizenship registers were posted in the tribes. However, the power of the pressure for citizenship is shown, in spite of punishment by slavery for violation, by the repeated necessity of revision of the registers. Before the end of the fourth century participation in public affairs was made possible for all classes of citizens by payment of members for attendance.

Among the powers of the assembly were the determination of foreign policy, legislation, the determination of political aspects of judicial power, the control of executive power, and the appointment and surveillance of all state offices. It appointed, instructed, and heard the reports of ambassadors. Military and naval matters were in its hands. In peace it heard reports on all matters of defense. In wartime it determined the contingents to be mobilized and the proportions of citizens serving in various capacities.

Economic Structure

The economy of Homeric Greece was semifeudal. That of Thessaly illustrates some of its potentials. In this largest plain of Greece the land was divided between families formed into tribes, the previous population being reduced or having fled. The lords possessed great estates (*kleroi*), cultivated by gangs of serfs (*penestai*) who owed their masters yearly service. The masters occupied themselves with horse-breeding, racing, and hunting. The free peasants and craftsmen were rarely prosperous in Thessaly. The middle class had no place. Even in such towns as appeared in Thessaly the family lists consisted primarily of horse-breeding nobles. The economic revolution of the seventh century B.C. shook the Greek world, but left much of the

[57] *Ibid.*, pp. 335 ff.
[58] *Ibid.*, pp. 200 ff.

Peloponnese, Boeotia and Phocis, Thessaly, Acarnania, Aetolia, and Epirus untouched.[59]

During this period colonization was in full tide, trade was developing, workshops multiplied in the ports, and markets were organized.[60] Ports by the dozen developed in Asia Minor, headed by Miletus. Euboea, Eretria, and Chalcis were engaged in colonization and commercial richness with the exchange of the products of the Lelantine plain and the neighboring mines. Mines and quarries were exploited by nobles. The *thetes* and slaves were gathered in workshops. A new, wealthy middle class was rising, recruited in part from the less-privileged members of the noble families, but also from persons of plebeian origin. The *nouveau riche* could not be ignored by the older aristocracy. In fact they frequently replaced it, and plutocratic political structures appeared. This commercial revolution, accelerated by the reception of electrum coinage from Lydia,[61] had also made possible the extensive oppression and increasing debt slavery of rural free peasants by urban creditors.

While the operation of feudal structures of Thessaly resulted in serfdom, the form of commercialization under way in urban centers made slavery more important. The ancient manufacturing establishments (*ergastria*)[62] were operated by slaves. Warfare was a profitable business, because it implemented the slave market. The primary method (other than war) of accumulating slaves was through debt oppression.[63]

The cities played a variable role in all this. Under aristocracies the cities pursued a policy of colonization, implementing the demands for new land on which the nobles could settle their offspring. Under plutocracies political structures were utilized to enforce commercial monopolies. For example, in Corinth traders and shipowners utilized the political forces at their disposal to seize first place in Mediterranean commerce. The Bacchiadae[64] maintained its commercial dynasty by permitting no alliance with other families. They kept the royal title and the chief offices in the family. A harbor was established on the Saronic Gulf, another on the Gulf of Corinth. A wooden road was laid between the two for portage of vessels. They established trade centers along the northwest coast of Greece, and founded the colonies of Corcyra and Syracuse.

The city increasingly emerged as the primary economic power. For one thing, the monopoly of coinage was usually reserved to the city. The wealth of Athens was in part due to her control over sources of silver. For another, the cities hired innumerable *thetes* as sailors. Moreover, under the

59 Zimmern, *op. cit.*, pp. 228 ff.
60 *Ibid.*, pp. 252 ff.
61 *Ibid.*, pp. 192–193.
62 Johannes Hasebroek, *Trade and Politics in Ancient Greece* (Chicago: University of Chicago Press, 1933), pp. 38 ff., 72 ff.
63 Zimmern, *op. cit.*, pp. 117–118.
64 Hasebroek, *op. cit.*, p. 20.

tyrants (for example, Pisistratus),[65] city construction projects were undertaken to give work to the otherwise increasingly helpless *demiourgoi.*

Outside the sphere immediately involved in this civic commercialization the trend was not always toward feudalization in the manner of Thessaly. Sparta showed the development of a militaristic form of state socialism. In Sparta the conquered populations were not serfs of individual estates but communal slaves—helots.[66] In the end, the agricultural labor of the helots supplied the community messes of the Dorian military camp. The individual estates of nobles were under the management of Spartan women (who achieved in this a unique freedom), and were worked by helots.

Religion

The earliest religion in ancestral Greece was dominated by functional deities.[67] In later times Zeus, Athena, and Apollo were personal deities, but in backward communities the worship of functional deities persisted: thunder and wind, the cult of Zeus Keraunos (thunder), at Mantineia and Zeus Kappotas (a meteoric stone) in Laconia. At this early stage, worship and festivals were agricultural. There were cults on mountaintops. A heaven god and earth goddess were recognized. There was both worship and appeasement of spirits of nature. That human sacrifice was practiced at one time was still known through the Delphic oracle. The Athenians later edited out of the Homeric poems references to human sacrifice.

The clan originally possessed its own religion. The phratries and tribes also worshiped common religious figures, probably normally the deity of the most powerful clan of the association. Through their conquests and migrations various Dorian deities once confined to special tribes or areas were diffused over Greek territories. As god of the sea Poseidon gained importance in the development of trade and commerce. In central Greece, Apollo, the god of flocks, was adopted by many Dorian communities. The various *amphictyones* which formed were characterized by worship at a common center. Such was the Tetrapolis of Marathon, the worship of Poseidon at Galuria. Delos was the center of Apollo worship.[68] Zeus was worshiped at Olympia. Zeus, Poseidon, Apollo, and Athena were gods of Thessaly.

The Homeric gods were like supermen, and were organized like a feudal family.[69] Their bickerings and intrigues paralleled the social phenomena of the day. Though Olympic religion remained a component in popular religion, in the city-states religion underwent extensive sublimation. The two

[65] Zimmern, *op. cit.*, pp. 141 ff.

[66] Chrimes, *op. cit.*, pp. 272 ff.

[67] Gilbert Murray, *Four Stages of Greek Religion* (New York: Columbia University Press, 1912).

[68] H. W. Parke and D. W. Wormell, *The Delphic Oracle* (Oxford: Basil Blackwell, 1956).

[69] Seymour, *op. cit.*, pp. 392 ff.

most significant religious developments in the sixth and seventh centuries B.C. were the elevation of Homeric religion as a state religion and the appearance of religious revivalism, Dionysus worship and Orphism being the two most famous examples.[70] The city-states brought the popular cults under civic supervision. Temples were erected to their deities. Processions and sacrifices were undertaken at state expense.

However, certain contrasts appear between the state religion and the religiosity centered in the figures of Demeter and Dionysus. Dionysus was a Thracian deity whose worship was orgiastic, characterized by torchlight processions on mountain tops, and dance ecstasy. Orphism developed early in the sixth century, and consisted in the establishment of communities practicing secret rites. The orphic sects were separatist. Orphism was diffused by mendicant priests reputed to be miracle workers who elaborated a salvation doctrine. One of the claims to importance of the tyrants was their advocacy of such popular religious movements. Typical was the reception under Pisistratus of Dionysus worship into the official state religion.[71]

THE COMMUNITY IN THE HELLENISTIC AGE

The death of Alexander the Great is conventionally regarded as the end of an era.[72] After this period the primary political powers in the Greek world, the Hellenistic monarchies, were formed. They were ruled primarily by kings of Macedonian birth and Greek culture, relying upon Greek and Macedonian mercenaries.[73] The Asian and Egyptian kingdoms were reinforced by numbers of Greek settlers who formed the highest class of well-to-do citizens and officials.[74] To be sure, the cities of the Hellenic world, remained in existence, but with a difference.

> The cities themselves remained, many of them, with a complete or almost complete self-government. But their pride was gone, and such independence as they retained was held on sufferance. They stood at the mercy first of Alexander, then of the military chief who happened to sway their region. To defy their Macedonian overlord was to court destruction. Their political ambitions, their party conflicts, their spasmodic efforts to assert themselves were mere eddies and splashes in a great stream whose new and mighty floods were wiping out and reshaping all the marks of the old bed.[75]

70 Botsford and Robinson, *op. cit.*, pp. 96 ff.

71 *Ibid.*, pp. 95 ff.; G. Lowes Dickinson, *The Greek View of Life* (New York: Doubleday, Doran, 1928), pp. 28 ff.

72 Cecil Fairfield Lavell, *A Biography of the Greek People* (Boston: Houghton Mifflin, 1934), p. 272.

73 G. T. Griffith, *The Mercenaries of the Hellenistic World* (Cambridge: Cambridge University Press, 1935).

74 Rostovtzeff, *op. cit.*, Vol. I, p. 364.

75 Lavell, *op. cit.*, pp. 272–273.

The new cities and capitals of the Hellenistic period (Alexandria, Antioch, Seleuceia, Pergamum, and Rhodes) were centers of industry and trade. An active cosmopolitan population intent on making money and enjoying itself held sway. At the pinnacle of the system was the king, officially deified and ruling over many different races. He was surrounded by a bureaucracy of considerable complexity.[76] The average citizens including wealthy persons found themselves increasingly depoliticized.

In the Hellenistic period the barriers between the cities broke down.[77] The Macedonians did not permit the cities of central Greece to develop an autonomous foreign policy, though they were allowed to administer their private affairs. The Macedonian kings, in fact, ruled only in the cities, where they maintained their own garrisons.[78] However, the city was ceasing to be a significant or even a distinct unit in the thinking of men. Athens largely lost her position as the primary market of the civilized world.[79] The place of Athens was largely taken over by Alexandria as the major port for grain, flax, glass, papyrus, and the produce from central Africa and the Red Sea. Alexandria also became a great manufacturing center for paper, glass, flax, jewelry, and cosmetics. In Asia Minor, Miletus, Ephesus, and Pergamum became important with secondary significance attaching to Cyzicus, Byzantium, Sinope, and Rhodes.[80]

The Hellenistic world became a great market controlled by Greek and Hellenized merchants and manufacturers. Industry and commerce were founded primarily by slave labor. As the slave establishments grew larger, an increasing number of persons were merely consumers. To their number as nonproductive consumers were added mercenary troops, sailors, and a growing body of government officials. Many of the cities were in a continual state of crisis because of inability to feed their urban populations. The factories operated by slave labor tended to squeeze out the independent artisans and domestic manufacturers, further aggravating the situation. While a small class grew rich in this process, the vast majority of the native population was impoverished.

By the end of the third century B.C. population and wealth had begun to leave Greece at an accelerating pace, and local institutions began to break down. The destruction was eventually completed by Rome. There was, meanwhile, a growing interest in the problems of a future life and the introduction of Eastern forms of worship in the Greek world. "Greek religion . . . becomes more and more spiritual and abstract, and at the same time loses its connection with special city-states."[81] As the classical sense of balance was lost, the extremes of spiritual experience were explored.

[76] Botsford and Robinson, *op. cit.*, p. 369.
[77] *Ibid.*, p. 379.
[78] Rostovtzeff, *op. cit.*, p. 368.
[79] For a detailed account of Athens in this period, see Ferguson, *op. cit.*
[80] Rostovtzeff, *op. cit.*, p. 368.
[81] *Ibid.*, p. 383.

> Side by side with religious mysticism, we find rationalism and materialism widely diffused in the society of the age. Agnosticism, which denies that man can know anything about God; atheism, which disbelieves in God; skepticism, and euhemerism, which explains away the supernatural part of religion—all these had plenty of partisans and followers, for whom religion was merely an artificial invention of the human mind. An instance of this tendency is the deification of Luck and Fortune—Tyché, *Fortuna*—powers whose worship was widely diffused throughout the whole Hellenistic world.[82]

The Hellenistic period in Greece has often invited moralizing. It has been viewed as a time of a general crisis of morality, of individualism, of the substitution of monetary for moral standards, of a corruption of the people by luxury and extravagance. The decline of Greece has been attributed to all these things: to the development of eroticism, the elevation of the courtesan, to the shunting of the responsibilities of fatherhood, to the extensive practice of abortion and exposure, leading to a declining birth rate. In antiquity Polybius phrased this:

> We see in our time throughout the whole world of Greece such a shrinking of the birth-rate and, in a word, such depopulation, that the towns are deserted and the fields lie waste, although there are neither continual wars nor epidemics. . . . The cause of the evil is manifest. . . . From vanity, from avarice, or from cowardice men are unwilling either to marry or to bring up children without marrying; at the most they will have only one or two in order that they may leave them a fortune and ensure for them a luxurious existence: thus the plague has rapidly assumed dangerous proportions. If once war or sickness comes to claim its tribute in these families of one or two children the line inevitably dies out and, just as with swarms of bees, the cities, becoming depopulated, quickly lose their power.[83]

Though figures from the period cannot be trusted, the birth rate does seem to have been declining. Athens averaging 30,000 population with 40,000 at its height was estimated at 21,000 a century later. In 480 B.C. the Spartans numbered more than 8,000; in 370 B.C. they numbered 2,000. Forty years later Aristotle computed their number at 700.

That there were changes in domestic manners and morals is clear. While the public treasuries were being depleted, there were increasing expenditures on private luxuries. Demosthenes observed that the splendor of private houses often rivaled or exceeded that of the temples. During this period monumental styles of sculpture were replaced by more individualized and realistic styles. In the drama the tragedy receded into the background, and comedy took its place in popular interest. Dramatic themes were increasingly taken from everyday life. In education the schools of the Sophists grew increasingly important. The theory of the relativity of custom, the concept of the law of the stronger, the notions of the subjectivity of judg-

82 *Ibid.*, p. 385.
83 *Pol.* XX, 6, 5–6.

ment were all popular. Sometimes all of these things have been summed up under the term "individualism" to which the decline of Greece is attributed. This, of course, is merely a euphemism for "decay."

During this period class tensions became tense. Free labor was in retreat before the competition of slavery. While there was a vulgar display of wealth at one end of the economic scale, there was intense poverty at the other. It has been estimated that in Athens in 431 B.C. the proletariat numbered approximately 19,000 out of 40,000 citizens. In 355 B.C. they were a majority, and four years later they numbered 12,000 out of 21,000 (57 per cent). Aristotle was so impressed by the problem that he made a special study of revolution. At Mitylene, debtors massacred their creditors. At Argos (370 B.C.), 12,000 of the rich were murdered and their property appropriated. Counterrevolution was also known. In Syracuse, there was intense clamor for the redistribution of land. In 371 B.C. Agathocles set his soldiers on the mass of the people. Within two days 4,000 citizens had died, and 6,000 had fled into exile.

A major explanation for the decline of Greece is found in the growth of slavery and the development of ruinous class struggles. The decline has also been attributed to the corruption of the political institutions. That political institutions of the city ceased to be progressive (and able to meet the problems facing them) is beyond doubt. Among the usual explanations in antiquity for political decline is the payment for office. To this was added the decline in standards of civic responsibility and the increased corruption of political leaders.

By conquest and voluntary clientage of the native kings, the Romans acquired Asia Minor. Ruined by the Roman civil wars, Greece found much of her wealth stripped by Roman generals. Large areas were depopulated. Though Athens remained a university town under the Romans, it was, like Greece as a whole, quite stagnant.[84]

SUMMARY

With its mountains, swift rivers, and steep valleys, despite the fertility of the plains of Aetolia, Boeotia, and Attica, Greece did not present an area permitting uniform agricultural exploitation. Nor could its rushing mountain streams sustain systematic internal transportation. From antiquity, the people of Greece were oriented outward toward the much divided coast and ocean islands, rather than inward toward the land.

Though a paleolithic culture has not been established in Greece, a thriving neolithic culture flourished at least by 4000 B.C. A Bronze Age civilization arose on this neolithic base with its primary center in the islands, particularly in Crete. The Cretan civilization developed a monarchical form of political structure with palaces, a developed religion, writing, administration by scribes, and a developed commerce. During the second mil-

[84] Botsford and Robinson, *op. cit.*, p. 455.

lennium peoples' movements from the north began to break against this civilization. They came in at least three major waves against the Mycenaeans on the Greek mainland, penetrating to the island cities.

Ancient Greek social history falls into three major periods: the Heroic period, the period of the formation of the city-states, and the Hellenistic period. As revealed in the Homeric epics, toward the close of the second millennium B.C. the Achaeans were in the process of consolidating into an uneasy confederation under Agamemnon. Sea-raiding and wars were frequent. The predominant community at the time was a semifeudal type of manorial structure resting on a base of peasant villages.

By the eighth century B.C. a formation of city-states was under way. In the time of Aristotle, when the school undertook the study of the constitutions of the Greek states, no less than 158 were surveyed. Two great epochs mark the period of the city-states which bear comparison with the problems of Palestine during its royal period. Greece, too, had problems arising from its foreign relations. In this case, however, the Persian power which dominated Palestine was turned back from Greece, giving the Greeks a space for free growth at a time when Palestine was being transformed into an ethnic community. Greece, too, had its internal problems. However, these took the form, not so much as a contest of rural towns and intercivic settled families against royal power, as a contest between one city and another. Throughout this period the city-state was the distinctive community of Greece.

In the end, the city-states proved unable to solve their problems, and first under the Macedonian empires of Philip and Alexander the Great, and later under the Roman Empire, an imperial system was clamped down on the world of Greek city-states. Though cities remained the primary communities of the Hellenistic period, they were converted into administrative units of the empire. Once their autonomy had been impaired, they went into a spiral of decay.

SELECTED BIBLIOGRAPHY

Botsford, George Willis, and Charles Alexander Robinson, *Hellenic History* (New York: The Macmillan Co., 1956).

Burn, Andrew Robert, *The World of Hesiod* (London: Kegan Paul, Trench, Trubner, 1936).

Evans, Sir Arthur, *The Palace of Minos at Knossos* (London: 1921–1935).

Glotz, G., *The Greek City*, trans. by N. Mallinson (New York: Alfred A. Knopf, 1930).

Jarde, A., *The Formation of the Greek People* (New York: Alfred A. Knopf, 1926).

Mylonas, George E., *Ancient Mycenae* (Princeton: Princeton University Press, 1957).

Rostovtzeff, M., *A History of the Ancient World* (Oxford: The Clarendon Press, 1925).
Schliemann, H., *Mycenae* (New York: 1880).
Weber, Max, *The City*, trans. by Don Martindale and Gertrud Neuwirth (Glencoe, Illinois: The Free Press, 1958).

14

THE CHANGING ROLES OF THE ANCIENT GREEK INTELLECTUAL

THE CIVILIZATION that preceded that of ancient Greece rested on variation of the city imperialisms such as were central to the Shang of China, the Indus Valley civilization, or the civilizations of Mesopotamia and Egypt. The only major difference was that Minoan civic imperialism dominated the eastern Mediterranean rather than a land area.

The Minoans possessed all the distinctive features of the early city imperialism: an indigenous system of writing, an organized religion (which presupposed religious schools and other related structures), an administration by learned administrators (either priests or persons who were priest-trained). If parallels with similar strata in other areas can be sustained, such priestly intellectuals were controlled by the hierocratic institutions to which they belonged. However, they must also have enjoyed a close identification with the political structure because of their virtual monopoly of writing skills and their ideological importance as bearers of the unifying religion.

Such Minoan priest intellectuals undoubtedly helped bring about the pacification of formerly independent groups in the areas of Minoan domination. Over and again this has been a primary function of the early civic religion—to create a new system of loyalties which makes the complex civic community possible. This function always has the incidental effect of exposing the subject population to conquest by barbarians from the outside, not because civilization makes men soft, but because the former institutions of self-help, particularly forms of tribal militarism, have been destroyed to make the city possible. If the city does not do this, it will be constantly torn by the conflicts of armed factions. However, when such a disarming of subgroups is carried through and war-making is reconsolidated in new specialized institutions, it is doubly important that they do their job. When one thus strikes down the control institutions of the city, it often appears as if the nerve center of the whole has been damaged. When the ancestral Greeks succeeded in this, the rest of the Minoan civilization easily collapsed before them.

Although the ancestral Greeks took over from the previous civilization in their own cultural synthesis far more than the Indo-Europeans did from the Indus Valley civilization, like them they did not directly take over its intellectual culture or receive former Minoan priest-intellectuals, even in changed status, into their own society (as seems to have been, in part, the case with the Chou in ancient China).

Thus, the distinctive forms of the ancient Greek society (and *milieux* for the intellectuals) begin with the semifeudal manorial communities of the Heroic period. The communities rested on a foundation of neolithic peasant villages and the fragments of destroyed Minoan-Mycenaean society. This was followed by a period of autonomous city-states which in Greece reached a scope and intensity without parallel in the other world areas. Finally, the Hellenistic period was characterized by the impairment of the cities as autonomous communities and the partial transformation of them into administrative divisions of the empires. The cities thereupon went into a slow social and spiritual decline which was only gradually terminated after some centuries by the emergence of religious communities and various forms of rural communities out of their ruins.

THE INTELLECTUAL IN THE HEROIC AGE

There were some differences between the semifeudal structures of Greece and their parallels in China and India. China's feudalism was preceded by the partial amalgamation of the Chou rulers with those of the Shang dynasty it displaced. In the course of this the Chou conquerors acquired literate and cultural traditions which established continuities with prior culture. In contrast to this, the waves of Indo-European migrants into Greece did not acquire the literate traditions of the Minoans. They were more like the Aryans of India, who failed to acquire the literate traditions of the Mohenjo-daro and Harappa civilizations. On the other hand, in contrast to the Aryans of India, the relations between the Indo-European invaders of Greece and the settled population were close and not, as seems to have been the case for the Aryans, sharpened by great racial and cultural differences. The one place in Greece where a near parallel to the Indian experience occurred was in the relation of the Spartans to the helots (which were very like the relation between the Aryans and Dasyus); however, the Spartans solved their relation to the helots in a manner quite different from the Indians—by a form of military socialism. Despite their differences, Homeric Greece and Vedic India were in many respects similar.

The Greeks were, of course, formed out of a branch of the same peoples' movement as the Aryans of India. The oldest form of religion of both shares many of the same deities. Indo-European religiosity was a form of nature worship; the Greek Zeus was the same deity as the Sanskrit Dasyus. Like the Vedic religion, religion of Greece was a sky cult. Zeus was the sky; his son Apollo was a ray of light. The storm wind, Hermes, was the messenger of the gods. The moon was Apollo's twin sister, Artemis. Castor and Pollux, the morning and evening stars, were the children of Zeus. The starry sky was the consort of the king of the gods enthroned on Mount Olympus.[1] Greek religion in the Homeric period offered a social situation for the emergence of the intellectual quite similar to that which in India led to the emergence of the Vedic priest.

The priest-intellectual, however, did not emerge in full relief in Heroic Greece as in Vedic India. While temples of the gods (consisting often of groves set apart for worship) were not numerous in the Homeric Age, they did exist. Vedic religion, by contrast, was bound more tightly to the house cult. Apollo's priest, Chryses, had a roofed temple at which fat thigh pieces of bulls and goats were burned. Athena had a temple in Troy. In addition to the Temple of Apollo at Chrysa, there were others at Pytho, Delphi, and Troy. The comrades of Odysseus proposed to erect a temple at Ithaca to Helios the sun god.[2] However, the temple did not undergo very extensive development. In the Homeric poems there is rarely any mention of statues to divinities and, in fact, altars are mentioned more frequently than temples.

The priests of the Homeric period formed neither a caste nor a hierarchy. Those of one temple had no relation to those of another. The only special item of clothing worn by priests when engaged in official duties was a fillet for the head. The only priestess mentioned is Theano who was the Trojan priestess of Athena. The priests were seers thought to have the power of foresight. However, priests were not necessary for proper performance of a sacrifice, as was the case among the Jews and Vedic Indians, nor was a complicated system of ritual observed.

The oracles at Dodona and at Delphi were mentioned once in the Odyssey. The prophet at Dodona interpreted the rustling of the leaves of the oak tree. Local oracles were consulted less frequently than seers or priests inspired by the gods, especially by Apollo. At Olympia Issus was thought to be able to hear the voice of Apollo. The blind seer of Thebes, Teiresias, had been granted knowledge of Hades by Persephone. Halitherses of Ithaca predicted Odysseus' departure from Troy and his return in the twentieth year. The Cyclops had a seer who foretold the blinding of Polyphemus by Odysseus. Achilles' horse, like Balaam's ass, was granted the power of speech just long enough to predict his master's death.

While the Homeric Greeks had no astrology or systematic auguries, a variety of omens from natural phenomena, especially thunder and lightning, were taken to be significant. Omens from the flight of birds were especially significant. Dreams were conceived to be familiar means by which the gods

[1] Weisenborn, *Homeric Life* (New York: American Book Co., 1903), pp. 43 ff.

[2] Thomas Day Seymour, *Life in the Homeric Age* (New York: The Macmillan Co., 1908), pp. 490 ff., contains an excellent summary of the religion of the Homeric era, which is followed here.

made their intentions known to men. At times the gods themselves appeared in dreams. The casting of lots was frequently employed to determine the will of the gods.

Thus, in contrast to India, the priesthood of Homeric Greece was not bound up intimately with the cult of the patriarchal household. Greek tradition has it that in primitive times there were a number of sacred bards, sons of gods and favorites of such muses as Orpheus, Linus, Musaeus, Pamphus, Eumolpus, and Thamyris.[3] These were the Greek counterparts of the Vedic priests. In historical times there remained cults requiring religious songs. In the time of Herodotus, for example, the Delian women sang songs attributed to the poet Olen.

From conditions similar to those of Vedic India a complex array of myths and heroic tales was developed. The Homeric poems wove these into unified epic form. Even in its earliest period Greece was moving away from the Indian pattern. Hence, while the oldest literature from India was represented by the Vedas, the oldest from Greece was the Homeric epics, transforming many similar types of materials to those of the Vedas into a much more secular form. The bard of Homeric times was a more free interpreter of his time than was the *purohita* of Vedic India.

The comparisons, of course, should not be drawn between the Homeric epics and the Vedas, but between them and the *Mahabharata* and *Ramayana*. The basic materials for the *Iliad* and *Odyssey*, like the basic materials for the Indian epics, came out of the Heroic period. Moreover, both were brought forth by later editors for semipropagandistic purposes: the Homeric epics, possibly by Pisistratus as a part of his demagogic self-representation as a public benefactor to counteract the illegal aspects of his tyranny; the Indian epics were brought into shape after the sixth century B.C. as part of the resistance of an embattled Hindu orthodoxy to the growing threat of heterodox religions.

The content of the two epics could be expected to differ somewhat, for the *Iliad* and *Odyssey* celebrate great military adventures of people without a major sense of ethnic difference, and also the various hazards of the sea trader and pirate of the Heroic Age, while the Indian epics relate somewhat more grim conflicts between a thin stratum of Aryan conquerors and the far more numerous native Dravidian tribes. It has been suggested that the account of the monkeys and their leader Hanuman, whose exploits alongside Rama are related in *Ramayana*, actually represent the Dravidian tribes brought into the fold of Aryan society by Rama and his holy men.[4] The undying hatred involved in the conflict between the Pandavas tribe and the Kurus in the *Mahabharata* seems inexplicable, unless the Pandavas were actually Dravidian founders of the Pandya kingdom forced by Aryan

[3] Alfred Croiset and Maurice Croiset, *An Abridged History of Greek Literature* (New York: The Macmillan Co., 1904), pp. 11 ff.

[4] Mariades Ruthnaswamy, *India from the Dawn* (Milwaukee: The Bruce Publishing Co., 1949), p. 16.

penetration to the south through the forest of Dekham. "The Mahabharata, it will be remembered, gives them a spell of exile in Kakshinaprastha."[5]

Because of their ethnic and racial aspects, the materials for the Indian epics may well have had dimensions of religious intensity from the beginning without equivalence in the materials of the Homeric Greeks. Moreover, the conditions of the editing of the respective epic literatures would have tended to emphasize somewhat different things. In any case, religion dominates the Hindu epic in a manner which has no parallel in the Greek epics. As Ruthnaswamy summarized it:

> The *Mahabharata* and the *Ramayana* are full of the doings of rishis and gurus. Although professedly recounting the wars and conquests and settlements of kings and peoples, they are replete with discussions on matters of religion, philosophy, and morality. Compared to Homer's *Iliad* or *Odyssey*, or any other national or popular epics of Europe, which speak of the loves and hates of women, the warlike and civic activities of kings, soldiers, judges, the *Ramayana* and the *Mahabharata* treat of these human affairs only incidentally. And even when they are treated *in extenso*, the religious motif creeps in every now and then. Debates and discussions on religion and philosophical subjects occur at frequent intervals. A whole section of the *Mahabharata* is occupied by the *Bhagavad Gita*, a compendium of Hindu moral philosophy.[6]

The same system of racial and ethnic tensions which seems to account for the quite different accent on religious materials in the Indian epics may have played an important part in the contrast between the quite secular Homeric bard and the sacred Vedic priest. Homeric religious practice, as might well be expected in tribes without major ethnic and racial tensions, tended to shift from the household cult to a community cult. However, the thin stratum of conquerors stretched over Indian society reinforced the cults of the household, particularly the noble household, against the cults of the tribes. The patriarchal conquest-families tended toward hereditary closure. The priests who served as house chaplains and as tutors within the household were pressed on a course toward hereditary closure as well. Indian conditions thus sharpened the roles of tribal and community priest and house priest and *guru* against one another, and sent them along different courses of evolution.

THE INTELLECTUAL IN THE PERIOD OF THE AUTONOMOUS CITY STATE

For its bearing on the intellectuals and their products, the period of the autonomous city in ancient Greece was comparable to the time of contending states in China, the civic patrimonial-state period in India, and the royal period in Israel. The Greek city of the classical period presented a distinct set of properties of importance for intellectual roles. What the intellectual did was always shaped by his service to his times. To some

[5] *Ibid.*, p. 19.
[6] *Ibid.*, pp. 60–61.

extent the Greek intellectual in the classical period was like the Chinese mandarin in that he played a direct political role in the affairs of his time. While the mandarin aspired to positions in the administration of feudal towns and later imperial bureaucracy, he was never a citizen in a self-governing community. Hence, while the thinking of both the Greek philosopher and the Chinese mandarin was politically relevant, their thoughts rested on different premises.

On the other hand, the Greek philosopher had some other points in common with the mandarin in contrast to the Indian *guru* and the Israelite priest and prophet. While the intellectuals of India and China (with certain notable exceptions) were primarily anchored in religious contexts, the Greek philosopher, like the mandarin, was a far more secular individual. The Greek city-state was, indeed, a religious community. However, in the very process of transforming the religion into an official civic cult, the philosopher was partly freed from religious concerns.

Since persons with roles equivalent to the Vedic priests in India and the Yahweh prophets in Palestine were present at the beginning of Greek development, it is of some value to trace the fate of persons occupying such priestly and prophetic roles through the classical period of Greek culture. To Murray, Greek religion developed through three stages:

> First, there is the primitive *Euetheia* or Age of Ignorance, before Zeus came to trouble men's minds, a stage to which our anthropologists and explorers have found parallels in every part of the world.
>
> Secondly, there is the Olympian or classical stage, a stage in which, for good or ill, blunderingly or successfully, this primitive vagueness was reduced to a kind of order. This is the stage of the great Olympian gods, who dominated art and poetry, ruled the imagination of Rome, and extended a kind of romantic dominion even over the Middle Ages. It is the stage that we know from the statues and the handbooks of mythology.
>
> Thirdly, there is the Hellenistic period, reaching roughly from Plato to St. Paul or the earlier Gnostics, a period based on the consciousness of manifold failure, and consequently touched both with morbidness and with that spiritual exaltation which is so often the companion of morbidness. It had behind it the failure of the Olympian theology, the failure of the free city-state, now crushed by semi-barbarous military monarchies; it lived through the gradual realization of two other failures—the failure of human government, even when backed by the power of Rome or the wealth of Egypt, to achieve a good life for man; and lastly the failure of the great propaganda of Hellenism, in which the long-drawn effort of Greece to educate a corrupt and barbaric world seemed only to lead to the corruption or barbarization of the very ideals which it sought to spread.[7]

The ancestral Greeks, like the Vedic Indo-Europeans, came as conquerors. The Homeric epics celebrate the kinds of military incidents which ac-

[7] Gilbert Murray, *Four States of Greek Religion* (New York: Columbia University Press, 1912), pp. 16–17.

companied this conquest and reflect the ideological reconstruction which accompanied the interadjustment of conqueror to conquered. According to Murray, the Olympian religion which developed from Homer at the Panathenaea produced a religious reformation. The religion of a northern conquering group organized on a patriarchal monogamous system displaced the religions of Aegean (Hittite) groups characterized by polygamy, polyandry, agricultural rites, sex emblems, and fertility goddesses.

> Contrast for a moment the sort of sexless Valkyrie who appears in the *Iliad* under the name of Athena with the Korê of Ephesus, strangely called Artemis, a shapeless fertility figure, covered with innumerable breasts.[8]

The Homeric tradition was borne by an aristocratic stratum scornful of popular superstition. The Homeric epics were based on poems recited at a *panegyris,* or official public occasion. Moreover, the poems were Ionian.

> We must remember that Ionia was, before the rise of Athens, not only the most imaginative and intellectual part of Greece, but by far the most advanced in knowledge and culture. The Homeric religion is a step in the self-realization of Greece, and such self-realization naturally took its rise in Ionia.[9]

The Olympian religion of the classical Greeks was characterized by three major elements: moral expurgation of previous moral and ethical practices, the development of a kind of rational order out of miscellaneous religious elements, and adaptation to new social requirements.[10] A great mass of preexisting mystical, superstitious, and orgiastic elements was rationalized, sublimated, and provided with mythical and symbolic interpretations by the classical Greeks. The high point in the attempt to rationalize the whole of this mass of material within the compass of Olympian religion was the poetry of Hesiod. All three of his poems were compiled under the influence of Homer and of Delphi. They attempted to integrate the elements of Homeric and folk religion into a single system.

> The *Theogony* attempts to make a pedigree and hierarchy of the gods; the *Catalogue of Women* and the *Eoiai* . . . attempt to fix in canonical form the cloudy mixture of dreams and boasts and legends and hypotheses by which most royal families in central Greece recorded their descent from a traditional ancestress and a conjectural god. *The Works and Days* forms an attempt to collect and arrange the rules and tabus relating to agriculture. . . . The Hesiodic system when compared to Homer is much more explicit, much less expurgated, infinitely less accomplished and tactful. At the back of Homer lay the lordly warrior-gods of the Heroic Age, at the back of Hesiod the crude and tangled superstitions of the peasantry of the mainland.[11]

[8] *Ibid.*, p. 78.
[9] *Ibid.*, pp. 79–80.
[10] *Ibid.*, p. 81.
[11] *Ibid.*, pp. 84–85.

The Olympian religion of the classical period was adapted to a different social situation from that of the Heroic period. The original religion of the ancestral Greeks had been one of tribes.

> In the age of the migration the tribes had been broken, scattered, remixed. They had almost ceased to exist as important social entities. The social unit which had taken their place was the political community of men of whatever tribe or tribes, who were held together in times of danger and constant war by means of a common circuit-wall, a polis.[12]

In the contest between city and tribe, the one great "negative" advantage of the Olympian gods was that they were neither tribal nor local.

> They were by this time international, with no strong roots anywhere except where one of them could be identified with some native god. . . . They were ready to be made "*Polioucboi*," "City-holders" of any particular city, still more ready to be "*Hellanioi*," patrons of all Hellas.[13]

The one-time tribal gods of the ancestral Greeks ceased to be tribal deities when the tribes were destroyed. The fact that the cities rose out of the fragments of tribes prevented the transformation of the former tribal deities into exclusive possessions of individual cities.

There was much in the early relation between the religion of the ancestral Greeks and that of the people they conquered to compare with the relation between the religion of the vedic Indians and the Dravidians. Many of the same contrasts between the religion of genteel conquerors and the orgiastic-ecstatic religions of the conquered appear. The Homeric bards and Vedic priests had many similar functions, in that both had to work out some relation between the religion of their hosts and that of native groups.

However, there were also many things in the socio-religious experiences of the Greeks in the Heroic Age similar to those of the Jews in the time of the confederacy. Like the ancient Jews, the Greeks in the Heroic period often consulted oracles, particularly during hazardous enterprises, such as military adventures. Moreover, like the ancient Jews, they frequently formed religious federations (*amphictyonies*) for purposes of conquest and defense. The linkage of the oracular center at Delphi with the fortunes of the northern *amphictyony* of Anthela and Pylae[14] raised the Delphic oracle into the nearest thing to a single religious center that the Greek world possessed. Delphi assumed a place in the religious life of Greece similar to that of Jerusalem to Israel. If the prophets and priests associated

[12] *Ibid.*, p. 86.

[13] *Ibid.*, p. 87.

[14] The members of this religious association were "dwellers around" the shrine of Demeter at Anthela, hence the name Amphictyones of Anthela. The league included the Locrians, Phocians, Boeotians, Athenians, Dorians, Malians, Dolophians, Enianes, Thessalians, Perrhaebias, and Magentes. Members of the league were sworn not to destroy any member city or cut off its water supply.

with Delphi had occupied a similar position to the prophets and priests of Palestine primarily as bearers of the socio-political thought of the time, one would have had a fairly exact replica of the situation in Palestine. However, it was fateful for Greek development that many of the primary currents of thought flowed outside it and without exclusive reference to Delphi and its priesthood.

According to a Homeric hymn, Apollo came to Delphi as a northern invader who slew a local she-serpent at the site. The place was named *Pytho* after the rotting corpse of the monster. The story has a ring of authenticity despite its legendary status, since it contains topographical matter and local traditions of northern Greece.[15] That the story is substantially correct seems confirmed by excavations at Delphi which show that the place had been occupied since late Minoan times as an ancient pre-Greek religious sanctuary.[16] The Greeks apparently overthrew the native fertility goddess as the legend suggests, installing in her place a prophet of their own. The original worship of an earth goddess[17] was replaced by that of Apollo. The tradition of Delphi itself was that, for the death of the serpent, Apollo had suffered nine years' exile in Thessaly.[18]

The methods of prophecy practiced at Delphi were quite similar to those found elsewhere in the ancient world from India to China.

> Legends associate many different methods of prophecy with Delphi. For instance, Parnassus, the eponymous hero of the mountain, was said to have discovered augury by means of birds, and Delphus and Amphictyon, the eponyms of the town and the Amphictyony, invented respectively the examining of entrails, and the interpretation of omens and dreams. One body of local priests were probably connected with divination by fire. The foretelling of the future by drawing lots is even more certainly evidenced in connection with Delphi. . . . In historic times all these methods had been displaced by the direct utterances of the Pythia.[19]

Moreover, prophetic and oracular guidance was sought in similar circumstances: military adventures, political reorganization, and personal accidents and misfortunes of all sorts.

As it emerged as a cult center for the Greek world, Delphi tended to absorb all major religious developments into its orbit. Dionysius was accepted into the circle of Delphi religions early in the sixth century. Another religious tradition located a woman prophetess other than the Pythia. At Delphi the sibyl was said to have prophesied from a rock which towered over the sacred route to the temple. Tradition represented the

15 H. W. Parke, *A History of the Delphic Oracle* (Oxford: Basil Blackwell, 1939), p. 6.

16 *Ibid.*, p. 8.

17 She was called Gé. Themis was associated with her as her daughter.

18 *Ibid.*, p. 11.

19 *Ibid.*, p. 13.

Delphic sibyl as a daughter of Poseidon, thus locating her in the pre-Apolline period.[20]

The Delphic oracle played a role in the shaping of the course of socio-political events. Among the types of public undertakings on which the Delphic oracle was usually consulted in advance by any Greek community was the sending out of a colony.[21] In the course of time the Delphic authorities must have assembled a considerable knowledge about distant lands which was invaluable for the success of colonizing ventures. However, before one assigns anything like exclusive importance to Delphi in the formation of the world of classical Greece, it must be noted that many of the traditions of oracular sanction of colonizing ventures were later inventions–they clearly served as legitimations of unprecedented activities. Though later traditions concerning the Messenian wars than those stemming from the poet Tyrtaeus (a contemporary) assign the Delphic oracles with a role in connection with them, Tyrtaeus himself does not mention Delphi. The oracles seem to have been inventions.[22] On the other hand, relation between Spartan policies and the utterances of the Delphic oracle is probable.

> The special position which that oracle held is shown by the fact that the kings had associated with each of them two Spartans elected as Pythii. These were sacred ambassadors who were appointed to go to Delphi, as required, and when in Sparta, they had their meals with the kings and shared with them the duty of preserving the oracles which had been delivered.[23]

In fact, until the third century B.C., once every nine years the *ephors* chose a clear, moonless night to watch for a shooting star from a certain quarter of the sky. If it came, the kings were put on trial for offending the gods and suspended from office until an oracular answer arrived from Delphi to reprieve or condemn the kings. Even the famous Lycurgan constitution of Sparta was reported to have been dictated by the Pythia.[24]

Though the Oracle at Delphi was consulted by many cities in connection with the founding of colonies and by the authorities of both Sparta and Athens on many issues in connection with the founding and changing of their civic constitutions before that time, the events of the first sacred war launched Delphi on its period of greatest prestige and influence. The sanctuary of Delphi lay near the Phocian town of Crisa, which sought to control the Delphians and levy fees on those who came to consult the oracle. The Delphians appealed to the Amphictyony of Anthela for assistance. Since the members of the Amphictyony espoused the cause of Apollo, they declared holy war (c. 590 B.C.) on the men of Crisa. The Delphic

20 *Ibid.*, p. 17.
21 *Ibid.*, pp. 47 ff.
22 *Ibid.*, p. 88.
23 *Ibid.*, p. 99.
24 *Ibid.*, p. 101.

shrine thereafter became a second meeting place of the league which came to be called the Delphic Amphictyony. The temple was protected by the league, and the property of the god was placed in the hands of the *hieromnemones* (sacred councilors) who met twice a year. The oracle and priestly nobles of Delphi found their prestige greatly enhanced. The Pythian games were organized (582 B.C.) and, like the Olympic games and the Panhellenic festivals which were instituted at Isthmus and Nemes (586 B.C. and 576 B.C.), became symbols of Greek cultural unity.[25]

The role that Delphi was able to play in events inside of the Greek cities is shown not only by the example of Sparta cited earlier but by the recourse Solon had to its authority in establishing his constitutional proposals.

> In view of Solon's particular mention of Delphi in the sanction of his legislation, it is likely that Apollo had given him some express encouragement, and that these lines come from the original oracle which has not been preserved complete. If so, within less than half a century Delphi had been associated with the establishment of the constitutions of both Sparta and Athens.[26]

It is not unfair to assume that the Delphic authorities played similar roles in many other city-states.

Since they were most closely associated with the traditional religious authorities, the Delphic priests were a conservative force. Parke feels that for this reason the Delphic authorities must have largely viewed the tyrants as a disturbing force.[27] However, generally they seem to have taken a caution tack, waiting to see how the whole enterprise came out before taking an explicit public stand on them. Apparently when the tyrants posed questions to the Pythia they received responses like any private petitioner. Moreover, that the same forces were acting on Delphi as on the city-states is shown by the acceptance of Dionysus at Delphi in the same period that Pisistratus was sponsoring his worship.

For a long time the Delphic oracle had an unusually close relation to Lydia. The Lydian kings, in turn, were most bountiful in their generosity to Apollo. This reached a high point in the relations between Delphi and Croesus. Hence with Lydia's destruction by Cyrus, the Delphic oracle suffered a serious blow. This defeat also permanently affected the Delphic judgment of the international situation. Thereafter

> No encouragement came from Apollo to the Greek cities of Asia Minor and no attempt was made to combine them to resist Cyrus.[28]

This policy of advising nonresistance to Persia was even maintained in the face of direct attack, though this would have meant incorporation of Delphi into the Persian empire. For their part, the Persians thoroughly

[25] J. B. Bury, *A History of Greece* (New York: Modern Library), pp. 149 ff.
[26] Parke, *op. cit.*, p. 130.
[27] *Ibid.*, p. 131.
[28] *Ibid.*, p. 159.

appreciated the value of having the religious authorities of a country they intended to take on their side. The Persians wooed the Delphic oracle in much the same manner that the Babylonians had wooed the Jewish scriptural prophets who were preaching nonresistance to the foreign powers. When the invasion of Greece actually began, the Delphic oracle continued to counsel nonresistance, but in the crucial hour of their history the Athenians refused to follow the oracle.

> Clearly on the arrival of the Athenian embassy the Delphians were already so convinced of the impending failure of the Greek cause that they could threaten Athens with destruction, and recommended the Athenians to remove their whole people to some colony. . . . But the Athenian ambassadors were not prepared to bring back this answer to their people, and they remained awaiting a second audience.
>
> Themistocles must have known in advance what opposition his plan would encounter and will have therefore instructed the ambassadors to Delphi to get what support they could from religious sources.[29]

After the Persian wars, though the Delphic oracle continued to be consulted, the decreasing reference to it indicates a general decline of influence on Greek affairs. In the Persian wars it and all cities which had followed its guidance were on the losing side.

Events in the Greek world thus tended to thrust the priesthood of Apollo at Delphi into a very different position from the priesthood of Yahweh at Jerusalem. Apollo worship was in no equivalent position to mount to unparalleled prestige in an hour of national disaster. However, that the Greeks had institutions that partly paralleled those of the Jews in the royal period is quite evident. Apollo was conceived as the national expositor whose work of exegesis was carried out by human instruments. In addition to the oracle at Delphi, he had ministers (*exegetai*) through whom he gave advice to states and private citizens.

> These *exegetai* are a curious institution, and an interesting example of the influence and methods of Delphi. Known to us from Athens, they probably existed in other cities as well, and at Sparta each of the kings chose two "Pythians," described as *Theopropoi* or prophets. They dined with the kings at public expense and interpreted the will of Delphi to the city. Their functions must have been similar to those of the Athenian *exegetai*, who were of two sorts, those named by the oracle . . . and those elected by the Athenian people. . . . The latter appear to have been chosen from one or two noble families who had a hereditary authority in certain matters of religious cult.[30]

The exegetes gave information on temples, cult procedure, sacrifices, and rules of purification to be followed in cases of homicide. At times, because of the close association of legal and religious matters, the exegetes acted as legal advisors to private citizens.

[29] *Ibid.*, p. 185.

[30] W. K. C. Guthrie, *The Greeks and Their Gods* (London: Methuen & Co., 1950), p. 186.

Both classes of religious experts—the exegetes of the Delphic oracle and those from families with hereditary religious monopolies (like the Athenian Eupatrids)—suggest an evolution of religious roles from the Homeric bards like the evolution of temple priests and Brahmans from the Vedic singers. From an early period, however, there were also free-lance religious experts. Some persons had made a practice of collecting oracles and prophecies often attributed by them to famous semimythical seers, for example, Bacis or Sibyl. These collectors were known as *chresmologi*. They intended to have ready at hand a prophecy for every contingency on which they might be consulted.[31] The work of establishing the completed Homeric text in writing was not done by philologists but by religious experts, who were comparable to persons who elsewhere collected the Sacred Books and utterances of ancient prophets.[32] Next in importance to the poetry of Homer and Hesiod among the religious literature gathered by such persons were the *chresmoi* (prescriptions of an oracle or wandering prophet) dealing with everyday problems of ritual propriety and special events. Collections of *chresmoi* in the name of Orpheus and Musaeus were made in the time of Pisistratus. However, Oliver notes that

> There is no evidence that the chresmologi, although they might serve as cooperating consultants, had a constitutional position like that of the four great Roman priestly colleges. They were called upon for advice or for special assignment, but when the assignment was over, their connection with the state was constitutionally no closer than that of other citizens of their class. They doubtless gave advice on sacred law and ritual propriety to private citizens, but there is no evidence that this implied anything more than the advice given by Roman aristocrats of the Hellenistic period on private law and legal procedure.[33]

During the fifth century B.C., from these three classes of chresmologists (the Delphic, traditional, and free-lance), boards of experts on religious problems were often set up and empowered to make recommendations on questions of traditional law. Examples are found in the Athenian decree regulating offerings of first fruits at Eleusis. An oracle from Delphi was also secured, concurring in this decree. During the fifth century B.C. some religious experts were still collecting *chresmoi* from such relatively unfamiliar authorities as Bacis and the wandering Sibyl of Euboea. However, these collections had much less authority than those made in the sixth century B.C. from Homer, Hesiod, Musaeus, and Orpheus. The latter "were not quite sacred books in the sense that the Bible was, but they had an authority far above that of standard works."[34]

As expounders of the Sacred Law in the fourth century B.C., the priests,

[31] Parke, *op. cit.*, p. 39.

[32] James H. Oliver, *The Athenian Expounders of the Sacred and Ancestral Law* (Baltimore: Johns Hopkins University Press, 1950), p. 4.

[33] *Ibid.*, p. 9.

[34] *Ibid.*, p. 10.

called *exegetes* were officials with recognized constitutional positions. The exegetes knew how far their right of authoritative exegesis extended, and were usually careful not to go beyond recognized limits.[35]

In the fifth century B.C. in Athens, the relation in the popular mind between traditional sacred law and *chresmoi* concerning religious matters was close. Hence the Eupatrid experts who pretended to monopolize authoritative interpretations of the *chresmoi* were widely respected. However, Themistocles' successful rejection of the interpretation of the *chresmos* from Delphi before the Battle of Salamis shows that such prophecies or oracles were not always heeded. Oliver believed, however, that Themistocles himself may have been a Eupatrid.[36] In any case, the care Themistocles took to get as favorable an oracle as possible was a tribute to public opinion on the matter. Though Aristophanes did not attack divination or deride the *chresmoi*, he questioned the pretensions of the chresmologists.

> Aristophanes derides chiefly three pretensions of the chresmologi-manteis, who are to be identified as the eupatrid experts in religious affairs: (1) that they can foretell the future, above all from exotic oracles, (2) that without waiting to be consulted they can intervene in public business to give commands, (3) that they receive maintenance in the Prytaneum.[37]

Thus while in fifth century Athens there were no colleges of expounding and divining priests, the Eupatrids were experts to whom recourse was had on occasion. Some Eupatrids who were experts in religious matters exploited this expertness for personal advantage, but they neither behaved toward other members of their circle as a caste, nor were they attacked except as presumptuous individuals.[38]

Thus there were many elements in the Greek world that suggest parallels with events in Palestine both in the confederation period and in the Jewish royal period. Here, too, the religious confederation played a role in the conduct of conquest. Delphi evolved into a kind of central religious institution with a role among the Greeks not unlike that of Jerusalem among the Jews. However, Delphi never enjoyed the same kind of linkage with a royal power superior to all Greeks as occurred under the Jewish kings. Though Delphi was consulted on many international matters, such as colonization adventures and wars, and on many types of internal political problems of the city-states, such as the constitutional reforms of Athens and Sparta and possibly many other cities, and though the Delphic oracle had official representatives in many of the city-states, the individual city-states were far too independent to permit any monopoly of their intellectual life by the Delphic oracle or its representatives.

[35] *Ibid.*, p. 11.
[36] *Ibid.*, p. 13.
[37] *Ibid.*, p. 13.
[38] *Ibid.*, p. 17.

Moreover, when Delphi backed the wrong horse in Lydia and seriously lost prestige with her defeat, its situation as the authoritative spokesman of Greek religious thought was weakened. When the Delphic authorities withdrew their religious support to the resistance of Persian aggression, they seriously weakened the league against Persia. While some city-states withheld support, the Athenians rejected the oracle in the hour of national crisis. Thereafter the prestige of the oracle and its right to remain the primary cultural and religious spokesman of the Greek world was shaken apparently beyond repair.

Thus there was rivalry between the experts in religious affairs who represented the Delphic oracle in the special cities and the *chresmologi* (collectors of religious oracles) who were not linked in the Delphic system. However, though the Eupatrids were called upon for interpretations of the sacred law, their interpretations were not always followed. They were largely confined to the status of only one kind of expert in the city-state.

In view of the multiple lines of conflict between the different kinds of religious authorities, those associated with Delphi, traditional religious authorities in the particular city-states, and various free-lance chresmologists, the monopolization of intellectual roles in the Greek city-state by any particular class of priests or prophets was quite out of the question.

The large majority of the Greek intellectuals were the offspring of eminent families. Perhaps if fuller information were available it would be clear that Socrates was not alone in finding it possible to be considered a major intellectual, though he was the son of a stonemason and a midwife. Perhaps others of comparatively humble origin, like Socrates, were influential, but unlike him had no Xenophon or Plato to describe them to posterity. In any case, the intellectuals were usually from eminent families. These were not days of mass public education. Only persons with sufficient wealth to pursue a life of leisure were generally able to achieve the equivalent of a present-day higher education.

In contrast to other world areas, there were few priests among the intellectuals. It was as if the main intellectual ferment in India had been confined to circles such as the Carvakaṣ or as if intellectual development in Israel was primarily in the hands of persons like the author of Ecclesiastes. Heraclitus of Ephesus was unusual precisely because of the fact that he was a sacrificial priest of the Eleusinian Demeter. While a member of the very highest aristocratic circles of Ephesus, he belonged to a group that was losing power.

In the Greek intellectuals one is not dealing with a priestly trained stratum. This does not mean that the intellectuals as a whole were irreligious. Heraclitus drew religious conclusions from his doctrine of flux. The Eleatics were religiously oriented. Pythagoras established a religious sect, and Plato took the core of Pythagorean religiosity for his own. In the case of Pythagoras and Plato, religious guilds or sects were formed and their schools had an almost monastic character with the observance of careful schedules, dietary practices, etc. They promoted the salvation religiosity of genteel intellectuals and not the formation of church structures and ministering priests.

Though the intellectuals were generally derived from high-status circles, they were by no means exclusively drawn from the landed aristocracy. Plato was an upper-class Athenian whose family was apparently from the landed gentry. Thucydides, too, came from property owners; his family possessed gold mines in Thrace. But the majority of the intellectuals came from commercial families. Thales was from a commercial family of Miletus; Herodotus was from a commercial family of Halicarnassus. Empedocles of Agrigentum and Democritus of Abdera, judging by the fact that he was widely traveled, were also from commercial families. There were many others.

The intellectual himself was not always wealthy. Plato, Thucydides, Herodotus, and some others were. Others of them became so. It was, however, not unusual for families to be suddenly depressed to poverty owing to the fortunes of either business or war. In a considerable number of cases one or other form of intellectual activity was in part taken up as a profession. Isocrates lost an inherited fortune, and began teaching rhetoric for a living. Demosthenes had a respectable inheritance, but he came into it as a minor and found it dissipated by his guardian by the time he reached his majority. He had inherited a sword-making and a bed-making factory. (His father appears to have been originally an ivory importer. Ivory inlay was used in the manufacture of both swords and beds.) The factories were taken over, because payment could not be made for credit in the form of advances of ivory to the establishments. Demosthenes went into legal practice to earn a living, and eventually made a fortune.

Not an inconsiderable number of the intellectuals were displaced persons of the Hellenic world who had lost their homes as well as their family inheritance, and assumed an intellectual trade in their new homes. Those displaced either by the Persian wars or by activities of local tyrants included Epicurus, Protagoras, Prodicus, Hippias, Thrasymachus, Xenophanes, and Pythagoras.

There were three general trades into which the intellectuals generally entered. As already indicated, Isocrates and Demosthenes, as well as many others, went into legal practice. Some of the displaced intellectuals became physicians. Under the tutelage of Pythagoras, an active "school" of medicine developed. Alcmaeon and Philolaus of Croton were physicians. Democedes of Croton was court physician of Polycrates. And it should not be forgotten that Aristotle's father had been a physician. Aristotle himself received training in his father's profession.

But by all odds the most important of the activities of the intellectuals was the founding of schools. Protagoras of Abdera taught in Athens. Prodicus of Ceos and Hippias of Elis also founded schools. Schools were founded by Pythagoras of Samos, Plato, Epicurus (son of an Attic clerouch), Zeno, and many others. Of all the founders of schools, the Sophists were most active. Their specialty was the teaching of rhetoric and the technique of argument, talents of tremendous importance in the city-state.

Of somewhat lesser importance than these possibilities was the appearance of the intellectual as a political advisor. Thrasymachus of Chalcedon on occasion served in such a capacity. Plato made repeated trips to Syracuse, and attempted to mold its political policy. Parmenides of Elis was said to have written a constitution for his city. Pythagoras in Croton was consulted by the political powers, and among the proposals made by himself and his school was a form of city-planning based upon their theory that numbers were the essence of all things. Anaxagoras and a number of others were called to Athens by Pericles, and presumably were consulted on occasion.

The plasticity of the intellectuals is noteworthy. Prodicus and Hippias served as ambassadors for their city-states. They were quick to set up schools in their various places of residence. Epicurus set up schools at Mitylene, Lampsacus, and finally at Athens. Aristotle served as a physician, tutor, and founder of schools. Isocrates first set himself up as a teacher of rhetoric, but soon found it more profitable to practice it.

The programs of the intellectuals profoundly reflect these diverse status orientations. The theories of Parmenides, Pythagoras, and Plato, for example, are addressed to the demands of a genteel religiosity. It was not without accident that the Sophists appear as sociologists, students of civilization, ethnologists, and were concerned with the customary determination of truth and the subjectivity of ideas. As a group they were displaced persons who had been forced to adjust to diverse customs. They made their living by cultivating in their students an urbanity on the one hand, and skill in dialectics on the other, so valuable to the citizens of city-states such as Athens. One segment of the Pythagoreans was oriented not only toward soul-healing but toward body-healing as well, quite in keeping with their situation as physicians and tutors in the households of royal and aristocratic families. The political orientations of those intellectuals who either entered into legal practice or trained others for it are equally clear.

TRANSFORMATIONS IN THE HELLENISTIC PERIOD

How radically the conditions of the Hellenistic period affected the intellectual and his product is reported by all students. To some extent the Greek intellectual acquired a new universalism, but lost the heightened intensity of old.

> Now, a citizen of the world, he might travel anywhere; the products of the world came to his door; but the high standards of taste, freedom, responsibility, and the intensity of Periclean life were definitely things

of the past. It is significant that the one great genius of the Age, Archimedes, came from Syracuse, a city-state.[39]

The loss of creativity has been observed many times. "The new dispensation produced no Aeschylus and no Sophocles, no Plato and no Thucydides."[40] In this period the intellectual ceased to be an independent agent in the autonomous city-state and, so far as he survived at all, was often a ward of the state.

> It is typical also of the Hellenistic Age that learning and the importance of learning were then for the first time recognized and appreciated by the state. The private philosophic schools still went on; but side by side with them rose the first public establishment for the encouragement of literature and science. The Museum (or "Home of the Muses") at Alexandria was the first learned society maintained by the state. It was a society of savants and men of letters who devoted their whole lives to science and literature. A great library was placed at their service, and also other appliances for study, for instance, a zoological garden. Pergamum could boast of a similar institution, and so sought to rival Alexandria in this field also.[41]

In the face of official patronage, thought outside of the museums went into an extensive decline.

The wide variety of roles available to the intellectual in the Hellenic period did not vanish all at once in the Hellenistic. However, from the beginning of the Hellenistic period the entire meaning of the intellectual's activity had been transformed. One of the most significant facts of the Hellenistic period was the disappearance of the autonomous city as one of the fundamental phenomena of the epoch. To be sure, many of the cities still enjoyed partial autonomy, but even when they did the ultimate determinants of the fate of Hellenistic man lay with the state and not with the city.

With this structural change in Greek society, the core of many of the intellectual skills was lost: there was no longer the need for the tutor in political techniques, and the founding of schools lost much of its meaning. So far as the older skills of the intellectual persisted, they were often isolated fragments. Often under the patronage of the state the intellectual survived as a mathematician, physicist, grammarian, librarian, literary expert, or something of the sort, but practically never as a fully equipped, well-rounded intellectual.

As the intellectual's message lost its function in a system of power, both comparatively and absolutely, it gained in moral and religious significance.

39 George Botsford and Charles Robinson, *Hellenic History* (New York: The Macmillan Co., 1956), p. 370.

40 Cecil F. Lavell, *A Biography of the Greek People* (Boston: Houghton Mifflin, 1934), p. 274.

41 M. Rostovtzeff, *A History of the Ancient World* (Oxford: The Clarendon Press, 1925), p. 395.

The new intellectuals of the Hellenistic world were either specialists supported by patronage or moral councilors. When their patronage was eventually withdrawn, the specialists tended to disappear.

In the Hellenistic world the role of the intellectual was transformed most fundamentally by the rise in importance of a variety of religious figures. A variety of mystery religions (mostly from the East, from Egypt, Syria, Anatolia, and Persia), often centering in the cult of a savior-god, competed for popular acceptance. The adherents of various mysteries built around Dionysus ate the flesh of a newly slain bull and engaged in sacred dances which evoked ecstatic states. Various sects arose in the name of Orpheus, the adherents of which practiced asceticism and vegetarianism and promulgated a doctrine of reincarnation. Other mysteries centered in the Great Mother who had brought about the resurrection of the Shepherd Attis after he had been slain by his enemies. Other cults arose around the Greek Adonis who presumably had died and risen again. Other mysteries concerned Osiris, the king, who had been killed by his brother and was revived by Isis, his wife, to become ruler of the dead. Developing out of the Eleusinian religion near Athens was a mystery dramatizing the death of vegetation in the fall and its reappearance in the spring. Mithraism (of Persian origin) was also widespread. Similar to the mystery religions was somewhat more intellectual Hermeticism, which proposed redemption of the spirit from the world of the flesh by means of ascetic practices and a curious blend of knowledge admixing polytheism, astrology, and other elements. In the same period the dominant philosophies–Stoicism, Epicureanism, and the older doctrines of the Peripatetics, the Pythagoreans, the Platonists, and the Cynics –all displayed a systematic displacement in mystical and moralistic direction. They became eclectic, and received many popular superstitions in their systems.

The effect of this increasing appearance of religious figures in the ranks of the intellectual strata was to bring about, in Murray's words, a new "relation of the writer to the world about him."

> Anyone who turns from the great writers of classical Athens, say Sophocles or Aristotle, to those of the Christian era must be conscious of a great difference in tone. There is a change in the whole relation of the writer to the world about him. The new quality is not specifically Christian; it is just as marked in the Gnostics and Mithras-worshippers as in the Gospels and the Apocalypse, in Julian and Plotinus, as in Gregory and Jerome. It is hard to describe. It is a rise of asceticism, of mysticism, in a sense, of pessimism; a loss of self-confidence, of hope in this life and of faith in normal human effort; a despair of patient inquiry, a cry for infallible revelation; an indifference to the welfare of the state, a conversion of the soul to God. It is an atmosphere in which the aim of the good man is not so much to live justly, to help the society in which he belongs, and enjoy the esteem of his fellow creatures; but rather, by means of a burning faith, by contempt for the world and its standards, by ecstasy, suffering and martyrdom, to be granted pardon for his un-

> speakable unworthiness, his immeasurable sins. There is an intensifying of certain spiritual emotions; an increase of sensitiveness, a failure of nerve.[42]

The role of the intellectual was in the slow process of being transformed primarily into that of the priest once more.

SUMMARY

When the ancestral Greeks swept down upon the Minoan-Mycenaean civilizations and helped bring about their collapse, they reenacted a drama that showed similarities to those of other areas of the ancient world. The three major types of communities to dominate Greek society in its various phases were: (1) the semifeudal communities of the Heroic period, (2) the city-states of the classical period, and (3) the semiautonomous cities of the imperial period.

These communities supplied the social foundation for very different kinds of intellectual roles. In the Heroic Age the intellectual was a bard, an expert in the interpretation of oracles, and a prophet of sorts. He bore great similarities to the Vedic priest. However, in contrast to the Vedic priest who was shaped by the social tensions between the Indo-European and Dravidian civilization into a house chaplain (*purohita*) and tutor (*guru*), the Homeric religious figure tended to evolve into a tribal or, at times, intertribal priest.

Religion played a role in the life of the Greeks of the Heroic Age which had many points of similarity with the religion of the Jews of the Confederation period. For Greece, too, it often supplied the foundation of intertribal confederations which had political and military functions. However, no consolidation of political and religious institutions occurred in Greece equivalent to that which was brought about in the Jewish royal period.

While Delphi came to serve as a kind of cult center for all of Greece, the city-states never lost their sovereignty to any political structure with which Delphi was identified. Hence, though Delphi had a hand in the colonization activities of the cities, and a voice in important internal affairs of many cities, its role remained only advisory. When Delphi supported the international politics of Lydia, its prestige suffered badly when Lydia lost its independence to Persia. It made a second mistake when it opposed the resistance of the Greek city-states to Persia. Thus in the decisive hour, the Greeks rejected their own religious authorities.

Meanwhile, traditional religious authorities, representatives of the Delphic oracle, and free-lance religious experts were variously employed in the city-states. However, they were never permitted to monopolize its intellectual life. Rather, the primary patterns of Greek thought were borne by the free citizenry of the cities, whether priestly or not.

In the Hellenistic period with the conversion of the city-states into only

[42] Murray, *op. cit.*, p. 103.

semi-autonomous entities, the primary context for the expression of the intellectual's talents had been basically changed. While a brilliant assemblage of scholars was collected from the various city-states and patronized officially at the Alexandrian Museum, it was by the same token withdrawn from the context of the city-state. The representatives of the old philosophies increasingly found themselves called upon to serve as moral and ethical councilors. Meanwhile, the ranks of the intellectuals were everywhere being penetrated by new types of religious figures.

SELECTED BIBLIOGRAPHY

Bury, J. B., and others, *The Hellenistic Age* (Cambridge: The University Press, 1923).

Cornford, F. M., *Greek Religious Thought* (New York: E. P. Dutton, 1923).

Guthrie, W. K. C., *The Greeks and Their Gods* (London: Methuen & Co., 1950).

Hamilton, Edith, *The Greek Way* (New York: W. W. Norton, 1930).

Kingsley, Charles, *Alexandria and Her Schools* (Cambridge: The Macmillan Co., 1854).

Murray, Gilbert, *Four Stages of Greek Religion* (New York: Columbia University Press, 1912).

More, Paul Elmer, *Hellenistic Philosophies* (Princeton: Princeton University Press, 1923).

Oliver, James H., *The Athenian Expounders of the Sacred and Ancestral Law* (Baltimore: Johns Hopkins University Press, 1950).

Parke, H. W., *A History of the Delphic Oracle* (Oxford: Basil Blackwell, 1939).

Tollinton, R. B., *Alexandrine Teaching on the Universe* (New York: The Macmillan Co., 1932).

15

SOCIAL THOUGHT AND CIVILIZATION IN ANCIENT GREECE

The three great periods in the development of ancient Greek society and civilization were the Heroic (from perhaps 1800 B.C. to 900 B.C.), the Hellenic (900 B.C. to 300 B.C.), and the Hellenistic (after 300 B.C.). Very different types of communities dominated each period. The Heroic period evolved semifeudal manorial communities, the conquest communities of warriors imposed on a world of peasant villages. By approximately 900 B.C. the kingships which arose in the Heroic period were occasionally subject to inner revolutions, during which the landed aristocrats took the administration into their own hands. The aristocrats were interested in full access to the trade opportunities which developed in connection with the sea castles. Though the cities evolved at different rates and in very different directions, the first step toward the city-state was almost everywhere similar—a revolt of the landed aristocrats against the monopoly of trade opportunities by the king. The aristocratic founders of the city usually confirmed their seizures of power in formal acts of synoecism. With the emergence of the city-state, ancient Greece entered upon its classical stage.

Despite a considerably cultural homogeneity, the Greek world never created communities more comprehensive than the city-state. At the same time, this world of city-states raised problems of an intercivic nature which the city could not solve. The devastating Peloponnesian War was one consequence. The empires (first of Macedonia, then of Rome) brought the intercity wars of the Greek world to an end, but transformed the cities into administrative units of the empires. Though they were still permitted much local autonomy, the nerve centers of the cities had been fatally impaired, and went into slow decline which continued until specialized rural and religious communities eventually took shape out of their ruins.

Each of these community forms produced its unique type of intellectuals. In the semifeudal communities of heroic times, the intellectuals were bards and augurers and oracle casters similar to the Vedic priests. They were also bearers of similar historical and religious traditions. However, in contrast to their Indian counterparts, they evolved in part into an intertribal priesthood suggesting the Yahwism of the Israelite Confederacy. At the same time, in most city-states until late times there were families of the *eupatridae* (nobles) which retained hereditary religious privileges and qualifications in a manner suggestive of the Indian Brahmans who emerged as a noble hereditary priesthood out of the Vedic singers. Finally, in addition to the Delphic priesthood and its representatives, hereditary religious families, various free-lance religious specialists appeared in the Greek world.

The various classes of religious specialists which emerged out of the Heroic period persisted into the classical period of the Greek city-state. However, all such priestly intellectuals underwent a systematic devaluation before the many types of secular intellectuals. The fundamental role of the secular intellectual was that of citizen. As citizens they were experienced in a wide variety of the major roles of the city-states—lawyers, administrators, judges, soldiers, etc. Their ranks were swelled by sophists who were largely displaced full citizens from other city-states who were forced to employ their learning as teachers in order to survive.

In the Hellenistic period the intellectual's status as a free citizen in an autonomous city-state melted away. On the surface, his status did not immediately change, but often appeared to improve. He became a specialist. Many of the best minds of the Greek world were siphoned off and patronized by the state at the Alexandrian Museum. However, the intellectual was being transformed from a fully free citizen into a state servant or moral councilor. Moreover, the ranks of the former secularized intellectuals were increasingly penetrated by various types of religious leaders.

THE MAJOR CONCEPTUAL PRODUCTS OF THE HEROIC PERIOD

The major intellectual products from the Heroic period were the texts of Homer and Hesiod. They were also the nearest things to sacred books for the Greeks of the classical period. The task of assembling them was carried out by chresmologists of the City period, not for aesthetic reasons, but for the ethical, mythological, and religious instruction they contained.

> Everything could be learned from Homer, and by no means least important, ritual propriety and the interpretation of omens. When the Athenians decided that in the interest of the state it was important to collect the sacred books, they thought first of all of Homer. The organization of the Great Panathenaic Festival in 566 B.C. provided the opportunity for musical contests with the participation by rhapsodists and the means to collect the text, which was collected as sacred literature, at, rather than for, the festival with the help of recitations by rhapsodists who appeared for the contests. The Attic black-figured pottery reveals a burst of Athenian interest in Homer beginning right after 566.[1]

[1] James H. Oliver, *The Athenian Expounders of the Sacred and Ancestral Law* (Baltimore: Johns Hopkins University Press, 1950), p. 4.

The *Iliad* and *Odyssey*, which came to be performed at the Panathenea at Athens every four years, were attributed to Homer, about whom almost nothing is known, though in the time of Aristotle a number of "lives" of Homer appeared, primarily deduced from the poems themselves. Estimates of Homer's date vary from 1159 B.C. to 685 B.C. The present text was not established till 150 B.C., when Aristarchus of Samothrace, at the time head of the Alexandrian Library, eventually published the edition recognized as authoritative. Solon may have started the movement for the recovery of Homer. A text was commissioned by Pisistratus at Athens between 560 and 527 B.C., at which time the poems were committed to writing.

As they now stand, the poems possess a unity imposed on originally different subject matter. Various strata of language are distinguishable: Attic on the surface, Ionic primarily in substance, with Aeolic elements and fragments of an ancient form of Greek hardly intelligible to the Athenians of the sixth century.[2] The poems describe a heroic age dominated by charismatic warrior adventurers with bodies of personal followers who entered upon plundering expeditions for booty. They burned their dead, worshiped at open altars, and sacrificed to feasting, singing, and conquering gods very like themselves.

As history, the Homeric poems are useless, but provide a general picture of the times. Some of the songs clearly go back to considerable antiquity, revealing the work of bards, the poet-bearers of an oral religious tradition. The bards were not priests in the same sense as the composers of the Vedic hymns, but poet entertainers of semifeudal courts.

The poems were songs of craft, war, plunder, and general adventure. It is the poetry of warriors whose gods were like unto them. Through them ran the moral presuppositions of an heroic age: *aidos*, the sense of personal shame (the honor of the feudal warrior), *nemesis*, the claims of one's companions (expectation of censure of others). These moral conceptions were not as yet depersonalized or turned into cosmological principles as later; they remained the demands of the individual of himself and the claims of others on him in a feudal order.

The compilation of the texts of Hesiod was brought about by chresmologists about the same time and under the same conditions as the text of Homer.

> To the sacred origins of the past the works of Hesiod belonged almost as preëminently as those of Homer. In later times his name used to be coupled with that of Homer as one of the great ethical and religious teachers whom the Athenians and other Greeks revered. Hesiod was the great promoter of what Nilsson calls religious legalism, of a severe ritualism such as is found among the Jews, and which was strongly marked among the Greeks precisely in the sixth century. . . . The story told by Heraeus of Megara that Pisistratus suppressed a line reflecting adversely

[2] Alfred and Maurice Croiset, *An Abridged History of Greek Literature* (New York: The Macmillan Co., 1904), pp. 11–48.

> upon Theseus would not by itself be enough to prove that a state copy of Hesiod was prepared by Athenian experts during the tyranny of Pisistratus, but since we have reason to infer approximately for that period the preparation of a complete text of Hesiod, the story has some corroborative value.[3]

The bard was one of the first of the intellectual types. Hesiod reveals some of the intellectual traditions of those groups who took part in the colonization movements from the eighth to the sixth century. Hesiod's father, apparently a free peasant in search of land, migrated from the Aeolic Cyme in Asia Minor to Boeotia. Hesiod and his brother Perses were born at Ascra near Mount Helicon. As a boy, Hesiod fed his father's flocks and looked forward to the life of a peasant. After the death of his father, Hesiod left his native land in disgust because of a lawsuit with his brother over the patrimony. He is said to have received his commission from the Muses to be their prophet and poet. The commission was acknowledged by dedicating to them a tripod won in a song contest at funeral games at Chalcis.[4]

Works and Days is a shepherd's calendar. It formulates the ethical value of honest labor and the disvalue of strife and idleness. It described rules of husbandry and presented a religious calendar of the months with observations on days most lucky for rural employments. The theme of the poem was Hesiod's reaction to the loss of his inheritance as a result of his brother's bribery of the judges. For all its didacticism, the poem analyzed the ills of the society from the standpoint of the free peasant squeezed by social changes.

In the *Theogony* Hesiod developed a cosmogony and recounted the legends of the dynasties of Zeus and Cronos. The contest of Zeus and the other Olympian gods with the Titans, and the description of the prison in which the Titans were confined with the giants reflects the conflict of Olympian religion with those religious forms it overcame. Throughout one finds a free peasant of Boeotia framing an ethical justification of the life of the small peasant and shepherd and attempting to bring order into the mythology of his day.[5]

INTELLECTUAL PRODUCTIVITY DURING THE CLASSICAL PERIOD

During the period of the autonomous city the ancient Greeks produced a volume and variety of thought greater than any of the other world areas at the same time. The most distinctive product of the Greek thinker of the classical period was philosophy. However, historians, poets, orators, and dramatists of the period also produced materials having few parallels elsewhere.

[3] Oliver, *op. cit.*, p. 5.

[4] Andrew Robert Burn, *The World of Hesiod* (London: Kegan Paul, Trench, Trubner, 1936); F. A. Paley, *The Epics of Hesiod* (London, 1861).

[5] Hesiod's *Theogony* (trans. by Norman O. Brown) (New York: Liberal Arts Press, 1953).

Greek philosophy in the classical period falls into a number of schools including the Milesians, Pythagoreans, Pluralists, Sophists, and Socratics. The most comprehensive and synthetic form of Greek philosophy appears in the work of Plato and Aristotle.

The Milesians

The three primary members of the Milesian school were Thales (624–546 B.C.), Anaximander (610–545 B.C.), and Anaximenes (585–528 B.C.). Thales was the son of a Carian father and a Greek mother. He is reported to have traveled in Egypt, where he calculated the height of the pyramids by the length of their shadows. He predicted an eclipse of the sun, and tried to explain the Nile flood. He constructed an instrument to determine the distance of ships at sea, and is said to have advised the Ionians to form a political combination against the threat of Persia. Anaximander is said to have led a Milesian colony to Apollonia. He constructed a sundial and a globe of the heavens, and carried on cosmological studies. Practically no biographical data are available on Anaximenes.

The Milesians are sometimes described as nature philosophers, for they presented a variety of interpretations of natural phenomena. Thales argued that water is the essence of all things, the earth floats upon it, and does not move because it is the center of everything. He viewed water as the vital substance of life itself. Anaximander posited a kind of protosubstance, the boundless, from which things arise. Were it not boundless, he believed, creation would exhaust itself, but motion is eternal. Warm and cold differentiated out the boundless; from them came the "moist." Further differentiation produced the earth and the air and the circle of fire, thought to surround the earth. In the beginning the earth was a fluid, which gradually dried up and brought forth living creatures. Men were first fishlike. Anaximander assumed the periodic creation and destruction in the universe and the existence of an infinite number of world systems. Anaximenes sought, too, for a primary substance, and found it in air. The two processes of rarefaction and condensation account for change. By rarefaction the air became fire; by condensation it became clouds, water, earth, and stones. In the process of creation the earth was formed; it was flat like a table top and sustained by air. Anaximenes thought the moon derived its light by reflection. He gave a naturalistic account of eclipses. Rainbows were explained as the effect of sunshine on clouds which the rays could not penetrate.[6]

The Pythagoreans

Pythagoras was a native of the Island of Samos (532 B.C.).[7] Either because of his dislike of the government of Polycrates or from fear of the Persian

[6] C. S. Kirk and J. F. Ravin, *The Pre-Socratic Philosophers* (Cambridge: University Press, 1957), pp. 73–215.

[7] *Ibid.*, pp. 217–262.

invasion, Pythagoras removed to Croton in Southern Italy, where he founded a society and influenced the affairs in the city. After a revolt of the citizens who established an administration negative to his influence, he moved to Metapontion.

The two primary conceptions of the Pythagorean system are the transmigration of souls and the notion that the essence of the world is number. Long before Sir James Jeans, God was thought to be a mathematician. The two ideas were linked in the closest possible way: for mathematical thinking was conceived as a form of contemplation that freed one from worldly entanglements. Things were viewed as composed of mathematical points: two for length, three for thickness, four for solidity. Since it consisted of $1 + 2 + 3 + 4$ dots arranged as a pyramid, the number 10 was sacred. The Pythagoreans were convinced of the mathematical harmony of the spheres. They discovered the numerical laws of vibrating strings, which was a great joy, and of incommensurables, which was a shock to them.

As a mystery religion, Pythagoreanism employed mathematical contemplation as an implement of spiritual purification. An elaborate catalogue of dietary and other ascetic prescriptions was also established. Their doctrines were carefully guarded. This combination of secret teaching, asceticism, the concept of transmigration of souls, belief in mathematics as the essence of the universe, and mathematical thinking as an implement of religious purification, are all well known from Indian culture.

The Pythagoreans were reputed physicians. Democedes of Croton was the court physician of Polycrates and later of Darius. Alcmaeon of Croton dissected animals, identified the brain as the organ of mental life, and discovered the optic nerve. He believed health depended on the harmonious distribution of the qualities of cold, dry, wet, bitter, and sweet. His distinguished between sense perception and thought. Philolaus of Croton, who was both a physician and a writer, wrote treatises on medicine, music, and the nature of the soul.

Perhaps the most striking innovations of the Pythagoreans were those in the field of medicine and their lively experimental work that led to empirical discoveries.

Early Monistic Philosophies

In contrast to the Pythagorean dualism of mind-body, monism was developed by the Eleatic school of philosophy founded by Xenophanes of Colophon (570–475 B.C.), who fled his native country at the time of Persian domination and, after many travels, settled in Elea, Southern Italy.[8] He was taunted because of his poverty, but he illustrates the self-reliance of the displaced intellectual for he made a living by his poetic skills as a rhapsodist. More important than Xenophanes for the school was Parmenides of Elea (540–470 B.C.), a rich noble who wrote a constitution for his city

[8] *Ibid.*, pp. 163–181.

and was otherwise involved in its political life.[9] Zeno,[10] a disciple of Parmenides, was the school's most able controversialist. He was forty years younger than his master. Melissus of Samos, who defeated the Athenian fleet in 441 B.C., also belonged to the school. Having the same objectives as the Eleatics, but holding quite different explanations of phenomena, was Heraclitus (544–484 B.C.), who was born in one of the noblest families of Ephesus. Heraclitus was sacrificial priest to the Eleusinian Demeter.

Xenophanes discovered fossils in the quarries of Syracuse, and drew conclusions about changes on the earth's surface and the origin of life. He attacked degeneracy and effeminacy of civilization, and criticized Homer and Hesiod because of their anthropomorphic religion. He argued for the spiritual unity of the cosmos, with the world itself as the deity. He taught that the stars were fiery clouds which glow at night, that the earth stretched downward to infinity, that the earth was originally covered with water, that living creatures were generated in the mud formed by earth and water, and that the sea was the source of water and the winds. Xenophanes was convinced of the mental progress of mankind. He regarded agriculture (particularly vine culture) and fire as the most important human inventions.

Though originally influenced by the Pythagoreans, Parmenides transferred his allegiance to Xenophanes. He attempted to prove the unity and essential changelessness of the world. Only two things were possible—"being" and "nonbeing." He argued that only being exists. Being cannot have a beginning or an end. It is continuous, undivided, motionless, unchangeable, everywhere identical with a rounded sphere having equal extension. Perception which presents us with a manifold, with creation and change, is the source of error. Though things are "seen" to change, our reason proves they cannot, for change involves notion of a thing moving from where it "is" to where it "is not." But there is no "is not." Being is also identical with thought. Zeno's importance lies in the cleverness with which he developed "proofs" of this doctrine of the essential changelessness of Being. Melissus also developed arguments against motion, change, creation, division, and mixture. Neither movement nor condensation nor rarefaction is possible. Xenophanes' pantheism was being turned into systematic devaluation of the world.

On the surface Heraclitus would seem to have asserted precisely the opposite. His basic doctrine, elaborated in many images, was that everything changes. However, he thought that in all change form was constant. Things were held together by a spiritual principle—*logos*. The essence of all things is fire. Everything is continually changing into its opposite. Strife is the justice of the world, war is father of all things, what is at war becomes united, what breaks up is fused. Homer was a fool for condemning discord. Primary substance passes through three fundamental forms: fire becomes

[9] *Ibid.*, pp. 263–285.
[10] *Ibid.*, pp. 286–297.

water, water becomes earth, and the reverse back to fire. The soul of man is part of the divine fire, and the purer the fire the more perfect the soul. When the soul leaves the body, it returns to the world fire. Morality, religion, ethics, as ordinarily understood, were all rather insignificant things to Heraclitus who saw only that all contradictions were resolved in absolute world harmony. The laws of world order were inviolable.

By different routes Heraclitus and the Eleatics presented fundamentally similar monistic and pantheistic positions.

Fifth-Century Pluralism

The solution to the problem of change developed by the Eleatics and Heraclitus was attacked during the fifth century by philosophers dissatisfied with it. Among the thinkers who attempted a new resolution of the problem on a pluralistic basis were Empedocles, Anaxagoras, and the atomists (Leucippus and Democritus).

Empedocles of Agrigentum (495–435 B.C.), a member of an upper-class family, whose grandfather had distinguished himself in horse-racing in the Olympic games, was active in local politics and had even been offered the kingship. Later he was forced into exile, and died in the Peloponnesse. Anaxagoras of Clazomenae (500–428 B.C.), though also of a noble and wealthy family, avoided politics. He cared little about the administration of his estates. He was brought by Pericles to Athens, where he lived thirty years, but when he joined the opposition against Pericles, he was accused of impiety, and migrated to Lampsacus. About Leucippus, founder of atomism, little is known. His teachings are indistinguishable from those of Democritus. Democritus, who was acquainted with Leucippus in Lampsacus, was born in Abdera (460–370 B.C.). He traveled extensively from Egypt to Babylonia and Persia, and eventually to Athens. The pluralists were displaced persons. It would have been difficult to persuade them that the changes that rocked their lives were illusions.

The clue to the problem of permanence and change (both motion and rest were accepted as real properties of events) was found by Empedocles in eternal substances. He held that substances are eternal and unchangeable; change and destruction arise from their mixture and separation. These substances are divisible into four elements, or roots–fire, air, water, and earth. None can be transformed into the other. Things are mixtures of them. Motion is produced by the antithetical forces that bring about mixture (love) and separation (hate). A sphere is a blissful circle from which all hate has been banished. The opposite is a complete separation of elements. The events of everyday life lie between these things: here individuals come into being, and then pass away. Love at first occupied the center of the present world, where it set up a vortex into which the substances were drawn. Ether first separated out to form the vault of heaven; next fire took its position; then water was pressed out from the earth by the rotation which, in turn, holds the parts of the universe in place.

Empedocles believed that plants and animals are generated from the earth through the unifying force of love. At first separate limbs came forth, which were combined in monstrous shapes. Eventually present-day animals and men appeared. Sense perception was made possible by effulgence of particles of the substance (like light) which activated an equivalent particle in the sense organ. Desire was produced by what was alike, dislike by difference. Beyond the realm of matter was a realm of spirits. Empedocles subscribed to the doctrine of transmigration of souls. In their lower stages souls (which assume forms according to merit and demerit of a previous life) find preferred dwelling places in plants and animals, such as laurel trees and lions. In a higher stage they occupy the bodies of priests and physicians. Meat-eating and blood sacrifice were prohibited.

Anaxagoras, too, viewed change as due to combinations of existing substances. However, he did not attribute change to love and hate but to the work of a thinking, rational mind. Matter is composite; mind is unmixed. Only mind exists for itself alone. Before the operation of mind, matter appears as an inert mass. Matter consists of innumerable imperishable, unchangeable particles of blood, flesh, bone, etc. Originally they were homogeneously distributed through the cosmos into which mind induced a rotary motion. The vortex initiated the process of world creation. Chaos first separated into the cold, moist, dark, and dense, and the warm, dry, light, and rare. Rotation produced the distribution of elements: the heavy elements of earth remained at the center; the light and warm were carried to the circumference. The earth was conceived to be a flat disk supported by air. The stars were formed of hot stone torn from the earth by rotation. The moon was like the earth, and inhabited. From mud fertilized by germs of the air and ether, living beings were produced. Their animating principle, mind, was shared in varying degrees. Sense perception was a function of mind, but was produced not by similars but by contraries. Among other things, he explained that the Nile River floods were due to melting snows in the Ethiopian Mountains. He objected to divination and miraculous intervention in nature. For his description of the sun as a hot stone, Anaxagoras was accused of impiety by the Athenians.

Democritus carried pluralism still further. Absolute creation and destruction of basic substance were impossible. Both being and nonbeing were ultimate properties of reality. He postulated the existence of innumerable particles too small to be perceived, which neither come into being nor cease to be. They are homogeneous in substance, distinguished only by their shape and size. Every kind of change is caused by their combination and separation. The qualities of things were established by the shape, size, position, and arrangement of the atoms. No outside forces (like love and hate) were necessary to account for their conjunction and separation. Because of their original size and shape, they were in rotary motion from the beginning.

Since motion is eternal, there is an infinite number of possible worlds—ours is only one. Its creation consisted of the formation of stars in the air, and their gradual drying up and ignition. The earth was a round disk in the air, hollowed like a basin—a view that accounted for the different places the sun and moon rise and set. Organic beings came from the earth's mud.

Democritus pressed the history of civilization into his theory. In the struggle for survival against beasts, men, out of necessity, were led to combine with each other. Then the need of understanding created language, and led to the gradual development of technical devices. The greatest civilized invention was fire, which lifted men out of barbarism.

The soul for Democritus consisted of small, round, fine atoms (fire). Though the soul is the noblest part of man, after death the soul-atoms are dispersed. Perception consists of changes produced in the soul by effulgences that come through the sense organs. Feeling is brought about by likeness of effulgences from objects with those of the organ of sense. Thinking is due to the right temperature of the movements of the particles of the soul.

> Atomism is in many ways the crown of Greek philosophical achievement before Plato. It fulfilled the ultimate aim of Ionian material monism by cutting the Gordian knot of the Eleatic elenchus. Much as it owed not only to Parmenides and Melissus, but also to the pluralist systems of Empedocles and Anaxagoras, atomism was not, however, an eclectic philosophy like that of Diogenes of Apollonia. It was in essence a new conception, one which was widely and skillfully applied by Democritus, and which through Epicurus and Lucretius was to play an important part in Greek thought even after Plato and Aristotle. It also, of course, eventually gave a stimulus to the development of modern atomic theory —the real nature and motives of which, however, are utterly distinct.[11]

Into this first period of Greek philosophy the fresh naturalism of the Homeric period was preserved, while its naïve theogony was lost. Cornford views it as the starting point for all European science:

> We have considered the Ionian science of Nature—the germ from which all European science has since developed—as marking the achievement of an attitude of mind in which the object has been completely detached from the subject and can be contemplated by thought disengaged from the interests of action. The fruits of this attitude were the first systems of the world that can claim to be rational constructions of reality.[12]

The Sophists

The sophists were a stratum of secular teachers. They moved from city-state to city-state, and amassed a quantity of information concerning com-

[11] *Ibid.*, p. 426.

[12] Francis Macdonald Cornford, *Before and After Socrates* (Cambridge: The University Press, 1932), p. 29.

parative custom. They appear as founders and teachers of special schools, as public lecturers, as physicians, as poets. They taught the art of dialectics of particular value in a legal order where every man had to defend himself.[13]

Among the more important sophists were Protagoras of Abdera (481–411 B.C.), Prodicus of Ceos, Hippias of Elis, Gorgias of Leontine (483–375 B.C.), Thrasymachus of Chalcedon (well known in Athens in 427 B.C.), and Antiphon of Athens.

Protagoras lived in the Periclean circle, and is said to have been chosen to draw up a constitution for the colony of Thruii. He was again in Athens in the first years of the Peloponnesian War, and lived through the plague. He was prosecuted for blasphemy, and met his death by shipwreck during his flight to Sicily.

Prodicus appears as a teacher in Athens, and is said to have been expelled from the Lyceum for conversing on improper subjects. He appears to have conducted diplomatic missions for his home city. Hippias came to Athens as an official ambassador, and for the same reason visited Sparta. Gorgias, too, initially came to Athens as an ambassador. He visited Boeotia and Thessaly, and in all these places formed schools. Thrasymachus, among other things, was known in Larisa for his defense of the city against the Macedonian king Archelaus' efforts at annexation, a fact which should be juxtaposed to the pure Machiavellianism attributed to him by Plato in *The Republic*.

To Protagoras is attributed the relativistic formulation, "man is the measure of all things." Protagoras transferred the problem of knowledge from the object to the subject. Morals and laws were conceived to be only relatively valid. They were binding in the community that formulated them only so long as it deemed them good. The basic law of the natural world was self-preservation. Man was superior to the animal in mental powers; his distinctness lay in his inventions, the most important being language, religion, and the state. Protagoras sketched a theory of education, based on natural gifts and practice. Consistent with his ethical relativism, he argued that punishment is necessary, but only as a means and a deterrent; it is useless as vengeance. He applied his relativism to every branch of knowledge. Mathematics, he asserted, is ideally and not really valid. He was interested in linguistics, and tried to found the science of grammar.

Convinced of the corruption of Greek society, Prodicus attributed it to a soft life. He admonished the young to assume the rigorous life of the hero. He advanced a theory of religious evolution beginning with a primitive fetishistic stage in which men worshiped as gods things useful to them—the sun, moon, rivers (he exemplified this by the cult of the Nile). In the second stage, the inventors of agriculture, vine culture, and metal work were worshiped (he illustrated with Demeter, Dionysus, Hephaestus).

[13] Mario Untersteiner, *The Sophists,* trans. by Kathleen Freeman (Oxford: Basil Blackwell, 1954).

When such views got him in trouble with the authorities, Prodicus busied himself with linguistic studies, and founded the science of synonyms.

Hippias was a widely read scholar interested in the history of the sciences. He made contributions to mathematics, perfected the mnemonic system invented by Simonides of Ceos, and developed numerous ingenious practical contrivances. In the course of studies of the history of civilization, he sharpened a distinction between divine, universal, and moral law and the rules of human morality based on it. This Natural Law was counterposed to *nomos*—law and usage in the conventional sense. He wrote that often *nomos* does violence to the law of nature. Conventional law can be measured and corrected by natural law. Foundations were being laid for social criticism. Hippias looked beyond the confines of the city-state to a community of mankind.

Gorgias seems to have been led into skepticism by Zeno's dialectic, for he accepted his arguments but not his pantheistic conclusions. He argued that nothing exists; if it did, it could not be known. If it were known, it could not be communicated. The subtle epistemology in which he presumably developed this nihilism has been largely lost. Gorgias also contributed to aesthetics and poetics. He discovered the psychology of suggestion which he viewed as a powerful instrument to sway men's minds. (Illusion could be a mechanism of social influence.) He distinguished justifiable deception in an ethical and in an aesthetic sense. Out of Gorgias' teaching on truth and morality, two opposed theories developed: the idea of natural law as the might of the stronger, and the laws are the work of weaker men who impose order on the stronger natures like beasts of prey; also the idea that law is at bottom a contract by which right is guaranteed. On the basis of the second interpretations, slavery was condemned.

The sophists' teachings mark a turning point in Greek thought. The method of the old physicalistic philosophies was deductive. By contrast, the sophists sought to amass knowledge from all departments of life as a basis for theoretical and practical conclusions

> . . . like those on the possibility or impossibility of knowledge, on the beginning and progress of human civilization, on the origin and structure of language; and partly of a practical nature such as on the appropriate and efficient arrangement of the life of the individual and society. Its method then was empirico-inductive.[14]

At times the sophists have been described as the world's first sociologists and anthropologists. In any case they were a component in the shift of emphasis from the divine and naturalistic to the human sphere.

> Many problems will be seen to have been inadequately dealt with by sophists. Thought has still a long way to go. But the sophists must still

[14] Eduard Zeller, *Outlines of the History of Greek Philosophy* (New York: Meridian Books, 1955), p. 94.

be given credit for having conceded man the right to a human life, human speech, and human thought.[15]

The Socratics

Socrates was born in 470 B.C.[16] His father was a sculptor, and his mother was a midwife. He learned his father's trade, and fought as a soldier in the Peloponnesian War. He appears to have preferred to stand around and argue in the market place rather than ply his trade. His criticism of the democratic constitution and his constant cross-examination of people in the streets made him many enemies. He was eventually impeached on the grounds of his corruption of the young. His defiance of the legal procedure and criticism of the judges were probably components in his condemnation. Socrates founded no school, set down no writing, and developed no consistent philosophy. His views must be inferred from the writings of Plato and Xenophon. The *Apology* of Plato and the speech of Alcibiades in the *Symposium* are the best sources of pure Socratic thought.

Aristotle attributed to him the development of the process of induction, definition, and the founding of ethics, which is an indication of the respect Aristotle had for Socrates rather than an adequate judgment. Socrates rejected natural science, and showed no inclination to employ inductive procedures in human affairs. He was preoccupied with the problem of self-knowledge to which his dialectical method of examination was addressed. Socrates' dialectic rested on an assumption of innate ideas. At the same time, in distinctly sophistic vein, he was critical of anything founded on tradition. These things hang together if one grants the assumption that there are innate truths intrinsic to the mind itself, not discovered by scientific study, but by self-examination. In the same manner, Socrates was convinced that behind morals there is a system of fixed principles for the communal life of man.

After Socrates' death a number of minor schools appeared that trace their lineage to him. The most important, the Cynic school under Antisthenes (445–365 B.C.), rejected science, insisting that virtue is all that is required for happiness. Virtue is a matter of action rather than of knowledge. The Cynics despised learning, mathematics, and natural science. Their mission was seen by the Cynics as the assistance of the morally corrupt. They became preachers and soul-healers, denouncing the folly of mankind (which included sophistication).

The Cyrenaic school of Aristippus of Cyrene (436–355 B.C.) followed a different lead from Socrates. Aristippus measured the value of knowledge by its practical utility. Mathematics was scorned, physical science was without value, epistemology was useful only as the basis of ethical systems. The crowning principle of his ethics was that all action should be directed to obtaining the greatest possible pleasure.

15 Untersteiner, *op. cit.*, p. xvi.
16 Cornford, *op. cit.*, pp. 29–53.

Plato

Plato (427–347 B.C.)[17] was born of aristocratic Athenian parents tracing descent to Codrus and Solon and relatives of Charmides and Critias. He received a genteel education, and possibly served in the cavalry. At an early age he displayed significant poetic talent, but came under the influence of Socrates at the age of twenty. He seems to have traveled to Egypt. He became friends with Philolaus and Archytas, and frequented the court of Dionysius I. Dionysius, however, was poor material for a philosopher king, and Plato returned in disappointment from his sojourn in Syracuse. On his return, Plato landed at Aegina, which was at war with Athens. He was seized and sold in the slave market, but was ransomed by friends. On his return, he set up the Academy. Plato paid two more visits to Syracuse in the hope of winning over the successor, Dionysius II, to his ideal of a philosopher king. This plan also proved in vain, and he finally returned permanently to his teaching and writing.

The Academy was organized along the lines of the Pythagorean order. Master and pupils formed a religious guild dedicated to the Muses. The pupils lived in small houses in the garden of the Academy. Study began in the early morning. Plato invented an alarm clock to summon the pupils to the lecture hall.

Plato's thought represented one culminating point of previous tendencies. Socrates, Heraclitus, the Pythagoreans, and Eleatics were among his more important sources. From Socrates was taken the ethical preoccupation with the good life; from Heraclitus the conception that the world of appearance is in constant change. From the Pythagoreans, Plato took over the fundamental dualism of spirit and matter. From the Eleatics (particularly Parmenides), he adopted the idea that true reality is timeless and unchanging. These were woven into an idealistic system of philosophy resting on the dualism of mind and matter, body and soul, god and the world. True reality inhered only in the mental; at best the material world was an imitation of the ideal.

Basic to Plato's theory of ideas was a sharpened distinction between conception and sense-perception, a distinction inspired by the search for knowledge of what is eternally unchangeable. The Heraclitan doctrine was applied to the world of sense; the doctrine of Parmenides to the world of thought. Plato's argument in *The Republic* was that we suppose the idea to exist when we give the same name to many things. In mathematics this is seen most clearly. However many examples there are of it, a mathematical form exists once and for all. Moreover, such forms cannot be derived from sense. We have an idea, for example, of a straight line. However, no actual line is ever precisely straight. Mathematical ideas are not supplied by sense

[17] Bertrand Russell, *A History of Western Philosophy* (New York: Simon & Schuster, 1945), 104–158; W. T. Stace, *A Critical History of Western Philosophy* (New York: St. Martin's Press, 1956), pp. 165–248; Zeller, *op. cit.*, pp. 133–171.

experience, but discovered by thought. They constitute a world of eternal and unchanging ideals.

How then, do we learn? Plato answered that all learning is recollection by the soul of ideas. This recollection is stimulated by perception of sensual things. Earthly phenomena are mere images of the world of ideas. In fact, they are real only insofar as they participate in the idea. The highest knowledge is mathematics. Thus the requirements of correct knowledge according to the Eleatics were fused with the Pythagorean conception of number as the essence of all things.

While his theory of ideas leaned toward the Parmenideans, Plato's religious orientation was Pythagorean. In the *Phaedo* he explored the dualism between reality and appearance, ideas and sensible objects, body and soul, with respect to its bearing on the problem of death. The soul was thought to be both pre- and post-existent to the body. The theory of recollection was taken as proof that the soul is at home in the world of ideas. In contrast to thinkers who argue that the soul is a mere harmony, which disappears like a musical composition the moment it is not being played, Plato argued that a soul has independent reality. Soul and body enter into only temporary combination. The soul *uses* the body as an instrument of perception. However, in this contact it tends to be dragged into the world of the changeable. By proper spiritual activity it is possible for the soul to return to itself and pass into the world of purity, eternity, immortality, and unchangeableness. Plato accepted the doctrine of the transmigration of souls. He believed that an impure soul will assume a lower status in the next life. It will become a ghost haunting the graveyard or enter the body of an animal according to its character. Only the true philosopher goes to heaven when he dies.

Plato's physics (or rather cosmogony) was an extension largely of Pythagorean doctrines. In *Timaeus* a Pythagorean astronomer relates the history of the world to the creation of man. The world being sensible cannot be eternal. The world was created by God, as a living creature having soul and intelligence. It rotated because circular motion is most perfect. The four elements—fire, air, water, and earth—were each represented by a number in proportion to the other; fire is to air as air is to water, etc. Being everlasting, the ideal cannot move, hence *time* was constructed as a moving image of eternity. It gave rise to days and nights. Time made possible the learning of numbers, for with the experience of day and night, months and years (knowledge of time) came the conception of number, and with this, philosophy.

There are four kinds of animals: gods, birds, fishes, and land animals. Gods are composed of fire. The fixed stars are divine and eternal animals. There is one soul for each star, and if a man lives well he goes forever to his star; if not, he is born again as some lower form of creature. One kind of cause is self-moved (intelligent), the other is moved by others. Space is intermediate between the world of essence and the world of transient sensible things. It is "a third nature" which is "eternal and admits not of destruction and provides a home for all created things."[17a]

The true elements of the material world are not earth, air, fire, and water, but two kinds of right triangles. Originally, before the elements were arranged to form the universe, everything was in confusion. God fashioned them by form and number. By means of the two triangles it was possible to construct four of the five regular solids. Atoms of earth are cubes: of fire, tetrahedra; of air, octahedra; and of water, icosahedra. The dodecahedron was used by God in the delineation of the universe. Man has two souls, an immortal soul and a mortal one. The mortal soul is subject to affections, pleasure, pain, rashness, fear, anger, hope; it is located in the breast. The immortal soul is located in the head.

If Parmenides and Heraclitus were primarily important for Plato's theory of knowledge, and Pythagoras for his cosmology, Socrates was most important for his theory of the state. While the nominal purpose of *The Republic* was to inquire into the nature of justice, on the theory that society is the individual writ large, Plato passes on to a discussion of the state. The ideal republic was visualized by Plato as a communistic society under a class of philosophic guardians. The primary objective of the guardians was to secure the proper education of the young. There are three classes in all: in addition to the guardians, there are warriors and common people. The primary requirement of each is that it behave strictly in accordance with its station.

Education in the ideal society consisted of music and gymnastics. Education was intended to inculcate decorum and courage. Homer and Hesiod were not to be allowed because of various immoralities contained in them. The theater was not to be allowed because of its portrayal of villains. Moreover, the actor and dramatist have no place in the good society. The capacity of the actor to assume a variety of parts makes him suspect. Lydian and Ionian music were to be excluded, because they expressed sorrow, tenderness, and sensuous delight. Only Dorian and Phrygian melodies were to be permitted, because they inculcated courage and temperance.

Economically and socially the society was communistic. The guardians were to have small houses and simple food; they were to dine at public messes; they owned no private property; gold and silver were forbidden. There were to be no families; women and children were to be shared in common. At various times the population was to be brought together to breed. However, though this was apparently by lot, the guardians were to keep a sacred record and manipulate the breeding on eugenic principles. Children were to be taken from their parents at birth and reared in common so no one would know his own children. Deformed children were to be disposed of. Among the principles of control in the society was the employ-

[17a] *Timaeus,* quoted by Russell, *op. cit.,* p. 146.

ment of official myths. The fundamental myth was that God created three kinds of men—of gold, of silver, and of brass. The first were fit to be guardians, the second soldiers, and the third the common people. Sparta strongly influenced Plato's social thought.

Aristotle

Aristotle of Stageira (384–322 B.C.),[18] the son of Nicomachus, physician of the Macedonian king Amyntas, learned the principles of his father's art. In his eighteenth year Aristotle came to Athens and remained in the Academy for twenty years and until the death of Plato. He then founded a branch of the Academy in Assus in the Troas, where he taught three years. In 343 B.C. Aristotle was invited to Pella by Philip of Macedon to supervise the education of Alexander. Aristotle continued as tutor and adviser to Alexander until the latter's expedition to Asia. In 335 B.C. Aristotle settled at Athens, and founded his own school, the Lyceum, under Macedonian patronage. It grew into a considerable organization with a library, a staff of teachers, and a regular system of lectures. He worked here until shortly before his death.

The phase of Aristotle's thought which even in antiquity was taken as authoritative was his logic. The most significant part of this was his theory of inference which he described as "a statement, in which something new is derived from certain hypotheses" (*Anal. Pr.* 1, 24b, 18). These hypotheses are expressed in premises or propositions. Categorical judgments are divided into affirmative and negative (quality) and particular and general (quantity). He distinguished two kinds of opposition—the contradictory and the contrary. Aristotle proposed to investigate the possible ways in which propositions can be linked to permit valid inferences. This work led to his doctrine of the syllogism, an argument consisting of three parts—a major premise, a minor premise, and a conclusion.

While Aristotle recognized that there are some inferences that can be drawn from a single premise, he thought the syllogism covered most valid forms of deductive inference. Aristotelian logic became almost as stereotyped in Western thought as Nyaya logic in India. In addition to the *Prior Analytics*, Aristotle wrote the *Categories*, "expressions which are in no way composite." He listed nine: substance, quality, quantity, relation, place, time, state, action, and affection.

In the *Posterior Analytics* he took up the basic problem of epistemological theory, how first premises are obtained, which Aristotle believed involved isolating the *essence* of a thing. The essence consists of those properties of a thing which it cannot change without losing its identity. Definition rests in part on proof and in part on immediate knowledge. Concepts denote

[18] Richard McKeon (ed.), *The Basic Works of Aristotle* (New York: Random House, 1941); Russell, *op. cit.*, pp. 159–207; Stace, *op. cit.*, 249–338; Zeller, *op. cit.*, pp. 172–224.

something general, a constant property of things of a class. If a concept expresses what is common to many things of a different kind, it is a generic concept. If the distinctive properties of the species are added, the species is defined. The concept of essence basic to Aristotle's idea of the nature of definition is bound up in the closest way to his analysis of the problem of universals and his metaphysics.

Aristotle vigorously rejected Plato's view that ideas, the universal forms of our concepts, are the real thing. His most important argument, the "third man" argument, had already been sketched by Plato in *Parmenides*. If a man is a man because he resembles an ideal man, then there must be a third man to whom the first two are similar. This idea leads, of course, to an infinite regress. Aristotle's critique is that the idea is not something real apart from things. Only the particular is real. The idea is imminent rather than transcendent.

Aristotle then proceeded to analyze the distinction between form and matter, in the course of which he was to restore the doctrine of ideas in disguised form. If a man makes a bronze sphere, the bronze is the matter; sphericity is the form. Also, in a calm sea the water is matter; smoothness is the form. However, form does not mean simply shape. Aristotle maintains that the soul is the form of the body. Form means the unity of purpose. We learn, furthermore, that the form is the essence of the thing and its primary substance. Things increase in actuality by acquiring form. This theory is bound up with a distinction between potentiality and actuality. Bare matter has a potentiality for form. The mathematical ontology of Plato is replaced by a biological type.

The relation of form to matter is a clue to Aristotle's idea of motion or change. Motion is the realization of the potential. Every motion presupposes a moving element and the thing moved. Where form and matter come into contact, motion necessarily arises. The ultimate cause of motion can only lie in an unmoved mover. For Aristotle the world was a uniform whole working toward a definite end. The first mover can be only one, the final cause of itself. The basis of all motion lies in the Deity as the pure, perfect, and inexhaustible mind. The thought of God is the "thought of thought." Metaphysics deals with the unmoved and incorporeal. Physics studies the moved and corporeal—that which has the cause of motion in itself. Nature is the cause of motion. (Aristotle here treats nature as the real power in the world.) Motion is every change, every realization of a potential. There are four kinds of motion: substantial—coming into being and passing away; quantitative—increase and decrease; qualitative—change of one substance into another; spatial—change of place.

Space was defined as a thing. Time, like number, presupposed a soul that counts. Spatial motion is circular and uniform and perpetual without beginning or end. The end and the aim of development are from potentiality to actuality, the incorporation of form in matter. The real ground of natural objects is in their final causes. Aristotle insisted on the eternity of the world. The earth and the heavens are composed of different materials. The heavens consist of ether, the fifth element capable of no change except position, and only circular motion. Earthly things are composed of the four elements—earth, air, fire, water—which stand to one another in opposition—light to heavy (fire, air, water, earth) and qualitative: dry (earth and fire) vs. moist (water and air) and cold (earth and water) vs. hot (fire and air). Because of this opposition, things constantly pass from one into another.

The earth was thought to be at rest in the center of the universe. It is spherical in shape. In concentric layers around it are water, air, and fire. Then come the heavenly spheres. The days are produced by the deity which encompasses the world without occupying space. The friction caused by the motion of the heavenly spheres, especially those beneath the sun, produced light and heat. These varied according to the season and the inclination of the sun's path.

Aristotle devoted much work to biology. He thought that life consisted of the capacity for self-movement: a form that moves and a matter that is moved. The purposive activity of nature appeared most clearly in living things. The resistance of matter was only gradually overcome. The life of plants consisted in nourishment and reproduction; animals had in addition self-perception and locomotion; man had these capacities in combination with thought. The progressive increase in vital activities corresponded to the scale of living things.

Man was distinguished by mind, which was combined with the animal soul. Among the activities of the soul was perception—the communication of the form of perceived objects to the subject. The individual senses were assumed to provide accurate information about the quality of things. The common qualities of things, however, were obtained through all the senses, the "common sensory," in which the images produced by the sense organs were united; this organ was the heart. When motion in the sense organ continued beyond the time of the actual perception, the result was a renewal of the image of phantasy. An image copying an earlier perception was a memory. All such functions belonged to the animal soul. Man had the additional faculty of mind or thought. Man's soul was eternal. It entered into the soul-germ transmitted from the father to the child.

In the *Nicomachean Ethics* the aim of human activity was conceived to be happiness. The criteria of happiness, however, were not subjective feelings, but the objective character of life activities. The good of a creature consisted in the perfection of its activities, and thus the *Ethics* was brought into line with Aristotle's metaphysics. In man this meant the perfection of human activity, that is, reason. Activity consonant with reason was virtuous. The content of ethical virtue was determined by the fact that it was a constituent of the will, keeping to the mean proper to our nature and fixed by reason in the manner of a wise man. While founded in natural capacities, human activities became virtues only when guided by wisdom. A will was moral when it preserved the correct mean between excess and defect; this was the business of practical wisdom.

The basic presupposition of Aristotle's *Politics* was that man was a political (social) animal. He assumed a communal impulse natural to man. Man needed the community both for self-preservation and for the fullest self-development. In this last sense, the state was more important than (prior to) the individual and the family. However, in time, the family and the village developed before the state. Nature led man and wife to establish the household; families developed into village communities, and village communities into city communities. Within the city, institutions still played a part. Aristotle objected to Plato's demand that private property be sacrificed to the state.

Among the preconditions of the state were the family (propertied and individualized), slavery (which was expedient and right as well as necessary for the appropriate leisure), a rigorous control of trade (retail trade was a necessary evil), and the elimination of usury. There were thought to be different kinds of government in terms of the character and needs of the people. The constitutions were of six types: kingdom, aristocracy, polity, democracy, oligarchy, and tyranny. The ideal state was an aristocracy. Only those citizens with appropriate position and education shared in government; all manual labor was to be done by slaves and metics. Such an ideal state would combine oligarchic and democratic institutions and sustain prosperous middle classes as the core of civil life.

Finally, Aristotle even wrote a treatise on aesthetics, resting on the doctrine that art is imitation. Such imitation was not interpreted to mean the simple reproduction of sensual reality, but of its forms, types, or general laws. Poetic license was not only possible but necessary. Art had the function of portraying good men. The highest of the arts was tragedy, the function of which was the expurgation of the emotions of pity and fear.

The Historians

However rich the ancient Greek intellectual was philosophically, the ferment was by no means confined to the construction of philosophical systems. An unusually fruitful tradition of historical writing also developed.[19]

Herodotus (484–425 B.C.) was born at Halicarnassus in Asia Minor, then dependent on the Persians. His family belonged to the upper rank of citizens. He left Halicarnassus in voluntary exile, and undertook wide-ranging travels to Rhodes, Cyprus, Delos, Paros, Thasos, Samothrace, Crete, Samos, Cythera, and Aegina. He visited Susa and Babylon. In the

[19] Francis B. Godolphin, *The Greek Historians* (New York: Random House, 1942), 2 vols.; Croiset, *op. cit.*, pp. 150 ff.; 265 ff.; 295 ff.

north he got as far as the estuary of the Dnieper. He traveled to Scythia, Thrace, and Palestine, and stayed for a time in Egypt.

Herodotus was not the first historian. The Ionian philosophers and Hecataeus had been interested in systematic geography and chronology. At first Herodotus seems merely to have intended to record his travel observations. However, before his narrative had progressed very far, the idea was born of giving a systematic account of the conflict between the Greeks and Persians which impressed him as the momentous fact in Greek experience of his day.

Among Herodotus' sources were works of previous writers–Dionysius of Miletus, Hecataeus, and Charon of Lampsacus, and Zanthus, the Lydian. He made frequent references to monuments, dedicatory offerings, inscriptions, and oracles. In some instances Herodotus was able to interrogate participants in events; in others he was only able to consult traditions about them. The moralizing tendencies recurring in Herodotus' work may in part be due to frequent use of information gathered from temple priests. He occasionally had access to written material.

At times Herodotus uncritically intermixed fact with myth. As a general explanation of historical events, he had frequent recourse to the concept of nemesis. For example, the fate of the Persian monarch was attributed to the sequence of prosperity, insolence, folly, and disaster. The same pattern appeared in the stories of Solon and Croesus, Atys and Adrastus, Polycrates and Cypselus. Herodotus' account of military events was notoriously weak. However, he was sensitive to the influence of climate and social custom, and employed myths to yield insight into the ideologies of the time. The major difficulty with his history was a lack of critical orientation to source materials.

Thucydides, born somewhere between 471 and 460 B.C., was from a wealthy Athenian family which possessed gold mines at Scapte Hyle on the Thracian coast. He states that he was banished by the Athenians in 424 B.C. for failure to relieve Amphipolis, indicating that he was one of the generals elected to direct political and military affairs. Thucydides recounts the motives that inspired his history. He was convinced that the Peloponnesian War would prove to be more important than any other event of which the Greeks had a record. The whole of the Hellenic world was involved in one or the other side of the contest. He thought his work would be permanently valuable as one of the lessons of history.

Thucydides carefully considered the problem of method. He divided his predecessors into two classes: the epic poets (for example, Homer) whose aim was to glamorize the past, and the Ionian prose writers, chroniclers, whose object was to diffuse knowledge of legends and written documents preserved in public archives. The second group published their documents without criticism. (Herodotus seems to have been included in the category of chroniclers whose aim was to be popular rather than trustworthy.)

Thucydides carefully scrutinized his materials, attempting to adhere to facts:

> As to the deeds done in the war, I have not thought myself at liberty to record them on hearsay from the first informant or on arbitrary conjecture. My account rests either on personal knowledge or on the closest possible scrutiny of each statement made by others. The process of research was laborious, because conflicting accounts were given by those who had witnessed the several events, as partiality swayed or memory served them.[19a]

Thucydides located all causes of human beings within the human sphere. It was the historian's task to isolate the causes of events. He rejected the semireligious social causation of Herodotus. He also opposed Herodotus' use of monocausal explanations. Myths likewise were not history. Thucydides presupposed a plurality of causes in which basic need and political-power aspiration replaced the Herodotean *nemesis.* Poverty and population were major keys to the political development of early Greece. He recognized the profound significance of chance factors in shaping history, for example, the plague in Athens (II, 47–52). Chance was contingent and accidental, not a hypostatized fortune or providence (as with the Romans later). He often analyzed individuals quite apart from their personal qualities (for example, Themistocles, in I, 138). He did not assume that the state was some kind of superindividual.

Much dispute has arisen over Thucydides' use of speeches. He himself denied that they should be interpreted as *verbatim* reports (I. 22). They functioned in his account primarily as vehicles for the general conceptualization of events (such as the discussion of the relation of imperialism and expediency [VI. 85] or the Melian debate as the right of the stronger [V. 85]).

The whole history is objective, value free, scientific in spirit. More important than the events he thought to set down for all time was the method by which he set them down. He is the father of scientific history.

The Orators

A particularly vigorous form of the socially and politically relevant thought of ancient Greece was found in the orators, whose interpretations were publicly presented before the law courts, and sometimes printed and widely read. Among the famous orators were Antiphon (411 B.C.), Lysias, Andocides, Lycurgus, Hypereides, and Deinarchus. Two examples may indicate the kind of form and direction oratorical thought could take.[20]

Isocrates (436–338 B.C.) was the son of Theodorus. Plato had prophesied a brilliant future for him. Under the Thirty he withdrew to Chios. Before this he taught rhetoric for a living, having lost an inherited fortune in the

[19a] *Peloponnesian War*, Book I, Par. 22.

[20] Alfred and Maurice Croiset, *History of Greek Literature* (New York: The Macmillan Co., 1904), pp. 350–391.

disorder at the end of the Peloponnesian War. He returned to Athens at the time of the restoration of democracy. He wrote speeches for the law courts, a task which he despised. Isocrates was an active publicist of the idea of uniting all Greece for a concerted attack on Asia. He reasoned that since in Greece there was peace neither within nor between the cities, a Panhellenic invasion would obliterate political differences. He sought a coalition between Athens and Sparta. This failing, he looked to Dionysius I, Agesilaus, and finally Philip of Macedon.

Demosthenes was born in Athens in 384 B.C. His father left him a factory for the manufacture of swords and upholstery. This patrimony was largely dissipated before Demosthenes came of age. He became a special writer of speeches for the law courts.

Long before Macedonia had become an immediate threat to Athens, Demosthenes was sensitive to it. He was an ardent nationalist. His speeches for public causes and defense of special cases had a major influence on political policy. He demanded that domestic administration be purified, that statesmen be made responsible to the state, that the misappropriation of public money by partisans be ended, that foreign policy be more clearly adjusted to Athenian interests, that warfare cease to be a matter of mass opinion, and that foreign policy reflect true political interests.

The Philippics show progressive despair. All of Demosthenes' effort proved in vain, and Philip progressively succeeded. However, with the loss of his cause Demosthenes' work was by no means over. He became a member of the commission for strengthening the fortifications of the city. He administered the festival fund. He organized public relief. He was chief of the sacred embassy to Olympia, and served in other important capacities.

There was an important, continuing interplay between the speeches of orators and the thought of the philosophers. The dialogue, as a philosophical form, was modeled after the oratorical contest. Plato followed Isocrates as a style model.

The Dramatists

The same intellectual themes which absorbed the philosophers and orators penetrated the drama.[21] While tragedy remained more traditionalistic in orientation, it showed a rationalization of the old semireligious conceptualizations of fate, destiny, the conflict of human and divine requirements, and the consequences of overweaning pride (Aeschylus and Sophocles). It underwent a progressive shift toward more psychologically subtle interpretations of personality and events (Euripides).

In comedy the bold, sophisticated critique of social and political ideas and conceptions was undertaken. Aristophanes (448–385 B.C.), the un-

[21] Whitney J. Oates and Eugene O'Neill, *The Complete Greek Drama* (New York: Random House, 1938), 2 vols.; Croiset, *op. cit.*, pp. 164–264.

questioned master, was a citizen of the tribe Pandionis, the deme Cydathene. His father was a landowner in Aegina.

The critique of political policy of thought and society runs through his comedies. *The Acharnians* (425 B.C.) deals with the attempts by an honest simple man, Dicaeopolis, who in despair at his fellow Athenians determined to make a private peace for himself and his family with the Spartans. The cry against demagogues speaks out in *The Knights* (424 B.C.). Demos, the state, is represented as an old man who has put himself in the hands of a rascally steward. The slaves of Demos contrive that the Paphlagonian be supplanted by a sausage seller. *The Clouds* (423 B.C.) was an attack on the new type of intellectual sophistic inquiry. A youth sent by his father to be cured by Socrates of his dissolute tendencies became so accomplished in dishonest and impious skills that the father prepared to destroy the philosopher.

The Wasps (422 B.C.) was a satire on the love of litigation so characteristic of Athens. An old man with a passion for lawsuits was finally controlled by his son by the device of turning the house into a law court and paying his father for absence from the public suits. *The Peace* (421 B.C.) presented arguments for peace with Sparta. This same desire for peace was an underlying motive of *The Birds* (414 B.C.), which seemed in part a protest against religious fanaticism, in part a desire for the revival of the Athens of the past. The *Lysistrata* (411 B.C.) ingeniously proposed a women's strike to bring peace. The administration of the state by women, since it appeared that peace could be achieved no other way, was proposed by *The Ecclesiazusae* (393 B.C.).

Aristophanes idealized the Athens of the past. He detested mob violence and vulgarity. He upheld the old forms of worship, and viewed the new ideas with alarm. The best of his comedies are vital, biting, journalistic satire.

THE GENERAL CHARACTER OF ANCIENT GREEK INTELLECTUALITY IN THE CLASSICAL PERIOD AND ITS RELATION TO GREEK CIVILIZATION

The varieties and internal differences in the forms of Greek thought in the Classical period hardly need be underlined. If anything characterizes the ancient Greek intellectual, it is the eagerness with which he seizes upon alternatives and the boldness with which he develops them. The Milesians explored the possibilities of a striking naturalism. While Heraclitus argued that all was flux, the Eleatics developed logical proofs that nothing could be more illusory than change, for all is rest.

The sophists arrived at the highly interesting concept of natural law which was quickly developed into alternatives: (1) since force was the first law of human nature (an argument profoundly important to Hobbes), conservatism of social forms, conventions, is needed to secure one's personal situation against assaults by superior force; and (2) convention is a social bond imposed by the weak to restrain the strong (an anticipation of Nietzsche's distinction between master and slave morality). Other sophists insisted that in nature all men are (within limits) equal, and individual freedom is the first law of nature. Slavery, a fundamental economic institution of antiquity, was attacked.

While the earlier philosophers approached human problems from the standpoint of nature, the sophists placed all emphasis upon human affairs. They were sociologists, ethnologists, and students of the history of civilization. While groups, for example, the Pythagoreans, approached social affairs from the point of view of religion, the sophists (at least some of them) approached religion from the point of view of social affairs. Formulations (man made god in his own image, and if horses could think they would perceive their gods as magnificent types of horses, etc.) were a product of their relativism. The utilitarian interpretation of religion (that man worships what happens to be most important to his continued well-being) was advanced. Hence the argument was presented that the first gods were personifications of natural forces, later the gods were personifications of the technical arts. It is not unfair to see this as an anticipation of Comte.

The variety of cosmological interpretations is also noteworthy. The earth was presented as a flat disk floating on water, as a disk floating on air, as a cylinder, as a sphere, etc. The heavenly bodies were interpreted at times as deities (divine animals), but also as masses of hot stone, and even as only apparently distinct bodies, the reality being simply an aperture of light through the atmosphere of what was in fact a wheel of fire. The physical world was at times interpreted as consisting of atoms and void, but also as a plenum and cosmological phenomenon produced by a vortex in the plenum. Evolutionary interpretations of biological development were current. They varied from the bizarre view that various special limbs appeared first, being combined into all sorts of monstrosities, to the views that life appeared first in the primeval mud, that water creatures appeared before land creatures, and that men had fish as ancestors.

While the notion that the soul is immortal was fairly widely diffused, the contrary notion, that the soul is to the body as music to the violin, also appeared. Contrary to the notion found in Homer that after death the soul goes to Hades, where it lives a rather miserable bloodless existence and can be evoked only by blood sacrifice, there appeared both the conception of the transmigration of eternal souls and the idea that the soul cannot survive the body, but is dissipated with its disintegration.

Conceptions of the utility of knowledge both for salvation and as the primary implement of betterment in this world were widespread. But this, too, had its critics, and the alternative view was that man was an irrational animal, and thinking more obfuscating than helpful.

Pantheistic theologies were opposed by theistic conceptualization. Philosophical monism was countered by dualism and pluralism. Vitalistic theories were opposed by rather thoroughgoing mechanistic positions.

A case in point of deliberate opposition is presented by the great summary philosophers, Plato and Aristotle. Aristotle quite evidently set out to modify the opinions of his teachers. Plato held a realistic conception of universals; Aristotle argued that universals can be found only *in res*. Knowledge for Plato was primarily an affair of recall. For Aristotle it was, in some contexts, primarily an affair of discovery. Plato presented arguments for a communistic ownership of property; Aristotle could not visualize an adequate society without private property. Plato argued for a community of wives; Aristotle for the individualized family.

Nor was the opposition confined to the persons identified later as philosophers. Among the historians, for example, while Herodotus looked for the interpretation of social events in single causes (like *nemesis*), Thucydides argued for pluralistic causal interpretations. While Herodotus specified climate and geography as important causal factors in history, Thucydides conceived of history primarily in terms of the imminent development of social processes, rejecting external causation. Opposition, too, was evident among the orators; and while Isocrates looked for the imperial integration of Greece, Democritus consistently fought for an Athenian nationalism.

The universal love of innovation was satirized by Aristophanes. He built a comedy around the notion that the women in complete despair at the inability of men to run the state smoothly decided to enter into a plot to take over the reins of government. He has one of the characters make the observation that at least this seems to be the only possible thing that has not been tried so far.

The common properties in Greek thought are not to be found in a system of concepts or even in a special problem to which it was addressed. One striking general feature of Greek mentality is the unusual role that observation played in their thought. The Greek intellectual was often a practically oriented person. To Thales, for example, is attributed the extension of the doctrine of similar triangles to the problem of the measurement of ships at sea. Another tale concerning him (related by Aristotle) is that in the off-season he rented all the olive presses and charged monopolistic prices when the olives came in season. This was presumably to prove, after being taunted for impracticality, that a philosopher can make a fortune any time he wishes. Everyday observation is quite evident in Anaximenes' interpretation of natural change. In central focus in his position was the assumption that physical changes were brought about by condensation and rarefaction. Air, he argued, under pressure becomes water, under still more pressure earth; rarefied, it becomes fire.

The Pythagorean discovery of the laws of vibrating strings rested on observation. According to the anecdote, Pythagoras chanced by a blacksmith shop when he heard chimes ring out from the hammers. And as the tale goes, he theorized first that the notes produced by the hammers were proportional to the strength of the men, but disproved that by having them exchange hammers. He then weighed them, and discovered them to be in the proportions of 12, 9, 8, 6. The fifth hammer bore no significant numerical relation to the rest, and was spoiling the perfection of the chime. The heaviest hammer was double the weight of the lightest, and produced the octave. The harmonic and arithmetic means were clues to the other fixed notes of the scale. Ignoring the confusions in the account and the apocryphal nature of the anecdote, Pythagoras or members of the school did apparently experiment on vibrating strings. In quite another area experimental discoveries were made. It is told, for example, of Alcmaeon of Croton (a physician of the Pythagorean school), that he performed dissection and vivisection. To him is attributed the discovery of the optic nerve.

The thinkers of Greece sometimes gave sources for their ideas that would have appeared scandalous elsewhere. Empedocles, for example, urged that the mixing of paints, the making of bread, and the sling were sources for his idea. He also experimented with the clepsydra, the water clock, and demonstrated that if the open end were put into the water while one closed the hole in the top of the cone, no water entered. He thus demonstrated that air was corporeal. This discovery was made during an attempt to demonstrate experimentally a theory of the movement of the blood.

Another type of use of demonstration of the corporeality of air was utilized by Anaxagoras. He filled bladders with air and tried to compress them. He urged that this proved the existence and corporeality of elements too subtle for the eye to perceive. This point was important for the development of atomistic theories in classical Greece.

Thoroughgoing naturalism is nowhere more evident than in the school of Hippocratic medicine. In the tract, *On Ancient Medicine*, an unknown writer argues:

> The fact is that sheer necessity has caused men to seek and to find medicine, because sick men did not, and do not, profit by the same regimen as men do in health. To trace the matter yet further back, I hold that not even the mode of living and nourishment enjoyed at the present time by men in health would have been discovered, had a man been satisfied with the same food and drink as satisfy an ox, a horse, and every animal save man, I mean the raw products of the earth—fruits, leaves, and grass.

In early times, he speculates, life must have been rough. He traces the origin of medicine to food experimentation:

> Formerly indeed they probably suffered less, because they were used to it, but they suffered severely even then. The majority naturally perished, having too weak a constitution, while the stronger resisted longer, just as at the present time some men easily deal with strong foods, while others do so only with many severe pains. For this reason the ancients seem to have sought for nourishment that harmonized with their consti-

> tution, and to have discovered that which we use now. So from wheat, by winnowing, grinding, sifting, steeping, kneading, and baking it, they produced bread, and from barley they produced cake. Experimenting with food they boiled or baked, they mixed and mingled, putting strong pure foods with weaker until they adapted them to the power and constitution of man. For they thought that from foods which are too strong for the human constitution to assimilate will come pain, disease, and death, while from such as can be assimilated will come nourishment, growth, and health. To this discovery and research what juster or more appropriate name could be given than medicine, seeing that it has been discovered with a view to health, well-being, and nourishment of man, in place of that mode of living from which came the pain, disease, and death?[22]

The same author draws distinctions between symptoms and their interpretation, viewing science as a fusion of theory and observation. He objects to arguments that start from a speculation rather than from observation. As against simplistic interpretations, he urges the complexity of empirical phenomena. He finds lack of knowledge of technique inexcusable.

There were, to be sure, strong forces operating against observational and experimental approaches to problems. These were formulated by the Eleatics, by the Pythagoreans (in spite of the above examples), and particularly by the great synthesists, Plato and Aristotle. However, Aristotle himself introduced the doctrine of fourfold causes, which would require observation for full understanding. He was a rather systematic observer himself, particularly in his biological studies. He is said to have commissioned Alexander to send back specimens of various things from his war campaigns.

In spite of strong forces to the contrary (forces which eventually prevailed), Greek thought shows greater observation and tendency toward experiment than has been observed hitherto. The demand to "get the facts" is evident in quite another sphere. Greece of the time showed an extraordinary growth of the disciples of ethnography, geography, biography, and history. Map-making progressed to a hitherto unparalleled degree and this, of course, poured back into practice, for such maps had commercial use. The demand for biographies flowed from the wish to know more about the important persons. Herodotus was himself something of a geographer and ethnographic student.

Thucydides took for granted that everyone would be interested for all time in the Peloponnesian War, and saw the reason for it not simply in that it involved the Greeks but a large number of the barbarians as well. He surveyed the conditions of the Greeks prior to the war, treating this survey as mere conjecture because of the state of the evidence. He indicated, incidentally, some of the primary principles of interpretation that he employed. Where the soil was barren there was ever a tendency for migration

[22] Quoted by Benjamin Farrington, *Greek Science* (Harmondsworth: Penguin Books, 1944), pp. 60–61.

(Thucydides, I, 2), whereas when the soil was good the original population tended to remain. He estimated, using Homer as a source, that there was no unity among the Greeks in early times, and that the name, Hellens, only became current later (I, 3). He believed early society was dominated by powerful chiefs, and the economy by piracy. He assumed that everyone at that time had to go about armed (I, 5–6). He viewed the accumulation of wealth and the establishment of fortified cities at ports as reactions to opportunities for trade and the danger of piracy (I, 7).

> Men do not discriminate, and are too ready to receive ancient traditions about their own as well as other countries. For example, most Athenians think that Hipparchus was actually a tyrant when he was slain by Harmodius and Aristogeiton; they are not aware that Hippias was the eldest of the sons of Pisistratus, and succeeded him, and that Hipparchus and Thessalus were only his brothers. At the last moment, Harmodius and Aristogeiton suddenly suspected that Hippias had been forewarned by some of their accomplices. They therefore abstained from attacking him, but wishing to do something before they were seized, and not to risk their lives in vain, they slew Hipparchus.[23]

Among the dangers to an adequate understanding of historical fact were myths and uncritical reports. The student

> . . . must not be misled by the exaggerated fancies of the poets, or by the tales of chroniclers who seek to please the ear rather than speak the truth. Their accounts cannot be tested by him.[24] (I, 21)

With respect to the presumed speeches of important persons introduced by Thucydides, concerning which there has been much dispute, he observed:

> As to the speeches which were made either before or during the war, it was hard for me, and for others who reported them to me, to recollect the exact words. I have therefore put into the mouth of each speaker the sentiments proper to the occasion, expressed as I thought he would be likely to express them, while at the same time I endeavored, as nearly as I could, to give the general purport of what was actually said.[25] (I, 22)

As to his own standards of fact, Thucydides stated:

> Of the events of the War, I have not ventured to speak with any chance information, nor according to any notion of my own. I have described nothing but what I either saw myself, or heard from others of whom I made most careful and particular inquiry. The task was a laborious one, because eye witnesses of the same occurrences give different accounts, as they remembered or were interested in the actions of one side or the other.[26] (I, 22)

A passion for facts and high standards of evidence was basic.

These two things, the inclinations toward a scientific method which,

[23] Francis Godolphin, *The Greek Historians* (New York: Random House, 1942, I, 20), Vol. I, p. 575.
[24] *Ibid.*, p. 576.
[25] *Ibid.*, p. 576.
[26] *Ibid.*, p. 576.

though abortive, were still distinct and the very positive trend toward a critical historical methodology, are major clues to the unifying element in Greek thought. It was most distinctive of the extent to which it was methodologically conscious.

In none of the other areas examined has there been such systematic survey of previous opinion in the development of thought systems. Theorizing develops in terms of a systematic examination of alternatives. Quite apart from other aspects of their philosophy, the Eleatics show the search for a standard proof. In this instance proof was taken as logical demonstration. The Eleatics discovered the logical principle of self-contradiction. The Socratic method was projected as an implement of truth. To be sure, it makes sense only on the theory of innate ideas which self-examination can reveal. In the contemporary age this method would be considered at best an implement for arriving at one's basic presuppositions, and such presuppositions would not for a moment be confused with empirical knowledge of the world. However, in its time it was famous for the search for a dependable method of knowledge. The investigations of language and the principles of rhetoric by the sophists were *not* just the work of cynics who cared about nothing more than "winning an argument" (or a case in court), but attempts to isolate a dependable intellectual implement. Aristotle's logic (which was in large measure the summary of previous theories) aimed at establishing the method of knowledge. Aristotle, moreover, carried to a high point the procedure of surveying previous opinion as a preliminary to the statement of problems and the projection of his own solutions. The common traits of Greek thinking are found in the fusion of bold speculation with sharpened methodological consciousness.

This is no place to trace the details of the civilizational synthesis of the classical Greeks, of which Greek thought was only a single, though most vigorous, part. Fortunately, so many brilliant studies have been made of special aspects of Greek civilization that almost any will suffice for our purposes. Over and again the students of Greek civilization have found in one cultural area after another the same general traits which are found in its social thought: a sense of form or order, an insistence on visualizing clearly the relation of parts to the whole, a dominance of reason over emotion, an ideal of balance.

> The sentences which Plato says were inscribed in the shrine at Delphi are singularly unlike those to be found in holy places outside Greece. *Know thyself* was the first, and *nothing in excess* the second, both marked by a total absence of the idiom of priestly formulas all the world over.[27]

As Edith Hamilton saw the matter, the Greeks were intellectualists with a passion for using their minds. This, she felt, was the central clue to their poetry as well as their philosophy.

[27] Edith Hamilton, *The Greek Way* (New York: W. W. Norton, 1930), p. 31.

> System, order, connection, they were impelled to seek for. An unanalyzed whole was an impossible conception for them. Their very poetry is built on clarity of ideas with plan and logical sequence.[28]

Greek art, she argued, "is intellectual art, the art of men who were clear and lucid thinkers."[29]

> The Greek temple is the perfect expression of the pure intellect illumined by the spirit. No other great buildings anywhere approach its simplicity. In the Parthenon straight columns rise to plain capitals; a pedimont is sculptured in bold relief; there is nothing more. And yet—here is the Greek miracle—this absolute simplicity of structure is alone in majesty of beauty among all the temples and cathedrals and palaces of the world.[30]

The same demand, according to Hamilton, gave Greek prose a stripped-down directness rarely seen elsewhere. And the same traits are found in the Greek drama as in its temples.

> They saw people simplified, because, just as in the case of their temples, they saw them as part of the whole. As they looked at human life, the protagonist was not human; the chief role was played by that which underlies the riddle of the world, that necessity which brings us here and takes us hence.[31]

Thus Hamilton feels that the accidental and the trivial dropped away, and only the universally human emerged.

Very similar estimates to those of Hamilton are made by Kitto, who maintained that logic and clarity are fundamental to the Greek sense of form.

> Equally obvious is the Greek love of symmetry . . . the irregularity of plan displayed by nearly every Gothic cathedral suggest to our minds the idea of dynamic energy, of life; to the Greek mind it would be abhorrent, suggesting only imperfection. . . . Or we may turn to Greek prose, with its passion for balance and antithesis, often indulged in to excess. . . . The Greek stylistic vice was not incapable shapelessness but bogus formalism.[32]

GREEK THOUGHT IN THE HELLENISTIC PERIOD

In the opinion of Stace, the most general property of Greek philosophy in the post-Aristotelian period is decay, a characteristic intimately related to the political, social, and moral events of the time.[33] He traces this decay in a new intense subjectivity and a decline of objectivity and uncommitted curiosity. "Philosophy only interests men insofar as it affects their lives. It becomes anthropocentric and egocentric."[34] All things in the new period

28 *Ibid.*, p. 35.
29 *Ibid.*, p. 158.
30 *Ibid.*, p. 60.
31 *Ibid.*, p. 203.
32 H. D. F. Kitto, *The Greeks* (Harmondsworth: Penguin Books, 1951), pp. 186–187.
33 W. T. Stace, *op. cit.*, pp. 339 ff.
34 *Ibid.*, p. 340.

tend to be subordinated to ethical concerns: "Metaphysics, physics, logic are not studied for their own sakes, but only as preparation for ethics."[35] The classical themes of rationality and balance decline in the face of a rising tide of intemperate mysticism.

> Hence the Neo-Platonists must needs cap all these tendencies by making out a drunken frenzy of the soul to be the true organ of philosophy, and by introducing into speculation all the fantastic paraphernalia of sorcery, demons, and demi-gods. Absence of sanity and balance, then, are characteristics of the last period of Greek philosophy.[36]

A lack of originality accompanied the subjectivism of Hellenistic thought. It ceased to advance along the lines laid down by the systems of the fifth and fourth centuries; and there was a tendency to revive old systems long discredited. One major trend was toward skepticism, the denial of knowledge, and the rejection of philosophy.

In contrast to the Golden Age of Greek philosophy, the Hellenistic world, in Russell's view, was inclined toward a specialization both in intellectual roles and in social thought. He notes that in the period of the autonomous city a Greek citizen could, on occasion, be called upon to play almost any of the civic roles: soldier, politician, lawgiver, or philosopher. Socrates had been a student of physics and a soldier, and was repeatedly involved in political disputes. Protagoras' activities varied from teaching aristocratic youths to drawing up a code of laws for Thurii. Plato, on occasion, tried his hand at practical politics, though he was primarily a leader of a genteel philosophic sect. Xenophon was a country squire, a general, and a writer. The Pythagorean mathematicians were also practical city planners. However, in the Hellenistic world, while there were "soldiers, administrators, physicians, mathematicians, philosophers . . . no one . . . was all these at once."[37]

The movements in Hellenistic thought can be marked by their step-by-step progress toward religious mysticism, tracing from Stoicism and Epicurianism through Skepticism to Neo-Platonism.[38]

Stoicism was founded by Zeno of Citium in Cyprus (343–262 B.C.).[39] From a Phoenician business family, he studied the doctrines of the Cynics (the Platonists accused him of plagiarism). Zeno was impatient of metaphysics. He developed a materialistic philosophy intended to cultivate virtue. Stoicism was preoccupied with cosmic determination and human freedom. Its general argument was that there is no such thing as chance;

[35] *Ibid.*, p. 341.

[36] *Ibid.*, p. 342.

[37] Bertrand Russell, *A History of Western Philosophy* (New York: Simon & Schuster, 1945), p. 224.

[38] See Paul Elmer More, *Hellenistic Philosophies* (Princeton: Princeton University Press, 1923); Zeller, *op. cit.*, pp. 207–315.

[39] More, *op. cit.*, pp. 65–94; Russell, *op. cit.*, pp. 252–270; Stace, *op. cit.*, pp. 344–353; Zeller, *op. cit.*, pp. 209–229.

events are determined by natural laws. God is not separate from the world, but is the soul of the world. Each man contains a part of the divine fire. In human life virtue is the sole good beyond health, happiness, or possessions. Freedom for man consists in emancipation of the self from mundane desires.

Epicureanism[40] was founded by Epicurus (341–270 B.C.), the son of an Attic *clerouch* born in Samos. He established schools at Mitylene, Lampsacus, and finally in Athens. Central to the Epicurean philosophy was the view that only pleasure is good. Knowledge, the pleasure of the mind, has some advantages over bodily pleasure. Virtue is either the prudent pursuit of pleasure or nothing. Justice consists in acting in such a way as not to incur the resentment of others. Active and passive pleasures were distinguished. The first consists in the attainment of a desire, the second in achieving a state of equilibrium. It is more prudent to pursue the second. The best of social pleasures is friendship. The Epicureans viewed, as the two greatest sources of fear, religion and the dread of death. They sought to disprove divine interference in human affairs. One need not fear death, they urged, because the soul perishes with the body.

Epicurus was a materialist. The world consists of atoms and void. Atoms have weight and are continually falling. The soul is material and composed of particles like breath and heat. Sensation is due to thin films thrown off by bodies which touch the soul-atoms. Epicurus accepted the existence of the gods, but was convinced they did not meddle with human affairs.

Skepticism is a form of doctrine denying the possibility of knowledge.[41] It was formulated as a school doctrine somewhat earlier than Stoicism and Epicurianism by Pyrrho, who had campaigned with Alexander in India. It sought not to advance but to disclaim thought. In this, Russell observes, it appealed to some groups:

> Skepticism naturally made an appeal to many unphilosophic minds. People observed the diversity of schools and the acerbity of their disputes, and decided that all alike were pretending to knowledge which was in fact unattainable. Skepticism was a lazy man's consolation, since it showed the ignorant to be as wise as the reputed men of learning.[42]

The skepticism founded by Pyrrho soon declined, but by then a similar doctrine was being taught at the school of Plato. Skepticism underwent a series of declines and revivals during the Hellenistic period.

> Without answering the arguments of the Skeptics, the ancient world turned aside from them. The Olympians being discredited, the way was left clear for the invasion of oriental religions, which competed for the favor of the superstitious until the triumph of Christianity.[43]

40 See Russell, *op. cit.*, pp. 240–251; Stace, *op. cit.*, 354–360; Zeller, *op. cit.*, pp. 230–241.
41 Russell, *op. cit.*, pp. 233–239; Stace, *op. cit.*, pp. 361–367; Zeller, *op. cit.*, pp. 241–245.
42 Russell, *op. cit.*, pp. 233–234.
43 *Ibid.*, p. 239.

Skeptics continued to be popular in special circles until the third century A.D.

Plotinus (205?–270 A.D.), the founder of Neo-Platonism, was the last great philosopher of antiquity. He was born in Egypt, and studied with the professors at Alexandria.[44] While Plotinus had great reverence for Plato (and for some others among the Greeks), he wrote in an atmosphere that was being transformed by the diffusion of Christianity then in its third century. Plotinus began the fusion of Platonic and Christian ideas which laid the foundations of medieval Catholic theology. The starting point for Plotinus' metaphysics was the Holy Trinity: The One, the Spirit, and Soul. The One is Supreme, followed by the Spirit, and the Soul. The first emanation from the One is *Nous* or thought, mind, reason. It is immediate intuition which thinks the One and thinks itself. From the *Nous* the World-Soul proceeds as a second emanation. It works rationally, though unconsciously inclining upward to the *Nous* and downward toward nature. Emanation is like light radiating from a center, shading into darkness. Matter is the basis for plurality and the cause of all evil. The object of all life can only be to escape from the material world by a process of liberation beginning with the freeing of one's self from domination of the body and senses by means of thought, reason, and philosophy acquiring an intuition of the *Nous*. These doctrines were elaborated and modified by later Neo-Platonists—Porphyry, Iamblichus, Syrianus. "The essential character of Neo-Platonism comes out in its theory of the mystical exaltation of the subject to God."[45]

> Plotinus is both an end and a beginning—an end as regards the Greeks, a beginning as regards Christendom. To the ancient world, weary with centuries of disappointment, exhausted by despair, his doctrine might be acceptable, but could not be stimulating. . . . The work of transmitting what could survive of his philosophy was performed by the Christian philosophers of the last age of Rome.[46]

The brightest part of the thought of the Hellenistic period belongs not to the trends in philosophy which move from individualistic subjectivism through skepticism toward religious mysticism, but in the specialized technical work under the patronage of the rulers of the Hellenistic world. With the first Ptolemy, the center of the scientific world shifted to Alexandria, where under the Library and the Museum the kings aimed at collecting a copy of every Greek work in existence. Many of the finest scholars of the Hellenistic world were attracted there, the greatest of whom, perhaps, was Archimedes (a Sicilian from a still free city-state). Eratosthenes was chief librarian. The notable array of specialists included Euclid, Aristarchus, Archimedes, and Apollonius. While many of these scholars brought the knowledge in their specialties into able synthesis, except for Archimedes of

[44] More, *op. cit.*, pp. 172–259; Russell, *op. cit.*, pp. 284–297; Stace, *op. cit.*, pp. 368–377; Zeller, *op. cit.*, pp. 290–315.

[45] Stace, *op. cit.*, p. 376.

[46] Russell, *op. cit.*, p. 297.

Syracuse and Hiero of Alexandria there was little original work done in the fields of physics, chemistry, and biology.

> Perhaps the largest part of the work of the Alexandrian scholars was in the fields of philology, grammar, and literary criticism. And in this atmosphere of analysis, research, and learning there was produced a vast literature. Alexandrian poetry consisted in the main of short, highly polished poems—epigrams, idylls, elegies, and the like—with few epics, nearly all poetry of erudition rather than of insight and inspiration.[47]

The philosophic traditions of Alexandria were typified by eclecticism.[48] Teachers from different places and with varied training and opinions met at Alexandria: missionary cynics, indifferent skeptics, heirs of the ancient creeds of Egypt, exponents of Eastern teachings, Jews settled in Egypt from the time of Jeremiah and later Christians, and many others.

> Amid all this interchange of ideas, schools of thought lost their rigidity and sharp definition. Plato could even be reconciled with Aristotle; the worship of Serapis with the worship of Christ.[49]

With the collapse of the autonomous city-state, the multiple-dimensioned role of the free citizen ceased to operate at the orienting point of Greek intellectuality. Intelligence was narrowed, specialized, personalized, and turned inward on itself. So far as it could assume general form, it became a jigsaw puzzle of eclectic fragments from many schemes and systems. The thought system of the Hellenistic period lacked the joyous excitement of the early intellectual adventures. They tended to be cheerless philosophies of despair, teaching resignation in the face of suffering or the pursuit of discretely ordered pleasures. Scholarship does not look forward to new conquests, but nostalgically backward to the past.

SUMMARY

In the three major historical periods of ancient Greek development the types of societies and social roles which dominated in each provided very different *milieux* for the development of social thought.

In the Heroic period within the semifeudal conquest communities a variety of semireligious, semihistorical materials were produced which reflected the facts of conquest and the amalgamation that was occurring between Greek and pre-Greek social and cultural elements. The epics, the *Iliad* and *Odyssey*, portray the increasing self-awareness of the Greeks during this time. They were assembled as semisacred books by the authorities and scholars of later times because of their capacity to instruct and inspire through heroic examples in ritualistic and oracular matters as well as in all affairs that involved the Greek as Greek. The religious poetry of Hesiod, which was collected for the same reason, portrays developments

[47] Lavell, *op. cit.*, p. 281.
[48] Tollinton, *op. cit.*, p. 14.
[49] *Ibid.*, p. 15.

toward the close of the Heroic period. Their major function was to rationalize a great mass of folk religiosity within the framework of the Olympic religion. Materials, such as those found in Homer and Hesiod, were created in the Heroic Age by semireligious figures: by bards and priests and prophets. The assemblage of these materials during the early classical period was the work of their heirs, the chresmologists.

Though the Greek conquest was in part implemented, as in Israel, by religious confederation (amphictyony) and though a cult center was established in Delphi which operated somewhat similarly to Jerusalem, no equivalent synthesis of religious and socio-political developments was achieved. An important move in that direction occurred at the time the Delphic oracle appealed to the Amphictyony of Anthela against the domination by the city of Crisa. The First Sacred War (590 B.C.) in transforming Delphi into a ward of the amphictyony launched it upon a career of unprecedented prosperity. For a time it appeared that the fusion of Delphi and the political structure of the whole of the ancient Greek world was in the making.

It is interesting to speculate on the kinds of developments which would have thrust Delphi into a situation fully equivalent with Jerusalem in the Jewish royal period. Perhaps if their fortunes had been linked with a city-state able to coordinate the Greek world (as was accomplished in China by the state of Ch'in), this might have occurred. As it was, Delphi backed the political aspirations of Lydia and suffered a major loss of prestige when it was destroyed by Persia. The Delphic authorities then drew the wrong conclusions from this setback and counciled nonresistance to the rest of the Greek world in the face of direct Persian aggression. A section of the Greek cities rejected their own religious authorities. Thereafter the Delphic oracle went into a slow spiral of declining prestige.

Events in Greece thus moved in a way which tended to minimize the role of religious authorities in intellectual life. Though a variety of chresmologists (representatives of the Pythia, noble [Eupatrid] families with hereditary religious prestige, and free-lance religious experts) appear, and though consulted with respect to problems of traditional law, the religious intellectuals suffered a general decline of prestige before a flowering secular intellectuality. In terms of comparisons with other world areas, it was as if the kind of thinkers represented by the She Che in China, the promulgators of the doctrines of Carvaka in India, or the kinds of writers that produced Ecclesiastes in Israel had become the primary bearers of intellectual development.

As a result of the displacement of the center of conceptual activity to the secular strata of the city-state, major properties of Greek thought in the classical period were fixed. The Greeks developed a system of social thought adjusted to the self-governing polis. The polis was the presupposed whole within which the relation of every part was sought. Clarity, logical interrelation, and balance within a clearly formulated whole were the traits most treasured in a system of thought or a system of social life. The same system of traits has been traced throughout all of the main features of the civilizational synthesis of Greece in the classical period—in the poetry, prose, literature, art, painting, and architecture.

Related also to the secular standing of much of Greek thought was the unusual extent to which it had to be established on the basis of internal criteria, that is, in terms of the manner of conduct of the thought process itself. This pressed Greek thought on a course that led to the isolation of the rational proof. The elements of rational clarity and methodological self-sufficiency were even applied by the Greeks to religion, and it was reported that over the entrance of the Delphic oracle the Greeks had inscribed two maxims: *know thyself* and *nothing in excess.*

In the Hellenistic period, the city ceased to be a fully autonomous community, being converted into a semiautonomous administrative unit of the empires. Intellectual life lost its brilliant amateur standing, and was converted into forms of expertness. Though Hellenism was transformed into an instrument of the cultural policies of the Macedonian and Roman emperors, it seemed to lose in depth what it gained in extension. It hardened into a shell from which its ancient spirit drained away. The social roles of the Greek intellectuals were increasingly penetrated once more by prophets and mystic religious types, and its thought was systematically displaced by many large and small formulas for salvation.

SELECTED BIBLIOGRAPHY

Cornford, Francis Macdonald, *Before and After Socrates* (Cambridge: The University Press, 1932).

Croiset, Alfred and Maurice, *An Abridged History of Greek Literature* (New York: The Macmillan Co., 1904).

Farrington, Benjamin, *Greek Science* (Harmondsworth: Penguin Books, 1944).

Hamilton, Edith, *The Greek Way* (New York: W. W. Norton, 1930).

Kitto, H. D. F., *The Greeks* (Harmondsworth: Penguin Books, 1951).

Kirk, C. S., and J. F. Ravin, *The Pre-Socratic Philosophers* (Cambridge: The University Press, 1957).

McKeon, Richard (ed.), *The Basic Works of Aristotle* (New York: Random House, 1941).

Oates, Whitney J., and Eugene O'Neill, *The Complete Greek Drama* (New York: Random House, 1938).

Russell, Bertrand, *A History of Western Philosophy* (New York: Simon & Schuster, 1945).

Tollinton, R. B., *Alexandrian Teaching on the Universe* (New York: The Macmillan Co., 1932).

Untersteiner, Mario, *The Sophists*, trans. by Kathleen Freeman (Oxford: Basil Blackwell, 1954).

Part VI

HUMANISTS AND SCIENTISTS IN THE WESTERN WORLD

Turning from the developments in the main cultural areas of the so-called Axial Period to the developments of society, the intellectual, and civilization in our own time, has both values and disvalues. Since we are still midway in the course of our own destiny, we cannot know for certain how it will come out; the eventual forms into which our civilization will finally crystallize are not yet fully clear.

Perhaps the most important disadvantage in the study of our own epoch is the lack of perspective that only time can give. In some respects, one's task is similar to that of attempting to choose the classics from the current crop of books which may turn out to be merely faddish or timely. The crises of the moment obscure the distinction between the trivial and the significant.

There are, on the other hand, great advantages in the analysis of our own times. We are dealing with facts that are a part of living experience. When one deals with the materials of a bygone age, he must not only be endlessly alert to separate interpretations of the facts from the facts themselves, but he must deal with distortions which tend to arise from the selective preservation of the facts themselves.

The greatest advantage of all to be gained by the application of the theory of social and cultural change to the present is the commitment of its propositions to an actual case of such change which is still in process. To ask the social scientist to make an exact prediction of the outcome of the present is as unreasonable as to ask a physical scientist to hazard a prediction as to exactly when and where a particular oak leaf will fall. There are unique as well as recurrent factors in the social and cultural developments of our times, just as there were between the developments of the various areas of the ancient world. Many of these uniquenesses defy all attempts at very definite predictions.

Our own times, however, are not without their prophets, oracles, seers, and soothsayers. Each year brings a new harvest of prophecies of the impending doom of Western civilization. Since we are armed with the tools of contemporary historical and social science, we are in a better position than the men of any previous period to estimate the potential scientific value of such prophecies, and more important, to establish with some exactness the recurrent and unique features of our own times.

It is already clear that there are numerous points in which our own development recapitulates features of the Axial Period. All of the axial civilizations had their origins in barbaric, semifeudal periods. So did our own. The critical movement toward a new civilization was heralded in the ancient world by the emergence of new communities; our own civilization first took shape with the rise of the Western city. The great creative period in the ancient civilizations lay in a time of community destruction and the formation of new communities. This process is paralleled and, in fact, is still under way in our own time.

16

THE CHANGING FORMS OF WESTERN SOCIETY

THERE were many similarities between the cycle of developments which came to a climax in classical Greek civilization and those which led to our own. The developments in ancient Greece opened with the movement of barbaric people against a more settled civilization; the development of recent Western civilization opened with the movement of Germanic peoples against the Greco-Roman world. The ancestral Greeks absorbed much of the culture of the world into which they moved; so, too, did the Germanic tribes which plundered Rome. In the interaction of tribes of ancestral Greeks and the more settled world they conquered, a semifeudal type of social system emerged. In the recent West, too, a feudal system forms the starting point for later developments. There were numerous other parallels which will appear in the course of the discussion.

AN OUTLINE OF HISTORICAL DEVELOPMENTS IN THE RECENT WEST

The Decay of Classical Society

The city-states of the classical Greek period were never able to solve the problem of living peaceably with one another, nor were they able to create stable political structures larger than the city-states. The empires put an end to this by reducing the cities to semiautonomous units within imperial structures. For a time, with the decline of intercivic conflicts and the creation of a new huge trade area coextensive with the Mediterranean world, an unusually high level of prosperity was realized. Moreover, Hellenism was employed as a deliberate cultural policy first by the Macedonians and then by the Romans. Such cultural policies were double-edged, and while a wide variety of primitives were "civilized," the Greco-Roman world was "barbarized."

> Kelts, Iberians, Rhaetians, Moors, Illyrians, Thracians were to some extent civilized by the culture of Greece and Rome, and achieved by its help a great advance in economic and civic organization as well as in education; Syrians, Egyptians, the inhabitants of Asia Minor only modi-

> fied to a certain extent their manners and views in order to meet the requirements of the Empire. But if the intermixture of tribes and their permeation by Graeco-Roman culture was in one sense a great progress, it was at the same time, but from another point of view, a decline; it was accompanied by a lowering of the level of the culture which exerted civilizing influence. While conquering barbarism and native peculiarities, Graeco-Roman culture assumed traits from its vanquished opponents, and became gross and vulgar in its turn.[1]

By the third century, however, a series of crises were added to the internal problem of culturally integrating the varied mass of barbarian peoples into the Roman system. Among these crises were the conflicts over the succession to the throne, conflicts between the armies and the provinces, and the barbarian invasions.

The great circuit of international trade in luxury goods produced in slave establishments of the Roman Empire was threatened from many sides. As the wars of conquest ceased, the prices of slaves began to rise so high as to threaten the slave industry. Moreover, the conflicts between various Roman forces on the one hand and barbarian invasions on the other jeopardized the security of the trade routes and also frightened away the capital and credit which would otherwise have been drawn into such commerce.

With a two-sided pressure on his activities, the mounting cost of production, and the increased cost from a hazardous commerce, the Roman merchant raised his prices so high that an edict of Diocletian attempted to establish maximum prices.

> The enactment itself dilates on the evil greed of avaricious producers and vendors, and declares in the name of the "fathers of human kind" that justice has to arbitrate and to intervene. The Emperors are especially incensed at the hard bargains which are extorted from soldiers quartered in the provinces or moving along the road: prices are screwed up on such occasions not to four or eight times the ordinary value, but to an extent that could not be expressed in words.[2]

Diocletian's measure failed to accomplish its objectives, as shown by the need for additional legislation to prevent the concealment of goods and to guard against interruptions of trade. An ancient Roman black market was the result. In the fourth century Julian tried to force the citizens of Antioch to fair-trade practices, but also failed.

> The emperors and their bureaucracy had come to look on the whole civilized world subject to their authority as upon a besieged city, in which all civil professions had to conform to military rule.[3]

A hardening was evident throughout civil and economic life. Legislation was designed to require corporations to restrict members to their occupa-

[1] Paul Vinogradoff, "Social and Economic Conditions of the Roman Empire in the Fourth Century," in *The Cambridge Medieval History* (New York: The Macmillan Co., 1929), Vol. I, *The Christian Empire,* p. 544.

[2] *Ibid.*, p. 549.

[3] *Ibid.*, p. 550.

tions for life. The abandonment by single members of their residences and usual work came to be punished by law.

> The codices are full of enactments against fugitives . . . and such legislation would prove, by itself, that a *regime* of caste was being gradually established throughout the empire.[4]

For example, the *navicularii* were persons who devoted themselves to the transport of goods for the state (corn, oil, and wood for the public baths). When such services turned into unprofitable burdens and at best began to return only honors which were increasingly experienced as worthless, the *navicularii* began to abandon these services. When the state could not even operate its own services, its authority came under a cloud. In the end the state began to compel rich men to join the *corpus naviculariorum*, making the service hereditary and confiscating the property of anyone who absconded.

Similar changes were evident in the civil service. In contrast to the situation which existed earlier when leading citizens competed for public service, there was increasing reluctance to assume such duties. Once it lost political significance, municipal self-government ceased to be a proud privilege. It was experienced as a burden. Civic administration became corrupt. Wealthy citizens were forced to operate the civic services by expenditures on pageants, distribution of charities, and extravagant philanthropies. When they began to avoid such service by any possible means, the emperors instituted curators of a different kind. This complicated the bureaucracy but did not remedy the evil.

The majority of the middle-class townsmen constituted the *curiales* from whose ranks the city senators (*decuriones*), executive officials, and justices were selected. The most burdensome of their obligations was tax collection. If a *curial* could not collect the required amount, he was forced to make up the difference from his own pocket.

> The Codex Theodosianus and the Codex Justinianus contain rules of enactments of forbidding the *curiales* to leave the place of their birth, condemning them to hereditary subjection to municipal charge (munera), in fact turning their condition into a kind of serfdom. All the sons of a *curialis* had to follow their father's career; they were deemed *curialis* from the date of their birth.[5]

The climax of such "legislation of servitude," as Vinogradoff describes it, was reached when for some crime or misdemeanor people were enrolled in a *curia* as punishment.

The Religious Ferment and the Rise of Christianity

Many explanations have been offered for the fact that at the same time that the civic communities of the Hellenistic world were disintegrating, a

[4] *Ibid.*, p. 552.
[5] *Ibid.*, p. 556.

great religious ferment was taking place. This has, at times, been explained as a "failure of nerve." It has also been explained as a product of cosmopolitanism:

> During the earlier centuries of the Roman Empire the process of disintegration was completed which had begun with the conquests of Alexander the Great. Instead of a system of self-contained societies, solidly united internally and fenced off from all external social, political, and religious influences, which characterized ancient civilization, this age saw a mixing of peoples and a cosmopolitan society hitherto unknown.[6]

Lindsay argues that such cosmopolitanism was a product of the admixture of families from all lands of differing religions and the appearance of social habits which tended to melt down national, social, intellectual, and religious differences and incline thinking to eclectic mixtures. Most of the oriental faiths which spread over the Roman world had been influenced by Greek mysteries, particularly those of Dionysus and Eleusis. Most of the major ones, except that of Mithras, had been Hellenized. Lindsay describes the situation in the third century, at the time of the triumph of Christianity, as follows:

> From Asia Minor came the worship of Cybele with its hymns and dances, its mysterious ideas of a deity dying to live again, its frenzies and trances, its soothsayings, and its blood-baths of purification and sanctification. From Syria came the cult of the Dea Syra, described by Lucian, the sceptic, with its sacred prostitutions, its more than hints of human sacrifices, its mystics and its pillar saints. Persia sent forth the worship of Mithras, with its initiations, its sacraments, its mysteries and the stern discipline which made it a favorite religion among the Roman legionaries. Egypt gave birth to many a cult. Chief among them was the worship of Isis. Before the end of the second century it had far outstripped Christianity and could boast of its thousands where the religion of the Cross could only number hundreds. It had penetrated everywhere, even to far-off Britain. A ring bearing the figure of the goddess' constant companion, the dog-headed Anubis, has been discovered in a grave in the Isle of Man. Votaries of Isis could be found from the Roman Wall to Land's End.[7]

The Isis cult typifies the oriental religions of the period which replaced the Olympic cults of the city-state. It possessed an organized clergy, a prayer book, a code of liturgical actions and requirements (specifying tonsure, vestments, and ceremonials), an inner circle of the religious elite, and a sharp distinction between adherents and outsiders.

While the oriental mystery religions and Christianity were rising in popularity, the philosophic heirs to the systems of the Greek classical period were losing their characteristics of rational synthesis; they were being submerged in moralistic and mystical preoccupations. The two

[6] T. M. Lindsay, "The Triumph of Christianity," in *The Cambridge Medieval History* (New York: The Macmillan Co., 1929), Vol. I, p. 87.

[7] *Ibid.*, p. 90.

types of transformation (in popular religiosity and in genteel philosophic outlook) were not unrelated. As the city-state lost its properties as an ultimate synthesis of social life, it ceased to be the reference point for both popular religion and philosophic understanding. The oriental mystery religions were replacing the Olympic religions of the polis; the new ecclesiastical salvation doctrines were replacing the rational philosophies of polis-based intellectuals.

To attribute both types of changes (in popular religion and in philosophy) either to a failure of nerve or to a new cosmopolitanism is rather unconvincing. In the first place, men seem to have been no less courageous (or more cowardly) in this period than in the period of the city-state. These sentiments merely took a different form. Moreover, to attribute the rise of the mystery religions to a sudden increase of sophistication (cosmopolitanism) is hardly convincing, for there was less rather than more genuine cosmopolitanism at this time. There is little doubt that *they were responses to the loss of autonomy by the city-state.*

It was also true that during the whole period there was a growing realization that communities which had held life together and assigned them meaning were decaying and all efforts to stay this process were of no avail. Under these circumstances, the estimation of the rise of the oriental mystery religions and Christianity on the one hand and the displacement of the Hellenistic philosophies in the direction of salvation religiosity on the other hand takes on a new meaning. They were constructive attempts to put the world of the city-state together in the very teeth of its evident decay.

It has been noted that members of Roman society in the early Christian centuries often tried successively or simultaneously a variety of the cults.

> The tombstone of Vettius Agorius Praetextatus, the friend of Symmachus, who took part in the *Saturnalia* of Macrobius, records that he had been initiated into several cults and that he had performed the *taurobolium.* His wife, Aconia Paulina, was more indefatigable still. This lady, a member of the exclusive circle of the old pagan nobility of Rome, went to Eleusis and was initiated with baptism, fasting, vigil, hymn-singing into the several mysteries of Dionysus, of Ceres and Koré. Not content with these, she went on to Lerna and sought communion with the same three deities in different rites of initiation. She travelled to Aegina, was again initiated, slept or waked in the porches of the small temples there in the hope that the divinities of the place in dream or waking vision might communicate to her their way of salvation. She become a hierophant of Hecate with still different and more dreaded rites of consecration. Finally, like her husband, she submitted herself to the dreadful, and to us disgusting, purification won in the *taurobolium.* A great pit was dug into which the neophyte descended naked; it was covered with stout planks placed about an inch apart; a young bull was led or forced upon the planks; it was stabbed by the officiating priest in such a way that the thrust was mortal and that the blood might flow as freely as possible. As the blood poured down on the planks and dripped into the pit the neophyte moved backwards and forwards to receive as

> much as possible of the red warm shower and remained until every drop ceased to drip. Inscription after inscription records the fact that the deceased had been a *tauroboliatus* or a *tauroboliate,* had gone through this blood-bath in search of sanctification.[8]

The growing frequency with which matters like this were occurring in all social ranks is a testimony to the search for significance in a society which everywhere was perceived to be in a state of decay. The full sociological explanation of why out of all the great mass of sects and cults Christianity alone survived has not been developed. The official Christian explanation is, of course, that this was because "it was the *one,* the only true, the universal religion."[9] However, this would be said by the adherents of whatever religions survived.

Tentatively it may be observed that Christianity seemed to be, by the accidents of its origin, more fitted to bring about the synthesis of the elements of popular religion and Hellenistic philosophy than any of its rivals. Christianity originated in an atmosphere of apocalyptic expectation of the imminent end of the world, turning the experience of evident decay of existing society into a powerful religious asset. In Christ it offered its adherents a Messiah at a time when every cult that offered its members saviors or messiahs could quickly win adherents. It spread in the lower classes of freedmen, particularly the newly enfranchised who were to prove to be the progressive stratum of the world that was to rise out of the ruins of ancient society.

At the same time, from its heritage of ancient Judaism Christianity had received a tradition of monotheism. This could not have been without an appeal, particularly to the upper classes, for it has often been observed that most of the oriental cults contained the idea of monotheism in germ. Moreover, it had a brilliantly simple religious philosophy of history; the conception of history was the unfolding of God's plan and of mankind moving toward a historical destiny in time. Christianity could thus potentially knit together the philosophies of the genteel intellectuals as well as appeal to lower classes of freemen searching for a Messiah and living in the apocalyptic expectation of the imminent end of the world.

In any case, as the decay of the city moved up the social and economic ladder, Christianity began to win adherents from progressively high social strata. In an atmosphere where many people tried one cult after another, it was a foregone conclusion that some would be won over to Christianity.

> The last decade of the second century witnessed the beginnings of a change. Men of all ranks and classes become converts—members of the Senatorial and Equestrian Orders, distinguished pleaders, physicians, officers in the army, officials in the civil service, judges, even governors of provinces. Their wives, sisters, and daughters accompanied or more frequently preceded them. Then the tone of society began to change,

[8] *Ibid.,* p. 93.
[9] *Ibid.,* p. 95.

> gradually and insensibly. Scorn and contempt gave place to feelings of toleration. Before the end of the third century no one gave credit to the old scandalous reproaches which had been flung at the followers of Jesus, even when an Emperor tried to revive them.[10]

The fact that Christianity was slowly turning into a competing point for the integration of Roman society to that offered by the Empire inevitably brought it into conflict with the Empire. There were periodic persecutions, but most were only sporadically and inconsistently carried out in the early period. When at last the systematic attempt was made to put the full weight of the Empire behind such persecutions, the change had gone too far, and a fair proportion of the ranks of the *curiales* had been converted to Christianity. Constantine decided, with considerable reason, that Christianity was what the Empire itself most needed, and transformed it into the official religion of the Empire.

The Invasions

It is interesting to contemplate what might have happened to the world once integrated by the Roman Empire if it had not been shaken and transformed by invasions from without. The disintegration of the city-state communities which had borne social and cultural life of the Hellenic period would have continued in any case. Moreover, the reconstructive forces of Hellenistic society manifest in the new religious ferment and the attempt to reconsolidate the world along religious lines would also have taken place. The transformation of Christianity into the official religion of the empire suggests that these various forces were moving toward a new religiously based synthesis. However, during what might otherwise have been a mere period of transition between two types of social integration, the invasions broke up the Empire.

The Teutonic Invasions

The Teutons played a major role both in the breakup of the Roman Empire and in the reconstruction of society and civilization afterward. Their earliest home was in the area around the western edge of the Baltic (south of Sweden, Jutland, Schleswig-Holstein). This Indo-Germanic cradleland was also the source of the peoples' movements manifest as the Indo-Europeans of India and the ancestral Greeks. These prehistoric Teutons possessed a Bronze Age civilization. After the original invasions a section of them remained behind to become the source of new peoples' movements two thousand years later.[11]

During the later Bronze Age (from 1000 to 600 B.C.), the Teutons took over the superior metal technology from the Celts and added to it a superior fighting organization. The Teutons began to expand at the expense of the

[10] *Ibid.*, p. 95.

[11] Martin Bang, "Expansion of the Teutons," in *The Cambridge Medieval History* (New York: The Macmillan Co., 1922), Vol. I, pp. 183 ff.

Celts, who occupied the territories to their west. By 200 B.C. they occupied the whole of northwestern civilization from the Rhine and the Main. By the middle of the second century B.C. they swept west of the lower Rhine as far as Ardennes and the Eifel, approaching the Romans ever nearer.

The first clash between the Teutons and the Greco-Romans took place far to the east in the course of the migration of Teutonic tribes to the shores of the Black Sea. In the west, toward the close of the second century B.C., a major clash came between the alliance of Cimbri and Teutons and the Romans. It shook the Western world. The Teutons administered a series of defeats to the Roman armies, and created a fluid and unstable situation until Caesar (58 B.C.) took command, and brought about a stable solution which lasted around two hundred years. In the third century A.D. unrest was manifest once again. The two powerful confederations of the Alemans and Franks thereafter dominated the Rhineland.

During the first centuries of the Christian era the various branches of the Germans were undergoing complex processes of assimilation and amalgamation within the Empire. Julian allowed the Franks (358 A.D.) to settle in Taxandria in return for military service. The Goth Ulfila took over Christianity from Byzantium, diffusing a form of Arian Christianity among the Eastern Goths. It had long been customary for barbarians to take service in the Roman legions. The last two great warriors of Western antiquity, Stilicho and Aetius, were barbarians. The invasion of Europe by the Huns (372 A.D.) set the various branches of the Teutons into motion, during which a series of conquest and plundering expeditions by various of the groups were released and Rome itself was plundered twice.

The Musulman Invasion

While the Teutonic invasions were breaking up the Roman world and laying the foundations for new kingdoms dominated by Germanic elements, other events were in the making on the other side of the Mediterranean. The capacity of the religion to unite the nomadic peoples into an effective war confederation was manifest once again in the rise and expansion of Islam in the seventh century.

Mohammed died in 632 A.D., but within seventy years the Islamic conquest had spread from the Atlantic to the Indian Ocean: the Persian Empire collapsed (637–644 A.D.), Egypt was taken (640–642 A.D.), Africa fell (689 A.D.), and Spain, in 711 A.D. The great movement halted at the threshold of Constantinople (717 A.D.), and before the soldiers of Charles Martel at Poitiers (632 A.D.). The invasions destroyed the ancient Mediterranean-based unity of ancient civilization. In Pirenne's words:

> For centuries Europe had gravitated about the Mediterranean. It was by means of the Mediterranean that civilization had extended itself; by means of the Mediterranean the various parts of the civilized world had communicated one with another. On all its shores social life was the

> same in its fundamental characteristics; religion was the same; manners and customs and ideas were the same, or nearly so. The Germanic invasion had not changed the situation in any essential respect. In spite of all that had happened, we may say that in the middle of the seventh century Europe still constituted, as in the time of the Roman Empire, a Mediterranean unity.[12]

Europe was transformed by the Musulman invasion into an inland society.

Major Developments in the European Middle Ages

The invasions destroyed the unity of the Roman Empire. Various states were formed independently of one another by the peoples who had carried out separate phases of the conquest. In time, however, all these states excepting the Anglo-Saxon kingdom of England and the Visigoth kingdom of Spain were integrated by the Carolingian conquest and the fusion within its politico-religious unity.[13]

During this period the most important social and economic process was the disappearance of the cities which had been the dominant communities of the ancient world and had served the empires as administrative units. With the disappearance of the cities, the international traffic in luxury goods produced in slave-operated establishments also vanished. In Gaul, urban life declined so completely that the kings no longer dwelt in towns, but in the country on their own estates. Kingly administration even, at times, became seminomadic.

> Ruined and depopulated though they were, the cities had not lost all their significance. Abandoned by the civil administration, they remained the centers of the religious organization. The episcopal see established under the Empire in the capital of each "city" was still extant, and the strong Roman scaffolding of the Church still rose from the ruins of the State. And so, in the heart of a purely agricultural society, something of the municipal character of the ancient State was preserved by the Church. It was owing to the Church that the cities did not disappear altogether, but waited for the still distant day when they would become the cradles of the new middle class.[14]

The disappearance of the towns, of international trade, of the money economy, of production by slave labor, shifted the economy to subsistence agriculture. In place of the rural latifundia operated by slave labor, there appeared manorial establishments operated by serfs. Each of such domains tended to develop into a small self-sufficient community with its own customs and laws subject to the patriarchal authority of a seigneur. Serfs worked the *demesne* of the seigneur for his profit, while they were permitted to work the mansionary land for their own support. The center of the domain was located in the seigneurial court (which housed the bailiff

[12] Henri Pirenne, *A History of Europe* (New York: University Books, 1936), trans. by Bernard Miall, p. 50.

[13] *Ibid.*, p. 128.

[14] *Ibid.*, p. 97.

and other officers with jurisdiction over the villeins). A chapel built by the seigneurs was served by a priest.

The great domains absorbed both the people and the land. Their productivity was applied to their own maintenance. The local aristocracy gained in self-sufficiency and power even as the resources of the state declined. Power slipped from the hands of the kings into the hands of the aristocrats who included the king's own officials. In the Merovingian epoch the state had been divided into counties. From the eighth century on, powerful counts (officials of the counties) began to dominate counties surrounding their own by means of strategic marriages, friendly alliances, and military power.

Prominent among the political events of the Middle Ages was the Investiture struggle, the struggle between the church and the Holy Roman Empire for ultimate secular authority. When the church won this struggle, it gained tremendously in prestige, but simultaneously lost in the sense that it no longer had the emperor as a general secular authority to counteract the effects of the feudal disintegration of political authority. Thereafter the church was exposed to the separate feudal powers. The other major political phenomenon of the Middle Ages primarily involving its feudal elements was the linkage of missionary Christianity and the military zeal of the feudal knighthood for adventure, booty, and land. The counterattack of the European world against Islam began with the petty Christian kingdoms of northern Spain, where poor soil and absence of natural frontiers created a natural tendency to enlarge their territories. At the same time, all over Europe the process of the expansion of feudal magnates at each other's expense had long been under way. As the contestants grew larger and more powerful, the game was tending to become more grim. The hardening of the rules of chivalry and the substitution of the tournament for warfare which were occurring at this time seem in part to have been attempts to prevent the increasingly costly interfeudal wars. The church took command of the militant expansive forces of feudalism, giving them the direction of a holy war.

> To begin with, [the First Crusade] . . . was purely and exclusively religious. In this respect it was intimately related, in respect of spirit that inspired it, to the great wave of Christian fervor of which the War of Investitures was another manifestation. It was further related to this movement by the fact that the Pope, who had instigated and waged this war was also the organizer of the Crusade.[15]

Pirenne observes that if the crusaders had merely wished to repel the Mohammedans, they would have helped the Spaniards and Normans. Their objectives were the Holy Places and Sepulcher of Christ in Jerusalem. There were as yet no states, though there was a military class, the Order of Chivalry, ready at hand with an army endowed from father to son by fiefs, which thus cost the Church nothing.

[15] *Ibid.*, p. 191.

> Western feudality acted in a body and, so to speak, of its own accord. No king took part in this crusade. The curious thing is that nobody gave any thought to the kings, to say nothing of the Emperor, who was the enemy of the Pope.[16]

With the single exception of Italy, whose commercial development the Crusades enormously stimulated, Pirenne observes that the whole formation of Europe can be explained without reference to the Crusades. However, the Crusades did have important consequences of another sort. From the time of the First Crusade, holy war was substituted for evangelization of the non-Christian world. It was also used against heretics. The heresies of the Albigensians and, still later, the Hussites were ruthlessly destroyed by force.[17]

LATE ROMAN AND EARLY CHRISTIAN CHRONOLOGY

Time	*Event*
200–189 B.C.	Rome breaks the power of Alexander's successors and turns eastern Mediterranean into a Roman protectorate
115–105 B.C.	Alliance of Cimbri and Teutons administers a series of defeats to the Roman legions
48–44 B.C.	Dictatorship of Caesar
312–313 A.D.	Constantine legalizes Christianity
325 A.D.	Constantine convokes the Council of Nicaea
372 A.D.	The Huns invade Europe
378 A.D.	The Revolt of the Visigoths
408 A.D.	The Visigoths march on Rome
455 A.D.	Vandals pillage Rome
476 A.D.	The Extinction of the Western Roman Empire
632 A.D.	The Death of Mohammed
711 A.D.	The Fall of Spain to the Musulman
768–814 A.D.	Charlemagne
1077 A.D.	Emperor Henry IV submits to the spiritual authority of Pope Gregory VII in the investiture struggle at Canossa
1099 A.D.	Jerusalem taken in the First Crusade

SOCIETY IN THE EARLY WESTERN MIDDLE AGES

When the cities of the ancient world collapsed, their place was taken by a variety of agricultural subsistence communities in the early Western Middle Ages. The three major forms were the peasant village, the manorial community, and the monastic community.

Peasant Villages

As the ancient cities decayed, one group after another was cast adrift within them to fend for itself. By contrast to the helplessness of the cities to take care of their own, the Germanic invaders were rooted in vigorous tribal communities, not only able to fend for themselves, but endowed with

[16] *Ibid.*, p. 193.
[17] *Ibid.*, p. 197.

an expansive power that permitted them to send out wave after wave of warrior adventurers to plunder. The Germanic tribes were self-sufficient village communities organized into patriarchal kin groups under a chief or headman. One source of their unusual expansive power lay in the wheeled plow invented in the Danube Basin in the early Iron Age. The Germanic peoples in this area found the wheeled plow drawn by the eight-ox team adapted to the heavy clay forest and swampy soils of northern Europe. They assembled their teams cooperatively, plowed and harvested in common, but retained individual ownership of the land. The success of their mastery of nature also gave them a sufficient margin over survival to launch their excess populations into conquests against the Roman world. Their vigor contrasts with the decadence of the socio-economic life of Rome, where the decline of urban populations was a major unalterable fact.

So long as soil fertilization was only incompletely understood, these Teutonic cultivating communities were seminomadic (this was, perhaps, also a component in the peoples' movements). A strip of ground continually planted, without adequate fertilization, will soon be exhausted. There is then nothing to do but abandon it and permit it to lie fallow until natural processes restore it to fertility once again. A precondition of community stability was inclusion of the fallowing process into the cultivating cycle. In the Middle Ages two major types of villages appeared, resting on agricultural partnerships and adapted to the more or less systematic fallowing which would permit continuous occupation of a single site.

Villages resting on one field cultivation grew up on poor soils, as in Scotland, Cornwall, and the central French highlands. Such villages were loosely organized. Each household cultivated a patch of soil until it was exhausted, then took up another. After some time it was able to return to the original piece. Such practices were wasteful and permitted only a fairly narrow margin above survival.

In most of England, in France, and in Germany to the Danube Basin, nucleated villages arose. Such villages were organized into a series of zones. At their core were dwelling lots. Around these were fenced land for kitchen gardens (*Wurt*). At times these two zones of dwellings and kitchen gardens were mixed. In a third zone was the arable land. In a fourth the pasture (*Alemand*), and finally, in a fifth zone was the village woods, where it was possible for the villagers to gather wood for fuel and for furniture and to pasture their pigs. In the three-field system of agriculture, the arable land was divided into fields which, in turn, were cut into strips. Every peasant possessed a strip in each field.

In contrast to the ancient scratch-point plow, the German plow with which these fields were cultivated consisted of a knife which cut the ground vertically, a share which cut it horizontally, and a moldboard which turned it over. The ox teams which pulled these heavy plows were animals owned by the peasant. Plowing was done in common. The arable land was divided into three fields: one seeded in summer grain, a second in winter grain, and the third was permitted to lie fallow. The farm belonging to the individual was hereditary. It was normally close to the 40 acres necessary, on an average, to support a family. It consisted of the dwelling lot, garden lot, and the family's share in the arable land.

Such villages had a herdsman. Clothing was made by village women. A variety of village specialists appeared, including bakers, brewers, and blacksmiths. The village elders and headman served as its political body. The usual medieval village had lost its ancient tribal religions and its priests (though these often lived on in the form of a local witch or wizard) and had replaced pagan customs with Christianity (though these had often been only thinly disguised as entertainments and transferred to various saints' days). The village priest was the official religious head of the village community.

Manorial Communities

The free, peasant-village community seems originally to have been native to northern Europe. The manorial or seigneurial community arose in the clash and integration of German and Roman institutions in the south of Europe, later spreading to the north and east. The manorial communities were also subsistence communities. They represented peasant villages in-incorporated into a system of seigneurial proprietorships, in which the ownership of the land was vested in persons who did not work it.

There were two primary and two secondary ways in which such seigneurial proprietorships arose in the early Western Middle Ages: (1) by conquest, (2) by internal differentiation, (3) by voluntary submission of free persons to the system, and (4) by deliberate founding of new manorial communities.

Property ownership was originally in the hands of the entire cultivating household. These were individual families, joint families, or clans. However, whenever new property was won by war chiefs and their followers, the requirement of the division of the land among the members of the clan or family was absent. On the other hand, everyone who participated in the conquest had a claim in the division of the land. Such land was often exploited directly by the war chiefs and their followers with the aid of the person occupying it at the time of the conquest. The Germanic conquests thus set up a class of seigneurs whose ownership claims fell outside the customary practices of the old cultivating community. Entire village communities taken over in this way, moreover, no longer consisted of members able to exercise the power of political self-determination over their community affairs. They were reduced to the status of serfs with, at best, hereditary claims to their serfdom.

A different kind of development with somewhat the same consequences occurred in the slave-operated *latifundia* of the old Roman agrarian economy. With the cessation of the wars and consequent drying up of the slave trade, that mode of wasteful economic production had to be abandoned. The *latifundia* were capitalistic enterprises which produced for sale in the market. The seigneurial domains that grew up in their place rested not on the capitalistic owners of slaves, but on land-owning proprietors and enfranchised slaves or serfs. Production was for the maintenance of the domain itself. The lord owned the property, though his ownership was limited by the hereditary rights of tenants. Each domain had its own law and was subject to the patriarchal authority of the lord. The lord possessed extensive rights over his serfs: they could not marry outside the domain or inside it without his consent, they owed work on his *demesne*, and they had to pay taxes and fees.

A third way in which the seigneurial proprietorship arose was through voluntary submission by the formerly free individual. With the decay of central political authority, the ordinary individual was subject to plunder from many quarters. Under these circumstances many persons voluntarily submitted to the emerging manorial system. If they had sufficient property, they could join the growing class of vassals enfeoffed, but owing war service to a lord. If not, they might be reduced to serfdom, but at least they were protected by the manorial authorities.

Finally, as time went by many powerful lords carved out new territories from the forests, on which they transplanted a *cadre* of peasants. In this way younger sons could also be set up as full proprietors on domains of their own.

The center of such a manor or seigneury was composed of the lord's court, the lord's officers, and various servants and companions in the household. In time, the court became surrounded by a palisade and moat, inside which the lord resided. His tables, barns, and granaries were also located in this protected area. Court was held in the enclosed area and presided over by the lord and his officials. The manor usually possessed its own chapel and priest. The lord often undertook various special enterprises, such as setting up his own baking ovens (part of each batch of bread baked in his ovens by his serfs was then extracted as a fee for the use of the facilities) or he built his own mill (in which the serfs were forced to grind their grain, again for a fee).

The feudal system of authority consisted of an elaborate series of contractual relationships between the lords of such domains and their various vassals enfeoffed with castles and estates for their sustenance and owing their lords, in return, military service. Warfare was the monopoly of this military class which spent its time in military training and tournaments, and, when not actually engaged in private wars or family feuds, semimilitary entertainment, such as hunting and falconry.

Monastic Communities

The third major type of agricultural subsistence community to appear in the early Middle Ages was the monastery. It was a special product of the forces for and against integration of ancient society. The Olympic religions had ceased to be an integrating element in the thoughts and feelings of ancient civic man in the Hellenistic period. His powers of self-determination in the no longer autonomous polis had been basically impaired. His abilities, by means of his own efforts, to solve the problems of his existence had been sharply curtailed. He experienced himself as a pawn (as he was) in the game played by distant emperors and depersonalized bureaucracies. He transferred his hopes for himself to the realm of the ideal and the future. His thoughts were absorbed in salvation from the very life he was leading. It was to the oriental mystery religions and to Christianity that he turned in order to put his life together.

It was certainly a brilliant *coup* by Constantine, who perceived that Christianity was integrating the world when the Empire could not and in the very teeth of persecution by the Empire, and hence made it the official religion of the Roman state. The last hope of holding the Empire together was thus placed on the Church. The Church, for its part, won the world but potentially at the cost of thorough secularization and the loss of the very thing that had made it important in the first place. This happened at the very time when the decay of the ancient city was casting one group after another upon its own resources. It was perhaps inevitable under these circumstances that, at the very time that the secularization of the church was being carried through, monasticism should arise among a small section of the religiously devout.

Christian asceticism has ancient roots. Celibacy, fasting, prayer, voluntary abandonment of material things, and philanthropy had always been conceived as religiously meritorious. However, the transformation of ascetic practices into a systematic way of religious life permanently withdrawn from the secular community was something new. In the times in which it arose, it represented a movement toward religious self-sufficiency in a world that was decaying.

The origins of Christian monasticism extend back to St. Anthony, born in Egypt (c. 250 A.D.), who practiced asceticism for a time and eventually withdrew to a height above the Nile (c. 285 A.D.) and spent twenty years in seclusion, prayer, and religious exercise. A number of disciples collected about him, following his precept and example.[18] A few years later Pachomius, who was born a pagan but became a Christian around 290 A.D., adopted the eremitical life at the age of twenty. He founded his first monastery at Tabennisi (c. 315–320 A.D.). Three hundred monks practicing

[18] E. C. Butler, "Monasticism," in *The Cambridge Medieval History* (New York: The Macmillan Co., 1929), Vol. I, p. 522.

various handicrafts collected there. They organized gardens, smithies, and bakeries. They practiced carpentry, tanning, basket-making, tailoring, and writing. They kept camels and herds of swine. They gathered in church four times a day. The fixed routine of life included church service, Bible reading, and religious study as well as routine work. The Pachomian monastery was a well-organized, self-supporting agricultural community.[19]

The philosophy of monasticism was brought together in Cassian's collations. These purported to be twenty-four conferences with desert monks in response to queries by Cassian and his friend Germanus (between 390 and 400 A.D.). The primary purpose of monasticism was stated to be the attainment of purity of heart, permitting the mind to dwell on God and divine things. Fasting, watching, meditation, solitude, and ascetic privations were instruments to the pure life rather than ends in themselves.

Egyptian monasticism reached its height in about 400 A.D. It was introduced to Palestine from Egypt early in the fourth century. It appeared in Syria and Mesopotamia around the middle of the fourth century. It entered Greek-speaking lands from the East, being first introduced in the Roman province of Armenia (about 330 A.D.). The father of Greek monasticism was St. Basil (c. 360 A.D.). In 339 A.D. monasticism was brought by St. Athanasius to Rome.

More than anyone else, St. Benedict of Nursia (c. 480 A.D.) adapted monasticism to Western ideas and needs. In contrast to Eastern monasticism, where asceticism was the normal procedure, St. Benedict, while recognizing the value of eremitical life, legislated only for cenobites. He established the principle that all should live by the rule and conform to the life of the community under the abbot's control, even during Lent. Work occupied more time in the daily monastic routine than church service or reading. Such work was in the field or about the garden and buildings. Six to seven hours a day were thus occupied. An unbroken fast was observed till midday. Other activities included the direct worship of God, reading (to which three to four hours a day were assigned), and the daily chanting of the canonical office in the choir, which took some four to four and a half hours a day. With their disciplined work and evident self-sufficiency, the Benedictine monasteries became object lessons as thriving rural communities.

> As Benedictine abbeys came gradually to be established more and more thinly in the midst of the wild Teutonic populations that were settling throughout Western Europe, they became object-lessons in disciplined and well-ordered life, in organized work, in all the arts of peace, that could not but impress powerfully the minds of the surrounding barbarians, and bring home to them the ideals of peace and order and work, no less than religion.[20]

The Benedictine form of the self-sufficient agricultural economy in the service of the religious life became the model for all later Western mo-

[19] *Ibid.*, p. 524.
[20] *Ibid.*, p. 539.

nasticism. These monasteries, and others formed on their plan, penetrated the wilderness and transformed it into cultivated garden land. There was no question as to the survival of Christianity in the face of the collapse of the Roman Empire with which it had become identified, for it was preserved in the self-sufficient monasteries of the period.

THE WESTERN CITY

The decline of culture and the weakening of large-scale political structures was so marked in the Middle Ages that it has often obscured the positive features of the period. Often the highest culture in an area was that of the castle-dwelling but illiterate aristocrats and their retainers. They were brutal and crude. The medieval Christian church was often little better off, for in the spread of Christianity over Europe a fusion occurred with elements of many local cults. At times there was little distinction between Christian and pagan.

Many of the destructive social trends of late Roman times, however, had been reversed. Slavery with all its attendant evils largely disappeared. The competition of slave with free labor ceased to be an issue. The technological backwardness associated with slavery was replaced by a more progressive attitude toward technology.

Among the signs of change in European society was the rapid clearing of the European forests. Systematic recovery of the swampland of northern Europe also began. Many inventions were introduced to improve the efficiency of routine labor: the wheelbarrow, the spinning wheel, the horse-collar, the nailed horseshoe. The windmill and watermill were used for such routine tasks as fulling cloth. With all its fanfare of knighthood, the Middle Ages was a time of comparative peace when human fortunes were improving. The decline of population evident in the Hellenistic world was reversed. The foundation was laid for a more extensive flowering of cities than had ever been seen before.

Much ink has been spilled over the problem of the origin of the Western city. It has been argued that it did not originate at all; it just grew from out of happily located rural villages. It has been maintained that the medieval city was simply continuous with the Roman-founded cities, largely arising in the same locations with basic continuities with Roman times; it has been asserted that the Western city evolved from the episcopal seats where the bishops of the church were located; it has been argued that the city grew up around the major fortresses and garrisons which extended protection to travelers; it has been insisted that the city originated by specific activity of secular or ecclesiastical authorities who granted charters and protection to the corporation so founded; it has been said that the city originated from the places of settlement of merchant strata or from the revolutions by new types of producers. Evidence has been gathered for each of these theories. The difficulty has been that all the evidence never fits any single one. Most of the theories were developed at a time of the popularity of evolutionism under the assumption that there had to be some single point of institutional origin for the city.

The city, however, is not simply an institution; it is a community, a system of institutions organized into a distinct way of life. A fully developed city had all the institutions which at one time or other were treated as the origin of the city: market, fortress and garrison, special social classes, political structure, legal structure, etc. In a world that has reached a stage of development where it is possible to support cities (sufficient agricultural productivity permanently to release large numbers of men from agricultural production) and where people have come to appreciate the new values made possible by the city, any of a variety of preliminary institutions can become the starting point for the formation of a complete city. The important thing is not where the city started—whether with a garrison, a settlement of foreign merchants, a river ford, the trade opportunities associated with a shrine, the sanctuary offered by a cathedral, the commercial activity associated with a monastic industry, the military protection offered by a fortress, the deliberate founding activity of a feudal prince or a monastic order or cathedral—but whether the new configuration gathered the system of institutions into a unity and acquired the autonomous self-determination which would make it into an independent community.

As a type of community finding its point of synthesis in secondary institutions, the city presupposed not only a level of economic development permitting large numbers of men to make a living off trade and industry rather than agriculture, but also an extensive weakening of kinship and neighborhood groups. Max Weber has pointed out that among the factors promoting the unusual flowering of urbanism in the West were the great peoples' movements at the dawn of the modern period. Such movements profoundly weakened the hold of the family, clan, and neighborhood groups over the individual. Weber also saw Christianity as a further significant factor in the growth of the city, for it substituted the *eucharist*, a cult of the community, for the family cult or clan religion as a primary basis for association. The extensive leveling of European forms by the Roman empire, by peoples' movements, by the spread of feudalism, by Christianity, laid the foundations for a far more extensive urbanism than was ever known in the ancient world. Besides, many urban traditions persisted as a heritage from the ancient world. Western urbanism first took shape in Italy on old grounds of Roman urbanism.

The ancient city was a religious community. The typical city had its city god, its temple, and its hierarchy of priests who carried out sufficient liquidation of tribal, clan, and family loyalties to form people into the new community of the city. When an appearance of cities was made possible in the late Middle Ages by the revival of Mediterranean trade (greatly promoted by the Crusades), the continuities of medieval with ancient urbanism were evident in the appearance of the city saint as symbol and protector of the city. To some extent, the city saint played a role for the early medieval city equivalent to the god of the ancient city. However, since the new cities grew up within a framework of Christianity, the city ceased to be a distinctly religious community in the ancient sense. As the wave of city formation spread north of the Alps, it even ceased to be necessary for the city to possess a civic saint. Religion operated in the West not as the peculiar binding force of the city but as a claim for more comprehensive loyalties.

Like the ancient city, the medieval city had to be able to defend itself against a surrounding world partly inimical to it. Hence, like its ancient counterpart, it developed civic armies and surrounded itself with fortress walls. However, here, too, the medieval city departed from its ancient model. Max Weber has argued that from the time of the creation of hoplite discipline the ancient city was a warriors' guild, creating trained hoplite armies out of their citizens. The thoroughness of discipline varied between the limits represented by Sparta and Athens. The ancient citizen was primarily a soldier. Beside the water wells, the market, and the official buildings, the gymnasium was a fundamental institution of the ancient city. The citizens' time was primarily spent in the market or the gymnasium. The citizens served jury duty in the courts, in the administration, and above all, in the military campaigns. The democratic polis laid its hands on any great aggregations of burgher wealth for military purposes. Such were the liturgies of the Trierarchy which outfitted and provisioned the commanders of warships. Moreover, the city pursued policies of conquest intended to accumulate booty and slaves. The conquest of a city usually resulted in the death or enslavement of its entire population and a sudden glut of the slave market.[21]

While there were some relatively close parallels to ancient development in the maritime cities of Venice and Genoa, where wealth was dependent on overseas colonial power, the industrial inland city of the Middle Ages was set upon quite a different course. Under the domination of the guild, the medieval city pressed in the direction of industry of a rational type. While there were individual cities (like Florence, which first established artillery) which made military progress, the medieval cities were not bearers of new developments in militarism. The source of the wealth of the medieval city lay in peaceful trade and industry, not in war and conquest.

> The knightly army remained equal to the city army in all essentials, and in the conquest of the countryside it was superior. The citizens had sufficient military strength to sustain the integrity of the island city but not to serve as a basis for economic gain.[22]

[21] Max Weber, *The City* (Glencoe: The Free Press, 1958), pp. 220 ff.
[22] *Ibid.*, p. 224.

At an early stage in the formation of the city, the relation between the citizens in their conflict with the countryside became self-conscious, and assumed the form of a sworn confederation.[23] When the city established itself as a distinct corporation, it sought control over its political administration and legal life,[24] as well as over its economic and financial situation.[25] During the early period of its formation, the city usually had a plutocratic structure, but the economic and political life of the city tended to develop through a series of revolutions into a more democratic structure.

The medieval city was no simple repetition of the ancient city, nor was it created as a finished artifact. It developed slowly with all the attendant difficulties and uncertainties of all newly formed communities. It broke through the floor of the feudal community; it freed new social forces; it was dependent on the creation of new institutions; it assembled new aggregations of wealth; it sustained new architectural styles and patronized new developments in art and letters. It was the foundation for a great new explosion of intellectual creation.

THE NATION-STATE

The rise of the nation-state in the modern world might at first appear similar to the triumph of the Empire over feudal China, or the establishment of the dynasties in India, or even the triumph of Babylonia over Palestine, and of Macedonia and, later, Rome over the Hellenic world. However, there is a most fundamental difference between these events. The various types of empires that brought an end to the Axial Period were not new communities representing a higher synthesis of the social forms that had preceded them, but a simplification and partial reversal of the communal trends they replaced. The many thriving feudal courts of the ancient Chinese feudal period were disbanded; there remained only a world occupied by the formalized imperial court, its administrative centers, and the peasant villages. In India a rich civic development was reversed, and finally under repeated foreign conquest older community forms were disintegrated, and Indian society was reformed into a regime of castes. The Jewish community was transformed into an ethnic community; the autonomous city-state of the Hellenic world disappeared, being replaced by far more rigid imperial cities which, in turn, underwent internal decay until almost every one, including Rome, was eventually sacked by barbarians. A variety of rural communities finally took their place.

The modern nation-state is a phenomenon quite distinct from the ancient empire. It has, to be sure, made profound inroads into such previous community forms as the rural community and the city, but it is not like the

23 *Ibid.*, pp. 96 ff.; pp. 107 ff.
24 *Ibid.*, pp. 181 ff.
25 *Ibid.*, pp. 186 ff.

ancient empire a product of the hardening and fixing of features of prior community forms but a genuine new community.

The modern state is often defined as that institution able to achieve a monopoly over the exercise of legitimate violence in a specific territory.[26] A nation is frequently defined as a commonality of sentiment which would adequately manifest itself in a state of its own.[27] However, the nation is not simply a commonality of sentiment; it is a community. The various things that Shafer has described as illusions of the nation[28] are not illusions at all, but ideologies, conditions, and institutions brought into synthesis by the national community: the ideology that the nation is a creation of God, nature, or mystical forces; the notion that it is an entity uniquely determined by soil, climate, and natural boundaries; the ideology that it is rooted in the biological and spiritual nature of man as manifest in tribe, race, blood, and instinct; that it represents a special configuration of economic and political institutions; that it rests on a common language; that it has a common history.

The modern nation-state arose out of the same medieval soil as the city. However, the city was not a stage in the development of the nation, but an alternative form of complex community, partly assisted by and assisting the nation-state, eventually to be reduced to a subordinate community within the nation-state. During the same period when the Western city flourished as an autonomous community, the nation-state was taking shape, eventually to provide a more comprehensive framework within which the autonomy of the city would be lost.

At first the formation of the state preceded the nation. Beginning in France and England, but later in Spain, Germany, Italy, and Russia, the feudal system began to break down under the aspirations of the more powerful and fortunate noble families. Through war, conquest, diplomacy, marriage, purchase, and good fortune, some feudal princes consolidated in their hands the powers that became the basis of the national monarchies. Hardly had the monarchies succeeded, however, when a series of revolutions within the growing states began to shift the location of power to more inclusive groups. As the states were made more democratic, they increasingly became the orienting point for contemporary institutions. Tocqueville observed that the French Revolution achieved greater concentration of power in a few years than the French monarchy had in centuries. Finally, by the twentieth century a stage in the evolution of the state was reached, when the totalitarian dream of the subordination of all institutions to the state could be envisioned.

[26] An extensive recent treatment from this point of view is contained in Harold D. Lasswell and Abraham Kaplan, *Power and Society: A Framework for Political Inquiry* (New Haven: Yale University Press, 1950).

[27] Max Weber, *From Max Weber* (New York: Oxford University Press, 1946), pp. 172 ff.

[28] Boyd C. Shafer, *Nationalism* (New York: Harcourt Brace, 1955), pp. 17 ff.

An important aspect of the consolidation of the power by the national state was the growth of its military forces. At first these consisted only of the retainers of powerful feudal princes. The feudal princes were interested in maximizing their money revenues in part to be able to keep professional soldiers permanently in their employ. In the early days of the monarchies, it was often necessary for the princes to float loans with private bankers to finance campaigns. In time most of the growing monarchies transferred the feudal knights into the employment of the state, and eliminated the military forces of the city. As the city ceased to be a military unit, it began to expand freely outside the walls of the original militarily autonomous form. Thus in one way or another both cities and countryside were disarmed, and the decisive military forces were consolidated by the state.

Economically, the rising states pursued those policies best fitted to put ready cash into their hands, which was necessary if they were to sustain their growing administrations and permanent armies. They often vigorously promoted the cause of the cities, since these were primary sources of cash income. The states also at times took the initiative in encouraging the Jewish financier and in the support of the international banker for the same reason. Moreover, the time was reached when it was to the financial advantage of the growing states to promote interlocal trade (which turned it against both the economic restrictions of feudalism and the economically self-directing city) and international commerce. Mercantilism was the first stage in the self-conscious formation of a national economic policy. This was followed by a series of economic revolutions which generalized the participation of groups other than the mercantilists in national economic policy. Capitalism and socialism were ideologies and programs which accompanied the successively more comprehensive generalization of the national economy; they are the economic counterparts of the political revolutions which generalized participation in national politics.

Religion played a variable role in the formation of the nation-state. Initially the universal church was a major force against the kind of parochialism represented by nationalism. However, once the ranks of the church had been divided by the Protestant revolts and the political landscape became divided between predominantly Roman Catholic and predominantly Protestant states, religion became a powerful force for establishing national identities. Moreover, the religious controversies waged through pamphlet duels in vernacular also helped fix the national languages and cultures. The states themselves quickly saw the advantages of promoting national religion, national customs, and a national language.

The formation of modern nation-states occurred, roughly, in three stages: in the first, the formation of the state preceded the appearance of an effective national community which, however, began to take shape around the states (England and France were the two major examples); in the second stage, nation formation occurred apart from the leadership of the state, and in this phase of cultural nationalism the nation often acquired sufficient shape to demand a state of its own (the chief examples were Germany, Italy, and the United States); in the third stage of nation formation (which is still taking place, though without the middle classes that were the bearers of the cultural nationalism of the middle stage), intellectuals often joined hands with other local political authorities to promote nationalistic programs. This last stage began in Eastern Europe, but continues throughout the world today. What is happening to the nation is somewhat like that which occurred in the formation of the city at an earlier period. Once conditions have sufficiently developed to make the state possible, and its advantages are seen, the national community may be formed out of many different initial materials.

BEYOND THE NATION

We seem to be in that stage in our own social history which is comparable to the last days of the Hellenic world. At the very time when the autonomous city-state of the ancient world had reached its fullest development, a level of problems appeared that could not be solved within its compass.

The units of our own world are not city-states but sovereign (politically autonomous) nation-states. At present the world is crystallizing into nations at an unprecedented rate. The national ferment throughout remote regions of Asia, Africa, and South America has never been greater. At the same time, the contemporary world seems to have reached a level of problems unsolvable within the framework of the nation-state. The major wars, for example, are no longer fought by single states but by great power-blocks to which no community corresponds. But whether we will move into a period of decline, as did the Hellenistic world, or to a new level of world community formation, we cannot know for certain.

SUMMARY

The development of recent Western society has many similarities with that of the various societies of the Axial Period. Like them, it arose out of the ruins of a previously civilized world. Like them, its bearers were persons more barbaric than those whom they displaced. Like them, its starting point was a feudal or semifeudal epoch. However, there were also differences.

The societies of the early Middle Ages, out of which and in terms of which modern societies developed, were three: peasant villages, manorial communities, and monastic communities. All were self-sufficient agricultural communities practicing forms of subsistence economy. Communities of the first two types also played a role in ancient China in the Chou period, in ancient India in the early Vedic period, and in Greece in the Heroic period. However, there does not seem to have been anything quite approximating the self-sufficient monastic community in either of them.

The rise of the Western city marks a stage in Western society which is quite directly parallel to some formations in the last stages of the Warring Kingdoms and the early Imperial period in ancient China, to the period of the patrimonial states in India, to the royal period in Palestine, and to the period of the city-state in Greece. However, once again there are differences.

The Western city found its key stratum not in a class of theologian-administrators or warrior citizens, but in commercial and industrial strata. Moreover, in contrast to the ancient Mediterranean city, it was not a warriors' guild or a religious community. It was an inland city rather than a city resting on international sea traffic. Its industrial foundation was composed of free rather than slave labor. Moreover, from the beginning its external situation was unique.

The full uniqueness of Western development, however, appeared most distinctly with the rise of a new community form, the nation-state, for which there was no ancient counterpart. The ancient empires which so often brought the Axial Period to a close have no counterpart in the nation-state. In contrast to them, it is a genuine community. We seem to be living at present in the last stage of the crystallization of the world into nation-states. The great ferment in Asia, India, South America, and Africa are aspects of the process.

One of the fundamental ways in which the development of the Western world is distinct from developments in the Axial Period is that, while the empires that so often terminated their development brought about a reduction of communities to a more primitive stage (peasant villages in imperial China, castes in India, the ethnic community in Palestine, and a variety of agricultural subsistence communities in the Roman world), our own society moved on to a community synthesis of a more complex character than the Western city.

SELECTED BIBLIOGRAPHY

Bang, Martin, "The Expansion of the Teutons," *The Cambridge Medieval History* (New York: The Macmillan Co., 1929), Vol. I, pp. 183–217.

Butler, E. C., "Monasticism," *The Cambridge Medieval History* (New York: The Macmillan Co., 1929), Vol. I, pp. 521–541.

Clarke, M. V., *The Medieval City-State* (London: Methuen & Co., 1926).

Lindsay, T. M., "The Triumph of Christianity," *The Cambridge Medieval History* (New York: The Macmillan Co., 1929), Vol. I, pp. 87–117.

Pirenne, Henri, *Medieval Cities,* trans. by Frank D. Halsey (Princeton: Princeton University Press, 1946).

Pirenne, Henri, *A History of Europe,* trans. by Bernard Miall (New York: University Books, 1936).

Stephenson, Carl, *Medieval Feudalism* (New York: Cornell University Press, 1942).

Vinogradoff, Paul, "Social and Economic Conditions of the Roman Empire in the Fourth Century," *The Cambridge Medieval History* (New York: The Macmillan Co., 1929), Vol. I, pp. 542–567.

Weber, Max, *The City*, trans. by Don Martindale and Gertrud Neuwirth (Glencoe, Illinois: The Free Press, 1958).

Weber, Max, *General Economic History*, trans. by Frank H. Knight (Glencoe, Illinois: The Free Press, 1950).

17

THE HUMANISTIC AND SCIENTIFIC POLES OF WESTERN INTELLECTUALITY

IN THE medieval world the classical spirit of Western thought went into eclipse: oriental mysticism walked the world, metaphysics and science were fused, and philosophy became the handmaiden of theology. In his reflections the typical church father combined daemoniac and miraculous elements along with fragments of ancient thought. The second-century compilation of Christian allegories, the *Physiologue*, or *Bestiary*, illustrate medieval knowledge of natural history. Typical of its doctrinal intent was the idea that the lioness brought her cubs dead into the world, breathing between their eyes on the third day so that they woke to life, thus symbolizing the Resurrection of the Lord, the Lion of Judah.[1] In the hands of the church propagandists, history was transformed into apologetics. The medieval historian did not hesitate to resort to outright forgery in the name of the faith, as illustrated by the false Decretals and the Donation of Constantine:[2]

THE MEDIEVAL SCHOLASTIC

The dominant intellectual of the ancient world in the Classical period was the philosopher. Though he might theorize profoundly about spiritual matters, he was a secular intellectual. His thought was dominated by the striving for a rational synthesis of ideas. He rested his case for acceptance

[1] Sir William Cecil Dampier, *A History of Science* (New York: The Macmillan Co., 1944), p. 72.

[2] Until the time of Gregory the Great, the supremacy of Rome over the local churches outside its immediate area was more theoretical than factual. Gregory's statesmanship greatly enhanced the papal prestige. His successors employed this prestige in their bestowal of the temporal crown on Charles the Great in reward for his defense of spiritual power. Charles, in turn, asserted that absolute obedience was due in spiritual matters to the see of Peter. The authority ascribed to Rome by Charlemagne was bolstered by the False Decretals whose object was to limit the absolutism of local metropolitans by exalting the prerogatives of the papal see. Earlier in origin than the False Decretals was the document known as the Donation of Constantine by which that Emperor was represented as bestowing upon the Popes his imperial dignity in the West, with a spiritual principate over other patriarchs and local churches. The principal aim of these fabrications was to transform the Roman see into the final court of appeal for Christians.

on adherence to standards of rational proof: the proper conduct of the thought process itself in terms of its own rules.

In the Hellenistic period all this began to change. Spokesmen, rivals of the philosophers, appeared among the leaders of popular sects, cults, and mystery religions. The heirs of the older philosophic positions, in turn, began to bend in the direction of these irrational popular faiths. Various forms of revelations and mystical intuitions began to take their place alongside the older rational arguments. The priest-theologians, the scholastics of the medieval world, who represented the end product of these developments and a starting point for modern developments, completed the amalgamation of faith and reason that was under way in the Hellenistic period by the subordination of reason to the requirements of faith.

The subordination of reason to faith is taken as the central clue to the scholastic and his thought by Sir Henry Slesser.

> The Catholic, perhaps, is the only modern man who can hope fully to appreciate the medieval scholastic philosophers, for he alone, like the Schoolmen whom we have here to consider, without qualification accepts the Beatific Vision of God as the final end of man. Moreover, it is not possible to understand, much less to accept, the medieval mode of thought unless we grasp firmly the fact that, in any event, wherever speculation might wander, it took place within the ambit of revealed faith as disclosed in the Scriptures, the Fathers, and the tradition and teaching of the Church.
>
> Whether we study St. Augustine and wonder at his remark: "Whence shall we begin? With authority or with Reason? Authority should precede Reason when we wish to learn anything" . . . or begin with St. Anselm and his "I believe that I may understand" . . . or St. Thomas who, when distinguishing between faith and philosophy, said, "it is necessary that there should be a doctrine according with divine revelation, besides the philosophical disciplines which are pursued by human Reason, because man was ordained towards God as towards an end passing his comprehension."[3]

Even philosophers who ran afoul the church, for example, Scotus Erigena and Abelard, subscribed to the primary of faith over reason. Erigena is quoted as stating: "The Scripture is the chief source of our knowledge of God. Reason establishes its data." And against the severe persecution of Abelard by St. Bernard for overstressing reason at the expense of faith stands Abelard's own formulation: "We set the faith of the blessed Trinity as the foundation of all good."[4] In this characterization of the scholastic, Slesser automatically locates the modern intellectual on the other side of his equation.

St. Augustine may be taken as marking the end of the evolution of the intellectual in the Hellenistic period from the philosopher to the scholastic.

[3] Sir Henry Slesser, *The Middle Ages in the West* (London: Hutchinson & Co., 1950), p. 197.

[4] *Ibid.*, pp. 197 ff.

He was also the greatest of the scholastics until the late Middle Ages. In his own life he epitomized much of the drama of the exploration of thought systems in the search for spiritual certainty which had come to dominate the learned men of the Greco-Roman world.

St. Augustine (Aurelius Augustinus, 354–430 A.D.) was born at Tagaste, Numidia, of Roman parents. His mother had been a Christian from childhood; his father was baptized late in life. At the age of twelve St. Augustine attended the grammar school at Madaura, where he became thoroughly acquainted with Latin literature and superficially acquainted with Greek. He formed a *liaison* with a concubine, and was a father before he had reached twenty years of age. Shortly thereafter he came under the influence of Manicheanism, which he studied for nine years. Because of conceptual problems with Manicheanism, he turned to the popular teacher, Faustus, but after a time cast off his influence as well, and fell back on the skepticism of the Academy (Neo-Platonism). In 384 A.D. he departed for Milan to teach, where he fell under the influence of its bishop, Ambrose. In 387 A.D. he was baptized a Christian. He was ordained a priest by the Bishop of Hippo in 391 A.D., and in 396 A.D. he himself became Bishop of Hippo.

Having worked his way through Manicheanism and Neo-Platonism to Christianity, St. Augustine was familiar with many of the currents of pagan philosophy. He was able to turn many of its formulations to account in his defense of the faith. No one has summarized his synthesis of Christian philosophy more compactly than Rudolf Sohm.

> On Easter Eve 387, at the age of thirty-three, he was baptized by the great Bishop Ambrose at Milan. The duty of his life was henceforth two-fold: to proclaim, first, the gospel of sin and grace, and then the glory of the Church. Against the British monk Pelagius he developed the doctrine of Original Sin and of the salvation of man by Grace alone, making the doctrine of Grace, as Luther at first also made it, equivalent to the doctrine of Predestination. Against the African Donatists, who would have made the effectual working of the sacraments dependent on the worthiness of the minister, he set up the idea of the Church as an institution for dispensing salvation, as an institution possessing *objective* sanctity. The supreme value of the church—even of the outwardly visible Church constituted as she is—he expressed in the statement that she represents the "City of God" (*Civitas Dei*) upon earth. From this commonwealth salvation flows forth upon the individual. To serve this commonwealth, and in particular to lead back the erring (the Donatists) by force into the Church is the highest duty of the State. Only by doing such service to the Church will the State attain a value which does not otherwise belong to it. The middle ages are dawning. Catholicism, at least Western Catholicism, in claiming supremacy for the Church over the world, is embodied for the first time in Augustine's mighty personality. Even in his monkish convictions he is a Catholic. Flight from the world into the cloister is to him the perfection of the Christian life.
>
> Yet this man has the Reformation—Luther's Reformation—in him too. Side by side with his conception of the Church as a hierarchy, he holds the opposite idea of the true Church as the invisible Church of the

predestined—the redeemed. In direct contradiction to his doctrine of the saving power of the Church, he lives by faith in grace freely given by God as the only source of salvation. He prepared a way for Catholicism by his doctrine of the Church, for Luther by his doctrine of Sin and Grace.[5]

St. Augustine worked elements of Hellenistic thought and Christian faith into a system of theology which was to remain the primary, uncontested framework of official church dogma for nearly a thousand years.

THE SCHOLASTIC DUEL WITH THE NEW URBAN INTELLECTUALS

St. Augustine brought many of the currents of ancient thought into a definitive synthesis within a framework of Christian faith at the very time the final collapse of the ancient city was imminent. The medieval heirs to the Greco-Roman intellectual were to be learned monks. In the Benedictine pattern of Western monasticism, from three to five hours a day were assigned to reading according to the season. As Butler observes:

> There can be little doubt that this reading was wholly devotional, confined to the Bible and the writings of the fathers, St. Basil and Cassian being recommended by name. Out of this germ grew in the course of ages those works of erudition and of historical science with which the Benedictine name in later ages became associated. . . . But the chief work of the monk was, in St. Benedict's eyes, neither field work nor literary work: all the services of Benedictines to civilization and education and letters have been but by-products.[6]

In the West there were long periods when the monastery was the only source of literacy. This was of inestimable value for the church, for again and again its literate popes and administrators were monastically trained. When new urban communities began to erupt through the floor of the medieval world and to displace its intellectuals, monasticism responded to the challenge with the development of powerful new orders:

> The "Four Orders" were (1) the Dominicans or Friars Preachers, often called Black Friars in England and Jacobins in France; (2) The Franciscans or Friars Minor, called in England Grey Friars, in France Cordeliers, and in Germany Barefoot Friars; (3) the Carmelites or Order of the Blessed Virgin of Mount Carmel, or White Friars; (4) the Austin Friars or Order of the Friar Hermits of St. Augustine. Many smaller Mendicant Orders also sprang up in the thirteenth century, but were suppressed, *i.e.*, forbidden to receive any more novices, by the Second Council of Lyons in 1274.[7]

The monastic orders rejected permanent endowments. Their members embraced a life of poverty, and undertook the reconciliation of secular and

[5] Rudolf Sohm, *Outlines of Church History*, trans. by May Sinclair (Boston: The Beacon Press, 1958), pp. 71–72.

[6] Dom E. C. Butler, "Monasticism," *The Cambridge Medieval History* (New York: The Macmillan Co., 1929), Vol. I, p. 538.

[7] A. G. Little, "The Mendicant Orders," *The Cambridge Medieval History* (New York: The Macmillan Co., 1929), Vol. VI, p. 727.

religious life. Many independent movements of this sort—organized groups of people devoting themselves to self-sacrifice, social work, and the imitation of Christ—appeared toward the end of the twelfth century. Among them were the Beguines and Beghars of the Low Countries, the Humiliati of Italy, and the Poor Men of Lyon. Between the Franciscans and the Poor Men of Lyon there was little difference other than the fact that the latter repudiated the Church. The Poor Men of Lyon were excommunicated as heretics, while the Franciscans were authorized as a religious order.

The Intellectual Ferment in the New Urban Communities

The conflict between the new urban communities and the church was inevitable. It was equally certain that the urban communities would give rise to a type of intellectual activity that would find its organization, in part, in opposition to the priest-theologian.

Pirenne has noted that as a general rule the lay princes favored the new urban communities. While they had nothing militarily or politically to fear from the *bourgeoisie*, it was to their economic advantage to protect them. The urbanites produced a new, taxable, moneyed wealth which helped the princes free themselves from dependency on the Church and the landed aristocrats. On the other hand, the bishops who remained on the sites of the once thriving Roman cities regarded with suspicion the struggles by the *bourgeoisie* to achieve autonomy.

> They were all the more suspicious because this autonomy was demanded by merchants. For the Church had an invincible objection to trade. It considered that trade endangered the salvation of souls, it accounted desire for gain as avarice, and in most commercial transactions it detected various forms of usury.[8]

The first struggle that cities arising in episcopal sees had to face was with the bishops. Pirenne has noted that the occurrences of insurrectional movements in episcopal cities were far too numerous not to be due to some common factor.

> The earliest mentioned occurred at Cologne in 1074; two years later in 1076 one broke out at Cambrai. Then about 1080 there followed a revolt at St. Quentin, one at Beauvais in 1099, one at Noyon in 1108–1109, one at Amiens in 1113, one at Laon in 1115. There is no doubt that this tendency to revolt was fomented by the merchants. The important part they played is definitely proved at Cambrai and Cologne; at Beauvais the insurrection movement was led by the cloth merchants. The subsequent insurrections at Noyon and Laon present a slightly different character. Here it seems that we are concerned with an agitation less obviously provoked by the merchant class. Serfs and even priests were involved.[9]

[8] Henri Pirenne, "Northern Towns and Their Commerce," *The Cambridge Medieval History* (New York: The Macmillan Co., 1929), Vol. VI, p. 517.

[9] *Ibid.*, p. 518.

However, where such insurrections are not directly traceable to the merchants, they were a precipitating factor. It is natural for class excitements to pull malcontents from other groups into their course.

These insurrections were no mere riots or occasions to let off steam, but directed movements. The merchants were determined to revise the laws and monetary arrangements sustained by the Church, which blocked the free exercise of their trade. They organized their movements into mutually sworn associations and proclaimed their communes in a revolutionary manner.

> The commune was, strictly speaking, the association of burghers, constituted by oath, who seized municipal power and undertook to defend both corporate and individual liberty against all attacks. It was the result of a conjuration and it sometimes even bore the name of Conjuration. Its members were conjurors (*coniurati*) and the same name *iuratus* or *jure* was adopted by the magistrates appointed at their head. It was thus essentially revolutionary, and it never appeared except in towns where self-government was gained as a result of a keen struggle. For this reason it is characteristic of episcopal cities, and especially of episcopal cities in Northern France.[10]

The aim of these revolutionary associations was to replace seigneurial law by an autonomous civic law and jurisdiction. When they succeeded, all inhabitants acquired similar status subject to the same courts and governed by the same council recruited from their members. The city became a distinct judicial territory. Their revolutionary origin did not prevent the communes from attaining a legal existence. Some revolutions were crushed, but many communes obtained charters from their overlord or king confirming their organization. Charters of communes such as were conceded only after insurrections in the eleventh century were frequently freely granted during the following century.

When the city so often arose as a revolutionary insurrection against the bishop, there is no question that it was providing an intellectual *milieu* for social roles other than that of priest. From the beginning the cities supported anticlerical types. Moreover, the city not only demanded different intellectual skills than a monastic or manorial community, but demanded them in far greater volume. In the monastic community the primary employment of literary skills was in devotional reading and study, and the keeping of monastic annals and records. In the manorial communities the amount of administrative work and record-keeping was so slight that all correspondence and records could be kept by the manorial priest who was, at times, the only literate person in the castle. The city, on the other hand, presented a great range of activities for which the routine application of literary skills was an absolute essential: business correspondence, record-keeping, administration of its many guilds, legal problems, and all the complete judicial, legislative, and administrative activities of the city itself.

[10] *Ibid.*, pp. 518–519.

The cities were seedbeds for voluntary associations of all sorts: for religious, welfare, health, economic, and political purposes. The cities were creating unprecedented needs in both quantity and kind for trained persons, which the existing monastic and cathedral schools were not equipped to supply. Besides, when active tensions with the bishops so often accompanied the establishment of the cities, the local clergy could hardly be expected to supply the trained persons who would make such revolts possible. At the same time, it was not altogether to the disadvantage of the bishops to have the cities grow up around them once again. Urban populations supplied a source of wealth undreamed of in the rural subsistence economy for the bishops as well as for lay lords. The cathedrals developed in size and wealth, undertook new building programs, developed administrative staffs, and incidentally developed new training schools, primarily to train their own personnel but also, at times, to serve the urban community and re-institute control over the urban population once again. However, whether these new educational institutions grew as voluntary guilds of students and teachers or by expansion of cathedral schools (the first was typical of southern Europe, the second typical of the north), an enormous expansion of secular education was under way to supply new requirements of the cities. Rashdall summarizes the basic patterns as follows:

> During the Dark Ages, whatever learning and education survived the barbarian cataclysm had their home almost exclusively in the monasteries and the cathedrals; and during this period the monastic schools were perhaps slightly in advance of the secular. The period has been called the Benedictine Age. In the cathedrals themselves some of the best-known teachers had been pupils of the monks. A marked feature of the intellectual new birth which took place in the twelfth century was the transference of the intellectual primacy from the monastic schools to those of the secular clergy. In the north of Europe the universities were an outgrowth of the cathedral schools, not of the monasteries. Anselm of Bec was one of the last great monastic teachers; the great Abelard—the introducer of a new era in the scholastic philosophy, the true father of the scholastic theology, out of whose teaching, though not in his lifetime, the University of Paris may be said to have grown—was a secular who lectured in the schools of the cathedral, though accidentally, as it were, he ended his days as a monk. At a later date, regulars played a great role in connection with the universities, but the universities themselves were essentially secular, *i.e.*, non-monastic, institutions. In Italy culture was never so completely the monopoly of the clergy as it came to be in the dark ages of northern Europe. The lay professions of law and medicine were never wholly extinguished; and, when the intellectual revival came, the movement was not so closely connected with the Church. And the universities to which it gave birth, though like all medieval institutions, they had close relations with the Church, may be looked upon, on the whole, not only as secular but as lay institutions. This was one of the great differences which from first to last distinguished the universities of northern Europe from those of the south, or at least of Italy. In the northern universities

> . . . the scholar was *ipso facto* regarded for many purposes as a clerk; he wore, or was supposed to wear, the tonsure and the clerical habit, while the Master was still more definitely invested with the privileges and subject to the restrictions of the ecclesiastical life, including the obligation to celibacy. In Italy the teacher was more often a layman than an ecclesiastic; the scholar was not necessarily a clerk, and the control which ecclesiastical authorities exercised over the universities was only of the kind which they exercised in all spheres of medieval life.[11]

The universities were the eventual institutionalization of a ferment of new ideas and the demand for new types of training at first supplied in the cities by voluntary associations of teachers and students. In the nature of the case, churchmen tried to take over or, at least, to guide the course of such movements, for if they did not, the control of society would slip out of their hands.

The Rise of the Universities

In the cities that had begun to take shape in Italy during the twelfth century, the typical institution of higher learning of the West was created—the university. Through Italy and Sicily in the twelfth century there was an influx of new knowledge into Europe from Arabic scholars, including the works of Aristotle, Euclid, Ptolemy, and the Greek physicians. The core of the new higher learning was made up of medicine and law.

In Salerno, south of Naples, in Lombard, and in Norman territory, the contact with the traditions of Greece was never completely lost. By the middle of the eleventh century, Salerno took shape as the foremost medical center of Europe around the teachings of Hippocrates amplified by developments in anatomy and surgery. In 1231 Frederick II regulated its degrees.[12] Meanwhile, in response to the revival of trade and the rise of town life, new demands were made for a law adequate to more complex social and economic conditions. Bologna became the center for the revival of Roman law as Salerno was for the revival of Greek medicine. By 1158 a student class of sufficient importance had appeared to receive a formal grant of rights and privileges from Frederick Barbarossa. The student corporation (university) was organized as a means of protection against the townspeople over the cost of rooms and supplies. The student organization was also employed to control the professors, who were put under bond and required to live up to detailed regulations guaranteeing the students their money's worth.[13]

Excluded from the universities of the students, the professors formed guilds or "colleges" requiring special qualifications ascertained by examina-

[11] Hastings Rashdall, "The Medieval Universities," *The Cambridge Medieval History* (New York: The Macmillan Co., 1926), Vol. VI, pp. 559–560.

[12] Charles Homer Haskins, *The Rise of Universities* (Ithaca: Cornell University Press, 1957), pp. 4 ff.

[13] *Ibid.*, pp. 7 ff.

tion for admission.[14] The professor's certification of attainment which gave him license to teach became the earliest type of academic degree. At an early period Bologna had already developed standard academic degrees, a university organization, and special officials such as the rector.

Bologna was the model of university organization for Italy, Spain, and southern France. Frederick II founded the University of Naples (1224) on its pattern. Padua was founded two years earlier as a secession from Bologna. In northern Europe the university originated around the cathedral school of Notre Dame in Paris. By the beginning of the twelfth century schools attached to cathedrals included Liège, Rheims, Laon, Paris, Orleans, and Chartres. Paris received its first royal charter in 1200; by this time there were four faculties each under a dean: arts, canon law, medicine, and theology. Paris was the model for the northern universities as Bologna was for the southern group. Oxford developed in the twelfth century; Cambridge somewhat later. By the end of the Middle Ages eighty universities had been founded in different parts of Europe.

This growth of universities was a direct or indirect response to the new demand for experts on the part of the new communities. The rise of medicine was a product of the requirements of more wealthy and sophisticated persons who broke out of the framework of medieval conceptions and limitations. The establishment of the faculties of civil and canon law was in response not only to the growth of legal problems in conjunction with the rise of the cities and the rapid development of trade, but to the increasing legal requirements of church and state. (It is noteworthy that as long as the University of Paris was under religious domination it had a college of canon law but not one of civil law.) The appearance of a theological faculty also testifies to the increased need of the church for trained persons in the face of accelerating social developments.

The Reopening of the Controversy between Classical Philosophy and Christian Theology

The transformation of urban-based voluntary associations for the acquisition of the knowledges and skills required by the changing times into the universities proper was accompanied by a reopening of the controversy between classical philosophy and Christian theology with which the ancient development had closed. Langlois phrased this succinctly:

> At the very moment when the new Aristotle and his Moslem commentators were introduced at Paris, the philosophical-theological system which was reigning in the schools was Platonic idealism or pseudo-Platonic, on the model of St. Augustine. Although St. Augustine had been almost dazzled by Greek metaphysics, yet he was one of the most violent contemners of reason: he subordinated the True to the Good, the Intelligence to the Will, and prostrated human thought in the dust. The disciples of this somber genius continued to maintain his funda-

[14] *Ibid.*, p. 11.

> mental theses, which were satisfactory to spirits inclined to obedience, to religious and mystical souls, to born defenders of orthodoxy, and to rhetoricians. For these reasons, Augustinianism has never ceased to have numerous partisans.[15]

Augustinianism represented a subordination of the classical philosophy to the requirements of faith; it was brilliantly adapted to a religious evolution on the threshold of withdrawal into agricultural subsistence communities. When the voluntary guilds of scholars and teachers emerged in the cities, it was because of a need for training in skills and knowledges not available in the monastic and cathedral schools. One must not be misled by the fact that some men associated with the church participated in the brilliant recovery of ancient thought which got under way in the twelfth century, the so-called twelfth century Renaissance. It arose in response to the requirements of the emerging urban *milieux*—not those of the monasteries. However, it was equally evident that if the Church was to remain in control of intellectual life, it must either destroy these trends or take them over.

> The rationalistic philosophy of Aristotle was received with distrust by theologians who followed the Augustinian tradition, because they judged it dangerous; but most scholars fell upon this new food with an avidity which is comparable only to the intoxication of the first humanists in the presence of the resuscitated Antiquity. Such a vigorous fermentation immediately set in that the ecclesiastical authorities attempted to stop it, in 1210 and 1215: "The Books of Aristotle on metaphysics and natural philosophy are not to be read." Nevertheless, the prohibition pure and simple could not be maintained. April 13, 1231, Pope Gregory IV gave absolution to the masters and students who had been excommunicated for having disobeyed orders by reading and interpreting Aristotle; in principle, he confirmed the prohibited decrees of 1210 and 1215, but "provisionally, until the books of the Philosopher had been examined and expurgated."[16]

The three major courses of study—philosophy, law, and medicine—of the primary university centers of the thirteenth century (Paris, Bologna, and Salerno) all had major nonreligious components in their origins. However, it was also true that at an early stage the religious authorities took cognizance of them. Speaking of this revival of intellectual activity in which the intersection of secular and sacred interests led to the institutionalization of the universities, Rashdall states:

> If the revived study of the Classics was prominent in the earliest phase of the movement—the phase represented by such teachers as Bernard of Chartres and such writers as John of Salisbury—these studies were never prominent at Paris, and were everywhere thrown into the background by the re-discovery of the lost works of Aristotle at the

[15] Adapted from C. V. Langlois, in Lavisse, *Histoire de France*, Vol. III, Part II, 1901, p. 387; Dana Carleton Munro and George Clarke Sellery, *Medieval Civilization* (New York: The Century Co., 1910), p. 460.
[16] *Ibid.*, pp. 460–461.

> beginning of the thirteenth century. In Italy the movement, though it began with a revival of literary study, and of Roman Law as a branch of ancient literature, soon concentrated itself on the study of Law which became increasingly scientific and professional. Broadly speaking, Paris was the home of scholastic Philosophy and Theology; Bologna was the great School of Law, and, in a subordinate degree, of Medicine. The contrast must not be overstated: there was a large body of canonists at Paris; Philosophy was studied at Bologna—though chiefly as a preparation for Medicine rather than Theology. And Medicine was studied in both; as a place of medical study, Bologna was inferior to Salerno, which was exclusively a Studium of Medicine. From a period considerably before the actual birth of the university organization, these three places —Paris, Bologna, Salerno—stood forth as the three great homes of highest culture. By the twelfth century they had come to be known as *Studia Generalia*, a term which at first meant simply, places of study resorted to by students from all parts.[17]

The rise of the orders of Mendicant Friars coincided with this great intellectual activity, one phase of which was the rediscovery of ancient learning, particularly Aristotle. After an outbreak of heretical teaching at Paris based on Aristotle, lecturing on Aristotle's natural philosophy was prohibited in the university by papal decree. However, the ancient learning was too brilliantly adapted to the new *milieu* to be put down, and the second phase of the interaction between ancient learning and Christian faith got under way. The reconciliation of Aristotle with Christian theology was taken over by the friars and carried through, particularly by the Dominicans. The two greatest thinkers of the Dominican Order were Albert the Great (c. 1200–1280) and Thomas Aquinas (1225–1274). The Dominicans reached their greatest power in Paris. The Franciscans, on the other hand, reached prominence at Oxford, where Robert Grosseteste became lecturer and produced the first of the *Summa* which were intended to synthesize the newly discovered Aristotle with Christian theology (1245). The greatest of the Franciscans were Roger Bacon, Duns Scotus (1270–1302), and William of Occam (c. 1320–1340).

Thus the Renaissance of the twelfth century was a major component in the stimulation of scholastic philosophy to the period of its most rapid evolution since the days of St. Augustine. The response of the church to it had roughly assumed three forms: the official recognition of the new intellectual movements by sanctioning the universities and, as far as possible, bringing them under church control; attempting by papal decree to prohibit that part of the new instruction deemed heretical; and encouragement of the great scholastic syntheses of the Franciscans and particularly the Dominicans.

From the beginning, in the rising universities there appeared essentially nonpriestly intellectuals. Such intellectuals were in the forefront of the reception of materials from classical antiquity which they immediately per-

[17] Rashdall, *op. cit.*, pp. 560–561.

ceived to be more directly adapted to their requirements than much of the traditional church theology. From the beginning, the universities were battlegrounds of the priest-theologian and the humanist. The thirteenth century victory of the Scholastics was only temporary, however, as the humanist—the first fully distinctive modern intellectual type—was emerging.

THE WESTERN HUMANIST

It has frequently been observed that the nearest point of contact between the ancient and modern intellectual is found in the Western humanist. Like his oriental counterpart, the Western humanist was equipped with secular literary learning and was the bearer of an ideal of cultivated deportment. There are sociological reasons for the similarity.

To Burckhardt goes the credit for the brilliant discernment of the changing character of self-consciousness that accompanied the movement from the feudal world into the city. Under feudal conditions, he urged, man was conscious of himself as a member of some general category—a race, people, party, family, or corporation. However, in the cities, corresponding to the change in his objective community, man became conscious of himself as a spiritual individual.[18] Dante's great poem would not have been possible in any European country of the time, for most of Europe lay under the spell of traditional rural communities. Only Italy evoked the treasures of individuality which the poet set forth.

Burckhardt believed that despotism was a major source of individuality, for being persons operating outside the sphere of tradition, the tyrant and the *condottiere* had to rely upon their personal resources. Their secretaries, ministers, poets, and companions were also forced to call upon their personal abilities to meet their problems. Individuality was also promoted by the new wealth, the new culture, and the conflict between church and state. Such conditions precipitated the emergence of the political individual. The private man indifferent to politics and busy with interests of his own also appeared, for members of defeated parties were involuntarily cast on their own resources. A heightened individuality inspired Agnolo Pandolfini (d. 1446) in his treatise on domestic economy which delineated the ideal of a private life more satisfactory than politics.

The cosmopolitanism emerging in cultivated circles of the city was itself a developed form of the individualism it expressed:

> Dante . . . finds a new home in the language and culture of Italy, but goes beyond even this in the words, "my country is the whole world," and when his recall to Florence was offered him on unworthy conditions, he wrote back: "Can I not everywhere behold the light of the sun and stars; everywhere meditate on the noblest truths, without appearing ingloriously and shamefully before the city and the people? Even my bread will not fail me." The artists exult no less defiantly in

[18] Jacob Burckhardt, *The Civilization of the Renaissance* (New York: Oxford University Press, 1945), pp. 81 ff.

> their freedom from the constraints of fixed residence. "Only he who has learned everything," says Ghiberti, "is nowhere a stranger; robbed of his fortune and without friends, he is yet the citizen of every country, and can fearlessly despise the changes of fortune." In the same strain an exiled humanist writes: "Wherever a learned man fixes his seat, there is home."[19]

The new individualism was manifest in the frequent appearance of many-sided personalities. Merchants also served as statesmen. Both merchants and statesmen often acquired both classical languages. Private education was vigorously promoted by middle-class strata for daughters as well as for sons. Educated men valued wide learning which could range from ethics to politics, from Aristotle to Pliny.

Learned men eagerly assembled collections of natural history, sought to apply the geography of the ancients to modern conditions, and established libraries and museums. It was quite possible for the same individuals to translate the comedies of Plautus, serve as their own stage managers, and act in the parts. One and the same person was often magistrate, secretary, and diplomat by turns. Typifying the many-faceted men of the time, in Burckhardt's view, was Leon Battista Alberti (1404–1472).[20] When young he achieved unusual gymnastic prowess, and was unsurpassed in walking and riding. He learned music without a master well enough to compose creditably. He studied both civil and canon law; he painted and modeled with facility. In Burckhardt's words, "Leonardo da Vinci was to Alberti as the finisher to the beginner, as the master to the dilettante."[21]

Under such circumstances men ceased to identify the highest ideal of life as the status honor of feudal man. Many men turned their highest energies to the pursuit of fame. Social recognition of this type of aspiration appears in the coronation of poets. Poets and men of letters were given honors formerly offered only to saints and heroes. The cult of the birthplaces of famous men was amplified by the cult of their graves. Cities engaged in rivalry with one another for possession of the bones of their own and foreign celebrities.

> By the side of these local temples of fame, which myth, legend, popular imagination, and literary tradition combined to create, the poet-scholars built up a great Pantheon of worldwide celebrity.[22]

As a counterweight to an often overdeveloped individuality, Burckhardt notes, was the appearance of ridicule and wit. Petrarch pioneered the collection of witty sayings. Among the cities Florence was particularly famous for the cynicism and sharpness of its wits. Eminent wits were themselves celebrities. No person or institution escaped their mockery, which ranged from the caricatures of the lovelorn wails of Petrarch to the parodies of the church

19 *Ibid.*, pp. 83–84.
20 *Ibid.*, pp. 85–86.
21 *Ibid.*, p. 87.
22 *Ibid.*, p. 91.

processions. Italy became, in Burckhardt's words, a school for scandal in a manner not to be approached again until the France of Voltaire.

The flowering of modern individuality in the cities of Renaissance Europe has many parallels in the princely courts of feudal China, in the royal cities of the Indian kingdoms and of the Jewish monarchical period, in the autonomous city-states of ancient Greece. In all times and areas an intensified individuality has accompanied the formative period of the community. The medieval priest-theologian is the Western counterpart to the religious hierarchs of the Shang and early Chou periods of China, to the Vedic priest of India, to the *ro'eh* and *seer* of premonarchical Judaism, and to the Homeric bard and soothsayer of the Greek Heroic period. The Western humanist was the counterpart of the mandarin, guru, of the Upanishadic period, and genteel, heterodox priest, prophet, Yahweh priest, and philosopher of the creative phase of the Axial Period.

The Western humanists were the creative bearers of an awakened intellectual life in the formative phase of the Western city. They formed a stratum of literarily trained, many-sided individuals. They shared a common set of values, problems, and status situations—positions and points of view rather than a special philosophy.

The humanists were often statesmen, merchants, diplomats, secretaries, administrators, poets, companions. They were almost as flexible as the citizen-intellectuals of the Classical Greek period. They were often self-taught, but above all in their circles the value of education was perceived. Many of them served as private tutors, and were often engaged in private teaching apart from the growing universities. They were all, though to varying degrees, learned in Latin and Greek antiquities. If they had a method of thought and life, it was the exploitation of ancient texts for guidance in their contemporary problems. They developed the methods of historical and philological criticism in the course of their researches and the promotion of an educational program based on the study of the classics. By the thirteenth century the humanists had established a distinctive point of view outside of, and partly in opposition to, the church and the scholastics who were fighting for control of the universities.

Humanism first became popular in the cities of Italy, spreading rapidly in cities and courts outside Italy and reaching its high point in the sixteenth century. The self-image of the humanist was clearly expressed by Petrarch (1304–1374). In a letter to Francesco Bruni, papal secretary in Avignon, he stated:

> "You make an orator of me, a historian, a philosopher, and poet, and finally even a theologian. . . . But let me tell you, my friend, how far I fall short of your estimation. . . . I am nothing of what you attribute to me. What am I then? I am a fellow who never quits school."[23]

[23] Ernst Cassirer, Paul Oskar Kristeller, and John Herman Randall, Jr. (eds.), *The Renaissance Philosophy of Man* (Chicago: The University of Chicago Press, 1948), p. 34.

Lorenzo Valla (1405–1457), who shared with many other humanists of his day an antipathy to Aristotle, to dialectic, and to the scholastics, illustrates the freedom of the humanistic mind in this early period in his cheerful attempt to reconcile reason and faith, philosophy and theology, paganism and Christianity. This, however, was quite distinct from the scholastic enterprise: faith was being subordinated to reason by Valla. More than any of his contemporaries he opened up the question of the philosophical basis of individual autonomy. This seems to have been his motive in freeing the problem of free will from Aristotelian and scholastic interpretations,[24] which led Ernst Cassirer to state:

> . . . for the first time since the days of the ancients the problem of Freedom was cited before a pure worldly forum, before the judgment chair of "natural reason. . . ." And still one traces above all in his work the power of the new critical-modern spirit which becomes conscious of its might and its intellectual tools.[25]

Marsilio Ficino (1433–1499) reveals the early Western humanist as reviver of a purified Platonism and as founder of the private school. With the patronage of Cosimo de Medici he established the Platonic Academy of Florence which became the center for the revival of Platonism throughout Europe.[26] Ficino actively promoted the idea of the unity and universality of human aspiration. Religion and philosophy were conceived by him as dual manifestations of man's spiritual life, each necessary for achievement of the highest good. In his five questions concerning the mind,[27] he reasoned that all human desire can have only boundless truth and goodness as its objective. The human soul is a middle essence with affinities with all things above and below.

Giovanni Pico della Mirandola (1463–1494) expressed the humanistic outlook in still another way in his ideal of the dignity of man and his desire to see a universal harmony among philosophers. He published in Rome in 1486 nine hundred theses inviting all scholars to a great public disputation. The latent tension ever present between priest-theologian and humanist here again became manifest after the earlier encounter in the university. Pope Innocent VIII suspended the debate, and appointed a commission to examine the theses. The commission condemned some of them as heretical. In the theses Pico advanced the proposition that the uniqueness of man consists of his lack of fixed properties, his power to share in the properties of other beings according to his own choice. The uniqueness of man lay not simply in his role as inventor of the arts and crafts, or even in his powers of speech

[24] Lorenzo Valla, "Dialogue on Free Will," *op. cit.*, pp. 155 ff.

[25] Ernst Cassirer, *Individuum und Kosmos in der Philosophie der Renaissance* ("*Studien der Bibliothek Warburg*"), Vol. X (Leipzig and Berlin, 1927), p. 82. Quoted by Charles Edward Trinkaus, Jr., in *The Renaissance Philosophy of Man, op. cit.*, p. 152.

[26] Josephine L. Burroughs in *The Renaissance Philosophy of Man, op. cit.*, p. 185 ff.

[27] *Op. cit.*, pp. 193 ff.

and reason, but in his ability to form his own nature by his own free choice.[28]

Humanism rises like a rainbow over the Western city in its formative period. Yet anyone who would seize it in its essence often finds that it dances tantalizingly out of reach. For the humanists did not fix a position; they pioneered an outlook. They were often anticlerical; originally they were rarely antireligious. They were often anti-Aristotle in considerable measure because he had been taken over by the Scholastics, but some humanists freed Aristotle and even Scholasticism for fresh application to everyday life. They were often preoccupied with the classics, but in the early period the classics were rarely turned into fetishes; they were freed for application to contemporary life and reinterpreted in terms of contemporary forms. The humanists reopened the question of the nature of man and freedom of the soul, but differed widely in their answers to the questions they propounded.

Humanism was a manifestation of the awakened intellectuality of the Western city. It was produced in these new communities by intellectuals cast upon their own resources for the solution of unprecedented problems. It was the self-confident view of men relying on their own talents and scholarship to solve the problems they faced.

Early humanism assumed recognizable shape in the twelfth century. By the thirteenth it fought and lost its first battle with scholasticism. It mounted rapidly to popularity in the Italian cities outside the universities, after having been partly blocked off within them, and soon spread to the cities and courts of northern Europe. It was not a point of view that could be permanently confined to private circles. It soon penetrated the upper ranks of the clergy and rallied its forces within the universities. By the sixteenth century early humanism had reached its height. Also, by the sixteenth century, powerful forces were at work which were to bring the early form of Western humanism to an end. The forces associated with the Protestant revolts (both in Protestant and Roman Catholic countries) created an atmosphere quite alien to the humanistic outlook. Besides, the institutions of the city were hardening in the face of extra-city forces.

It was of great significance to the West that at the very time the city had begun to lose its elasticity, the new community represented by the nation had begun to assume distinct enough form to take up where the city left off. One of the fundamental contrasts between the social roots of ancient and modern creativity is that while ancient creativity rested on one wave of community formation, modern creativity rests on two. The nation-state was not like the empire of ancient China, or like the Indian caste system, or the pariah community of Jewry, or the Macedonian or Roman Empires which represented in considerable measure a reduction and hardening of prior community elements. Rather, the nation-state was a genuine new community of greater complexity than the city. However, the nation-state was not

[28] Kristeller, in *The Renaissance Philosophy of Man, op. cit.*, p. 219.

merely a higher stage of the city, for though the city was a component in its growth, it sprang from independent roots, eventually coming into conflict with and partly supplanting the city.

Like the city before it in its formative period, the nation-state faced unprecedented problems. At the very time when the freedom of the individual was narrowing, within the city, it was expanding within the nation-state. In this new, more comprehensive framework, the creative individual was encouraged in a self-reliant manner to call upon his own nature as he did earlier in the city. To be sure, in this second phase, Western humanism was somewhat changed. Remnants of the older humanism had been taken up in theological circles and the universities, where classical learning had been transformed from a fresh approach to the contemporary social order into a basis for reaction. Hence the true heirs of the humanistic position in the new period were often disinclined to accept the classics (though much of the old humanistic nostalgia remains). When the issues were drawn, the humanists of the new period remained true to the critical spirit of early humanism. Moreover, the second phase of humanism enjoyed the strategic possession of a far richer cultural heritage than their predecessors, a heritage which included that of the early humanists.

By the seventeenth century the new intellectual ferment associated with the rise of the nation-state had as definitely gotten under way as was true for early humanism of the twelfth century city. By the eighteenth century it had achieved its classic fullness and a name of its own—*The Enlightenment.* The early humanists had raised the problem of the autonomy of the individual under the form of the problem of freedom of the will. The thinkers of the *enlightenment* take as unquestioned that the human understanding is capable, by its own power and without recourse to the supernatural, of understanding and controlling the world.[29] The base values of the eighteenth-century humanists were the same as those of their Renaissance predecessors: hatred of ignorance and superstition, love of intelligence and learning, conviction of the innate dignity of the individual. Moreover, like their Renaissance predecessors, they shared an outlook rather than a fixed position. This was formulated clearly by Lecky:

> By the spirit of Rationalism . . . I understand not any class of definite doctrines or criticisms, but rather a certain caste of thought, or bias of reasoning. . . . It leads men on all occasions to subordinate dogmatic theology to the dictates of reason and of conscience. . . . It predisposes men, in history, to attribute all kinds of phenomena to natural rather than miraculous causes; in theology to esteem succeeding systems the expressions of the wants and aspirations of that religious sentiment which is planted in all men; and, in ethics, to regard as duties only those which conscience reveals to be such.[30]

[29] Carl Becker, *The Heavenly City* (New Haven: Yale University Press, 1932); W. E. H. Lecky, *Rationalism in Europe* (New York: D. Appleton & Co., 1891).
[30] Lecky, *op. cit.,* Vol. I, pp. 17–18.

The enlightenment thinkers often wore an impudent air of skepticism which was only the flimsiest of disguises for bubbling optimism and, at times, moral smugness. They were never more secure than in the conviction that they needed only to consult their own minds to arrive at the truth.

Corresponding to the cosmopolitan universalism of the earlier humanists was the international character of enlightenment culture; there was also a corresponding flexibility of roles. French and Latin were used everywhere. Hume and Adam Smith were familiar in Paris salons; Montesquieu, Voltaire, and Rousseau spent time in England. Even scholars who did not travel (for example, Kant and the young Goethe) were usually in correspondence with leading scholars of the day, and familiar with all main intellectual developments in other circles.[31]

Their intellectual products have little national identification. Rousseau's *Social Contract*, for example, and More's *Utopia* avoid frontiers and national identifications. Voltaire's *Candide* presents a philosopher's progress in the world, and ends with the advice to mind one's own business, but between individual self-sufficiency and philosophic universalism there is no stopping point.

The highest ideal of cultivation is that of the universalistic scholar, not the specialist. This ideal inspired the French scholars to undertake with assistance of the Académie and royal government to compile an encyclopedia, the prospectus of which was published in 1750. Goethe and Voltaire each in his particular way came close to approximating the condition of the universal scholar. Goethe practiced law for a period before the imperial law courts; for ten years he was an official of the Duchy of Weimar. He hated war, and thought revolution was not worth the price in blood. His private loyalties were to learning and culture rather than to the state. His study and work ranged the entire field of letters and science. Voltaire was twice sent to the Bastille, where he spent his time writing plays. During his three years in England he earned his way by his pen. He spent some time in many of the courts of Europe. He was careful with his earnings, and planned to secure his own freedom by purchasing land in three European states. Condorcet observed that it would have required a league of the major European powers to silence him. Voltaire wrote plays, histories, and popular science, and in his way covered most of the world of letters.

Whatever the spirit of rationalism touched, it naturalized and tried to reduce to rational principles. In *De jure belli ac pacis* (1625) (*The Laws of War and Peace*), Hugo Grotius contemplated a system of universal jurisprudence resting on principles as self-evident as mathematical axioms. So unconditionally valid, he thought, was his scheme of natural law to be as to hold for all reasoning beings including God. In *De Veritate* (1624) Lord Herbert of Cherbury visualized a rational theology resting not on authority

[31] R. B. Mowat, *The Age of Reason* (Boston: Houghton Mifflin, 1934), pp. 36 ff.

and revelation but on universal principles immediately evident to the understanding of all men. Lord Herbert's study was a major influence in the development of a rational psychology and empiricist epistemology. Just as Grotius' influence was transmitted to Leibnitz and Christian Wolff, that of Lord Herbert was transmitted to theological rationalists (such as John Hales and Chillingworth), the Cambridge Platonists (Whichcote, John Smith, Cudworth, and Henry More) and the deists and freethinkers generally (John Toland, Anthony Collins, Herman Samuel Reimarus, Voltaire, Diderot, d'Alembert). In *Leviathan* (1651) Thomas Hobbes visualized the rational organization of the state by way of a formal contract to end the state of "war of each against all," which he assumed would characterize man in his natural condition. Hobbes' views had general influence on most later political thinkers, including Locke, Rousseau, and Kant. In the *Spirit of the Laws*, which has at times been described as the greatest book of the eighteenth century, Montesquieu (1689–1755) accepted the rationalistic theory of human nature of his contemporaries and went beyond it to develop a natural and social environmentalism to explain why an identical human nature should in fact display such varied forms. In numerous special treaties the physiocrats laid the foundation for the first general form of the classical economic doctrines of Adam Smith's *Wealth of Nations* (1776). The physiocrats and classical economists conceived economic behavior as a natural product of rational human activity. In *Outlines of an Historical View of the Progress of the Human Mind* (1795), Condorcet synthesized the historical theories of the enlightenment in his conception of the progress of the human mind as the central law of society.[32]

Like their humanistic predecessors, the men of the enlightenment were a product of an open period of community formation. Like them, they found the point for the synthesis of their lives and philosophies in their own hearts and minds, in their intellectual and scholarly skills. Like them, they carried out the liquidation of traditional social forms, standing in the way of new community formation. Like their predecessors, they partly originated outside the universities and other formal institutional hierarchies, but helped create the social forms of new communities and the dogmas of new academic disciplines. The early humanists were spokesmen for the cities, the later humanists for the nation. Each in his way helped to create the community that made their own situation impossible.

The humanists pioneered one form of the intellectual life of the free Western man. By and large they were optimists, confident in the abilities of the human reason to solve the problems of man's destiny. Society, to them, was not the end of man, but his instrument. Institutions were made for people, not people for institutions. The highest objective of society was

32 In addition to the various particular works cited, for other references see Ernst Cassirer, *The Philosophy of the Enlightenment*, trans. by Fritz C. A. Koelln and James P. Pettigrove (Boston: The Beacon Press, 1951).

the fullest possible development of human personality. In this form humanism represents the general foundation of Western liberalism.

THE WESTERN SCIENTIST

The debt of the West to the humanists is very great, for they presided over the birth of its two major community forms: the city and the nation-state. They helped free these communities from the dead hand of the past, provided the justifications for their expansion, indicated their aspirations, and helped to implement their new institutions. But in the end the humanists were not destined to give their signature to the epoch. We live not in an age of humanism, but in an age of science.

There is fairly widespread recognition of the fact, despite denials, that the humanist and the scientist are to some extent contrasting intellectual types. It hardly need be added that the contrast is not absolute, nor does it extend to every point. The very examples of a happy fusion are instructive—as when a humanist is also a scientist, or when a scientist wins recognition as a humanist. The point of gravity of the humanist is in the world of letters, in scholarship, in learning; the point of gravity of the scientist is in the world of experimental research. When a scientist is said to be a humanist, it is usually because over and beyond his successful conduct of research (laboratory or other), he is also a man of erudition; when a humanist is said to be a scientist, it is because over and beyond his scholarly achievements he is at home in research (usually experimental). At the other extreme from the scholarly man of letters who abhors the laboratory is the experimental-minded individual who is inclined to dismiss the world of letters as mere untested balderdash until such time as it has been processed through the laboratory.

The contrast between the humanist and the scientist, however, is more extensive than the mere location of the center of their activity between the world of letters and the laboratory. The fundamental difference between humanism and science is that between a normative and an empirical discipline. Humanism is a system of values and modes of conduct designed to secure them; science is evaluatively neutral pursuit of knowledge, renouncing all claims to prescribe what ought to be. At times, this difference has been confused by the evident fact that same types of social *milieu* negative to humanism are also negative to the pursuit of scientific objectivity. Hence, it is sometimes stated that science has at least that minimum value program which would make science itself possible. However, the only scientific proposition is: "if you wish to promote science, then certain specifiable social conditions are necessary." The further proposition, "science ought to be promoted," is not scientific.

Humanism locates ultimate value in the fullest self-realization of the human personality. This aspect of its theory was never more brilliantly formulated than by Kant in his various explications of the categorical imperative: so act that one's action can become a universal law. This meant, for Kant, that a type of individuality was the ultimate good. Nothing, he maintained, is more ultimately good than the good will. Hence the categorical imperative was capable of being reformulated: so act that one never uses other persons as means, only as ends. This formulation of the humanistic and enlightenment theory of individuality in its relation to society was not, as Kant knew, a scientific statement. It belonged not to the sphere of science but to the sphere of ethics. Kant was convinced that the nonscientific category of freedom was as crucial to the sphere of ethics as the category of causality was to the sphere of scientific explanation. This, however, was no grounds for confusing them.

Western humanists immediately strike us as the counterpart of the ancient intellectual because their knowledge, too, was always ultimately normative. The Western humanist is the transitional intellectual type from the ancient to the modern intellectual. The reason why the Western scientist immediately strikes one as different from the ancient intellectual (and from the humanist) is that his knowledge always rests on empirical rather than normative considerations.

It is not unfair to describe scientific knowledge as instrumental, if one does not construe this too narrowly. It is certainly wrong to describe scientific knowledge as practically instrumental, though much of it is. The pure or theoretical scientist is concerned with the solution of problems arising out of the growing body of scientific knowledge in its relation to empirical events. Often the pure scientist will give for his studies a practical justification, as it were, at second remove. So, for example, one often hears that, when one develops applied science at the expense of pure science, in the long run the sources from which applied scientists draw their ideas disappear. Thus, pure science is being justified by its value for practice after all; it is merely a prudent long-term annuity. This is not very satisfactory, since it also rests on the promise of results, though not very immediate results. Most persons prefer the bird in hand. In the face of this rather lame justification for science, many theoretical scientists maintain that they want to know for the sake of knowing, and that science is the pursuit of knowledge for its own sake. However, since science is never a knowledge which prescribes human ends, this seems to put the scientist in a position comparable to that of the miser toward his money; he too has converted a purely instrumental form of power into an end in itself. In any case, the ultimately instrumental character of scientific knowledge remains. In the argument that science increases man's ability to predict, to control, to master nature either immediately or in the long run remains the more convincing justification of scientific knowledge. That the possessor of instrumental knowledge should give his signature to an entire epoch is a most extraordinary fact. How and why this came about contains the ultimate mystery and paradox of the West.

Without pretending to solve the mystery of the rise of the Western scientist to a position of dominance over other intellectual types, some of the characteristics of the process of establishing empirical knowledge and the change in the intellectual's role that made it possible will be noted.

The roots of empirical knowledge are as deep as life itself. Every living creature contains sufficiently effective response-potential to the world around it to survive, or it does not exist long. Very often the instinctive adaptation of a creature to its environment is so subtle as, almost spontaneously, to evoke the characterization of it as a kind of biological wisdom. In the more complex creatures the location of the response potential of the creature tends to move to the higher brain centers, to be intellectualized. What is lost in instinctive fixity in this process is more than gained in adaptability.

In an address delivered on the occasion of the centennial celebration of the organization of the United States Patent Office, Otis T. Mason called up the image of what man must have been like before the rise of civilization:

> But, I ask you now, . . . go with me to that early day when the first being, worthy to be called man, stood upon this earth. How economical has been his endowment. There is no hair on his body to keep him warm, his jaws are the feeblest in the world, his arm is not equal to that of a gorilla, he cannot fly like the eagle, he cannot see into the night like an owl, even the hare is fleeter than he. He has no clothing, no shelter. He had no tools or industries or experience, no society or language or arts of pleasure, he had yet no theory of life and poor conceptions of the life beyond.[33]

The all-important property of man, as Mason sees it, that could change all this is his faculty for invention:

> Through this faculty of invention, the whole earth is man's. There is no lone island fit for his abode whereon some Alexander Selkirk has not made a home. For every mineral, plant, and animal so far known a place has been found . . . in his *Systema Naturae*. Every creature is subject to man; the winds, the seas, the sunshine, the lightning do his bidding. Projecting his vision beyond his tiny plane; this inventing animal has cataloged and traced the motion of every star.[34]

His faculty for inventing, together with his capacity to retain what he has learned in his habits, potentially turns every invention, in Mason's phrases, into the very nursery of future inventions, into the cradle of a future Hercules. The original ancestors of the major nineteenth century inventions were often quite humble: the ancestor of the steam plow was the digging stick sharpened and hardened by fire; the ancestor of the steam harvester was the stone sickle; of the thresher the roasting tray; of the cotton gin and power loom crude frames to aid the human fingers; of the

[33] Otis T. Mason, *Proceedings and Addresses,* 1891, pp. 403–412.
[34] *Ibid.*, p. 403.

sewing machine the needle or bodkin of bone with a leather cap over the ends of the fingers for a thimble.

The aspiration for more exact empirical knowledge is as old as human culture. Mason is quite correct: the basic process in the mastery of nature is invention or discovery. Moreover, for every invention or discovery there are perhaps a hundred tentative probings or accidents of thought which fail to work. An invention or discovery is an idea which practice has confirmed and society has accepted.

One should not think of inventions and discoveries as only, or primarily, material in nature. The greatest of all complexes of inventions is language, which lifted all others to a higher plane of generality and became the mechanism of all higher forms of civilization. A new form of social organization is as much an invention as a new kind of arrowhead, and may be more significant. However, an invention, material or nonmaterial, acquires significance only when accepted. If there are at least a hundred trial ideas for every one confirmed as an invention, there are at least a hundred inventions delayed in reception or by-passed for every one accepted into the conserving complex of community formation.

Thus we are brought back to a point noted before: every community has a body of empirical knowledge about nature and man appropriate to it; new discoveries or inventions proceed from this base, being impeded or spurred on by the basic forces sustaining the particular community. Invention is possible in any community, but only a highly specialized community elevates the scientist to a key position among its social types.

The comparatively open periods of community formation are usually marked by extensive gains in the stock of empirical knowledge of mankind, though different types of communities vary in this. In the neolithic peasant village, the gains in empirical knowledge included domestication of plants and animals, many new features of weaving and spinning, pottery-making, the invention of the wheel and its adaptation to both vehicles and pottery-making. While there was a considerable extension of the empirical knowledge of the peasant village in the world's first cities, their more impressive inventions were of a nonmaterial nature—writing, the beginnings of science, the first foundations of mathematics, new forms of social organization (religion, government, etc.). There were also significant gains in empirical knowledge in the Axial Period, particularly in Greece.

The occurrence of fresh empirical observation in the formative period of the Greek city-state has been traced by Farrington. In the pre-Socratic period, he observed, the ancient thinkers never lost sight of the fact that they were trying to understand nature. The Pythagoreans experimented with the relation between the pitch of tones and the length of string. Empedocles demonstrated the corporeal nature of air by thrusting a funnel into water with the upper end closed, proving that water could not enter until the hole was uncovered and the air released. Anaxagoras demonstated the limits of accuracy of sense perception by taking two vessels, one filled with white liquid and one with black, and mixing them drop by drop until the eye could no longer discern a difference. "These and similar experiments show that they had taken the first step to a real technique of systematic experimental investigation, although they did not get very far with it."[35]

However, the time rapidly approached in ancient Greece when the fresh observation of nature was seen as endangering the state cult. Farrington takes the most striking indication of change to be the expulsion of Anaxagoras from Athens. Anaxagoras was "an ideal embodiment of the spirit of Ionian science."[36] However, his naturalistic account of the heavenly bodies made him suspect. Plato by contrast defended the divinity of the heavenly bodies. However, to some extent "Aristotle saved his scientific soul by a break with Platonism."[37] The devaluation of empirical knowledge continued until "the very understanding that there was such a thing as science, except for a few languishing techniques such as medicine or architecture, almost died out under the Empire."[38]

As Sarton was to phrase the problem:

> However much one may admire Greek science, one must recognize that it was sadly deficient with regard to the (experimental) point of view which turned out to be the fundamental point of view of modern science.[39]

The experimental philosophy has been compactly and clearly summarized as follows:

> Establish the facts by direct, frequent, and careful observations, and check them repeatedly one against the other; these facts will be your premises. When many variables are related find out what happens when only one is allowed to vary, the others remaining constant. Multiply such experiments as much as you can, and make them with the utmost precision in your power. Draw your conclusions and express them in mathematical language if possible. Apply all your mathematical resources to the transformation of the equations; confront the new equations thus obtained with reality.[40]

The splendid triumphs of modern science are due to the application of the experimental method.

The real contribution of the Greeks to the development of modern science was not to be found in the many original experiments carried out by them or even in the brilliant syntheses of the scientific knowledge of the

[35] Benjamin Farrington, *Science and Politics in the Ancient World* (New York: Oxford University Press, 1940), p. 58.
[36] *Ibid.*, p. 74.
[37] *Ibid.*, p. 230.
[38] *Ibid.*, p. 232.
[39] George Sarton, *The History of Science and the New Humanism* (New York: George Braziller, Inc., 1956), p. 100.
[40] *Ibid.*, pp. 101–102.

Hellenistic world by the Alexandrians. It lay rather in their discovery and preservation of the rational proof. Euclid (330–260 B.C.), who was trained at Athens probably by a pupil of Plato, carried out his synthesis of Greek mathematics in the *Elements of Geometry* at Alexandria. It was one of the primary monuments to, and future sources of, the influence of the rational proof. The Greeks were well aware of the fact that the rational proof was an important and unique development. Beside it, empirical knowledge seemed second-rate. This dominance of the rational proof over empirical considerations appears even in Archimedes (312–287 B.C.) of Syracuse, perhaps the nearest approach of a modern scientist in antiquity—with his mathematical conception of knowledge and extraordinary talent in handling mechanical problems. However, though Archimedes often made brilliant use of mechanical devices in arriving at his logical and mathematical demonstrations, he did not consider such knowledge on a plane with logical proofs. He usually presents his proof, but does not explain how he reached it. Hence, despite brilliant syntheses of earlier science like Aristarchus of Samos' (310–230 B.C.) heliocentric theory of the planetary system and attempts to measure the distances of the sun, moon, and earth, despite Archimedes' invention of the screw, and his studies of specific weights of metals and experiments with the lever, despite Eratosthenes' (276–194 B.C.) measurement of the earth, or Hipparchus' (190–120 B.C.) original astronomical investigations, and Ptolemy's (–170 A.D.) final astronomical summary of ancient knowledge and his experiments in optics, Singer still speaks of the entire Alexandrian period in science as "a failure of nerve."[41]

The first ingredient of science is this same rational proof. Though it was partly thrust aside by medieval thought, and in the form of scholastic logic for a time made subordinate to theology, it was never completely lost in the West after the Greeks. Whenever the conception of rational proof was freed from extraneous influences (such as theology), it tended to evolve rapidly toward a mathematical conception of knowledge. As applied to science, it pointed toward the ideal of the concepts formulated with exactness and of proofs as certain as mathematical demonstrations—in fact, if possible, cast into the form of mathematical demonstrations.

Science only emerges, however, when the rational proof is subordinated to the achievement of empirical knowledge, a subordination requiring a special kind of social atmosphere. The domination of the pursuit of new empirical knowledge over the intellectual ethos was not possible in any of the world areas during the Axial Period. Though the mandarin intellectuality of ancient China was plastic and free in its sphere, that sphere of application was socially and politically expedient. Nature was not an object of study on a par with the study of man; the naturalization of man was the violation of his essence. The thought of the Indian *guru* was confined within a narrow

[41] Charles Singer, *A Short History of Science* (Oxford: The Clarendon Press, 1941), pp. 56 ff.

range of religious and moral concerns; it was concerned with *atman*, not *maya*, with timeless spiritual essences, not the snares and betrayals of spirituality by time-bound experience. The priests and prophets of Israel were dominated by political, religious, and ethical problems of another type which were also remote from systematic experimentalism.

Only in the secularized speculation of the citizens of the autonomous Greek city-states was there a near approach to the scientific ethos. One major effect of the elevation of the rational proof into central focus in Greek thought was democratization, the process of truth establishment, for the basis of truth became the conduct of the thought process in terms of the criteria of thought itself. While this was not yet science, from this standpoint one can phrase the general conditions for the domination of science over the intellectual ethos: *it is possible for science to dominate the intellectual ethos only if a generalization of the procedure of empirical proof is carried through in a manner equivalent to the generalization of the rational proof of logical and mathematical thought.*

The two major institutional complexes of ancient Greece which prohibited the rise of science in the modern sense were militarism and slavery. In the time of its dominance, the autonomous city-state of the eastern Mediterranean was the bearer of the highest military technology of the world. The hoplite on land and the sailor on the seas were each unsurpassed in their spheres. The city-state was a warrior's community. In the long run military and political considerations had the decisive voice in events. When political and military considerations supply the authenticating badge of significance, thought is turned away from systematic experimentalism in non-military spheres. Insofar as it may appear at all, experimentalism on everyday problems was primarily confined to lower social strata: metics, peasants, and slaves. Meanwhile, not all but significant blocks of the technology of the autonomous city-state were in the hands of slaves. Slavery inclines toward technological backwardness. The two systems—militarism at the top and slavery at the bottom—of ancient society were mutually self-supporting. The wars were always in considerable measure slave raids. The only technology of the classical city that was progressive was that of warfare. The presence of slavery required war and at the same time impeded non-military technical advance.

Only among practitioners of the practical and fine arts could a progressive attitude toward the advance of empirical knowledge be anticipated, and these strata in the ancient city were trapped between the slaves from below and the soldiers from above. There was, however, in the ancient city a stratum revealing this progressive pattern. The ancient city had a stratum of enfranchised persons. A large number had been former household slaves. The suggestion has been advanced that the number of persons enfranchised increased in economically troubled times, and declined in times of prosperity. Enfranchisement was one way in times of economic hardship by which a lord could reduce expenses of the household and shift the risk of bad times onto the former slave.[42]

The economic activity of enfranchised persons of antiquity was quite similar to that of the modern *bourgeoisie*. Enfranchised persons did not have full access to civic office, the priesthood, nor did they enjoy full connubium with the highest civic strata, though they were at times called to arms. However, the slave who was permitted through his own free economic activity to buy his freedom was driven by unusually powerful incentives. While the master now had only limited liability for him, the former slave was inclined rationally to exploit every economic opportunity as fully and effectively as possible:

> Thus the enfranchised were the most important bearers of those economic forms which best display a character corresponding to modern petty capitalism. Under the circumstances, however, it signified the accumulation of wealth in a middle class in contrast to the typical *demos* of full citizens in the Hellenic city which monopolized political conditioned rents: state rents, daily allowances, mortgages, and land rents. The industrial schools of slavery operating under the possibility of the achievement of freedom were as powerful an incentive for rational economic conduct on the part of the unfree in antiquity as it has been in modern Russia.[43]

As a special stratum, the enfranchised appeared only for a short time in the precity period of the European Middle Ages. Serfdom and grades of semifree persons vanished in the city in accordance with the principle that city air makes men free. In contrast to antiquity, the medieval guild reached its full development by ignoring nonurban status differences. The progressive attitude toward empirical knowledge and of a rational economic technology became a property of the entire urban community.

In the Western city, strata associated with the practical and fine arts were in a position to set the style for all the rest; in fact, to sound the keynote of its civilization. Moreover, the stratum in central position during the formative period of a community is not only able to impose its outlook on all others, but is freest of all the strata for self-development. In the Western city, industrial and merchant strata had their unparalleled opportunity for development.

The patricians who rose to power in the cities attained their positions by their successes in trade, commerce, and industry rather than by religious excellence, military prowess, or aristocratic family ties. They might occasionally adopt a feudal conception of rank in the course of their inner civic competition, and even aspire to own rural villas or castles and stables for horse-racing, but the fundamental content of their status striving was that of merchant adventurers. They imported art objects from distant places, turned their merchant talents to good effect in the creation of libraries and

42 Max Weber, *The City* (Glencoe: The Free Press, 1958), p. 216.
43 *Ibid.*, p. 218.

museums. They knew good craftsmanship when they saw it, and formed the perfect patrons for a brilliant flowering of art. When the fine arts emerged, that is, the production of objects to be enjoyed for their own sake or to be pressed into the decoration, enhancement, and celebration of life, it was in terms of clear standards of craft quality. The work of the better artists was known, valued, and sought after.

Two properties of the arts in the formative period of the Western city had considerable bearing on the rise of science: (1) the line between the practical and fine arts was not sharply drawn, for fine art was of a continuity with practical art, being, in considerable measure, merely a qualitatively superior example of it; (2) the lines between the different arts were not sharply drawn, making it quite possible for a given artist-craftsman to display excellence in a variety of fields. When a given person is skilled in a number of areas, he may draw inspiration for the solution of problems in one area from another.

The artist is a bearer of a peculiar kind of knowledge—knowledge of characteristics of materials, of the nature of skills, of tools, and of mechanical processes. In the Western city, the many-sided artist was the counterpart in a different sphere to the many-sided citizen intellectual of the ancient city. The ancient Greek intellectual was often a soldier, administrator, diplomat, teacher, lawyer, and school founder. The artists of the early Western city were often craftsmen, painters, sculptors, metal workers, engineers, fortification experts, stage designers, architects, and even musicians.

The work of the fine-artist is particularly noteworthy, for it presents the artisan as creator. It requires the highest level of information of the properties of materials, skills, tools, and mechanical processes—naturalistic, empirical knowledge. At the same time, the fine artist is expected to innovate. His situation is thus one involving a synthesis of empirical knowledge, demanding a high level of devotion, and yet with creativity at a premium. When the fine artist achieves something new, it will rarely be sheer accident —at least not by this alone. New results will usually only be obtained by projecting a new idea into an empirical situation and trying it out.

The essence of the Greek in contrast to the modern achievement is the pursuit of certainty in the world of thought in contrast to the pursuit of certainty in the world of experience. The Greeks solved their problem by the rational proof; the modern world solved its problem by systematic experiment. The distinction lies between the certainties of mathematics and those of experience. Leonardo da Vinci had already arrived at the view that in its sphere mathematics provides certainty:

> He who blames the supreme certainty of mathematics feeds on confusion, and will never impose silence upon the contradictions of the sophistical sciences, which occasion perpetual clamor.[44]

[44] Edward MacCurdy, *The Notebooks of Leonardo da Vinci* (New York: George Braziller, 1956), p. 83.

However, experience also gives certainty its sphere:

> Experience is never at fault; it is only your judgment that is in error in promising itself such results from experience as are not caused by our experiments.[45]

In the workshops of the Renaissance artists, firsthand observation and experiment were generalized as a method of knowledge and applied to almost every conceivable problem. Leonardo was not alone among the artists of the time, though without question he was the most able. His notebooks read like a continuous never-ending system of laboratory notes and he records observational and experimental knowledge turned up by his own reflections and work and that of others. To Sarton, Dürer and Leonardo epitomize the artist-scientist of the Renaissance:

> Dürer was a businessman, a man of substance, living in his own comfortable house; he was capable of taking some interest in scientific questions, but he was not a man of science. Leonardo, on the contrary, was a pure artist, a disinterested inventor, a man of science, a cogitator, a Bohemian; he was decidedly not a businessman or an administrator. He was anxious to obtain not money, or power, or comfort, but beauty and truth. He wanted to understand God, nature, art, himself, and other men. I admire them both, but I love Leonardo.[46]

In the sixteenth and seventeenth centuries the spread of the scientific point of view to ever wider spheres is evident. Nicolaus Copernicus (1473–1543) renovated the heliocentric theory from antiquity. Belon (1517–1564), Rondelet (1507–1564), Salvini (1514–1573), Gesner (1516–1565), and Androvandi (1525–1608) opened the modern study of animals. Andreas Vesalius (1514–1564) made the first significant advances in anatomy since Galen. William Gilbert (1546–1604) in his work, *On the Magnet and on Magnetic Bodies and Concerning the Great Magnet, the Earth, a New Physiology*, made the first great original contribution to science in England. Giordano Bruno (1547–1600) raised the demand for a new level of precision of observation.

For the full emergence of science, however, it was necessary not only to develop systematic observation and experiment, but to subordinate the establishment of rational proof to them. This was accomplished in the course of the transformation of mathematics into an instrument of physical investigation. François Viete (1540–1603) employed letters to represent numbers, and applied algebra to geometry in a manner anticipating analytical trigonometry. Simon Stevin (1548–1630) introduced the decimal scheme for representing fractions. He also experimented on the relative rates of the fall of bodies, and computed the pressure of liquids on any given point of a vessel, laying the foundation for hydrostatics. John Napier (1550–

45 *Ibid.*, p. 64.
46 George Sarton, *Six Wings: Men of Science in the Renaissance* (Bloomington: Indiana University Press, 1957), pp. 232–233.

1617) discovered a general rule for roots of all degrees in the course of his attempt to systematize algebraic knowledge. He conceived the principles of logarithms, and computed the table of logarithms. Kepler developed the mathematics of conic sections. In his analytic geometry, Descartes introduced the conception of motion into the geometric field, displaying the basic correspondence of number and form. Blaise Pascal (1623–1662) advanced the theory of probability, and invented one of the first mathematical machines. John Wallis (1616–1703) anticipated differential calculus. Newton read Wallis' *Arithmetica infinitorum* (1655) and derived the binomial theorem from it. Wallis wrote the first mathematical work on the tides. Mathematical development and the advance in scientific knowledge were beginning to move hand in hand.[47]

In the work of Galileo Galilei (1564–1642) systematic experimentalism and the mathematical ideal of scientific knowledge were fused. Though trained in scholasticism and Aristotelianism, he soon began to modify this heritage in the course of his experimental researches. He worked from the conception of a world of calculable forces and measurable bodies. The whole modern science of dynamics was laid by Galileo. In the words of Bertrand Russell:

> Scientific method, as we understand it, comes into the world full-fledged with Galileo . . . and, in somewhat lesser degree, his contemporary, Kepler (1571–1630).[48]

As the first modern scientist, Galileo was destined to clarify another aspect of science over and beyond the synthesis of a mathematical conception of nature and experimentalism. For championing the Copernican theory of planetary motions in 1632, he came under censure of the Inquisition. In its censure the Inquisition called attention to its earlier criticism of Galileo in 1615. In its document the Inquisition indicated its own conception of the proper way to establish truth:

> The two propositions of the stability of the sun, and the motion of the earth, were qualified by the Theological Qualifiers as follows:
>
> 1. The proposition that the sun is the center of the world and immovable from its place is absurd, philosophically false, and formally heretical; because it is expressly contrary to the Holy Scriptures.
>
> 2. The proposition that the earth is not the center of the world, nor immovable, but that it moves and also with a diurnal action, is also absurd, philosophically false, and theologically considered, at least erroneous in faith.[49]

For offenses against the faith, the Inquisition declared:

> That the book Dialogues of Galileo Galilei be prohibited by a public edict, and We condemn you to the formal prison of This Holy Office

[47] Charles Singer, *A Short History of Science* (Oxford: The Clarendon Press, 1941), pp. 189–195.

[48] Bertrand Russell, *The Scientific Outlook* (Glencoe: The Free Press, 1931), p. 20.

[49] Quoted by Russell, *Ibid.*, p. 25.

> for a period determinable at Our pleasure; and by way of salutary penance, We order you during the next three years to recite, once a week, the seven penitential psalms, reserving to Ourselves the power of moderating, commuting, or taking off, the whole or part of the said punishment or penance.[50]

The mode of establishing truth by the new science was at the opposite pole from the truth-establishment of the medieval church. Scientifically established truth could come into conflict with religion. The Inquisition stamped out the beginnings of science in southern Europe.

Of considerable importance for the further development of science was the Reformation which broke the monopoly of the medieval ecclesiastical hierarchy and opened a new era in European culture as well as in church history. The Reformation reached its climax in the sixteenth century, but it had roots deep in the Middle Ages in sacred and clerical groups opposed to religious centralization. The Reformation reached particular intensity in the towns where the new urban freedom encouraged the emergence not only of free thinkers and nonconformists but a new, more individualized religious intensity. In place of the traditional primacy of the sacraments and ministrations of the priesthood, the Reformation offered a nonsacramental theory of the church which placed great emphasis on the religious conscience of the individual. In its area the Reformation eliminated the monastic ideal of religious life for a religious elite, while it imposed a new, more rigorous religious interpretation on the everyday life of lay religious persons. This new ideal of lay religiosity has often been described as inner-worldly asceticism. The role that the Reformation played in enhancing those trends in the cities and in the national economies that led on to modern capitalism, has been brilliantly traced by Weber.[51]

The Reformation not only broke up the spiritual monopoly of the church, thus establishing areas where the Inquisition was unable to carry out its opposition to science and other forms of modernism, but intensified those religious sentiments of Western civilization that were most nearly akin to the emerging scientific spirit. To a considerable degree the Reformation, modern capitalism, and modern science were simply different, though closely interrelated, aspects of the same process. Robert Merton has traced the relation between Protestantism and science in seventeenth century England in a manner directly parallel to Weber's study of the interrelation between Protestantism and capitalism.[52]

[50] *Ibid.*, p. 30.

[51] Max Weber, *The Protestant Ethic and the Spirit of Capitalism,* trans. by Talcott Parsons (New York: Charles Scribner's Sons, 1948).

[52] Robert K. Merton, *Science, Technology, and Society in 17th Century England* (Bruges, Belgium: St. Catherine Press, Ltd. Osiris: Studies on the History and Philosophy of Science, 1938). Merton also carried out a number of shorter studies of this interrelation. See the bibliography of Robert K. Merton's *Social Theory and Social Structure* (Glencoe: The Free Press, 1949), pp. 409 ff.

Western science was to reach its highest development in the Protestant countries of northern Europe. If Merton is correct, science was borne primarily by the new Protestants. Moreover, the attitudes and norms of inner-worldly asceticism, which Weber was to find central to the formation of the capitalistic ethos where also capable of being transmuted into the scientific attitude and philosophy of experimentalism.

Humanism made its appearance as a form of intellectuality in the early period of the Western city. However, as the city developed and increasingly realized its potential, the point of gravity of its intellectuality tended increasingly to shift toward science. Moreover, leadership in the new science taking shape within the city was transferred to the newer community of the nation-state. This was observed by Butterfield:

> The whole story of the Renaissance shows within the limits of the city-state how the exhilarating rise of an urban civilization is liable to issue in a process of secularization—the priest as well as the noble loses the power that he was able to possess in a more conservative agrarian world. Something parallel has happened over and over again in the case of nation-states when not only have towns become really urban in character—which is late the case of England, for example—but when a sort of leadership in society has passed to the towns, and literature itself comes to have a different character.[53]

At the height of the early phase of the Renaissance, it has been noted, philosophy was considered the queen of the sciences,[54] but this was rapidly undergoing change toward the end of the Renaissance. Francis Bacon complained about the divorce between observation and explanation. In the seventeenth century, when the autonomous Western city had passed its height and the nation-state was beginning to take shape, the new science got thoroughly under way.

> Not only did the science of mathematics make a remarkable development in the seventeenth century, then, but in dynamics and in physics the sciences give the impression that they were pressing upon the frontiers of mathematics all the time. Without the achievements of the mathematicians, the scientific revolution, as we know it, would have been impossible.[55]
>
> It is not until the seventeenth century that the resort to experiments comes to be tamed and harnessed, so to speak, and is brought under direction, like a great machine getting into gear.[56]

Science was rapidly becoming the distinctive thought of the West. Yet in the nature of the case, this was a growth outside the institutional thought of the day. Ornstein has advanced the thesis that the science of the seventeenth century received little help from the university. Rather, the new

[53] H. Butterfield, *The Origins of Modern Science* (London: G. Bell & Sons Ltd., 1949), p. 183.
[54] *Ibid.*, p. 66.
[55] *Ibid.*, p. 77.
[56] *Ibid.*, p. 79.

science was its own sponsor in the scientific societies which supplied indispensable aid.[57]

The seventeenth century produced the microscope, telescope, machinery for grinding lenses, time-measuring instruments, thermometer, barometer, air pump, the apparatus of the modern physical laboratory, places and conditions where experimentation could be carried on, the modern observatory, and many other things necessary to exact observation and experimentation. Ornstein maintains that the leadership in promoting these technical developments, creating the conditions for scientific work, and publicizing their findings were unions of scientific workers which became the dominating feature of scientific activity after 1650.

These societies concentrated groups of scientists in single places, performed experiments and investigations impossible to individuals, became centers of scientific information, published and translated scientific works, promulgated scientific efforts, coordinated the scientific effort of different countries, concerned themselves about the application of science to trade and commerce, tools and machinery, and sought to dispel popular errors about science by means of lectures.

> But first and foremost they developed the scientific laboratory, devised, perfected, and standardized instruments, originated and insisted on exact methods of experimentation, and thus established permanently the laboratory method as the only true means of scientific study.
>
> The conclusion is thus inevitable that the organized support which science needed in order to penetrate into the thought and lives of people was not obtained from universities, but was derived from those forms of corporate activity which it had created for itself, the scientific societies.[58]

The major trends from the seventeenth century to the present have consisted in the institutionalization of science first in modern industry, second in the universities within which it has become a dominating influence, and finally the increased support of scientific research by the modern state. Step by step the contemporary world has been transformed into an age of science.

SUMMARY

Three major communities organized the medieval world out of which the contemporary world developed: peasant villages, manorial communities, and monasteries. Two of these, the manorial and monastic communities, sustained intellectual traditions of sorts: the epic and romantic literatures of chivalry and the theological literatures of the priest-theologians. The dominant intellectuals of the period were the priest-theologians who had replaced the philosophers of the ancient world and whose intellectual

57 Martha Ornstein, *The Role of Scientific Societies in the Seventeenth Century* (Chicago: University of Chicago Press, 1928).

58 *Ibid.*, pp. 260–261.

products reversed the order of elements of ancient thought, transforming reason into the handmaiden of faith.

When the cities arose in the eleventh century they provided *milieux* to which the priest-theologians on the one hand and the bearers of the feudal chivalric traditions on the other were ill adapted. The basic tension between the requirements of the church-dominated communities of the Middle Ages and the new urban communities is revealed by the frequency of the conflicts which occurred whenever a new city began to rise on the site of the old episcopal sees. The bishops perceived the rising *bourgeoisie* as a threat, and evaluated major phases of their commercial activities in religiously negative terms. For their part, the merchants perceived the ecclesiastics as an obstacle, and often formed sworn confederations which carried out revolutionary seizures of power from the ecclesiastical authorities. No communities which found it necessary to acquire power against the priests were going to find the priestly intellectual fully adequate to their needs.

The range of new intellectual requirements of the urban centers were first satisfied by voluntary organizations of students and teachers or by an expansion of the curriculum of the cathedral schools. The three great centers of learning which emerged in the early period were: Salerno, Bologna, and Paris, specializing in medicine, law, and philosophy respectively. For at least two centuries before the universities were formally organized, these centers continued to grow, drawing students from all parts of Europe and evolving into the highest centers of culture of the time. In connection with the growth of these intellectual centers a great recovery of ancient science, at first primarily from Moslem and Jewish sources, got under way.

So many medieval institutions, such as the urban administrations, the state, and eventually the church itself, began to look at these voluntary associations of teachers and students for a supply of trained persons that a competition for their control emerged. In the course of this competition the formal organization of the universities was carried through. Moreover, within the universities at an early stage a struggle broke out between the secular intellectuals and the monastically trained men. This pressed the scholastics to the highest level of intellectual activity to be seen in the West since the days of St. Augustine. The twelfth-century Renaissance was thus the foundation for the thirteenth-century scholastic synthesis of classical learning and Christian theology. Of the various *Summae* which were undertaken, the most famous was that of the Dominican, Thomas Aquinas, which was to become the official point of view of the Roman Catholic Church.

However, despite the fact that the final form of scholasticism was in part a product of the very forces which were lifting the city into the central experience of early modern man, the scholastics were destined to be the last of the medieval intellectuals though, to be sure, they still have heirs in the contemporary world. The intellectual patterns of contemporary man were destined to achieve their distinctive properties in the Western humanist and the scientist. Though a variety of priests and scholastics play a part in the contemporary world, humanist and scientist demark the two major poles of its distinctive intellectual life.

SELECTED BIBLIOGRAPHY

Becker, Carl, *The Heavenly City* (New Haven: Yale University Press, 1932).

Burckhardt, Jacob, *The Civilization of the Renaissance* (New York: Oxford University Press, 1945).

Butler, E. C., "Monasticism," *The Cambridge Medieval History* (New York: The Macmillan Co., 1929), pp. 521–542.

Cassirer, Ernst, Paul Oskar Kristeller, and John Herman Randall, Jr. (eds.), *The Renaissance Philosophy of Man* (Chicago: The University of Chicago Press, 1948).

Dampier, Sir William Cecil, *A History of Science* (New York: The Macmillan Co., 1944).

Haskins, Charles Homer, *The Rise of Universities* (Ithaca, New York: Cornell University Press, 1957).

Lecky, W. E. H., *Rationalism in Europe* (New York: D. Appleton & Co., 1891).

Little, A. G., "The Mendicant Orders," *The Cambridge Medieval History* (New York: The Macmillan Co., 1929), Vol. VI, pp. 727–762.

Munro, Dana Carleton, and George Clarke Sellery, *Medieval Civilization* (New York: The Century Co., 1910).

Pirenne, Henri, "Northern Towns and Their Commerce," *The Cambridge Medieval History* (New York: The Macmillan Co., 1929), Vol. VI, pp. 505–527.

Rashdall, Hastings, "The Medieval Universities," *The Cambridge Medieval History* (New York: The Macmillan Co., 1929), Vol. VI, pp. 559–601.

Sarton, George, *The History of Science and the New Humanism* (New York: George Braziller, 1956).

Slesser, Sir Henry, *The Middle Ages in the West* (London: Hutchinson & Co., 1950).

Sohm, Rudolf, *Outlines of Church History*, trans. by May Sinclair (Boston: The Beacon Press, 1958).

18

SOME PROBLEMS OF WESTERN SCIENTIFIC CIVILIZATION

THE COMMUNITIES which more than any other serve as vehicles of Western civilization are nation-states. The intellectual roles standing at their core are those of humanist and scientist. At the basis of all distinctively modern developments lies a fabulously effective mastery of nature. Moreover, having displayed unparalleled powers to transform physical nature, science has been applied to ever-widening spheres of life outside the strictly material. All the great general processes of modern society rest in considerable measure on the application of the methods of science: the industrial revolution, capitalism, the development of scientific warfare, the bureaucratization of administration, the coordination of men and machines through scientific management, the development of electronic computers which have taken over routine clerical and calculation functions of all types.

Even the arts, as Walter Benjamin has pointed out, have been transformed. In an era of technical reproduction made possible by science, a great revolution in the arts comparable to that carried out for writing by the development of printing has occurred. The reproduction of visual and auditory stimuli by modern electronic and photographic techniques has made possible arts which destroy the ancient uniqueness (the characteristic of being created as a unique thing once and for all) of the art object. Uniqueness and individuality lose their ancient meaning for an art which by the very nature of its production exists only in copies. Moreover, in the new distinctly modern arts an analysis of experience occurs which, in Benjamin's opinion, is as distinct from that of the traditional artist as the work of a contemporary scientifically trained medical doctor is from that of a medicine man.

The medicine man accepted people as they were in their natural condition. He approached them from the outside as complete individuals and oriented his treatment to the person as a whole. The scientifically trained doctor approaches the patient impersonally and professionally with attitudes which do not require that he be any different than a thing. He does not proceed by the "laying on of hands," but penetrates the very body of his patient with his knowledge, tools, and skills. In similar fashion the person armed with modern electronic and photographic equipment penetrates the structure of everyday sense experience with enlargements, close-ups, slow motion. He is able to tape-record natural sounds, run them backward, slow them down to one-half or one-fourth or one-eighth speed, and reveal a world of sound no man has ever been able to experience outside of science. He is able to take a visual event apart and reassemble it from a point of view no natural person could ever occupy, for it is from the point of view of the apparatus.

No era of contemporary life has remained permanently free from the application of the skills, techniques, and orientations of science. Moreover, science brings revolutionary changes in any sphere to which it is applied. In the course of such revolutions the traditional values which give the sphere its significance are systematically destroyed. One of the externally recurrent questions concerns what values, if any, science permits to rise in the place of those whose destruction it speeds.

The tension between the systematic instrumentalism of science and all traditional configurations of value appears in the first place in the latent tension between the two most fundamental intellectual roles of modern man, the humanistic and scientific.

THE LATENT TENSION BETWEEN HUMANIST AND SCIENTIST

The peculiar dilemma of Western thought has come into view whenever science has come into conflict with the other main pole of Western thought, humanism. There is much kinship between Western humanism and science: they were born in the same atmosphere, both flourish under conditions of freedom, they have often supported one another. However, in the end science and Western humanism have come into conflict. Western humanism is a value program devoted to the achievement of the full development of the cultivated man. Its theory of society is normative: the only end of society is the fullest possible promotion of personality. Science, on the other hand, is not a value position, and its theories are never normative. It has only one objective, the achievement of the most general empirical knowledge possible. How this knowledge is used is often of great interest and importance to particular scientists as individuals, but is of no concern to science as such.

Occasions have repeatedly arisen when scientists have been called upon to reject as nonscientific those very values which the humanists hold most dear. On the other hand, these same occasions have been perceived by humanists as demonstrating the ultimate amorality if not immorality of science. This dilemma does not appear merely negatively, but at the positive core of science when one examines it as an activity capable of providing meaning to life.

Every society permits some individual freedom to its members. The kind of individuality a society supports is concentrated in its intellectual and artistic types. This was also evident in both the Western humanist and the scientist; these intellectual roles appealed to types of persons with relatively high demands for personal autonomy. The study of the contemporary scientist by Anne Roe seems to confirm this selectivity. In her social-psychological research on sixty-four outstanding research scientists, she found them to be persons whose work typically never ends, for they characteristically pursue their science on week-ends, Sundays, holidays, and even vacations.[1]

Though the amount of reading they did varied, most read nothing but professional literature. Only four played an active part in civic or political organizations. None spontaneously mentioned church activities as important. Of the total group of sixty-four scientists, five came from Jewish homes and all but one of the rest had Protestant backgrounds. There were none from Roman Catholic families. They were primarily recruited from professional families. They valued learning for its own sake. Thirty-nine of the sixty-four were the oldest child. The next greatest number, thirteen, were second children. Roe concluded: "The development of personal independence to a high degree is an extremely important factor in the production of a research scientist."[2]

These findings of Roe are reinforced by other studies[3] which have shown that among mathematicians and physicists an unusually high proportion have lost a father or mother before the age of fourteen. Such losses seem to have been factors which establish the kind of life in which the demand for personal autonomy is strong. Of the sixty-four scientists studied by Roe, a large number had trouble while growing up because of some exceptional physical condition. Some were abnormally tall, some abnormally small.

> More than is usual, these men were placed on their own resources. It happened in different ways, in different cases. Some lost a parent early in life; some had serious physical problems; many were eldest sons, although the bearing of this is not clear. Even as children, though, most of them had intense private interests, and except among the social scientists, these were usually shared by only a few friends. Most of them were inveterate readers, and most of them enjoyed school and studying.[4]

The need for independence, for autonomy, for personal mastery of the environment was unusually strong. Roe reports that they were not altruistically motivated by the urge to contribute to the welfare of humanity. "This in my experience is not really the basic motivation for any of them, and as

[1] Anne Roe, *The Making of a Scientist* (New York: Dodd Mead & Co., 1952), pp. 158 ff.

[2] *Ibid.*, p. 72.

[3] E. T. Bell, *Men of Mathematics*, cited, p. 86.

[4] Roe, *op. cit.*, p. 231.

additional motivation it is more absent than present."[5] This finding confirms Weber's judgment that "in the field of science only he who is devoted *solely* to the work at hand has 'personality.' "[6]

The fact that science recruits to its service persons with strong demands for personal autonomy (a fact which it shares with humanism) has at times been permitted to obscure the latent tension between scientist and humanist. However, the moment one's attention shifts to the content of their respective enterprises the tension emerges between the fundamental ethical orientation of the humanist and lack of it by the scientist. While humanist and scientist both value personal autonomy, to the former it is an end in itself and an aspect of his assignment of significance to life; to the latter it is a personal requirement and an instrument in his achievement of control over man and nature.

THE SCIENTIFIC DISENCHANTMENT OF THE WORLD

The scientist, of course, may recognize the humanistic striving for autonomy as a personal value. There is, moreover, little doubt that to the individual scientist the ultimate appeal of scientific work with great frequency is as a sphere primarily for autonomous self-realization. However, when science is examined as an intellectual activity capable of giving meaning to life, its full dilemma is manifest. Here, Weber notes, it stands in extreme contrast to art:

> Scientific work is chained to the course of progress; whereas in the realm of art there is no progress in the same sense. It is not true that the work of art of a period that has worked with new technical means, or, for instance, the laws of perspective, stands therefore artistically higher than a work of art devoid of all knowledge of these means and laws—if its form does justice to the material, that is, if its object has been chosen and formed so that it could be artistically mastered without applying those conditions and means. A work of art which is genuine "fulfillment" is never surpassed; it will never be antiquated.[7]

By contrast there is nothing accomplished in science that will not be antiquated in a comparatively short time. Though some scientific works live on for a time as gratifications because of their artistic quality (for example, Darwin's *Origin of Species* which continues to be read for its literary excellence rather than for its scientific arguments), or because they remain important for training, they will be surpassed scientifically.

For the scientist directly, but also in the long run for a world resting on science, scientific progress is an aspect of the process of intellectualization which has been going on for thousands of years. This statement does not,

[5] *Ibid.*, p. 232.

[6] Max Weber, *From Max Weber: Essays in Sociology*, trans. by H. H. Gerth and C. Wright Mills (New York: Oxford University Press, 1946), p. 137.

[7] *Ibid.*, pp. 137–138.

indeed, mean that modern man necessarily knows more than the savage about the general conditions under which he lives. The savage knows incomparably more about his tools. He knows enough to get his daily food by means of them, while any single modern man only knows a fragment of what his society requires. Rather, it means that for modern man no mysterious incalculable forces come into play and one can, in principle, master all things by calculation. The world, in Weber's terms, is disenchanted, for one no longer needs recourse to magic in the attempt to control the world.

The disenchantment of the world by science has never been phrased with more poetic force than by Nietzsche in his famous passage on *The Madman:*

> Have you ever heard of the madman who on a bright morning lighted a lantern and ran to the marketplace calling unceasingly: "I seek God! I seek God!" As there were many people standing about who did not believe in God, he caused a great deal of amusement. "Why! Is he lost?" said one. "Has he strayed away like a child?" said another. "Or does he keep himself hidden? Is he afraid of us?"—the people cried out laughingly, all in a hubbub. The insane man jumped into their midst and transfixed them with his glances. "Where is God gone?" he called out. "I mean to tell you! *We have killed him,*—you and I! We are all his murderers! But how have we done it? How were we able to drink up the sea? Who gave us the sponge to wipe away the whole horizon? What did we do when we loosened this earth from its sun? Whither does it move? Whither do we move? Away from all suns? Do we not dash in unceasingly? Backwards, sideways, forwards, in all directions? Is there still an above and below? Do we not stray, as through infinite nothingness? Does not empty space breathe upon us? Has it not become colder? Does not night come on continually, darker and darker? Shall we not have to light lanterns in the morning? Do we not hear the noise of the grave-diggers who are burying God? Do we not smell the divine putrefaction?—for even gods putrefy! God is Dead! God remains dead! And we have killed him! How shall we console ourselves, the most murderous of all murderers? The holiest and the mightiest that the world has hitherto possessed, has bled to death under our knife,—who will wipe the blood from us? With what water could we cleanse ourselves? What lustrums, what sacred games shall we have to devise? Is not the magnitude of this deed too great for us? Shall we not ourselves have to become gods, merely to seem worthy of it? There never was a greater event,—and on account of it, all who are born after us belong to a higher history than any history hitherto!" —Here the madman was silent and looked again at his hearers; they also were silent and looked at him in surprise. At last he threw his lantern on the ground, so that it broke in pieces and was extinguished. "I come too early," he then said, "I am not yet at the right time. This prodigious event is still on its way, and is travelling,—it has not yet reached men's ears. Lightning and thunder need time, the light of the stars needs time, deeds need time, even after they are done, to be seen and heard. This deed is as yet further from them than the furthest star, —*and yet they have done it!*"—It is further stated that the madman made his way into different churches on the same day, and there intoned his *Requiem aeternam deo.* When led out and called to account, he

> always gave the reply: "What are these churches now, if they are not the tombs and monuments of God?"[8]

If the process of disenchantment carried out by modern science meant no more than the destruction of the ancient conception of life as a magical garden, it would be all to the good. However, it does not stop here, but raises the question of whether man can have any meanings that go beyond the practical and technical. This, Weber believes, was what Leo Tolstoy (1828–1910) had in mind when his broodings came to center on the question: Can death be a meaningful phenomenon for modern man? His conclusion was that for civilized man death has no meaning. Since his life is placed in a series of infinite progress, in terms of its internal meanings it should never come to an end, for there is always a further step. One cannot, like the patriarchs of old, whose lives were ordered on an organic cycle, die in the full completion of one's life.

While rejecting theological and all other intrinsic meanings, science leaves only self-clarification as an ultimate value:

> Science today is a 'vocation' organized in special disciplines in the service of self-clarification and the knowledge of interrelated facts. It is not the gift of grace of seers and prophets dispensing sacred values and revelations, nor does it partake of the contemplation of sages and philosophers about the meaning of the universe. This . . . is the inescapable condition of our historical situation.[9]

It must never be forgotten that self-clarification is not at all the equivalent to self-realization which glides outside the proper sphere of science. Science instrumentalizes the individual life without providing it with any final end. It places it on a ladder rising to nowhere.

A similar instrumentalization occurs in philosophies based on science. When the philosophers of the modern world search the scientific process for clues as to the ultimate meaning of life, no very satisfactory results are achieved. Among the products of this enterprise are instrumentalism, pragmatism, operationalism, scientism, and some forms of positivism. The common property of all such positions is their attempt to make science itself the ultimate criteria of worth, presumably under the assumption that science, like virtue, is its own reward. However, such philosophies so far have managed to satisfy no one, for either they lead to a reification of the scientific process and the determination of value from the instruments to achieve them, or they disguise some set of values as scientific propositions. The result is either a metaphysics of instruments, as if the end of man were to make machines possible, or a corruption of science.

At the same time, while it is incapable of supplying ultimate significance to life, science has unparalleled capacity to implement the interests that

[8] Friedrich Nietzsche, *The Joyful Wisdom*, trans. by Thomas Common (New York: Frederick Ungar Pub. Co., 1960), pp. 167–169.

[9] *Ibid.*, p. 152.

employ it. Like the genie of the magical lamp of mythology, science has no control over its owners, but brings its fabulous powers to the service of whoever rubs the lamp. When the Atomic Energy Commission brought about its Inquisitionlike condemnation of Oppenheimer, it was determined that motives of political expedience, rather than humanism, shall preside over government-sponsored science.

The fundamental issue in the West has increasingly centered on the question: Who shall be master of the genie? There is deep penetration into the predicament of the West in Julien Benda's *The Betrayal of the Intellectuals*,[10] for Benda perceived that the two poles of Western intellectuality lie in humanism (which is nearest to the intellectuality of antiquity) and science. For a time it appeared that science would be brought into the service of humanism. The enlightened thought of the eighteenth century was the nearest approach to a synthesis of the two poles of Western thought ever achieved. However, the synthesis was never very complete, and as its powers were gradually revealed, science was promoted far more vigorously in nonhumanistic circles than it had ever been by the humanists. So it came to pass, the science began to evolve with ever-accelerating speed in the service of industry and warfare—circles to which the humanists had never looked for full realization of the potential of man. The industrial and military scientist, for his part, was inclined to dismiss humanism as archaism. Science, the distinctive thought of modern man, has moved to the service of political and material goals. Benda, to be sure, was mistaken in treating this as a betrayal by the intellectuals. It was not. They could no more have prevented it than they could by reason have reversed the direction of the wind.

Because of its superior mastery of the material conditions of life, science gravitates to the configurations of power in society. An idealist like Nobel might dream of the great benefit that dynamite could bring to the peaceful pursuits of mankind, but military interests took the lead in supplying the laboratories, materials, and funds for research for its development into a new war material.

Moreover, since science renounces the claim to establish ultimate values, a vast liquidation of traditional wisdom occurs whenever science is made into the norm of correct thinking. All that is instrumental in traditional wisdom is taken over into the growing body of science, while all that is not instrumental is cast on the scrap heap. Science is no different in this that other bodies of thought that have preceded it. It assumes authorship of that part of traditional knowledge that fits its requirements. It is novel in always claiming the instrumental as its own.

The simultaneous movement of science toward the centers of power and

[10] Julien Benda, *The Betrayal of the Intellectuals*, trans. by Richard Aldington (Boston: The Beacon Press, 1955). See the discussion of his general argument in Chapter 2.

destruction of configurations of knowledge in conflict with it (traditional common sense, magic, religion, much traditional philosophy) accelerates in proportion to the arbitrariness of the power complex involved. Modern capitalism, for example, grew up outside the framework of both the city economy and the traditional feudal economy. It became the automatic sponsor of the new technical efficiencies made possible by the application of science to industrial process. By pressing science into its service, capitalism shattered opposing forms of economy. Similarly, in its consolidation of power the modern state increasingly pressed science into its service. In the course of the national wars of modern times the occasions have repeatedly arisen when the national states have not stopped with ordnance research, research in chemical warfare, in quartermaster supplies, in logistics, in transportation, in military engineering, and the like. Periodically, the occasions have presented themselves when the total nation has been mobilized for war and the total scientific facilities have been mobilized as well for the promotion of military and civilian needs relevant to the war effort.

The liquidation of traditional values which occurs when one area after another is systematically instrumentalized by the application of science thus tends to clear the ground for the emergence of configurations of power. Inevitably, the institutions of socialization, particularly educational institutions, are affected by the process.

SCIENCE IN THE UNIVERSITIES

As the major complexes of power in modern times (the economy and the state) began to depend on science for their efficiency, they turned naturally to the universities for their supply of scientists. The universities were then pushed through their third major internal reorganization, giving them the form they have today.

At the time of their origin in the late Middle Ages, the universities were primarily designed to supply the increased need for persons with specialized training arising out of internal changes in the new civic communities. The four fundamental colleges of the early universities were theology, canon law, civil law, and medicine. After their early humanistic excitement they became battlegrounds of the new spirit and old theology, and were subordinated to the scholastic mode of thought.

The new communities of the city and the nation, however, continued to grow. They required a new outlook on life and a whole series of subject-matter specialties falling outside the official scholasticism ensconced in the universities. A new flowering of extrauniversity humanism was the response to these new needs, arising first in the city and later in the early stages of the nation. Arising anew outside the universities, humanism soon allied itself with kindred elements in the university and began to force its way to a position of dominance in the university curriculum and to bring about a transformation of its dominant mode of thought. Scholastic methods ceased to be exclusively distinctive of university thought, being rivaled or replaced by philology and historical criticism.

The rise of science brought about the third major revolution in university instruction. As late as the seventeenth century science was still developing primarily outside the universities. Not only did science receive little assistance from the universities, but often, active opposition. However, by the eighteenth century a serious beginning of the introduction of science into university curriculums was being made. The mode of thought was also changing, and when in the nineteenth and twentieth centuries the scientific revolution was complete, direct observation and laboratory research had become the distinctive methods of university thought. Philology and historical criticism have declined so far in importance that they are primarily areas for specialists rather than the general symbol of the university-trained scholar. In America even for the degree of doctor of philosophy the language requirement has been modified; many universities now accept one language besides the candidate's own as qualification for the highest academic degree, with a variety of technical substitutes for the former rigid humanistic requirements.

In the schematization of the university's development into the three phases (scholastic, humanistic, and scientific), it is not intended to imply that these stages have followed one another in exact order. The actual development has been complex and confused. After its original dominance, humanism suffered serious reverses before the scholastic mode of thought, and fought its way only with great difficulty back into a position of dominance in the universities. The conflict between humanism and scholasticism lasted for centuries. Similarly, there have been and continue to be pitched battles between the humanistic and scientific wings of the modern university, even though the liberal arts everywhere decline in the face of the institutes of technology.

Meanwhile, the same forces that pulled science into the spheres of power continue to operate on it in the university setting. Science provided superior mastery of the material conditions of life; industry and government found science to be an invaluable instrument. Since industry and government look to the universities for their supply of trained personnel, the movement of science into them was a foregone conclusion. In industry and government, however, there is always an inclination to apply science to the tasks of the hour. Though lip service is paid to pure science, it tends to be an ideal rather than a practice. There is a playback of this displacement toward technology on university training in science. In *The Higher Learning in America*[11] Veblen traced this displacement in the American universities. In his view, learning was being transformed. He maintained that, as corporations and trusts, the American universities have increasingly been trans-

[11] Thorstein Veblen, *The Higher Learning in America* (New York: Sagamore Press, 1957).

formed in accordance with business norms. In their colleges and professional schools the universities cultivate the genteel and the purely vocational, not in the service of science and scholarship, but to promote the arts of the market place:

> Business principles take effect in academic affairs most simply, obviously and avowedly in the way of a businesslike administration of the scholastic routine; where they lead immediately to a bureaucratic organization and a system of scholastic accountancy.
>
> The underlying business-like presumption . . . appears to be that learning is a merchantable commodity, to be produced on a piece-rate plan, rated, bought, and sold by standard units, measured, counted, and reduced to staple equivalence by impersonal, mechanical tests. . . .
>
> Intimately bound up with this bureaucratic officialism and accountancy, and working consistently to a similar outcome, is the predilection for "practical efficiency"—that is to say, for pecuniary success—prevalent in the American community.
>
> It appears, then, that the intrusion of business principles in the universities goes to weaken and retard the pursuit of learning and therefore to defeat the ends for which a university is maintained.[12]

Veblen worked out his formulations in the early 1900's, though they were not published until 1918. Writing in 1959, Jacques Barzun, Dean of Faculties and Provost of Columbia University, made essentially the same indictment of American intellectuality, though he accounted for it differently. The products of the intellect, he maintained, were never more valued nor was intellect itself ever more despised:

> The expert, the Ph.D. or his equivalent, is everywhere—in government, industry, labor unions, banking, philanthropy, city planning, written and spoken journalism, espionage, national leadership, and international councils—as well as in the hobby that makes the whole world kin, preparing for war.
>
> To understand our situation, this paradox must be kept whole. Both halves are true. Intellect is despised and neglected. Intellectuals are well paid and riding high.[13]

While Barzun's indictment of higher learning is similar to Veblen's, his explanation for this condition is different. "The truth is that commercialism is not *per se* the enemy of intellect, but something deeper."[14] This disrepute of the intellect, he believes, is caused by naïve anti-intellectualism which universally experiences the intelligence as the enemy of emotional freedom and spontaneity.

> The truth is that Intellect can be diminished in its own eyes only with its own consent; its troubles become obsessions, its presence a canker, only from within: the real disaster haunting the intellectual today is

[12] *Ibid.*, pp. 162–165.

[13] Jacques Barzun, *The House of Intellect* (New York: Harper & Bros., 1959), pp. 1–2.

[14] *Ibid.*, p. 7.

> that the alienation, the disinheriting, the loss of authority have occurred, not between the intellectuals and the rest—the commercial rump—of society, but among intellectuals themselves and as a result of their own acts. As will appear again and again, they have abdicated but live on self-exiled. Hence the mutual recriminations, the contempt for life, and the search for scapegoats.[15]

Barzun maintains the foremost enemy of the intellect is science. Science is rivaled as an intellectually alien force only by art and philanthropy. The orgiastic dispersal of the work of contemporary artists is said to leave them angry and gloomy, making them "the most persistent denouncers of Western civilization."[16] From its early symbolic period Western art is seen as a displacement of what is common and its "replacement by the singular and indefinable." Moreover, "for many people art, displacing religion, has become the justification of life." Barzun argues that art values perception and its qualities, which he sees as at war against intellect.

> The cant words of modern criticism suggest what these qualities are: *ambiguity*, *sensibility*, *insight*, *imagination*, *sensitivity*, *creative irony*. All these in art, declare the undesirability, perhaps the impossibility, of articulate precision and thus defy, counteract, or degrade the chief virtue of intellect.[17]

Finally among the enemies of intellect, along with art and science, is "a third and closely related enemy, which is Philanthropy." This is any action based on "the liberal doctrine of free and equal opportunity as applied to things of the mind."[18] This view in Barzun's opinion leads in the long run to the liquidation of all standards of excellence.

Barzun's indictment of higher learning in America is essentially similar to Veblen's: the pursuit of pure thought everywhere is shifted to second place. However, his explanation (or as he describes it, the truth) is different. He would have us believe that the intellectuals have brought it all on themselves. Whether or not one accepts Barzun's judgment as to what ails the modern intellect, there is not the slightest doubt that he is right about the current popularity of the attacks on the modern intellectual and, in particular, on academic man by academic men. This point can be illustrated by the studies of Logan Wilson and Caplow and McGee.

Wilson's portrait of the academic man provides many rationalizations of popular negative stereotypes of the professor. An old saw expressing negative reaction to the teacher is that "those who can do, those who can't teach." Wholeheartedly agreeing, Wlison suggests that many persons are recruited to the academic profession simply because they are without goals. "Many individuals still lack vocational orientation upon completing a general education, and simply go into the graduate school as the next obvi-

[15] *Ibid.*, p. 9.
[16] *Ibid.*, p. 15.
[17] *Ibid.*, p. 17.
[18] *Ibid.*, p. 21.

ous step at hand."[19] Moreover, once he gets into graduate school, the individual often endures the rigmarole only because he is mediocre.

> The mediocre quality of many Ph.D.'s attests the fact, moreover, that by persistent plodding the poorer students often master the elaborate rigmarole of credits, examinations, theses, and other measures designed to sift them out.[20]

When the graduate student completes his work, favoritism is the basis of four out of five appointments to a university staff.

> An investigation in a more or less typical university of middle rank revealed that personal elements account for at least four-fifths of all appointments, leaving only a small proportion of vacancies to be filled through open competition.[21]

Once on the staff, a disproportionate accent on success leads to an extensive competition. "Warped results and distorted organization personalities are bound to develop."[22] One product is the faculty politicians who "swarm into the committees, with the result that the least intelligent professors are very often the most powerful."[23] While lip service is paid to good teaching, no one knows what it is.

> Universities profess to desire good teachers, but will admit having no infallible means of developing or detecting them. For these and other reasons, superior teaching is neither demanded nor rewarded in the same way as distinction in research.[24]

The principle that holds sway over the status competition of the academic man is "publish or perish."

> In many places today, only a modicum of efficiency is demanded in teaching, and even meritorious achievement in performance seldom brings the prestige awarded for outstanding research.[25]

A man's research success is therefore said to be everywhere rewarded as a matter of course, while success in teaching is not.[26] Professional recognition is achieved "through activities engaging a minor portion of the average man's energies."[27] This results in mass production, popularization, and the substitution of quantity of output for quality.

> There is often a confusion of notoriety and fame, a feeling that quantity of output is more important than quality, that one's name must

[19] Logan Wilson, *The Academic Man* (New York: Oxford University Press, 1942), p. 16.
[20] *Ibid.*, p. 36.
[21] *Ibid.*, p. 55.
[22] *Ibid.*, p. 173.
[23] *Ibid.*, p. 176.
[24] *Ibid.*, p. 179.
[25] *Ibid.*, p. 188.
[26] *Ibid.*, p. 191.
[27] *Ibid.*, p. 195.

> be kept constantly in print—hence the common phenomenon of the textbook writer who turns out a volume almost annually.[28]

Moreover, in his research the academician gains more "by riding one idea hard rather than by being eclectic," and if the professor "lacks the creativeness to achieve in his 'own right' he may gain minor renown by attaching himself as a satellite to some already established school of thought and filling in gaps left vacant by the master."[29]

While adding no generalization not already contained in Logan Wilson's study, Theodore Caplow and Reece J. McGee in *The Academic Marketplace* study reduce their picture of the academic man purely to the factors involved in his mobility, further documenting Wilson's argument. With some violence they reinforce Wilson's contentions that favoritism is a major component in university appointment, that the least intelligent professors become faculty politicians exercising more power than the good ones, that no one knows what a good teacher is in the first place, that publication is valued more highly than teaching, and that most of the publications are second-rate. In reinforcing the statistics gathered in the name of such contentions, Caplow and McGee assembled a considerable volume of quotations by professors concerning faculty colleagues who were changing positions.

The big schools, according to Caplow and McGee, often resort to any stratagem to place second-rate or undesirable individuals.

> We took him on the basis of the enthusiastic support of an outstanding professor at Harvard. That's very important. If Princeton pushes a man, I know it means I'll have to look somewhere else. I don't trust Columbia either, or Chicago. With one or two exceptions in each department, those bastards are shysters; they'll say anything about anyone to get a man placed. There's one man at Harvard and one at Yale that I know I can trust. I won't take a man from either place without their say-so.[30]

The most important qualities in a candidate for an academic appointment are said to be prestige and adaptability. "The biggest thing is that other people think well of him. It's like choosing a wife; you want one that other people will admire too."[31]

> He had to have a good background in the subject, a Ph.D., some experience, research-oriented, bright, hard working. Good social person, nice person, happily married. Those last two are important; you let some shit in, or someone with marital problems, Christ knows what'll happen. We have trouble enough with the things that happen normally without a paranoid around or someone's wife trying to lay everybody. We hire men to keep; we think personality is tremendously important.[32]

[28] *Ibid.*, p. 201.
[29] *Ibid.*, p. 208.
[30] Theodore Caplow and Reece J. McGee, *The Academic Marketplace* (New York: Basic Books, 1958), p. 153.
[31] *Ibid.*, p. 158.
[32] *Ibid.*, p. 160.

Among factors which were said to play an important part in evaluation and selection of professors were personal traits and domestic relations: "His wife was a quarrelsome, gossipy, shallow woman. He was interested in Milton."[33] And, "He played the record. That was the reason we hired him."[34]

The place of teaching was said to be incidental: "Our requirements are purely mathematical. No one gives a damn if you can teach."[35]

> He did a really tremendous job. It caused the rest of us to decide that if this kind of activity was not what was honored—and he'd led them to several national recognitions—then we'd do what was honored—namely, sitting in the library and writing weighty papers, and let their goddamned student group go to hell, which it has.[36]

In his foreword to the Caplow and McGee study, Barzun observed: "Like most anatomies, it does not present a pretty picture."[37]

> He goes on to observe that in his opinion the chief limitation of the study "consists in the authors' proper unwillingness to take up the cultural conditions of the repeated failures of mind, ethics, and dignity which they report.[38]

In fact, it is difficult to escape the impression that the only basis on which the researchers were willing to quote the remarks of one professor about another was the fact that they were ungrammatical, vulgar, vicious, or obscene.

Of course it requires hardly a moment's reflection to realize that this is only the worst side of a profession, the best side of which the authors chose to ignore. It seems that, in the minds of its practitioners, the academic profession has suffered an extensive loss of romance. One is reminded of the anti-intellectualism in the attacks by the skeptics on philosophy in the declining Hellenistic period of ancient thought. Surely, Barzun is to be forgiven if he views the crisis of the contemporary intellectual to be due primarily to the lack of faith by the intellectual in his own activity.

The formula for the successful *exposé* of the academic man seems to run as follows: (1) List the main stages in the career of the academic man, (2) imagine what can go wrong at any stage, (3) find a few examples of the negative possibility, envisioned, and if possible arrange them in a statistical table, and (4) support the finding by a quotation or two from dissatisfied colleagues. One could visualize an *exposé* of the medical profession along equivalent lines. One might inquire into how many persons are possibly motivated to enter the medical profession by sadistic or other psychologically destructive motives; one could make a statistical study of how many

[33] *Ibid.*, p. 92.
[34] *Ibid.*, p. 165.
[35] *Ibid.*, p. 159.
[36] *Ibid.*, p. 83.
[37] *Ibid.*, p. vi.
[38] *Ibid.*, p. vii.

doctors do not keep up with all the latest medical research; one could study how mnay operations are performed that need not have been performed; one might gather opinions as to how many instruments or other foreign matter are left in the patients after operations have been performed; one could study fee-splitting with druggists, and perhaps conclude with a study of what doctors think of one another when they lose patients to each other.

The frequency and popularity of recent *exposés* of the academy must be considered in connection with the areas of strength of the universities if they are to be understood. In the first place, it must be stated emphatically that the standards of professional selectivity in the universities do work after a fashion. When one considers all the things that can go wrong, the surprising thing is how high the level of competence is. Moreover, the formula, "publish or perish," is not nearly the terror it is often presented to be. For one thing, surprisingly little research or writing is necessary for a professor to maintain the reputation for being an active and productive scholar—a good article a year will do it. Many of the academic men who protest that one must publish or perish seem, in fact, to be employing the formula in a manner equivalent to the complaint against "greasy grinds" by undergraduates as a protest formula against productivity norms. In any case, it is an amazing spectacle to see persons who pay lip service to productivity and creativity complaining because they are in a situation in which they are encouraged and rewarded for creating.

It is surprising to find that the same persons who protest that teaching and research functions are contradictory, usually also protest most vigorously against the writing of textbooks. Offhand it would seem to be the ideal fusion of functions of the academic man as writer and teacher. Yet nothing seems more quickly to elicit scorn. This is despite the fact that there has, perhaps, never been a textbook writer who did not become a better teacher as a result of the serious attempt to integrate his field. Moreover, many of the great literatures of the world have been essentially textbooks: many of the writings of the ancient Chinese, practically all of Aristotle, the classics of Judaism, and the codifications of Roman law are a few examples.

Finally, there is a curious assumption that the mobility of the academic man is somehow bad. Yet all the evidences of the creative periods of mankind seem to show that when physical mobility is lost, other types of freedom are eventually lost as well. Mobility permits the scholar to find an environment fitted to his personality rather than force him to fit his personality to any single environment.

While from within the universities major attacks on the academic man have been launched, the universities have seemed to some students outside to be declining as havens of comparative freedom for scholarly research, primarily because of forces external to them. In his brilliant study, *The Organization Man*, William H. Whyte devoted a section to "The Organization Scientist,"[39] which he opens with a chapter on "The Fight against Genius." As Whyte sees it, under the old-fashioned Protestant ethic which Merton described in his study of science in seventeenth century England, the scientist was largely self-determined. This autonomy, Whyte believes, is being lost and group-needs, or a so-called social ethic, increasingly determine the course of scientific work. This results in concentration on practical applications of existing ideas rather than the discovery of new laws. Scientists increasingly work as units in scientific cells, in which organization loyalty is more important than brilliance, and well-rounded team-players are more valuable than creative but potentially disruptive men. Of the four billion dollars currently spent annually on research and development by industry, government, and the universities, less than 4 per cent (one hundred fifty million) is spent for creative research. The majority of scientists engage in supervised team research. Of the more than 600,000 people involved in scientific work, less than five thousand pick their own problems.

America's industrial research budget of $1.6 billion is now concentrated in the laboratories of corporations. Yet in a study[39a] of nominations of young men as top scientists, of 225 names nominated, only four were from industry. The universities seem overwhelmingly to present environments more favorable for pure science than do business or government. Moreover, of the top scientists nominated from industrial laboratories, the majority came from two—General Electric and Bell—which encourage pure research as a matter of policy. No scientist from Du Pont had been named more than once, and except from American Cyanamid, no other leading chemical firm had a scientist named to the top group. Chemists were able to name only one new chemical reaction discovered by an American chemical company in the last fifteen years. The reason for this is industrial policy:

> By their own statements of policy the majority of corporations make it plain that they wish to keep their researchers' eyes focused closely on the cash register. Unlike GE or Bell Labs, they discourage their scientists, sometimes forbid them, from publishing the results of their work in the learned journals or communicating them in any way to scientists outside the company preserve.[40]

Company policy is often explicitly opposed to virtuosos. Inhibiting the scientist, Whyte believes, also inhibits the flow of good ideas.

> Go down the list of commercial inventions over the last thirty years: *with very few exceptions the advances did not come from a corporation laboratory*. Kodachrome, for example, was perfected in Eastman's huge laboratories, but was invented by two musicians in a bathroom. The jet engine is an even clearer case in point. As Launcelot Law Whyte

[39] William H. Whyte, *The Organization Man* (New York: Doubleday Anchor Books, 1957), pp. 225–265.
[39a] By Whyte for *Fortune*.
[40] *Ibid.*, p. 231.

points out, none of the five earliest turbo-jet developments in Germany, Britain, and the United States was initiated within an established aircraft firm.[41]

The trends toward the bureaucratization of the scientist so pronounced in corporation research are found also in academic research for

> . . . the people in the foundations and the universities are reinforcing these values, and by reinforcing them further molding the scientists to the organization image.[42]

Government money is considered to be primarily responsible for altering the structure of academic research. With government contracts the direction of research has tended to slide from university control. Of 225 colleges and universities receiving research contracts, 5 received as much as the other 220, making research into big business. There was an increase in the number of papers written by two people, an even greater number written by teams of three, four, or five. Committees are increasingly used to plan, supervise, and carry out interdisciplinary research.

> The Ford Foundation gave $50,000 apiece to each of five universities for a self-study of their work in the behavioral sciences. For a year committees and subcommittees and visiting committees met and correlated, and at last five massive documents were produced. The result was thoroughly conventional: in most cases, the really tough issues were noted rather than explored, and the strong implication was that few things were wrong that more financial support couldn't cure. The only trenchant analysis that $250,000 produced was a supplementary report. It was written by one man.[43]

According to Whyte, the foundations as well as government are intensifying the trend toward bureaucratization. In government, of the $38 million given for projects, all but $22 million goes to applied, large-scale team projects. For the foundations, of the $11.5 million a year given to social science only $2.8 million goes to individual projects or fellowships, while $8.7 million, or 76 per cent, goes to big team projects and institutions. It is noteworthy that while Whyte agrees that the universities are being pressed into the trend away from pure research, he is convinced that the pressures arise primarily from the outside. Whyte's analysis thus follows more closely that of Veblen than those of Barzun, Logan Wilson, or Caplow and McGee.

If one studies the negative responses by such insiders as Veblen, Barzun, Logan Wilson, and Caplow and McGee to what is happening in the universities, and positive responses by such outsiders as William H. Whyte, together with the general transformation of the universities as, in their course of adaptation to the external milieu, they have been thrust from

[41] *Ibid.*, pp. 237–238.
[42] *Ibid.*, p. 240.
[43] *Ibid.*, p. 246.

scholasticism, through humanism, to scientism, the confused pattern that they at first seem to present falls into perspective. The major event in the universities in recent times has been the rise of the scientific outlook to a position of dominance and the transformation by science from within. The major conflict, still extant in modern times, has been between humanism and science. However, in the long run the conflict has tended to tip in favor of science. When it does, the liquidation of traditional values tends to be carried through, leading also to a displacement within scientific activity itself toward pure technology. This history led Veblen to deplore the decline of the humanistic point of view, which terminates in the substitution of the institutes of technology for the liberal arts college. Barzun was responding to the identical process, differing from Veblen only in placing responsibility for the change on the intellectual himself rather than, as did Veblen, on the rise of modern business civilization. Barzun's arguments are like those which accounted for the change from the ancient philosopher to the medieval mystic by a failure of nerve. Finally, Logan Wilson and Caplow and McGee shifted attention away from the general process of the conflict between humanism and science which has occurred in the universities, to description of the qualities of an intellectual *milieu* from which the humanistic spirit has been drained away, leaving only an atmosphere of instrumentalism, of expediency, and of Machiavellian power-seeking.

Whyte, on the other hand, was calling attention to the systematic instrumentalism which arises in *any* area in which science emerges into dominance. As an outside observer, his perspective was fixed by the comparison of science in business to science in the universities. From the point of view of this comparison, university science remains immensely closer to the old spirit of pure science which was at its height at the time when the roles of the humanist and scientist were most nearly fused.

The main weight of the evidence, however, seems to suggest that the humanistic spirit in the universities will continue to decline and that the influence of government and business-sponsored science will continue to rise. As it does, the systematic instrumentalism which occurs whenever science enters an area will increase.

SOCIAL SCIENCE AS THE SYNTHESIS OF WESTERN THOUGHT

The great drift in modern times has been toward the increasing conquest of one area after another by science. Social life fell within the sphere of science in the nineteenth century, making it the great century of the rise of the social sciences. Anthropology, economics, geography, jurisprudence, political science, psychology, and sociology emerged from the spawning bed. At the time of their origin, the social sciences were welcomed as the great syntheses of modern thought. This was the view of Comte, Herbert Spencer, and Lester Ward—the founders of sociology.

As observed, however, wherever the scientific point of view is established, the inner transformation of knowledge into instrumental form soon gets under way. What had been heralded as the great synthesis soon began to take on a more ominous mien. At a comparatively early stage in the development of the social sciences representatives of the humanistic disciplines began to react to them as the latest abomination of science. The reaction against the social sciences has repeatedly arisen in recent times, even on the part of social scientists themselves. Recent studies by two of America's foremost sociologists may illustrate this.

In his book on *Fads and Foibles in Modern Sociology*, Sorokin has brought the major trends of modern social science under sometimes witty and almost always violent attack. The very titles of his chapters indicate that he primarily has positivism, scientism, and operationalism in social science under attack: *Amnesia and New Columbuses; Verbal Defects: Obtuse Jargon and Sham-Scientific Slang; The Illusion of Operationalism; Testomania; The Fad of Intelligence Tests; Quantophrenia; The Grand Cult of "Social Physics" and "Mental Mechanics"; The Wonderland of Social Atoms and Small Groups.* No one who reads Sorokin's study with adequate discount for its often intemperate language can doubt the penetration of its insight or the legitimacy of many of its charges.

Sorokin's positive solution to the predicament of the social sciences has some startling novelties. The creative Renaissance of social science, he maintains, requires a reconstruction of our notion of what constitutes psycho-social reality.

> Prevalent psycho-social science views psycho-social reality as purely sensory phenomena; an adequate knowledge of it as a systematized body of propositions, describing sensory observations and sensory perception in all its forms—plain observations, clinical, experimental, statistical—assisted by logico-mathematical reasoning as the only way in which cognition of the total psycho-social reality can be gained.[44]

These "invalid assumptions" must be replaced according to Sorokin by an "integralist conception" of reality and truth:

> The integralist conception views psycho-social reality as a complex manifold in which we can distinguish three different aspects: sensory, rational, and supersensory-superrational.
>
> The supersensory-superrational aspect of psycho-social reality is manifested by the highest creative activities and created masterpieces of genius in all fields of cultural reality.
>
> There should be the closest cooperation and unification of all three methods into one integral conception of reality, an integral system of truth, and an integral method of reason.[45]

Sorokin's solution to the problems of social science is the subordination of science as a body of theory produced by systematic experimentalism

[44] Pitirim A. Sorokin, *Fads and Foibles in Modern Sociology and Related Sciences* (Chicago: Henry Regnery Co., 1956), p. 315.

[45] *Ibid.*, pp. 316–317.

(as an inferior form of truth) to the requirements of a superscientific point of view and a transrational intuition. It seems that Sorokin has his reasons that reason knows not of.

The most recent attack on the main drift in social science by one of its top figures is C. Wright Mills' *The Sociological Imagination*.[46] To estimate the significance of his contentions, it is necessary to realize that of his generation Mills is probably the number one sociologist in America. There are other sociologists who are more popular with sociologists proper; there are others who have greater access to foundation funds. Of the members of his generation, however, Mills is read perhaps by more professionals in and out of social science, both in America and in Europe, than any other sociologist. And whatever their defects, *The New Men of Power*, *White Collar*, and *The Power Elite* are among the major sociological works of America of the 1950's.

The starting point for Mills' attack on the main traditions of current sociology is the assumption, as old as August Comte, that sociology is the truly modern synthesis of knowledge. He contends "that journalists and scholars, artists and publics, scientists and editors are coming to expect . . . what may be called the sociological imagination."[47] Its nature is described in terms reminiscent of Marx's concept of dialectical materialism as a tool for distinguishing true and false consciousness.

> The sociological imagination enables its possessors to understand the larger historical scene in terms of its meaning for the inner life and the external career of a variety of individuals. It enables him to take into account how individuals, in the welter of their daily experience, often become falsely conscious of their social positions.[48]

The sociological imagination, Mills contends, enables the individual to understand his experience and gauge his fate by locating himself in his period. It is the capacity to shift perspectives from the single family to the comparative national budgets of the world, from theological to military establishments, from the oil industry to contemporary poetry. It is "the most fruitful form of self-consciousness." It is Mills' view that sociology is the truly modern synthesis of intellectuality:

> I believe that the social sciences are becoming the common denominator of our cultural period, and the sociological imagination our most needed quality of mind.[49]

As Mills develops his thesis, however, it is not long before he makes clear his desire to separate social from physical science.

[46] C. Wright Mills, *The Sociological Imagination* (New York: Oxford University Press, 1959).

[47] *Ibid.*, p. 5.

[48] *Ibid.*, p. 5.

[49] *Ibid.*, p. 13.

> The cultural meaning of physical science—the major older common denominator—is becoming doubtful. As an intellectual style, physical science is coming to be thought of by many as somehow inadequate.
>
> Many cultural workmen have come to feel that "science" is a false and pretentious Messiah, or at the very least a highly ambiguous element in modern civilization.[50]

The primary targets for Mills' guns are what he describes as the three major trends in sociology today: "grand theory" (primarily illustrated by the works of Talcott Parsons), "abstracted empiricism" (illustrated by the works of Bernard Berelson, Samuel Stauffer, Paul Lazarsfeld, and many others), and "illiberal practicality" (which seems to include both the work of the group-dynamics theorists and industrial sociologists). His primary criticism of the work of Talcott Parsons is that it is "drunk on syntax, blind to semantics."[51] It is, he asserts, on such an abstracted level of generality that it never gets down to facts. Mills' chief critical device is to translate passages from Parsons into simpler English.

> Is grand theory, as represented in *The Social System*, merely verbiage or is it also profound? My answer to this question is: It is only about 50 per cent verbiage; 40 per cent is well-known textbook sociology. The other 10 per cent, as Parsons might say, I am willing to leave open for your own empirical investigations. My own investigations suggest that the remaining 10 per cent is of possible—although rather vague—ideological use.[52]

It is perhaps significant that Mills does not care to discuss the 10 per cent of Parsons' work which he indicates may represent some novelties.

By abstracted empiricism Mills seems primarily to mean the various statistical studies of social events. His most general criticism of it is that it is bound by a "methodological inhibition" which "stands parallel to the fetishism of the Concept."[53] It is, he feels, a pseudo-exactness whose "thinness of . . . results is matched only by the elaboration of the methods and care employed."[54] Its use (as illustrated by the American soldier studies during World War II) proves "that it is possible for social research to be of administrative use without being concerned with the problems of social science."[55] Abstracted empiricism, according to Mills, "is not characterized by any substantive propositions or theories."[56] In the following phrases Mills reiterates his views of it.

> The adherents of abstract empiricism . . . provide employment for semi-skilled technicians on a scale and in a manner not known before;

[50] *Ibid.*, pp. 15–16.
[51] *Ibid.*, p. 34.
[52] *Ibid.*, footnote p. 49.
[53] *Ibid.*, p. 50.
[54] *Ibid.*, p. 52.
[55] *Ibid.*, p. 53.
[56] *Ibid.*, p. 55.

> they offer to them careers having the security of the older academic life but not requiring the older sort of individual accomplishment. (p. 54)
>
> Probably no one familiar with its practitioners would care to deny that many of them are dominated by concern with their own scientific status; their most cherished professional self-image is that of the natural scientist. (p. 54)
>
> Because of the expensiveness of The Method, its practitioners have often become involved in the commercial and bureaucratic uses of their work, and this indeed has affected their style. (p. 65)
>
> In the many ways indicated, as well as in others, it is possible to cling to The Method and yet attempt to cover up the triviality of its results. (p. 71)
>
> Those in the grip of the methodological inhibition often refuse to say anything about modern society unless it has been through the fine little mill of The Statistical Ritual. (pp. 71–72)

Once again it is noteworthy that Mills declines to discuss any substantive propositions of such sociologists though he admits, with some reluctance, that they do offer some after all.

However, it is the third branch of contemporary sociology in Mills' classification that incurs his most biting scorn. He describes it as illiberal practicality, by which he seems to mean the position of the bootlicks, lackeys, and sycophants of modern power complexes.

> The new practicality leads to new images of social science—and of social scientists. New institutions have arisen in which this illiberal practicality is installed: industrial relations centers, research bureaus of universities, new research branches of corporation, air force and government. They are not concerned with the battered human beings living at the bottoms of society. . . . But . . . with enlightened circles of business executives and with generals having sizable budgets. For the first time in the history of their disciplines, social scientists have come into professional relations with private and public powers as well above the level of the welfare agency and the county agent.[57]

The aims of exponents of illiberal practicality are to serve their masters: to formulate the problems of administrators, to mold the lives of workers who are restless and low in morale, to serve commercial and corporate ends of the communications and advertising agencies.

According to Mills, work in the abstracted empirical manner is so expensive that only large institutions can afford it: the army, state, corporations and their organs for advertising, promotion, and public relations. Hence the idea of a university as a body of colleagues and apprentices is replaced by a set of research bureaucracies. The key types are intellectual administrators and promoters (who in "large foundations tend to encourage large-scale bureaucratic research into small-scale problems") and younger recruits describable as research technicians. As in other bureaucratic structures the control of competition, Mills insists, tends to fall into the hands

[57] *Ibid.*, pp. 95–96.

of cliques. Academic cliques regulate competitions and assign rewards, give friendly advice to younger men, control job offers, recommend promotions, assign books to favorable reviewers, secure acceptance of articles and books for publication, allocate research funds, arrange for honorific positions within professional societies and on the editorial boards of professional journals.[58] Between the cliques appear statesmen whose work is that of a broker, dealing in the allocation of prestige for both teams:

> The prestige he has accumulated is so disproportionate to what he has actually accomplished, the promise that he has held out is so grand, that he is often quite inhibited from getting down to 'The Study': and when he does have a major part in some study or book, he is reluctant to finish it or to publish it, even when others think it is finished. He complains then about the committees and other statesmanlike burdens he is carrying. . . . He is trapped . . . but also he really must continue to trap himself—else his very role as a statesman will be recognized by others and by himself as a mere excuse.[59]

Like Sorokin, Mills has primarily turned his artillery on the positivistic traditions of sociology. It is also interesting to see how considerably their positive proposals correspond. Social science, according to Mills, deals with the problems of biography, history, and their intersection in social structure.[60] All the productions of the historians are conceived as a great file indispensable to social science.[61] Mills argues that there is no law stated by any social scientist that is transhistorical and capable of being understood as having to do with no specific structure of a specific period.[62] If this is true, the whole basis of the present study is called into question. The task of the social scientist, Mills states, can only be to understand the present epoch. This understanding rests on values selected from those of Western society:

> They are simply values proclaimed by men and within limits practiced in small circles. What a man calls moral judgment is merely his desire to generalize, and so make available for others those values he has come to choose.[63]

These values Mills insists are three: the value of truth ("In a world of widely communicated nonsense, any statement of fact is of political and moral significance");[64] the second value consists of "the role of reason in human affairs; along with it is the third value of human freedom."[65] The

[58] *Ibid.*, pp. 107–108.
[59] *Ibid.*, p. 111.
[60] *Ibid.*, p. 143.
[61] *Ibid.*, p. 145.
[62] *Ibid.*, p. 150.
[63] *Ibid.*, p. 178.
[64] *Ibid.*, p. 178. This is an intriguing statement which I hope to understand some day.
[65] *Ibid.*, p. 179.

task of the social scientist, Mills urges, is "intellectually to transcend the milieux in which he happens to live."[66]

> As social scientists we locate ourselves. By the nature of our work, we are aware of social structure and somewhat aware of the historical mechanics of its movement. But clearly we do not have access to the major means of power. . . .
>
> It is, I think, the political task of the social scientist who accepts the ideals of freedom and reason, to address his work to each of the other three types of men I have classified in terms of power and knowledge.
>
> To those with power and with awareness of it, he imputes varying measures of responsibility for such structural consequences as he finds by his work to be decisively influenced by their decisions and their lack of decisions.
>
> To those whose actions have such consequences, but who do not seem to be aware of them, he directs whatever he has found out about those consequences. He attempts to educate and then, again, he imputes responsibility.
>
> To those who are regularly without such power and whose awareness is confined to their everyday milieux, he reveals by his work the meaning of structural trends and decisions for these milieux, the ways in which personal troubles are connected with public issues; in the course of these efforts, he states what he has found out concerning the actions of the more powerful.[67]

Though his arguments are somewhat more skillfully phrased, Mills' position seems remarkably close to that of Sorokin. Like Sorokin, Mills takes a powerful antipositivistic stand which at times becomes outright antiempiricism.[68] While he brings his stinging language to bear on the field, he has criticized very few substantive issues of contemporary sociology. Like a heavy wind that shakes a forest, this may only bring down a few dead limbs.

In his positive program Mills is far closer to Sorokin than appears on the surface. He denies the capacity of social science to discover laws of social life, insisting that it can only comprehend a particular time. He asserts that sociology has a built-in value program. In fact, only its moral judgments are general, giving the social scientist ability to transcend his milieu. The final task of the social scientist is said to be to complain against those in power and to inform those who are not in power as to what those who are in power are up to. All in all, this is not very dissimilar from Sorokin's transrational integral truth, for it abandons sociology as a strictly scientific enter-

[66] *Ibid.*, p. 184.

[67] *Ibid.*, p. 185.

[68] "In our situation, empirical work as such is for beginning students and for those who aren't able to handle the complexities of big problems: it is also for highly formal men who do not care what they study so long as it appears to be orderly. All these types have a right to do as they please or as they must; they have no right to impose in the name of science such narrow limits on others. Anyway, you ought not to let them bother you." C. Wright Mills, "On Intellectual Craftsmanship" in *Symposium on Sociological Theory*, edited by Llewellyn Gross (Evanston: Row, Peterson & Co., 1959), p. 35.

prise and transforms it into a sociopolitical program. To sociology is left the ultimate task of evaluating the epoch, which seems to be precisely what Sorokin intends by establishing integral truths.

The views of Sorokin and Mills have an importance over and beyond their great intrinsic interest, for it was the rise of social science in the nineteenth century that tipped the balance in the contest between humanism and science in favor of science. It was by the route of the social sciences that many humanists for the first time found their way to science. It may be noted that in countries where humanism was most entrenched, such as England, France, and Italy, the social sciences made slowest headway in the universities. In countries where the humanistic tradition was less firmly rooted, Germany and the United States, the social sciences have tended to sweep all before them. Moreover, the humanistic disciplines suffered the most serious inroads from the expansion of the social sciences. It is little wonder that the exponents of the older humanistic studies have viewed the social sciences with suspicion.

On the other hand, the rapid evolution of the social sciences is in large measure explainable by their promise of fusing the two poles of Western thought: implementing the humanistic outlook with science and encouraging the scientific analysis of areas which were hitherto the exclusive property of the humanities. However, when leading students, such as Mills and Sorokin, experience the trends as a betrayal, this cannot be dismissed as a mere eccentricity of publicity seekers. Sorokin was one of the foremost figures of his generation; Mills is one of the most prominent figures, if not the most prominent, of his generation. Once again one is brought face to face with the fact that wherever the scientific point of view is introduced and permitted to follow its natural course, it achieves its efficiencies by the instrumentalization of the body of knowledge to which it is applied. This is not a betrayal; it is the consequence of the scientific process. In reaction Sorokin and Mills are attempting to transform the social sciences from empirical to normative disciplines, moving them from the field of science to that of ethics.

The rejection of social science from within by certain leading social scientists is important for another current trend. Many scientists and scientific-minded philosophers who have retained full awareness of the general trends in the modern world have grown alarmed at the apparent evolution of the scientist into a mere technologist. Repeatedly such persons have advocated the fusion of the two poles of modern intellectuality into scientific humanism. An extensive literature has developed around this theme: Haldane's *The Philosophy of Humanism*,[69] Sarton's *The History of Science and the New Humanism*,[70] and Lamont's *The Philosophy of Human-*

[69] Viscount Haldane, *The Philosophy of Humanism* (London: John Murray, 1922).
[70] George Sarton, *The History of Science and the New Humanism* (New York: George Braziller, Inc., 1956).

ism[71] are typical. The proposals for a scientific humanism do take into account the two major poles of modern thought. However, when these poles are actually fused, they result in social science. But then, if Sorokin and Mills can be taken as an accurate index, in the end the scientific aspects of social science will set aside its humanism as nonscientific, or the humanistic will abandon science.

Meanwhile, in all branches of science, the same processes that led to the institutionalization of science in industry, government, and the universities tends to displace the intellectual by the technician. As Julien Benda put it, realistic and practical motives tend everywhere to dominate the modern intellectual. The notable list of modern students who have perceived and reacted against the trend includes: Thorstein Veblen, Jacques Barzun, Logan Wilson, George Sarton, Corliss Lamont, Pitirim Sorokin, C. Wright Mills, and many, many others who were not mentioned.

Where will it all end? No one can say for certain, for the destiny of contemporary man has not run out. It may perhaps be significant that the three greatest Utopias of the twentieth century, Zamiatin's *We*, Huxley's *Brave New World*, and George Orwell's *1984*, all project the transformation of science into a terrifying new instrument of social control. Huxley puts in the mouth of Mustapha Mond, Resident Controller of the Western World, the attitudes of the scientific caste system in control of the *Brave New World* toward various areas of life including science:

> We have our stability to think of. We don't want change. Every change is a menace to stability. That's another reason why we're so chary of applying new inventions. Every discovery in pure science is potentially subversive; even science must sometimes be treated as a possible enemy.
>
> Truth's a menace, science is a public danger. As dangerous as it's been beneficient. It has given us the stablest equilibrium in history. . . . But we can't allow science to undo its own good work.
>
> "Art, science—you seem to have paid a fairly heavy price for your happiness," said the Savage, when they were alone. "Anything else?"
>
> "Well, religion, of course," replied the Controller.[72]

SUMMARY

The distinctive contemporary community is the nation-state. The civilization which has grown up in connection with it, unlike any other that humankind has created, is scientific. Modern scientific culture made its first brilliant gains in the transformation of physical nature. From here it was extended to one social and cultural sphere after another including the arts, where its reanalysis of experience by means of modern electronic, photographic, and

[71] Corliss Lamont, *The Philosophy of Humanism* (New York: Philosophical Library, 1957).

[72] Aldous Huxley, *The Brave New World* (New York: Modern Library, 1946), pp. 269, 272, 276.

mechanical equipment destroyed the ancient individuality and uniqueness of the art object and substituted a quantity of mechanically reproduced copies suited to the scientifically implemented perception of contemporary mass man. For the first time, in the opinion of some students, the arts have been completely removed from the sphere of cultic observance and relocated in that of politics. In a world in which science carries out dramatic revolutions in every sphere it touches and from which no area is permanently removed, civilization seems most appropriately approached from problems which arise for science.

No one doubts that by its analysis science conflicts with traditional social and ethical evaluations of experience. The critical question—which cannot be answered for certain—is: Does science conflict in the end with all values, except those which are purely instrumental?

The systematic instrumentalism of science brings the humanist (the bearer of one of the distinctive intellectual roles of contemporary man) into conflict with the scientist (the other). While scientist and humanist have both flourished under conditions of freedom, and while they have often supported one another, in the end they have come into conflict. While the Western humanist developed a value program in the name of the fullest possible development of the cultivated man, the scientist has been forced to renounce this kind of theory-making as normative and without scientific standing.

It is not alone between the roles of humanist and scientist and their immediate intellectual products, however, that tension is felt. The scientific explanation of the world had transformed it from magical garden into a world without ultimate mysteries in which everything is at least in principle explainable. The scientific disenchantment of the world (that is, destruction of traditional ways of determining significance) does not, in the opinion of many serious students, stop with the elimination of magic, but tends to uproot all ultimate values whatsoever. So, it has been argued, that in a scientific world even human life and death are rendered insignificant. Having been placed on an endless rising ladder of scientific advance, man's life provides no point from which it may be said to have been fulfilled. There is always a next step. Moreover, in a world in which this is true, one traditional way of assigning significance to life after another is shattered. Science itself gravitates as a most powerful tool toward those configurations of power most willing to use it, with no other consideration than the expediency of the moment.

Since these same configurations of power which increasingly assume command of science look to the universities for their supply of trained scientists, the universities are pushed on to their third great internal revolution which historically moved from scholastic through humanism to scientism. As the humanistic claims upon the modern university-trained mind declined, some scholars (like Veblen and Barzun) saw it as a disaster for which they tried to account. Others (like Wilson and Caplow) have devoted themselves to the description of what they conceive to be the *milieu* of Machiavellian machinations which characterizes academic life. It is often outsiders (for example, William H. Whyte, Jr.) who most clearly see that despite a transformation of the universities by a systematic instrumentalism which abandons all ultimate ends, the universities still remain the strongest traditional centers of pure science.

The tendency for the various spheres of modern life (from the arts to the university disciplines) to be transformed into *milieux* in which all values are relativized and only the rules of a purified expediency prevail, makes important a renewed examination of the social sciences. The social sciences epitomize the hope and the fear of contemporary man. When the social sciences burst like a shooting star on the nineteenth-century horizon, they seemed to many persons like the promise of an ultimate fulfillment for Western civilization. The basis of this promise and source of appeal of the social sciences lay in the fact that they were presumed to fuse the roles of humanist and scientist and the programs and methods of each. However, the actual course of this marriage of true minds plunged many sensitive humanists into dismay. For it has often seemed that the integration of humanism and science in the social sciences was only the prelude to the invasion of one more sphere by science and its gradual reduction by systematic instrumentalism. This has led certain leading contemporary social scientists (for example, Sorokin and Mills) to the tacit abandonment of social science and the substitution for it of politico-ethical programs.

SELECTED BIBLIOGRAPHY

Barzun, Jacques, *The House of Intellect* (New York: Harper & Bros., 1959).

Benda, Julien, *The Betrayal of the Intellectuals*, trans. by Richard Aldington (Boston: The Beacon Press, 1955).

Caplow, Theodore, and Reece J. McGee, *The Academic Marketplace* (New York: Basic Books, 1958).

Gross, Llewellyn (ed.), *Symposium on Sociological Theory* (Evanston: Row, Peterson & Co., 1959).

Haldane, Viscount, *The Philosophy of Humanism* (London: John Murray, 1922).

Lamont, Corliss, *The Philosophy of Humanism* (New York: Philosophical Library, 1957).

Mills, C. Wright, *The Sociological Imagination* (New York: Oxford University Press, 1959).

Roe, Anne, *The Making of a Scientist* (New York: Dodd, Mead & Co., 1952).

Sarton, George, *The History of Science and the New Humanism* (New York: George Braziller, Inc., 1956).

Veblen, Thorstein, *The Higher Learning in America* (New York: Sagamore Press, 1957).

Weber, Max, *From Max Weber: Essays in Sociology*, trans. by H. H. Gerth and C. Wright Mills (New York: Oxford University Press, 1946).
Whyte, William H., Jr., *The Organization Man* (New York: Doubleday Anchor Books, 1957).
Wilson, Logan, *The Academic Man* (New York: Oxford University Press, 1942).

Part VII

SUMMARY AND CONCLUSION

19

THE COMPARATIVE STUDY OF SOCIETY AND CIVILIZATION

SINCE the late nineteen twenties the comparative study of society and civilization has not enjoyed very high repute among social scientists. There have been a variety of reasons for this, some of which have some interest for us.

Because of various licenses taken by early social scientists[1] with the so-called comparative method, the procedure itself was brought under suspicion. The habit had grown up of assuming in advance some course of social development which was then used as a kind of chain along which "facts" torn from the context of various societies were strung. Social science was being rapidly turned into an art of illumination in which the only criterion of correct procedure was the comparative attractiveness to the person concerned with the end products.

Partly in response to the collapse of early forms of the comparative method, the formalistic school of sociology arose, which made the rejection of the comparative method a fundamental plank in its program.[2] This gave theoretical reinforcement to the disrepute of the comparative method produced by the babble of competing schemes of social development which arose in the heyday of the comparative method.

Another trend which tended, more by default than by positive intent, to bring the comparative use of historical data into disrepute was the rapid evolution of the statistical method which was popularized by the works of Tarde in France and Giddings and Ross in America. To be sure, Tarde listed as the proper methods of sociology archeology (comparative history) and statistics.[3] However, in his own work and still more among those students of pluralistic behaviorism stemming from Tarde and Giddings, the task of gathering statistics eclipsed the comparative analysis of historical data. However, the most able members of the school of pluralistic behaviorism, for

[1] See Don Martindale, "Sociological Theory and the Ideal Type," in Llewellyn Gross (ed.), *Symposium on Sociological Theory* (Evanston: Row, Peterson & Co., 1959), pp. 59 ff.

[2] See Don Martindale, *The Nature and Types of Sociological Theory* (Boston: Houghton Mifflin, 1960), pp. 211 ff.

[3] *Ibid.*, p. 306.

example, Chapin, continued to insist on the employment of comparative historical methods along with statistical methods.[4]

More important than any of these reasons for the disrepute of comparative studies of society and civilization was the substantive collapse of early forms of progress theory which had dominated sociology since its origin. The early sociologists had assumed that mankind evolved in a unilinear manner from some primitive form into its most complex forms. They had also assumed that all societies—though at varying rates—are undergoing the same evolution. This convenient assumption had legitimized their special use of comparative methods. One needed only to see the various primitive societies of the world as travelers on the same route to high civilization as one visualized himself to be on, and to take them as reference points for one's description of the course as a whole.

Among the critical difficulties with unilinear evolutionism were: the concealed value premises in what various thinkers took as the lowest and highest stages of civilization (different value premises gave different results); the failure to set up scientific criteria for proof or disproof of the given theory; the increasingly evident fact that the evidence would not fit any single form of the theory of unilinear evolution. Human societies have varied from the beginning, and even when they were somewhat similar they have developed in different ways. These differences can be reconciled only by doing violence to the facts.

Finally, most of the studies of comparative society and civilization, such as Spengler's *Decline of the West*, Sorokin's *Social and Cultural Dynamics*, Toynbee's *Study of History*, and Jaspers' *Origin and Goal of History*, have usually been, at best, thinly disguised evaluative studies rather than scientific studies proper. They have been the work of special pleaders intent upon the ethical evaluation and the spiritual interpretation of various historical events rather than explanation of them.[5] No one has made more unmistakably clear certain of the elements of special pleading in Toynbee's account, for example, than Samuel.

> When we collate the numerous and often repetitious passages on the Jews in *A Study of History*, we discover, behind the arabesques of erudition, three familiar and rather shopworn ideas:
>
> 1. That there has been only one episode of value in Jewish history—the Prophetic;
> 2. That the spiritually fatal mistake of the Jews was their rejection of Christianity;
> 3. That it was by this rejection that they condemned themselves to everlasting sterility.[6]

[4] F. Stuart Chapin, *Cultural Change* (New York: The Century Co., 1928).

[5] See the discussions of Toynbee and Jaspers in Chapter 3.

[6] Maurice Samuel, *The Professor and the Fossil* (New York: Alfred A. Knopf, 1956), p. 73.

Samuel made a brilliant assault on these suppositions, and annihilated them. However, it should be noted that Samuel was himself a special pleader (though *for* traditional Judaism rather than against it) and deliberately and self-consciously lifted his study outside the framework of social science. He imagines an adversary who "is a composite of all the pessimists I have encountered,"[7] and, among other things, places in his mouth the interpretation of Judaism from the standpoint of social science:

> There are many rabbis who find their justification of Judaism in Westermarck and Malinowski and Margaret Mead and Ruth Benedict. They talk, as rabbis, a professional technical language drawn from anthropology, sociology, psychology, and social service. They explain Jewish needs in terms of "ego-satisfaction," of "the father motif," "*rites de passage*," and the couvade. They find more comfort in the literature stemming from *The Golden Bough* than in the Bible; indeed, they tend to regard the Bible as an illustration of the views set forth by Frazer and the later anthropologists rather than as the unique utterance of a people's struggle to hold on to God.[8]

Against all such sociological interpretations of Judaism, Samuel uncompromisingly takes his stand and turns his face. The Jewish ethos, he insists,

> Is based on the One God who made everything, the universe and man, light and darkness, good and evil.
>
> The moral laws shall not be deduced from sociological or anthropological study; they do not have to be, and in fact they cannot be; for they are not relative things.[9]

In the end one gathers that for Samuel no comparisons with the history of the Jews are tolerable, for of all people they alone are chosen by God. And in the end their experience defies all sociological explanation, for it is a product of the interaction of the Jews with God through time according to the ancient terms of the Covenant.

The comparative study of society and civilization must move from the sphere of the special pleader, whether he be of a traditional type (like Samuel) or of a special type (like Spengler, Sorokin, Toynbee, and Jaspers), if it is to be undertaken by social science. However, when it does, the task of assigning evaluative significance must be abandoned. Evaluation is not the task of the sociologist. Meanwhile, it may be noted that in the failure of social science to undertake the comparative study of society and civilization from a value-neutral position, the field has tended to be occupied and obscured by various traditional and nontraditional forms of special pleading. From a scientific point of view, one has less to fear from the traditional moralists than from the various nonstandard, self-appointed spiritual interpreters of comparative society. The traditionalists are far less inclined to disguise moral evaluation in factual propositions. However, another basic

[7] *Ibid.*, p. 170.
[8] *Ibid.*, p. 168.
[9] *Ibid.*, p. 179.

reason for the low repute of the comparative study of society and civilization is found in the number of problems produced by various traditional and nontraditional forms of special pleading.

A primary objective of the present study has been to open up the comparative sociological study of society and civilization once again, since it offers the greatest hope for a new attack on the theories of social and cultural change which have been in crisis. The three major positions that have been advanced by current social science to explain social and cultural change are: (1) the culture-lag theory (by certain pluralistic behaviorists), (2) organic cyclical theory (by certain recent organicists), and (3) the intrusive disturbance theory (of the functionalists). For all three of these positions the comparative study of society and civilization is essential.

The crisis in the explanation of social and cultural change has arisen from the fact that although the early progress-evolution theory collapsed, the contemporary positions have not been altogether satisfactory. The culture-lag theory rested on a distinction between material and nonmaterial culture and the notion that inventions in the material realm are progressive, while those in nonmaterial realm are not. As a crudely accurate description of contemporary scientific civilization, the culture-lag theory was plausible. Moreover, it was a disguised form of the theory of progress. However, when one examined the distinction between material and nonmaterial culture carefully, it tended to melt away. The idea of a technical process, for example, is no more material than the idea of a new school curriculum. Furthermore, when one studied other cultures, it quickly became apparent that many waves of civilization have formed without an appreciable change in the basic material culture. Should one not explain classical Greece as a fine example of the "lag" of material culture behind an inventive nonmaterial culture? There were many additional difficulties, but these may illustrate the fact that there were both theoretical and empirical problems for the culture-lag theory.

The various cyclical theories of social and cultural change projected by the organicists who appeared when positivistic organicism disintegrated[10] suffered from the fact that they were dominated by doctrinaire intentions. This inclined them arbitrarily to select from the evidence, and even to distort it to fit their moral and ethical intent.[11]

Finally, the functionalists, who were the heirs of the positivistic organicists, found themselves in a rather curious predicament. Their organismic theories of society inclined them to the position that functionally interrelated social wholes were the primary causal factors in interhuman behavior. From this standpoint social and cultural change could have one of two possible origins: from intrusive events outside the organismic system or from the imminent evolution of the forces within the system itself. The

[10] See the *Nature and Types of Sociological Theory, op. cit.,* pp. 110 ff.
[11] See the discussion in Chapter 3.

fact that contemporary functionalism did not embrace until very recently imminent evolutionism can only be explained by the historical disaster this theory of change suffered in early sociology. Hence, by fairly general admission the single most significant difficulty with contemporary functionalism has been its failure to develop an adequate theory of social change.

A notable characteristic of all three of these positions on social and culture change is that they refer to fairly large-scale social units. If nothing else, only the study of entire societies and civilizations is adequate to the genuine test of their hypotheses or in the search for substitutes for them. The argument often advanced that the study of events of this scale only makes limited generalizations possible is beside the point. It is the task of explanation to discover how far they can in fact be generalized.

THE SOCIAL BEHAVIORISTIC THEORY OF SOCIAL AND CULTURAL CHANGE

Since the theory of change is concerned with the manner in which social and cultural forms originate and are destroyed, the description of these forms is a logically prior requirement to an explanation of them. In other words, the theory of change is the capstone of sociological theory. Moreover, social behaviorism seems at present to hold out more promise than other current explanations.

Social behaviorism is the view that at bottom all human social events may be reduced to interhuman behaviors which are meaningful to the parties involved. It assumes that the peculiarity of man is his lack of instincts and correspondingly extended capacity for learning. Man is not born social; he learns to be social. However, he is so dependent on others for survival (having the longest period of dependency of all creatures) that he is unavoidably shaped in terms of the particular patterns of the social unit which rears him. Everything he does or becomes is through learning and the modification of one learned pattern by another. Though men have an almost endless capacity for modification, the collective survival of any plurality of men requires (if a society is not to destroy itself as a result of its own inner contradictions) that some few more or less consistent systems of interhuman behavior shall prevail in the social life of a given time and place. Such structures of interhuman behavior exist at various levels of generality: social groups and institutions, communities, and civilizations.

The social behavioristic theory of social groups and institutions accounts for the manner in which first-order structures of behavior arise. The social behaviorist assumes that these first-order structures arise in response to two fundamental problems which must be solved if men are to survive: the mastery of nature and the establishment of working arrangements of man with man. The three major subforms in which these two general problems are encountered are *socialization* (the transformation into social beings of men who are not born social), the *mastery of nature* (the development of collective arrangements of behavior in response to physical nature, such as food-getting, which make group survival possible), and *social control* (the concentration of decision-making and development of structures which make decision-making and execution possible). No system of social life is possible without a solution to these three types of problems. Institutions are the solutions to them; social groups are the going concerns in which these solutions are put into practice.

The theory of community is the account of the processes involved when the various specific groups which represent first-order structures to social life are formed into more or less consistent total ways of life. A community is a system of groups formed into such a complete way of life. The three processes at work to bring communities into existence are *stability* (the tendency for successful solutions to collective problems to be learned and repeated), *consistency* (the bringing of the institutional solutions to problems in one area of life into a sufficient harmony with those of another area to make both possible), and *completeness* (the forming of the stable and consistent solutions to the problems of collective life into a completed set). A community forms a complete set of groups in a twofold sense: it possesses a set of groups sufficiently comprehensive to bring a plurality of people through the cycle of a year and sufficiently comprehensive to bring it through the cycle of a normal life from the birth to the death of an individual. After the completion of either of such cycles, the set repeats.

The formation of a community out of first-order groups and institutions creates problems that do not occur in the formation of groups and institutions in the first place. The solution to the problems of socialization (say of a special kind of family) can easily come into conflict with the solution of the problems of the mastery of nature (such as a special kind of economic arrangement). When, for example, the machine production of many kinds of economic goods moved their manufacture from the home to the factory, the meaning of the family (which had formerly been something of an industrial establishment) was changed. Women who had formerly manufactured textiles in the home left it to take jobs in the textile mills. A revolution in other aspects of the family was, in part, brought about by such changes.

The formation of communities thus brings about a modification and reconstruction of groups and institutions of first order. In some instances groups and institutions are strengthened; most of the time they are impaired. Communities form somewhere within the range of possibilities (unique to the given case) of sufficient modification of first-order institutions to make the community possible, but not so drastic a modification of first-order institutions that the basis of social life itself is impaired.

Thus every community is a triumph and a tragedy. It is a triumph in that it sets up a working set of the interhuman behaviors which permits a plurality of men to survive and which guarantees them an array of socially produced values over and beyond mere survival. It is a tragedy in the sense that around every community hangs the haunting specter of lost hopes, the realization that it contains only one tiny part of the vast potential of man. Moreover, it is a tragedy in the sense that human creativity always exceeds the requirements of any time and place, and every community must continually censure those innovations which, however attractive in the area of first-order institutions, would destroy the community formula itself.

The particular forms of social life, the culture, which includes not only the social institutions of the community but all other social forms that arise, tend also to be integrated. The social behavioristic theory of civilization accounts for the manner in which the total stock of cultural forms of a people is woven into more or less consistent systems complementary to the community. Three basic processes were tentatively identified in the formation of a civilization: *playfulness* (the tendency of man to vary, transform, and develop the patterns of his behavior), *aesthetic receptivity* (the sensitivity to forms and the enjoyment of arrangements of forms), and *sublimation* (the tendency to cast unsolved problems arising in the sphere of group and community formation to ideal realms, where they are supplied with ideal solutions). Whenever communities are brought into a synthesis there is a shift of the creative impulses of individuals to the formation of the styles that compose a given civilization.

While the theory of social and cultural change is eventually concerned with all three of these areas (the establishment of groups and institutions, community formation, and civilization synthesis), the present study has primarily been concerned with the process of community formation and has not undertaken the systematic investigation of the formation of groups and institutions or of the synthesis of civilizations. The formation of communities was taken as particularly significant for the theory of social change since no community can arise without the reconstruction of basic institutions. Moreover, without going into detail, again and again it appears that the most basic initial factor in the syntheses of civilization is the crystallization of a basic type of community. Social changes of first-order structures (groups and institutions) are a proper subject of research by institutional specialists—family sociologists, industrial sociologists, and the like. Civilizational synthesis—which the present study did systematically not undertake—properly awaits the prior study of community formation. The present study has concentrated on community formation, which has always been central to the theory of social change.

While every man, according to social behavioristic theory, is a potential innovator, the formation of communities which reconstructs first-order institutions and integrates them into the completed set, making up a total way of life, casts into central consideration those persons who operate, not in the special institutional areas, though they may have an anchorage in a particular institution, but who act to bring about the integration of the total set. In the study of these more comprehensive structures, these system-innovators or integrators—the intellectuals of the particular society—occupy a strategic role. It is not assumed for a moment that the intellectuals are the sole creators. However, it is in their roles that the tensions of the whole are peculiarly manifest. Moreover, the intellectuals play an important role in the civilizational synthesis: they *are* responsible for one vigorous part of the civilization—its social thought.

If one is to study the interrelations between community, the intellectual, and civilization, his empirical examples must be of sufficient scope to comprehend the wave of development which covers the rise and decline of a community. Communities are slow to form and hard to destroy. The total process may extend over centuries. The five major case histories which constitute the empirical testing ground of our study (ancient China, India, Israel, Greece, and the recent West) illustrate this possibility. However, it must not be assumed that every single event that has happened in such spans of time is relevant to community formation and destruction. Such an assumption would remove community formation from the sphere of practicable studies. It is only necessary to consider the changes in the community formula. Since the community formula changes only very slowly, this is not as difficult as has, at times, been assumed.

The social behavioristic theory of community formation seeks to establish as precisely as possible the relation between intellectual activity, community formation, and civilization synthesis. Four major hypotheses concerning these relations were advanced and tested in the five particular case histories.

1. Creative epochs of humankind are the periods of formation of new communities. At such times the sphere for manifestation of individuality is widened and its products are rewarded.

2. The quality and quantity of creativity are related to the type of community in which they occur. In general, the brilliant creative periods of human culture have coincided with the creation of the more complex human communities.

3. During the period of maturity of a community the encouragement of free creativity declines. The sphere of social life left open for the free construction of individuals is narrowed, and a restrictive array of intellectual forms is fixed.

4. The standards of the acceptability of thought or truth in this restrictive sense varies as between the creative and conformist epochs of human civilization: (a) during creative epochs there is a strong tendency to determine truth in terms of standards and criteria established in the proper conduct of the thought processes; (b) during conformist epochs of human civilization there is a tendency to establish socially acceptable truth by institutional procedures.

THE CREATIVE PERIODS OF HUMAN CULTURE

There are evidences of great creative periods in human culture before the time period of our study. Some time between 14,000 and 8000 B.C. mankind moved out of a world of tribal communities of hunters and food-gatherers into a world of peasant villages within which active food-production was carried on. In these neolithic peasant villages of the Old World the domestication of plants and animals was carried out, pottery-making was discovered, a great advance in the manufacture of textiles was made, social units of larger size than hitherto were created, and a new differentiation of institutions was achieved.

A second great creative period of human culture, one conventionally identified with the rise of historical civilization, was carried out between 5000 and 3500 B.C., when the first cities of the ancient world were formed as new kinds of communities on a foundation of neolithic peasant villages. The new urban communities were synthesized around secondary rather than primary institutions. They provided the context for the emergence of many new social groups of men—priests, administrators, specialized craftsmen, mercenaries, and others. A new specialization of institutions produced city religions, city governments, complex economic institutions, and social classes. New developments in the arts, in architecture, and in literature occurred. With the invention of writing, written history dawned. However, in time the first cities of the world reached a kind of internal limit in their development, and began to crystallize into comparatively inelastic forms.

The specific period of four of our case studies, the so-called Axial Period of human history, represents the third great wave of human cultural creativity or the second wave of civilization. This figure of speech for the period—the axis or hub of civilization—is, of course, only appropriate from the standpoint of the present. Like spokes of a wheel, the underlying forms of contemporary civilization have been said to spring from the solutions to the institutional problems of this period. Though there is some truth in this formulation, there are certain misleading aspects of the figure, for it suggests that the period from around 900 to 200 B.C. was the starting point of all civilization. However, the Axial Period was itself preceded by the earlier wave of civilization accompanying the early city formation which terminated in the civic imperialisms of the river valleys. These, in turn, were preceded by the world of peasant villages. Every wave of social and cultural creativity works with social and cultural materials already in existence, as did the Axial Period. Moreover, the conception of the period as axial suggests a unity which did not exist in fact.

The comparative review of the social structure and the intellectual and his product in the four major areas of the ancient world supplies strong evidence for the general hypotheses of our study. The Axial Period opened in all areas with the bankruptcy of the previous civilizational movements. In ancient China the empire of the Shang which is discernible in the last half of the second millennium, while supporting a civilization of considerable refinement, had passed its apex. It was not able to maintain itself in the face of more vigorous barbarians on its frontiers. When it was eventually conquered by the Chou, the deterioration of the empire into feudal particularism progressed at a rapid rate.

Similarly the ancient Mohenjo-daro and Harappa civilizations of Northern India seem to have grown so rigid and inelastic that it required only a minor push by the more barbaric invading Indo-Europeans from the north to complete their destruction. A period of cultural backwardness followed in which even the techniques of writing were lost.

On the borders of Palestine at the time of the opening of Jewish history, the ancient civilizations of Babylonia and Egypt were bogged down in their own internal problems. The deterioration of the great powers had gone so far that they were even unable to protect their frontier outposts in the Palestine area against the uprisings and conquests of confederations of peasants and stock-breeders or against new invaders like the Philistines from the sea coast.

In the eastern Mediterranean at the time of the opening of Greek history, the ancient civilization of Crete had passed its peak. It, too, found itself in such a state of decay as to be unable to defend itself effectively against the piratical raids of barbaric sea raiders who roved the Mediterranean in search of booty.

The early history of the recent West presents a similar picture. The empires which destroyed the autonomy of the ancient urban communities and transformed them into imperial administrative units set in motion processes of internal decay. The time came when the Roman Empire had to resort to compulsory legislation to force performance of essential services, converting them into hereditary obligations. The low point in the deterioration of the ancient city was certainly reached when legal enactments made enrolment in the corps which performed essential civic tasks a punishment for various categories of crimes. A distinction that had once been the eagerly sought prerogative of freemen was converted into a legislation of servitude. Again a once mighty empire was unable to defend itself against the barbarians who invaded its borders.

In all areas the Axial Period opened up on a world partly structured by preexisting civilizations which, though possessing refined culture and writing, had reached some inner structural limitations. In all areas the forces for particularism seemed at any moment ready to triumph over the forces for universalism. New institutions were needed, but the creativity to fashion them was prevented from emerging from their midst. In all areas the future lay in the hands of more primitive peoples lacking the refinements of the old centers of culture but free of their limitations as well. There was a freshness, a dawn quality, a naïve self-confidence about the more barbaric peoples who created the high civilizations of the Axial Period.

In similar fashion in the period of the decay of the ancient empires of the West the forces for particularism were everywhere manifest. In fact, in the once integrated cities, one social group after another was cast upon its own resources and forced to fend for itself. And in the society that replaced the imperial cities of Rome, the great domains gathered the complex of economic, military, political, judicial, and administrative powers into their own hands. Three major kinds of communities, peasant villages, seigneurial manors, and monastic communities which dominated the early medieval period produced only for themselves. At the same time, in these self-sufficient agricultural communities the negative features of the decaying empire vanished. Population ceased to decline. A progressive attitude toward technology had replaced the unprogressiveness of a slave economy. The communities tended to expand, at first only nibbling at the wasteland around them, but eventually entering upon an enthusiastic colonization, forest-clearing and land-clearing enterprise which transformed Europe, between the fifth and the fifteenth centuries, from a land of forests and fens, swamps and moors, into a cultivated garden.

That the creative epochs of mankind are times of community destruction and reformation is borne out by all of the cultural areas of the Axial Period and by the recent West. China's creative period lay in the time of the competing courtly communities of the feudal princes. India's creative period lay in the time of the formation of the cities and patrimonial kingdoms. Israel's most creative period lay in the time of the civic formation of Israel's Royal period. The most highly creative period of ancient Greece was that of the autonomous city-state. The Western world is still in the midst of its wave of creativity.

In all areas at this time the intellectual's skills were at a premium. Although this situation varied from place to place, plasticity and diversity were the keynotes to the social roles of the intellectual at such times. The intellectual appeared in the various guises of clerk, administrator, political advisor, the founder of schools, the founder of sects, priests, prophets, sophists, philosophers, humanistic scholars, and scientists. It was a time of competing intellectual centers and the not infrequent appearance of the displaced person whose detachment (voluntary or involuntary) from a particular place provided him with comparative social experience and encouraged the universalization of his theories. In all areas the skills of the intellectual were pressed into social use and his new ideas were often rewarded.

THE RELATION BETWEEN COMMUNITY TYPE AND KIND OF CREATIVITY

The second major hypothesis of the present study, that quality and quantity of creativity are related to the type of community in which they occur with peaks of development occurring in complex communities, also finds confirmation in the Axial Period and in the recent West. Some students of civilization have not bothered to distinguish the mere occurrence of creativity from the form this has taken. In fact, at times the fact of creativity has been attributed to the peculiar form this creativity has taken. For example, the creative excitement of the ancient Greeks is attributed to the fact that they were philosophers. Under such circumstances, theory assumes an unrealistic quality, for the relation between individual freedom to create and the community under which it is manifest vanishes from view. All in all, fewer assumptions are involved if one keeps these two phenomena separate: creativity occurs at a time of the formation of new communities, when considerable space is left for the free expression of individuality; the form that creativity takes is related to the peculiarities of the given community type.

Creative innovation bubbles up whenever there is social space for it. However, there is never absolute freedom. Only those innovations relevant to the problems of the particular time and place are encouraged or, at least, seen to be relevant. Innovations which appear to have negative consequences may be prohibited or brushed aside as irrelevant. Moreover, it is difficult for most men, including most creative men, to maintain interest in problems which their times define as irrelevant. Thus, both positively by awards and negatively by the withdrawal of interest or even by punishment, the operations of creativity are steered upon a path by forces in the social *milieu.*

While creativity occurred for the same general reason in the main cultural areas of the ancient world, the *milieux* were distinct. Chinese creativity in the late Feudal period was provided by the courtly society of the feudal princes; that of the ancient Indians by the cities and seats of the patrimonial princes; that of Palestine by the royal cities and rural towns of the monarchy; that of Greece by the autonomous city-states. The *milieu* for the creative activities of the recent West was provided first by the Western city and then by the nation-state.

The qualitative uniqueness of the intellectual products of each area is beyond doubt. The thought of ancient China is appropriate to the social requirements of educated administrators. It is practical, sophisticated, secular, always avoiding the extreme forms of abstract speculation on the one hand and magic on the other. The intellectual product of India is adapted to the status situation of genteel priests and moves primarily within the compass of the house priest and the *guru* of the religious school. It is subtle, abstract, esoteric, metaphysical, magical, and other-worldly. In some respects it is at the other end of the scale from the pragmatic time-bound practicality of the mandarin.

The intellectual product of Israel ranges through the compass points demarked by the priest and the prophet: the priest expressing the religious conscience of the monarchical city, the prophet expressing the strong traditional conscience of the old confederacy as it survived in the towns and in the rural clans. All problems, including those of international politics, were cast in religious form. Throughout, the linkage of politics and religion is maintained in a manner impossible in China or in India.

In contrast to all these other areas, the intellectual product of the Greek philosophers has a speculative, bold, secular freedom always appropriate to the status situation of the free citizen of the autonomous city-state. Greek thought has a kind of political relevance approximated only in China, though its character is distinct. It has a secularity never quite possible in Palestine. It has a speculative boldness only matched in India, but without the Indian inclination toward mysticism and magic.

The intellectual product of the recent West also has a character quite its own. It arose as a humanistic protest against the priestly and monastic mentality with which the ancient Greco-Roman world had closed. From the time of its origin, it was thus thrust more in the direction of Chinese or classical Greek mentality than that of India or Palestine. In its early humanistic phase, it combined both Chinese and Greek properties. It was literary, style-conscious, and pragmatic like the Chinese mentality, but it was also formally rational and speculative like the Greek.

The mentality of the recent West, however, had other properties which were to thrust it along another course. It was powerfully influenced by the artist in a manner not paralleled in any of the cultural areas of the Axial Period. This link with the practical as well as the fine arts and with economic enterprise sent it along a route toward science. In time the scientific impulse dominated all others, giving the intellectual products of the recent West a powerful impetus toward a systematic instrumentalism which liquidates every traditional configuration of value with which it comes in contact. It carries through a process described by Weber as disenchantment, a process which led Nietzsche to his formulation that for modern man "God is dead!" Thus in a unique manner the intellectuality of the West tends to establish a sphere of pure expediency. Science itself tends to glide into the hands of those institutions inclined to employ it most ruthlessly.

COMMUNITY STABILITY AND CULTURAL STEREOTYPING

The third major hypothesis around which our study was organized states that in the late phase of a community's development the sphere of creativity narrows.

In the final phase of a community's development the hardening of forms is often, though not always, brought about by the development of forces internal to the community itself. This is not always apparent, since the *coup de grace* often comes from the outside—as in the case of the Greek cities or in the role of the Jewish Exile in the formation of the ethnic community. However, the internal hardening of its structure exposes a community to such outside forces. If it comes, the blow from the outside only accelerates forces already in motion.

The radical narrowing of the sphere of free expression of individuality in the closing days of the societies of the Axial Period has been noted. In China it was dramatically signaled by the burning of the books under Shih Huang-ti. Under the Empire, Chinese thought was canonized and some versions maintained as official. In India the beginning of a reaction which established orthodoxy began with bloody persecutions of the heterodox faiths under the Sunga dynasty. While the process did not acquire the same clear official form as in China, the increasing canonization of Indian thought was beyond any doubt. As the caste system developed, the magical stereotyping of thought was carried through with greater thoroughness than the traditional stereotyping of China. In Palestine the stereotyping of thought suggested during the Exile was implemented in the restored community. Thereafter, the canonization of thought proceeded very rapidly. The time came when the elders officially declared that the age of prophecy was ended. Creative adaptation of the religious tradition to the changing times did not cease but had to take the form of comments and interpretations of the law. In Greece the end of the creative period came more slowly as the classical sense of balance was lost and by degrees the tradition moved from the subordination of all objective judgment to moral and practical requirements, through skepticism, toward Neo-Platonic mysticism, eventually to be stereotyped as Christian theology.

The decline of creativity which accompanies community closure can easily be overestimated. Riencourt, for example, argues that the Shang and early Chou periods of China were characterized by the creation of many new forms and styles. These were said to have been simplified in the period of the Warring States in the Han period:

> The organic development of Chinese art came to an end. The same forms, canons, symbols were used over and over again, preserving an eternal freshness of inspiration but remaining in the deep furrows dug out during China's great cultural period. Even so, art was beginning to show definite signs of exhaustion.[12]

Riencourt maintains that only the collapse of the Han and the penetration of Buddhism into China prevented immediate and permanent stereotyping:

> By now, a final synthesis was needed before Chinese civilization could enter its final slumber. A compromise had to be worked out intellectually and embodied in a firm, workable doctrine—just as Shankara's final formulation of the Vedanta doctrine crystallized Hinduism for all times or al-Ghazali formulated the final synthesis of Islamic thought.[13]

This final synthesis, Riencourt believes, was brought about by Chu Hsi. The peasant village, he believes, fixed its social life.

[12] Amaury de Riencourt, *The Soul of China* (New York: Coward-McCann, 1958), p. 94.
[13] *Ibid.*, p. 100.

> By now, the final form of China's civilization had matured. While the tenacious energy of the peasant shaped the immense garden which is China, the cultured intellectuals and artists no longer created anything new and original. . . . The Chinese world-outlook congealed, no inward development took place, and the fixity of death seized the Chinese soul. . . . From an intensely *historical* epoch the Chinese relapsed into *zoological* eras in which centuries passed uneventfully like the dream of a second. The great Chinese comet had now become a slow-moving star, revolving around this petrified cultural center, waiting for a new, profound shock to explode the fetters of old age.[14]

Equivalent to Riencourt's judgment of the complete lack of creativity in China in the period of community consolidation is Toynbee's characterization of the Jews as fossils. Samuel summarizes Toynbee's view as follows:

> Whatever Professor Toynbee may mean with regard to the other specimens in his showcase, he means that the Jewish people are spiritually and intellectually a fossil, an inert and petrified form devoid of any living juices, a lifeless and unproductive, though perhaps instructive, curiosity, a simulacrum of genuine peoplehood.[15]

Such extreme characterizations of societies and cultures during their periods of consolidation and conservatism seem to arise and assume their extremist and inflexible form as a product of reification. A culture is not creative or uncreative; people are. Moreover, there is no reason, from a social behavioristic point of view, to assume that the *potential genius* of a people is greater during one period than during another. However, it is also true that a price must be paid if one is to stabilize one kind of community. To do so, it is necessary to bring under control all things that would destroy the community formula. This, and only this, is the foundation for drawing a distinction between creative and noncreative epochs.

The canonization of texts which accompanies the attempt to consolidate the ideological supports of a community do not stop the course of social change. It may, however, give the process of innovation special character. In Judaism, for example, the establishment of the Old Testament canon pressed the adjustment to changing times into the form of comments on and interpretations of the text. The literature that formed the Talmud arose in this manner. The Talmud, in turn, was canonized, but again the process of interpretation set in.

The very nature of the Jewish community as an ethnic community gave it properties which prevented it from crystallization into any single final form. As an ethnic community, it flowed into many sorts of underprivileged minority situations within the framework of various alien communities. Objective survival depended upon its members taking up occupations in the majority community, which over and again represented the less privileged,

[14] *Ibid.*, pp. 105–106.
[15] Samuel, *op. cit.*, p. 20.

hazardous, or despised trades. Social survival depended on the maintenance of a tough core of traditional Judaism. This ever and again encouraged tendencies to integrate Judaism with cultural elements of the surrounding community and as often to react against such syntheses.

The first important example of this appears in the work of Philo Judaeus of Alexandria, who attempted to synthesize Judaism with Hellenism. The Greek philosophical teachers at Alexandria had employed allegorical interpretations of the poetry of Homer and Hesiod in the adaptation of it to the changing times. Under Greek influence some Jews had tentatively explored allegorical explanations of their own Scriptures. Eventually two factions appeared in the Jewish community of Alexandria; the group of fundamentalists opposed all allegorical explanation of the Scriptures, while the other group of liberals denied the Scriptures any but allegorical meanings.

> Between these two sections, which have had their counterparts in two attitudes of mind at every epoch of Judaism, there was the section of the conservative intellectuals who, while eager to acquire the best products of the Greek intellect, and to show the harmony between Hebraism and Hellenism, at the same time held fast to the Mosaic law and the traditional customs of their ancestors. . . . Of this section Philo is the supreme exponent, as he is also the one great writer of the Jewish Hellenistic philosophical school. He is the outstanding figure of the Alexandrian-Jewish community, whose function it was to combine the religion of the Bible with the reflective thought of the Greek philosophers, and give to Judaism a philosophical doctrine.[16]

It is also noteworthy that the orthodox section of the community rejected Philo. However, from the days of Philo to the present, similar cycles of response and resistance to outside intellectual currents have occurred. India and China did not have similar external factors to tempt their members to violate their community and civilization formulas.

Meanwhile, the underprivileged situation of the Jew and the necessity to take over marginal situations in the majority community in order to survive have made the Jews pioneers of new thoughts, new techniques, new ideas, new enterprises in the classical manner of the marginal man.

> There was always a section of the Jewish community which was attached to the faith more or less loosely; and thus, exactly like the Biblical Jewish communities, those of the Middle Ages were forever throwing off into the outside world contingents drawn from the decaying elements. One might speak of these as emigrant groups. . . . Just as a strong people on its own soil may send out, generation after generation, sons and daughters who became assimilated into other lands, so the medieval Jews—and still more the modern—yielded up, generation after generation, to persuasion or compulsion, their tribute of "emigrants."[17]

[16] Norman Bentwich, "Philo Judaeus of Alexandria," in *Aspects of Hebrew Genius*, edited by Leon Simon (London: George Routledge & Sons, 1910), p. 7.

[17] Samuel, *op. cit.*, p. 159.

Except for the fact that they had no equivalent outside situation to stimulate new departures, there is no basis whatsoever for not assuming that in China and India in the period of community closure there was not an equivalent occurrence of innovating activity. In China and in India innovating activities were simply reabsorbed into the system. We may recall an example cited earlier. Kabir, the most famous of the disciples of Ramananda, was the founder of the sect of Kabir Panthis. According to Hopkins, the Kabir Panthis are unsectarian Unitarians who conform to no rites, or *mantras*. Kabir attacked idolatry, ridiculed the authority of the Scriptures, and insisted that only the inner man was important. However, the Hindu process of the deification of *gurus* which made them into living saviors worked even on Kabir. "He who rejected idolatry became himself a deity. And in fact every Teacher, Guru, of the sect was an absolute master of thought, and was revered as a god."[18]

THE CHANGING CRITERIA OF THOUGHT

The final broad hypothesis that guided this study was concerned with the standards for the acceptability of knowledge. The establishment of truth in the sense of acceptable or authoritative knowledge varies between creative and conformist epochs. In the creative epoch, the very free space for individuality inevitably leads to a plurality of points of view. The time comes when the attempt is made to defend one's own point of view and to refute others. At such times the manner of conducting the thought process itself is appealed to as the foundation of truth.

In all the main areas of the ancient world during the creative period, the problem of truth was raised, though in quite varying degree. The competing schools of Chinese thought challenged the grounds of truth of one another. Some of the Taoists advanced the view that the knowledge of other schools was vain and contradictory. And Motse even formally raised the problem of method which he resolved by a form of pragmatic historicism. In India the disputations between the various sects sometimes reached unusual intensity. Particularly between the heterodox (Carvakas, Jain, and Buddhists) and orthodox positions did the attack on rival claims of truth become severe. Epistemological questions were raised by most major schools and advances were made in the theory of formal proof at least equivalent to that of Aristotle's logic. In Palestine as in China, epistemological questions were unusual. However, the beginnings of methodological inquiry were present. Particularly in the conflicts between the prophets of the king and the free prophets did the problem become intense. In the theories of true and false prophecy, a start on the road toward epistemology was made. Greece, with the richest development of alternative intellectual positions of all, came to be dominated by the elaboration of rational methodology in all spheres from

18 Edward Washburn Hopkins, *The Religions of India* (Boston: Ginn & Co., 1895), p. 511.

philosophy to history. In fact, at times the world-historical contribution of classical Greece to civilization has been described as its discovery of the rational proof. The two monuments to this discovery were Aristotelian logic and Euclidean geometry.

The Greeks of the Classical period were unique not in the kind of things they did, but in the profundity of their fulfillment of a possibility implicit in all periods of creativity when the establishment of truth tends to glide into the hands of the intellectuals themselves. Under such circumstances the means are sought to establish truth by application of the principles of the thought process itself. The Indians had a clear glimpse of this possibility, but only the Greeks in antiquity fully realized it.

The recent West took over the problem of truth from the Greeks, and carried it to undreamed of lengths. The two monuments to the Greek discovery of the rational proof were Aristotelian logic and Euclidean geometry. In mathematical logic the contemporary West has advanced enormously beyond Aristotle and achieved what the Greeks could not, that is, the integration of logic and mathematics. Moreover, the branches of contemporary mathematics have been enormously extended. The Greeks dreamed of integrating geometry and arithmetic, but were frustrated by their poor algebraic notation and their discovery of irrational numbers (for example, the square root of 2). The West not only solved this problem of integrating geometry and arithmetic, but transformed mathematics into a powerful tool for the investigation of nature.

It is not only in the enormous extensions of logic and mathematics, however, that the recent West differed in its solution to the problem of truth. Unique was its development of the scientific method which occurred when experimentation was generalized into a systematic procedure for the verification of empirical propositions. By contrast, the ancient Chinese only offered pragmatic workability. The Indians recognized the value of experience for supplying certain kinds of information, but did not appear to have established any criteria for verifying empirical propositions. The Greeks intermittently experimented, but never systematized experimentation into a general rule of empirical procedure.

In periods of community closure the ascertainment of truth shifts, or is taken from the hands of the intellectuals, and located on grounds other than the proper conduct of the thought process. It is no longer left to individual decision, but placed under institutional control. In China the decisive voice as to acceptable knowledge was placed in the hands of the official censor. On special occasions imperial councils of major literati were called to settle questions concerning the classics. In India, truth determination for the heterodox faiths slipped into the hands of the church council, and for the orthodox Hindus it lay in the hands of the caste *panchayats* and the school authorities or *pundits*. In Palestine the determination of truth eventually shifted into the hands of the council of priests and elders. In the Mediterranean world, though it took time, the establishment of truth eventually fell into the hands of the imperial lawyers of Rome and the theologians of the Christian Church and, above all, the church councils at times. This location of truth in institutional decisions was implemented by the distinction between different kinds of truth: secular truth established by means of Aristotelian-scholastic logic and higher truth of the faith. Eventually to the church council were added the Inquisition and Index.

The extent to which the determination of truth in the recent West will, if at all, be shifted from logical and scientific to institutional grounds cannot yet be known. The nation-states which are the primary bearers of social life in our time seem at present to be moving toward closure, though this result is far from accomplished. Periodically in the modern nation-states various kinds of censorship have been clamped down on the intellectual life of the nation concerned. All nations resort to it as a necessity in wartime, but with especial frequency it is employed as an implement of social control by the totalitarian countries in peacetime as well. Inquisitionlike procedures have sporadically appeared among the legislative and administrative bodies of many modern nations and, at times, indexes of dangerous books and periodicals have been compiled. In the United States after both world wars, widespread discontent was manifest about leaving the problem of truth in the hands of the individual.

All three of the major Utopias of the twentieth century, which employ the device of projecting an imaginary future state of society in which practices of the present are carried to their logical conclusions, envision the institutional determination of truth as a basic feature of social life. Zamiatin's *We* visualizes the control of thought by means of constant discipline, a system of guardians, and finally a scientific invention which will permit the destruction of the human imagination. Huxley's *Brave New World* imagines a behavior exactingly controlled through biological and psychological conditioning, through the use of tranquilizing drugs which induce artificial euphoric states, and the device of exile to isolated islands for persons who still persist in thinking for themselves. Orwell's *1984* envisions forms of continuous spying by means of monitoring television screens, constant propaganda, and carefully designed "cathartic" hate periods, and the terrifying operations of a "ministry of truth" to keep thought under control.

Such evidences and projections of the emergence of institutional criteria of truth suggest that in the West, too, the day may come when they no longer represent sporadic phenomena but dominate the whole.

THE CONTINUING CLASH OF HUMANISM AND SCIENCE

The two major poles of Western thought continue to be humanism and science. Again and again sensitive persons who have not thought about the matter before seize upon the possibility like an illuminating lightning flash that could modern man only bring his humanism and science together into a single formula his mentality need no longer be torn by internal conflicts. This recently was the thesis of C. P. Snow in the Rede Lecture for 1959, published as *The Two Cultures and the Scientific Revolution.*[19] The lecture touched a theme so important to contemporaries that the book went through four printings in a year. The most fundamental problem of the modern mind, Snow argues, is the tension between the humanist and the scientist:

> I believe the intellectual life of the whole of western society is increasingly being split into two polar groups. When I say the intellectual life, I mean to include also a large part of our practical life, because I should be the last person to suggest that the two can at the deepest level be distinguished.
>
> Literary intellectuals at one pole—at the other scientists, and as the most representative, the physical scientists. Between the two a gulf of mutual incomprehension—sometimes (particularly among the young) hostility and dislike, but most of all lack of understanding.[20]

The nonscientist, Snow urges, believes that "scientists are shallowly optimistic, unaware of man's condition."[21] On the other hand, many scientists are convinced that

> . . . the literary intellectuals are totally lacking in foresight, peculiarly unconcerned with their brother men, in a deep sense anti-intellectual, anxious to restrict both art and thought to the existential moment.[22]

It is Snow's opinion, however, that there is nothing so very wrong that a little discussion cannot cure. "On each side there is some of it which is not entirely baseless. It is all destructive. Much of it rests on misinterpretations."[23] Snow then argues from the strong psychological demand for personal autonomy which seems to be powerful in most[24] persons, that every scientist is a natural humanist.

> Each of us is solitary; each of us dies alone; all right, that's a fate against which we can't struggle—but there is plenty in our condition which is not fate, and against which we are less than human unless we do struggle.[25]

In fact, he argues that only science holds out the possibility of real improvements in man's condition. However, inasmuch as science liquidates traditional culture, its opponents respond in blind reaction.

> If the scientists have the future in their bones, then the traditional culture responds by wishing the future did not exist. It is the traditional

[19] C. P. Snow, *The Two Cultures and the Scientific Revolution* (New York: Cambridge University Press, 1959).
[20] *Ibid.*, p. 4.
[21] *Ibid.*, p. 5.
[22] *Ibid.*, p. 6.
[23] *Ibid.*, p. 6.
[24] See Roe, *op. cit.*, and the discussion in Chapter 18.
[25] Snow, *op. cit.*, p. 7.

> culture, to an extent remarkably little diminished by the emergence of the scientific one, which manages the western world.[26]

Snow believes that the "intellectuals, in particular the literary intellectuals, are natural Luddites."[27] Snow, it may be observed, has embraced a form of the culture-lag theory—the gap between humanist and scientist has replaced that between nonmaterial and material culture, and the former lags behind the latter.

Unfortunately, the problem is not so simple that it can be exorcised by a little "understanding," nor does Snow seem aware of the fact that the original great appeal of the social sciences was their presumed synthesis of humanism and science. Within his own personality Snow seems to have sealed off a system of humanistic convictions from the consequences of his scientific training. However, the existence of an occasional personal compromise between these orientations cannot change their nature: humanism is a system of normative theory; science is not. In the end, science does not and by its nature cannot supply ultimate values. The penetration of science into a sphere of life tends to bring about the systematic instrumentalism which led Weber to speak of the scientific "disenchantment of the world." It led Nietzsche to his formulation that for modern man "God is dead." For Snow, as for many of us, the words of Nietzsche's madman ring out.[28]

When modern man's *Book of Job* is written, the counterpart of the attempt of a just man to reconcile the meaninglessness of human suffering with the conception of a merciful God will, perhaps, consist of incidents reporting the attempt by sensitive men to reconcile humanism and science. Over and again, as science has been eagerly embraced, the systematic instrumentalism it tends to carry out has brought the individual face to face with the void. This fact seems to account for the number of persons who, sensing themselves to be faced with the alternatives—gaining the world but losing its meaning, or winning a sense of significance and losing the world—have suddenly, midcareer, embraced one of the traditional faiths or even one of the Eastern religions.

The conflict between control and significance buried in the alternatives of science and humanism also seems to be a component of the rise in popularity of points of view which move outside the sphere of Western thought encompassed by humanism and science. The popularity (significantly, in part outside Roman Catholic circles) of Neo-Thomism seems to arise from an attempt to return to the scholastic compromise between medievalism and modernity which temporarily occupied the scene before the rise of the contemporary polarity of humanism and science.

Moreover, the popularity of existentialism seems to rest on similar grounds —the attempt to establish a point of view outside the sphere circumscribed

26 *Ibid.*, p. 12.
27 *Ibid.*, p. 23.
28 See Chapter 18 above, pp. 463–464.

by humanism and science. The existential formula, man's existence precedes his essence, seems for most existentialists to be an attempt to establish man's significance on anti-intellectual grounds. It appears to be a contemporary way of covertly returning to the formula which places faith in control of man's reason. This seems to be a primary component in the existential philosophies of Kierkegaard, Heidegger, and Jaspers. Kaufmann summarizes Kierkegaard's position as follows:

> Kierkegaard takes no pride in the progress of freedom of science. Modern man's achievements, far from solving our basic problems, are distractions. All men, except true Christians—if there be any—are in despair. . . . Only Christian faith can save us from despair.[29]

Kierkegaard's emphasis on individuality is misleading if it is confused with individual self-determination and responsibility in the manner of the humanist or scientist. It is the complete antithesis of these. Kierkegaard demands an absolute individual subordination to authority, more extreme even than anything demanded by the traditional church. In his *Journals* from 1847 he maintained:

> They would have us believe that objections against Christianity come from doubt. This is always a misunderstanding. Objections against Christianity come from insubordination, unwillingness to obey, rebellion against all authority. Therefore they have hitherto been beating the air against objectors, because they have fought intellectually with doubt, instead of fighting ethically with rebellion. (Lowrie, p. 122; *Journals*, Par. 630)[30]

Kaufmann sums up Kierkegaard as a solipsistic moralist who demands blind obedience on the basis of an authoritarianism which extends beyond religion.

Heidegger, too, seems bent on abandoning the sphere of Western thought contained within the compass of humanism and science. Kaufmann notes that over and again many statements that Heidegger makes about "Being" are meaningless until it is realized that Being is substituted for what the theologian calls God. "While theologians speak of our alienation from God, Heidegger suggests that our tragedy consists in the oblivion of Being."[31] This arouses associations of estrangement from God without committing Heidegger to any particular belief.

> Like Faulkner, Heidegger seems to feel that technology has estranged as, not only from poetry, but from the world itself. The two men share a rather murky, if generous, hatred of machines, science, and clarity; an anti-intellectualism that on occasion makes a virtue of reaction; a self-made theology that, however sincere, is a pretty muddy affair compared to the Book of Genesis. The lack of clarity and contempt for grammar that are functional and admirable in Faulkner's communication of unclear states of consciousness in his novels, but offensive

[29] Walter Kaufmann, *From Shakespeare to Existentialism* (Garden City: Doubleday Company, 1960), p. 205.

[30] Quoted by Kaufmann, *ibid.*, p. 177.

[31] *Ibid.*, p. 363.

in some of his pronouncements, border on obscurantism in Heidegger's philosophy of Being.[32]

The degree to which Jaspers, in similar manner, abandons both science and humanism for a peculiar faith of his own was indicated earlier.[33]

To be sure, not all of the existentialists have employed the position as a device for placing faith in the saddle over reason or as a covert return to religion. Sartre, for example, in "Existentialism Is a Humanism," makes it the vehicle for the affirmation of an atheistic form of humanism:

> Atheistic existentialism, of which I am a representative, declares . . . that if God does not exist there is at least one being whose existence comes before essence, a being which exists before it can be defined by any conception of it. That being is man. . . . If man as the existentialist sees him is not definable, it is because to begin with he is nothing. He will not be anything until later, and then he will be what he makes himself. Thus, there is no human nature because there is no God to have a conception of it. Man simply is. Not that he is simply what he conceives himself to be, but he is what he wills, and he conceives himself after already existing—as he wills to be after that leap toward existence. Man is nothing else but that which he makes of himself.[34]

This statement was such a shock to Jaspers and Heidegger that they not only disowned Sartre's description but existentialism as well.

The contest between the humanist and the scientist thus continues, and it is complicated by numerous reactions (such as those of the Neo-Thomists and certain existentialists). However, it should not be thought that the older type of humanistic point of view finds support only from Sartre and his followers. Perhaps the most brilliant formulation of a humanistic outlook by any contemporary writer is that of Walter Kaufmann in *From Shakespeare to Existentialism.*

Kaufmann reformulated the old humanistic argument in the teeth of what he feels is "a deep dissatisfaction with the time in which it is their lot to live" by many contemporary writers, for example, T. S. Eliot.[35] He feels that a manifestation of the same sort appears in the "thousands of writers who feel sorry for themselves and some who" though they "do not greatly admire Eliot believe Gertrude Stein when she blamed society for her inability to write better and when she told them that they were a lost generation."[36] These defeatist and self-pitying attitudes even lead men to destroy history by, for example, turning Socrates and Shakespeare into honorary Christians or sentimentalizing Dante and Aquinas. To Kaufmann the true essence of the modern mind is found in its older forms of self-confident individualism.

32 *Ibid.*, p. 363.
33 Refer to the discussion in Chapter 3.
34 Jean-Paul Sartre, "Existentialism as a Humanism," in *Existentialism from Dostoevsky to Sartre*, edited by Walter Kaufmann (New York: Meridian Books, 1960), pp. 290–291.
35 Kaufmann, *op. cit.*, p. 1.
36 *Ibid.*, p. 1.

> Shakespeare's poetry is the poetry of abundance. There is laughter in it and despair but no resentment or self-pity. He was not even intent on fame and did not see to it that his works were painstakingly committed to print. He knew the view that man is thrown into the world, abandoned to a life that ends in death, with nothing after that; but he also knew self-sufficiency. He had the strength to face reality without excuses and illusions.[37]

The view that life ends in death, after which there is no reward, Kaufmann feels, inspired Prospero's speech in *The Tempest:*

> Like the baseless fabric of this vision,
> The cloud-capp'd towers, the gorgeous palaces,
> The solemn temples, the great globe itself,
> Yea, all which it inherit, shall dissolve;
> And like this insubstantial pageant faded
> Leave not a rack behind. We are such stuff
> As dreams are made on, and our little life
> Is rounded with a sleep.

This, however, in Kaufmann's view did not mean, for Shakespeare or any other humanist, that one must abandon one's self to resigned pessimism. The significance of life was not found in the tortured hopes for compensation in a hereafter, but in making the most of the here and now, in the achievement of self-mastery, in securing the highest degree of autonomy of which one is able. He feels that Sonnet XCIV more than any other expresses Shakespeare's basic philosophy:

> They that have power to hurt and will do none,
> That do not do the thing they most do show,
> Who, moving others, are themselves as stone,
> Unmoved, cold, and to temptation slow
> They rightly do inherit heaven's graces
> And husband nature's riches from expense
> They are the lords and owners of their faces,
> Others, but stewards of their excellence.[38]

This ideal of self-mastery, Kaufmann feels, also lay at the core of Nietzsche's outlook. Nobility of soul is most fully manifest in those who have power to hurt, but freely choose not to do so. Nietzsche observed:

> Verily, I have often laughed at weaklings who thought themselves good because they had not claws.

And in *Measure for Measure* (II, ii) Shakespeare observed:

> . . . O, it is excellent
> To have a giant's strength; but it is tyrannous
> To use it like a giant.[39]

37 *Ibid.*, p. 3.
38 *Ibid.*, p. 5.
39 Quoted by Kaufmann, *ibid.*, p. 6.

The Western literary tradition, as Kaufmann sees it, was inspired at its best by the humanistic ideal of the autonomous individual: facing life as he found it without illusion; demanding from it no compensation from the beyond; finding such significance as life is capable of in self-overcoming; rising to nobility of soul to the degree one was able to act out of freedom rather than expediency, and refraining from doing such hurt to others as was in one's power. In his brilliant critical essays on the Western philosophic and literary figures, Kaufmann turned this renewed vision of the humanistic outlook against many trends in contemporary criticism:

> Nietzsche, the first great philosopher to celebrate the tragic outlook that pervades the work of Shakespeare and the first in modern times to celebrate the great-souled man of Aristotle's *Ethics*, is now viewed as a half-mad, eccentric critic of "tradition" who attempted, single-handed, to turn all things upside down.
>
> Rilke, the greatest pagan religious poet since Hölderlin, is posthumously christened; Kafka is turned into a misty mystic, and then Heidegger confronts us all at once with an allegedly distinctly modern philosophy of alienation. The critics who have given us this picture are themselves alienated from a magnificent tradition that culminates in Heidegger—"not with a bang but with a whimper."[40]

Against all such trends Kaufmann gallantly recovers the essence of the humanistic point of view as he sees it.

But in the end, the man determined to face life without illusions must also face this question: Can the humanistic outlook long be maintained in a world, where the growth of giant organizations ever narrows the sphere over which an individual is permitted to exercise self-control? When the capacity for self-determination was lost in the ancient polis, thoughtful men step by step moved through Stoic and Epicurean philosophies of consolation and despair onto a route that only terminated with the complete embracing of faith. Our own times must answer the question whether the humanistic outlook will inevitably decay in the face of the systematic instrumentalism and disenchantment brought about by science and the continuous curtailment of the sphere of individual self-determination by the growth of mass institutions.

SELECTED BIBLIOGRAPHY

Heinemann, F. H., *Existentialism and the Modern Predicament* (New York: Harper & Bros., 1958).

Huxley, Aldous, *Brave New World* (New York: Modern Library, 1946).

Jaspers, Karl, *The Origin and Goal of History*, trans. by Michael Bullock (New Haven: Yale University Press, 1953).

Kaufmann, Walter (ed.), *Existentialism from Dostoevsky to Sartre* (New York: Meridian Books, 1960).

[40] *Ibid.*, p. 9.

Kaufmann, Walter, *From Shakespeare to Existentialism* (New York: Doubleday Anchor Books, 1960).
Orwell, George, 1984 (New York: Signet Books, 1949).
Snow, C. P., *The Two Cultures and the Scientific Revolution* (New York: Cambridge University Press, 1959).
Weber, Max, "Science as a Vocation," in *From Max Weber,* trans. by Hans Gerth and C. Wright Mills (New York: Oxford University Press, 1946), pp. 129–158.
Whyte, William H. Jr., *Is Anybody Listening?* (New York: Simon & Schuster, 1952).
Zamiatin, Eugene, *We* (New York: E. P. Dutton, 1924).

Index